Black Baseball Entrepreneurs, 1902–1931

Sports and Entertainment
Steven A. Riess, *Series Editor*

OTHER TITLES IN SPORTS AND ENTERTAINMENT

Abel Kiviat, National Champion: Twentieth-Century Track & Field and the Melting Pot
ALAN S. KATCHEN

Beyond Home Plate: Jackie Robinson on Life after Baseball
MICHAEL G. LONG, ED.

Black Baseball Entrepreneurs, 1860–1901: Operating by Any Means Necessary
MICHAEL E. LOMAX

Blacks at the Net: Black Achievement in the History of Tennis, Two Volumes
SUNDIATA DJATA

Fair Dealing and Clean Playing: The Hilldale Club and the Development of Black Professional Baseball, 1910–1932
NEIL LANCTOT

My Los Angeles in Black and (Almost) White
ANDREW FURMAN

The Rise of American High School Sports and the Search for Control, 1880–1930
ROBERT PRUTER

Sport and the Shaping of Italian American Identity
GERALD R. GEMS

The Sport of Kings and the Kings of Crime: Horse Racing, Politics, and Organized Crime in New York, 1865–1913
STEVEN A. RIESS

BLACK BASEBALL

The Negro National and Eastern Colored Leagues

ENTREPRENEURS, 1902–1931

Michael E. Lomax

Syracuse University Press

Photographs courtesy of National Baseball Hall of Fame Library, Cooperstown, NY.

Copyright © 2014 by Syracuse University Press
Syracuse, New York 13244-5290

All Rights Reserved

First Edition 2014

14 15 16 17 18 19   6 5 4 3 2 1

∞ The paper used in this publication meets the minimum requirements of the American National Standard for Information Sciences—Permanence of Paper for Printed Library Materials, ANSI Z39.48-1992.

For a listing of books published and distributed by Syracuse University Press, visit www.SyracuseUniversityPress.syr.edu.

ISBN: 978-0-8156-3363-1 (cloth)
978-0-8156-1039-7 (paper)
978-0-8156-5282-3 (e-book)

Library of Congress Cataloging-in-Publication Data

Lomax, Michael E.

Black baseball entrepreneurs, 1902–1931 : the Negro national and Eastern Colored leagues / Michael E. Lomax. — First edition.

pages cm.

Includes bibliographical references and index.

ISBN 978-0-8156-3363-1 (cloth : alk. paper) — ISBN 978-0-8156-1039-7 (pbk. : alk. paper) — ISBN 978-0-8156-5282-3 (ebook) 1. African American baseball team owners—History—20th century. 2. Baseball—United States—History—20th century. 3. African American business enterprises—History—20th century. 4. Entrepreneurship—United States—History—20th century. 5. Negro National League. 6. Eastern Colored League (Baseball league) I. Title.

GV863.A1L67 2014

796.3570922—dc23

[B]   2014012834

Manufactured in the United States of America

In Loving Memory of Donald and Ollie Scott

MICHAEL E. LOMAX is an associate professor of sport history in the Department of Health and Human Physiology at the University of Iowa. His primary research focus is on the African American experience in sport and the rise of sport entrepreneurs. He has written several articles on race and sport, labor relations in sport, and Major League Baseball's expansion era. His book, *Black Baseball Entrepreneurs, 1860–1901: Operating by Any Means Necessary*, examines the ways in which African American entrepreneurs transformed baseball into a commercialized amusement.

Contents

List of Illustrations ◆ *ix*

Introduction ◆ *xi*

Part One.
Independent Ball, 1902–1920

1. Continuity and Change ◆ *3*
2. Black Professional Baseball's Growth and Expansion, 1906–1907 ◆ *28*
3. Striving for Professionalism ◆ *72*
4. Years of Transition, 1911–1913 ◆ *104*
5. Black Baseball and the Separate Black Economy ◆ *138*
6. The War Years: *Toward the Rise of the Negro Leagues* ◆ *171*

Part Two.
The Rise and Fall of the Negro National and Eastern Colored Leagues, 1920–1931

7. Pitfalls of Baseball: *The Rise of the Negro National League* ◆ *241*
8. Black Baseball War: *The Rise of the Eastern Colored League* ◆ *271*

9. Pursuing Peace • *309*
10. Caught in a Rundown • *342*
11. Before the Fall • *371*
12. The End of an Era • *404*

Notes • *429*
Bibliography • *471*
Index • *477*

Illustrations

Photographs appear following page 214.

1. John Henry Lloyd.
2. Philadelphia Giants with co-owner and player-manager Sol White.
3. Philadelphia Giants with H. Walter Schlichter, Sol White, and Harry Smith from the Giants' management team.
4. Lincoln Giants in their inaugural season.
5. Harrisburg Giants with C. W. "Colonel" Strothers.
6. Leland Giants with Frank Leland and Andrew "Rube" Foster.
7. Indianapolis ABCs with Charles Isham "C. I." Taylor.
8. Brooklyn Royal Giants.
9. Bacharach Giants with John Connor.
10. Chicago American Giants.
11. Promotional flyer, Harrisburg Giants and a white semiprofessional club.
12. Hilldale club.
13. Souvenir program from the 1924 Colored World Series.
14. Hilldale club.
15. Chicago American Giants, 1926 and 1927 Negro National League pennant winners and Colored World Series champions.
16. Oscar Charleston.

17. Rube Foster and Cap Anson.
18. Dave Malarcher.
19. Jose Mendez.
20. Baltimore Black Sox.
21. Cuban Stars East.
22. St. Louis Giants.
23. St. Louis Stars.
24. Kansas City Monarchs.

Introduction

In the late nineteenth and early twentieth centuries, baseball had been a special game among African Americans. The black game's institutional development evolved as part of African American community building in the pre–Civil War era. It was transformed into a commercialized amusement by a generation of African American entrepreneurs who attempted to work within the parameters of a biracial institutional structure. Volume I of this history, *Black Baseball Entrepreneurs, 1860–1901: Operating by Any Means Necessary*, analyzed the forces that led to black baseball becoming a commercialized amusement and traced the ways the sport's business development was part of blacks' overall struggle to compete within the framework of the US economy.

The second volume continues the story from 1902 to 1931. These first three decades for black professional baseball were in many respects an era of triumph and disillusionment. Despite a costly trade war, an inequitable relationship for some black club owners with whites, and other vicissitudes, the black baseball business consolidated its position as the leading team sport among African Americans. Overall attendance and profits increased, allowing the black game to travel along the same path the white Major Leagues traveled to form leagues and develop a postseason championship series. Increased newspaper coverage led to the emergence of new heroes like Rube Foster, Oscar Charleston, Dick Redding, and John Henry Lloyd, who won the acclaim of the public and the press. In spite of black baseball's significant progress, the collapse of the Negro Leagues by 1931 symbolically represented a dream deferred in the overall African American pursuit for freedom and self-determination.

This volume utilizes the analytic framework implemented in the first one. I pay particular attention to the black baseball magnates' decision-making process, the ways in which they marketed and promoted their clubs and leagues to their target audiences, and the way they endeavored to develop their leagues and simultaneously maintain their symbiotic business relationship with white semiprofessional teams. This study will naturally pay close attention to social and cultural developments, particularly how race intersected with black baseball's institutional development and how it shaped the business relationship with white baseball clubs and park managers, Cuban club owners, and among themselves. This point will be important not only to clarify black baseball's submission to some wider *mentalité* but also to examine the ways in which these African American magnates may have insulated themselves from the forces external to the decision-making process and thereby either filtered, misread, or distorted the arguments of their constituents. Therefore, in this volume, I examine the choices that confronted black baseball entrepreneurs to show why the Negro National League and Eastern Colored League took on the organizational and structural development that they did.

At the forefront was the continued effort by a new generation of black baseball entrepreneurs to transform the sport into a commercial enterprise by working within the parameters of a biracial institutional structure. They operated their segregated enterprises (black and Cuban teams) within the fabric of the mainstream economy (professional baseball). These entrepreneurs continued their symbiotic business relationship with white semiprofessional teams at a time when the respective club owners were attempting to develop a more stable institutional structure to maximize revenues. Simultaneously, black baseball entrepreneurs continued to develop their own rivalries and championships and began to transform their unconventional playing style to embody a more competitive game on the field that reflected the white Major Leagues. Transforming the game on the field represented the pursuit by African American entrepreneurs to form black baseball as a business enterprise in their own way of operation, as opposed to emulating the white game. This new generation of black baseball entrepreneurs perpetuated the legacy of nineteenth-century African American efforts to create business enterprises to advance their own economic interests. They were not merely passive victims, allowing internal and external forces to influence their business development; they imposed themselves on the internal and external forces that came their way.

Black baseball experienced tremendous growth and expansion in the opening decade of the twentieth century. Several black, as well as Cuban, teams emerged to challenge established teams like the Philadelphia Giants, the Leland Giants, and the Cuban X Giants for players and gate receipts. Black team owners confronted challenges similar to those that conventional black businesses faced, most notably the ways in which a separate black economy was being imposed on them. Ballpark ownership remained the biggest obstacle to the black game's growth and development. Major League owners enjoyed the advantage of being able to build or remodel ballparks to sustain a fan base and maximize revenues that African Americans never enjoyed. This resulted in several African American club owners entering into partnerships with white businessmen to gain access to suitable playing facilities and maintain business ties with white semipro teams.

The growth spurt that black baseball experienced sparked efforts to form leagues and associations. League formation represented the overall attempt to place the black game on a sound economic footing, and the African American team owners used the white Major Leagues as their model for organization. However, black baseball entrepreneurs did not embrace the fact that while they were competitors on the field, they were also partners in business who had to cooperate to a much greater degree than entrepreneurs in more conventional business enterprises. Instead, they sought to maintain their symbolic business relationship with white semipro clubs and concurrently schedule games that were regional and national in scope while ideally expanding their network internationally to Cuba.

The early efforts to form leagues and associations produced several teams that were black owned and operated and functioning as full-time enterprises. Five teams—the Bacharach Giants, Chicago American Giants, Hilldale Athletic Club, Indianapolis ABCs, and St.

Louis Giants—utilized the same mode of operation that black baseball entrepreneurs had employed in the late nineteenth century to transform their clubs into top independent teams. They began by assembling and sustaining a team of talented players and gained access to a ballpark within close proximity to a large urban area to in order to build a fan base. To sustain rivalries that would stimulate spectator interest, these black clubs scheduled more games among themselves than with other black teams and white semipro and Cuban clubs. Scheduling exhibition games with all-star teams composed of major and minor league players served to heighten a black team's prestige. Embarking on extended barnstorming tours not only elevated a black team to the ranks of an elite touring team; the tours also served as a means of market expansion.

Efforts at market expansion illustrated that black baseball clubs did not rely solely on a separate black economy for their economic viability. The Chicago American Giants and the Indianapolis ABCs tapped into their respective black consumer markets while maintaining their business ties with white semipros that allowed them to exploit the white baseball market. Access to their respective ballparks allowed the American Giants club owner Andrew "Rube" Foster and ABCs magnate Charles Isham "C. I." Taylor to develop and maintain a fan base in Chicago and Indianapolis and expand into new markets in the West and South nationally and internationally to Cuba.

As the United States entered World War I, the Great Migration—the mass movement northward of African Americans—dramatically expanded the black consumer market, particularly in large urban centers in the North. Several black baseball magnates attempted to tap into this growing market by creating civic ties with the black middle class and developing a business relationship with the black press. They used the race rhetoric of self-help and racial solidarity to promote their clubs as symbols of race respectability and racial uplift. Race rhetoric served in fact to promote a sense of respectability, and the success of black clubs on the diamond provided a sense of heightened prestige for their respective communities.

By the end of the 1910s, Rube Foster had emerged as the premier black baseball owner, and his Chicago American Giants became the benchmark that African American team owners attempted to emulate. Operating in the largest market in the Midwest allowed Foster to develop a booking service to maximize revenues and heighten his prestige. He created a barnstorming network that enabled him to book games for midwestern black clubs throughout the Midwest and East. Creating this network was plausible because several black teams operated on a full-time basis, and in many ways these barnstorming tours represented a dry run for the formation of a Negro League.

In the 1920s, several forces combined to make league formation plausible. The Great Migration dramatically expanded the black communities where several black baseball teams resided. The expansion of the black press provided the means for these club owners to tap into this growing market. League formation coincided with remarkable US economic growth. Baseball's market expanded through the accelerated growth of cities and small towns as the US changed from a rural society to an urban one. Combined, these factors allowed Rube Foster to form the Negro National League (NNL) and Hilldale club owner Ed Bolden, along with Brooklyn Royal Giants magnate Nat Strong, to organize the Eastern Colored League (ECL).

Throughout the NNL's and ECL's existence, black club owners operated their respective leagues in what can best be described as the business alliance model. This approach was based on the supposition that black club owners would have maximum control over their players under contract and over the franchise, meaning the team name and logo, which could be commodified. As associations with a few club owners in certain cities enabled them to collectively eliminate players jumping their contracts, giving the owners tighter control over black baseball's player force. The business alliance model allowed owners to form loose associations among themselves to ensure that their clubs secured the best playing dates and parks in which to play. This arrangement, however, came at the expense of some of the league clubs. In most cases, several of them became reliant on Rube Foster and Nat Strong to book additional games to generate gate receipts. This arrangement led to constant franchise shifting in the NNL, with the American Giants, Kansas City Monarchs, Detroit Stars, and St. Louis Stars being the only teams to operate consistently throughout the league's existence. In the East, a peculiar business arrangement evolved where Bolden sought to maintain an alliance with Strong to schedule lucrative weekend games in New York. Two teams, the Lincoln Giants and the Baltimore Black Sox, refused to schedule weekend games away from their ballparks. Weaker franchises like the Bacharach Giants either scheduled their own weekend games or used Nat Strong's booking agency for contests in Gotham.

The business alliance approach was in stark contrast with the black press's vision of how the Negro Leagues should operate. From the outset, African American sportswriters advocated that the NNL and ECL follow the pattern of the white Major Leagues. This vision was grounded in the race rhetoric of the era that became the mantra of the black middle class: racial solidarity and uplift through self-help. African American club owners were in a position to provide opportunity for black people, most notably by hiring black umpires. A pennant race and postseason championship would stimulate interest in the black game. If the Negro Leagues operated on the same level as the white Major Leagues, they would, theoretically, elevate the race from its political, economic, and social plight. Symbolically, the Negro Leagues would represent assimilation into the mainstream of US society.

By the mid-1920s, the business alliance approach had begun to unravel. Rube Foster, Ed Bolden, and Nat Strong placed their economic interests above their respective leagues' interests. From their point of view, it was not in their best economic interests to pattern their leagues after the white Major Leagues. They refused to recognize that their leagues' overall economic interests and their interests were one and the same. The separate black economy being impose on them and the decline of white semiprofessional baseball meant that these club owners were becoming more reliant on the black consumer dollar. The illnesses of both Foster and Bolden resulted in both leagues losing what effective leadership they had. When the United States entered the Great Depression, the NNL and ECL fell into the dustbin of history.

In spite of their demise, the Negro National League and Eastern Colored League left their imprint on the African American experience specifically and American baseball in general. The Negro Leagues inform us of the ways African Americans strived to compete within the framework of the US economy, and simultaneously they represented the overall pursuit of freedom and self-determination. The black baseball business evolved into a commercial enterprise at a time when segregation shaped the relationship between black and white people. African Americans made it clear that despite their exclusion from mainstream America, they would develop their own institutions and shape their own sporting patterns. Rube Foster, C. I. Taylor, Ed Bolden, and to a lesser degree John Connor, Henry Tucker, and Thomas Jackson, operated by any means necessary to advance their economic interests in the national pastime. The members of this new generation of black baseball entrepreneurs were not merely passive participants responding to forces that impacted on them. They sought to form the Negro Leagues as a business enterprise in their own image.

In this study, I employ what I call inferential economics to highlight a black baseball club's ability to produce revenue in the opening decades of the twentieth century. Inferential economics is an approach I used in the first volume to help overcome the problems created by the lack of financial data on early-twentieth-century black baseball. Although there was no complete set of data for any one team, there was a sufficient amount of economic information on black baseball teams in the late nineteenth century to create reliable and useful estimates of the generated revenue of black baseball clubs. My fundamental assumption was that I could infer a black baseball club's ability to generate revenue. Essentially, three factors contributed to my comfort in making what I believed to be a good educated guess. First, it was tied to the gestalt I created by immersing myself in the conventional primary sources. Second, I erred on the side of caution as I expanded expenses and limited income. Finally, I was concerned with constructing realistic estimates, not reconstructing truth.

I envision inferential economics as a vehicle to aid in constructing a more textured analysis of the black baseball clubs rather than creating a precise financial assessment. I was most confident in the numbers when

I dealt with teams like the Philadelphia Giants, since there was more hard data on them than on any other black club, with the exception of the Hilldale Baseball and Exhibition Company. Gate receipts constituted the lifeblood of professional black baseball teams. To generate a black club's take for its games, I needed the following information: game attendance, admission price, and a breakdown of the visitor's share. Attendance figures, however, must be viewed with a healthy skepticism, as padding the numbers was a common practice for black, as well as white, clubs that sought to place their teams in a favorable light. Since the numbers were inflated, I used a set ticket price of twenty-five cents to present a conservative estimate of generated revenue. Ticket prices for the better managed and financed clubs like the Philadelphia Giants ranged from twenty-five to fifty cents. In addition, in some places black baseball clubs did not received a share in the revenues generated from the grandstand and concessions; normally, they went to the park manager or owner. Therefore, the lower ticket price was used to provide what I considered a safe estimate. In regards to the division of gate receipts between home and visiting clubs, black clubs used the formula developed by the Major Leagues: for the visitor, a percentage of the gate receipts (normally 40 percent) or a "heavy guarantee" (normally $250). To err on the side of caution, I divided the gross revenue in half to determine net revenue for both the home and visiting clubs.

No work of this scope is accomplished without assistance. But first, I want to give honor to my Lord and Savior Jesus Christ. Without Christ operating in my life, none of what follows would have been possible.

Billy Hawkins, Stephen Hardy, Steven Riess, and Darren Rhym have been involved, providing their expertise in devising the book's framework and thorough line-by-line edit of the initial manuscript. Anthony Grant has reviewed the manuscript at one stage or another and compelled me to think through ideas and conclusions in need of revision. My mentor, Fred Mims, an assistant athletic director at the University of Iowa, shared his experiences as an African American administrator at a Division I school, and that was very instrumental in shaping my perspective in this study. Special thanks go to Jim Gates and the library staff at the Baseball Hall of Fame, who located numerous sources for this study. I would also like to thank the staff at the Afro-American Historical and Cultural Museum in Philadelphia, where the Lloyd Thompson-Bill Cash Collection resides. Finally, special thanks go to the College of Liberal Arts and Sciences at the University of Iowa, which provided funding for this study. Without the encouragement and support of all of the aforementioned, this book would have never seen the light of day.

Part One

Independent Ball, 1902–1920

1

Continuity and Change

On April 23, 1902, the Philadelphia Giants played the Camden City club at Columbia Park, the home of the American League's Philadelphia Athletics. The Philadelphia *Evening Item* claimed the Giants possessed "some of the best players in America [today], and were it not for the fact that their skin [was] black, some of them would be . . . drawing fancy salaries in one or the other big leagues." The Quaker club broke the game open with a six-run rally in the second inning. Led by shortstop and manager Sol White, who collected three hits including a triple, the Giants coasted to a 12 to 4 victory.[1]

The formation of the Philadelphia Giants represented the continued efforts of African American entrepreneurs to develop businesses to serve their own economic interests. These black entrepreneurs exhibited a willingness to work within the parameters of a biracial institutional structure. Early black baseball entrepreneurs recognized that in order to conduct business in the United States, they had to negotiate with the white power structure. This meant transacting business with white semiprofessional club owners; park managers; and occasionally, a white entrepreneur who would serve as a business partner. The Giants scheduled games against white semiprofessional, African American, and Cuban teams. At times, they also played against major and minor league teams. Moreover, the Giants' phenomenal success reflected both the continuity and change that black professional baseball underwent in the early twentieth century. The owners utilized the business practices established by the successful black baseball clubs of the late 1880s and 1890s, like the Cuban X Giants and the Chicago Unions. The Quaker club followed the fundamental strategy of going where the money was and creating a demand for its team in several locales. By 1905, the Philadelphia Giants were the premier semiprofessional baseball club in the East.

Black baseball in New York experienced a reshuffling period. In 1904, the Cuban X Giants lost the World's Colored Championship to the Philadelphia Giants along with a certain degree of prestige. However, the X Giants were still one of the elite black clubs in the United States, and its management team of Edward B. Lamar and Clarence Williams attempted to expand the team's barnstorming network to Cuba. They entered into a partnership with Almendares Blues manager Abel Linares to establish an All Cubans team to tour the United States. Players for the All Cubans were chosen when the Cuban X Giants toured Cuba. Under Lamar and Linares' management, the All Cubans team toured the southern states of Florida and Louisiana, traveled up the Eastern Seaboard to New York and New Jersey, and then barnstormed throughout the Midwest.

Chicago's black baseball scene was chaotic. Three teams—the Chicago Unions, the Chicago Union Giants, and the Columbia Giants—competed for players and gate receipts in the Windy City. The competition for players resulted in a feud between the leading black baseball entrepreneurs in the city, Frank Leland and William Peters. The bad blood between the two men occurred at the same time as two white semiprofessional organizations began to operate as booking agents to compete for local clubs to join their circuits. One of these organizations, the Intercity Baseball Association, became involved in a dispute between Leland and Peters over the use of the name Union Giants. In 1905, Frank Leland renamed his club the Leland Giants and his team embarked upon the most successful season in its young history. The successful season resulted in Leland emerging as the leading black baseball entrepreneur in the Midwest. As the 1906 season approached, black baseball entered a period of growth and expansion that ushered in a new era for the sport.

The Birth of a Quaker City Enterprise

Solomon (Sol) White, Harry Smith, and H. Walter Schlichter formed the Philadelphia Giants. White was the driving force behind the Giants.

Born in Bellaire, Ohio, on June 12, 1868, White began playing baseball at age fifteen for the Bellaire Globes, a white amateur club. He supposedly got his opportunity to play when the Globes' regular second baseman injured his hand prior to a game against Marietta College. The captain and second baseman for the Marietta club was Byron Bancroft "Ban" Johnson, who went on to become president of the American League. In later years, White took great pride in having played against the Marietta captain. It appeared that White began his professional baseball career in 1886 with a club in Louisville, Kentucky. According to the *Wheeling Daily Intelligencer*, White was "making himself a great name in Louisville." This could possibly have been on the Falls City Club, a black club that operated in the Bluegrass state in the 1880s. On July 26, 1886, the *Intelligencer* reported that the local Wheeling club could strengthen its outfield by acquiring White. By late August, White had made his debut with the Wheeling Green Stockings as the team's second baseman. In October, the Green Stockings played an exhibition game against the National League's St. Louis Maroons. White unfortunately went hitless in four at bats as the Maroons demolished the Green Stockings, 14-6.[2]

In 1887, White began the season on the roster of the Capital City club of Washington, D.C., in the National League of Colored Base Ball Players (NCL). Several investors sought to establish a Negro League patterned after the National League, limiting membership to clubs in leading cities. By March, the Capital City club had failed to pay its entry fee and was dropped from the league. White joined the Pittsburgh Keystones and played for that club until the NCL collapsed in May. In July, White rejoined the Wheeling Green Stockings of the newly created Ohio League. He went on to have a fine season, finishing the year with a .381 batting average.[3]

In 1888, White's professional baseball career coincided with the changing racial climate in minor league baseball. On February 29, the *Sporting Life* reported that the Ohio League had expanded to ten teams and become the Tri-State League. At the same time, the reorganized league repealed a provision allowing league clubs to sign black players, and White was dropped from the Green Stockings' roster. From

1889 to 1894, White played on all-black clubs that included the Gorhams of New York, York Colored Monarchs, Pittsburgh Keystones, Boston Monarchs, and Cuban Giants. In 1895, he returned to white Organized Baseball, playing for Fort Wayne in the Western Interstate League. When the league disbanded in June, White joined the all-black Page Fence Giants and played for all-black clubs in the latter half of the 1890s. In 1901, White was on the Cuban X Giants' roster.[4]

Little is known regarding the backgrounds of Harry Smith and H. Walter Schlichter. As sports editor of the *Philadelphia Tribune*, Smith served on what eventually became the oldest continuously circulating black newspaper in the United States. Smith, evidently, had also worked in the hotel industry. The *Evening Item* referred to him as the former chief bellman of the Mercantile Club. He would also serve as the Giants' first baseman in their inaugural year. According to White, it was Smith who conceived the idea of a black club representing the City of Brotherly Love, and the latter undoubtedly contacted Schlichter to form this partnership.[5]

Schlichter, on the other hand, was the sports editor of the Philadelphia *Evening Item*. White characterized Schlichter as the "instigator" behind the formation of the Giants and was his "ideal of an owner of a colored baseball team." The *Cleveland Advocate* reported in 1901 that Schlichter organized an exhibition game between the Cuban X Giants and the American League's Philadelphia Athletics. This contest "brought Walter Schlichter into the business," as he apparently saw black baseball as a potentially lucrative undertaking. The Giants-Athletics game led Schlichter to declare "his intentions to organize a Colored baseball team." In addition to his interest in baseball, Schlichter, known also as "Slick," supposedly had some managerial experience, managing boxing clubs and boxers.[6]

The Giants' organizers formed their club around the business strategy of economic cooperation. The roots of cooperative enterprises in the black community went back to the late eighteenth century. Early black entrepreneurs recognized that if they were to attain any success in developing black business to an appreciable level in the black community, that success would come only through economic cooperation. It was obvious to them that no concrete help in obtaining capital and credit could be expected from white America. Therefore, African American entrepreneurs would pool their resources together to create a successful business enterprise. The Giants' organizers, however, were willing to operate within the framework of a biracial institutional structure. White and Smith, apparently, sought a partnership with Schlichter because business dealings went smoother with white semipro clubs and park managers with a white partner as part of the management team.[7]

The Philadelphia *Evening Item* listed H. Walter Schlichter as the manager of the Giants, Harry Smith as the assistant manager, and Sol White as captain, but White was the prime mover behind the ball club. There was no evidence that either Schlichter or Smith had played on or managed a ball club previously. White, on the other hand, had been in baseball for fifteen years, and he had played on the Cuban X Giants when the players formed a cooperative enterprise with E. B. Lamar. According to White, the players hired Lamar to perform administrative functions like keeping the books and issuing press releases. He undoubtedly drew from the experiences of such previous managers of the Cuban Giants and the Cuban X Giants as Clarence and George Williams and Frank Grant. Therefore, Sol White managed the club on the field, located and developed talented players, and scheduled games with white and black clubs. Schlichter and Smith performed administrative roles like bookkeeping, issuing press releases, and generating publicity. They also provided the start-up capital necessary to form the ball club. The Giants benefited tremendously from the increased press coverage the *Item* provided. In many ways, White's business relationship with Schlichter and Smith was similar to Philadelphia Athletics' manager Connie Mack's relationship with Benjamin Shibe and Albert Reach. Mack assumed field management and partial ownership of the A's; Shibe purchased the majority of the club's stock and Reach became a minority partner.[8]

Three factors were essential to ensure that the cooperative business enterprise strategy was successful. Organizing a team of talented black players who could compete at an elite level constituted the first factor. The Philadelphia Giants had several prominent black baseball veterans and some promising young stars. Three of the veteran players had previous managerial experience. Clarence Williams was an original member of the Cuban Giants, the most accomplished black club of the late nineteenth century. Williams was the Giants' catcher and he possibly assisted White in managing the club and scheduling games. Williams's brother, George, was the team's shortstop, who may have also aided White in some managerial duties. Frank Grant was the Giants' second baseman and was considered one the best baseball players, black or white. John Nelson and Charles "Kid" Carter, both of whom had played previously for the Cuban X Giants, bolstered the pitching staff. Andrew "Jap" Payne began as a nineteen-year-old outfielder with the Quaker club and in the next seventeen years developed a reputation as a player who could help a team in many ways. White placed the club on salary, paying the players from sixty to ninety dollars per month.[9]

Securing a good playing facility represented the second factor. The ballpark was essential if a black professional team was to build and maintain a fan base. The park had to be easily accessible to city transit and located within or in close proximity to a large urban area. Philadelphia had a reputation for being a baseball town, given its substantial population (1,549,008), and its having been represented in the white Major Leagues since the 1880s. The Giants secured a working agreement with the Philadelphia Athletics to play their games at Columbia Park, located at Twenty-Ninth Street and Columbia Avenue. The ballpark seated 9,500, mostly on uncovered wooden bleacher benches, and the Giants played their home games there when the Athletics were on the road.[10]

Mastering the scheduling process known as barnstorming constituted the third and final factor needed to ensure that the cooperative enterprise strategy was successful. Black baseball entrepreneurs would schedule games with white semipros, black, and Cuban teams during the season at home and throughout the United States. Games were scheduled regionally with clubs that were within approximately a one-hundred-mile radius of a team's home base of operation. When a club developed a reputation as a good gate attraction, black teams would expand their scheduling commitments to other regions of the country, particularly the Midwest. Ideally, a black club would seek to expand its barnstorming tours internationally to Cuba. They would play there during the winter months, return to the US, and barnstorm their way to their home base prior to the beginning of the regular season. Successful black clubs scheduled from approximately 120 to 144 games per year. In their inaugural years, the Philadelphia Giants focused on developing a regional barnstorming schedule, touring the states of Pennsylvania, New York, Delaware, and New Jersey.

In 1902, the Philadelphia Giants got off to a fast start in their opening season. After defeating Camden City in their season opener, the Giants won fifteen out of nineteen games. They played in one of the first night games in baseball history. On June 3, the *Item* reported the Giants would play John O'Rourke's Cosmopolitans under the lights at Columbia Park. The grounds would be illuminated by "an engine . . . mounted on a track on wheels, with detachable poles, wires, and lamps which [could] be put up and taken down in a few hours." Evidently, the fans were not amused by the spectacle. A reported four hundred fans journeyed to Columbia Park, and they "did not go crazy over the game." The six-inning contest was a fiasco, as both clubs committed fifteen errors, with the Giants winning 15-13.[11]

Throughout their opening season, the Giants issued several challenges to the Cuban X Giants for the World's Colored Championship. The Colored Championship Series served as a way in which black baseball entrepreneurs marketed and promoted the black game in the late nineteenth century. To compete for the colored championship, a black club from the East, for example, would have to defeat all the black clubs within its region of the country. It would then issue a challenge to play against the top black clubs from another region. Once a black club defeated the top black clubs from each region of the country, it could proclaim itself as the World's Colored Champion. Although this informal means of determining the colored champion would lead to controversy, it did generate a lot of publicity for the black game.[12]

The Cuban X Giants' manager, E. B. Lamar, snubbed the upstarts, supposedly claiming the Giants' players had been "knocking" the X Giants, and that if both clubs played in an actual game, the latter would be "injured." A more plausible explanation would be that since several of Lamar's former players played for the Quaker club, the Cuban X Giants' reputation would be tarnished if they lost the series. On June 23, the *Item* reported that the Giants challenged the Cubans again for the colored championship. The challenge went unanswered.[13]

By the end of September, the Philadelphia Giants had compiled an 81-43-2 won-lost record. They culminated their opening season with a two-game series against the American League champion Philadelphia Athletics. The Athletics' pennant-winning season was marred by controversy. In the midst of a bidding war for players with the National League, A's manager Connie Mack lured second baseman Napoleon Lajoie from the National League Phillies, along with pitchers Chick Fraser and Bill Bernhard. The Phillies secured a court order enjoining Lajoie and the two pitchers from playing with the Athletics. American League president Ban Johnson switched Lajoie and Bernhard to the Cleveland Americans to remove both players from the jurisdiction of the Pennsylvania courts while preserving them for the junior circuit. Fraser, on the other hand, returned to the Phillies.[14]

Despite losing these players, Mack still had a good ball club. Midway through the season, he offset the loss of Lajoie with the acquisition of Danny Murphy and Rube Waddell. Murphy filled the void at second base and provided batting strength. Waddell became the A's pitching ace, winning twenty-four and losing seven. Known for his idiosyncratic behavior, Waddell was an overhand pitcher with tremendous speed and an excellent curve ball who was virtually unbeatable when he concentrated on his work. Eddie Plank was a left-handed pitcher whom Mack had signed right out of college; Plank won twenty games and gave the A's a formidable one-two pitching combination. The Athletics boasted six .300 hitters—an unusual number in the early twentieth century—including Socks Seybold, who led the American League with sixteen home runs.

Before the series began, both teams were honored with a big parade to commemorate the clubs' successful seasons. Two hundred escorts and a brass band accompanied the clubs, and several of the city's leading politicians took part in the parade. The Athletics acquired Boston Red

Sox outfielder Buck Freeman to play in the series; he had had an outstanding season, leading the Red Sox in doubles (37) and triples (20) and leading the American League with 121 runs batted in. However, in the first game, Freeman did not perform well against the Giants' pitcher Charles "Kid" Carter. The *Item* reported that Freeman struck out five times! Carter's performance was not enough to stop the American League champions, as the Giants lost, 8-3. The second game was no contest. The Athletics took a 13-3 lead into the eighth inning. Despite scoring four runs in the eighth inning and two in the ninth, the Giants lost, 13-9.[15]

In 1903, White bolstered his club by signing Harry Buckner, William Binga, Robert Footes, and John Patterson. Buckner was one of the leading pitchers in the 1890s. He played for the Chicago Unions and the Columbia Giants, and he was also an excellent hitter, shortstop, and outfielder. William Binga began his career with the Page Fence Giants and was regarded as one of the top third baseman in the black game. Veteran catcher Robert Footes had played previously with the Chicago Unions and the Chicago Union Giants. John Patterson was a versatile player who could play second base and the outfield. He was a member of the Page Fence Giants team that defeated the Cuban X Giants for the 1896 colored championship.[16]

The Giants' management team sought to maximize the club's revenues by creating rivalries with semipro clubs throughout Pennsylvania, New York, and New Jersey. Baseball entrepreneurs tried to create rivalries with other semipro teams to sustain their economic viability. A seasonal rivalry, particularly on Sundays, meant a big payday for semipro clubs. Club owners tried to develop seasonal rivalries with at least three or four independent clubs throughout the year. Furthermore, rivalries in conjunction with the Colored Championship Series became the means by which a top black club tapped into lucrative baseball markets like New York and Philadelphia.

In addition to rivalries, several separate-admission doubleheaders were scheduled throughout the season, particularly on Saturday. Pennsylvania Blue Laws prohibited the scheduling of Sunday games in Philadelphia. To maximize revenues in the Quaker City, the Giants' management team scheduled a morning and twilight game on several Saturdays throughout the season. On May 31, the *Item* reported a doubleheader between the Giants and the Wilmington Base Ball team. In the first game, Kid Carter held the Wilmington club to five hits en route to a 4-0 shutout win. In the second game, Giant's pitcher William Bell was equally tough, holding the Wilmington team to five hits and coasting to a 3-1 victory.[17]

Another response to Pennsylvania Blue Laws was to schedule Sunday games in New York and New Jersey. This strategy was not without controversy, however. On May 11, the *Item* reported the Giants game against the Bayside club was a test to determine whether the local police would stop the contest. Bayside players were reportedly arrested a week before the Giants game, but the charges were dismissed. The police did not interrupt the game and the Giants demolished the Bayside club, 15-2.[18]

In 1903, attendance at Giants games revealed the club was making progress toward its goal of maximizing revenues. The average attendance at Giants games was 4,199. With ticket prices set at twenty-five cents, the Giants' gross revenue was $1,049.75, with a net revenue of $524.88. The Giants developed a rivalry with the Harrisburg Athletic Club throughout the season. Of the ten games reported in the press, six listed attendance figures. A total attendance of 21,400 generated a gross revenue of $5,350 and a net revenue of $2,675. The largest reported attendance was in Philadelphia against the Harrisburg AC at Columbia Park. Approximately 12,800 fans witnessed a pitcher's duel. Harrisburg took a 2-1 lead into the ninth before the Giants rallied with three runs in the bottom of the frame and won, 4-2.[19]

In September, the Philadelphia Giants again challenged the Cuban X Giants for the World's Colored Championship. Apparently, Lamar felt enough confidence this time to accept the challenge after acquiring marquee players Andrew "Rube" Foster and Charlie Grant. He also reacquired Clarence Williams and lured Jap Payne from the Quaker club. Ten games were scheduled between the two clubs in New York, Philadelphia, Camden, Trenton, and Harrisburg. Unfortunately, only five games were reported in the press. In the first game, Rube Foster baffled the Quaker club, holding it to two hits in the first seven innings.

The Giants scored two runs in the eighth inning before bowing in defeat, 4-2. On September 13, the clubs played a doubleheader at Ridgewood Park in New York. A reported crowd of seven thousand fans watched the Cubans thwart the Giants, 8-1. In the second game, Philadelphia scored five runs in the fourth inning on the way to a 5-2 victory. It was the Giants only win, as the Cubans swept the final two games.[20]

Despite the Giants' poor performance against the Cuban X Giants, White continued to strengthen his ball club. He induced pitching nemesis Rube Foster to move from the X Giants and added pitcher Danny McClellan, outfielder Pete Hill, and catcher George "Chappie" Johnson. Concurrently, the Giants' management team signed a lease to play Giants' home games at Broad Street and Jackson Avenue in the Quaker city. This move, no doubt, was predicated on the Giants playing more games in Philadelphia to maximize revenues. They were no longer required to schedule home games around the Philadelphia Athletics' schedule. Evidently, additional games were booked at Broad and Jackson either while the Giants were on the road or as part of a doubleheader. Throughout the season, the *Item* reported several games played by the Morrow club at the Giants' new grounds.[21]

The Philadelphia Giants scheduled more games in New York and New Jersey to create a demand for their club in several locales. Rivalries were created with the Murray Hills in New York; the Ridgewoods of Long Island, New York; and the All Cubans team from Cuba. On April 11, the *Evening Item* reported a doubleheader involving three teams: the American League New York Highlanders, the Ridgewoods, and the Philadelphia Giants. A reported twelve thousand fans watched the Highlanders crush the Ridgewoods, 14-2, in the first game of the doubleheader. In the second game, Rube Foster of the Giants gave up six hits and struck out eleven Ridgewood batters in a 6-3 win. On July 31, former National League pitcher Bill Duggleby took the hill for Murray Hill against Kid Carter. In 1901 Duggleby had won twenty games for the Philadelphia Phillies, but he was no match for the Giants' hitters. Led by Bill Monroe's three doubles, the Giants coasted to an 11-4 win. In August, the All Cubans played the Giants in what was promoted as an "international contest." Kid Carter gave up seven hits in a 6-1 Giants win. A second game was scheduled between the two clubs for August 17. In a pitcher's duel, All Cubans' hurler Jose Munoz prevailed over Giant's pitcher Will Horn, 3-2.[22]

On July 28, the *Item* reported that the Giants had opened the home series in the recently formed Tri-County League. This league appeared to be more of a booking arrangement rather than an established circuit playing for a pennant and a championship. Press coverage for the league was sporadic and no league standings were printed. The league, apparently, consisted of four teams: the Giants, Pottstown, Brandywine, and Oxford. The league could have emerged out of a rivalry between the Giants and the Pottstown club. Of the league games reported in the press, the Giants-Pottstown rivalry received the most attention.[23]

In September 1904, the Philadelphia Giants challenged the Cuban X Giants again for the World's Colored Championship. A best two-out-of-three-game series was scheduled in Atlantic City, New Jersey. In the first game, four thousand fans witnessed Rube Foster put on a spectacular performance. He struck out eighteen batters, scattered seven hits, and defeated the Cubans by 8-4. Foster also collected three hits, including a triple, and scored one run. The Cuban X Giants turned the tables in game two as Harry Buckner outlasted Will Horn, 3-1. Rube Foster pitched the rubber game for the Philadelphia Giants. The X Giants took a 2-0 lead into the fourth inning; then, the Quaker club scored one in the fifth and two in the seventh. Foster struck out six batters, gave up only three hits, and defeated the Cuban X Giants, 4-2. Foster's performance in the series was impressive. In eighteen innings, he struck out twenty-four batters while giving up six runs and ten hits. According to the *Item*, the Giants' defeat of the Cuban X Giants was a "big surprise even to their strongest admirers." The Philadelphia Giants became only the second team to defeat the Cuban X Giants for the World's Colored Championship.[24]

The Philadelphia Giants culminated their successful season with two contests with the All Cubans team, and they also attempted to schedule a series with a Major League club. The *Item* proudly proclaimed the Giants "made good their claim for the colored championship" by defeating the All Cubans, 13-3. The game was played as a benefit for a building fund for the Frederick Douglass Hospital. The Douglass Hospital was founded in 1895 by Nathan Mossell, black Philadelphia's leading physician and a prominent member of the African American community. It was one of the first institutions to be staffed wholly by blacks and functioned as an important training center for doctors, nurses, and pharmacists. Several fund-raising drives were conducted throughout the late 1890s to pay off the hospital's substantial mortgage. The Giants' game with the All Cubans was apparently one of those fund-raising efforts. The *Item* reported that all the "colored aristocracy" was present to witness the Giants break the game open with a six-run rally in the eighth inning behind the heavy hitting of Pete Hill and Bill Monroe. Foster outpitched All Cubans ace Jose Munoz, striking out fourteen batters and giving up only five hits. By the end of September, rumors were circulating that the Giants had issued a challenge to play the American League's New York Highlanders, who were in a close pennant race with the Boston Red Sox. The challenge went unanswered, no doubt because the Highlanders lost the pennant on the last day of the season! The Giants did receive some consolation by defeating the All Cubans at Ridgewood Park before a reported crowd of 4,500 fans.[25]

The 1905 season was the Giants' best one in the team's young history. It began with a three-game series with the Eastern League's Newark Eagles. Formerly known as the International League, the Eastern League was a high-level minor league, and Newark was one of its strongest clubs. They were managed by Ed Barrow, who would later serve as president of the International League and general manager of the New York Yankees. The series was marked by the awesome performance of the Giants' new shortstop, Grant "Home Run" Johnson. In 1895, Johnson—and Bud Fowler, one of the best black players of the late nineteenth century—formed the Page Fence Giants and served as the team captain. Prior to becoming the Giants' shortstop, Johnson was a member of the Cuban X Giants. In the first game, Johnson lived up to his nickname by belting two home runs and batting in four runs, leading the Giants to a 5-3 victory. In game two, Danny McClellan scattered eight hits and defeated the Eagles, 6-4. Grant Johnson led a nine-hit attack in the final game, hitting his third home run of the series as the Giants won, 8-4. The Giants' three-game sweep of the Newark Eagles was impressive.[26]

On May 12, the *Item* reported a contest between the Giants and "Johnson's Pets." Jack Johnson, who in 1908 would become the heavyweight boxing champion of the world, sponsored the club and played first base in the game. Johnson reportedly played first "in fairly good style" but had trouble at the plate, although he managed to get two hits. Fans were entertained by the Giants' third baseman Bill Monroe's "antics," as he apparently teased Johnson throughout the game. Johnson's Pets were no match for the Giants, losing by the lopsided score of 13-4.[27]

Attendance at Giants' games grew dramatically, in part because of an increase in Sunday games played in New York and New Jersey. Their attendance reached 77,027, which averaged out to 3,501 fans per game. These numbers, however, do not reflect attendance at weekday games, but nonetheless, the increase was still substantial. Attendance ranged from as low as 500 to as high as 8,352. Gross revenues ($19,256.75) were almost twice their 1903 total.[28]

Attendance figures for games in New York and New Jersey showed that the Giants were in much demand there. Attendance at New York games were 58,502, with an average of 4,875 fans per game. They amassed a gross revenue of $14,625.50 and a net of $7,312.75. In New Jersey, attendance reached 16,025, with an average of 2,003. The Giants collected a gross of $4,006 and a net of $2,003.[29]

Total attendance and the revenue accumulated against two white semiprofessional teams—the Ridgewoods of New York and the Atlantic City club of New Jersey—were equally striking. Four games with the Long Island Ridgewood club amassed a total attendance of 15,100 and a gross of $3,775. A grand total of 11,525 fans watched six games between the Giants and the Atlantic City club. Both clubs realized a gross of $2,881.25 and a net of $1,440.63. The numbers reveal that the Philadelphia Giants could generate revenue and had the potential to be a lucrative enterprise.[30]

On August 3, the *Item* reported that the Cuban X Giants had issued several challenges in the newspapers to arrange a series with the Philadelphia Giants. According to Walter Schlichter, Lamar declared that the public demanded a series between the two clubs and that he was motivated "solely by the love of the sport in endeavoring to force me to play [the Giants] in a series of games." Schlichter agreed to arrange a five-game series in New York and Philadelphia with Lamar—the winner to take all the gate receipts. The winner-take-all stipulation was nonnegotiable. The following day Lamar responded to Schlichter's terms. He would agree to a series of nine or ten games, the winner to receive 60 percent of the gate receipts and the loser forty percent. The chances of the series happening were unlikely because of Lamar's unwillingness to agree to the winner-take-all edict. Supposedly, several members of the Quaker club stated the X Giants wanted "to get on the loser's end [of the gate receipts] in the hope of getting a little money out of an unsuccessful season." Since Lamar had snubbed the Giants three year earlier, it was apparent that animosity existed between the two management teams. The series never took place.[31]

In September, the Brooklyn Royal Giants challenged the Philadelphia Giants for the colored championship. A three-game series was scheduled in Atlantic City, New Jersey. In the first game, twelve hundred fans watched Giants' pitcher Emmett Bowman shut out the Royals, 2-0. The second game was tied at six in the ninth inning before the Royal Giants went down in defeat, 7-6. Danny McClellan gave up two runs and eight hits in a 7-2 victory as the Giants went on to sweep the series and defended their colored championship title in a second straight championship win.[32]

The Philadelphia Giants mastered the cooperative enterprise strategy that had made black baseball clubs successful in the late nineteenth century. They followed the fundamental approach of going where the money was and creating a demand for their club in several locales. By 1905, the Giants were in much demand. Defeating the Cuban X Giants for the colored championship and defending it the following year heightened the Quaker club's prestige in the black baseball world.

Black Baseball's US-Cuban Connection

Although they had lost their colored championship to the Philadelphia Giants, the Cuban X Giants were still one of the elite clubs in the black baseball world. They were the first club to utilize the cooperative business enterprise strategy, and they became the model that other black clubs sought to emulate. As the United States entered the twentieth century, the Cuban X Giants' management team attempted to establish barnstorming tours to Cuba.

In 1902 Clarence Williams was the last original member of the Cuban Giants of the late 1880s. He became a player-manager upon joining the team in 1885 and remained so for the Cubans throughout his baseball career. Williams was born on January 27, 1868, in Harrisburg, Pennsylvania. He began playing baseball in Harrisburg in 1882 as a left fielder for the local club. The following year, he was a catcher for the Middleton baseball club of Pennsylvania and in 1884 moved on to the Williamsport club. In 1885 Williams joined the Cuban Giants as a backup catcher and first baseman. An excellent hitter and a fine base runner, Williams was known for his vaudevillian flair on the diamond, entertaining the fans with his antics.[33]

In 1896 Williams and several other Cuban players entered into a partnership with Edward B. Lamar and formed the Cuban X Giants. The Cuban X Giants were established due to a rift between the players and Cuban Giants' owner, John "J. M." Bright. Several former players bolted the Cuban Giants team to form a cooperative enterprise with Lamar. Throughout the latter half of the 1890s and the opening decade of the twentieth century, Lamar's Cuban X Giants and Bright's Cuban Giants barnstormed the US for prestige and gate receipts. Lamar served in an administrative capacity, keeping the books, issuing press releases, and generating publicity. Formation of this cooperative enterprise was based on the premise that business dealings went smoother with semipro magnates and park managers when a white business associate was at the helm. It was a concession these black players were willing to make to advance their economic interests.[34]

The Cuban X Giants operated as a traveling team in the opening decade of the twentieth century, barnstorming the nation for gate receipts. They established a rivalry with the Ridgewood club, one of the leading white semiprofessional teams in New York City. After losing the colored championship to the Philadelphia Giants in 1904, the Cuban X Giants played the Chicago Union Giants the same year for the "colored championship of the world." The *Chicago Tribune* erroneously mistook the X Giants for J. M. Bright's Cuban Giants and incorrectly stipulated that the Cuban Giants had arranged a three-game series with the Union Giants in the Windy City. A close examination of the box scores in the *Tribune* shows it was the Cuban X Giants who had arranged the series. Fans watching the first two games witnessed excellent pitching performances by the Cubans' hurler Walter Ball. Ball held the Union Giants to five hits in the first game on the way to a 6-1 Cuban victory. He was equally impressive in the second game, giving up only two hits and striking out four batters in a 3-1 Cuban win. The Union Giants won the third and rather meaningless game, 3-2. Since the Cuban X Giants had lost to the Philadelphia Giants previously, they could not lay claim to the World's Colored Championship, according to its informal parameters. Nevertheless, the Cuban X Giants' performance against the Union Giants was outstanding.[35]

While the Cuban X Giants continued their barnstorming ways in the United States, its management team began to make inroads into Cuba. On January 2, 1902, *Sporting Life* reported that the All Cubans club would tour the US in 1903 under the management of E. B. Lamar. The article, written by Cuban baseball entrepreneur Abel Linares, stated the club would be composed of star players from the Cuban National League (CNL). The Cuban X Giants would reportedly travel to Havana in October and play a series of games against CNL clubs. Undoubtedly, the Cubans' visit to Cuba served as a scouting tour to determine who would play on the All-Star team.[36]

The 1903 All Cubans' barnstorming tour of the US would set the pattern for future excursions of the early twentieth century. Abel Linares would form a partnership with a black baseball manager like E. B. Lamar to schedule games throughout the United States. The All Cubans team would leave Cuba after the end of the Cuban League season in March and barnstorm the US until after Labor Day. US teams and players were welcomed to play in Cuba in late November and December before the start of a new Cuban season.

The 1903 barnstorming tour was evidently the fourth trip organized by Abel Linares. Little is known about Linares's early background. In addition to his role as a club owner and organizer of barnstorming tours of Cuba by black and Major League teams, Linares wrote a column titled "Cuba's Chapter" for *Sporting Life* from 1902 to 1904. In 1899 he organized a barnstorming tour of the US that started in July and lasted through early September. During this tour, the All Cubans played the Cuban X Giants in a two-game series. This series of games may have marked the start of the business relationship between Linares and Lamar. In 1900, the Cuban X Giants embarked on a tour of Cuba, playing a reported fifteen games and winning thirteen. According to *Spalding's Official Base Ball Guide*, Linares organized two additional tours in 1900 and 1902. During the 1902 season, the All Cubans compiled a reported 77-22-1 won-lost record. More important, these tours may have served to solidify business ties between Linares and the Cuban X Giants' management team.[37]

The timing of the tours coincided with the rallying of white and black Americans behind the cause of *Cuba libre* (free Cuba). Interest in seeing Cubans perform was due, in part, to a desire to transplant American cultural success to territories freed from Spanish colonialism. The US baseball world was also caught up in the euphoria, as sporting newspapers reported the support of North American ballplayers for liberating Cuba from Spanish rule. Reports in *Sporting Life* and other sporting newspapers stated that professional players like Clark Griffith expressed their willingness to bear arms to defend *Cuba libre*. Griffith and other players had participated in tours of Cuba, and they were exposed to the ideals of the nationalist movement, the articulation of a nonracial national identity espoused by Cuban nationalists, and the political conditions there. US intervention brought an end to Spanish colonial rule. Policies enacted during the US military occupation created a favorable climate for baseball to flourish. According to historian Adrian Burgos, spectators attending games of the All Cuban team included Cuban émigrés who sought to reestablish links with their countrymen, capitalizing on the tours' strategic stops in towns with enclaves of Cubans and other Latinos like New York, Chicago, New Orleans, and Tampa. The All Cubans would barnstorm their way up the Eastern Seaboard to New

York and New Jersey and then make a swing throughout the Midwest. The tours usually lasted until Labor Day.[38]

Organizing these international tours required a lot of administrative work. Linares not only had to schedule games, he also had to secure visas for the players to enter the US and post bonds with US immigration officials to gain travel clearance. As Burgos has pointed out, these bonds ensured that the team had sufficient residuals to return to their native land and that the players would not remain in the US or become public charges.[39]

The All Cubans toured the US from 1903 to 1905 and finished the 1903 season with an 89-28-1 won-lost record. They played the top white semipro clubs, like the Murray Hills, and the top black teams, like the Philadelphia Giants. On August 21, 1904, the *Evening Item* reported that the All Cubans defeated John O'Rourke's Camden club behind the excellent pitching of Jose Munoz. The Cuban hurler gave up only two hits and struck out four batters in a 3-0 shutout victory. On October 27, 1905, the Cuban X Giants prevailed over the All Cubans, 8-6, with a team composed of several members of the Philadelphia Giants. Rube Foster, along with Danny McClellan and Pete Hill, played for the X Giants.[40]

The Lamar-Linares partnership was not only important in regards to scheduling games, but also in negotiating with both white semipro teams and park managers. Much like black baseball entrepreneurs who preceded him, Linares undoubtedly recognized that business transactions went smoother with a white business partner as part of the negotiation process. He acknowledged early that in order to do business in the United States, he had to deal with the white power structure. Nonetheless, with the Philadelphia Giants emerging as the elite black club in the East and the Cuban X Giants' management team making inroads into Cuba, black baseball in Chicago was in utter chaos.

A STATE OF DISARRAY

Since the early 1890s, William Peters and Frank Leland had been black baseball's leading entrepreneurs in Chicago. Peters began as a first baseman with the Chicago Unions in 1887 before forming a partnership with Leland and several other members of Chicago's black community to transform the club into a full-time operation. Leland was born in 1868 in Memphis, Tennessee. In 1887 he was on the roster of the Washington Capital City Club of the National Colored League. When the Colored League collapsed, Leland moved to Chicago, where he first became an umpire for the Unions. By the mid-1890s, he was the Unions' traveling manager and, along with Peters, mastered the barnstorming pattern that made the team the premier semipro club in the Midwest. The Unions toured the midwestern states of Indiana, Michigan, Ohio, and Wisconsin during the week and returned to Chicago for Sunday games. They would schedule as many as two or three games on Sunday to maximize the Unions' revenues. Peters and Leland developed several promotional schemes, like a winner-take-all series and substantial side bets to generate interest and stimulate competition among the leading white semipro clubs. By 1898, the Unions had created what could best be described as a barnstorming rivalry with the Cuban X Giants. Both clubs played Sunday games and billed them as colored championship series, and they concurrently barnstormed the midwestern states during the week. Creating this rivalry with the Cubans served to heighten the Unions' prestige in the latter half of the 1890s.[41]

In 1901, Leland split with Peters and formed the Chicago Union Giants. The breakup stemmed from several factors. One was that the Unions lost their lease on their home grounds on Thirty-Seventh Street and Butler Avenue, resulting in the club being relegated to a traveling team. Peters began to alienate many white semipro club managers with his questionable and bizarre behavior. For example, Peters canceled a three-game series with the Marquette club because he had inadvertently scheduled the Cuban X Giants on the same days. He made unusual statements in the press, like saying Marquette manager Jack Keary would get the "best players" in the city to defeat his Unions, who had played the previous day and had traveled all night. The rationale was that the Unions were not in the best condition to play because the players did not "get their proper rest." By breaking his contract with Keary, Peters irritated the Marquette manager and injured the Unions' credibility.[42]

To further exacerbate matters, both the Unions and the Union Giants competed for players and gate receipts with a third black club—the Columbia Giants. The Columbia Giants consisted of former members of the Page Fence Giants, who had defeated the Cuban X Giants for the colored championship in 1896. The Giants relocated to Chicago in 1898 under the management of Alvin H. Garrett and Julius Avendorph. The following year, the Giants challenged the Unions for the colored championship and defeated them in five straight games. They went on to challenge the Cuban X Giants for the World's Colored Championship but fell short, winning only four of eleven games. In 1901, the Columbia Giants negotiated an agreement with White Sox owner Charles Comiskey to play in his American League park when the White Sox were on the road. They finished that season playing a two-game series with the Union Giants, winning both games and proclaiming themselves the "colored champions of the world."

In 1902, Peters and Leland were engaged in another competition for players. The *Chicago Tribune* reported that Peters had signed several players who would make the Unions a formidable foe. He acquired pitcher and future black baseball magnate Andrew "Rube" Foster from Fort Worth, Texas. Foster was at the beginning of what would be a spectacular career. Peters also signed Andrew Campbell, who had played for the Cuban Giants the previous year, to serve as Foster's catcher. To round out his acquisitions, Peters signed Dave Wyatt as the Unions' new shortstop along with pitcher Clarence Lytle. Wyatt had played briefly for the Unions in 1898, and after his baseball career was over, he became a sportswriter for several black newspapers, most notably the Indianapolis *Freeman*. In 1901, Lytle pitched for the Chicago Union Giants.[43]

Peters apparently could not hold on to some of these new players. On June 23, the *Tribune* reported that Rube Foster pitched for the Union Giants against the Jefferson Grays and that Wyatt played center field. Foster struck out seven batters and hit a double in a 12-5 victory. He was equally impressive against the Columbia Giants, striking out ten batters and scattering five hits en route to a 7-3 win. Inducing players to jump their contracts only added to the bad blood that already existed between Leland and Peters. To add insult to injury, the players that made the Unions the top black club in the Midwest were now on the Union Giants' roster. Harry Buckner, William Binga, Robert Footes, and John Patterson made Leland's Union Giants an exceptional club.[44]

Both the Chicago Unions and Union Giants benefited from Chicago's semiprofessional infrastructure that had existed since the 1880s. In 1882, the Chicago Amateur Baseball Association (CABA) was formed. The CABA served essentially as a booking agent, securing leases on several playing grounds throughout the Windy City. It scheduled games for the various independent clubs and weekend leagues throughout the city. In Chicago, several amateur leagues were sponsored by business and industry, such as the Commercial League, the Mercantile League, and the Board of Trade League. League clubs in these circuits rarely played the independents due to their high caliber of play. In 1898, CABA collapsed, and from that time on, several amateur associations tried to take its place.[45]

One such organization was the Amateur Manager's Baseball League (AMBL). It was unclear when the AMBL was formed. On April 7, 1903, the *Chicago InterOcean* reported that William Peters was named treasurer of the league and George S. Cusack, former president of the CABA, became its vice president. Much like the CABA, the AMBL functioned as a booking agent. There is no evidence that the league was granted the authority to impose penalties or fines. There was also no indication of the league sanctioning a pennant race or sponsoring a championship series at the end of the season. Moreover, there was no evidence to suggest the Chicago Union Giants club was an AMBL member.[46]

The Columbia Giants evidently did not join the AMBL. For reasons unclear, the Giants moved to Algona, Iowa, and renamed themselves the Algona Brownies. In essence, the club relocated out of the largest baseball market in the Midwest and into a small rural town in northern Iowa. It evidently operated as a traveling team, barnstorming the Midwest for gate receipts. The 1903 season was the final one for a club that was originally the brainchild of Bud Fowler.[47]

In 1904, the AMBL found itself competing for semipro teams and leagues with a rival organization, the Intercity Baseball Association (IBA). On April 3, the *Chicago Inter Ocean* reported that 164 clubs had joined the organization, which aspired to increase its membership to 250 teams. Amateur loops like the Mercantile, Commercial, West End, and South Athletic Leagues affiliated with the IBA. Several teams outside the Windy City reportedly sought to join the organization. The IBA would offer a banner inscribed "Amateur Champions of the Intercity Baseball Association" to the best amateur team at the end of the season. It was unclear how the best team would be chosen, however.[48]

The IBA became involved in a dispute between Peters and Leland over the use of the name Union Giants. The *Chicago Tribune* reported that Peters had apparently retired from black baseball and handed control of the club over to Leland. However, this assertion appears to be inaccurate, given the fact that Peters fielded teams for the 1902 and 1903 seasons. A more reasonable explanation is that Peters did not field a club in 1904 because of his inability to hold onto top-level players like Rube Foster and Dave Wyatt. Nevertheless, Peters supposedly traveled to Springfield, Illinois, and incorporated a club under the name Union Giants. His actions resulted in the IBA prohibiting its member clubs from scheduling games with Peters's Union Giants. In addition, Leland supposedly sought restitution in the courts, and the IBA supported him.[49]

Apparently, Leland did not follow up on his court litigation. In 1905, he renamed his club the Leland Giants while Peters continued to call his club the Union Giants. Subsequently, William Peters never regained the prominence he had achieved in the mid and late 1890s. He seemed content to operate a traveling team, passing the hat to meet expenses. Peters would eventually turn the Union Giants over to his son, Frank, who would manage the club in the 1910s.[50]

The Leland Giants had its finest season in its young history. They played a reported 122 games and lost only 10. In one stretch they won 48 straight games. Leland constructed the same managerial configuration the Unions had used in the 1890s. He served as manager of the club and William Brown performed the duties of the team's traveling manager. Leland obtained a lease for a playing grounds on Seventy-Ninth Street and Auburn Avenue. On the field, the Giants were led by their captain and second baseman, Nate Harris, who had begun his baseball career in 1900 as a third baseman for the Smoky City Giants, a club organized by Bud Fowler. In 1901, Harris joined the Columbia Giants, and the following year he coached a football team at Prepatory [sic] College in Grand Rapids, Michigan. In 1903 and 1904, Harris traveled east and played for the Cuban Giants and the Philadelphia Giants before returning to Chicago to manage the Lelands. Charles "Joe" Green was the Lelands' catcher; he had begun his career in 1903 with the Union Giants. Green would later become owner of the Chicago Giants club, a charter member of the Negro National League in 1920. After playing one season with the Philadelphia Giants and the 1904 season with the Union Giants, William Binga returned to play third base for the Lelands. Billy Holland bolstered the Giants' pitching staff. Holland was a member of the Page Fence Giants, who defeated the Cuban X Giants for the colored championship.[51]

Amid this chaotic situation, Frank Leland emerged as the leading black baseball entrepreneur in the Midwest. Lack of evidence makes it difficult to determine the Leland Giants' ability to generate revenue. The fact that they played over 120 games in 1905 indicates that the potential to generate revenue was promising. The Lelands' successful 1905 season caught the attention of the Philadelphia Giants and the Cuban X Giants, both of whom would barnstorm the Midwest during the 1906 season. Leland would also benefit from the successful efforts of several entrepreneurs to form a semiprofessional league.

From 1902 to 1905, black baseball experienced what could best be described as a reshuffling period. Through the efforts of Sol White, H. Walter Schlichter, and Harry Smith, the Philadelphia Giants emerged as the premier black baseball club in the East. The Cuban X Giants' management team of E. B. Lamar and Clarence Williams made inroads into Cuba, creating a black baseball–Cuban barnstorming network. The chaotic state of baseball in Chicago resulted in Frank Leland emerging as the leading black baseball entrepreneur in the Midwest. These black baseball entrepreneurs perpetuated the business practices developed by their predecessors of the late nineteenth century. They developed and sustained talented teams over a period of time and secured suitable playing facilities to build a fan base. They followed the fundamental strategy of going where the money was and creating a demand for their clubs in several locales. Also, they developed rivalries with at least three or four clubs throughout the season. As the 1906 season approached, black baseball would enter a period of unprecedented growth and expansion.

2

Black Professional Baseball's Growth and Expansion, 1906–1907

Beginning in 1906, black professional baseball experienced tremendous growth and expansion. Several black clubs emerged in the East to challenge established teams like the Philadelphia Giants and Cuban X Giants for players and gate receipts. Many of these new teams, like the Brooklyn Royal Giants, were run by African American entrepreneurs who epitomized the new black middle class that arose in the early twentieth century. This black business and professional class left its mark in the development of business ventures, institutions, and organizational politics. This growth spurt of eastern black baseball clubs led to the creation of the National Association of Colored Baseball Clubs of the United States and Cuba (NACBC). While this new organization was supposedly modeled after the white Major Leagues, it did not operate in the traditional sense of competing for a pennant and sponsoring a season-ending championship series. Rather, the primary focus of the NACBC was to tighten control over the player force, maintain the teams' symbiotic business relationship with white semiprofessional teams, gain access to the better parks to generate more gate receipts, and develop extended barnstorming tours nationally and internationally. The NACBC set out to accomplish this by concentrating power in the hands of a few individuals and gaining control of decision-making process.

The Leland Giants, on the other hand, experienced a dismal 1906 season, and Frank Leland made several decisions to improve his ball club the following year. Leland lost several of his players to eastern black clubs and, in 1907, he retaliated by signing Rube Foster away from the Philadelphia Giants. Foster lured several black players from the East to Chicago and transformed the Leland Giants into a top-notch black club.

Simultaneously, Leland made an alliance with several members of Chicago's new black leadership and formed the Leland Giants Baseball and Amusement Association (LGBBA). The LGBBA was an enterprise designed to cater to Chicago's growing black consumer market and concurrently to maintain the Giants' symbiotic business relationship with white semipros. Leland also attempted to expand his influence in the Midwest by organizing a National Colored League of Professional Ball Clubs. While the proposed baseball league ended in failure, its demise did in no way diminish the LGBBA's significant progress within a short period of time.

The growth of black baseball in the early twentieth century coincided with the dramatic change in patterns of urban life. The growing population alone was staggering, as the total number of inhabitants in the United States expanded from 75 million in 1900 to 100 million during World War I. The urban city became the focus of the new America. Rural villages became small towns. Towns and trading centers grew into medium-sized cities like Minneapolis, Cleveland, Pittsburgh, and Detroit. In the urban-industrial heartland of the Northeast–North Central region, an entirely new type of city emerged: the modern industrial metropolis.[1]

Technological innovations and industrial expansion also contributed to this era of dramatic change. Instead of walking to work, people could now travel by horse car and beginning in the 1890s by electric streetcar. These new modes of transportation made possible the emerging exodus to the suburbs or to outlying areas of the city, allowing urban populations to arrange themselves by racial, ethnic, or socioeconomic groups. Furthermore, the expansion and diversification of large industries resulted in a more rigid system of zoning regulations than had existed before. These factors were instrumental in the emergence of huge urban centers linked by an interconnection of economic relationships but divided into numerous commercial, industrial, and residential districts.

It was within this context that John W. Connor formed the Brooklyn Royal Giants. Organized in 1904, the Royal Giants club was the first in New York that was exclusively black owned and operated since the late 1880s. The Royal Giants began their inaugural season playing games primarily on the weekends. Connor represented the new black leadership that emerged in the early twentieth century that became involved in the management and ownership of black baseball teams. Connor was born in 1878 in Portsmouth, Virginia, and after spending a short time in school, he ran off and joined the United States Navy and served in the Spanish-American War. Unlike Sol White or Clarence Williams, Connor was not a former ballplayer. He migrated to Harlem after the war and entered the restaurant business. Connor was one of the first African Americans to own and operate a nightclub in Harlem, Connor's Inn. He owned a restaurant called the Royal Café and was also affiliated with several fraternal lodges, including the Brooklyn lodge of Elks, the Kapaganda lodge of Masons, and the Odd Fellows.[2]

Connor personified the new black middle class that began to emerge in the early twentieth century. Between 1890 and 1920, the imposition of segregation and intensification of discrimination were pivotal in the creation of a petit bourgeoisie of professionals and businessmen relying primarily on the black masses for their livelihood. They were primarily self-made men of humble origins, the majority of them darker-skinned than the old upper class. This meant they were less likely to be descendents of antebellum house slaves or from free people of color. The new leaders rarely articulated a racial ideology like the old elite, and many of them shunned racial activities altogether. These men left their imprint not by writing or speaking, but in business ventures, institutions, and organizational politics. To the extent to which they were involved in the ideological battles of their era, they leaned towards Booker T. Washington's philosophy of self-help and economic independence. However, the Tuskegee ideology did not determine their actions. It merely validated what they were already doing. The new black elite formed an ambitious and aggressive middle class, and the more successful among them achieved upper-class status before the First World War.[3]

It was no coincidence that black entrepreneurs within the ranks of the new black middle class would be attracted to the business of baseball. Black radical economist Abram L. Harris found that African American businesses fell primarily within four main categories: (1) amusement and recreation enterprises, (2) real estate, (3) retail trade, and (4) personal service. One reason recreation and amusement enterprises were attractive was that the funds demanded to start such an endeavor were both short and long term in character. In other words, they did not require a substantial financial investment, and if they were successfully managed could yield a high return. Black baseball exemplified the gradual progression in the growth of black businesses in the early twentieth century. Vishnu V. Oak found that black businesses increased in number from 40,445 in 1900 to 74,424 in 1920. In that period banks had increased from 4 to 51, undertakers from 450 to 1,000, and retail merchants from 10,000 to 25,000. In New York, by 1910 there were more African American printing companies, whereas only two had existed in 1899. The number of real estate companies increased from 4 in 1899 to 16 in 1910.[4]

Although his nightclub and restaurant relied chiefly on black patronage, John Connor operated his Royal Giants like previous black baseball magnates—within the parameters of a biracial institutional structure. He ran the Royal Giants around the familiar concepts of going where the money was and expanding the club's market potential to several locales. The Royal Giants began as a local club, playing most of its games in New York and New Jersey. In the first of their games reported in the press, the Royal Giants defeated the Elm Field Club in Jersey City, 13-9. In 1905, the Royals challenged the Philadelphia Giants for the colored championship, losing to the Quaker club in three games.[5]

In 1906, Connor secured the services of Grant "Home Run" Johnson to manage the Royal Giants, and the club embarked upon its first midwestern barnstorming tour. Prior to becoming the Royals' manager, Johnson was a member of the Philadelphia Giants. Connor and Johnson assembled a solid ball club, signing former Philadelphia Giant Andrew "Jap" Payne to play left field. They lured Billy Holland from the Leland Giants to pitch and play third base. Gus James, a solid hitter and fielder, was the Royals' second baseman. Al Robinson played first base, entertaining the fans with his "humorous catching." The pitching staff was bolstered by Jack Emery and Lefty "Pop" Andrews.

On May 7, the *Chicago Tribune* reported a three-team doubleheader between the Royal Giants, Leland Giants, and Chicago Union Giants at Auburn Park. The first game, between the Royals and Union Giants, featured the strong pitching of Jack Emery, who gave up five hits in a 2-0 Royals win. The second game, with the Royals pitted against the Lelands, was billed as a colored championship contest. The Lelands took a 2-0 lead into the seventh inning before the Royals scored two in the seventh and one in the ninth to win, 3-2.[6]

During the 1906 season, the Brooklyn Royal Giants established a rivalry with the Philadelphia Giants. On May 31, Lefty Andrews and Rube Foster engaged in a pitchers' battle that ended in a 1-1 tie. Four days later, the clubs faced each other in Trenton, New Jersey. The game was tied at four before Philadelphia scored three runs in the ninth inning and won, 7-4. Although the Philadelphia Giants held the upper hand in their rivalry against the Royal Giants, the series, in conjunction with their midwestern barnstorming tour, exemplified the progress Connor's club had made in a short time.[7]

The emergence of the Brooklyn Royal Giants in New York occurred simultaneously with the efforts of white semiprofessional teams to form leagues and associations. The rise of white semiprofessional leagues and associations illustrated the impact of the changing attitude of business toward baseball. Industrial supervisors responded to their workers' need to improve the quality of their lives not by altering the industrial system, but through approved channels outside the workplace or in conjunction with it. Business accomplished this through what became known as welfare capitalism, an attempt to improved morale and increase productivity by adding recreation and other programs and services to the workday. Both industrial and business baseball grew as a part of a paternalistic and manipulative system of recreation designed as a means of social control. The motive of business was to further its self-interest by increasing production; reducing employee turnover; and above all, eliminating unions and avoiding strikes.[8]

In the 1890s, baseball play among workers changed from self-generated play to play generated by company-sponsored teams. At the same time, there was a shift from rural life to industrial life, where factories and neighborhoods replaced extended families as the centers of allegiance. This created the potential to form a new locus of a worker's social life, which meant the possibility of organizing factory or neighborhood baseball teams. By 1900, department stores, hotels, insurance companies, newspapers, railroads, mills, and other small businesses began sponsoring baseball teams and leagues, with games often scheduled during lunchtime or other nonworking hours.

Two other factors contributed to the rise of semipro leagues and associations. The first was the impact of new technology that was changing the face of urban cities. Newly built trolley lines linking towns and neighborhoods heightened league formation in the city and the suburbs. In 1905, for example, a plethora of independent clubs emerged in Philadelphia that included Morrow, Elmwood F. C., Haddington, and the Philadelphia Professionals. A semiprofessional league that included each police precinct in the Quaker City operated at this time.[9]

The impact of the Playground Movement represented the second additional factor influencing the development of semipro leagues and associations. Throughout the Progressive Era, municipal support for baseball grew. City governments began to view organized recreation and sports as a means to curb juvenile delinquency and as a way of "Americanizing" immigrant children. The increasing number of public parks and playgrounds available for ball playing compensated for the rapidly declining sandlots victimized by subdivision.[10]

In 1906, approximately one hundred clubs in New York and New Jersey formed the Intercity Association (IA). The formation of the IA demonstrated the importance of Sunday ball for semipro clubs. Before the Blue Laws in those states were abolished in 1919, professional ball clubs were forbidden to schedule games on Sunday. To circumvent these laws, it was customary for professional and semiprofessional clubs not to sell tickets of admission to games. Instead, they admitted fans free if they purchased programs or magazines for fifty or seventy-five cents or if they volunteered a "donation." Baseball magnates generally received cooperation from the police, who rarely convicted anyone tried in its courts.[11]

F. D. Baldwin, the Association's first president, had indicated the previous year that semipro ball had deteriorated to such a state of chaos that "playing would entirely cease on Sundays." On March 26, 1905, for example, the Cuban X Giants faced the Cedars at Bronx Oval in Brooklyn. The *New York Times* reported that four players were arrested and the game was stopped to the dissatisfaction of two thousand spectators. The contest was stopped because of a ruling the previous year that stated a game, "although not professional, but played on Sunday, which had been previously advertised, was a violation of the Sunday law."

Thus, the IA's primary goal was to make the semipro games respectable so Sunday ball could continue. To accomplish this, Baldwin stated three objectives: (1) secure better playing facilities, (2) induce Park Commissioners to lay out diamonds in various parks, and (3) develop better relations with police authorities regarding Sunday games. For a club to become eligible for entry into the IA, a team had to be "regularly organized, officered, and uniformed."[12]

The formation of the Intercity Association in 1906 created an opportunity for an entrepreneur to create a lucrative enterprise by booking semiprofessional games. The key to the autonomy of booking agents was their ability to gain control of several ballparks. This control enabled them to schedule clubs they deemed the most attractive to the public and that could also generate the most revenue. The booking agent could also determine which clubs got the better dates—primarily Sundays or holidays—and charge a 10 percent fee for their services. Because of this control over several parks, booking agents could virtually make or break a semipro club by either keeping a club very busy or very idle. Because of this control of several parks, most black and white semipro clubs were relegated to traveling status, making it almost impossible for a local owner to compete on equal terms against the booking agent.

In New York, Nathaniel Colvin (Nat) Strong saw the opportunity to create this type of lucrative enterprise. Strong was born on January 4, 1874, in New York City. He attended the College of the City of New York and got his start in baseball by becoming part owner of the Bushwicks Baseball Club. Strong was a sporting goods salesman by trade, and one of his first successful teams was the Murray Hills club, which played the Philadelphia Giants in 1903. Strong owned the Ridgewoods baseball club, and he was also a member of the New York Athletic

Club. In March 1907, Strong succeeded F. D. Baldwin as president of the Intercity Association.[13]

Both scholars and contemporaries recognized Nat Strong as the booking power in New York. What is often not addressed, however, is how this relatively small-time operator gained so much autonomy. Part of the answer lies in the connection between professional baseball and New York politics in the early twentieth century. No such control over several parks in New York could have possibly occurred without some political affiliation with Tammany Hall. This citywide political machine had been intimately involved in local baseball affairs since the late 1860s. Andrew Freedman, former owner of the National League's New York Giants from 1895 to 1901 and a rising young realtor, had been a Tammanyite since 1881. He was also a close friend of Richard Croker, the machine's political boss. Throughout the 1900s, Freedman controlled most of the suitable locations for baseball fields through leases or options. If a ball club had managed to secure a good lot, Freedman would use his political clout to run streets through the property or disrupt its transit facilities. Clearly, Strong could not have operated in New York without some kind of alliance with Freedman and the Tammany machine. Moreover, American League president Ban Johnson made concessions to the Tammany machine by placing one of its members as the owner of the New York Highlanders franchise so the Highlanders could place a league club in Gotham. Therefore, it is likely that Strong needed to make some concessions, too.[14]

A second factor linking Strong to Tammany Hall was tied to the American League's New York Highlanders, later the Yankees. Throughout the prewar era, Strong booked several black baseball games in the Highlanders' home park. Frank J. Farrell, a big-time gambler, and William Devery, a former police chief, owned the Highlanders, and both men had strong Tammany Hall connections. Strong clearly had no control over this American League park. This suggests that he had created several political alliances with the Tammany machine to enable him to gain his autonomy over several parks in the prewar years. No such autonomy could have possibly been attained without such connections. Moreover, both black and white semiprofessional clubs would have to deal with Strong to have games scheduled at the best parks and to secure the best playing dates so they could maintain some semblance of profitability.[15]

As president of the Intercity Association, Nat Strong began his twenty-eight-year reign as the booking power in New York. His primary focus was on white semiprofessional baseball. However, the ambitions of Sol White and H. Walter Schlichter in Philadelphia and John Connor in Brooklyn to expand their clubs' market potential led to Strong's becoming involved in scheduling black baseball games as well. An opportunity to expand his booking control internationally also emerged when several Cuban baseball clubs began to barnstorm the United States. Strong's initial involvement in black baseball resulted from the formation by Philadelphia entrepreneurs of an international league of black and Cuban teams.

League Formation and the Rise of a "National" Organization

In 1906 several entrepreneurs made efforts to organize black and Cuban baseball clubs into leagues and associations. These attempts were in response to the emergence of several black baseball clubs that were organized throughout the year. It also marked the start of efforts by magnates to centralize power by gaining control of the decision-making process regarding the scheduling of semipro games, obtaining access to the best ballparks to generate gate receipts, and gaining a hegemony over their player force.

The 1906 season witnessed a virtual explosion of independent black baseball teams in New York, New Jersey, and Pennsylvania and within a hundred-mile radius of those states. Several black clubs emerged, including the Quaker Giants of New York, Wilmington Giants, New York Giants, Baltimore Giants of Newark, and Keystone Giants of Philadelphia. Abel Linares's tours of the United States resulted in several Cuban clubs barnstorming the nation for gate receipts. According to Sol White, "Of the many Cuban teams that have visited America, the strongest was the Cuban Stars of Santiago de Cuba. They were organized in 1905 and composed of all Cuban players. Their American manager is Manuel Camps of Brooklyn, N. Y." These clubs—along with the established black clubs like the Philadelphia Giants, the Genuine Cuban Giants, the Cuban X Giants, and the Brooklyn Royal Giants—became the catalysts for the formation of the International League of Colored Baseball Clubs in America and Cuba (ILBCAC).[16]

William Freihoffer and John O'Rourke formed the ILBCAC. An advertisement in Sol White's *History of Colored Baseball* indicated that Freihoffer owned a bakery. In 1902, O'Rourke's Cosmopolitan club was the same team that played the Philadelphia Giants in that forgettable night game. Press reports at the time suggested that ILBCAC headquarters resided in Philadelphia. According to the Philadelphia *Item*, several league games were scheduled on the playing grounds of the National League Phillies and the American League Athletics. The ILBCAC consisted of six clubs: the Cuban X Giants, Philadelphia Quaker Giants, Cuban Stars, Havana Stars of Cuba, Philadelphia Professionals, and Riverton Palmyra. The league was culturally diverse, consisting of two black, two Cuban, and two white teams. These semipro clubs continued to play other independent teams and league games. The winner of the ILBCAC pennant received a championship cup donated by Freihoffer.[17]

On July 24, 1906, the *Item* reported that the Philadelphia Giants and the Wilmington Giants had replaced the Cuban Stars and the Philadelphia Quaker Giants. The change was in response to the Stars' and the Quaker Giants' failure to appear for scheduled league games. The Philadelphia Giants and Wilmington Giants assumed the expelled clubs' places in the standings and their league schedules.[18]

The Philadelphia Giants' entry into the ILBCAC coincided with another spectacular season for the club. In April, the Giants played Connie Mack's team in Atlantic City, New Jersey. Mack's team featured three players who were members of the American League's Athletics: pitcher Bill Bartley, outfielder Harry Armbruster, and catcher Jim Byrnes. Bartley took a 12-8 lead into the eighth inning when the Giants erupted for five runs in the top of the frame and took a one-run lead into the ninth inning. Mack's team tied the score in the bottom of ninth before the game was stopped because of darkness.

Several exhibition games were scheduled with clubs from the Tri-State League, a low-level minor league. This Pennsylvania-based circuit consisted of teams from Harrisburg, Johnstown, Lancaster, Altoona, York, and Williamsport. On April 17, a total of 966 fans watched the Giants lose to Harrisburg, 6-2. The Quaker club lost a three-game series against Altoona then but rebounded with a victory over the Williamsport club.[19]

In May, the Giants began their first extended barnstorming tour, traveling through the states of Illinois, Ohio, and western Pennsylvania. The tour occurred simultaneously with the rise of several top white semipro clubs in Chicago. The Gunthers, Logan Squares, and Jake Stahl's South Chicagos formed the nucleus of the resurgent semipro infrastructure in the Windy City. Undoubtedly, the Leland Giants' excellent 1905 season encouraged the Philadelphia Giants to travel to Chicago. On May 19, the Giants suffered a tough defeat at the hands of Jimmy Callahan's Logan Squares. The game was tied at three going into the tenth inning, when the Squares scored a run in the top of the frame to win the game. The following day, the Giants played a doubleheader against both the Union Giants and the Leland Giants. The first game was a hard-hitting affair, with the Union Giants took an 8-0 lead in the first inning. The Quakers rallied with four runs in the seventh inning and six runs in the eighth to win, 10-8. The second game was effectively over in the third inning, when the Philadelphia Giants scored six runs. With Rube Foster holding the Lelands to three hits, his team won, 9-1. In Dennison, Ohio, the Philadelphia club won 9-2, as Emmett Bowman held the locals to only four hits.[20]

Upon their return to the East, the Philadelphia Giants played the Cuban X Giants for the World's Colored Championship. Concurrently, both clubs played for the Freihoffer Cup to determine the winner of the ILBCAC pennant. On August 19, the *Item* reported the Cubans were tied with the Giants for first place, each having a 6-1 record. On September 2, the Giants defeated the Cubans and won the Freihoffer Cup. Three days later, the Giants played the Cubans for the colored championship. The Giants scored three runs in the top of the ninth inning and defeated the Cuban X Giants, 5-3, successfully defending their colored championship.[21]

The Philadelphia Giants compiled an impressive 108-31-6 record. H. Walter Schlichter issued a challenge to Major League teams, calling for a best two-out-of-three game series to determine "who can play baseball the best—the white or black American." The Philadelphia Athletics answered the challenge. Connie Mack's Athletics had experienced a dismal season, finishing in fourth place in the American League. In the first game, going into the ninth inning the Athletics led 5-1 behind the excellent pitching of Eddie Plank. The Giants rallied with three runs in the bottom of the ninth before bowing in defeat, 5-4. In the second game, the Giants were no match for the eccentric Rube Waddell. He pitched a two-hit shutout en route to a 5-0 win. Despite this disappointing series loss, the Philadelphia Giants had had a spectacular season.[22]

On October 22, 1906, the National Association of Colored Baseball Clubs of the United States and Cuba (NACBC) was formed in Brooklyn, New York. The *Item* reported the Association would be modeled after the American and National Leagues of Major League baseball. The NACBC elected the following officers: H. Walter Schlichter, president; John Connor, vice president; J. M. Bright, treasurer; and Nat Strong, secretary and business manager. Manuel Camps and E. B. Lamar were placed on the Board of Trustees, along with Schlichter. The organization included five of the top black baseball teams in the East: the Philadelphia Giants, Cuban X Giants, Brooklyn Royal Giants, Cuban Giants, and Cuban Stars. The NACBC's broad objective was to ensure "the perpetuation of colored baseball" by fostering "absolute public confidence in its integrity and methods and maintaining a high standard of skill and sportsmanship in its players." The Association tried to safeguard "the property rights of those engaged in colored baseball as a business, without sacrificing the spirit of competition in the conduct of the game." Finally, the NACBC sought to promote "the welfare of colored ballplayers as a class by perfecting them in their profession and enabling them to secure adequate compensation and expertness."[23]

Forming the NACBC was supposedly in response to the "financial results of the 1906 season." Every black baseball club owner in the East reportedly lost money because of high player salaries and "the keen competition among the various clubs." In other words, club managers competed against each other for the best players, resulting in increased salaries that diminished revenues. Thus, the organization attempted to place the black game on a sound economic footing and prevent players from jumping from one club to another, which had apparently became rampant during the 1906 season. The NACBC was also organized to protect member clubs "from unscrupulous and unreliable managers of independent clubs who engage the colored clubs and unceremoniously cancel the dates at the last moment if so inclined." The new association intended to "cut out" clubs that engaged in such practices.[24]

The name chosen by the group for the new organization—National Association of Colored Baseball Clubs of the United States and Cuba—was highly significant. Due to the emergence of black and Cuban clubs in the mid-1900s, NACBC organizers endeavored to protect their investment by introducing certain collusive practices to tighten control over black players by imposing salary limits and denying bookings to uncooperative teams or managers. Using the white Major Leagues as their model, these entrepreneurs tried to establish a monopoly organization, based on what can best be described as the competitor-partner model. Like any other businessmen, the baseball owners were interested in turning a profit. Club owners had to market their product successfully, and their teams had to approximate each other in skill to accomplish that outcome. Contests have to be sufficiently interesting to attract fans; people would hardly pay to see a champion Boston Red Sox club play a high school team. This is why no single owner could sell the product by himself. He had to market in cooperation with his fellow owners. Within this context, black baseball club managers were not only competitors but also partners who had to cooperate with each other to a much greater degree than in more conventional enterprises.[25]

Several factors were essential for NACBC organizers to be able to form their organization within the parameters of the competitor-partner model. First, these club managers had to gain a hegemony over the black baseball player force by acquiring and keeping the best players. Securing the best playing facilities that provided easy access for fans and had a seating capacity substantial enough to generate gate receipts was vital to the success of the enterprise. The owners would have to minimize competition among themselves with regard to bidding for talented players to keep salaries at a reasonable level and maximize revenues. Finally, centralizing the decision-making process into the hands of a few individuals would, theoretically, result in the NACBC gaining tighter control over the potentially growing industry of black professional baseball.

The surplus of black baseball teams in the East resulted in competition among black baseball managers to secure the best playing talent. The success of teams like the Philadelphia Giants and the Cuban X Giants was contingent upon a manager's ability to keep a nucleus of talented players together for a long period of time. As John Henry Lloyd, often referred to as the black Honus Wagner, later said, "Where the money was, that's where I was." In his *History of Colored Baseball*, Sol White contributed an entire section highlighting the obstacles confronted in the player-manager relationship. He lamented that "with twelve or fourteen men under his command, twelve or fourteen different minds and dispositions to control and [center] on the intricate points of play, with no National League of [baseball] clubs behind the rules and regulations, with the many complaints and threats of quitting ringing in his ears day after day, he passes many sleepless nights and will often ask for that 'Patience he needs.'" Such remarks reinforced the call for the formation of the NACBC and the introduction of restrictive practices designed to foster the development of a monopoly organization. Undoubtedly, White, Connor, and Lamar paid higher salaries to keep their talented teams together, and with this investment they searched for ways to protect it. The higher salaries could possibly explain why the *Item* reported that the majority of club owners lost money during the 1906 season.[26]

The growth of black baseball resulted in NACBC organizers endeavoring to apply certain restrictive practices to control consumer markets and impose salary restrictions. The fact that they used the Major

Leagues as the model to form their organization suggests they wanted to gain a hegemony over the black baseball business. In the following years, NACBC organizers would seek to expand their market potential by establishing barnstorming networks to the Midwest and Cuba. The resurgence of black baseball in Chicago and the plethora of Cuban teams made this ambition plausible.

THE LELAND GIANTS BASEBALL AND AMUSEMENT ASSOCIATION

The Leland Giants did not repeat their spectacular performance of the 1905 season. A significant turnover in their player force resulted in a mediocre year for Frank Leland's Giants. Simultaneously, a restructuring of Chicago's semiprofessional infrastructure occurred, leading the Giants to join the newly formed Park Owners Association (POA). Leland strengthened his team by luring Rube Foster away from the Philadelphia Giants to manage the club and at the same time creating civic ties with black Chicago's emerging new leadership. By the end of the 1907 season, the Leland Giants would be merged into a recreation enterprise—the Leland Giants Baseball and Amusement Association—and Frank Leland would make his only attempt to form a black professional league.

Before the start of the semipro season, the Leland Giants played a benefit game to raise funds for the victims of the 1906 San Francisco earthquake. On April 24, the *Chicago Tribune* reported that the Intercity Baseball Association had scheduled several benefit games and that the gross receipts would be donated to the California relief fund. The seismic earthquake, which was felt from southern Oregon to south of Los Angeles and as far inland as central Nevada, resulted in an estimated seven hundred deaths in and around the San Francisco Bay area. The Lelands played Jack Keary's Marquettes at the White Sox's American League park and donated their receipts to the earthquake relief fund.[27]

The Leland Giants' 1906 season was a dismal one. Of the thirty-three games reported in the press, the Giants won only fourteen. A significant turnover in the Lelands' player force appears to have been the reason for the team's unspectacular year. Leland lost captain Nate Harris, third baseman William Binga, and pitchers Billy Holland and Will Horn. Although the team acquired talented players like second baseman Danger Talbert, catcher Bruce Petway, and pitcher Bill Gatewood, the Lelands played poorly.[28]

The one bright spot of the 1906 season was the Lelands' return engagement with the Cuban X Giants, billed as a Colored Championship Series. The first game was a hard-hitting affair, with the Cubans taking a 10-0 lead into the sixth inning. The Lelands rebounded with two runs in the sixth, three in the seventh, and four in the ninth before bowing in defeat, 11-9. The second game was played in Dekalb, Illinois, and the game was tied at three before the Lelands scored one run in the ninth inning to win, 4-3. In the final game, the Lelands took an 8-1 lead into the sixth inning before the Cubans rallied with three runs in the bottom of the sixth and three in the seventh before losing, 8-7. The Leland Giants got some satisfaction in avenging their 1904 series defeat at the hands of the New York team.[29]

Prior to the Cuban X Giants series, the Leland Giants played the Philadelphia Giants and the Brooklyn Royal Giants. It appears that these series were costly for Leland because several of his former players had ended up on the rosters of these clubs. Captain Nate Harris was a member of the Philadelphia Giants and Billy Holland played third base for the Royal Giants. By the latter half of the season, Leland had lost pitcher Bill Gatewood and outfielder Sherman Barton to the Cuban X Giants. In an ironic turn of events, these eastern black clubs would form an organization in 1906 designed to prevent players from jumping from one club to another at the end of the season. This could possibly explain why the Leland Giants performed poorly during the 1906 season.

White semipros in Chicago evidently had trouble with players jumping from one team to another. On September 27, 1906, the *Chicago Tribune* reported that several club owners of the leading small parks would form an organization with the purpose of imposing salary limits. These clubs would reserve the current players on their rosters until April 1, 1907, rather than give them their release, which had been the standard practice. Each club would post one thousand dollars "to insure good faith," and they would not play any traveling teams the following season. The action taken by these teams were reportedly independent of the Intercity Baseball Association, which was expected to oppose the new organization.[30]

The new organization appeared to be the Park Owners Association. The POA consisted of ten teams: Anson's Colts, Artesians, Gunthers, Lawndales, Leland Giants, Logan Squares, Normals, Rogers Park, South Chicagos, and West Ends. These clubs represented the top independents in the Windy City. The Gunthers were organized in 1899 and were destined to become one of the most prominent semipro clubs in Chicago. Charles F. Gunther, a businessman, was serving as an alderman of the Second Ward in Chicago at the time of the club's organization. By 1904, the Gunthers were competing against the top clubs of the city. On June 13 of that year, the *Tribune* reported the Gunthers defeated the Chicago Union Giants, 8-7, by scoring six runs in the eighth inning.[31]

In 1903 Jimmy Callahan formed the Logan Squares. A Massachusetts native born on March 18, 1874, James Joseph Callahan possessed exceptional athletic ability, excelling at the plate and on the mound. He began his baseball career playing semipro ball on the weekends and concurrently working as an apprentice for a plumber. In 1894 Callahan was signed by the Philadelphia Phillies but was given his unconditional release at the end of the season. The following year he played for Springfield in the Eastern League, winning thirty-two games and batting .321. In 1897, Callahan was drafted by Kansas City in Ban Johnson's Western League, and in the following season, he played for Cap Anson's Chicago White Stockings. In 1903, Callahan managed the American League Chicago White Sox, leading them to a seventh place finish. He was replaced by Fielder Jones midway into the 1904 season after compiling an overall 83-95 won-lost record in 1903–1904. In 1906, the Squares' lineup included several semipro and Major League players like Jack McCarthy, Jimmy Ryan, Fred Schmidt, and "Long" Tom Hughes. Callahan also secured enough capital to build a new enclosed ballpark at the corner of Diversey and Milwaukee on the North Side. The same year his team played exhibition games against barnstorming teams composed of Cubs and White Sox players and won both games.[32]

Two other clubs emerged that would be instrumental in the formation of the POA. In 1907, Jake Stahl formed the South Chicagos. A versatile athlete from the outset, Stahl was a catcher on the University of Illinois baseball team, and he also played football. He began his Major League career in 1903 as a backup catcher and outfielder for the Boston Red Sox. In 1905 and 1906, Stahl was a player-manager for the American League's Washington Senators, leading the club to consecutive seventh place finishes and compiling an unimpressive combined 119-182 won-lost record. Stahl secured a lease to play home games at South Chicago Park. Former Major League star Adrian Constantine "Cap" Anson formed Anson's Colts. Out of baseball since 1898, Anson was pressured out of his job as the city clerk of Chicago during an employee payroll scandal. In 1907, he formed the club and, after watching from the bench the first season, he returned to the field the following year at age fifty-seven.[33]

As the 1907 season approached, Chicago's semiprofessional baseball infrastructure was significantly altered. Both the Intercity Baseball Association and the Amateur Managers Baseball League served as the official schedulers of weekend semiprofessional games. Semipro clubs that either owned or leased their own parks used either the IBA or the AMBL to publicize the games they booked for a particular weekend. Teams without ballparks scheduled their games through the Traveling Managers Association, which would then submit these games to either the IBA or AMBL for publication. Weekend leagues like the Lake Shore League, the Columbia League, or the Royal League also used the IBA to announce upcoming games. Finally, the AMBL created a commission to serve as an arbitrator for disputes among semipro teams or leagues.

While the POA prepared for its first season, Frank Leland made efforts to strengthen his ball club. His attempt to rebound from the dismal 1906 season occurred simultaneously with the Philadelphia Giants losing several of its key players. Despite their phenomenal success on the field, several Giants players were unhappy with the salaries they made. According to Rube Foster, the Giants' monthly payroll was approximately $850 per month. Although the Giants played on a full-time basis, Foster pointed out that the team had trouble meeting its monthly payroll, saying "The owner of the Philadelphia Giants could get but $100 for a game" in New York City.[34]

Most of Foster's assessment, however, appears to have been self-serving. Using the 1905 estimates of average attendance for Sunday games in New York (4,875), one game could amass a gross revenue of $1,219, with the Giants receiving $609.38. After subtracting the 10 percent booking fee ($122), the Giants realized a profit of $487.38. Average attendance for weekday games was roughly four hundred fans, generating an additional $250. The Giants' weekly revenue would be $737.38, and their monthly take roughly $2,949.52. The average monthly salary for fifteen players was sixty dollars, making their monthly payroll $900. Undoubtedly, star players like Foster received more, and the estimates do not reflect added expenses like travel, accommodations, park rental, and equipment purchases. Yet the estimates reveal that the Philadelphia Giants did exhibit an ability to generate enough revenue to meet their monthly payroll.[35]

A more reasonable explanation for the departure of players from the Philadelphia team would be the salary limits the NACBC sought to impose and Rube Foster's ambition to become a player-manager. In addition to lowering player salaries, the NACBC would allow players only two meals at fifteen cents a day. Also, the players would have to furnish their own uniforms. These imposed limits were in response to NACBC clubs' supposed loss of money during the 1906 season. Much of this ostensible loss was because players like Bill Gatewood and Billy Holland were induced to leave the Leland Giants and join the Cuban X Giants and Brooklyn Royal Giants, respectively. These players may not have received the higher salaries promised to them, which possibly led to some player unrest. In any event, Foster, along with Harry Moore, Pete Booker, and Nate Harris left the Quaker club and traveled to Chicago. Brooklyn Royal Giants shortstop George Wright also jumped ship and headed for the Windy City.[36]

Rube Foster was primarily responsible for the Leland Giants' rise to prominence. His ascendancy as both their player-manager and booking agent marked the start of his dominance of black baseball in the Midwest. Foster was born in Calvert, Texas, in 1879, the son of a presiding elder of Calvert's Methodist Church. Devoutly religious, Foster neither drank nor allowed anyone to consume spirits in his household, but he otherwise tolerated it from others. Foster exhibited his organizational skills at a young age, operating a baseball team while in grade school. He left school in the eighth grade to pursue a career in baseball. By 1897, Foster was pitching for the Waco Yellow Jackets, a traveling team that toured Texas and the bordering states. In the spring of 1902, William Peters invited him to join the Chicago Unions, but as he sent no travel money, Foster remained in Texas. Simultaneously, Leland invited Foster to join the Chicago Union Giants, initiating a stormy relationship between the two men. By midspring, Foster had quit the Union Giants to join a white semipro team in Michigan. When its season ended, he headed east to play for the Cuban X Giants. From 1904 to 1906, Foster played for the Philadelphia Giants and was instrumental in the team's phenomenal success. Before the start of the 1907 season, Foster traveled to Cuba to play for the Fe club. Upon his return to the US, he led a players' revolt that resulted in four players leaving the Giants.[37]

Frank Leland restructured the Leland Giants' management team when, to keep Foster on the club, he offered a pay increase, which Foster accepted. Leland served as the team's general manager, but due to his failing health and his responsibilities as the newly elected Cook County commissioner, he allowed Foster to assume control of booking Giants' games. From that time on, Foster established a business arrangement whereby either gate receipts would be divided in half or he would ensure a substantial guarantee to attract the top teams.

Foster's first act as field manager was to release the players of the previous year despite Leland's opposition. It was obvious that the Lelands' new manager wanted his own players, as he had just brought five players from the East to serve as the club's nucleus. Given the Lelands' poor 1906 season, the move was understandable. Foster did, however, re-sign Danger Talbert from the previous year to play third base. Nicknamed "Old Reliable," Talbert was considered one of the best defensive third baseman in the opening decade of the twentieth century. In addition to bringing Harry Moore, Nate Harris, Pete Booker, and George Wright from the East, Foster also signed pitchers Bill Gatewood and Walter Ball from the Cuban X Giants and the Quaker Giants respectively. Finally, Foster signed Jap Payne from the Brooklyn Royal Giants to play center field and Haywood Rose to serve as the backup catcher. The club Foster assembled in his first year as player-manager was impressive.[38]

In the 1907 season, Rube Foster began perfecting the barnstorming schedule that would be his trademark for the next decade. On February 20, the Indianapolis *Freeman* reported the Leland Giants would embark on a spring training tour. The proposed tour was in response to the organizing of white semipro clubs in Milwaukee, Chicago, and Joliet, Illinois, into a league and supposedly receiving "protection" from the National and American Leagues. Apparently, this involved an agreement by each league to respect each others' players under contract. This proposed league led the *Freeman* to speculate that the Lelands were "about to break that strong barrier of race prejudice." Therefore, the Leland Giants would have to be in top form. More important, the proposed tour indicated that for the first time, a semiprofessional club that was black owned and operated had accomplished this feat.[39]

The Leland Giants would also have to be in the best of form to begin their first season in the Park Owners Association. The POA did not operate as a league in the traditional sense of a pursuit of a pennant and a season-ending championship series. The association did not publish league standings in the press, nor did it maintain statistics for the players. The POA functioned essentially to formalize a scheduling system among the member clubs that would maintain their rivalries and generate gate receipts. Rivalries then existed between the Leland Giants, the Logan Squares, and the Gunthers. With Jake Stahl's South Chicagos and Anson's Colts composed of top semipro and former Major League players, the POA was the cream of the Windy City's semiprofessional crop.

Several black baseball clubs from the South barnstormed the Midwest during the regular season. The Louisville Giants and the Birmingham Giants, for example, made Chicago part of their travel itinerary. On July 6, 1907, the *Broad Ax* reported the Lelands would play the Louisville Giants in a two-game series. A five-hundred-dollar side bet was placed on the series to stimulate interest. The Leland Giants swept the series and won the bet.[40]

On August 6, the Leland Giants began the first of two three-game series with Mike Donlin's All-Stars at Charles Comiskey's American League park. Also known as "Turkey Mike," Donlin was a former Major League player who had begun his career in 1899 with the National League's St. Louis Cardinals. In 1901 he played with the American League's Baltimore Orioles, who later became the New York Highlanders. Donlin's best season in the Major Leagues was in 1904 with the Cincinnati Reds, when he led the club in hitting (.351), runs scored (110), and triples (18). He later appeared on the vaudeville stage and would marry Mabel Hite, a well-known actress and vaudeville performer.[41]

Donlin organized a team composed of former Major League, semipro, and college players. Logan Squares' manager Jimmy Callahan and South Chicagos skipper Jake Stahl played left field and first base respectively. Center fielder Jimmy Ryan began his Major League career in 1885 with Cap Anson's Chicago White Stockings. After a brief stint with the Chicago club in the Players League, Ryan returned to the White Stockings and played for the team throughout the 1890s. He finished his Major League career in 1903 with the Washington Senators, compiling a .309 lifetime batting average. Arthur "Doc" Hillebrand was the team's right fielder, and he also pitched. From 1903 to 1905, Hillebrand coached the Princeton baseball club, amassing a 27-4 won-lost record. Former Dartmouth pitcher Percy Skillem and local semipro star hurler Gus Munch rounded out Donlin's All-Star team. Prior to the series on July 11, Donlin's All-Stars demolished the Leland Giants, 11-1, at Logan Square Park.[42]

A side bet of $1,500 was riding on the first three-game series between the two clubs, which turned out to be the Rube Foster show. In the first game, Foster engaged Percy Skillem in a pitcher's duel. The game was tied at two when the Lelands scored one run in the top of the seventh inning to win, 3-2. The All-Stars rebounded in the second game with a 6-2 victory behind the excellent pitching of Gus Munch. In the final game, six thousand fans watched Foster scatter five hits and shut out the All-Stars, 1-0. The Giants won the series and the side bet.[43]

The second three-game series began on August 27 at Charles Comiskey's American League park. Five thousand fans watched Rube Foster in top form as he held the All-Stars to five hits in a 3-1 victory. Once again, Gus Munch held the Giants in check in the second game, holding the Lelands to two hits and striking out seven batters in a 3-1 win. Controversy surrounded the final game. Jap Payne reportedly disputed a call that resulted in the center fielder punching the umpire. Payne was ejected from the game but refused to leave the field, resulting in a ten-minute delay. When play resumed, the Lelands coasted to an 8-4 victory. Rube Foster had won four of the six games between the two clubs.[44]

The second three-game series provided the best evidence of the Leland Giants' ability to generate revenue. The total attendance for the series was 13,500 fans. With ticket prices set at twenty-five cents, both teams amassed a gross revenue of $3,375 and a net of $1,687.50. There was no evidence that a side bet was placed on the second series. Nevertheless, the estimated revenue for the series was substantial.

The black press applauded the Leland Giants' spectacular performance against Donlin's All-Stars. Understandably, the spotlight shined bright on Rube Foster. The *Broad Ax* proclaimed Foster as "one of the greatest [baseball] players in this country." Under the pseudonym "Frederick North Shorey," a black sportswriter for the *Freeman* stated, "As for Rube Foster, well, if it were in the power of the colored people to honor politically or to raise him to the station to which they believe he is entitled, Booker T. Washington would have to be content with second place." The accolades Foster received were warranted. He pitched four complete game victories, giving up only seven runs in thirty-six innings pitched. Foster struck out eighteen batters and compiled a 1.75 earned run average.[45]

The Leland Giants' series victories were also touted as a symbol of race pride through self-help. In the race rhetoric that epitomized the era of Booker T. Washington, black sportswriter and former Union Giants player Dave Wyatt stated that the series showed how baseball was a "common leveler" in regards to race relations. "There was no color line drawn anywhere," Wyatt added, "our white brethren outnumbered [blacks] by a few hundred, and all bumped elbows in the grand stand, the box seats, and bleachers." Interracial spectatorship had always been the norm at black baseball games, however. The early black baseball entrepreneurs promoted their teams to cater to a white clientele. Economic factors made this strategy a necessity and not a luxury. Wyatt's comments did, however, reveal the impact of early black migration on northern cities in the early twentieth century. Migration would not expand the black consumer market significantly on a national basis until the war years. Yet in Chicago, migration had expanded the Windy City's black consumer market to the point that baseball magnates could no longer ignore it. Chicago's black population grew continuously between 1900 (30,150) and 1920 (109,455). Thus, Wyatt, promoting the supposed racial harmony among blacks and whites, might have advance the economic interests of the black baseball entrepreneurs. Nevertheless, the series victories over Donlin's All-Stars marked the beginning of the Leland Giants' dominance in the Midwest and heightened Rube Foster's status to almost legendary dimensions.[46]

Wyatt's editorial illustrated the willingness of African American businessmen to work within the parameters of a biracial institutional structure to advance their economic interests. His rhetoric was consistent with the self-help economic initiatives commonly attributed to Booker T. Washington and W. E. B. Du Bois, although they differed sharply on political strategy. Black businessmen were not to isolate themselves from the larger society by selling only to blacks, nor were black fans expected to patronize black baseball games only because the teams were black. African Americans were to advance themselves by free competition on the open market. Much like Washington, Leland and Foster's ultimate goal was not to build a black counterculture. Even in the nineteenth century, Frederick Douglass recognized that "a nation within a nation is an anomaly." The purpose of self-help and racial solidarity was to encourage black unity and self-assertion on a political level, while encouraging cultural and economic assimilation. This would, theoretically, result in the integration of blacks into the mainstream of American society. In the case of black baseball, that meant white Organized Baseball.[47]

In a short period of time, Rube Foster transformed the Leland Giants into one of the top black baseball teams in the United States. He demonstrated an ability to lure the top black players to Chicago to accomplish this task. The Lelands' spring training tour would be the first of many barnstorming tours to create a demand for the Giants in several locales. As a member of the POA, the Lelands were able to maintain their symbiotic business relationship with white semipros and continue to operate within the parameters of a biracial institutional structure. While Foster ran the baseball operations, Frank Leland was forging civic ties with black Chicago's business leaders and concurrently laying the groundwork for organizing a black professional league.

The Leland Giants Baseball and Amusement Association

Frank Leland's alliance with Chicago's new black leadership resulted in an effort by these men to gain control of the Windy City's growing African American market. The expansion of northern black communities—a direct result of migration—facilitated the emergence of a new market that black baseball entrepreneurs attempted to exploit. These African American entrepreneurs, or "Race men," typified the business leaders who deemphasized the fight for integration and dealt with discrimination by creating black institutions. The widening discrimination in Chicago and other northern cities resulted in the emergence of the physical ghetto. Chicago's African Americans, for example, were excluded from most white-owned recreation and leisure venues. Many theaters seated blacks only in the balcony, and bartenders frequently refused to serve black patrons. Illinois state law prohibited racial discrimination in public accommodations and municipal services. However, it was difficult to obtain a conviction under it. In 1905, a jury decided in favor of a theater that had turned down an African American who was trying to buy tickets for the main floor. The plight of Chicago's African Americans forced them to make decisions limited by their exclusion from a host of social and economic institutions. Increased separation, however, did open new opportunities for entrepreneurship.[48]

It was within this context that Robert R. Jackson and Beauregard F. Moseley figured prominently in consolidating Leland's ball club into a commercial amusement and recreation enterprise. Robert Jackson was born on September 1, 1869 in Malta, Illinois. He left school at age twelve and began working at various jobs in a department store and dental laboratory and as an errand boy in a retail store. In 1888, Jackson became a clerk in the US postal service and maintained one of the highest efficiency ratings during his fourteen years on the job. Jackson was a member of several fraternal orders like the Pythias Lodge, the Prince Hall Lodge, and the Grand Lodge, and he also established his own printing and publishing business.[49]

Beauregard Moseley was born in Georgia and moved to Chicago in the early 1890s. Upon his arrival, Moseley established the *Chicago Republic* newspaper. He left the newspaper business in 1896 to pursue a career in law. Moseley was admitted to the bar that same year, and within six years he had built a lucrative practice worth approximately eight thousand dollars annually. The *Broad Ax* reported that Moseley represented some of Chicago's foremost businessmen, and he was also chief counsel of the Olivet Baptist Church, Chicago's largest African American congregation. When asked to what he attributed his success, Moseley replied, "Close attention to business and the happy faculty of knowing no one except my client in a lawsuit."[50]

Leland, Moseley, and Jackson combined to form the Leland Giants Baseball and Amusement Association (LGBBA). Incorporated in 1907, the LGBBA was more than just a baseball team; it was also a summer resort, skating rink, and restaurant, and the venture represented the black response to white discrimination in amusement venues and public accommodations. On October 19, the Indianapolis *Freeman* reported the LGBBA had increased its capital to one hundred thousand dollars and secured a lease on the Columbia Dance Hall, an old building located on Fifty-Third and State Streets. Stock options were offered to the public at ten dollars a share to raise funds for remodeling the old building. The *Broad Ax* reported the LGBBA would open a roller-skating rink under the management of Robert Jackson, Frank Leland, and Rube Foster. They also planned to open a dance pavilion, a restaurant—known as the Grill Room—and a bowling alley called the Bowling Emporium. A contest was proposed to determine a name for the amusement hall. The first three contestants to send in the most appropriate name would receive the following prizes: first prize, five dollars in gold; second prize, a pair of roller skates; and third prize, a season pass to Auburn Park and the skating rink. The amusement hall was named the Chateau De La Plaisance—the House of Pleasure.[51]

On November 2, the Chateau De La Plaisance opened its doors to the public. From the outset, the Chateau was promoted to cater to Chicago's black elite. The *Broad Ax* listed several members of black Chicago's professional and business class—such as County Commissioner Edward H. Wright, Dr. Bert Anderson, and *Broad Ax* editor Julius Taylor—as attending the opening day festivities. The Chateau De La Plaisance served as an expression of racial uplift, an ideology that became the mantra of the African American elite in the early twentieth century. The amusement hall was a race enterprise created by blacks that sought to fulfill the wants and needs of a black consumer market. As *Broad Ax* editor Julius Taylor explained, "Every enterprise which is not intended to degrade the Negro conducted by Afro-Americans, tends to raise every worthy member of the race up in the business world." Taylor concluded that as long as the Chateau was managed in a first-class manner, "it should receive the patronage of the decent amusement loving public."[52]

Simultaneously, Frank Leland made his only attempt to organize a black professional league. On November 9, 1907, the *Freeman* reported that a movement was being put forward to form the National Colored League of Professional Ball Clubs. The proposed league was clearly based on the cooperative business philosophy. Leland, *Freeman* editor Elwood C. Knox, and Indianapolis ABCs club owner Randolph "Ran" Butler were the prime movers behind the enterprise.[53]

The primary focus in the early days of league planning was raising enough capital for the venture and scheduling the first organizational meeting. League organizers encouraged Race men and white capitalists to form a stock company as a means of consolidation. The circuit was to be an eight-team league with the possible cities to include Cincinnati; Cleveland; Louisville; Pittsburgh; Chicago; Indianapolis; Kansas City, Missouri; Toledo, Ohio; Detroit; Milwaukee; Memphis; Nashville; and Columbus, Ohio. The cities would be chosen according "to what showing they [would] make after a trial contest." However, it was unclear what constituted this trial contest. On December 18, preliminary plans to form the National Colored League were made. According to the *Freeman*, a "large body of Representatives" met in Elwood Knox's office and elected the following officers: Frank Leland, president; Edward Lancaster of the Louisville Giants, vice president; Edward S. Gaillard of the Indianapolis ABCs, corresponding secretary; Cary B. Lewis of the Louisville Giants, secretary; William Roberts of the ABCs, treasurer; and Charles Marshall, a *Freeman* sportswriter, organizer. A committee was selected to draft a constitution for the next meeting. There were no indications in the *Freeman* of who would serve on it.[54]

From December 28, 1907, to January 25, 1908, the league directors established guidelines for league entry. For a club to be considered for admission it had to (1) be represented by a stock company fully organized and incorporated under state law, (2) secure a bond, the amount unspecified and to be determined by the league's board of directors, (3) pay fifty dollars into the league treasury to cover the expenses for league operations, and (4) secure a suitable ballpark and have the full support of the press. A small percentage of the gate receipts from each city would be placed in the league treasury. The season would run from May to September.[55]

Despite the organizers' efforts, the league died stillborn. From the beginning, the organizers had no clear direction regarding how to place the league on a sound economic footing. In contrast to the NACBC, there was no indication of whether organizers would pattern their circuit after the white Major Leagues. Throughout the organizational phase, the league directors asked for suggestions "from every person interested under the sun" on how the league should function. This lack of direction could possibly explain why prospective entrepreneurs were slow to commit to the enterprise. The *Freeman* reported that only Chicago and Indianapolis made commitments to the proposed league.[56]

Also, there apparently were not enough clubs in the Midwest to compete with the Leland Giants. From 1902 to 1907, press reports indicated that of the cities under consideration for league entry, only two—the Indianapolis ABCs and the Louisville Giants—made barnstorming tours to the Windy City. A third club, the Topeka Giants, played the Lelands in 1906, but they were not under consideration. Furthermore, there were several black baseball magnates who were against league formation, fearing it would damage their business. Evidently, several of the club managers felt that operating in a league format could lead to losing lucrative games with black and white semipro teams within their respective regions of the country. It could also mean that clubs would have to make extended barnstorming tours outside their respective regions. If, for example, clubs from Pittsburgh and Nashville were members of the league, the travel and overhead expenses of the midwestern clubs would increase because of these cities' distance from the other cities. It would create an unworkable format, since most of the prospective cities were in the Midwest.[57]

A final factor involved Frank Leland's poor health. On February 15, 1908, the *Freeman* reported that Leland had suffered from heart failure. He did not attend the league meeting in Indianapolis on February 16, but he did send a letter stating that he would abide by any steps the league might propose. Leland apparently had spread himself too thin, fulfilling his duties as Cook County commissioner, managing a skating rink, serving as general manager of the Giants, and organizing a black professional league. It was evident that the league lost what little direction it had when Leland's health turned for the worse.[58]

The failure of the league did not deter the attempts by the organizers of the Leland Giants Baseball and Amusement Association to build their recreation enterprise. In the following years, LGBBA organizers continued to expand while Rube Foster maintained the Giants' competitiveness on the diamond. While the LGBBA continued to tap into Chicago's black consumer market, NACBC organizers took the initial steps to create their barnstorming network.

Creating the Network

In 1907 the National Association of Colored Baseball Clubs of the United States and Cuba implemented its objective of expanding its booking network to the Midwest and internationally to Cuba. Benefiting from the resurgence of semiprofessional baseball in Chicago, the All-Havana baseball club of Cuba barnstormed the Windy City for gate receipts. In October 1907, the Philadelphia Giants embarked on its first and only tour of Cuba, playing primarily against the Almendares Blues and the Havana Reds. Another way these black baseball entrepreneurs sought to reach the objective of advancing their business interests was through barnstorming. Sol White's *History of Colored Base Ball* was published in 1907 to expand black baseball's appeal to a popular audience. The NACBC supposedly modeled its organization after the white Major Leagues. However, in its inaugural year, its primary focus was to develop its booking network to expand its member clubs' market potential.

On May 28, 1907, the All-Havana baseball club invaded Chicago. The team played against the top white semipro teams like the Oak Leas, Logan Squares, Anson's Colts, and South Chicagos. The All-Havanas typified the type of baseball club that played during the dead ball era. Pitching, defense, base running, and timely hitting were the keys to the Cuban club's success. They were led by their shortstop Luis Bustamente, who according to New York Giants manager John McGraw, was the "perfect shortstop." Bustamente was known for his superb defense on the field and was also considered a good clutch hitter. Rafael Almeida played third base, catcher, and pitched for the Havanas. He possessed good speed and average power and would later play three seasons with the National League's Cincinnati Reds. Jose Figarola was the team's catcher and first baseman; he was an excellent defensive player behind the plate and a light hitter. Hector Magrinat played left field and was considered one of the best Cuban outfielders in the early twentieth century. An outfielder, Carlos Moran was an excellent hitter and base stealer. These players made the All-Havanas a formidable opponent.[59]

The All-Havanas performed admirably against Chicago's white semipros. In their opening game, they surprised the Oak Leas by 5-2, scoring five runs in the seventh inning to ensure victory. On May 30, the Havanas played the Logan Squares in the second game of a three-team doubleheader. The Cuban team got off to an early 3-0 lead and never looked back, winning easily by 6-1. The *Chicago Tribune*, however, was quick to point out that the Squares were handicapped by the loss of one of their top players, manager Jimmy Callahan. On June 8, the Havanas squared off against Anson's Colts. It took fourteen innings before the Cuban nine defeated the Colts, 7-5. The following day, however, the All-Havanas were no match for Jake Stahl's South Chicagos, falling behind early in the game and losing, 5-1. Interestingly enough, the Chicagos secured the services of Logan Squares' manager Jimmy Callahan, who played center field and collected two hits and scored one run. Nevertheless, of the six games reported in the press, the All-Havanas won four. As the *Tribune* astutely noted, the All-Havanas demonstrated "that baseball [was] no joke in Cuba."[60]

While the All-Havanas made a favorable impression in the Midwest, Sol White's *History of Colored Base Ball* was released. Arguably, guidebooks represented one way by which early sports entrepreneurs commodified the sport product. Karl Marx defined a commodity as an "object outside us, a thing that by its properties satisfied human wants of some sort or another." Yet not all products are necessarily commodities. "To become a commodity," Marx explained, "a product must be transferred to another whom it will serve as a use-value, by means of exchange." Thus, as historian Stephen Hardy points out, sport becomes a commodity when its producers transfer it, via exchange, to a separate group of consumers. Guidebooks served this purpose, as organized leagues resorted to published rule books, purchased annually by officials, administrators, coaches, players, and fans. In the 1860s, *The Beadle Dime Baseball Player* sold fifty thousand copies annually and was instrumental in making the New York Game the National Pastime. By the 1880s, a guide—including rules and statistics—for all sports comprised a substantial segment of Albert Spalding's empire, which amassed vast profits and supported the influence of governing bodies whose rules Spalding published.[61]

From the outset, White's guidebook was targeted to a mass audience in order to stimulate spectator interest in the black game. In the preface, White stated the book's primary focus: "I have endeavored to follow the mutations of colored base ball, as accurately as possible, from the organization of the first colored professional team in 1885, to the present time, in the trust that it will meet the approbation of all who may peruse the contents of this book." White highlighted the factors that led to the formation of the Cuban Giants and accentuated the exceptional players of which the club was composed, like Clarence Williams, Ben Boyd, and Abe Harrison. He also shed some light on the various owners of the club who included S. K. Govern, Frank Thompson, John Lang, Walter Cook, and John "J. M." Bright. Three other teams that received attention included the Gorhams of New York, the Chicago Unions, and the Page Fence Giants. The fundamental premise of this historical overview was to highlight the significant progress black baseball had made by the opening decade of the twentieth century.[62]

Two sections that illustrated White's effort to connect with a popular audience dealt with the "Championship Contests" and the "Notable Feats of Colored Pitchers." Local or regional championship contests were "bitterly fought," but this intensity did not exist "when the teams are from distant points of the country." He provides examples of these intense regional series that began in 1887 between the Cuban Giants and the Gorhams of New York. The Gorhams defeated the Cubans in this series. The Giants reclaimed the colored championship the following year in a tournament that included the Gorhams; the Keystones of Pittsburgh; and the Red Stockings of Norfolk, Virginia. Chronicling the colored championship contests illustrated the importance of rivalries and championships as the lifeblood of the black baseball business.[63]

Several outstanding pitching performances were chronicled throughout. A particular focus was on the Philadelphia Giants' pitchers Danny McClellan and Rube Foster. As a member of the Cuban X Giants, for example, McClellan pitched a no-hitter against the Penn Park club in York, Pennsylvania. On September 1, 1904, Rube Foster gave up no hits to the Camden club in Atlantic City, New Jersey. Foster's spectacular pitching performance in the 1904 colored championship against the Cuban X Giants was also highlighted.

In the sections "Colored Base Ball As a Profession" and "Manager Troubles," Sol White sought to make his case that black baseball was a legitimate profession. White began by advising black ballplayers that they "should always look before [they leap]," an obvious reference to the constant player jumping that had supposedly become rampant and, undoubtedly, in reference to his own career as a player. Although black players could not command the same salaries as their white counterparts, the pay scale had increased significantly since the late 1880s. In 1906 black baseball employed roughly 150 players, with club owners paying over $70,000 in salaries, an average of roughly $466 per player. This represented a 78.5 percent increase from 1886 to 1906, or an average pay increase of 39.25 percent per year. White was quick to point out that these figures were substantially lower than what white players received. He estimated the Major Leagues paid over $600,000 per season for more than 300 ballplayers. The minor leagues, on the other hand, paid two million dollars to 3,500 players.

Although White's assessment was valid, he didn't consider the wide salary differential among players and clubs. To be sure, rising attendance in the opening decade of the twentieth century stimulated several sharp salary increases. The first came when the American League challenge abolished the $2,400 limit and escalated salaries to new levels. By 1906 Bobby Wallace, a star infielder for the St. Louis Browns, was the highest-paid player at $6,500. Yet recognized stars like Hal Chase received only $2,500 and Joe Tinker a paltry $1,500. On average, a rookie in the majors could receive from $1,500 to perhaps $2,000. Detroit Tigers' outfielder Ty Cobb, for example, received $1,500 in his first full season. An established Major League player made roughly $3,000 in this era. Less affluent clubs maintained a low salary scale. For instance, Connie Mack was praised for keeping his total payroll at $36,000 for 1903. The more prosperous clubs like the New York Giants were more generous. By 1909 Giants' pitching star Christy Mathewson made $6,000. As Harold Seymour indicated, a wide salary differential among players of comparable skill existed because of the disparity in club markets. In other words, the salaries of players were based on the consumer market in which they played. That was why, for example, New York was so generous in paying its players and St. Louis so frugal. This disproportion in salary distribution was concealed as they were in territorial rights, a disparity that increased as the population in the US shifted.[64]

The wide salary differential in player salaries was also evident in the minor leagues and white semiprofessional baseball. Historian Robert Burk has estimated that semipros might get five dollars a game, or ten dollars on Sunday, or one hundred dollars a month. Minor leaguers at a Class D level could earn less than the top semipros and at the Double AA level as much as a Major League rookie. Regional variations, however, in minor league wages meant that although a veteran minor leaguer in the Northeast made $300–$400 a month, or $1,500–$2,000 a year, in the Southern Association the scale was $100 a month lower. Based on White's analysis, the salaries of top-level black clubs were comparable to those of the low-level minor leagues.[65]

In his "Manager Troubles" section, White stressed the need to establish an organizational structure like Organized Baseball's and to gradually eliminate a "vaudevillian" style of baseball that featured comic antics to maintain fan interest. Independent teams were difficult to manage as opposed to clubs under the jurisdiction of the National Agreement, by which both the major and minor leagues collectively agreed to abide by certain stipulations, like playing rules and market considerations. This agreement bound both the majors and minors into the industry that became Organized Baseball. An organized league with established rules would generate player respect for authority. It would allow managers to maintain discipline and, with the sanction of owners and administrators, give them the authority they needed over their player force. The focus on establishing rules and creating a governing body provided the rationale for forming the NACBC.

In addition to calling for the establishment of a governing body, White pointed to the decline of vaudevillian baseball in the black game. Vaudevillian baseball represented the unconventional playing style developed by black clubs in the late nineteenth century. It was based on the premise that baseball must stimulate interest to maintain consistent patronage. The sport's unpredictable outcome has always been its most appealing characteristic. Because independents at times had to schedule contests with teams that were not of high caliber, alternative measures were obviously developed to stimulate fan interest when a game became too one-sided. The Cuban Giants developed a series of comedy routines, including a pantomime that would later be referred to as "shadow ball." This act involved simulating an imaginary game on the field without the use of a baseball.[66]

By the early twentieth century, the fans had become more sophisticated. They "were [once] content with being amused and the game developed comedians. . . . But now they demand faultless play," White said. "The funny man in colored base ball is becoming extinct. Where every man on a team would do a funny stunt during a game back in the eighties and early nineties, now will be found only one or two on a team who essays to amuse the spectators of the present day."[67]

Although vaudevillian baseball would never completely disappear from the black game, White's assessment illustrates the use of public relations to broaden the sport's appeal to a popular audience. Sport management scholar Bill Sutton argues that public relations play an essential role in the marketing mix because of its long-term focus and direction and due to its limited organizational control and its reliance on public perception and interpretation. Thus, a public relations campaign is critical in positioning the product in the consumer's mind through an image-building and enhancement program. There is, nevertheless, no guarantee a consumer will accept the positioning of the product a marketer may present. White highlighted the gradual elimination of vaudevillian baseball from the black game to show the sport was progressing in toward being on par with the Major Leagues.[68]

The game on the field was critical to this image-building/enhancement program, and black baseball would embody the style of play that characterized the sport in the dead ball era. It was based on the playing style of one of the most successful teams in the National League: John McGraw's New York Giants. In 1904, the Giants won a record 106 games with a team built on speed, defense, and pitching. It was also built on McGraw's mastery of what would eventually be called "inside baseball." As one commentator accurately defined it, inside baseball was "merely the outguessing of one team by another." It featured the manager's signaling from the bench or the coaching box for particular plays: base-stealing attempts, pitchouts to keep opponents from stealing, sacrifice bunts, squeeze and hit-and-run plays, even what one's pitcher should throw or whether one's batter should swing. In White's view, transforming the black game from its clowning antics to the "scientific" style of inside baseball served to legitimize black baseball as a profession. Transforming the black game on the field also served to convey a more subtle message: black baseball's embodiment of the white game could only be accomplished within the context of an organization patterned after the Major Leagues.[69]

Finally, Sol White assessed professional baseball's race relations. He began by stating, "In no other profession has the color line been drawn more rigidly than in base ball." White briefly chronicled the plight of black players who played in the major and minor leagues, such as Bud Fowler, Fleet and Weldy Walker, and Frank Grant. He then shifted his attention to the person who was most instrumental in erecting the color barrier, Cap Anson. In White's view, Anson's "repugnant feeling, shown [at] every opportunity, toward colored players, was a source of comment through every league in the country, and his opposition, with his great popularity and power in base ball circles, hasten[ed] the exclusion [of] the black man from the white leagues."[70]

White's animosity towards Anson is understandable. White's professional baseball career began when African Americans were slowly being phased out of the white leagues. Yet given the constant presence of racism, the elimination of blacks from Organized Baseball could not simply be attributed to the onset of Jim Crowism or to men such as Cap Anson. The shift in Organized Baseball's race relations happened at the same time as the industry confronted several trade wars that shaped its labor relations. Although not assured victory in any of these conflicts, the National League gained the upper hand in these player wars, allowing its club owners to gain tighter control over the labor force. These practices also impacted Organized Baseball's race relations. While the owners fought wars over the services of white players, they appeared more than willing to use their collusive behavior to exclude blacks from the Major Leagues.[71]

To be sure, white racism was a critical factor in excluding blacks from the Major Leagues. The 1890s was a period of increased racism and competition from white immigrants for several occupations, including baseball players. The National League operated as a cartel organization by virtue of gaining a hegemony over the labor force. Establishing the minor leagues as a cheap labor pool, the National League magnates felt no pressure to broaden the player force's racial base. They sought a stable, profitable equilibrium, in this case an ethnocultural and socioeconomic profile for the player force that catered to the ethnic middle class's growing spectatorship. At the same time, league owners also attempted to maintain a wasplike respectability regarding the players' image and conduct as expected by the Victorian fan. While fifty-five blacks managed to play in twenty different white leagues between 1884 and 1898, none entered the majors in the 1890s. With the collapse of the talent demand after the players' revolt, from 1891 to 1898 only four white minor leagues employed a total of three different African American players.[72]

By the turn of the twentieth century, White claimed "on good authority that one of the leading players and a manager of the National League is advocating the entrance of colored players in the National League with a view of signing 'Matthews,' the colored man late of Harvard." The identity of the leading player was unclear, but the manager appeared to be John McGraw. White was referring to William Clarence Matthews, an outstanding shortstop-outfielder who played for Harvard University. Matthews left Harvard and signed with the Burlington club in the Vermont League, an independent minor league. He confronted racial hostility from the league's white players, which led to his exodus from baseball. Despite Matthews's predicament, White was cool to the idea of African Americans entering the Major Leagues (although he held onto the ultimate goal of integration). He used the experience of Charlie Grant to validate his reservations.[73]

In 1901, then Baltimore Orioles manager John McGraw tried to circumvent the color line by signing Grant. Interestingly enough, Grant's signing occurred simultaneously with the American League's war over players with the National League. Grant was a well-known black player when McGraw discovered him working as a bellhop at the Eastland Hotel in Hot Springs, Arkansas. To undermine the color barrier, McGraw figured that a change in name and heritage might accomplish his objective. Because of his light complexion, Charlie Grant became Charlie Tokohoma, a full-blooded Cherokee.

Despite the effort to "pass" Charlie Grant off as a Cherokee Indian, the black second baseman's reputation proved his undoing. He had debuted professionally with the Page Fence Giants in 1896 and had played for the Columbia Giants in 1900. Grant was well-known in Chicago baseball circles, and his identity was inadvertently revealed by black fans who publicly congratulated him. Chicago White Sox president Charles Comiskey recognized Grant from previous appearances in Chicago as a member of the Columbia Giants. Grant never played for McGraw's Orioles, but he had come closer than any other black player to crossing the color line at the turn of the twentieth century.[74]

Sol White's analysis of the color line in professional baseball further illustrated the need for black baseball to develop an organization patterned after Organized Baseball. The comparison of black and white player salaries served to stress the importance of protecting the club owners' investment. This pro-owner stance was understandable, given White's position as a player-manager and co-owner. Therefore, the black game should "be taken seriously by the colored players, as honest effort, with his great ability[,] will open an avenue in the near future wherein he may walk hand-in-hand with the opposite race in the greatest of all American games—baseball." This would only occur, in White's view, when black professional baseball got its proverbial house in order.[75]

Sol White's *History of Colored Baseball* represented the continued efforts of African American entrepreneurs to advance their economic interests in the National Pastime. It should be noted that the creation of an all-black baseball organization did not mean that these entrepreneurs would sever their business ties with white semipros. Economic factors—and the way race influenced them—made this option unreasonable. In fact, they tried to solidify these business relationships. The formation of the NACBC coincided with the efforts of semiprofessional clubs to organize into leagues and associations. To protect their investment, the owners of the leading black clubs responded in kind. Establishing an organization that provided a sense of professional legitimacy was in these black baseball entrepreneurs' best economic interests. Furthermore, attempting to legitimize black professional baseball represented their continuing efforts to operate their segregated enterprise within the fabric of the mainstream economy. In other words, the segregated enterprise (the NACBC) would operate within the fabric of white semiprofessional baseball. Ultimately, this new organization would, the owners anticipated, be integrated into the structure of Organized Baseball.

Maintaining a competitive club was one way to attempt the integration of black baseball into Organized Baseball's structure. Despite losing several players to the Leland Giants, Sol White managed to field a competitive team for the fifth straight year. Pete Hill, Bruce Petway, Billy Francis, William Binga, Emmett Bowman, and Danny McClellan continued to dominate black and white semipro clubs in the East. They were the NACBC's flagship club.

White exhibited his uncanny ability to lure talent to the Philadelphia Giants by signing John Henry Lloyd from the Cuban X Giants. Often referred to as the black Honus Wagner, his applied knowledge of baseball in the dead ball era allowed him to develop a variety of skills. Lloyd would become a first-rate hitter and a dangerous base runner. He was also an excellent defensive player with exceptional range and good hands at shortstop. Born on April 25, 1884, in Palatka, Florida, Lloyd gravitated toward baseball at an early age, playing for a team called the Jacksonville Old Receivers and working as a porter for the Southern Express Company. In 1905 Lloyd was a catcher for the Macon, Georgia, Acmes, a team too poor to have such luxuries as a mask and chest protector for their backstops. In the winter, Lloyd joined other players waiting on tables at Florida resort hotels and playing baseball to entertain the guests. It was in Florida where Lloyd was supposedly seen by E. B. Lamar, who signed the talented shortstop to play for the Cuban X Giants in the 1906 season. Lloyd's first season with the X Giants marked the start of his twenty-six-year career as both a marquee player and manager in black professional baseball.[76]

The Philadelphia Giants' tour of Cuba exemplified the NACBC's efforts to centralize the scheduling of games among their elected officials. Ironically, Sol White did not accompany his Giants to Cuba. According to the Philadelphia *Item*, the Giants were under the management of E. B.

Lamar, and Clarence Williams managed the team on the field. Lamar, undoubtedly, was better suited to handle the administrative duties of securing visas for the players to travel to Cuba. His business arrangement with Abel Linares enabled Lamar to make schedule arrangements with the Cuban teams. Moreover, Lamar had previously organized several tours in Cuba.[77]

The Giants played the majority of their games against the Almendares Blues and the Havana Reds. The Blues were undoubtedly Cuba's marquee team. On April 21, 1907, the *Item* reported the Blues won the Cuban League championship. They then embarked on a barnstorming tour of the US. Much like the All-Havanas, they were built around solid pitching, defense, base running, and timely hitting. Their star hurler, Jose Munoz, "the premier pitcher of Cuba," led the club. Munoz toured the United States with the All Cubans, baffling hitters with his fastball and screwball. When he was not pitching, Munoz exhibited his athletic prowess by playing in the outfield and batting second or fifth in the batting order. Heliodoro Hildalgo and Rogelio Valdes were two light-hitting outfielders who were both excellent defensive players with outstanding speed. Armando Marsans was the Almendares' star player. He played several positions and was touted as "the Cuban answer to Ty Cobb." Like Rafael Almeida, Marsans would also play for the National League's Cincinnati Reds. The Havana Reds, on the other hand, were the same team that played as the All-Havanas in the United States.[78]

The Philadelphia Giants got off to a slow start. In their opening game against the Almendares, Jose Munoz held the Giants to four hits and shut them out, 6-0. The Blues went on to defeat the Giants the next three times they played. On November 7, the Giants finally prevailed against the Blues, but not without a struggle. The Giants took a 3-2 lead into the seventh inning before breaking the game open with a four-run rally on the way to an 8-2 win. The Giants then won four out of the next six games. Out of the thirteen games reported in the press, the series was tied with six wins, six losses, and one tie.[79]

The Havana Reds were equally tough. After losing their first two games to the Giants, the Reds won six out of the next seven games. Each game was closely contested, however. For example, on December 29 the score was tied at six going into the ninth inning, when the Reds scored three runs in the top of the frame. The Giants scored two runs in the bottom of the inning, and with a man on third and two outs, Jap Payne stepped to the plate. He grounded out hard to Bustamente at short and the Giants lost, 9-8. Overall, the Reds won the series with six wins and five losses.[80]

The Giants' on-field performance was mediocre. Of the games reported in the press, the Quaker club won fourteen, lost twelve, and tied two. The Almendares Blues' and the Havana Reds' performances against the Philadelphia Giants showed that Cuban baseball was on par with the black game in the States. More important, the Philadelphia Giants' tour of Cuba elevated its status to the rank of an elite touring team. Despite their subpar performance, the Giants were head and shoulders above the rest of the clubs in the North American black baseball world.

Economically, the Cuban tour appeared to be a lucrative one. Attendance at Giants' games ranged from as low as 80 to as high as 8,000. Total reported attendance was 46,320, which averaged out to 2,336 a game. With ticket prices estimated at twenty-five cents, the Giants generated gross revenues of $12,262.50. The Giants' share of the gross was $6,131.25. Revenue generated in games against the Almendares Blues was equally impressive. Total attendance at Giants-Blues games was 22,980 fans, amassing total revenue of $5,745 and net of $3,241.25. Total attendance at Giants-Reds games was 13,940, generating a gross of $3,485 and a net of $1,653.75. Barnstorming Cuba for gate receipts seemed to be a lucrative enterprise.[81]

The NACBC had made inroads toward establishing its booking network to the Midwest and internationally to Cuba. However, attempting to pattern its organization after the white Major Leagues would be problematic. Undoubtedly, NACBC organizers sought to emulate Organized Baseball's restrictive practice of territorial rights—the division of consumer markets among the clubs, giving each a monopoly within the area in which it operated. As Harold Seymour explained, territorial rights were based on the supposition that consumer demand for professional baseball was limited. Therefore, if only one club exploited a given area, it would have a better chance to prosper than if several clubs competed for the same market. While the concept of territorial rights was commendable in theory, the ideal did not match the configuration of the clubs that made up the National and American Leagues. The Major Leagues in the early twentieth century had three clubs in New York and two each in Philadelphia, Boston, Chicago, and St. Louis.[82]

Much like their Major League counterparts, NACBC organizers faced the predicament of having the majority of its clubs residing in one market. Three of five clubs, the Brooklyn Royal Giants, Cuban X Giants, and the Cuban Giants, relied primarily on the New York market for their economic viability. The Cuban Stars was a traveling team that also sought to tap into this market. A primary reason why the Philadelphia Giants formed the NACBC was to schedule more Sunday games in the New York-New Jersey area.

The NACBC's club configuration was further complicated by the fact that none of these association clubs possessed their own home grounds, making the development and maintenance a fan base problematic. Also, there were no strong black clubs on par with the Philadelphia Giants in urban cities like Detroit, Cincinnati, or Cleveland.

Finally, much like the black baseball clubs of the 1890s, NACBC officials underestimated the importance of consistent press coverage to generate publicity and stimulate fan interest. Although semipro clubs began to receive better press coverage, the Major Leagues still received top priority in terms of media attention. Therefore, it was still a semipro club magnate's responsibility to ensure his team remained on the sport pages. (Some did not fulfill their responsibility because their teams lost most of their games, although there were other reasons as well.) For reasons unclear, the Philadelphia Giants' press coverage began to decline after the 1906 season. This could possibly have been the rationale for the publication of White's guidebook: to keep the black game before the general audience. The primary means of generating publicity for a league—a pennant race, rivalries, and championships—were the furthest things from the minds of NACBC officials.

The overwhelming focus of the NACBC in its opening year was to establish a booking network to expand its member clubs' market potential. It should be noted that the attempt to form this association began in Philadelphia and not in New York. Prior to 1910, NACBC treasurer Nat Strong had little or no interest in operating black baseball clubs. His primary focus was running his Ridgewood and Murray Hill clubs and, as president of the Intercity Association, maintaining his booking control in New York. Black and Cuban clubs were well aware that if they wanted a big payday in Gotham, they would have to deal with Nat Strong. Conversely, given the large crowds the Philadelphia Giants generated for Sunday games, it made good business sense for Strong to schedule games with them. Since eastern black clubs did not have their own home grounds and top-level clubs did not exist in Cleveland, Cincinnati, or Detroit, focusing on the development of a booking network was both practical and understandable.

Black professional baseball's growth spurt led entrepreneurs among the leading black clubs in the East to form leagues and associations. Their primary motives were to tighten control over their player force, maintain their symbiotic business relationships with white semipros, gain access to the best parks to generate maximum gate receipts, and expand their member clubs' market potential through the creation of extended barnstorming tours nationally and internationally. The All-Havanas' tour of Chicago and the Philadelphia Giants' excursion to Cuba marked the initial steps the NACBC took to create such a network. The NACBC did not establish a baseball organization in the traditional sense of including competition for a pennant and sponsoring a season-ending championship series. The owners created an association based on the premise of centralizing power by gaining control of the decision-making process.

The resurgence of the Leland Giants in Chicago resulted from Frank Leland's efforts to strengthen his ball club and simultaneously exploit Chicago's growing black consumer market. He accomplished this by hiring Rube Foster to run the baseball operations and establishing an alliance with the Windy City's new black leadership. The Giants' successful 1907 season became the cornerstone for maintaining their symbiotic business relationship with white semipros and initiating a recreation enterprise to cater to Chicago's growing black consumer market. The baseball team, skating rink, restaurant, and bowling alley were promoted by the black press as a clear expression of racial uplift through self-help. Leland's endeavor to expand his influence in the Midwest through the creation of a black professional league ended in failure, however. The failed league did not, however, diminish the success the LGBBA achieved in a short period of time.

In the following years, both the LGBBA and the NACBC continued to enhance their organizations to maximize revenues. LGBBA organizers expanded the recreation enterprise significantly, while Rube Foster made the Leland Giants the elite black club of the Midwest. The NACBC would send several of its member clubs to the Midwest while, at the same time, H. Walter Schlichter set out to develop a baseball empire. Although these organizations would make tremendous progress toward achieving their goals, forces both internal and external were at work that would lead to the organizations' demise.

3

Striving for Professionalism

H. Walter Schlichter sought to expand his influence in both black and white professional baseball. In 1908, Schlichter became the manager of the Philadelphia club in the newly created Union League. The Union League was a minor league that operated outside of Organized Baseball's structure and was classified as an "Outlaw League." Club owners within the circuit attempted to sign several star players like Ty Cobb from the Major Leagues. Failure to sign them and the disbanding of its three clubs by early June led to the league's collapse. Schlichter then turned his attention back to black baseball. He promoted the sport's tremendous progress and along with Sol White organized a tournament among the leading eastern clubs to determine the colored champion. Simultaneously, the NACBC sent three of its member clubs to the Midwest to barnstorm the region for gate receipts. The tour culminated in a controversial series between the Philadelphia Giants and the Leland Giants for black baseball supremacy.

Despite their significant progress, conflict emerged among the NACBC organizers. Centralizing power by gaining control of the decision-making process led to an internal conflict between Schlichter and White, resulting in the Giants' manager leaving the team. White's departure marked the start of the Quaker club's fall from prominence. When the NACBC refused to book games with White's new club, the Quaker Giants, he attempted to persuade Brooklyn Royal Giants' magnate, John Connor, to withdraw from the NACBC and form a new association. By July 1909, the NACBC was split into two factions.

The rift among the NACBC club owners continued to plague the organization during the 1910 season. The NACBC's top-heavy administrative approach marginalized managers like White and Grant "Home Run" Johnson who were instrumental in their teams' success. The scheduling system Nat Strong created began to break down as Cuban Giants' club owner J. M. Bright began booking his own games. A breach occurred between Brooklyn Royal Giants' magnate John Connor and his manager, Grant Johnson, which resulted in several players leaving the team. Connor also pondered leaving the organization. As the 1910 season drew to a close, the NACBC was in a state of chaos.

The Leland Giants Baseball and Amusement Association continued its significant progress, although like the NACBC, it would experience a split among its officials as a result of its success. The Giants became members of newly formed Chicago City League and finished their excellent 1908 season with a six-game series against the American Association's Minneapolis Millers. At the same time, LGBBA organizers expanded their recreation enterprise to include a movie theater, dance hall, and a second restaurant. In 1909, the Lelands continued their success on the diamond. They embarked upon a barnstorming tour of the South, competed in the Chicago City League championship, and played a three-game series with the National League's Chicago Cubs. Their accomplishments were promoted as a symbol of race pride and racial solidarity through self-help.

The LGBBA's progress led to a rift between Frank Leland, Beauregard Moseley, and Rube Foster. In a hostile takeover, Moseley aligned with Foster to force Leland out of the organization. In response, Leland, along with former association members Robert Jackson and Alvin Garrett, formed the Chicago Giants to compete against his old club for players and gate receipts and contend for the Chicago City League championship. Leland confronted several obstacles to transforming his Giants into an elite touring team, one of which was that the LGBBA took him to court to prohibit him from using the name Leland Giants, and another was the City League's ban on scheduling games with NACBC clubs. These obstacles did not prevent Leland from obtaining his goal. The Giants' spring training tour of the South, and its participation in the California Winter League, allowed Frank Leland to reemerge as one of black baseball's leading entrepreneurs.

The breakup in leadership did not hinder Beauregard Moseley's aspirations for the LGBBA. It purchased a ballpark located within a close proximity of the growing Black Belt and continued to make its imprint upon black community development. To stimulate fan interest, Moseley issued a challenge to determine the "best baseball team in the world." The Leland Giants embarked upon an eastern barnstorming tour and made their first trip to Cuba. Concurrently, Moseley attempted to organize a black professional league around the familiar concept of economic cooperation. Despite the enthusiasm the proposed league generated, it still died without a pitch thrown. The failed league illustrated the fundamental flaw that plagued these black entrepreneurs' organizational efforts: the stronger, better-financed clubs operated primarily in New York and Chicago.

An Outlaw League and Promotion of Black Baseball

On December 16, 1907, the Union League of Professional Baseball Clubs was formed. The Union League initially began with six clubs: Baltimore; Brooklyn; Newark, New Jersey; Paterson, New Jersey; Philadelphia; and Reading, Pennsylvania. The league expanded to eight teams by adding Wilmington, Delaware, and Elizabeth, New Jersey, while a club from Washington replaced the Newark franchise. Al Lawson was elected president, and from the outset claimed the Union League had no intentions of antagonizing "in any way organized baseball." The Union League was committed to elevating the game for the benefit of the players and the public. Lawson asserted that he intended "to keep faith with the public at all times, and by doing so reap the benefits that [the players and fans] would justly deserve." No contract jumpers would be permitted to play in the new league. Moreover, league clubs would not use the reserve clause in player contracts to bind them to their respective teams.[1]

Two club managers had a different agenda than their league president. The Washington club signed Arthur Irwin to serve as its manager. In the 1880s, Irwin had played shortstop for the National League's Boston Beaneaters and had supposedly introduced the padded fielder's glove. He was actively involved in the Brotherhood War of 1889—a revolt of players against the reserve clause binding them to a team—serving as an alternate on the committees that negotiated with the owners. Published in 1895, his book, *Practical Ball Playing*, was a manual on how to play the game, providing tips on "scientific" fielding, batting, and base running. The Philadelphia *Item* reported that Irwin attempted to sign two of Major League Baseball's top stars: Pittsburgh Pirate outfielder Tommy Leach and Detroit Tiger outfielder Ty Cobb. Cobb was offered $5,500 to play for Washington, and the Tigers outfielder supposedly said he would accept the offer if he could not come to terms with his American League club. Cobb, however, re-signed with Detroit and led the Tigers to the American League pennant in 1908.[2]

Schlichter also attempted to sign several minor and Major League players. He signed left-handed pitcher Frank Coveleski, who would later play nine seasons in the Major Leagues, winning eighty-two games and losing fifty-five. Schlichter aggressively pursued Pittsburgh Pirates' star shortstop Honus Wagner, offering him an unheard of ten thousand dollars to play for the Quaker club. Wagner had apparently "retired from baseball" (perhaps as a ploy to get more money), which undoubtedly led Schlichter to offer the Pirates star this generous offer. Wagner rejected the proposition, stating that if he did play baseball it would be for the Pirates. The thirty-four-year-old shortstop played for Pittsburgh, leading the National League with a .354 batting average and driving in 109 runs.[3]

Despite its inability to sign these star players, the Union League began the season with high aspirations. In early June, however, it collapsed. Two factors contributed to the Union League's demise. First, the Unions competed for gate receipts with Brooklyn, Washington, and Philadelphia in the Major Leagues, Baltimore in the Eastern League, and Reading in the Tri-State League. Having failed to sign Cobb, Leach, and Wagner, it would be extremely difficult to compete against the Major Leagues and their star players like Christy Matthewson, Eddie Collins, and Walter Johnson. The *Item* indicated that several Union games would conflict with these clubs throughout the season. A final factor was the economic instability of three of the Union League clubs. By the end of May, Baltimore, Wilmington, and Paterson had dropped out of the league. A team from Allentown replaced one of the disbanded clubs, and the Union League operated as a six-club loop. A little over two months into the season, the Union League disbanded.[4]

H. Walter Schlichter's brief stint as Philadelphia's manager was a dismal one. Any success the club may have had was thwarted when Wagner rejected Schlichter's contract offer. Despite signing several supposed top minor league stars, the Quaker club was in fifth place by early June with a dismal 10-24 won-lost record.

The Union League's demise led Schlichter to focus his attention on promoting the black professional game. Much like Sol White the previous year, 1907, Schlichter highlighted black baseball's significant progress since the 1880s. He pointed to the performances of several top-level teams like the Leland Giants, Indianapolis ABCs, and St. Paul Gophers in the Midwest and the Brooklyn Royal Giants, Philadelphia Giants, and Cuban Stars in the East. At the same time, Schlichter claimed that black baseball has had "an overcrowded market of [baseball] talent, and the demand has never been so great but that the supply was greater." It was because of this glut of black players and teams that he called for a National League of Colored Base Ball Clubs. "If interest continues as great in the next few years as it has since 1904," Schlichter added, "we can look for colored leagues along the same lines [as] the American and National League organizations." League formation would enable the NACBC club owners to maintain a salary cap, gain a hegemony over black baseball's consumer markets, gain access to the better parks to generate greater gate receipts, and deny bookings to uncooperative managers.[5]

Schlichter and White organized a baseball tournament to determine the colored champion of the East. The Quaker club, Brooklyn Royal Giants, Cuban Giants, and Cuban Stars agreed to play five-game series against each other. The team that won the most games would become the colored champion. The Philadelphia Giants won a series from each club and claimed the colored championship of the East. It was an excellent recovery for White's club after its mediocre performance in Cuba.[6]

While the Philadelphia Giants continued their dominance in the East, the NACBC sent three of its member clubs to barnstorm the Midwest for gate receipts. On May 30, the All-Havanas embarked upon their second midwestern tour. The tour marked the debut of Cuba's legendary pitcher Jose Mendez. Also known as *el diamante negro* (the Black Diamond), Mendez began his baseball career at age sixteen. Five years later, he pitched for Havana and in his first game in the United States, he shut out the Brooklyn Royal Giants, 3-0. During one stint, Mendez compiled a scoreless inning streak of twenty-five innings against the Cincinnati Reds (1908) and the Detroit Tigers (1909). Mendez did not fare well in his first game against Chicago's Riverview club. He relieved Emilio Palomino in the sixth inning and gave up three runs in the seventh in a 7-4 loss.[7]

On June 2, the *Chicago Tribune* reported the All-Havanas played the "first game in the series for the colored championship" against the Leland Giants. The Lelands took a 5-3 lead into the eighth inning before the Cuban club erupted with three runs in the eighth and two in the ninth to win, 8-7. According to the *Tribune*, the Lelands eventually won the series, seven games to four.[8]

In July, J. M. Bright's Cuban Giants made their way to Chicago. The first game set the tone for the rest of the series. Rube Foster squared off against John Nelson, and the Lelands' manager took a 2-1 lead into the fifth inning. The Lelands went on to score three runs in the sixth, four in the seventh, and six in the eighth and won in a rout, 15-3. From that time on, the Cuban Giants were listless as they proceeded to lose their next four games. After defeating the All-Havanas and the Cuban Giants, the Leland Giants awaited the arrival of the Philadelphia Giants.[9]

On July 27, the Philadelphia Giants began a seven-game series with the Leland Giants. The Lelands hit Giants' pitcher Danny McClellan early and often and took a quick 6-0 lead. It would be all Emmett Bowman needed, as he scattered five hits and defeated his former club, 6-4. The Philadelphia Giants evened the series at one game each with a 5-4 win that took eleven innings to complete. The third game was a pitcher's duel between Walter Ball of the Lelands and a left-handed pitcher named Fisher for the Giants. The game was tied at two going into the ninth inning when Leland's catcher, Pete Booker, singled and went to third base on Walter Ball's single to center field. Leland's left fielder,

Bobby Winston, singled to left and Booker came home with the winning run. The Lelands crushed the Giants in the fourth game, 11-1, and took a 3-1 lead in the series.[10]

The Philadelphia Giants rallied to stay alive in the series. Led by John Henry Lloyd's four-hit attack, the Giants knocked Rube Foster out of the box, taking an early 6-2 lead and winning game five, 8-2. Lloyd led the Giants to victory in game six, collecting two hits, batting in two runs, and scoring three runs en route to a 7-4 win. The seventh game was not played. It is unclear why the two clubs did not complete the series. Clearly, the Leland Giants would have benefited from defeating the Quaker club. Not only could they have claimed the colored championship; a series victory would also have highlighted the Lelands' significant progress since Rube Foster became their manager. Defeating the All-Havanas, Cuban Giants, and the Philadelphia Giants in the same year would have been a remarkable accomplishment. Even had Philadelphia defeated the Lelands, the Giants would have ranked among the elite in the black baseball world. The Philadelphia Giants, on the other hand, could have maintained their claim as black baseball's marquee club, given their victory in the colored championship in the East. Defeating the Lelands could also have provided further consolation for their mediocre performance in Cuba. Given Foster's defection from the Giants in 1907, it was apparent that bad blood still existed between the two clubs. Therefore, when the Quaker club tied the series, Foster and White could have let their personal animosity toward each other cloud their business judgment.[11]

Despite the controversial ending to the Colored Championship Series, Sol White and H. Walter Schlichter remained as the leading black baseball entrepreneurs of the East. In the midst of competition for players—a direct result of black baseball's tremendous growth—White continued to exhibit an ability to keep a competitive ball club intact. The Giants' continued success allowed Schlichter and White to focus attention on market promotion to spread the black game nationally and internationally and broaden the sport's appeal to a popular audience. Although the NACBC did not operate in the same manner as the white Major Leagues, it did maintain the standard business practices that had sustained black baseball clubs since the 1880s. It had effectively created a demand for its product in several locales. Barnstorming tours remained the lifeblood of the black baseball business, and through its administrative efforts, the NACBC had created a network to the Midwest and Cuba. It continued its symbiotic business relationship with white semipros and simultaneously created new rivalries with black and Cuban clubs. The NACBC's progress reflected Schlichter and White's vision that black professional baseball was progressing in the right direction for developing black leagues that would be on par with the white Major Leagues. However, as the 1909 season approached, internal dissension within the NACBC's ranks was beginning to surface.

The Decline of the NACBC

Although the evidence is limited, it appears that the International League of Colored Baseball Clubs in America and Cuba was absorbed into the NACBC. The same clubs that made up the ILBCAC were also NACBC members. There were no indications to suggest that William Freihoffer and John O'Rourke remained in their positions as ILBCAC officials. League clubs played in the ILBCAC in the East, while they functioned under the umbrella of the NACBC during their barnstorming tours in the Midwest and Cuba.

Despite the Philadelphia Giants' phenomenal success on the field and their elevation to the ranks of a touring team, Sol White, the manager, had become disgruntled. White apparently recognized his diminished role as the Giant's co-owner. With the scheduling of games in the hands of NACBC treasurer and business manager Nat Strong, White lost a significant degree of administrative control. Nothing illustrated this better than the Giants' tour of Cuba. E. B. Lamar and Clarence Williams ran the club while it was in Cuba, and this undoubtedly irritated White. After all, it was White who had transformed the Quaker club into one of the top black teams in the United States and had managed to keep a nucleus of star players together to maintain its competitiveness. He had also created a demand for his club in a new locale by barnstorming to the Midwest prior to the NACBC's formation. White's

History of Colored Base Ball had served to broaden black baseball's appeal to a popular audience and made the case that the sport was a legitimate profession.

On April 8, 1909, the *New York Age* reported that White had officially broke with Schlichter and become the new owner of the Quaker Giants. Controversy arose when the ILBCAC allegedly agreed not to schedule games with White's new team. Strong supposedly told White and Brooklyn Giants' manager, John "Pop" Watkins, that booking dates were not available to them. In response, White visited the various park managers in New York City and apparently received promises that they would schedule the Quaker Giants regardless of the ILBCAC's objections.[12]

The effort to exclude White's Quaker Giants from playing ILBCAC clubs illustrated how Nat Strong benefited from the NACBC's attempt to centralize power by gaining control of the decision-making process. From White's perspective, the alliance between Schlichter and Strong turned out to be a bad marriage. Strong from the outset had little or no interest in black baseball clubs. His primary concern was to maximize his profits through his Ridgewood and Murray Hill clubs and to establish his booking autonomy in New York City as the president of the Intercity Association. The Ridgewoods, for example, were permitted to play regularly at a certain park, allowing them to build a fan base. According to African American sportswriter Doc Lambert, Strong refused to play his team in other parks unless he received either from 35 to 40 percent of the gate receipts or a substantial guarantee. Strong devised a system whereby 10 percent of the clubs' gate receipts went to him, 65 percent to the club owners, and no more than twenty-five percent to the players. Conversely, black clubs received no more than five hundred dollars for any game regardless of how substantial the gate receipts were. To offset this, black clubs would schedule doubleheaders in the New York area, but if Strong booked the game they still had to pay a 10 percent fee, whereas other park managers charged 5 percent.[13]

Although this business relationship was an inequitable one, black baseball teams still generated a substantial amount of revenue, particularly in New York. For example, a black club could arrange a three-team doubleheader whereby they would play a morning game in New York and an afternoon game in Hoboken, New Jersey. The morning game in Gotham drew 8,000 fans, amassing a gross revenue of $2,000. After deducting Strong's booking fee ($200), both teams could receive a net of $800, with 65 percent going to the owner ($520) and the rest to the players ($280). An afternoon game in Hoboken could hypothetically amass an attendance of 5,500 fans. Both teams generated a gross of $1,375 and net of $687.50. After subtracting the 5 percent booking fee ($68.75), the owners' take would be $402.19 while the players received $216.56. Overall, a doubleheader in New York and New Jersey could realize a net of $1,418.75, with the owners receiving $922.19 and the players $496.56.

Operating in the nation's largest baseball market provided Strong with considerable advantage and leverage. With Strong scheduling games for the Philadelphia Giants, the Brooklyn Royal Giants, the Cuban Giants, the All-Havanas, and the Cuban Stars in New York, booking fees alone could be quite lucrative. Yet by the same token, black and Cuban clubs still benefited from the gate receipts they could generate from Sunday games in Gotham. This was one reason why Schlichter sought an alliance with Strong in the first place—to tap into the New York market. However, this association came at the expense of black baseball clubs making concessions that white clubs never had to make. It was a compromise black baseball entrepreneurs were willing to make to advance their economic interests.

In addition to consulting the various park managers in New York City, White attempted to persuade Brooklyn Royal Giants' owner John Connor to withdraw from the ILBCAC. At first Connor was reluctant to bolt from the league, but by July the *Age* reported the Royals' owner believed his team was not being given proper consideration in regards to booking dates. White tried to convince Connor, Pop Watkins, and J. M. Bright to form a new association. Bright was also at odds with Strong, leading the Cuban magnate to book his own games. The NACBC was split into two warring factions. On one side, Schlichter, Strong, and E. B. Lamar sought to maintain the status quo. On the other, Connor and Bright were seriously considering forming a new association.[14]

The division within the NACBC did not change its aspiration to expand the market potential of its members' clubs. The Cuban Stars embarked upon a three-month tour of the Midwest that went through the states of Indiana, Kentucky, Illinois, and Wisconsin. The majority of their games were played against Chicago's top semiprofessional clubs. Stars' manager E. B. Lamar had assembled one of the most talented Cuban teams to that time. It was led by a pitching combo that could compete against any Major League club in the dead ball era: Jose Munoz and Jose Mendez. Shortstop Luis Bustamente and second baseman Manuel Govantes provided the Stars with some stellar defense up the middle. First baseman Augustin Parpetti was not only an excellent defensive player; he was also considered one of the best Cuban hitters of all time. The Stars' left fielder, Hector Magrinat, was regarded as one of the best Cuban outfielders in the opening decades of the twentieth century.

The Cuban Stars toured the aforementioned states during the week and returned to Chicago for Sunday games. They also played weekday games in the Windy City as part of a series with the Logan Squares, Gunthers, and Leland Giants. White semipro magnates like Jimmy Callahan and Charles Gunther who owned or leased their ballparks benefited economically from these series by renting out their grounds to stage these contests. Callahan, in particular, profited from the plethora of black clubs from the East and Midwest who began to barnstorm to Chicago for weekend games.[15]

On June 14, the Cuban Stars began a five-game series with the Logan Squares. The *Chicago Tribune* reported that several Cub players in the Major Leagues, including Frank Chance, Johnny Evers, and Frank "Wildfire" Shulte, watched the Squares' pitcher Will Torrey pitch a no-hit, no-run game. The Squares scored two runs in the first inning, one in the second, and one in the seventh in a 4-0 victory. The following day, Jose Mendez was equally impressive. He gave up one run, two hits, and struck out seventeen batters in a 5-1 win for the Cubans. In game three, Torrey was locked in a pitcher's duel with Jose Munoz. The two pitchers battled to a 2-2 tie over fifteen innings before the Squares scored one run in the sixteenth to win the game. The Cubans won the final two games and won a closely contested series by three games to two.[16]

The Cuban Stars then turned their attention to Rube Foster's Leland Giants. The Lelands were having another spectacular season and were on their way to winning the Chicago City League pennant. Jose Mendez bested Bill Gatewood in the first game of the seven-game series. The game was tied at one going into the seventh inning when the Cubans broke the game open with a four-run rally on the way to an 8-2 win. Rube Foster evened the series at one game apiece with an impressive 7-0 shutout victory. In game three, the Giants committed six errors in the first two innings and the Stars scored four runs as they coasted to a 4-1 win. The fourth game matched Rube Foster against Jose Mendez. The game exemplified the kind of classic pitchers' battle that occurred during the dead ball era. The Giants scored the only run in the game in the second inning when Hector Magrinat dropped Pete Booker's fly ball in left field. Booker went to second on an error, stole third base, and scored on Harry Moore's single. The 1-0 heartbreaker evidently took the life out of the Stars, as they lost the next two games and the series, four games to two.[17]

The Stars culminated their midwestern tour in an eleven-game series with the Kansas City Giants and a seven-game series with the Philadelphia Giants. The games were played on City League parks, with the majority of them staged at Logan Squares Park. Two players who were beginning their long and productive careers in black baseball—Tully McAdoo and Bill Pettus—led the Kansas City Giants. The first game set the tone for the series. Jose Munoz struck out seven batters and scattered eight hits in a 2-1 Cubans' win. The Stars won the next three games before the Giants prevailed in game five with an 8-1 victory. The Cubans won the three out of the next five games and took the series, seven games to four.[18]

The Stars awaited the arrival of the Philadelphia Giants. Despite the turmoil that surrounded the team, the Giants were still a competitive bunch. John Henry Lloyd, Danny McClellan, Spotswood Poles, and Billy Francis made the Quaker club an awesome opponent. The Quaker club began its second Midwest tour with a three-game series against the Leland Giants in Detroit, Michigan. After the Giants suffered a 3-1 defeat in the first game, their pitcher, Charles "Bugs" Raymond, held the Lelands to one run and four hits in a 5-1 victory. The third game was no contest as the Giants scored six runs in the first two innings and coasted to a 9-1 win. The series was not promoted as a Colored Championship Series, but the Quaker club got some satisfaction in defeating the best club in the Midwest after their series the previous season ended in controversy.[19]

The Philadelphia Giants' seven-game series with the Cuban Stars in Chicago told a different story. Their series with the Stars showed that a changing of the guard had taken place in black baseball in the East. Ironically, this change became apparent in the Windy City. The Stars took the first three games of the series before the Giants rebounded in game four with a 9-5 win. The clubs split the next two games before the Giants collapsed in game seven. They got off to a 6-3 lead before the Stars scored two in the fifth, three in the sixth, four in the seventh, and four in the eighth and routed the Quaker club, 16-6. The lost typified the roller-coaster ride the Giants endured during the 1909 season.[20]

On August 24, the *Chicago Tribune* reported the Cuban Stars were "ordered" to return east, evidently by NACBC officials. Upon their return, the Stars were challenged by John Connor's Brooklyn Royal Giants for black baseball supremacy in the East. Connor and manager Grant Johnson assembled the strongest Royal Giants team in its brief history. Captain Frank Earle was the Royals' versatile star performer, pitching and playing in the outfield. Harry Buckner was the Royals' workhorse on the mound, while Bill Monroe, Jules Thomas, and Gus James rounded out a team that dominated black and white semipro teams in the East. The Royal Giants still operated as a local club, playing the majority of their games in New York, New Jersey, and Pennsylvania.[21]

On September 2, the *New York Age* reported that the Brooklyn Royal Giants would meet the Cuban Stars for the colored championship. A best three-out-five game series was scheduled on consecutive weekends throughout the various parks in New York City controlled by the NACBC. A second game followed each series game, the second one being between the Royal Giants or Cuban Stars against either a top white semipro club like the Ridgewoods or the Philadelphia Giants, who had just returned from the Midwest. The colored championship turned out to be the Frank Earle series. A reported crowd of six thousand fans packed Bronx Oval to watch Earle defeat Stars' pitcher Luis Padron, 5-3. Padron took a 2-1 lead into the sixth inning before the Royals scored four runs to win the game. In the second game, Earle defeated Jose Mendez 2-1, although the latter struck out ten Royals batters. Padron prevailed in the third game with a 4-2 victory, but the reprieve was short-lived. Earle triumphed for the third time with a 5-3 win over Padron, and the Royal Giants won the colored championship. The Royals' captain put on an impressive performance.[22]

However, the Royal Giants' claim to the colored championship was premature. According to the informal parameters that governed the colored championship, the Royal Giants would have to defeat the top black clubs in each region of the country. It wasn't necessary to play the colored champion of the South because of the Stars' defeat of the Louisville Giants. However, the Stars had lost to the Leland Giants during their midwestern barnstorming tour. Since the Royal Giants did not play the Leland Giants or tour the Midwest during the 1909 season, they could only lay claim to being the eastern colored champions.

More important than the colored championship was the NACBC's ability to withstand the internal conflict that plagued the organization. The 1908 and 1909 barnstorming tours to the Midwest and Cuba illustrated that centralizing the scheduling process was an effective mode of operation. This booking system was successful in exploiting baseball's two largest consumer markets—New York and Chicago—and simultaneously extended NACBC's market potential internationally to Cuba. But the attempt to centralize black baseball's business practices came at the expense of marginalizing the African American entrepreneurs who shaped the product (the game on the field); created a demand for that product (through barnstorming); and developed the symbiotic business relationship with white semipros.

On the Verge of Collapse

Internal conflict continued to plague the NACBC during the 1910 season. Much as with the Philadelphia Giants, a wedge emerged between

Brooklyn Royal Giants' owner John Connor and his manager, Home Run Johnson. It began with the Royals' winter tour of Florida. Beginning in 1909, Johnson led the Royals to the South to represent the Breakers establishment in the Hotel League at Palm Beach, Florida. Much like the Cuban Giants of the late 1880s and 1890s, the Royals were hired as waiters, but they were essentially there to entertain the guests with their ball-playing skills. In 1910, the Royal Giants competed against the Leland Giants, who represented the Royal Poinciana Hotel. The clubs played each other eight times—each team winning three games while they tied two.[23]

When the Royal Giants returned north, Johnson sought a partnership with Connor, but was refused. Apparently, when the Royals were in Florida, the *Age* reported that Connor attempted to trade Johnson to the Philadelphia Giants for John Henry Lloyd. Connor charged Johnson with unsuccessfully encouraging other players to leave the club. No doubt this alleged insurrection was in response to Royals' owner refusing to grant Johnson a partnership. As Connor explained, "For the last two years I have spent thousands of dollars trying to furnish New York with a champion team, and did not think that I should give any one interest at this time." As a result, Johnson left the Royals and signed with the Leland Giants. In addition to Johnson leaving the club, Giants' first baseman Al Robinson signed with the Cuban Giants. Connor, nevertheless, was able to keep together a strong team that included Frank Earle, Bill Monroe, Emmett Bowman, Harry Buckner, and Gus James. To replace Johnson, Connor named Sol White as the Royals' new manager.[24]

Connor's assertion that his financial investment was a key to making the Brooklyn Royal Giants a successful enterprise was a valid claim. However, he could not have accomplished this without Grant Johnson's managerial expertise. Connor was not a former ball player and he had no previous experience managing a black baseball club. Johnson, on the other hand, had served in a managerial capacity since the 1890s, when he assisted Bud Fowler in forming the Page Fence Giants. Therefore, Connor had to rely on Johnson with regard to talent acquisition and the scheduling of games with black and white clubs, vital elements to ensure the Royal owner's return on his investment. Once the Brooklyn Royal Giants became a member of the NACBC, Johnson lost a great deal of autonomy within the administrative process. As a co-owner, Johnson undoubtedly recognized that he would be able to maintain some influence over the decision-making process, but because Nat Strong was the business manager, he took over the scheduling duties from Johnson. Therefore, Johnson was marginalized to managing the game on the field. When Connor refused to take on Johnson as a partner, it marked the end of a successful business association between the two men. It also exemplified the wedge between ownership and management that evolved within the NACBC.

A split emerged within the NACBC's ownership ranks. On May 5, 1910, the *Age* reported that the NACBC had expelled the Leland Giants and the Cuban Giants. In other words, the association would refuse to schedule games with these clubs, and the NACBC would use its influence to ensure that neither club would get the best playing dates with top-level semipro teams. The Lelands' expulsion was undoubtedly in response to Rube Foster's signing of Grant Johnson. To add insult to injury, Foster lured John Henry Lloyd from the Philadelphia Giants. Lloyd reportedly did not want to play with the Giants anymore and had been contemplating going to Chicago anyway. Since one of the NACBC's broad objectives was to impose salary limits and minimize constant player movement, breaking its business ties with the Leland Giants was predictable. The Cuban Giants' banishment, on the other hand, was probably due to J. M. Bright's fall into disfavor the previous year when he began to book his own games.[25]

In the midst of this turmoil, the NACBC managed to send two of its member clubs on their annual midwestern barnstorming tours. The Cuban Stars and the Philadelphia Giants made a tour of the Midwest for the third consecutive year. However, neither club played the Leland Giants. Abel Linares accompanied the Stars to the Midwest instead of E. B. Lamar, and of the thirty-seven games reported in the press, the Stars won twenty-three of them. Conversely, the Philadelphia Giants performed poorly. They began strong by winning six of their first eight games, but from June 11 to June 25, the Giants lost eight of their last nine games. The Philadelphia Giants were once the centerpiece of the NACBC, but their fall from prominence was swift.[26]

While the Cuban Stars and the Philadelphia Giants toured the Midwest, John Connor continued to confront internal problems within his player force. On August 18, 1910, the *Age* reported that several Royal players were entertaining offers to jump their contracts and sign with a "certain New York baseball fan, who is also interested in theatricals." In response, Connor gave notice to all his disgruntled players that they could leave and said that he would find new players. Evidently their differences were temporarily resolved, because the disgruntled players finished the season with the Royals.[27]

As the 1910 season came to a close, the National Association of Colored Baseball Clubs of the United States and Cuba was in a catastrophic state. The NACBC experienced a crisis in leadership because H. Walter Schlichter's attention was diverted with dreams of building an empire in black and white professional baseball. Internal division emerged within the ownership and managerial ranks of the Philadelphia Giants and the Brooklyn Royal Giants. Interestingly enough, the fall from prominence of the NACBC's flagship club the, Philadelphia Giants, coincided with Sol White's departure. The NACBC's team owners created further division when J. M. Bright began booking his own games and John Connor contemplated leaving the association. While the NACBC was in a state of collapse, the Leland Giants Baseball and Amusement Association would experience a period of both continued progress and lost opportunities.

AT THE PEAK OF ITS PRESTIGE

The Leland Giants continued their spectacular success on the diamond, enlarged its recreation enterprise, and restructured its management team. LGBBA organizers expanded the Chateau De La Plaisance to include a Moving Picture Show, a dance hall called the Terpsichorean Parlors, and a restaurant. It sponsored several promotional events, including a potato race, a One Mile Handicap race, and a skating competition in which contestants had to skate the entire rink backwards in ten minutes to win a prize. The Association made plans to open a summer amusement park called the Summer Garden and Peruvian Gallery that included a restaurant and an Out Door Music Emporium. The LGBBA revised its management structure by electing the following members to hold office: Frank Leland, president; Robert Jackson, vice president; Beauregard Moseley, secretary and treasurer; and Rube Foster, manager and captain of the team. Whereas the LGBBA expanded its recreation enterprise to include a movie theater, dance hall, and summer garden, the Leland Giants baseball team continued to be the foundation on which the venture was built.[28]

The Lelands began the 1908 season as a member of the newly created Chicago City League. A war with the Park Owners Association over players was fought during the City League's organizational phase. Forming the new league was further complicated when the stockholders of one its member clubs, the West Ends, split into two factions. Some of its stockholders favored joining the City League, while the others preferred remaining in the POA. Tensions between the leagues heightened when two POA clubs, the Logan Squares and the South Chicagos, defected to the new league. The Chicago City League began the season with eight teams: the Leland Giants, Logan Squares, West Ends, South Chicagos, Riverviews, Marquettes, Athletics, and Spauldings.[29]

While the Chicago City League began the season with high hopes, the circuit collapsed in the middle of the season. The City League operated as a weekend league and allowed the Lelands to continue their barnstorming pattern of playing weekday games throughout the Midwest and returning to Chicago for Sunday games. Unlike the POA, the Chicago City League published league standings, but there were no indications that it would sponsor a season-ending championship series. By the end of June, the Leland Giants had won all of their league games. Trouble surfaced within the league, however, when the Riverviews failed to play the Marquettes in a scheduled league game. The *Chicago InterOcean* reported that the gates at the ballpark were locked when the Marquettes arrived. The Riverviews were dropped from the circuit, and the City League operated with seven clubs. On August 1, 1908, the Indianapolis *Freeman* reported that the Chicago City League had disbanded.[30]

At the end of September, the Leland Giants concluded their regular season with a six-game series with the American Association (AA) Minneapolis Millers. The American Association was a double A minor league in Organized Baseball, the minors' highest classification. Formed in 1901 as an outlaw organization, the AA would prove more stable than any other minor league over the first half of the twentieth century. The AA had franchises in eight cities: Columbus, Indianapolis, Kansas City, Louisville, Milwaukee, Minneapolis, St. Paul, and Toledo. The Millers played in what Neil Sullivan described as the AA's most remarkable facility, Nicollet Park. From 1896 to 1955, players tried to adjust to the dimensions that ran from 279 feet in right field to 435 in center to 328 in left. The park included a right-field wall similar to Fenway Park's Green Monster in left field.

After losing the first game of the series, the Lelands rebounded in the second game by scoring three runs in the eighth and two in the ninth on the way to a 6-4 victory. The Millers took a 3-1 lead into the sixth inning in game three before the Giants erupted with four runs in the seventh inning and one in the ninth to win, 6-3. In game four, Giants' pitcher Emmett Bowman gave up only five hits and shut out the Millers, 4-0. Unfortunately, the final games were not reported in the press. Nevertheless, the Giants' performance against the Millers was outstanding.[31]

The Leland Giants' excellent showing in the Chicago City League and their season-ending series with the Minneapolis Millers served to heighten the club's prestige within Chicago's black community. On October 15, several members of Chicago's black middle class sponsored a banquet on behalf of the Lelands. Nothing illustrated the rhetoric of racial uplift better than the praise bestowed on the Leland Giants in the *Broad Ax*: "This team of Colored ballplayers have by their abilities won a place in the forefront of America's greatest past time baseball and have taken the whole race with them[;] nothing has contributed to the lessening of race prejudices in this community more than this gallant manly scientific gentlemanly aggregation of ball players, who have wrung from the throats of our enemies more praise than was ever showered upon us and have thereby served as a deterrent to the avalanche of hate that oftentimes comes our way." Such praise illustrated the significance the

Chicago's black middle-class citizenry placed upon the Leland Giants' tremendous success on the diamond in a sport that most Chicagoans respected and even glorified.[32]

The Leland Giants continued to succeed throughout the 1909 baseball season. On May 15, 1909, the Indianapolis *Freeman* reported the Leland Giants had traveled 4,465 miles playing black and white teams in Memphis, Birmingham, Fort Worth, Austin, San Antonio, Prairie View (Texas), and Houston. Foster supposedly received a hero's welcome upon his return to his home state of Texas. He reportedly received a welcome in Forth Worth that would "have done honor to the President of the United States." In Houston, the Lelands played to the "largest crowd ever at a baseball game" in that city, where the Giants swept the local Texas club in three games. A large contingent from Foster's hometown in Calvert attended one of the games there. The Leland Giants traveled by Pullman car to illustrate their reputation as an elite black independent club. This mode of traveling also served as a response to the widening discrimination that African Americans confronted in the early twentieth century. The Pullman car not only provided a means of transportation, it was also the team's living quarters. Black teams did not have to deal with white hotel managers and their prejudice when they traveled on the road, particularly in the South.[33]

Chicago's semipro baseball season was notable for the Chicago City League's completion of its first regular season. Six teams formed the revised league, which included the Logan Squares, Gunthers, Anson's Colts, West Ends, Milwaukee White Sox, and Leland Giants. By July 4, the Logan Squares, the Leland Giants, and the Gunthers were locked in a close pennant race. On September 4, the Lelands clinched the City League pennant with a 5-3 win over the Logan Squares. They finished the season with thirty-one wins and nine losses. The Giants' pennant-winning season led a *Chicago Tribune* sportswriter to state that "while undoubtedly it is galling to many persons to see a colored nine take honors from five white teams, the Leland Giants are entitled to a place in the league by their drawing powers." The writer went on to describe how the Lelands had such talent that "at least five of them would be in the major league if white."[34]

The Leland Giants culminated their 1909 season with a three-game series against the National League's Chicago Cubs. The Cubs were the best team in the National League. They won the NL pennant three years in a row in 1906, 1907, and 1908, and finishing second in 1909. They won a National League record 116 games in 1906 only to lose to the Chicago White Sox in the World Series. In 1908 the Cubs defeated the Detroit Tigers for the World Series championship. From 1906 to 1909, the Chicago Cubs won 426 games. The Cubs possessed the legendary double play combination of Joe Tinker, Johnny Evers, and Frank Chance and boasted an outstanding pitching staff that included Mordecai "Three Finger" Brown, Orvie Overall, and Ed Reulbach.

The Leland Giants and Chicago Cubs played three tightly contested games. In game one, 2,344 fans watched the Cubs defeat the Lelands, 4-1, behind the excellent pitching of Three Finger Brown. The game featured a courageous effort by Giants' center fielder Joe Green, who tried to score from first base on a broken leg. He was thrown out at home plate and collapsed to the ground under excruciating pain. In the second game, the Lelands took a 5-2 lead into the ninth inning before the Cubs scored four runs and won, 6-5. The game ended on a controversial play when Foster, trying to slow down the Cubs' momentum, left the mound to consult with pitcher Pat Dougherty to determine whether the latter should relieve Foster. This obvious stalling tactic irritated the Cubs and the home plate umpire. When Dougherty approached the mound, the umpire refused to let him enter the game. Amid this confusion, Cubs' right fielder Frank "Wildfire" Schulte stole home and was called safe by the umpire to the dismay of Foster and the Lelands. The final game was a pitcher's duel between Three Finger Brown and Pat Dougherty. The game was called in the seventh inning because of darkness with the Cubs ahead, 1-0.[35]

Despite losing the series to the Cubs, the Leland Giants Baseball and Amusement Association had made tremendous progress. They expanded the Chateau De La Plaisance and made plans to open a summer resort. The Leland Giants' barnstorming tour of the South and its capture of the Chicago City League pennant heightened the club's prestige. When it appeared the LGBBA was ready for bigger and better things, however, the enterprise exhibited signs of internal dissension among its leadership.

Internal Conflict and the Rise of the Chicago Giants

The progress made by the Leland Giants Baseball and Amusement Association produced a conflict of interest within the team's management. Although Frank Leland was elected president of the LGBBA, its secretary and past president, Beauregard Moseley, was the driving force behind the enterprise. Acknowledging his diminished role within the organization, Leland attempted to wrestle control of the Giants away from Rube Foster. However, the Association's investors felt it was in the corporation's best interests to retain Foster as manager. As a result, Moseley and Foster united to force Leland out in a hostile takeover. Foster's alliance with Moseley made the split inevitable.

In response to being forced out, Leland formed the Chicago Leland Giants in partnership with former association members Robert Jackson and Alvin H. Garrett. His goal was to make his Giants a top touring team to compete against the Leland Giants and simultaneously to contend for the Chicago City League championship. To accomplish this, Leland raided his former club for players. He signed Nate Harris to serve as team captain and added Harry Moore, Joe Green, George Wright, Bobby Winston, Chappie Johnson, and Walter Ball. Leland also signed black players from several other clubs, like Bob Marshall, Felix Wallace, and James Taylor, all three from the St. Paul Gophers.[36]

Leland's pitching staff would be led by a tall, hard-throwing right hander from Seguin, Texas, Joseph Williams. Referred to either as "Smokey Joe" or the "Cyclone," Williams's blazing fastball allowed him to become one of the most dominant pitchers for the next twenty-two years. In addition to his fastball, Williams had exceptional control and was a smart pitcher who in his later years compensated for his loss of velocity with cunning and know-how. He began his playing career in 1905 with the San Antonio Bronchos, amassing a five-year won-lost record of 95-29. During one stretch of his Texas career, the Cyclone is reported to have won twenty straight games. On May 2, 1910, Williams made his debut against Chicago's semipros, defeating Donahue's Red Sox, 7-2, at Auburn Park.[37]

In April, the Chicago Leland Giants embarked upon a barnstorming tour of the Deep South. They toured the states of Texas, Louisiana, Mississippi, Tennessee, and Florida. Robert Jackson accompanied the club as the traveling manager. The tour began on April 4 against the Black Buffalos of Houston, Texas. The Giants lost a 3-2 contest that took fourteen innings to complete. However, the Black Buffalos, according to Jackson, needed the assistance of the umpire to ensure victory. For the rest of the tour, the Giants went on a tear, winning their next ten games.[38]

The Chicago Leland Giants' successful spring training tour evidently led to a conflict with Leland's old ball club. On April 23, 1910, the *Broad Ax* reported that the Leland Giants Baseball and Amusement Association had taken Leland to court to prohibit him from using the name Leland Giants. The court ruled in favor of the LGBBA and stated, "No person or persons acting for Frank Leland shall in any way use the name Leland Giants, as it rightfully belongs to the Leland Giants Baseball and Amusement Association. The other persons were an obvious reference to Leland's business partners, Robert Jackson and Alvin Garrett. From that time on, the Chicago Leland Giants were the Chicago Giants.[39]

To further complicate matters, conflict emerged for a second time between the Chicago City League and the Park Owners Association. The Gunthers withdrew from the league over a dispute with the other semipro club owners when, apparently, one of the Gunthers' players jumped his contract. The *Chicago Tribune* reported that the City League and the POA met to devise a plan to respect each others' players under contract. At the same time, the City League was also involved in the lawsuit between the Chicago Giants and the Leland Giants. The City League sided with the Chicago Giants, and the league replaced the Leland Giants in the circuit. It was unclear why the City League favored the Chicago Giants over the Lelands.[40]

Both the Chicago City League and the Park Owners Association began the season under a cloud of controversy. The City League started the season with the Chicago Giants, Rogers Park, Logan Squares, Spauldings, West Ends, and Donohue's Red Sox. The Gunthers and Lelands became members of the Park Owners Association. The POA consisted of twenty-two clubs that included Auburn Park, Mutuals, Illinois Giants, and Normals. The POA also added a Cuban club to its circuit. The *Chicago Tribune* reported that the Stars of Cuba, under the management of A. M. McAllister, left the island for the United States to play in the Chicago circuit. The team featured pitching ace Jose Mendez. Eight clubs in the POA possessed their own parks, with the remaining teams operating on a traveling basis. Despite the disparity of some teams having their own park and others not, the Chicago *Defender* claimed that the clubs with enclosed grounds made the POA "twice as strong as the City League."[41]

Semiprofessional baseball in the Windy City was further complicated when the Chicago City League issued a ban prohibiting the scheduling of games with black and Cuban clubs. The reason given by the City League was that local patrons complained about the lack of contests scheduled with local teams. The ban did not apply to the Chicago Giants, since they were a member of the City League. The aspirations of the eastern-based National Association of Colored Baseball Clubs of the United States and Cuba apparently produced a conflict of interest. The *New York Age* speculated that the prohibition could have emerged because some of the top Cuban teams—like the Cuban Stars and the All Havanas—had been invading the area for the past two years. For the remainder of the 1910 season, City League clubs scheduled no games with NACBC teams.[42]

The Park Owners Association did not issue a ban against games with black and Cuban clubs. NACBC teams could still schedule games with POA clubs, which kept their barnstorming network to the Midwest intact. However, when the Leland Giants signed Grant Johnson and John Henry Lloyd, the NACBC severed its business ties with the LGBBA. The NACBC would schedule games with POA clubs like the Gunthers, Normals, and Artesians.

Neither the LGBBA's lawsuit nor the controversy surrounding Chicago's semiprofessional leagues hindered Frank Leland's efforts to make his Chicago Giants a top touring team. They maintained the standard midwestern barnstorming pattern of touring the surrounding states during the week and returning to Chicago for Sunday games. They competed in the City League and occasionally scheduled doubleheaders on Sundays. To obtain community support, Leland and Jackson organized the Chicago Giants Rooter's Club, which participated in an opening festivity known as Flag Raising Day. That Day was similar to the opening day activities that occurred at Major League baseball games. As Harold Seymour explained, "There was always the march of the two teams across the field to the flagpole in centerfield, where the opposing captains hoisted the flag, then the return march to the dugouts, followed by the throwing out of the first ball by some dignitary." In June, the Giants relocated to Red Sox Park located on Sixty-First Street and Lawrence Avenue. The move was made because the Giants' old grounds, Auburn Park, had been sold by court order to satisfy the heirs of the property. The Giants' new grounds were in a closer proximity to the growing Black Belt on Chicago's South Side, so Leland was in a better position to tap into the Windy City's growing black consumer market.[43]

In late August, the Chicago Giants played an eight-game series with Jimmy Callahan's All Star team. The creation of all star teams at the semipro level had become commonplace by 1910, and Chicago's black clubs benefited by scheduling these exhibition games. On August 22, Callahan's All Stars invaded Red Sox Park, and they hit Giants' pitcher John "Steel Arm" Taylor early and often on the way to a 12-7 victory. The second game ended in a 4-4 tie called in the eleventh inning because of darkness. Unfortunately, games three and four were not reported in the press. The Giants prevailed 6-2 in game five with a four-run rally in the eighth inning. The following day, Joe "Cyclone" Williams held the All Stars to three runs and five hits while striking out ten batters in a 5-3 Giants win. Bobby Winston and Harry Moore led a fifteen-hit attack in game seven as the Giants demolished the All Stars, 12-4. In the final game, Walter Ball held the All Stars to three hits in a 4-1 win, and the Chicago Giants took the series, five games to three.[44]

On August 10, 1910, the Chicago *Defender* reported that Frank Leland had negotiated a deal with the officers of the California Winter

League (CWL) to represent the city of Los Angeles in the circuit. The CWL was a collection of teams made up of former and current major and minor league players. The league began in 1906 with a variety of teams from Santa Barbara, Los Angeles, San Diego, Pasadena, and San Bernardino. Prominent Major Leaguers like Fred Snodgrass, Walter Johnson, and the controversial Hal Chase played in the loop. The *Los Angeles Times* reported that the Giants' entry into the CWL "aroused the greatest amount of interest." The *Times* added, "The Coast League could do no better [than] to draft some of them Chicago Giants] for they shine."[45]

The California Winter League did not operate in the traditional sense of having a pennant race and a season-ending championship. The league consisted of four teams: the Giants, San Diego Griefers, Doyles, and McCormick Shamrocks. Because the CWL operated as a weekend league, the Giants barnstormed the West Coast for weekday games. The Giants began the winter league season with a doubleheader against the Doyles. The Doyles destroyed the Giants in the first game, 11-1, but Leland's club rebounded in the second game with an 11-7 win.[46]

Overall, the Chicago Giants fared well in this competitive league. Of the games reported in the *Los Angeles Times*, the Giants won ten, lost seven, and tied one. The winter season was notable for two pitching performances, one from Joe Williams and the other from Frank Wickware. On January 8, 1911, the *Times* reported that the Cyclone struck out nineteen batters and gave up three hits in a 7-0 win. The *Times* added that Williams's accomplishment was something to be proud of, "because the Doyles were composed of 'real professionals,'" including Elmer Rieger, who had pitched for the St. Louis Cardinals. On January 22, Frank Wickware was equally impressive, giving up two runs and six hits and striking out nine batters in a 4-2 win.[47]

The 1910 season represented a comeback for Frank Leland. Despite the failed attempt to organize a professional league, his expulsion from the LGBBA, and his participation in the troubled Chicago City League, Leland rebounded by making the Chicago Giants one of the leading black baseball clubs in the Midwest. Winning recognition as Comeback Player of the Year (although he was not a player) meant Leland was still one of black baseball's leading entrepreneurs

While the Chicago Giants enjoyed an outstanding first season, the LGBBA made plans to move into its new ballpark, located at Sixty-Ninth and Halsted Streets. The new park had a seating capacity of 5,000, with 400 box seats and 1,600 bleacher seats. The park was easily accessible via the trolley lines or the South Side L. Since the LGBBA owned the enclosed park, it served as a symbol of racial advancement through self-help. The *Broad Ax* hailed the new grounds as "the prettiest and most comfortable park in the city," and it allowed the LGBBA to maintain its symbiotic business relationship with white semiprofessional clubs while at the same time attempting to corner the black consumer market on the South Side.[48]

The LGBBA continued to make inroads into Chicago's black community in order to tap into its growing black consumer market. To invoke community pride and team spirit, the LGBBA created the Leland Giants Rooters Club and elected former Chicago Unions co-owner Al Donigan as president. The Association contributed annually to Provident Hospital, founded by Daniel Hale Williams, the country's best-known African American physician and one of the outstanding surgeons of the day. Provident Hospital was a hugely ambitious African American civic undertaking in Chicago. In 1891, Williams formed a coalition of black community leaders and several of his white medical colleagues with the intent of organizing the first interracial hospital in the United States. Unlike any other hospital in the city, Provident received blacks on an equal basis and provided opportunities for black doctors and nurses. In its early years, Provident received its major financial support from wealthy white Chicagoans like Philip Armour and Florence Pullman. The hospital also solicited and received contributions from the black community. Exhibition baseball games represented one way these funds were raised. On August 6, 1909, for example, the Leland Giants played a benefit game for the hospital at Comiskey Park. The *Chicago Tribune* reported that over six thousand fans had witnessed the game and that $2,500 had been raised for the Provident.

While this gesture was based on a profit motive, as were all public relations campaigns, it also served as a means for the LGBBA to make its imprint upon black community development.[49] Raising funds for Provident Hospital illustrated the use of public relations as an integral part of the LGBBA's strategy to maximize revenues. They used PR to sway public opinion in the Association's favor, which thereby promoted the Leland Giants baseball club while also advancing the popularity of the LGBBA's various recreation enterprises that catered to the needs and wants of black Chicagoans. On May 14, 1910, the *Defender* published an article written by "an observer" who praised the LGBBA's yearly contributions to Provident and also highlighted its yearly donations to the "Old Folks" home. The observer added that the LGBBA was "deserving of patronage on the part of those who wish to see a genteel, scientific ball game as well as those who believe in paying honor to whom honor [was] due." Public relations was used to wage another, more subtle kind of battle. Through the creation of the LGBBA, Chicago's African Americans attempted to prove to the white world (and no doubt to their doubting brothers and sisters) that they were worthy of all the things they fought for. As Vincent Harding has pointed out, blacks sought to "bind up the wounds of their own community, to improve the quality of its life, to serve its needy, to demonstrate their capacity for self-determination, self-improvement, and freedom." They built the black community from within, preparing it for the continuing stages of its struggle toward a new humanity.[50]

Moving into a new ballpark and raising funds for Provident Hospital was part of the higher ambitions that Beauregard Moseley had for the LGBBA. Despite Leland's raiding his club for players, the Leland Giants remained a competitive club. Foster secured the services of top players like Pete Hill, John Henry Lloyd, Grant Johnson, Pete Booker, Bruce Petway, and Jap Payne. Pat Dougherty, Billy Norman, and Rube Foster made the Giants' pitching staff awesome. On August 27, the *Broad Ax* reported that Moseley had issued a "world challenge" to determine who was the best baseball team. "In order to put at rest all doubt as to what Baseball Club is the champion of the world," Moseley added, "the Leland Giants will begin a tour of the world." They would "meet all comers" to compete for a one-thousand-dollar side bet plus the gate receipts for a series of three or more games. If this challenge was not accepted by September 15, then the Leland Giants would proclaim themselves the "Champions of America."[51]

Several clubs answered the challenge. On September 23, the Leland Giants began an eastern and southern barnstorming tour that took them through the states of New York, New Jersey, and Florida. The tour culminated with a series of games in Cuba. The Giants defeated every club they played. The Lelands' game against Nat Strong's Ridgewood club illustrated their dominance. The Giants took an 11-5 lead into the fifth inning before they broke the game open with a seven-run rally in the ninth to win, 21-7. This game appeared to be a slap in the face of the NACBC, which had expelled the Giants from its barnstorming network. In any event, the Leland Giants had won twenty straight games by the end of September. On October 1, the Leland Giants embarked upon their first tour of Cuba. Along with the American League's Detroit Tigers, the Lelands played the top Cuban clubs, including the Havanas and the Almendares. While the Giants won the majority of their games, they lost a tough series to the Almendares.[52]

While the Leland Giants barnstormed the East and Cuba for gate receipts and prestige, Moseley urged blacks to organize their own professional league. He recognized that the raiding of player rosters was a destructive practice that had to be eliminated. The proliferation of black teams from the South and Midwest made it feasible, in Moseley's view, to form a black professional league. The proposed league was another exposition of the doctrine of self-help. In his statement of purpose, Moseley indicated that blacks "are already forced out of the game from a national standpoint" and find it increasingly difficult to play white semiprofessional teams locally. This "presages the day when there will be [no opportunities for black baseball players], except the Negro comes to his own rescue by organizing and patronizing the game successfully, which would of itself force recognition from white minor leagues to play us and share in the receipts." Moseley added, "Let those who would serve the Race assist it in holding its back up . . . organizing an effort to secure . . . the best club of ball players possible."[53]

The prospective owners first met on December 30, 1910. Moseley was elected temporary chairman and Felix Payne of Kansas City temporary secretary. Eight cities were represented: Chicago; New Orleans; Mobile; Louisville; St. Louis; Columbus, Ohio;, Kansas City, Missouri;

and Kansas City, Kansas. Unlike Leland, Moseley had devised a detailed plan, consisting of twenty-points that explained how the league should operate. Using the cooperative business philosophy, Moseley suggested that eight Race men in each city pool their resources and form a stock company. The league was projected to have an operating capital of $2,500, with each club paying roughly $300. Half the league's umpires would be black and paid five dollars a game. A reserve list would be developed, and players who jumped their contracts would be banned from the league. Finally, an effort would be made to limit the league to one franchise per city.[54]

The prospective league generated a lot of enthusiasm the following year and rumors persisted of other cities joining the loop, but it still died stillborn. As with the previous organizational efforts, investors did not come forth. At its inaugural meeting, only Chicago, New Orleans, and Kansas City, Kansas, were represented by investors. The remaining five were represented by fans, and there was no evidence to indicate that possible financiers existed in these cities. Second, it appeared that no semiprofessional baseball infrastructure existed in the aforementioned cities that was comparable to Chicago's. In addition to the City League and the POA, Chicago also had several other leagues and associations, like the Suburban League and the Inter-City League. Also operating in the Windy City were several independent clubs that did not belong to any league. This infrastructure was pivotal to black baseball teams functioning competitively and economically. Finally, Chicago's population of 2,185,283 was exponentially larger than that of any city in the proposed league. The next closet city was St. Louis, with a population of 687,029. This market imbalance might explain why no comparable semiprofessional baseball infrastructure existed in cities aside from Chicago prior to World War I. Attempting to maintain a symbiotic business relationship with white semipros and simultaneously tap into the black consumer market also proved problematic. For example, Kansas City, Kansas's total population in 1910 was 82,331. Its black population was 9,286, hardly comparable to Chicago's African American population of 44,103. The unwillingness of black baseball entrepreneurs to venture too far outside their respective territorial regions was understandable.[55]

Although the proposed league ended in failure, it did reflect both the continued progress and lost opportunities underwent by black professional baseball. The calls for organizing black professional leagues, patterned after the white Major Leagues, in the East and Midwest was understandable, given the proliferation of black teams since the middle of the new century's first decade. As H. Walter Schlichter accurately pointed out, black baseball had "an overcrowded market" of baseball talent, with supply greater than demand. Yet upon a closer examination, black professional baseball did not have enough teams operating at a high caliber to organize leagues on par with the white majors. Black baseball needed strong clubs in the bigger urban cities like Boston, Detroit, Pittsburgh, and Cincinnati. By 1910 the stronger, better financed, clubs operated largely in New York and Chicago.

The Leland Giants Baseball and Amusement Association continued to make significant progress in spite of the internal divisions its success created. The LGBBA continued to expand its recreation venues and make its imprint upon black community development. The Leland Giants emerged as one of the elite touring teams with their extended barnstorming tours of the South and East and to Cuba. Their exhibition games with the Minneapolis Millers and Chicago Cubs and winning the Chicago City League championship heightened the club's prestige. Furthermore, the LGBBA moved into a new ballpark it purchased, and the organization was promoted as a symbol of race pride and racial solidarity through self-help.

The LGBBA's progress, however, produced a conflict of interest among its leadership, resulting in Frank Leland's expulsion from the enterprise. To add insult to injury, the LGBBA took Leland to court to prohibit him from using his name for his new club, the Chicago Giants. The Chicago City League's ban on scheduling NACBC clubs meant Leland would lose some lucrative weekend games. None of these obstacles prevented Leland from making his Chicago Giants a top touring team. The Giants' spring training tour of the South and their participation in the California Winter League allowed Frank Leland to serve notice that he was still one of black baseball's leading entrepreneurs.

The National Association of Colored Baseball Clubs of the United States and Cuba made similar progress in the East. It continued to advance toward Sol White and Walter Schlichter's goal of making black baseball a legitimate profession. The centralization of power through control of the decision-making process proved effective in maintaining a barnstorming network to the Midwest. White and Schlichter promoted the game in the sporting press to appeal to a mass audience. The Philadelphia Giants, Brooklyn Royal Giants, and Cuban Stars emerged as the premier black baseball clubs in the East.

However, as with the LGBBA, the NACBC's accomplishments produced a conflict of interest among its leadership. Schlichter's efforts to expand his influence in black and white professional baseball resulted in a leadership crisis. The NACBC's top-heavy administrative approach marginalized managers who, like White and Grant Johnson, were instrumental to their teams' success. The scheduling system that Nat Strong created began to break down when J. M. Bright started booking his own games and John Connor contemplated leaving the association. As the 1911 season approached, the NACBC's collapse was inevitable.

4

Years of Transition, 1911–1913

The 1911 season marked the beginning of a transition in the ownership of eastern and midwestern black baseball teams. Sol White left the Brooklyn Royal Giants and became the manager of the newly created Lincoln Giants. White assembled one of black baseball's strongest teams, and it dominated black and white semipro clubs throughout the season. Turmoil among the Lincoln's management team, however, resulted in White leaving it in September. Despite losing some of his best players, John Connor maintained a competitive club, and his Royal Giants embarked upon their first extended tour of the South and Midwest. When the Royals returned to New York, Connor secured a lease on a playing grounds in Harlem where the team would play its home games. The formation of the Lincoln Giants and the acquisition by Connor of a playing grounds ended the National Association of Colored Baseball Clubs of the United States and Cuba's booking control.

The state of confusion that characterized eastern black baseball at the end of the 1911 season continued the following year. Amid the chaotic 1912 season, the Brooklyn Royal Giants set out on their second extended tour of the Midwest. They played the top black and white semipro clubs, with the tour including a six-game series with Rube Foster's Chicago American Giants. Simultaneously, the turmoil that continued to surround the Lincoln Giants' management team and the collapse of the NACBC resulted in a competition for players by several black baseball magnates seeking an opportunity to capitalize on the national game. The competition for players resulted in the temporary departure from black baseball of John Connor and the assumption of control of the Brooklyn Royal Giants by Nat Strong. On the other hand, the Lincoln Giants emerged as the top touring team of the East, but their financial problems placed the club on economically shaky ground.

While eastern black baseball underwent its transitional period, midwestern black baseball in Chicago was also in turmoil. Rube Foster left the Leland Giants Baseball and Amusement Association and formed the Chicago American Giants. Foster's defection heightened tensions between Chicago's leading black baseball entrepreneurs, who competed against each other for players, gate receipts, and preeminence in the Midwest. The Chicago American Giants and Chicago Giants competed against each other in a series of games for midwestern supremacy that was marked with controversy. Despite their squabbling, a second series was scheduled between the two clubs. The Leland Giants, on the other hand, suffered through a dismal season. Beauregard Moseley failed to recognize the importance of maintaining a symbiotic business relationship with white semiprofessional teams and sustaining consistent press coverage. In its competition for players with the American Giants and the Chicago Giants, the Lelands lost several of their best team members. When the 1911 season ended, the Leland Giants club was a shell of its former self.

Rube Foster took his American Giants on extended barnstorming tours of the East and West. The extended tours represented Foster's goal from the outset: to make his club a touring team. The American Giants made two tours to the East, and in 1912 they made their first appearance in the California Winter League. The winter tour continued into the 1913 season, and Foster's club played a reported 104 games. Foster concurrently urged black baseball club owners to organize a league patterned after the white Major Leagues. The call for an organized league was in response to the decline of white semiprofessional baseball in Chicago and the need for club owners to protect their investments. He envisioned a circuit composed of teams in Chicago; Detroit; Indianapolis; Kansas City, Missouri; Louisville; and St. Louis. Foster expressed his willingness to organize a league with the purpose of placing the black game on a sound economic footing.

Eastern Black Baseball's Rocky Transition

At the end of the 1910 season, Sol White broke with John Connor, and along with white sports promoters Roderick "Jess" McMahon and his brother Ed, formed the Lincoln Giants. The *New York Age* reported the McMahon brothers were "well-known promoters of sporting events in New York," and they supposedly organized several fight promotions in Gotham. The McMahons secured a lease on Olympic Field, located on 136th Street and Fifth Avenue, and stated they would not give a percentage to anyone to book their games. This assertion was obviously directed at Nat Strong.[1]

At the same time, Sol White assembled one of his strongest teams. He lured catcher Phil Bradley as well as pitcher Harry Buckner from the Royals and signed pitcher Danny McClellan, catcher Pete Booker, and shortstop John Henry Lloyd. White also signed Billy Francis, who was considered the best third baseman in the opening decades of the twentieth century. Spotswood "Spot" Poles was the team's center fielder and leadoff batter; he was a sharp hitter with incredible speed. Poles was reportedly clocked under ten seconds in the 100-yard dash.[2]

The 1911 season marked the start of the career of one of black baseball's legendary pitchers: Richard "Cannonball Dick" Redding. Born in Atlanta, Georgia, in 1891, Redding began pitching with local clubs in his home city. In early 1911, the Philadelphia Giants spotted him there and took him north. Redding was a big, fun-loving Georgian who stood six feet four inches, and along with his speed, he utilized a no-windup delivery and developed a "hesitation pitch" long before Satchel Paige appeared on the scene. In his first game with the Lincoln Giants, Redding shut out the St. Louis Giants, 2-0, giving up only one hit and striking out six batters. By August, Redding had reportedly won seventeen straight games.[3]

The Lincoln Giants began their season with an exhibition game against Mike Donlin's All Stars, who were no match for the Lincolns. Led by Spot Poles and John Henry Lloyd, the Giants took a 6-0 lead into the seventh inning before breaking the game open with a five-run rally on the way to an 11-1 victory.[4]

The McMahons aggressively marketed the Lincoln Giants to appeal to a mass audience. Using sports celebrities to umpire games had been part of black baseball promotions since the late 1880s. On June 18, the *New York Times* reported featherweight champion Abe Attel would umpire the second game of a doubleheader between the Lincolns and the New Londons. On July 2, African American boxer Sam Langford served as an umpire in a three-team doubleheader that included the Giants, Central Islip, and the New Londons. The use of boxers as umpires highlighted the McMahons' connection to fight promotions and represented an elementary form of brand equity—the value added to a product by virtue of name recognition.[5]

The McMahons promoted several Ladies Days throughout the season. Ladies Day promotions had their roots in the late 1860s. The Knickerbockers club established the last Thursday of each month as Ladies Day. Club members were requested to invite their wives, daughters, and girlfriends and appointed a committee to ensure that "suitable seats or settees" were available for them. When the professionals took over the game, the owners adopted the practice. Ladies were usually admitted free if accompanied by a gentleman. On July 17, the McMahons organized a Ladies Day event that included a band concert before and during the game.[6]

Throughout the year, the Lincoln Giants developed a rivalry with the St. Louis Giants. The St. Louis Giants began as a sandlot team that eventually evolved into a touring team. They were managed by Charles Mills, a local saloonkeeper, who organized a club composed primarily of youngsters wearing cheap, nonmatching uniforms and earning less than sixty cents a game. In 1907, the Giants leased Kuebler's Park at 6100 North Broadway in St. Louis and played primarily against white semipros on weekends. The Giants soon became a gate attraction, outdrawing the local white Trolley League. In 1910, the Giants journeyed to Chicago to challenge the top semipro clubs there. Mills signed several talented players who made his St. Louis team a competitive club. Shortstop Joe Hewitt was an outstanding base stealer who used his speed to expand his range at shortstop. Center fielder Jimmie Lyons also had exceptional speed and was a good hitter. Veteran pitcher Bill

Gatewood bolstered the Giants' pitching staff. On September 24, 1910, the St. Louis Giants played a two-game series with Frank Leland's Chicago Giants. The Chicago Giants took the first game 6-3, as John "Steel Arm" Taylor held St. Louis to five hits. In the second game, Bill Gatewood trailed Chicago pitcher Walter Ball, 3-1, before the St. Louis club scored three runs in the top of the ninth inning and won, 4-3.[7]

In 1911 Mills made the initial efforts to elevate his Giants to the ranks of a touring team. He entered into a partnership with local black businessmen and formed the St. Louis Giants and Amusement Association (SLGAA). The SLGAA was another expression of the cooperative enterprise strategy used by baseball entrepreneurs since the late nineteenth century. This black-owned-and-operated enterprise consisted of Mills, manager; Noah Warrington, president; Ollie Jackson, treasurer; and Felix Wallace, team captain. The SLGAA apparently provided Mills with the capital necessary to acquire veteran black baseball players. He signed Chappie Johnson, Steel Arm Taylor, Ben Taylor, and Tully McAdoo to the 1911 squad.[8]

The St. Louis Giants embarked upon their first extended tour of New York. They played a five-game series with the Lincoln Giants that consisted of two doubleheaders and a single game. The St. Louis club provided the Lincolns with some stiff competition. The *Age* reported that the Lincolns' 10-7 loss to St. Louis was their first defeat of the season. A reported crowd of ten thousand fans watched Jimmie Lyons, Felix Wallace, and John Taylor lead a seventeen-hit attack. The Lincolns evened the series with a 12-1 shellacking of the Giants in a game that was called after six innings because the overflow crowd was spilling onto the field of play. The third game was played at Inlet Park in Atlantic City, New Jersey, with St. Louis winning by a score of 3-2. A slugfest ensued in the first game of the second doubleheader. The Lincolns took a 5-4 lead into the sixth inning before St. Louis broke the game open with two runs in the sixth, two in the seventh, and one run in the eighth and ninth innings en route to a 10-5 win. St. Louis was no match for Dick Redding in the second game, as the Cannonball shut the Missouri team out, 2-0.[9]

Despite losing their series with St. Louis, the Lincoln Giants were having a spectacular season. By mid-August the Lincolns had won sixty-two out of seventy-one games. They defeated some of the top semipro clubs like the Philadelphia Professionals, Loughlin, and Cuban Stars. On September 6, a reported twelve thousand fans witnessed the Lincolns defeat Rube Foster's Chicago American Giants, 6-4, at the New York Highlanders' American League park.[10]

The Lincoln Giants' excellent season was marred by some unexpected turmoil within the club's management team. On September 14, the *New York Age* reported that Sol White had "been deposed as [the] manager" of the Lincolns and replaced by John Henry Lloyd. It was unclear why White was replaced by the Giants' shortstop. The general impression was that the McMahons and White had a harmonious relationship, given the Giants' performance on the field. The *Philadelphia Tribune*, on the other hand, reported that some "indifference" existed within the management team. White undoubtedly was irritated at being relegated to managing the game on the field. While the Lincolns' skipper assembled a competitive club, the McMahons held the lease on Olympic Field and the players' contracts, giving them considerable leverage. Therefore, White might have left the Lincoln Giants because of the limited influence he had on the decision-making process.[11]

The Lincoln Giants club was Sol White's last hurrah as one of black baseball's leading entrepreneurs. White sought to legitimize black baseball as a profession by assembling the Philadelphia Giants, one of its most successful teams, and placing the players on a salary rather than the co-op plan, by which the owners and players had divided the gate receipts among themselves. His guidebook served to preserve black baseball's history to that time, promote the game to a mass audience, and highlight the progress the black game had made since the mid-1880s. Furthermore, Sol White exemplified the African American entrepreneurs who developed business enterprises not only to advance their own economic interests, but as a civil rights strategy. White continued to manage black independent teams in the 1910s and made a brief appearance as a manager in the Negro National League in the 1920s.

However, he would never regain the influence he had in the opening decade of the twentieth century.

Despite losing White as their manager, the Lincoln Giants continued to play excellent baseball. They culminated their season with a game against the All Leaguers at Olympic Field. The All Leaguers consisted of Major League stars and future Hall of Famers Walter Johnson and Honus Wagner. Danny McClellan dueled the Big Train to a 3-3 tie for six innings before the All Leaguers scored one run in the seventh and one in the ninth to win, 5-3. Despite losing to the All Leaguers, the Lincoln Giants finished the season with 88 wins and 17 losses.[12]

While the Lincoln Giants made their impact upon eastern black baseball, John Connor maintained a competitive club in spite of losing several of his top players. Frank Earle, Bill Thomas, Bill Monroe, and Emmett Bowman served as the catalyst that elevated the Brooklyn Royal Giants to the ranks of a touring team. Connor signed Sam Crawford, a lanky hurler with a good fastball and knuckleball, and Jesse Shipp to bolster the pitching staff. The Royal Giants barnstormed the South and Midwest from April to mid-May. Connor booked games in Jacksonville; New Orleans; Mobile; Birmingham; Pensacola; Memphis; and Hot Springs, Arkansas. In Jacksonville, the Royal Giants defeated Rube Foster's Chicago American Giants. Connor's tour culminated in the North with games in West Baden and French Lick, Indiana; Detroit; and Buffalo, New York. The Royals defeated Charles Mills's St. Louis Giants, and by the end of the tour, the Royal Giants had played a total of forty-six games, winning forty-three and losing three.[13]

On July 20, 1911, the *New York Age* reported Connor had secured a lease on Harlem Oval, located at 142nd Street and Lenox Avenue. Procuring a five-year lease, Connor began renovations by covering the grandstand and expanding the seating capacity to handle 2,600 people. In addition to booking games, Connor envisioned sponsoring athletic events "conducted under the auspices of colored athletic organizations." According to the *Age*, the deal marked the first time in the history of New York City that an African American had complete possession of an "up-to-date ball grounds." Despite the turmoil he faced, the 1911 season was John Connor's finest hour in black baseball to that time.[14]

Connor's securing of a lease on Harlem Oval coincided with the increase in New York's African American population, most notably in Harlem. From 1900 to 1910, Gotham's black population rose from 60,666 to 91,709. New York's blacks were in a constant state of movement, settling essentially in the Tenderloin district, San Juan Hill, and Harlem. The Tenderloin district extended from the west twenties to the west fifties and lured a large number of blacks. By the 1900s, however, the San Juan Hill area in the west sixties had grown so rapidly that it became the largest black community in Manhattan. Yet neither the Tenderloin nor San Juan Hill could compete with the tremendous growth that occurred in Harlem. Better living facilities were available to blacks on 122nd Street, between Fifth and Lenox Avenue, and from 124th to 126th Streets, between Eighth and Tenth Avenues. From 1900 to 1910, other blocks in Harlem were slowly filled by blacks. By 1915, the growth of black Harlem was so great that 60 percent of all blacks living in Manhattan resided between 118th and 144th Streets, from the Harlem to the Hudson River. Undoubtedly, John Connor held aspirations to tap into this growing black consumer market, and since Olympic Field was located at 136th Street and Lenox Avenue, Jess McMahon held similar aspirations.[15]

The forming of the Lincoln Giants and Connor's acquisition of a lease on Harlem Oval ended the NACBC's booking control. The organization began to unravel. J. M. Bright had continued to book his own games after leaving the Association the previous year. On August 3, the *Age* reported the Philadelphia Giants had disbanded. Rumors circulated that E. B. Lamar would book games for the Royal Giants. On August 10, the *Age* said that Nat Strong would represent the Cuban Stars in arranging a five-game series with the Lincoln Giants for the colored championship.[16]

The state of confusion that characterized eastern black baseball at the end of the 1911 season continued into the following year. In the midst of the chaotic 1912 season, the Brooklyn Royal Giants set out on their second extended tour of the Midwest. They began the tour with a three-game series with the St. Louis Giants and single game with the Kansas City Giants. Three tightly contested games ended in a 2-1 series win for Charles Mills's Giants. The SLGAA was so happy with the outcome it agreed to a second series in New York with the Royals in July. The Royals received some satisfaction in Missouri with their 13-6 defeat of the Kansas City Giants.[17]

On May 18, the Royal Giants began their six-game series with the Chicago American Giants. From the outset, the series was a disaster for John Connor's Royals. In the first game, Royals' pitcher Hurly McNair's wildness, along with the timely hitting of Bruce Petway, Bill Pierce, and Bill Monroe, resulted in an 8-3 American Giants win. The Royals were their own worst enemy in game two. A costly error in the fifth inning and another in the sixth led to six runs for the American Giants, who coasted to a 7-0 victory. Brooklyn pitcher John Goodgame took a 1-0 lead into the six inning of game three before the Royals fell apart, committing six errors and losing 4-1. Then the Royal Giants lost the final three games.[18]

The Brooklyn Royal Giants received some consolation in their games against some of the other semipro clubs in Chicago. In a doubleheader against the Gunthers, John Goodgame pitched extremely well, striking out thirteen batters and giving up four hits in a 7-1 win. The second game was no contest. The Royals scored seven runs in the first two innings and cruised to an 11-1 victory. The Royals apparently took out all of their frustrations on Charles Gunther's club because of their poor performance against the American Giants. On June 2, the Royal Giants completed their midwestern tour against the Chicago Giants. Frank Earle and Al Robinson led a twelve-hit attack as the Royals broke the game open with a five-run rally in the fifth on the way to an 8-3 win. Although the Brooklyn Royal Giants' performance overall was subpar, their second extended barnstorming tour elevated them to the ranks of a touring team.[19]

During the course of the Brooklyn Royal Giants' midwestern tour, turmoil continued to plague the Lincoln Giants' management team. The *New York Age* reported that John Henry Lloyd had resigned as the Lincolns' player-manager. Some of his teammates supposedly had not given him "proper support" as the club's manager. In a letter to the *Age*, Lloyd claimed, "There are some players who believe in doing their best for any man they are under while there are others who do not even mean themselves any good. I never expect to be at the head of another team as long as I am in baseball, regardless of what kind of salary is offered me." Lloyd expected to return as a player for the Giants or with "some other good colored club."[20]

When the 1912 season began, Lloyd apparently changed his mind. On April 11, the *Age* reported that he would serve as captain and manager of the Lincolns. However, the *Philadelphia Tribune* asserted, his return was contingent on certain "open agreements," which included cuts in player salaries, no bonus for "special games," and the release of Harry Buckner and Phil Bradley with no explanation for their dismissal. Evidently, these players did not give Lloyd the "proper support" he expected.[21]

To further complicate matters, a conflict about the lease on Olympic Field surfaced. The *Age* reported the McMahons had lost the lease on the grounds. Supposedly "other parties had secured the park for baseball purposes," and a team from Brooklyn, managed by Sol White, would play its games there. However, Jess McMahon evidently came to some agreement, because the Lincoln Giants would reportedly play their home games at Olympic Field for another year.[22]

Despite the continual problems surrounding the Lincolns' management team, the Giants assembled another strong club. Although they lost Buckner and Bradley, the Giants retained Billy Francis, Spot Poles, George Wright, and Danny McClellan. Louis Santop began his second season as the team's catcher. Also known as "Big Bertha," Santop was a strong-armed catcher who excelled at blocking the plate but was better known for his power hitting. Bill Pettus was signed to play first base. Pettus had begun his career with the Kansas City Giants in 1909, before moving on to play for the Chicago Giants the following two seasons. He was a power hitter who could steal bases when the situation called for it. Finally, Jess McMahon lured Cyclone Joe Williams from the Chicago Giants, the hurler with a blazing fastball and exceptional control. The Lincoln Giants began the season with an awesome pitching staff that included Williams, McClellan, and Dick Redding.[23]

The Lincoln Giants became one of several teams competing for players to capitalize upon the national game. On May 2, 1912, the *Age* reported that Dick Cogan had made plans to organize a black team called Cogan's Smart Set to represent Paterson, New Jersey. Cogan was a former Major League pitcher who played three seasons for three different teams, compiling a 2-3 won-lost record. With "a nice piece of money" in his hands, Cogan made overtures to various players on the Lincoln Giants and the Brooklyn Royal Giants. He was successful in landing Danny McClellan and Jude Gans from the Lincolns. Gans was a good all-around player who could hit, field, and had good speed on the bases. He would become one of black baseball's best outfielders in the 1910s. Cogan also signed Harry Buckner and Phil Bradley, the two players who had supposedly caused trouble on McMahon's club. Finally, Gus James was signed away from the Brooklyn Royal Giants.[24]

On August 12, 1912, sportswriter Lester Walton observed that there was a high degree of "kidnapping" occurring among black clubs. Spot Poles having become disgruntled with the McMahons, in May he jumped to the Royal Giants. By late July, the Royals were set to meet the Lincoln Giants at American League Park. The following day, Poles returned to the Lincoln Giants. A week later, the Lincolns played a doubleheader with Cogan's Smart Set and the St. Louis Giants at Olympic Field. When the Lincolns played St. Louis, Jude Gans was returned to McMahon's club. Players jumping their contracts also took their toll on J. M. Bright's Cuban Giants, who disbanded at the end of the season. This constant player movement led to distrust among the baseball moguls.[25]

The tumultuous 1912 season left a bitter taste in John Connor's mouth. Since 1910 he had tolerated internal conflict with his player force and disputes with his managers. Connor's assertion that his Royals were not given proper consideration regarding playing dates was valid. As a NACBC member, the Royal Giants never embarked on an extended barnstorming tour of the Midwest or Cuba. It should be noted that Connor, and not the NACBC, booked the Royals' extended tours. During the Royals' second tour, rumors circulated that efforts were made to have all New York black clubs controlled by white owners. To accomplish this, white owners would coerce Connor to accept a flat guarantee instead of sharing gate receipts. As Lester Walton noted, "The *Age* does not believe that colored fans should loyally support teams [simply] because they are managed by colored men." However, Walton was quick to point out that black fans "should resent any attempt to put a colored manager out of business. To see Manager John Connor get the worst of a raw deal would not only be a rank injustice to him, but a gross piece of discourtesy to the colored fans."[26]

White owners supposedly attempted to compel Connor to accept a flat guarantee. Connor threatened to schedule no more games with McMahon's club because the Royals' owner believed he had received an inadequate share of the gate receipts in a game against the Lincoln Giants. The two men must have changed their minds, because the Royals and the Lincolns played a doubleheader later that year. Dealing with players threatening to jump their contracts, the substantial investment to renovate Harlem Oval, and coercion by white managers to make him accept a flat guarantee was more than Connor could endure. On July 19, 1913, the *Age* reported a transfer in the ownership of the Brooklyn Royal Giants to a contingent headed by Nat Strong. Temporarily, John Connor was out of black baseball.[27]

The Lincoln Giants, on the other hand, finished their season with a series of games against all star teams composed of Major League players and a tour of Cuba. On October 31, the *New York Age* reported a contest between the Lincoln Giants and the New York Giants. The New York club was led by National League Giants' second baseman, Larry Doyle, who organized a team featuring Hal Chase, Red Murray, and Louis Drucke. The Lincolns bolstered their lineup by adding Grant Johnson and Harry Moore. Cyclone Joe Williams dominated Hal Chase's All Stars, giving up only four hits and striking out nine batters in a 6-0 victory. In a second game with the All Stars, Williams displayed his brilliance on the mound. The Cyclone held the All Stars to four hits in a second 6-0 shutout victory. The Lincolns finished their season in Cuba, playing against the Almendares Blues and the Havana Reds. Only one game was reported in the press. In a game against Havana, Frank Wickware held the Reds to three hits and cruised to a 3-0 win. The tour of Cuba elevated the Lincoln Giants to the ranks of a touring team.[28]

When the Lincoln Giants returned to New York for the start of the 1913 season, their management team was involved in another controversy over the use of Olympic Field. Jess McMahon was unable to negotiate with local authorities for the use of the ballpark. The lease on Olympic Field was supposedly linked to a graft and corruption scandal involving New York police inspector Dennis Sweeney. The *New York Times* reported Sweeney assessed a fifty-dollar tax for use of the grounds for Sunday games, but after his indictment, local authorities allowed the Lincolns to play their home games at Olympic Field.[29]

The constant confusion that defined the Lincoln Giants' management team reached its nadir during the 1913 season. As of August, the players reportedly had not been paid for weeks. Several judgments had been rendered against the McMahons, but there was little or no chance that the players would be paid. The McMahons were supposedly involved in several business ventures yielding little or no return. Whereas huge crowds attended Giants' home games, it was reported that the majority of the revenues were used to pay the McMahons' non-baseball debts. Brooklyn Royal Giants' magnate Nat Strong refused to play his club at Olympic Field until he received the money from a "recent engagement."[30]

Through all their financial woes, the Lincoln Giants maintained their status as a touring team. They played the Chicago American Giants for the World's Colored Championship, and in October competed in a three-team doubleheader with the Brooklyn Royal Giants and the National League's Philadelphia Phillies. The Phillies finished second to John McGraw's New York Giants in the National League pennant race. They were led by pitching ace Grover Cleveland Alexander, who won 22 games, and hard-hitting outfielder Gavy Cravath, who led the National League with 19 home runs and 128 runs batted in. A reported crowd of eleven thousand fans watched the Lincoln Giants hit Alexander early and often. They scored three runs in the third inning and three runs in the fourth and seventh innings to win, 9-2. The winning pitcher was Joe Williams, who turned in another masterpiece for the Giants, giving up eight hits and striking out nine batters.[31]

The Lincoln Giants finished their season with a three-game series against Earl Mack's All Stars. Earl Mack was the son of Connie Mack, the Philadelphia A's manager and owner. In the first game, Philadelphia

Phillies' hurler George Chalmers out dueled Joe Williams, 1-0, scattering seven hits and striking out ten batters. Even in defeat Williams shined, giving up only six hits and striking out thirteen All Stars. Chalmers and Williams faced each other in game two. Led by Spot Poles and Jude Gans, the Lincolns rapped out nineteen hits and coasted to a 7-3 victory. In the rubber game, the Cyclone faced All Stars' top pitcher Charles "Chief" Bender. Williams dueled Bender to a 1-1 tie until the Chief was replaced in the fifth inning. The Lincolns scored a run in the ninth inning to win the game and the series from the All Stars, two games to one. The Lincoln Giants' performance against these All Stars teams composed of Major League players was spectacular.[32]

As the 1913 season came to a close, eastern black baseball remained in a state of confusion. Despite elevating the Brooklyn Royal Giants to the ranks of a touring team, John Connor relinquished control of his Royals to New York booking agent Nat Strong. The Lincoln Giants would also emerge as a touring team, but the constant turmoil within its management team placed the club on financially shaky ground. While eastern black baseball experienced its rocky transition, midwestern black baseball also underwent a period of change.

THE RISE OF ANDREW "RUBE" FOSTER: A BLACK BUSINESSMAN

With eastern black baseball in a state of flux, Rube Foster left the Leland Giants Baseball Amusement Association and formed the Chicago American Giants. In a letter to the Indianapolis *Freeman*, Foster highlighted his reasons for forming the American Giants. He began by providing his view of black baseball's evolution since 1905. According to Foster, the National Association of Colored Baseball Clubs of the United States and Cuba failed to obtain the cooperation of the midwestern promoters in its efforts to control consumer markets and gain hegemonic control over the player force. The failure to obtain this cooperation led to what Foster referred to as a "guerilla campaign" in black baseball. In other words, club owners induced players to jump their contracts to place a competitive team on the field. These tactics resulted in the Philadelphia

Giants losing several of their best players, who went to Chicago to join the Leland Giants.[33]

Foster turned his attention to the reasons the LGBBA broke up. In Foster's view, the primary reason for the organization's demise was a desire of one man to control the entire operation in order to satisfy his ego. Foster was referring to Frank Leland, who the former saw as the man primarily responsible for the LGBBA's decline. In an obvious personal attack, Foster stated that Leland's "low, dirty, undermining tactics, against me, and his ambition to exterminate me from baseball, dug a grave for him in baseball, and he is now a detriment to the game." What Foster conveniently neglected to mention was his alliance with Beauregard Moseley to force Leland out of the organization and their lawsuit prohibiting their former president from using the name Leland Giants. In addition, Leland's successful 1910 season and the Chicago Giants' appearance in the California Winter League could also have led to Foster's personal attack against his former boss. The Chicago Giants were a legitimate threat to Foster's aspirations to obtain midwestern supremacy in black baseball.

Throughout his letter to the *Freeman*, Foster portrayed himself as the victim in an obvious attempt to sway public opinion in his favor. He wrote of the ways in which Leland and his partner, Robert Jackson, tried to diminish his credibility with white and black semipro managers. During the season, Foster supposedly approached Leland and Jackson to secure an agreement to respect each other's players under contract. He was turned down. The Chicago Giants refused to play the Lelands during the regular season, and Leland and Jackson used their influence to dissuade white semipros from scheduling games with Foster's club.

Virtually absent from Foster's evaluation of black baseball in Chicago were his primary reasons for leaving the LGBBA. There was also no discussion about his relationship with his former boss, Beauregard Moseley. Evidently, baseball was taking too much time from Moseley's law practice. In a conference with Foster, Moseley reportedly told the Giants' field manager, "You know baseball, I know law [;] you take the team and do whatever you see fit, and I will go back to my law practice." Two reasons make this assertion problematic. First, at the time

Foster left the LGBBA, Moseley was attempting to form a Negro baseball league. Second, Moseley formed a coalition of businessmen and professionals to run the LGBBA and compete against Foster's American Giants and Leland's Chicago Giants. A more plausible explanation would be the internal division within the LGBBA's leadership and the failure of attempts to form two black professional leagues, leading to Foster's exit from the organization. The men who made the Leland Giants a successful baseball team, Frank Leland and Rube Foster, were no longer within the ranks of the LGBBA.[34]

It was within this context that Rube Foster entered into a business relationship with John M. Schorling and formed the Chicago American Giants. Schorling had operated a sandlot club in Chicago for several years. He leased the grounds of the old White Sox Park on Thirty-Ninth and Shield after the American League team moved into its new ballpark. The White Sox had torn down the old grandstand, and Schorling built a new one with a seating capacity of nine thousand. He approached Foster with an offer of a partnership that reportedly operated on a fifty-fifty basis. In other words, both men had a 50 percent controlling interest in the enterprise that became the Chicago American Giants.[35]

Foster put together what would become the first of several great American Giants teams. They were led offensively by their outstanding catcher, Bruce "Buddy" Petway, and their center fielder, Pete Hill. Born in Nashville, Tennessee, in 1883, Petway began his professional career in 1906 with the Cuban X Giants. As a member of Foster's Leland Giants, he developed a reputation as an excellent hitter. In 1910 Petway played for the Havana Reds in Cuba, and in a series against the Detroit Tigers, he reportedly threw out Ty Cobb twice attempting to steal. Preston "Pete" Hill was a left-handed batter who hit both for power and average. He began his career in 1899 with the Pittsburgh Keystones, leaving after two seasons to join the Cuban X Giants. In 1903, Hill joined the Philadelphia Giants and along with Foster led the club to three colored championships from 1904 to 1906. He rejoined Foster and the Leland Giants in 1908 and held down the center field position throughout the 1910s with the American Giants. Leroy Grant, Jap Payne, and Frank Duncan rounded out a solid American Giants team.[36]

As with the majority of strong black teams of the dead ball era, pitching made the American Giants awesome. Although he was not the dominant hurler of the previous decade, Rube Foster was still one of black baseball's premier pitchers. Pat Dougherty was the Giants' star left-hander who lost a 1-0 heartbreaker to Mordecai "Three Finger" Brown in the three-game series with the Chicago Cubs in 1909. Bill Lindsay began his career in 1910 with the Kansas City Giants, earning the nickname, "the Kansas Cyclone." After Lindsay pitched against the Leland Giants in late June of that year and struck out seven batters in a losing cause, Foster was so impressed with the hard-throwing right-hander that he signed him for the remainder of the season. Although his career was short-lived, Lindsay became the American Giants' dominant hurler.[37]

While Rube Foster organized his team for its inaugural year, Frank Leland's Chicago Giants continued to ride the wave of its successful 1910 regular season and its appearance in the California Winter League. The team beat the majority of the clubs it faced and in late June had won twenty-one straight games. The Giants' pitching staff was magnificent, as Cyclone Joe Williams began his second season as the staff ace. Williams was challenging Rube Foster as black baseball's premier pitcher. On May 28, Williams faced Dick Redding, who had pitched for the Philadelphia Giants before moving on to play for the Lincoln Giants. The Chicago Giants scored two runs in the first inning, and it was all the Cyclone needed as he defeated Cannonball Redding, giving up only three hits and striking out eight batters in a 2-0 shutout victory. Walter Ball continued to be brilliant on the mound, and Bill Gatewood rounded out a Giants pitching staff that could compete against the best baseball clubs, black or white. Veteran players Harry Moore, Bobby Winston, Joe Green, and Bill Pettus gave the Chicago Giants a solid hitting attack.[38]

On July 2, the Chicago American Giants and Chicago Giants began the first of a series of games for midwestern supremacy. The series was also a vehicle for a subtle and hidden agenda. According to Foster, "Supremacy in baseball was the watchword, but extermination was the aim, and to the latter end not a stone was left unturned in its accomplishment." Whereas Foster's rhetoric sounded melodramatic, the series was fiercely contested. Bill Lindsay faced Cyclone Williams in the first game. The American Giants led 1-0 into the sixth inning before they broke the game open and coasted to an 8-0 win. Lindsay gave up four hits, struck out eight batters, and collected three hits in the game. The Chicago Giants evened the series, hitting Rube Foster early and often en route to a 7-3 victory. Games three and four were part of a Fourth of July doubleheader. In the first game, Walter Ball scattered five hits and shut out the American Giants, 7-0. Lindsay and Williams squared off in the nightcap, and the American Giants knocked the Cyclone out of the box for the second time. Pete Hill led an eleven-hit attack including a home run, and the American Giants evened the series with a 7-5 win. Game five was a twelve-inning affair. The American Giants took a 5-1 lead into the eighth inning, when Frank Wickware relieved Pat Dougherty and promptly gave up two runs. The Giants went on that inning to load the bases, and Bobby Winston hit a triple to left field to give Leland's club a 6-5 lead. The American Giants tied the score in the ninth inning. In the twelfth, Bruce Petway singled, stole second base, and scored on Fred Hutchinson's "Texas league" single to give the American Giants a hard-fought 7-6 win. The American Giants led the series, three games to two.[39]

Controversy surrounded the sixth game. With the American Giants leading 4-2 in the eighth inning, Giants' shortstop William "Bubber" Parks reached second base on Fred Hutchinson's throwing error. After Bill Pettus struck out, Harry Moore hit the ball back to the pitcher, who threw to second and trapped Parks in a rundown between second and third base. The umpire called Parks out, claiming he had interfered with the ball. Leland's Giants protested the call and immediately walked off the field. The home plate umpire gave the Chicago Giants five minutes to return to the field. When they refused, the umpire forfeited the game to the American Giants.[40]

Cooler heads eventually prevailed, and both teams resumed the series. On July 29, Pat Dougherty held the Giants to four hits, striking out nine batters and shutting out Leland's club, 1-0. The Chicago American Giants won the series and could lay claim to the midwestern colored championship.[41]

On August 13, the two teams began a second series. A best two-out-of-three set of games was scheduled at Schorling Park. The Giants took an early 5-0 lead in the first game behind the hitting of Sherman Barton and their newly acquired shortstop, Home Run Johnson. It was all Walter Ball needed, as he gave up seven hits and struck out seven batters on the way to a 5-1 win. The second game was a closely contested affair. The Giants took a 6-5 lead into the ninth inning. The American Giants' first baseman, Bill Pierce, led off the ninth with a single. After Lindsay walked, left fielder Frank Duncan scored the base runners with a screaming line drive to right field that gave the American Giants a 7-6 victory. The fans had to wait until September 17 to see the final game between the two clubs. The third game was never in doubt as the American Giants got off to an early 6-0 lead and Pat Dougherty gave up only five hits on the way to a 6-1 win.[42]

The Chicago American Giants' defeat of the Chicago Giants marked the end of Frank Leland's career as a baseball club owner. On April 18, 1912, the *New York Age* reported that Leland would not organize a team for the regular season and that he had "ceased to be a baseball manager." Several factors contributed to Leland's leaving black baseball. First, Leland lost the lease on the playing grounds on Sixty-First Street and Lawrence Avenue. The Giants played as a traveling team during the 1911 season, and several of their Sunday games were booked at Schorling Park. Second, Leland's partner, Robert Jackson, left the club to pursue a career in politics. Jackson was a significant investor in the enterprise, and his loss made it difficult to pay the high salaries of star players like Joe Williams, Walter Ball, and Bill Pettus. Finally, Leland's health was the most critical factor influencing his decision to leave the black game. After 1907, when Leland attempted to organize a black professional league, his health became an issue and was, undoubtedly, influential in the LGBBA's retaining Rube Foster as player-manager and booking agent. Leland's career in black baseball had been a roller-coaster ride, but his Chicago Giants' successful 1910 season at least allowed him to end it on a high note. In 1914, Frank Leland died at the age of forty-five.[43]

Riding the momentum of their series defeat of the Chicago Giants, the Chicago American Giants set out on their first barnstorming tour of the East. The tour reflected Foster's objective from the outset: to make his American Giants a touring team. That explains why the third game of the second series with the Chicago Giants was played in September. From August 29 to September 6, the American Giants played a series of games with the Cuban Stars in Atlantic City, New Jersey, and a three-team doubleheader with the Stars and the Lincoln Giants at Olympic Field in Harlem. A reported crowd of twelve thousand fans watched the American Giants lose a close game to the Lincolns, 6-4.[44]

While the Chicago American Giants and the Chicago Giants battled for midwestern supremacy, the Leland Giants endured a gruesome season. Following the break with Foster, Beauregard Moseley organized a booster coalition drawn from the black community. The Leland Giants Booster Club (LGBC) was an aggregation of black middle-class businessmen and professionals. The formation of the LGBC represented the cooperative enterprise philosophy and race rhetoric prevalent among the new black leadership that emerged in the early twentieth century. LGBC president Jesse Bolling was a restaurant owner who donated his Burlington Buffet as the club's official headquarters. Thomas W. Allen, the club's secretary, was a city inspector. Other coalition members included the editors of Chicago's two leading black newspapers, Robert Abbott of the Chicago *Defender* and Julius Taylor of the *Broad Ax*.[45]

The LGBC served to promote the businesses of its member coalition and represented an elementary form of brand equity by associating the members with a popular team. The effort of Chicago's black businessmen to create a brand with the Leland Giants' past success was both practical and ideological. The LGBC staged an event that consisted of a touring car, known as the Red Devil, which paraded through the streets to the ballpark. The event served to stimulate group pride among Chicago's black citizenry and increase spectatorship of Leland Giants games. Moreover, the LGBC was an expression of the philosophy that combined self-help and racial solidarity with an economic ideology that emphasized the acquisition of middle-class virtues and African American support of black businesses.[46]

The LGBC brought more attention to the members of the booster coalition than to the baseball club. Throughout the pages of the *Broad*

Ax and the *Defender*, a particular spotlight was focused on who among Chicago's black elite attended games. The *Broad Ax*, for example, stated: "Race present were Dr. A. W. Williams, R. T. Motts of the Peking [restaurant], Thomas W. Allen, City Inspector [and] Jesse Bolling." The *Broad Ax* also pointed out that the "ladies were also present and looked as cute as ever" and encouraged its readership to attend the game the following Sunday. The *Defender* repeatedly stated that the LGBC members were the "fun makers of the baseball world." The race rhetoric of the early twentieth century was used to promote the enterprise. The *Defender* indicated that Professor William Emanuel and Artist Johnson "were among the race building characters at Sunday's game who believed in patronizing [a] race enterprise." Press coverage of the Leland Giants' games themselves was sporadic in both papers. The LGBC failed to recognize that baseball fans came to see the players and not the members of Chicago's black elite.[47]

Press coverage in the white dailies—most notably the *Chicago Tribune*—also was skimpy. Nineteen games were reported in the press and the Lelands won eight of them. It appeared the Giants were still a competitive team on the field. Veteran players Nate Harris—who also served as captain—Danger Talbert, Harry Moore, Sherman Barton, and Frank Wickware formed a solid nucleus for the club. However, competition from the American Giants and the Chicago Giants for players made it difficult to retain these veterans. Barton and Moore would end up on the Chicago Giants' rosters, and Wickware defected to the American Giants late in the season. Moseley failed to recognize the importance of maintaining a symbiotic business relationship with white semiprofessional teams. Of the games reported in the press, only three were against Chicago's leading white semipro clubs (two with the Gunthers and one with the West Ends). The Lelands played the Chicago Giants only twice during the season, losing both games, and there was no evidence of any games with the American Giants. Consistent press coverage was the lifeblood of baseball promotions in the early twentieth century. Maintaining rivalries throughout the year was one way to ensure consistent press coverage. The lack of games with the leading black and white clubs in the Windy City made this difficult for Moseley's Leland Giants to achieve.[48]

Moseley confronted other obstacles as the LGBBA began to unravel. He was engaged in several business endeavors in addition to organizing a baseball league and booking games for the Lelands, and he probably neither delegated authority to booster club members nor had an adequate management team to supervise his many operations. When the LGBBA began operations in 1907, the majority of its facilities were located outside the Black Belt, where increased white hostility made venturing outside the black community unpleasant for Chicago's African Americans. In 1910, when the Leland Giants moved into their new ballpark on Sixty-Ninth and Halsted, Moseley had just renovated it, no doubt at large expense. The obstacles were more than the LGBBA could withstand. As the 1911 season came to a close, the skating rink closed for good, and the Leland Giants were relegated to a local club for the remainder of the decade.

At the end of the 1911 season, Rube Foster evaluated the state of semiprofessional baseball in Chicago and called for black teams to organize into a professional league. White semiprofessional baseball in the Windy City had reached a saturation point, leading to the disbanding of several teams and to park closings. There were only two parks on the North Side, one on the West Side, and one on the South Side. A closer examination revealed that the five parks still in operation housed Chicago's top semipros: Schorling Park, Gunther Park, West End Park, Normal Park, and Rogers Park. The *Chicago Tribune* reported park managers charging high rents as a result of a rise in property values, which may have led to the park closings.[49]

Foster's assessment of semiprofessional baseball in Chicago was valid. Of the semipro clubs that played in the Chicago City League and the Park Owners Association, only six clubs fielded teams for the 1911 season: the West Ends, Gunthers, Spaldings, Rogers Park, Normals, and Eclipse. In addition to reaching a saturation point, internal division among the club owners of the two leagues placed their circuits on shaky ground. Two of the prominent club owners left the semipro scene. James Callahan disbanded his Logan Squares in 1910 and returned to manage the Chicago White Sox. The South Chicagos disbanded when Jake Stahl retired from baseball to return to his banking business in Chicago. In

1912, Stahl became the manager of the Boston Red Sox and led them to the American League pennant and the World Series championship. The decline of white semiprofessional baseball in the Windy City resulted in black clubs scheduling fewer games with them, which impacted adversely on their symbiotic business relationship with white semipros.[50]

In response, Foster urged midwestern black teams to organize into a professional league. He also called for a new way for black clubs to conduct business: "The old-time methods and ideas, which being nothing but disruption and discord should be forgotten, and twentieth century policies, the methods that bring success, should be inaugurated. The wild reckless scramble under the guise of baseball is keeping [blacks] down, and we will always be the underdog until we can successfully employ the methods that have brought success to the great powers that be in baseball of the present era." It was evident that the "great powers" to which Foster referred were the white Major Leagues. Much like his counterpart Sol White, Rube Foster argued for a black professional league patterned after the Major Leagues, limiting club membership to one team per city to control consumer markets and gaining a hegemony over the player force. Foster proposed a league consisting of six teams, to be located in St. Louis; Kansas City, Missouri; Louisville; Indianapolis; Chicago; and Detroit. He pointed out that black teams "make the same jumps without a league and it is a certainty we could with a league." This statement was in obvious reference to the barnstorming tour the American Giants and the St. Louis Giants made. The formation of a black league would legitimize black baseball as a profession that, in Foster's view, "could force, by public sentiment, the same as Jack Johnson forced [Jim] Jeffries, the winner of the white league to meet us for the championship." If an African American could force a white man to compete for the heavyweight title in boxing, Foster surmised, then why not the champion of the black leagues do the same and play the World Series champion of the Major Leagues? Foster concluded his letter by stating his willingness to organize a black league. However, he pointed out he was not for any "wildcat schemes." "But I know this to be the best way," Foster added, "and when I say I know, those who know me know I am not guessing."[51]

Julius Taylor provided a somewhat similar evaluation about the plight of black baseball in Chicago. In an editorial in the *Broad Ax*, Taylor concluded that black baseball in Chicago was hopeless. This conclusion was in response to the Leland Giants' fall from prominence. What irritated Taylor the most was the unwillingness of blacks to make the commitment to organize a professional league. The effort to form a black league ended in failure because of an unwillingness of investors to make a commitment to the enterprise. With regard to the Leland Giants, their success led to their downfall. "Rivalry and a desire to control," Taylor added, "brought about the formation of other clubs to compete for the patronage and prowess of the Leland Giants." This assertion was in reference to the rise of Chicago Giants and the American Giants. Taylor acknowledged the Chicago American Giants' spectacular success in a short period of time. However, he bemoaned the fact the American Giants played at Schorling Park and that they paid "the money to John M. Schorling that should be received by the Race to which the patrons of the game belong."[52]

Taylor's frustration about Chicago's black baseball predicament was understandable. Yet his declaration concerning the American Giants "paying the money to John M. Schorling" was somewhat problematic. Black baseball clubs had never been marketed exclusively to an African American consumer market. From the beginning, black baseball teams were targeted toward a white middle-class spectatorship because it constituted a more viable consumer market. The prewar migration of blacks to Chicago, however, offered a new market on which black entrepreneurs could capitalize. The rise of several midwestern black clubs outside of Chicago provided an additional incentive to exploit this new market. However, since the late 1880s, the black community had yet to demonstrate an ability to support a commercialized amusement without the support of white spectatorship. After all, a substantial majority of this new black market was economically depressed.

Another factor that made Taylor's assessment problematic was the fact that black baseball entrepreneurs did not own the ballparks in which their teams played. The *Chicago Tribune* reported that Schorling owned the lease on Auburn Park when the Leland Giants played there.

Thus, the Giants paid rent to Schorling. However, Taylor conveniently neglected to mention that when the Giants played a white semipro club, money from the "other race" went into the Lelands' coffers. In 1910, the Leland Giants did move into their own ballpark on Sixty-Ninth and Halsted. But the opportunity to maximize revenues was short-lived because of the internal division within the LGBBA leadership. Park ownership would remain the Achilles heel of black baseball throughout its history, and this would impact significantly upon its ability to place the game on a sound economic footing.[53]

It was because of these circumstances that Andrew "Rube" Foster became a businessman first and a Race man second. Foster had demonstrated his ability to run a baseball operation, and from his perspective the club would run smoother with another baseball man as his partner. For all intents and purposes, Foster's partnership with Schorling was a business decision. Two factors made this business association a wise move on Foster's part. First, it allowed him to maintain his symbiotic business relationship with white semipro managers, and it allowed him to continue to capitalize on the white consumer market. Second, Schorling Park's close proximity to the black community on the South Side permitted Foster to tap into this growing consumer market.

Simultaneously, Foster's business relationship with Schorling allowed him to serve Chicago's black community. He maintained the practice of playing benefit games to raise funds for Provident Hospital. Community organizations were permitted to use the ballpark for fund-raising events. The *Defender* reported a fund-raising event for the Old Folks' home. A doubleheader was played between the Grace Sunday School and the "U. P." team in the first game, and the Doctors and Dentists faced the Emergencies in the nightcap. More important, Foster had achieved the objectives spelled out in the race rhetoric commonly attributed to Booker T. Washington that advocated building a segregated enterprise within the fabric of a national economy. In other words, the segregated enterprise, here the Chicago American Giants, operated successfully within the framework of the national economy—in this case, semiprofessional baseball—through the creation of annual booking arrangements with black, Cuban, and white semipros.[54]

Nothing illustrated Foster's motivation as a businessman first and Race man second better than his emergence as a booking agent. The decline of Chicago's semiprofessional infrastructure resulted in Foster scheduling more games at Schorling Park during the week and on Sunday. He scheduled more games with black and Cuban clubs like the Cuban Stars, West Baden Sprudels, French Lick Plutos, and St. Louis Giants. Throughout the season, the Chicago Giants and Cuban Stars played several games at Schorling Park. On July 4, the Cuban Stars faced the Chicago Giants in a four-game series, with both teams winning two games.[55]

The Chicago American Giants set out on their second extended barnstorming tour, further illustrating Foster's businessman-first approach. The American Giants made their first appearance in the California Winter League. The CWL consisted of four teams: the American Giants, McCormicks of Los Angeles, Tuft Lyons of Pasadena, and a club from San Diego. The CWL's 1912 season was noteworthy for the plethora of major and minor league players on club rosters. Four players came from the National League champion New York Giants. John "Chief" Myers was the Giants' catcher; he led the club with a .358 batting average. Fred Snodgrass finished third in the NL with forty-three stolen bases. Playing in the CWL was a homecoming for Snodgrass because he owned a farm in California. Tillie Shafer was a utility infielder who batted .288 with twenty-two stolen bases. Fred Merkle was the Giants' first baseman who will long be remembered in baseball folklore for the infamous "Merkle boner."[56]

The American Giants opened the CWL season in a three-game series with the McCormicks. The McCormicks knocked Pat Dougherty out of the box in the sixth inning and defeated the Giants, 8-5. *Los Angeles Times* sportswriter Harry Williams proclaimed, "The Caucasian race, particularly that wing of it originating in Ireland continues to reign supreme in all things pertaining to baseball." Game two told a different story. The American Giants had developed a reputation of winning closely contested games. Foster's players had an uncanny ability to get timely hits or make big plays with the game on the line. With the game tied at three in the tenth inning, Bill Monroe walked and reached second base on Bruce Petway's sacrifice. Pat Dougherty was sent in to pinch hit for Fred Hutchinson and grounded out to second base, advancing Monroe to third. Utility fielder James Parks was sent in to pinch hit for the pitcher and hit a line drive down the right-field line that brought home the winning run. Game three belonged to Giants' ace Bill Lindsay. The Kansas Cyclone gave up one run on four hits and struck out ten McCormick batters in a 3-1 win.[57]

However, the American Giants' overall performance in the California Winter League was subpar. According to William McNeil, the Giants won six games and lost seven, although the complete standings for the league were not published. Given the caliber of talent in the CWL, however, it must be said that the American Giants exhibited an ability to compete with some of the top players in professional baseball.[58]

The Chicago American Giants remained on the West Coast throughout the winter months and concluded their tour in April with a series of games with minor league clubs. On April 14, 1913, the American Giants began a three-game series with the Seattle Steelheads of the Northwestern League. *Seattle Post-Intelligencer* sportswriter Pontus Baxter stated it was no surprise that "[Pacific] Coast League clubs avoided battle with the American Giants (colored) of Chicago." The American Giants had reportedly amassed an 85-10 won-lost record during the winter. In the first game of the Steelheads series, Fred Hutchinson, Jesse Barber, and John Taylor led a twelve-hit attack and defeated Seattle, 10-5. The second game was shortened by rain, with the American Giants leading 5-3 after six innings. Game three was a hard-fought contest until the Giants erupted for ten runs in the ninth inning and won, 17-7. Pete Hill, John Taylor, and Bill Gatewood hit home runs and Bill Pierce hit a pair of doubles in the lopsided game. The American Giants' sweep of Seattle was impressive.[59]

Press reaction to the Chicago American Giants' success was mixed. Writing in the Chicago *Defender*, former Columbia Giants' club owner Julius Avendorph stated that the American Giants' entry into the CWL came "with a great deal of gratification." On April 26, 1913, the *Defender* added that the American Giants were respected everywhere they went and praised Rube Foster for being one of the "headiest men in the business, white or black." The *Freeman* described the American Giants as a "piece of perfect machinery that can only be put together by a master and in this case the mastermind is Mr. Foster." The *Freeman* extolled the conduct of the American Giants on the field, saying that they always behaved "as gentlemen should act."[60]

By the middle of the 1913 season, the *Defender*'s view of Foster and his American Giants had begun to change. Much like *Broad Ax* editor Julius Taylor, the *Defender* began to take jabs at Foster because it was upset over the revenue "going over to the other race." The black newspaper insisted this was "why so many are pulling against Rube." In addition, the *Defender* in particular was critical of the supposed lack of support given by the American Giants to black institutions in the black community. This claim, however, was erroneous in light of the fact that Foster perpetuated the LGBBA's practice of scheduling benefit games for the purpose of fund-raising. It appears that the *Defender*, and undoubtedly former LGBBA members, were the prime movers in an attempt to sway public opinion against the American Giants' magnate.[61]

This opposition in no way swayed Foster from his businessman-first approach. His objective was to present the best product possible, and he accomplished that by using the business practices devised by the black baseball entrepreneurs of the 1880s and the 1890s. Rube Foster went where the money was and created a demand for his American Giants in several locales. He secured and maintained a talented club and developed a winning reputation. Foster's partnership with John Schorling accorded him a ballpark to develop and sustain a fan base. Schorling Park allowed Foster to generate extra revenue by booking additional games either as part of either a three-team doubleheader or when the American Giants were on the road. But reaching his objective with a white business partner made Rube Foster an unpopular man among some of Chicago's black citizenry.

On July 5, 1913, the *Defender* announced a championship series between the Lincoln Giants and the Chicago American Giants. This series marked the first time a home-and-home series was arranged to determine the colored champion. In other words, the games would be played in both teams' home ballparks. The Lincolns and the American Giants were head and shoulders above the rest of the black and Cuban teams, and the time was right to determine the true World's Colored Champion.[62]

The championship series began in New York, and it started under a cloud of controversy. Originally a best three-out-of-five game series was scheduled, but only three games were played. The New York Age reported that Jess McMahon signed pitcher Frank Wickware from the Mohawk Giants and paid him one hundred dollars to pitch against the American Giants. McMahon had made it a practice to sign top players for an important series and then return them to their former club once it was completed. When the first game was about to begin, Wickware was in an American Giants uniform. McMahon informed Foster that he paid Wickware to pitch for the Lincolns. Foster insisted the hurler remain with the American Giants, and this led to a squabble between the managers that ended with the game being canceled. The series eventually began, and it became the Joe "Cyclone" Williams show. After winning the first game 8-3, Williams needed a ninth-inning rally to edge out a 5-4 win in game two. The Lincolns took a 5-3 lead into the ninth inning of game three, but then the American Giants scored three runs to win, 6-5.[63]

The final game of the series was canceled due to Foster's objection to McMahon's borrowing of Brooklyn Royal Giants captain Frank Earle to play for the Lincolns. Earle was signed to replace the injured Jude Gans. *New York Age* sportswriter Lester Walton scolded the black baseball managers for habitually borrowing players from other clubs: "The sooner the managers of colored teams get together and agree upon a working basis for their mutual protection the better." Nonetheless, the Lincoln Giants left New York with a 2-1 series lead.[64]

The series moved to Chicago, and Lincolns' pitcher Lee Wade scattered seven hits; that and the timely hitting of Spot Poles and John Henry Lloyd led to an opening game 3-1 victory. The American Giants won the second game on what the *Chicago Tribune* called "the closest kind of a decision." In the ninth inning, the American Giants led 6-2. They scored an additional run in the ninth. They had Frank Duncan on first base and Bill Kindle on third. Kindle was caught in a rundown between third and home on an attempted double steal. Kindle scored when Lincoln's first baseman Leroy Grant mishandled a wild throw to the plate. The run proved crucial when the Lincolns rallied with four runs in the bottom of the ninth inning before losing, 7-6. The third game was a hard-hitting affair with the Lincolns taking a 4-3 lead in the first inning. Led by Bruce Petway, Bill Kindle, and Fred Hutchinson, the American Giants continued to hammer away at Cyclone Williams and won, 9-5. Lincoln Giants' catcher Louis Santop's throwing error in the fourth inning and Bill Lindsay's superb pitching gave the American Giants a 2-1 win in game four. Overall, the American Giants led the series by four games to three.[65]

In the first of the last four games, the Lincolns defeated the American Giants 11-6 to even the series. The Lincolns then split a doubleheader, leaving the series even at five games each. In the final and deciding game, the Lincolns made an interesting move, sending outfielder Jude Gans to pitch the deciding game against Bill Gatewood. The Lincolns took a 1-0 lead into the eighth inning, but the Giants erupted for three runs in the top of eighth to seal a 4-1 win. The Lincoln Giants had won the World's Colored Championship, six games to five.[66]

The Chicago American Giants' extended tour of the West Coast and World's Colored Championship Series brought Foster accolades from a prominent member of Chicago's black middle class. Writing in the *Defender*, Julius Avendorph extolled the American Giants for "their high class baseball playing . . . [and] for their gentlemanly conduct on the ball field." The American Giants were "an example that lots of white clubs can take pattern from." When some of Chicago's black patrons berated Foster for raising the ticket prices, the *Defender* switched its earlier position and came to Foster's defense. Chicago's black fans, the newspaper said, would "have to pay for quality and they [the fans] have certainly got their money's worth lately," referring to the colored championship. Moreover, the *Defender* reminded its readers that many of the Windy City's black fans had "never [known] what it was to see a game among those of their race unless forced to go to 79th Street. . . . Now it is a stone's throw from their homes."[67]

AFTERMATH: RUBE FOSTER'S REVIEW OF BLACK BASEBALL

On December 13, 1913, the Indianapolis *Freeman* published an article by Rube Foster that reviewed the 1913 season and for a second time urged black baseball owners to organize a professional league. He began by stating that the past season had generated more interest than previous ones. The high caliber of play by several clubs resulted in an increase in attendance and enthusiasm. It also led to unrest and uncertainty among the club owners who controlled the destiny of their teams. Fans demanded "first class attractions," and this led club owners to pay higher salaries for players that diminished the amount of revenue a team could earn. Foster highlighted the St. Louis Giants, the Mohawk Giants, and Cogan's Smart Set as teams whose payrolls were higher than the gate receipts they generated. These teams either disbanded or played on the co-op plan.[68]

Foster then turned his attention to the criticism he received from the press and the fans. Several fans and press members questioned his judgment in taking his club on extended barnstorming tours. The year-round play supposedly "broke down a winning combination of the best club that ever represented the West." Foster replied that "no man can go on winning forever, and especially be successful without encouragement from the fans of the city he represents." Fan support was needed for the Chicago American Giants to continue their winning tradition.

Much as in his 1911 letter to the *Freeman*, Foster presented himself as a victim to sway public opinion in his favor. He did this in response to what he said were the many in Chicago placing "obstacles in my way" in an effort "to tear me down." It is unclear what obstacles Foster was referring to. Undoubtedly, one of the roadblocks was the negative press he received, and another was the disgruntled fans who complained about higher ticket prices. Foster reminded the readers of the Chicago American Giants' accomplishments since the 1911 season: Chicago's black fans had a ballpark within a close proximity of their community; on the West Coast tour in the American Giants had defeated clubs in the Pacific Coast League, the Northwestern League, and the Union Association; and the Giants had compiled an overall 94-10 won-lost record. In

Foster's view, these accomplishments alone should serve as a source of race pride for Chicago's black community.

Foster concluded his article by making another plea for black baseball clubs to organize. His argument for organization was similar to the one he had made previously: "We have the players," Foster added, "and it could not be a failure, as the same territory is traveled now by all the clubs with no organization or money." Organization was black baseball's means for legitimacy. It was also vital for black baseball's salvation: "[Organization] would give us a rating and a standing in the daily papers which would create an interest and we could then let the best clubs in our organization play for the world's championship with [the champion of other leagues]. Public sentiment would compel them to do it. Every little city, where they can draw $100 gate receipts per day, among the whites, has a league, leaving no city where any money can be made outside of an organization." Foster pointed out that every "hamlet and village" in the US had a team, and it would be a "crime for the Negro who has such an abundance of talent in such a progressive age to sit idly by and see his race forever doomed [in] America's greatest and foremost sport."

Rube Foster's perspective regarding the need for press and fan support was somewhat self-serving. To be sure, Foster did have his detractors, but he also received some positive press. Even the *Defender* changed its view of Foster after the completion of the World's Colored Championship Series. Foster, however, apparently perceived he had more detractors than supporters. What is clear is that Rube Foster recognized the importance of the press in influencing public opinion in his favor. Portraying himself as a victim, focusing attention on his accomplishments and the American Giants' success on the field, and providing a vision for black baseball's future served as a public relations campaign that conveyed an image of Rube Foster and his Chicago American Giants as a symbol of race pride.

Foster's call for an organized black league appeared to be overly optimistic. Since 1902, eight clubs had made extended barnstorming tours either nationally or internationally: the Brooklyn Royal Giants, Chicago American Giants, Chicago Giants, Cuban Stars, Leland Giants, Lincoln

Giants, Philadelphia Giants, and St. Louis Giants. Three teams had barnstormed in Cuba: the Leland Giants, Lincoln Giants, and Philadelphia Giants. With the exception of the St. Louis Giants, all these teams played the majority of their games in New York or Chicago. By 1908 the Philadelphia Giants had become a traveling team, and they played the majority of their games in New York or Atlantic City, New Jersey. Since the Quaker club and the Cuban Stars did not have their own ballparks, they relied on Nat Strong's booking agency to schedule games in the better parks. Joe Green assumed the ownership of the Chicago Giants upon Frank Leland's retirement. Under Green's management, the Giants became a traveling team, barnstorming the Midwest for gate receipts.

Foster's aspiration for a black league was further compromised by the performance of the other black clubs in the Midwest and East not mentioned previously. The majority of black teams of the era were essentially local clubs who played on the co-op plan. Cogan's Smart Set did make an extended tour of the Midwest that included a four-game series with the Chicago American Giants. However, by 1913 the Smart Set had disbanded. There was no evidence to indicate whether teams like the Mohawk Giants, Indianapolis ABCs, West Baden Sprudels, Kansas City Giants, or French Lick Plutos made extended tours.

Yet Rube Foster's call for an organized league was valid. Foster and, undoubtedly, other black baseball club owners recognized the need for the introduction of restrictive business practices to protect their investment, control consumer markets, obtain access to the better parks to generate gate receipts, and gain a hegemony over the player force. Inducing players to jump their contracts, or borrowing players for important series, made it difficult to place the black game on a sound economic footing. It should be noted that since independent teams did not sanction a governing body to enforce rules and impose penalties, these practices, albeit unethical, were not illegal. More importantly, the leading black baseball club owners would have to cooperate to a much greater degree to expand the black game into large urban cities outside of New York and Chicago. In essence, black professional baseball was experiencing the same kinds of growing pains the white Major Leagues had undergone. By the same token, however, the black game confronted obstacles the white leagues had never had to endure.

As the 1914 season approached, black professional baseball would enter a new period. Several new baseball entrepreneurs would emerge who would be instrumental in making Rube Foster's vision of an organized black league a reality. But the black game would still have to travel a long and rocky road to get there.

5

Black Baseball and the Separate Black Economy

The rise of black professional baseball in the early twentieth century occurred simultaneously with the emergence of black corporate America. The period from 1900 to 1930 witnessed the rise of major black capitalists who achieved millionaire status and established million-dollar enterprises. Their wealth exemplified their success within a black economy that developed despite the exclusion of African Americans from the substantial supply of capital flowing from investment banks, foreign interests, and massive government subsidies. Although black business activity expanded during this period, most African American businesses established during this time, with the exception of banks, insurance companies, independent baseball teams, and the hair care industry, did not survive the Great Depression. Black business remained on the fringes—a virtual shadow economy—and its profits were diminished by the financial giants of the period. At the turn of the twentieth century, the total wealth of black America was seven hundred million dollars. That amount was less than the nation's first billion-dollar corporation, United States Steel, organized in 1901.

Black baseball epitomized the expansion of business activity among African Americans during this period. Much like the owners of more conventional businesses, black team owners dealt with the ways in which a separate black economy was being imposed upon them. Ballpark ownership remained the biggest obstacle to black baseball's business development. African American owners did not enjoy the advantages the Major League owners had in regards to building or remodeling ballparks to sustain a fan base and maximize revenues. Their direct and indirect connections with urban politicians allowed Major League owners to obtain valuable information on matters like transportation plans and real estate developments. In response, several African American club owners entered into partnerships with white businessmen to gain access to suitable playing facilities and maintain business ties with white semiprofessional teams.

Business partnerships with whites did not always work in African Americans' favor. Obtaining the leases to the better ballparks in New York and signing the best black players in the East gave Nat Strong and James Keenan a considerable advantage in Gotham. They maintained a business alliance that made it difficult for a black owner to operate there. Moreover, black players were content to play for these owners because of their ability to schedule games against the top white semipros, Major League clubs, and all-star teams composed of Major League players.

In the Midwest, the Indianapolis ABCs emerged to challenge Rube Foster's Chicago American Giants for black baseball supremacy in that region of the United States. C. I. Taylor assembled a strong club, and by 1916 he had elevated his ABCs to the ranks of a touring team. They played against the leading black clubs, including the Cuban Stars and the Lincoln Stars, and scheduled several postseason series with all-star teams composed of Major League players. The ABCs' rivalry with the Chicago American Giants, however, proved to be a mixed blessing. On the one hand, the rivalry led to increased coverage from the black press, which generated interest in the black community. Concurrently, though, increased press coverage revealed black baseball's shortcomings. Rowdyism, the potential violence in the stands, at black baseball games had the potential to detract fan interest from the sport. The rivalry led to a feud between Rube Foster and C. I. Taylor. Ford perceived Taylor as a threat to his midwestern autonomy, and he used the black press to ruin the ABCs magnate's reputation. Taylor, in response, used the opportunity to call for the organization of a black professional league. A league would serve to remedy the negative influences of rowdyism and petty quarrels by establishing an arbitration procedure to clarify rules and settle disputes. It would also protect the club owners' investment in the sport, and Taylor urged Foster to take the lead in organizing the league.

Rube Foster was reluctant to do that. His winter tour of 1915–1916 could possibly explain this resistance. Black baseball owners had ignored Foster's previous calls for league formation, so and the American Giants' magnate focused on mastering the year-round barnstorming tour. The 1915–1916 tour was the longest one a black club had ever embarked on, and it exemplified the modern marketing principles used by sport organizations in the latter half of the twentieth century. The year-round barnstorming tour served Rube Foster's economic interests better than an organized black league.

The Rise of Black Business Districts

Prior to 1915, the leading black economic nationalists were William E. B. Du Bois (1868–1963) and Booker T. Washington (1856–1915). Whereas their philosophies differed regarding education, civil rights, and black political participation, both were persistent in believing that black business was vital for the survival of the race. Washington warned African Americans that "agitation of questions of social equality is the extremist folly." However, at the same time, he stated, "No race that has anything to contribute to the markets of the world is long in any degree ostracized." Likewise, Du Bois stressed the importance of black business as a springboard for racial toleration: "We must cooperate or we are lost. Ten million people who join in intelligent self-help can never be long ignored or mistreated."[1]

Du Bois sought to encourage the development of a national black consensus in support of black business. He called for "the organization in every town and hamlet where colored people dwell, a Negro Business Men's Leagues, and the gradual federation from those state and national organizations." In 1900, Booker T. Washington organized the National Negro Business League (NNBL) at a meeting in Boston with the purpose of encouraging more African Americans to go into business. By 1905, membership had grown from five thousand to forty thousand people, with over six hundred chapters in the U.S., and the Gold Coast of West Africa. Several national business organizations were founded in conjunction with the NNBL. For example, the National Bankers Association and the National Association of Negro Insurance Companies met each year with the NNBL, and their members were affiliated with the parent organization.[2]

Throughout this period of growth and expansion of black business and professional associations, Washington and Du Bois continued to argue that a separate economy was being forced on blacks so there was no choice for them but to work within this framework. Both were convinced that business expansion was critical to black economic survival. Du Bois further emphasized that cooperative efforts were needed by blacks in developing business enterprises. In outlining the principles of the Niagara Movement that he founded, Du Bois stressed in 1905 that the denial of equal economic opportunities to blacks tended "to crush . . . small business enterprise"; blacks, therefore, had to push for "business cooperation." Although Du Bois promoted black business in the spirit of capitalism, he also underscored that the extreme poverty of blacks required them to ally themselves with labor rather than capital.[3]

The promotion of a black economic nationalist ideology combined with migration and statutory and institutional racism to contribute to the development of black business districts in American cities. The most significant event was the Great Migration of World War I, when blacks moved in great numbers from the rural South to large industrial centers in the North and the South. In northern and southern urban centers, increased black populations were concentrated in segregated residential areas, encouraging the development of black business districts. In the North, the influx of blacks led to the development of the physical and institutional ghetto that locked them into distinct and separate sections of those industrial centers. Black business districts in those cities, as in the South, developed on major streets in the center of the black population. In Chicago these districts were geographically separated from the central business district, often by light industrial areas. In New York, on the other hand, while residential segregation in Harlem increased, as late as 1912 a few traditional black businesses continued to serve whites even as they began to rely more on black customers. In Philadelphia, white resistance to national changes enabled the old black service-sector economy to hang on longer than elsewhere.[4]

Several innovative enterprises emerged as the number of black businesses increased in black business districts. In Chicago, Sandy Trice opened a small haberdashery to supplement his income as a porter for the Illinois Central Railroad. The store did well enough for him to leave the railroad in 1905 and devote full time to his business. Trice put in a complete line of men's, women's, and children's clothing. He incorporated the store, bringing into management such prominent South Side figures as Archibald Carey and Richard Wright Jr. The Trice Company prospered for a few years but found it increasingly difficult to compete with white stores in the Black Belt and went out of business in 1909.[5]

Several businessmen attempted ventures on a larger scale. Some of the more successful entrepreneurs taking on ambitious undertakings were real estate developers. As middle-class African Americans sought to escape the slums by moving into previously white neighborhoods in Chicago, real estate agents seized the opportunity to profit by buying property and obtaining leases on flats on the edge of the Black Belt. Jesse Binga, for example, employed a number of assistants, and his "Binga Block" at Forty-Seventh and State Streets was billed as "the largest tenement row in Chicago." In 1908, Binga used his profits to form the Binga Bank, the first black-owned institution in Chicago.[6]

Phillip A. Payton Jr. was New York's pioneer African American realtor. In 1904, he founded the Afro-American Realty Company, capitalized at half a million dollars, with fifty thousand shares offered at ten dollars each. The company was permitted to "buy, sell, rent, lease, and sub-lease, all kinds of buildings, houses . . . lots, and other . . . real estate in the city of New York." Ten of the eleven original members of the all-Negro Board of Directors subscribed to five hundred shares each. Emmett Scott, Booker T. Washington's personal secretary, sat on the board, providing Payton with a base for expanding his influence in New York and eventually the entire East Coast.[7]

Madame C. J. Walker's enterprise earned her a million dollars. Her wealth was still intact when she died in 1919, leaving generous endowments to the black community. She began manufacturing hair preparation products and sold them door-to-door in St. Louis in 1905. Walker's improvement on the hair straightening comb, in conjunction with her hair preparation products—which collectively became known as the Walker System—provided the foundation for her great financial success. In 1911, the Walker Manufacturing Company was incorporated, with Walker as the sole stockholder. With five hundred agents, monthly sales grew from four hundred dollars to one hundred thousand dollars. In 1916, she moved to New York and built a million-dollar mansion. By then the company had more than seventy-five different hair and skin preparations and other cosmetic products.[8]

With the increasing urbanization of African Americans in American racial ghettos, black business activity became more reliant on the development of a separate economy. In both North and South, however, enterprises owned by native whites and immigrants, Europeans, and Asians were also located in black business districts. Combined, they represented [a group] economy based on the consumer purchases of blacks. Consequently, while African American businesses relied essentially on a black consumer market, they did not exist in a wholly separate economy. White businesses, in fact, captured most of the black consumer dollars that came primarily from wages paid by whites. As historian Juliet E. K. Walker has pointed out, the surplus value of the labor of twentieth-century black wage earners was returned to whites in much the same way the surplus value of slaves' labor was absorbed by their masters. Therefore, the black purchasing dollar in black business districts circulated back into the white community. This is commonly referred to as economic detour, and black baseball would exemplify this phenomenon in many ways.[9]

Baseball and the Emergence of Black Corporate America

The rise of black baseball is an example of the increased business activity among African Americans in the early twentieth century. Entrepreneurs attempted to capitalize on the baseball craze made possible by the success of the Philadelphia Giants, Chicago American Giants, and

Lincoln Giants. Unlike the more conventional businesses in which African Americans engaged, black baseball did not rely solely on a separate black economy for its economic viability.

The exclusion of African Americans from white professional baseball in the late nineteenth century led to the creation of all-black teams. Professional black clubs in the North emerged at a time when the majority of the African American population resided in the South. Therefore, northern black teams sought to compete within the fabric of a professional baseball economy. Because only a handful of teams—like the Cuban Giants, Cuban X Giants, Page Fence Giants, and Chicago Unions—operated on a full-time basis, they benefited by being "the only game in town."

By the turn of the twentieth century, the growth and expansion of black baseball led to attempts to organize leagues and associations. The purpose of league formation was to protect the club owners' investment in the sport, secure the best playing facilities to generate gate receipts, maintain a hegemony over the best players, and deny bookings to uncooperative managers. Their pattern for organization was the white Major Leagues. Given the fact that the National League had been in business since the 1870s, emulating the majors was practical and understandable. Only the National Association of Colored Baseball Clubs of the United States and Cuba operated for a brief time. May we say "The only black baseball association operating at the time [at what time period?] was the NACBC, and it lasted for only a brief while. Furthermore, it did not operate like a league in the traditional sense . . ." That may not be accurate because the ILBCAC functioned as well. I only speculate the ILBCAC was absorbed into the NACBC. Yet it did not function like a league in the traditional sense, with a pennant race and a season-ending championship series Rather, NACBC organizers developed a scheduling system to enable their member clubs to barnstorm nationally to the Midwest and internationally to Cuba.

It was within this context that the black baseball business operated within the framework of a group economy. Several factors contributed to the functioning of black baseball teams within this economic environment. First, of the three tangible assets that constituted a professional ball club—the franchise, contracted players, and the ballpark—African Americans had a greater autonomy over the first two than the third. Throughout its history, the ballpark remained the Achilles heel in black baseball's business development.

The proliferation of black teams came at the same time that several Major League owners either remodeled their ballparks or built new ones. The old wooden structures of the late nineteenth century were becoming ramshackled and unattractive. Several ballpark fires and other disasters occurring between 1894 and 1911 also fueled the demand for new and bigger facilities. Some of the ballparks endangered fan safety. The city of Cincinnati's building inspector in 1907 and again the following year presented a bill of particulars about the unsafe conditions of the park. The building commissioner in St. Louis badgered the Cardinals' management about the grandstand, which dated back to the Union League of the 1880s, being in constant danger of collapse.[10]

In response, Major League owners began constructing fireproof stadiums. The technology needed to build safer buildings was developed by engineers in the late nineteenth century. The material, concrete, was cheaper and stronger than stone, reduced the amount of steel needed for construction, and fireproofed the steel. The building program enabled the owners to install more boxes and high-priced seats to increase profits. Some owners realized that reinvesting profits into larger, more elaborate plants might deter possible competitors, who would think twice before risking the big investment necessary to have any hope of success in the business.

To protect their investment, club owners attempted to develop business relationships with local politicians by liberally distributing passes, donating fields for political functions, and making politicos their partners. From the outset, nearly all professional baseball teams had direct and indirect connections to urban politics. The politicos were typically professional politicians seeking to capitalize from baseball by using their connections to build stadiums and simultaneously picking up votes from grateful fans who would appreciate their sponsorship of a popular entertainment. In towns like New York, Philadelphia, and Chicago, politicians operated their ball clubs like their other enterprises. They were in an advantageous position to assist and secure valuable information on matters like transportation plans and real estate developments. They also obtained preferential treatment in fees, taxes, and police protection. In Chicago, White Sox owner Charles Comiskey purchased a lot in the Armour Square area on the edge of the Bridgeport neighborhood to construct his new ballpark. He used his political clout to get the city council to close off a key avenue to street traffic to enable him to build his park in the white ethnic neighborhood that was the heart of White Sox fandom. Brooklyn Dodgers owner' Charles Ebbets received considerable assistance in planning and implementing the building of Ebbets Field. Ebbets and his primary contractor, Steve McKeever, were both well-connected former politicians. Building supervisor John Thatcher assisted in the matter of digging sewers, while Park Commissioner M. J. Kennedy advised on landscaping.[11]

Both the huge investment in constructing and remodeling stadiums and the direct and indirect connections with urban politicians gave the Major League owners a considerable advantage and leverage over black and white semiprofessional teams. This dual advantage represented the second factor that led to black baseball clubs operating in a group economy—forming business partnerships with whites as either co-owners or negotiating with park managers to gain access to suitable playing facilities. Historians generally define black cooperative enterprises as exclusively black owned and operated and as essentially catering to and reliant on a separate black economy. However, this was not always the case with black baseball. Prior to 1915, the Chicago Unions was the most successful black owned and operated ball club to use the cooperative enterprise approach. Whereas the Leland Giants Baseball and Amusement Association and the St. Louis Giants Amusement Association operated effectively for a short time, both were out of business before the start of the 1914 season.[12]

The majority of African American entrepreneurs eventually functioned as businessmen first and Race men second because of the need for a suitable playing facility. Rube Foster's partnership with John Schorling gave him access to a ballpark in the midst of a growing Black Belt on Chicago's South Side. Foster could tap into this growing black consumer market and, by maintaining his business ties with white semipros, continue to exploit the white baseball market. In this way, a black independent club exemplified an elementary form of market segmentation, the process of dividing a large heterogeneous market into more homogenous groups of people with similar wants or needs to which the product may be targeted. Market segmentation went beyond the Chicago baseball market. Obtaining a ballpark enabled Foster to develop and maintain a fan base in the Windy City and spread the American Giants' brand to the West and the South nationally and internationally to Cuba. From Foster's view it made good business sense to form his partnership with Schorling, who had access to a ballpark and had previous experience running a semipro club in Chicago.[13]

In St. Louis, Charles Mills entered into a business arrangement similar to Foster's. The *St. Louis Argus* reported that Mills "close[d] the deal" to "manage and act as business manager of the St. Louis Giants Baseball Club." Mills added that he could "truthfully state that it is the first time since handling baseball that I have been given a free rein." The Giants co-owner entered into a partnership with local businessman Conrad Kuebler, who had access to a ballpark located at 6100 North Broadway. Kuebler remodeled the park, adding 192 box seats, extending the bleachers along the third base side to the left-field foul line, and refurbishing the outfield fences. Mills's partnership with Kuebler evidently made for smoother business dealings with white semipro teams. The Giants played their opening game in the new park against the Maroons of the local Trolley League. A reported crowd of 4,300 fans watched the Giants demolish the Maroons, 14-3.[14]

Operating as a businessman first and a Race man second, however, did not always ensure that African Americans would serve as co-owners of a ball club. From 1914 to 1916, the three leading black clubs in New York—the Lincoln Giants, Lincoln Stars, and Brooklyn Royal Giants—were owned exclusively by whites. African Americans served as either playing managers or field managers, who do not play. These blacks represented the African American businessmen who operated business establishments rather than owning them. On April 9, 1914, the *New York Age* reported that the baseball situation in Harlem was "very much muddled ... as the McMahon brothers ... [were] managing the Lincoln Stars, while Charles Harvey [had] secured control of the Lincoln Giants and Olympic Field." It is unclear why Jess McMahon left the Lincoln Giants and formed the Lincoln Stars. His past problems in maintaining the lease on Olympic Field could have been a factor. McMahon was able to obtain a lease on the Lenox Oval ballpark, located at 145th Street and Lenox Avenue, which allowed him to continue to tap into Harlem's growing black consumer market. The Lincoln Giants, on the other hand, would have a new owner before the start of the 1915 season. On March 4, the *Age* reported that James J. Keenan had assumed ownership of the Lincoln Giants and obtained the lease on Olympic Field. Keenan would remain the Giants' owner for the next fifteen years.[15]

Difficulty in securing the leases on the best ballparks in Harlem illustrated the kind of competition black businessmen faced in the separate black economy. The Lincoln Giants were in an ideal location to exploit Harlem's black market. The historian Seth Scheiner has pointed out that on Fifth Avenue between 131st and 138th Streets, blacks constituted 98 percent of the consumers, but they owned only 12 percent of the stores. Olympic Field, located on 136th Street and Fifth Avenue, placed Keenan in the heart of this large black consumer market. Both McMahon and Keenan kept their parks busy on the weekends, scheduling Sunday doubleheaders against black, white, and Cuban semipro teams. Both men were able to eliminate the competition by maintaining the leases on Olympic Field and Lenox Oval and sustaining rosters of some of the best black talent in the East.[16]

Neither James Keenan nor Jess McMahon involved themselves in philanthropic activities to serve the needs of Harlem's black community. Yet both men created a demand for their clubs by scheduling some of the best teams at both the semipro and Major League level. Scheduling these games undoubtedly satisfied the players, who could expect to receive better financial remuneration by generating gate receipts. Throughout the period from 1914 to 1916, the Lincoln Giants and Lincoln Stars scheduled several games with Major League clubs or all-star teams composed of big league players. McMahon continued to send his Lincoln Stars on barnstorming tours of the Midwest.[17]

While Keenan and McMahon operated in Harlem, Nat Strong became more active in the black baseball business in the 1914 season. As the owner of the Brooklyn Royal Giants and president of the Intercity Association, he had access to the best ballparks in Gotham. As a consequence, several black and Cuban clubs used his booking service to schedule games throughout the Greater New York area. From 1914 to 1916, both the Cuban Stars and the Philadelphia Giants used his booking service to play the best semipro teams, black and white. It is unclear whether Strong assumed the ownership of the Philadelphia Giants after H. Walter Schlichter and Sol White dissolved their partnership. Press reports suggest that Grant "Home Run" Johnson managed the Quaker club and probably sought out Strong for games. Booking games for his Royal Giants, and providing the same service for the Philadelphia Giants and the Cuban Stars, provided Strong with some considerable leverage in the business of black baseball. With Strong, Keenan, and McMahon controlling the best playing facilities, along with having some [of] the best players on their respective rosters, it became extremely difficult for African American entrepreneurs to operate a ball club in New York.[18]

It appears that Nat Strong made a business alliance with James Keenan to force Jess McMahon out of black baseball. From the beginning, Strong had an antagonistic relationship with McMahon and refused to schedule games with the Stars' owner. Understandably, Keenan wanted to oust McMahon from Harlem to have the growing black market to himself. Press reports revealed that neither the Lincoln Giants nor the Brooklyn Royal Giants scheduled games with McMahon's Lincolns. The Philadelphia Giants and the Cuban Stars did not play games with the Lincoln Stars either. Nonetheless, Strong and Keenan kept their clubs busy by scheduling doubleheaders at Ridgewood Park in Brooklyn and Olympic Field in Harlem. The Cuban Stars were booked as part of three-team doubleheaders with either the Royals or the Lincoln Giants. Despite this exclusion, McMahon managed to keep his Stars active. This was due, in part, to his willingness to embark on barnstorming tours to the Midwest. However, by 1916 the Lincoln Stars were hanging on by a shoestring.[19]

Attempts to force Jess McMahon out of black baseball could explain why no midwestern black club traveled to New York for games during this period. Nat Strong exhibited a willingness to boycott teams that scheduled games with McMahon's Lincoln Stars. To remain in good standing with the Royals' owner, black teams that used his booking service refused to play these teams too. For reasons unclear, the Cuban Stars appeared to be the exception to this rule, since they did play the Chicago American Giants and the Indianapolis ABCs on their midwestern barnstorming tours. To maintain his alliance with Strong, James Keenan scheduled no games with teams that played the Lincoln Stars. Furthermore, given the previous experience of the St. Louis Giants, midwestern club owners did not want to lose their top players to Strong and Keenan and face possible ruin.[20]

By the middle of the 1910s, the black baseball business exemplified the kinds of challenges African Americans confronted in a group economy. While Rube Foster and Charles Mills ran successful operations in the Midwest, white autonomy in New York illustrated the lack of opportunity black businessmen had in baseball. Park ownership was a significant limitation on such opportunity. The result was that African American entrepreneurs made business ties with whites which did not always work in the formers' favor. Nevertheless, the limited opportunities did not deter African American entrepreneurs from attempting to break into the black baseball business. Before the start of the 1914 season, an African American entrepreneur in Indianapolis would seek to challenge Rube Foster's supremacy in the Midwest.

C. I. Taylor and the Indianapolis ABCs

On February 21, 1914, the *Indianapolis Ledger* reported that C. I. Taylor had bought half interest in the Indianapolis ABCs. Taylor's partnership with Thomas Bowser, a white businessman, marked the beginning of the ABCs challenge to Rube Foster's Chicago American Giants for midwestern black baseball supremacy. From the beginning, Taylor ran his ABCs as a full-time operation, following the typical midwestern barnstorming pattern of touring the surrounding states during the week and returning to Indianapolis for Sunday games. The highlight of the ABCs' regular season was a home-and-home series with the American Giants, and it marked the start of a fierce rivalry between the two clubs. In 1914, Taylor culminated the ABCs' regular season with a two-game series against an All-Star team composed of Federal League players. Additionally, the ABCs represented the Royal Poinciana Hotel in Florida during the winter months. In 1915, Taylor continued to pursue his goal of elevating the Indianapolis ABCs to the ranks of a touring team.[21]

Charles Isam Taylor was born on January 20, 1875, in Anderson, South Carolina. He attended Biddell and Clark Universities and served in the Spanish-American war. In 1904 Taylor, along with his brothers—Ben, "Candy" Jim, and "Steel Arm" John—organized the Birmingham Giants. After five years in Birmingham, Taylor moved the team north to West Baden, Indiana, where he served as a player-manager. Taylor assembled a competitive team, and on June 28, 1913, they stunned the Chicago American Giants with a 7-5 win. In many ways, C. I. Taylor's management style was like that of the Philadelphia Athletics' club owner Connie Mack. He was patient in dealing with players and allowed them to think for themselves during the course of a game. He held regular team meetings after the game to discuss how a game was won or lost. Taylor epitomized the black middle-class professional that emerged in the early twentieth century. He was a member of both the Bethel AME Church and the Persian Temple of the Mystic Shrines. As a member of the Masonic Lodge, Taylor held the honor of being a thirty-third degree Mason.[22]

Taylor assembled a strong ABCs club in his inaugural season as co-owner. Many of his players had played previously for him with the West Baden Sprudels. C. I.'s brother, Ben, was the team's first baseman; he was considered the best at that position prior to the arrival of Buck Leonard. Ben was also an excellent pitcher who reportedly won thirty games with the St. Louis Giants in 1911. He would eventually become one of the leading field managers in black baseball. Left fielder George Shively was one of the fastest men in black baseball. He was also a solid defensive outfielder and an excellent bunter. The club's pitching ace was John "Steel Arm" Taylor, who earned his nickname because of his durability. Taylor pitched on average thirty to forty games a year and never lost more than seven games. Possessing a blazing fastball and an excellent curve, in 1908 he outdueled Cyclone Joe Williams, 1-0, in a game in San Antonio, Texas.[23]

C. I. Taylor's partnership with Thomas Bowser typified the business relationship African American baseball entrepreneurs entered into with whites. A bail bondsman by trade, Bowser purchased the ABCs in 1912 from Randolph "Ran" Butler, a local tavern owner. He obtained the lease on Northwestern Park, located at Eighteenth Street and Canal Avenue. Taylor, on the other hand, located and developed player talent, managed the team on the field, and scheduled games with leading black and white semipro teams in the Midwest. Having access to Northwestern Park allowed Taylor to tap into the Indianapolis baseball market and concurrently create a demand for his club in several locales.[24]

Prior to the start of the 1914 season, Taylor made his first of several calls for black teams to organize into leagues and associations. In what he referred to as his "maiden effort at writing for the newspapers," Taylor assessed the state of black baseball for the Indianapolis *Freeman* and began by highlighting black players' exclusion from Organized Baseball: "Whatever may be the qualifications of the Negro, or however well-known the fact of those qualifications might be, the Negro is out of the present system of organized baseball, and according to the present indications, he is out to stay." Exceptional playing ability was not enough "to be a wedge by which the Negro can pry the gate of organize baseball open." Taylor's remedy was for blacks to organize into a professional league.[25]

Taylor's call for black club owners to form a professional league reinforced W. E. B. Du Bois's assertion that a separate economy was being forced on blacks. Much like the African American activist, Taylor stressed the need for economic cooperation among blacks in developing business enterprises. He highlighted the need to protect the owners' investment in baseball by eliminating the jumping of contracts by players and to protect the public's interest by placing a quality product on the field. "Protection through organization of a Negro league," Taylor concluded, "[would] come to the thousand of patrons of the present day independent colored teams."[26]

By 1913, press reports revealed that African American and Cuban teams were beginning to schedule more games between each other. This represented a challenge to those clubs operating in a group economy. On the one hand, scheduling more games against each other highlighted the ways in which a separate economy was being imposed on them. Racial prejudice undoubtedly led some white semipro teams to schedule fewer games with black and Cuban clubs. However, the rise of the Federal League in 1913, which lured white semipro players to its teams, impacted upon the business relationship between black and white clubs. By the same token, it was difficult to exclude black and Cuban teams because of their ability to generate gate receipts. Because there was a growing number of quality black and Cuban teams operating on a full-time basis by 1913, scheduling more games among themselves was done by design. Black baseball entrepreneurs exhibited an ability to create a demand for their product among the public.[27]

In his attempt to protect the public's interest, Taylor scheduled games against the leading black and white semiprofessional teams. On May 30, the Indianapolis ABCs began a four-game series against the Chicago American Giants at Schorling Park. American Giants' hurler Horace Jenkins held the Hoosier club to five singles en route to a 7-1 win. The ABCs rebounded in the second game with a 7-2 victory behind the four-hit pitching of Louis "Dicta" Johnson and a thirteen-hit attack led by George Shively. The Hoosier club was no match for Rube Foster in game three. Foster scattered three hits in a 2-0 shutout victory. The final game was no contest, as the American Giants destroyed the ABCs, 13-1.[28]

On July 27, the home-and-home series between the Chicago American Giants and the Indianapolis ABCs began. The *Indianapolis Ledger* reported that the largest weekday crowd ever at Northwestern Park watched the American Giants take a 4-1 lead into the seventh inning and then break the game open with a three-run rally in the eighth to win, 9-5. The second game was a closely contested affair. The American Giants took an 8-5 lead into the ninth inning. After walking the catcher,

Russell Powell, Giants' pitcher Lee Wade gave up a single to a pinch hitter named O'Neil. ABCs pitcher Tom Williams moved Powell to third on a single, and the catcher scored on George Shively's groundout to second base. With two outs and two runners on base, second baseman George Brown hit a three-run home run to win the game for the ABCs, 9-8. The third game was also a close encounter. Giants' first baseman Jess Barber hit a home run with a man on base to give the Windy City club an early 2-1 lead. The Hoosier club rallied with three runs in the fifth inning and went on to defeat the American Giants, 5-2. The *Indianapolis Ledger* hailed the series win as "the greatest victory ever played by the locals."[29]

The second series began on August 24 at Schorling Park. The home field advantage for the American Giants was evident as they hit ABCs pitcher Tom Williams early and often in the first game and coasted to a 9-1 victory. The Hoosiers lost a heartbreaker in the second game when Rube Foster hit a double in the bottom of the ninth to win the game, 7-6. The ABCs turned the tables on the Giants in game three, as Ben Taylor outlasted Foster, 4-3. The Hoosier club was no match for Frank Wickware in the final game. Wickware pitched a no-hit, no-run game on the way to a 1-0 victory. Overall, the Chicago American Giants defeated the Indianapolis ABCs, seven games to four, but the home-and-home series illustrated C. I. Taylor's ability to assemble a competitive team to attract the Midwest's leading black and white semipro clubs.[30]

Taylor finished his inaugural season as co-owner with a two-game series against an All-Star team composed of Federal League players. In 1913, the Federal League emerged as an independent league not under the protection of the National Agreement. In the League's opening season, its teams did not sign Major League players, instead recruiting exclusively from the talent pool in white semiprofessional baseball. During the winter, Federal League president James Gillmore sought National Agreement protection but was rebuffed by American League president Ban Johnson, who claimed there wasn't enough room for a third major league. The Federals denounced the National Agreement and began luring Major League ballplayers with contracts that not only paid more money but left out the reserve clause.[31]

Federal League All-Star shortstop Joseph "Ownie" Bush assembled the Federal All-Star team, many of whose players had previous Major League experience. An Indianapolis native, Bush began his Major League career in 1908 with the Detroit Tigers. He would play several more years in the majors after the Federal League had disbanded. Center fielder Benny Kauf earned the nickname "The Ty Cobb of the Feds" and would later play for John McGraw's New York Giants. Charlie French, the team's second baseman, had played previously for the Boston Red Sox. George Daus anchored the pitching staff, and he would later win 221 games as a hurler for the Detroit Tigers.[32]

To compete against the Federals, Taylor recruited several players from the Chicago American Giants. Jess Barber, John Henry Lloyd, Bruce Petway, and Frank Wickware bolstered the ABCs' lineup. For seven innings, the first game typified the classic pitchers' duel in the dead ball era between George Daus and Frank Wickware. The All-Stars won the game with a three-run rally in the eighth inning. The ABCs reversed their fortune in the second game. Leading 2-0 going into the seventh inning, the Hoosiers erupted for six runs behind the heavy hitting of Ben and John Taylor. Tom Williams gave up four hits and fanned seven batters on the way to an 8-0 victory. The *Ledger* declared the contest as "the classic of the season."[33]

The Indianapolis ABCs barnstormed their way to West Palm Beach, Florida, to once again represent the Royal Poinciana Hotel during the winter months. They played several exhibition games against a team representing the Breakers Hotel, a team composed of players from the Lincoln Giants and the Lincoln Stars. In March 1915, the Hoosier club embarked on a tour of the South, playing games in Birmingham, Alabama; Holy Springs, Mississippi; and Memphis, Tennessee. The home-and-home series with the Chicago American Giants, the two-game series with the Federal League All-Stars, and the southern barnstorming tour represented a remarkable accomplishment by the ABCs under the ownership of C. I. Taylor and Thomas Bowser.[34]

At the beginning of the 1915 season, Taylor made several moves to strengthen his ABCs. First, he obtained a lease to Federal League Park, which had been vacated by the Indianapolis Feds, who relocated to

Newark, New Jersey. Taylor would schedule games there and continue to use Northwestern Park. Next, he signed three players who would eventually become among the top stars in early-twentieth-century black baseball. Elwood "Bingo" DeMoss was the team's second baseman and would eventually become one of the great players at that position. Born on September 5, 1889, in Topeka, Kansas, DeMoss began his career in 1905 with the Topeka Giants. He was on the West Baden Sprudels team from 1912 to 1914, with a brief stint on the Chicago Giants. DeMoss was a well-rounded player, with excellent speed and great hands. William "Dizzy" Dismukes strengthened the Hoosier club's pitching staff and was regarded as one of the best pitchers in the 1910s and 1920s. He began his career with the West Baden Sprudels in 1910 and played for several clubs, including the St. Louis Giants, Philadelphia Giants, and Brooklyn Royal Giants. His submarine delivery baffled opposing hitters, along with his variety of breaking pitches.[35]

Taylor signed arguably the greatest player in black baseball history. Oscar McKinley Charleston was a barrel-chested, spindly legged power hitter who was often compared to New York Yankees' slugger Babe Ruth. Defensively, his excellent play from shallow center field was reminiscent of Cleveland Indian star outfielder Tris Speaker. Born on October 14, 1896, Charleston was the seventh of eleven children, and as a youngster, he served as a batboy for the ABCs. He left home at age fifteen and served in the army, where he ran track and played basketball while stationed in the Philippines with the Twenty-Fourth infantry. As a member of the ABCs, Charleston was at the beginning of a career that saw him emerge as a fearless competitor who could not be intimidated and whose on-and-off-the-field fights were as legendary as his playing skills. By the same token, Charleston developed a reputation of protecting younger players and possessing a charisma that made him an idol of many fans.[36]

Obtaining a lease on Federal League Park and signing these talented players allowed C. I. Taylor to schedule more games against the leading black clubs. He scheduled a series of games throughout the season with the Cuban Stars, marking the start of a fierce rivalry between the two clubs. The Stars' lineup was emblematic of the club's nickname. Veteran players Pelayo Chacon, Jose Figarloa, Augustin Parpetti, and Herman Rios made the Cubans a formidable foe. Stars' left fielder Christobal "Carlos" Torrenti was at the beginning of a stellar career in black baseball. The left-handed power hitter was also an excellent defensive player with great range and a strong throwing arm. On June 14, the ABCs began a four-game series against the Stars at Northwestern Park. In the first game, Paleyo Chacon's solo home run off Dizzy Dismukes in the first inning proved to be the margin of victory in a 4-3 Stars win. The Hoosier club won the next two games before the Cubans won the finale to split the series at two games. Of the games reported in the press, the Cuban Stars held the upper hand in the rivalry, winning nine games and losing five.[37]

A second home-and-home series was scheduled between the Indianapolis ABCs and the Chicago American Giants. The American Giants maintained their home field advantage by defeating the ABCs three games to two at Schorling Park. However, controversy surrounded the series in Indianapolis. The Chicago *Defender* and *Indianapolis Ledger* gave conflicting accounts about what occurred in the first game. The American Giants took a 3-2 lead into the eighth inning when their pitcher, Frank Wickware, began to struggle. Foster replaced Wickware with Dick Whitworth, who promptly gave up a single to George Shively and walked Bingo DeMoss. Bill Gatewood relieved Whitworth and walked Oscar Charleston and Ben Taylor to force in the tying run. At this point, the *Defender* reported that a windstorm occurred, blowing up dust and making it difficult for the players to see. An argument ensued for reasons unclear, as both teams left their benches and came to the plate. The paper added, "Both teams grabbed bats, the umpire and Pete Hill [the American Giants' team captain] had an argument and the umpire jerks out a gun and hits 'Pete' over the nose. It [was] reported that his nose was broken." The *Ledger* told a different story. It said that after the ABCs tied the score, Foster began to engage in stalling tactics "in an effort to stay hostilities until rain should descend in sufficient quantity to declare the contest off." It reportedly began to rain after the dust storm. Supposedly, the umpire forfeited the game to the ABCs because of Foster's stalling tactics.[38]

On July 31, both the *Defender* and *Ledger* printed Rube Foster's version of the events surrounding the controversial series. During the course of the windstorm, he wrote, play was interrupted to allow the ABCs' management to get a hose and water down the infield. Then, when rain began to fall, Thomas Bowser allegedly told the umpire to continue play. Foster objected because the area between first and second had yet to be watered down. He added, "I reasoned still further with [the umpire], pleading [with] him that [since] there was so much money at stake on the result of the game how much fairer it would be to all to permit the weather to calm, and if the grounds were not in condition to play in thirty minutes . . . the result would be a draw." The umpire ignored Foster's plea and forfeited the game to the ABCs.[39]

The following day, Foster was subjected to "the most complete humiliation both for my ball club and myself." With the score 6-4 in favor of the Hoosier club in the third inning, Foster proceeded to the coach's box on the first-base side. Reportedly, a police officer came on the field and verbally abused the Giants' magnate, supposedly wanting to know who had started the dispute between the two clubs the previous day. At the same time, Foster sent Giants' infielder Harry Bauchman to coach third base. Bauchman noted the third-base bag was out of line and kicked it back into position. C. I. Taylor saw this and ran out onto the field, pushed Bauchman aside, and reportedly called the police onto the field. The police began to beat the Giants' infielder over the head. When cooler heads prevailed, the ABCs went on to defeat the American Giants, 7-4. To add insult to injury, the American Giants lost the final two games.[40]

Foster placed the blame for these two events on Taylor and Bowser. Because there was neither a fight nor an argument in the second game, the police could not come on the field unless the management instructed them to, he asserted. "There can be but one answer to it," Foster added, "the owner, Bowser, being in with the police and a bondsman had directed them to do so." Foster concluded his response using his usual press tactic: portraying himself as a victim. "It was the complete humiliation of a life's effort to advance and promote baseball among our people, and I can forgive the many hard words that may have been said."

He assured the public that he had presented the facts surrounding the controversial series, and the Giants' owner hoped that his explanation would meet with their approval.[41]

Foster continued his attack on Taylor and his ABCs in the black press. After reviewing the events surrounding the series, Foster focused on Taylor's character, portraying him as an ingrate and a "stool pigeon." The Giants' manager alleged that Taylor had been assaulted on the field by his own players and that "his low tactics ruined baseball at West Baden." Foster claimed he gave Taylor's brothers—Jim and Ben—money to cover their travel expenses, and he also wrote that he covered the expenses of eastern clubs like the Lincoln Stars, who supposedly received $594.50 to travel to the Hoosier city. "This [was] merely mentioned, not as a boast," he added, "but to prove that all my efforts has always been to try and help, and not tear down, and advance colored ball." In other words, Foster attempted to craft an image that depicted himself as one who attempted to place the black game on a solid foundation. Taylor, on the other hand, was described as a club owner who made efforts to destroy black baseball.[42]

On August 14, C. I. Taylor responded to Foster on the pages of the Indianapolis *Freeman* and the *Ledger*. Taylor made it clear that it was not his intention to deny what he referred to as "the many malicious and libelous statements as in the 'Signed Statement' of the self-styled 'Greatest Manager' the game has produced." Rather, he offered his perspective on the events surrounding the controversy and simultaneously stated his goals and aspirations as the ABCs' co-owner. He denied the allegations that the American Giants' captain Pete Hill's nose was broken by the umpire, and no other players were injured in the "melee." Taylor admitted that the Giants' infielder Harry Bauchman was attacked by the police but said he did not approve of the officer's actions. He did not explain why the police were called onto the field in the first place. The ABCs' mogul took issue with Foster's labeling him a "stool pigeon" and the latter's claim that he had "ruined" baseball in West Baden, Indiana. Such allegations could have been the basis of a lawsuit, but Taylor expressed no intention of filing one. He wrote that he had no connections with the police department and absolved himself of the police action. Taylor added what "hurt Foster most was that he legitimately lost four straight games."⁴³

Taylor devoted the remainder of the article to what would be his mantra throughout the 1910s: the need for black clubs to organize into a professional league. He had written several letters making the case for a Negro baseball league. Taylor claimed he was "met with all sorts of opposition from sources which would be a great surprise to the baseball public of the United States." To validate his assertion, Taylor produced two letters he wrote to Rube Foster at the start of the 1915 season. In his first letter, Taylor stated that Foster should lead in organizing a league and that he would serve as Foster's lieutenant in league affairs. Organization was the salvation for African American club owners if they were going to survive. A league would eliminate player raiding and the bidding war among club owners to keep their teams intact. Undoubtedly, a black league would minimize the kind of controversial events surrounding the Giants-ABCs series in Indianapolis. An "equalization of strength" among league clubs "was important to maintain fan interest, and to ensure the organization's success." Taylor acknowledged that Foster agreed with the aforementioned stipulations for maintaining a league's stability. Yet Taylor claimed that Foster was reluctant to take the lead in organizing the league. This represented an ironic turn of events, given the fact that as early as 1911 Foster was promoting the need for a black professional league.⁴⁴

The second letter provided some insights regarding Foster's reluctance to take the lead in league organization. Evidently, animosity had existed between the two men prior to the Indianapolis series: "You will find that it is not [in] the best interests of you or anybody else to threaten to wipe somebody off the map in baseball every time somebody happens to ask to have the privilege of having something to say and do with affairs that concern them as well as yourself. I note carefully that almost every letter you write me, provided we are differing on some matter[s], that you offer a threat to annihilate me forever from baseball." Such behavior was not in Foster's best interest. The ABCs were a competitive club, and as a gate attraction they generated revenue. Finally, Taylor expressed his desire to run a successful baseball operation, and "any fair minded man would not object to me having my own idea of things and having the manhood and courage to let my ideas be known." It was his purpose, Taylor concluded, to operate a good ball club and concurrently to place no obstacles in front of anyone with the same aspirations.[45]

Sportswriter Billy Lewis of the *Freeman* challenged the carefully crafted image Rube Foster sought to create for himself. Lewis began by acknowledging Foster's accomplishments in the black game. At the same time, some in black baseball circles perceived that Foster had allowed "his reputation" to cloud his better judgment. "They hold that he was all right," Lewis continued, "as long as he feared no competition." Lewis saw Foster as the "overlord of the business" and that this standing would not be contested if he would simply cooperate with his fellow black club owners. C. I. Taylor, Lewis believed, was one of those owners Foster should cooperate with in good faith. Lewis countered Foster's portrayal of Taylor by characterizing the latter as "studious in every detail" and a "pleasant but earnest and thorough going individual of great business affairs."[46]

Lewis presented additional information that reflected negatively on Foster and his American Giants. On August 23, the American Giants began a series with the Cuban Stars that was marred by controversy. The series revealed how rowdyism had become problematic at black baseball games. In the first game, the Stars' left fielder, Carlos Torrenti, was called out by the umpire when he attempted to steal third base in the fourth inning. Angered by the decision, Torrenti hit the umpire, and the Giants' pitcher, Sam Crawford, came to the umpire's rescue, landing a "crushing blow" to the outfielder's jaw. The police came onto the field and restored order. The debacle led the Stars' owner, Augustin "Tinti" Molina, to state, "We have been treated very badly here by the American Giants."[47]

Foster's claim of paying the travel expenses of eastern black clubs was challenged by Brooklyn Royal Giants' owner Nat Strong. In a letter to the *Freeman*, Strong stated the Royal Giants "never received a dollar for transportation from Foster, never requested it, although it was offered to us, and paid the entire expenses myself." He added that the Cuban Stars never received a dollar from the American Giants' magnate either. The Royals' owner added that in 1911 he had advanced sixteen round-trip tickets Foster requested for the American Giants to travel to New York. In conclusion, Strong said he was writing the letter to show that he was responsible for all his business dealings, which undoubtedly served to keep his reputation intact. Lewis presented these materials in the *Freeman* to show "how far the controversy extended and how hurtful it was."[48]

The reason why Rube Foster went to such great lengths to injure C. I. Taylor's reputation is unclear. In any case, the tactic almost backfired. The Chicago American Giants' extended tour during the winter of 1915–1916 would somewhat overshadow the feud he had instigated with Taylor. Certainly, the carefully crafted image Foster attempted to construct of himself was tarnished. The feud revealed that Foster viewed Taylor as a threat to his autonomy in the Midwest, and it also revealed the importance a black club owner placed on being seen as having the leading black baseball team in a particular region of the country.

On the other hand, the controversial series between the American Giants and the ABCs marked the beginning of several challenges for C. I. Taylor that made it difficult for him to run a successful baseball operation. Several factors contributed to Taylor's difficulties. The boycott of an exhibition game with the American Association's Indianapolis Indians represented the first challenge. On September 25, the *Ledger* reported that the Indianapolis manager had prohibited his club from playing the ABCs "under any circumstances." Evidently, this was an eleventh-hour decision, because the *Ledger* stated the Indians' manager "should have made this fact known publicly before this late date." His decision could have been influenced by the ABCs' shellacking of another Association club, the Columbus team, 12-0. To counter this decision, Taylor scheduled postseason games with an All-Star team composed of American League players and Ownie Bush's Federal All-Stars club.[49]

A near riot at a game between the Hoosier club and the Bush All-Stars formed the second challenge. On October 30, the *Freeman* reported that a "race riot of serious proportions was narrowly averted at the Federal League Park" between the two clubs. In the fifth inning, with the All-Stars at bat, Bush attempted to steal second base and was called safe by umpire James Scanlon. Second baseman Bingo DeMoss reportedly ran after Scanlon and punched him in the face. Center fielder Oscar Charleston supposedly ran in from the outfield and attacked Scanlon too. Both benches emptied to stop the assault, and fans ran onto the field as well. The police came onto the field to disperse the crowd and restore order. Both DeMoss and Charleston were arrested and charged with assault and battery but were released in time to accompany the ABCs for their winter tour of Cuba.[50]

Two months later, the *Freeman* reported that the Indianapolis police would prohibit games between black and white clubs. The decision was in response to the assault on Scanlon in the ABCs game with the Bush All-Stars. "It occurs to me that it [was] time to call a halt in baseball playing between whites and blacks when two teams of mixed colors can not play a game without trouble," said an Indianapolis police captain by the name of Burmfuhrer: "It [was] not the fact that one or more of the colored players struck Umpire Scanlon, but it [was] the principle of the whole argument that had caused this action. I have talked to several witnesses, and there [was] no doubt but what the two colored players [Charleston and DeMoss] incited trouble which might have been more serious than it was." Apparently, the police captain had no concern over his own officers' behavior in the American Giants–ABCs series. Given the fact that the problems that occurred in the ABCs contest with the Bush All-Stars was the exception rather than the rule, the police chief appeared to exaggerate the supposed trouble that occurred at games between black and white clubs. At any rate, the police apparently did not follow through on its proposed prohibition. Throughout the 1916 season, the Indianapolis ABCs continued to schedule games with white clubs.[51]

Taylor had a more pressing concern than the proposed prohibition of games between black and white clubs. A rift between Taylor and his business partner, Thomas Bowser, constituted Taylor's third challenge. On March 25, 1916, the *Freeman* reported that Bowser stated Taylor would not be connected with the ABCs for the upcoming season. The announcement was made while Taylor accompanied the club during its barnstorming tour of the South. Bowser added that he would "direct the affairs of the club" and the team would play its home games at Northwestern Park. Billy Lewis was puzzled by the split, particularly at a time when the Hoosiers had entered the ranks of a touring team. Lewis pondered whether race contributed to this breach in management, although he did not pursue this assertion. The upshot was that there would be two ABCs clubs competing for gate receipts in Indianapolis for the 1916 season.[52]

A second series with the Chicago American Giants ending in controversy represented the fourth and final challenge. In spite of his breakup with Bowser, C. I. Taylor kept together the nucleus of players that made the Indianapolis ABCs one the top touring teams in black baseball. Ben and John Taylor, Bingo DeMoss, George Shively, Oscar Charleston, and Dizzy Dismukes made the ABCs a tough opponent. On October 21, the *Defender* reported that a series of games was scheduled between the ABCs and the American Giants at Federal League Park in Indianapolis. Supposedly, "thousands of dollars" were waged on the outcome, and Taylor arranged for four umpires to work the series instead of the customary two. The series was for the World's Colored Championship.[53]

Declaring the winner of the colored championship became the source of controversy. On November 4, the *Freeman* proclaimed the ABCs the colored champion after defeating the Giants, 12-8. One week later, a *Defender* sportswriter—writing under the pseudonym Mr. Fan—erroneously stated that C. I. Taylor claimed his team won the championship. Mr. Fan pointed out that each team had won four games, with one game "under protest." At the start of the seventh inning in the third game, Rube Foster walked out to the first-base coach's box, picked up a glove lying on the ground, and placed it on his hand. ABCs first baseman Ben Taylor reportedly asked the umpire to make Foster remove the glove from his hand. Foster refused and told the umpire he was not breaking any rules. Foster related the incident to the umpire-in-chief, who supposedly told the base umpire that the Giants' skipper was not breaking any rules. With Foster refusing to remove the glove, the base umpire ordered him to leave the coach's box. The incident resulted in Foster pulling his team off the field, and the base umpire forfeited the game to the ABCs.[54]

On November 18, both C. I. Taylor and Rube Foster presented their interpretations of the confusion over the Colored Championship Series in the *Defender* and the *Freeman*. From the outset, Taylor stated the ABCs were not the colored champions. The series was contracted for twelve games, he said, and one club would have to win seven games to be declared the champion. There was no stipulation that the team that won the "majority of games would be the champion." As the series stood, Taylor maintained, the American Giants had won three games and the ABCs one game, with and a fifth game ending in a tie.[55]

Rube Foster refuted much of what Taylor said. He began by acknowledging both the *Indianapolis Ledger* and *Freeman* as "respectable newspapers" and that their sportswriters were "reliable." Since they relied on the ABCs management for information, however, both papers had been "hoodwinked" into reporting that the Hoosiers won the championship. The ABCs won five games, the American Giants four, with three games to play, Foster asserted. Foster placed the blame for the controversy on C. I. Taylor's shoulders. He questioned the competency and the motives of the umpires Taylor had hired. What was of interest was the way Foster used "the rules of baseball" to justify his actions in the third game, forfeited to the ABCs. If "the ruling of the umpire was wrong," Foster claimed, "the officials of the league [would] throw the game out and order it played over." Apparently the rules he referred to were the ones that govern Organized Baseball. Unlike Organized Baseball, however, independent clubs did not have an arbitration procedure to clarify rules or settle disputes. With no national commission to hear appeals, it was clear that Taylor and Foster were at an impasse.[56]

The fierce rivalry between the Chicago American Giants and the Indianapolis ABCs proved to be a mixed blessing. As the increased coverage from the black press showed, the bitter rivalry between the two clubs generated interest within the black community. Although the coverage was sporadic, it was substantial enough to allow these African American entrepreneurs to tap into the growing black consumer market. The rivalry and the World's Colored Championship became the means to do this. At the same time, the increased coverage revealed black baseball's shortcomings. Rowdyism had the potential to mar the product on the field. The absence of an arbitration procedure to clarify rules and settle disputes could conceivably impact adversely on a black baseball owner's investment in the sport. In other words, petty disputes could diminish fan interest and lead club owners to induce players to jump their contracts, resulting in the destruction of an independent club. These consequences seemed to validate C. I. Taylor's call for an organized black league.

The ABCs–American Giants rivalry highlighted the challenges Taylor faced to elevate his ABCs to the ranks of a touring team. His split with Bowser resulted in two ABCs clubs competing for gate receipts in the Indianapolis baseball market. The negative press, which often portrayed his club as a rowdy bunch, did not bode well for Taylor. Yet none of his challenges deterred Taylor from running an effective baseball operation. He survived the challenges he faced and kept his Indianapolis ABCs intact.

Rube Foster, on the other hand, perceived C. I. Taylor as a threat to his midwestern dominance in black baseball. His actions would suggest that he sought to force Taylor out of baseball. The carefully crafted image Foster attempted to construct revealed the dark side of public relations. Foster endeavored to convey a message that his motives and actions were in the best interests of the sport while his competitor, in contrast, sought to destroy it. It was a tactic the Giants' magnate was willing to use to advance his economic interests. Much of the Foster-Taylor feud was overshadowed, however, when the Chicago American Giants embarked upon the longest barnstorming tour a black club had made to that time.

Rube's Tour

The Chicago American Giants' winter tour of 1915–1916 represented an ambitious undertaking. The American Giants crisscrossed the United States, beginning in the California Winter League, then barnstorming through the Deep South and landing in Cuba. After spending a month in Cuba, the Windy City club embarked on a second tour of the South and finished its winter tour on the West Coast.

The 1915–1916 winter tour exemplified the modern marketing principles commonly used by sport organizations later, in the second half of the twentieth century. Branding, for example, is a means to achieve product differentiation. Brands can be created or fixed in the mind of the consumer through the names, marks, designs, or images of any one or more of the product elements. A brand name refers to the element of the brand that can be vocalized. Many black clubs in the early twentieth century used the nickname "Giants" to identify their team. Previous scholars of black baseball have suggested that the overused nickname was deployed because of the popularity of the New York Giants. Clearly, the Cuban Giants established this brand among black clubs due to their phenomenal success in the 1880s and 1890s. The nickname took on a particular significance following the success of the Cuban X Giants, Page Fence Giants, Philadelphia Giants, and Leland Giants. Early-twentieth-century black clubs aspired to be the next great "Giants" team.[57]

The name Chicago American Giants suggests that Rube Foster sought to differentiate his team from the other Giants clubs. Certainly, the extended barnstorming tours contributed to the plausibility of placing the name "American" in front of "Giants." Combined with their spectacular success on the diamond, the Chicago American Giants had developed a national reputation in black and white baseball circles.

Another means to build the Chicago American Giants brand was through the reputation of the team's successful owner/pitcher, Andrew Rube Foster. Foster established his reputation as black baseball's premier pitcher as a member of the Cuban X Giants, Philadelphia Giants, and Leland Giants. He further built on his standing by assembling one of his strongest teams for a 1915–1916 winter tour. John Henry Lloyd, Jude Gans, Pete Hill, Bruce Petway, Joe Williams, Frank Wickware, and Dick Whitworth could compete against any Major League club of the era. Foster solidified his stature by continually donating Schorling Park for philanthropic activities and maintaining good press relations.[58]

Market reach represented another modern marketing principle illustrated by the American Giants' winter tour. Reach refers to the accessibility of the target market. Spectators attending the games translate into reach. Press coverage and barnstorming provided the American Giants with a significant degree of market reach. Throughout the pre–World War I years, the Windy City club received consistent press coverage in the *Chicago Tribune* in the form of published box scores. Other white dailies like the *Indianapolis Star*, *Seattle Post-Intelligencer*, and *Los Angeles Times* provided press coverage when the team was in their respective regions of the country. The Indianapolis *Freeman* granted Foster a forum to call for the organization of a black league. During the war years, he attempted to develop better relations with the black press, and most notably the Chicago *Defender*.[59]

Foster's efforts to develop good press relations occurred at the same time as the *Defender* was becoming the largest-selling black newspaper in the United States as World War I approached. As historian James Grossman has stated, "Fearless, sensationalist, and militant, the *Defender* advertised the glories of Chicago so effectively that even migrants headed for other northern cities drew their general image of the urban North from its pages." Two-thirds of the "World's Greatest Weekly's" circulation was outside the Windy City. Robert Abbott, editor of the *Defender*, built his wide circulation through an association with black railroad men during the newspaper's struggling years. The *Defender*'s circulation was astounding, reaching 33,000 by 1916 and skyrocketing with the northward migration of blacks during the war. By the early 1920s, approximately 160,000 to 250,000 customers read the Windy City paper. The *Defender* was instrumental in providing invaluable publicity—as the winter tour demonstrated—for Foster and his American Giants throughout the Midwest and South.[60]

The extended barnstorming tours represented another way the American Giants obtained a significant degree of market reach. It also elevated the perceived quality of the American Giants' brand. As a member of the California Winter League, Foster's club played against teams composed of players from the major and minor leagues, such as William "Pol" Perrott, who won ninety-two games in his nine-year Major League career, and Charlie French, a member of the Federal League All-Stars team that played the Indianapolis ABCs. The American Giants won the CWL pennant and further heightened their prestige.[61]

After winning the winter league title, the Chicago American Giants began what was referred to as their "spring training tour." The tour began with a series of games in Havana, Cuba. On March 18, 1916, they left Cuba and barnstormed through the Deep South, playing games in New Orleans; Gulfport, Mississippi; and Mobile, Alabama. By the end of March, Foster's club had toured through the West Coast, making stops in Portland, Oregon, Oakland, California, and Sacramento, California, winning fifty-seven games and losing fifteen. When the local season began in May, the American Giants had traveled over twenty thousand miles. It was during this tour that *Defender* sportswriter Frank Young made the somewhat exaggerated claim that "the Rube" had brought Chicago more promotion than all other city enterprises combined.[62]

The success of the 1915–1916 winter tour could possibly explain Rube Foster's reluctance to take the lead in organizing a black league. Foster's early efforts toward league formation were ignored by black baseball club owners. Undoubtedly, this led the American Giants' magnate to focus primarily on mastering the year-round barnstorming tour. The lack of attendance figures makes estimating the revenue these tours generated problematic. Given the fact that the American Giants went on these tours for five consecutive years, however, would suggest that they were lucrative. In Foster's view, the year-round barnstorming tour served his economic interests better than an organized black league.

Conclusion

The rise of black baseball was an example of the increased business activity among African Americans in the early twentieth century. Black independent teams highlighted the challenges African American entrepreneurs confronted in an attempt to function in a group economy. Much like the more conventional businesses, black team owners had to deal with the constraints that a separate black economy imposed on them. They could not capitalize on the advantages Major League owners enjoyed in regards to building or remodeling a ballpark to sustain a fan base. To overcome this difficulty, several black baseball owners established business ties with whites to gain access to suitable playing facilities and scheduled games with white semipro teams. Partnerships with whites did not always work in an African American entrepreneur's favor. Nat Strong's and James Keenan's ability to monopolize the better ballparks in New York made it extremely difficult for a black owner to operate a club in baseball's largest consumer market. Black players were content to play for these white owners because of their ability to schedule games with the leading white semipros, Major League clubs, and all-star teams composed of Major League players. Their behavior was in line with John Henry Lloyd's claim that wherever the money was, he would be there.

Concurrently, African American entrepreneurs sought to make inroads into the growing northern black consumer market—a direct result of black migration. Rivalries and championships became the means to achieve this objective. Although rivalries and championships generated interest in the black community, they also revealed black baseball's shortcomings. As the Chicago American Giants–Indianapolis ABCs rivalry illustrated, the black game received increased press coverage from the black press, which further stimulated fan interest. At the same time, increased press coverage also showed how rowdyism and petty disputes could negatively impact on a black baseball owner's investment in the sport. The absence of an arbitration procedure to clarify rules and settle disputes could lead to diminishing fan interest, and the destructive practice by club owners of inducing players to jump their contracts.

Nevertheless, by the end of the 1916 season, several black clubs emerged that would serve as the catalyst for the rise of the Negro Leagues in the 1920s. The Lincoln Giants, Brooklyn Royal Giants, Cuban Stars, Chicago American Giants, and Indianapolis ABCs would become the foundation on which these leagues would be built. Before this could happen, however, the black game would have to experience the US entry into World War I, the emergence of a black baseball entrepreneur in Philadelphia, the unexpected return of John Connor, and a change in Rube Foster's views regarding black league formation.

6

The War Years

Toward the Rise of the Negro Leagues

The United States had never prepared in advance for the wars it fought. For a year after the nation entered World War I, it contributed little to the manpower of Great Britain and France, the unofficial allies of the US against Imperial Germany. On May 18, 1917, Congress enacted a conscription law that affected all able-bodied American males between the ages of twenty-one and thirty-five. June 5 was declared National Registration Day, yet it wouldn't be until early in the next year that the Wilson administration's programs for mobilizing manpower and resources began to take effect. Eventually the draft board registered over 24 million men, and of these approximately 2.8 million would be inducted. Roughly 2 million more volunteered, bringing the total to about 4.8 million who saw service.

In most respects, neither the Major Leagues nor black baseball were affected by the American entry into the Great War during the 1917 season. The Chicago American Giants embarked on a winter tour of the South that began in Palm Beach, Florida. The American Giants were hired as waiters to represent the Royal Poinciana Hotel on the diamond. The winter tour marked the start of Rube Foster's construction of barnstorming tours to the East and Midwest in an attempt to open new markets for midwestern black baseball teams. Foster scheduled games for his club, the Indianapolis ABCs, and the Cuban Stars to be played in Atlantic City, Philadelphia, Pittsburgh, Cincinnati, and Detroit.

Despite this ambitious undertaking, several challenges, both internal and external, confronted the black teams in the Midwest and East.

The St. Louis Giants, plagued by a constant turnover in ownership, found themselves in the middle of controversy with the St. Louis Browns owner Phil Ball over the use of a ballpark. C. I. Taylor continued to compete with a second ABCs club for gate receipts in Indianapolis. By 1918, rumors were circulating that Taylor was considering moving his ABCs to another city. In New York, Jess McMahon quit black baseball, and several of his former players, along with the Brooklyn Royal Giants, formed the Grand Central Terminal Baseball Club, known as the Red Caps. James Williams, the team's manager, attempted to obtain the services of Nat Strong to schedule games in New York. Strong refused, leading Williams to accuse the Royals' owner of discrimination.

In the midst of this challenge to the black clubs' operational autonomy, the Great Migration dramatically expanded the African American population in the North, particularly in urban centers. Black baseball entrepreneurs could no longer marginalize the significance of this growing black consumer market. Club owners like Rube Foster and C. I. Taylor began forging civic ties with their respective black communities and concurrently establishing a business relationship with the black press. Foster further capitalized on the opportunity brought by the migration through the development of a booking service to maximize his revenues by keeping Schorling Park busy. Foster's goal of maximizing the use of Schorling Park led him to engage in a more ambitious undertaking. By scheduling games for his American Giants, the Indianapolis ABCs, and the Cuban Stars, Foster established a midwestern barnstorming network by making business relationships with Major League owners like Frank Navin in Detroit and August Herrmann in Cincinnati. Finally, Foster formed the Detroit Stars, transferred several of his players to the team, selected John "Tenny" Blount as the club's business manager, and named Pete Hill as its field manager.

Foster benefited from the emergence of a club in Philadelphia and John Connor's return to black baseball. Although getting their start in the prewar years, the Hilldale Athletic Club evolved from a sandlot team to one the top black teams in the East. Hilldale owner Ed Bolden was the chief architect of the team's transformation. He followed the fundamental pattern of acquiring top-level players, securing a playing facility to build a fan base, and spread the Athletic Club's brand to other regions of the country through barnstorming. By 1916, the club had been incorporated into the Hilldale Baseball and Exhibition Company (HBEC), and Bolden began signing professional players. Much like Foster and Taylor, Bolden acknowledged the importance of community support, and he devised a marketing strategy to attract the black middle-class spectator. By 1919, the HBEC had become the most successful baseball club that was exclusively black owned and operated.

While Ed Bolden transformed his HBEC, John Connor's return to black baseball resulted from the migration of a club from Jacksonville, Florida, to Atlantic City, New Jersey. In 1916, two African American politicians, Tom Jackson and Henry Tucker, lured the Duval Giants to the Seaside City. The team was renamed the Bacharach Giants after the Atlantic City's mayor, Harry Bacharach. After playing as a local club for three years, Tucker entered into a business relationship with Connor and Baron Wilkins, one of Harlem's renowned restaurant owners. This business relationship would allow the Bacharach Giants access to Harlem's black consumer market, in spite of Nat Strong's and James Keenan's stiff opposition. The Bacharach's management team was able to circumvent the Strong-Keenan alliance by obtaining ballpark leases in Harlem and Atlantic City. This allowed Tucker to schedule games with all-star teams made up of Major League players and made it possible for midwestern black clubs to play in New York for the first time since the prewar years. In 1920, Connor entered into a business agreement with the Brooklyn Dodgers' owner Charles Ebbets to use Ebbets Field when the National League team was on the road. Access to three ballparks to schedule games minimized Nat Strong's ability to exclude the Bacharach Giants from playing in Gotham.

Revisiting Old Markets and Exploring New Ones

Since the 1880s, Florida had been on the barnstorming itinerary of black and Cuban teams during the winter months. The touring of black and Cuban teams in Florida coincided with the rise of the hotel resort system in the Sunshine State. In 1885, Henry Morrison Flagler, a railroad magnate, decided to build the Ponce de Leon Hotel in St. Augustine, Florida. This plush hotel integrated a network of leisure activities designed to attract and entertain a wealthy clientele. The resort system created an opportunity for Cuban Giants' entrepreneur Frank Thompson to bring black baseball southward during the tourist season. The players were hired as waiters, but their primary responsibility was to entertain the guests with their baseball skills.[1]

By 1894, St. Augustine's share of tourist patronage began to decline, and Flagler began to turn his attention further south to Palm Beach. Palm Beach's reputation as a winter resort area originated in 1886, when Robert R. McCormick, a railroad entrepreneur from Denver, purchased property and built a cottage on the east side of Lake Worth. Others became involved in resort activities. One of the area's original settlers, Captain E. N. Dimick, added rooms to his house and named it Cocoanut Grove House. Prior to Flagler's arrival, Dimick sold his fifty-room hotel to Pittsburgh millionaire C. T. Clark. Flagler rented the hotel from Clark in 1893 and used it as his headquarters during the construction of his first Palm Beach hotel.[2]

In May 1893, Flagler began construction of the Royal Poinciana Hotel. He spent a total of three hundred thousand dollars for the one-hundred-acre hotel site. The Poinciana was a six-story colonial-style wooden building that faced Lake Worth, with rear wings for dining rooms, kitchens, servants' rooms, and a large ballroom. The hotel contained 125 private baths and had electricity throughout, including its three elevators. Several additions were made to the building from 1900 to 1905. Upon final completion, the Royal Poinciana became the world's largest hotel, whose value increased from less than one million dollars in 1898 to almost two million dollars in 1913.

The Poinciana was an immediate success, and rumors began to circulate that Flagler would build another hotel on the ocean side of Palm Beach. During the summer of 1895, he began construction of the Palm Beach Inn, which opened for the following winter season. Although it was not as large as the Poinciana, the Inn had a sizable following, leading Flagler to double its size before the 1901 season. He also renamed it the Breakers. Flagler hired Fred Sterry to manage both hotels, and he was responsible for hiring black baseball players as waiters.

It was within this context that the Chicago American Giants and several players from the Lincoln Giants and Cuban Stars represented the Royal Poinciana and Breakers Hotels in what was commonly referred to as the Hotel League. The Chicago *Defender* reported the American Giants were hired by the Poinciana management because "of the runaway contests of the past year" when the Indianapolis ABCs represented the Breakers. Rube Foster assembled one of his strongest Giants teams. John Henry Lloyd, Oscar Charleston, Pete Hill, and Bingo DeMoss would pound the baseball during the winter tour and in the regular season. The pitching staff was bolstered by Tom Johnson, Luis Padron, and Ruby Tyree. The Breakers' roster constituted a formidable opponent. Spots Poles, Louis Santop, Joe Hewitt, and Bill Pettus provided the Breakers with an awesome hitting attack. Cannonball Dick Redding and Cyclone Joe Williams anchored the Breakers' pitching staff.[3]

Both teams played the competitive brand of inside baseball rather than the vaudevillian style of their predecessors. The biographer Edward N. Akin stated in 1907 that the guests were entertained by the stereotypical behavior of the players. In a letter to his mother, Arthur Spalding, an organist at Flagler's Whitehall mansion, claimed that "the third baseman on the Poinciana team was a wonderful ballplayer and kept the whole crowd roaring with his horseplay and cakewalks up and down the sidelines." But this kind of behavior was no longer part of the game in 1917. On February 17, the *Defender* reported that Tom Johnson held the Breakers to no runs and no hits for eight and two-thirds innings. The no-hitter was broken up by Blainey Hall's pinch-hit single down the third base line. The Poinciana club scored first when Oscar Charleston walked and stole second base. He went to third when Pete Hill flied out to right field and scored on John Henry Lloyd's sacrifice fly. The Poinciana team scored three more runs and won a 4-1 victory. On February 23, both teams played another closely contested game. This time the Breakers prevailed, 3-1, behind the solid pitching of Cyclone Williams and the five errors committed by the Poincianas.[4]

The Chicago American Giants concluded their winter tour with an excursion through the Deep South. In a telegram to the *Defender*, Rube Foster highlighted the team's stops in cities like Tampa and Jacksonville, Florida; Atlanta, Georgia; Mobile, Alabama; Gulfport, Mississippi; and New Orleans, Alexander, and Shreveport, Louisiana. The American Giants' southern tour was an indicator of the increased press coverage black baseball was beginning to receive from the black press. The growing press coverage received by the Giants occurred simultaneously with the successful efforts of several black entrepreneurs in creating a number of politically influential newspapers. In his examination of black political journalism during the era of the Harlem Renaissance, Theodore Vincent has suggested that "the prime of the black American press covered the years of the US involvement in World War I and the height of the Great Depression of the 1930s." The size of the press blossomed as journalists capitalized on the dramatic story of the Great War, on the mass migration of blacks from the rural South to northern cities, and on the rediscovery of black culture. Several black newspapers—including the Indianapolis *Freeman*, *New York Age*, and *Philadelphia Tribune*—began covering the American Giants' winter tours.[5]

From 1917 to 1919, Rube Foster began taking steps to expand his booking control in the Midwest and concurrently to build civic ties with Chicago's black community. Much like Nat Strong, Foster established a booking service designed to maximize his revenues by keeping Schorling Park busy. He began to book as many as three games on a single Sunday, regardless of whether the Chicago American Giants were at home or on the road. Benefiting from the increased press coverage Foster and his American Giants received from the black press, local politicians—seeking to address the needs of the black community—acknowledged the benefits derived from a close association with the team.

The emerging Cuban Stars club was one of several clients with whom Foster had to, given the decline of the white semipro infrastructure in Chicago, establish his booking service. To avoid confusion with the eastern-based Cuban Stars, the new club was commonly referred to as the Cuban Stars West. The Stars were under the management of P. S. Valdez (president) and A. M. Soto (secretary and manager). They were composed of several veterans plus promising young players. Luis Padron anchored the pitching staff along with Jose Junco. Junco began his career in 1912 with Tinti Molina's Cuban Stars and became one of the top pitchers during the last decade of the deadball era, which ended in the 1910s. Bernardo Baro was the team's center fielder, a left-handed batter who could run, field, throw, and hit for average and power. Geravacio "Strike" Gonzales was the Stars' first baseman. He also doubled as a catcher and excelled in all defensive skills but was most noted for his strong and accurate throwing arm. He was also a good base stealer and hit well in clutch situations. Jose Rodriquez was the team's catcher and began his career with the Fe club in Cuba, although he played most of his years with the Almendares Blues. Although Rodriquez lacked consistency at the plate, he exhibited excellent speed on the base paths and was an accomplished defensive player.[6]

The Cuban Stars played several games in Schorling Park during the 1917 season. On June 17, the *Chicago Tribune* reported a three-team doubleheader between the Stars, the American Giants, and the Indianapolis ABCs. Because of the Stars' 6-1 victory over the ABCs in the first game, they faced the American Giants in the nightcap. Cannonball Dick Redding faced the Stars' hurler Bernardo Baro, whose wildness in the fourth inning resulted in two hit batters and a walk, which allowed the American Giants to score before they got a hit off him. The Giants added three runs in the seventh to win, 4-0. On August 19, the Stars faced the Chicopee Falls club in what the *Tribune* claimed was "one of the best games of the season." Luis Padron held Chicopee to six hits, and a three-run Stars' rally in the eighth resulted in a 3-0 victory.[7]

Foster's aim of keeping Schorling Park busy led him to attempt a more ambitious undertaking. On May 12, the *Freeman* reported that Foster had invited managers from several midwestern clubs to meet him at the *Freeman*'s office. Club owners were invited from the Indianapolis ABCs, Flemings' ABCs, the All Nations of Kansas City, and the St. Louis Giants. Foster represented the Cuban Stars; the Havana Cubans; and the "Hicaugo" Giants club, another Cuban team. The intent of the meeting was to attain two objectives. First, Foster attempted to amalgamate the two ABCs clubs and to lease Northwestern Park. This would eliminate the competition between these teams for gate receipts in the Hoosier city. Second, efforts were made to ensure more cooperation among the club owners. The *Freeman* claimed Foster was finding out "there [was] more in the game than the mere fact of playing ball": "Contest [was] the thing, and with various cities making the whole thing stand as an idea above the mechanical. Something must be done by way of organized baseball, that the proper spirit of rivalry maintains and grows. The rotation of clubs [was] essential; good clubs of good reputation and ability [were vital to black baseball's success] or the game [would] become stale, flat, [and] unprofitable." Although several club owners had reservations, the *Freeman* proclaimed the meeting a success because there were indications the owners would endeavor to cooperate with each other.[8]

The owners' meeting led several midwestern black clubs to embark on an eastern and midwestern barnstorming tour, which had been a goal of Foster's when he called the meeting. The Chicago American Giants, Cuban Stars West, and Indianapolis ABCs played several games in Cincinnati, Pittsburgh, and Detroit. The tour began with the American Giants and the Cuban Stars playing a single game at Cincinnati's Redland Field and a three-games series between the ABCs and Joe Green's Chicago Giants at Detroit's Navin Field. On September 1, the American Giants played a doubleheader with the ABCs at Navin Field. The American Giants reestablished their midwestern dominance by sweeping the ABCs by scores of 7-0 and 6-3.[9]

The Great Migration undoubtedly influenced the decision to barnstorm throughout the Midwest and East. The migration of blacks from the rural South to the urban North became, after 1916, a mass movement. The exact number that migrated in these few war years is unknown. What is clear, however, is that in the decade of the 1910s, the North experienced a net migration gain of over half a million blacks. The cities in which black teams played illustrated this influx of African American migrants. During the decade, Cincinnati's black population increased from 19,639 to 30,079; Detroit's from 5,741 to 40,838; and Pittsburgh's from 25,623 to 37,725. This expanding black consumer market became too important for black baseball entrepreneurs to marginalize.[10]

Foster's attempt to build civic ties with Chicago's black community further exemplified his efforts to tap into this growing market. Beginning in the 1916 regular season, a ritual emerged that remained a constant at American Giants' home openers. A pitcher-catcher battery of Windy City politicians or businessmen would throw out and catch the first ball at the opening games of the local season. The first battery consisted of Alderman Oscar DePriest (the pitcher), who was later elected to the US House of Representatives, and former Leland Giants secretary Beauregard Moseley, the mayor of Idlewood, a local satellite community. Such gestures illustrated Foster's recognition of the importance of middle-class support in conjunction with Schorling Park's becoming a platform where local politicians could be seen as well as heard.[11]

Foster made other concessions to African American politicians. In 1917 Foster reserved a special box for Chicago's black elite. At the opening of this local season, Alderman Louis Anderson and Chicago *Defender* editor Robert Abbott served as the ceremonial battery. Along with Abbott and Anderson, Alderman Edward H. Wright and local businessmen George Holt and Harry Basken watched Foster's American Giants defeat Jake Stahl's Chicago City League club, 5-3. Prior to the game, a New Orleans jazz band entertained the Chicago faithful.[12]

Market expansion and penetration continued the following year. However, World War I would served as somewhat of a brake. Both the draft and the so-called work-or-fight-order—a government directive that set July 1918 as the deadline for men to get essential work or face induction into the armed forces—impacted black baseball's player force. On September 8, 1917, the *Defender* highlighted the draft's impact, as the American Giants lost six players, including Dick Redding, Leroy Grant, and George Dixon. During their eastern trip on July 18, the American Giants lost Frank Wickware and Judy Gans to the armed forces. The Indianapolis ABCs also felt the sting of the draft, losing Dave Malarcher, Oscar Charleston, and Dizzy Dismukes. Star shortstop John Henry Lloyd turned in his bat and glove to work for the quartermaster's department of the United States Army.[13]

In spite of losing these star players, the midwestern black clubs launched a second tour of the Midwest and East. The Chicago American Giants and several players from the Lincoln Giants and Cuban Stars played a second season in the Hotel League. The American Giants and ABCs scheduled several games against each other in Washington, D.C.; Pittsburgh; Detroit; and Philadelphia. The American Giants played in Atlantic City; New York; and Darby, Pennsylvania. Like their Major League counterparts, black baseball teams finished their season on Labor Day because of the war.[14]

The midwestern and eastern barnstorming tours highlighted Rube Foster's endeavor to open new markets by spreading the midwestern brand of black baseball and simultaneously build civic ties with Chicago's black middle class. The Great Migration undoubtedly influenced this decision to spread the black game into both new and familiar territories in the Midwest and East. While World War I somewhat hindered the objective of market expansion, several problems—both internal and external—among black clubs outside of Chicago also slowed progress.

Trouble in the Midwest and East

Midwestern black clubs outside of Chicago confronted several challenges to their operational autonomy within their respective cities. Since their formation in 1907, the St. Louis Giants had to deal with a constant turnover in its ownership ranks. Charles Mills remained the sole constant within the Giants' management team, and it was a testament to his business acumen that the club experienced some degree of success. Before the 1917 season began, the *Freeman* reported that Mills would not manage the Giants, but that the club would be run by a "syndicate of well known Colored men." On April 6, the *St. Louis Argus* reported that a Mr. Brock would serve as the Giant's club owner.[15]

Problems in obtaining a suitable playing facility could have possibly explained the Giants' constant turnover in ownership. The *Argus* reported that St. Louis Browns' owner Phil Ball sought to prohibit the Giants from using Federal League Park, located at Grand Avenue and Laclede Street. Philip De Catesby Ball made his fortune selling ice-manufacturing plants. He became involved in baseball as a result of the sport's recent prosperity. Ball was the principal owner of the Federal League St. Louis Terriers. When the Federal League disbanded, Ball was allowed to purchase the Browns as part of a "peace settlement" designed to maintain Organized Baseball's monopoly. Ball held the lease on Federal League Park, and it was due to expire on April 9. Brock, on the other hand, had signed a five-year lease on the park that was scheduled to begin the following day. To prevent the Giants from using the park, Ball removed the seats in the grandstand area.[16]

On May 4, the *Argus* reported the Giants would not open their season at Federal League Park. In addition to removing the grandstand seats, Ball filed suit in municipal court to prevent Brock from exercising his new lease. This posed a problem, because Brock had already spent three thousand dollars to refurbish the park. The repairs reportedly broke the Giants' owner, who relinquished control of the club. A man named Richard Barnett and J. H. Haynes assumed ownership, and they obtain the services of Charles Mills to run the ball club. The St. Louis Giants limped through the 1917 season as a traveling team and disbanded the following year. Mills would manage to assemble the Giants for the 1919 season. This constant turnover in ownership and the inability to secure a ballpark made it difficult for the St. Louis Giants to maintain a symbiotic business relationship with white semi-pros. It undoubtedly rendered problematic efforts to tap into St. Louis's growing black consumer market and could also explain why the Mound City club was not a part of Rube Foster's barnstorming tours of the Midwest and East.[17]

Whereas Charles Mills struggled to keep his St. Louis Giants on the diamond, C. I. Taylor's plight in Indianapolis was bittersweet. On the one hand, Taylor was recognized as a prominent citizen in Indianapolis's black community. The *Freeman* characterized Taylor as a "wizard of the game" and said he had earned the respect of the Hoosier city's black elite. On the opening day of the 1917 season, Taylor organized a civic parade before the game. The parade consisted of thirty automobiles "with prominent Colored people" riding through the main streets of the black community on their way to Washington Park. Much like

Rube Foster, C. I. Taylor recognized the importance of black middle-class support at a time when migration was expanding Indianapolis's black consumer market.[18]

On the other hand, Taylor faced several predicaments that led him to contemplate leaving Indianapolis. First, he found himself competing with a second ABCs club for gate receipts. Apparently, Rube Foster was unable to get the two ABCs clubs to amalgamate. It was difficult to determine who owned the second ABCs club. The *Freeman* had referred to it as Fleming's ABCs but would later call it Jewel's ABCs. The situation confounded *Freeman* sportswriter Billy Lewis, who pondered whether Taylor's former partner and now nemesis Thomas Bowser was behind the debacle. However, unlike Charles Mills's situation in St. Louis, Taylor held the lease on Washington Park, which allowed him to maintain a symbiotic business relationship with white semipros and to exploit Indianapolis' growing black consumer market.[19]

A second problem involved a two-game series with the American Association Indianapolis Indians. Evidently, both the black press and black fans were spoiled by the ABCs' success on the diamond, because on September 29, 1917, in an open letter in the *Freeman*, Taylor explained why his club had performed so poorly against the American Association pennant winners. The ABCs, he wrote, were in a crippled state when the series began on September 22. Paul Powell, Oscar Charleston, Dave Malarcher, and John Taylor suffered from a variety of injuries that included a broken rib, sprained ankle, and a "charley horse." The first game was over in the first inning when the Indians erupted for five runs on the way to a 13-6 victory. The second game was never in doubt, as the Indians took a 6-1 lead into the fifth inning and coasted to a 7-2 win. Taylor pointed out that his letter was not intended as an alibi for his club's poor performance. Rather, he accepted "defeat as a true sport" and acknowledged Rube Foster's Chicago American Giants as the "greatest Colored aggregation in the business." He was, Taylor said, "sportsman enough to proclaim to the world that I have been beaten, and the Foster's team was master of the situation [during the 1917 season]."[20]

By October 6, the *Defender* printed a telegram Taylor had sent in response to an article printed in the *Indianapolis Ledger* titled "A. B.

C. Got First Ledger Roast." A primary focus of the *Ledger*'s "Roast" was that Taylor did not make a concerted effort to prepare his ABCs to face the Indians. Taylor indicted the *Ledger* for not investigating thoroughly the team's predicament prior to the series and provided a more in-depth explanation for his club's poor performance. Taylor's response stipulated the kinds of "manager troubles" Sol White would highlight in his *History of Colored Baseball*. Several players left the club during the season, including Dizzy Dismukes and George Shively. The rash of injuries illustrated what an independent club endured during the course of year-round barnstorming. Taylor pointed to twelve different players who experienced some type of injury during the season. In response, Taylor wrote, he hired an athletic trainer to treat the various ailments. His club, according to Taylor, was the only black team to have a trainer on the payroll.[21]

Taylor accentuated other ways he tried to get his ABCs ready for their series with the Indians. It was customary for black and white clubs to recruit extra players for postseason series. The Indians lured first baseman Jay Kirke from the Association Louisville club. Kirke was pivotal in the Indians' series sweep, collecting six hits in ten at-bats, including three doubles, a home run, and three runs scored. Taylor, on the other hand, sent a telegram to Rube Foster to recruit several of his players. Foster replied that he had just scheduled a series of games in Beloit, Wisconsin, and that the American Giants would not return in time to provide the Hoosier club with players. During the ABCs' eastern tour, Taylor attempted to entice players from eastern-based black clubs including Cyclone Joe Williams, Louis Santop, and Spots Poles but was unsuccessful in his endeavor. Taylor sought to convey a message to the public that he made every effort to maintain the Indianapolis ABCs as one of the leading touring teams in the US. He found it disheartening that "a leading journal [the *Ledger*] which stands for the uplift of the Race, would be the first to suggest that the support of the people should be withdrawn, [which] is more than even a prejudiced mind should conceive."[22]

A final factor involved rumors that Taylor was considering a move to another city. On July 6, 1918, Billy Lewis claimed the Hoosier city's black community was "considerably wrought over C. I. Taylor's announcement that the ABCs . . . would be transferred to some other city." Allegations that the fans were rooting for the visiting club was, from Taylor's view, "a repudiation of his team, [and] of his splendid effort in building it up." Lewis emphasized the ABCs magnate's accomplishments over the preceding three years. He extolled Taylor for being a prominent member of the black community, for his business acumen and quiet demeanor, and for his philanthropic activities. Taylor purchased bonds and thrift stamps to support the war effort and made numerous contributions to charitable organizations. Yet Lewis claimed the ABCs' magnate was misperceiving the fans' cheers for the visiting team, stating Taylor was "a bit over sensitive." To the contrary, Lewis wrote, the Indianapolis fans had exhibit considerable support for the ABCs. The Hoosier city faithful, Lewis said, championed a high caliber of play on the diamond so that, in essence, the supposed fan support for the visiting team was an acknowledgment of the high level of competition which teams like the Cuban Stars provided for the ABCs.[23]

On July 20, the *Freeman* printed Taylor's response to the rumors of his club's supposed departure to another city. He began by stating that his ideal was to create an enterprise in which black people could take pride. His actions and rhetoric reflected the aspirations of the new black middle class to create institutions that were symbols of race pride and racial solidarity. Along with the *Indianapolis Ledger*, Taylor mounted a public relations campaign to eliminate drinking, gambling, and rowdiness from the ballpark: "There [was] no club in the country that has made a more enviable reputation for clean sport and good conduct on and off the field." Taylor then indicted the fans for their disreputable behavior at ABCs games. He had never played in a city where the fans rooted more for the visitors than the home team, which led to disruptive behavior from unruly fans and certain clubs. He was extremely critical of the Cuban Stars, whose rowdy behavior was a direct result of the crowd's pulling for them. The Cubans, Taylor asserted, had become especially astute at arousing the fans by disputing every decision of the umpire.[24]

Even more significant was the scheduling problem Taylor confronted. The fans, he reported, asked him when either the Cuban Stars or the American Giants were coming to town, a clear indication that they would only patronize the ABCs when these clubs were scheduled. But as Taylor pointed out, the ABCs could only play the Cuban Stars three Sundays out of the season and the American Giants once. That left eight Sundays out of the season in which the ABCs had to play other clubs. What resulted was the haunting legacy of the Cuban Giants' early years in Trenton, New Jersey. The fans showed little interest in patronizing games in which either the Cubans or the American Giants were not the opponent. In 1919, C. I. Taylor did not organize the ABCs for a local season.

While C. I. Taylor and Charles Mills dealt with several challenges to their operational autonomy, several players left the Brooklyn Royal Giants and joined the Grand Central Baseball Club. Throughout the war years, Nat Strong and James Keenan maintained their hegemony over New York's black baseball consumer market. Strong's booking service, along with his alliance with Keenan, made it difficult to run a ball club there. Maintaining control over their respective parks and having some of the best players on their rosters provided both men with a considerable advantage and leverage. In addition, Strong booked games for the Cuban Stars East and the Philadelphia Giants. These business arrangements allowed Nat Strong to eliminate any competition that might come his way.

On April 6, 1918, the *New York Age* published a photo of three leading players from the Brooklyn Royal Giants who had joined the Grand Central Baseball Club, along with their manager, James H. Williams, who worked in the railroad industry. Frank Earle, the Royals' captain, led this player exodus to the team also known as the Red Caps. Earle was the center fielder and captain of the team who doubled as a pitcher. In 1909, Earle single-handedly defeated the Cuban Stars for the eastern colored championship. Frank "Lefty" Harvey was the Red Caps' leading pitcher. In 1912, Harvey began his career with the St. Louis Giants and joined the Royals the following year. Pearl "Speck" Webster began his career as a catcher with the Chicago American Giants. He joined the Royal Giants in 1912, where he developed into a solid hitter. Bill Hardy played second base and shortstop for the Royals, where he earned a reputation as a good hitter and exceptional defensive player with excellent speed on the base paths.[25]

Scheduling games in New York proved to be difficult for the Grand City club. On June 8, Williams complained to the *Age* that Strong was doing everything he could to keep the Red Caps from securing dates. Williams's accusation was like the one John Connor had made in the prewar era. Sportswriter Lester Walton reinforced this claim, stating that Connor insisted he had been discriminated against in regard to obtaining desirable dates for his Royals. Walton added that the charge should be investigated and that if it was found valid, the fans should rally around the Red Caps. Williams charged Strong with trying "to corner all the colored ballplayers." Walton took a neutral position on this claim and acknowledged that such an aspiration was "an honorable ambition." However, he asserted that warnings were being made that any attempt by Strong or any white manager to discriminate against a black manager would jeopardize black patronage. Walton pointed out that it was "well known to white amusement promoters that in Harlem . . . the colored people are not as keen for patronizing their own as in Chicago and other cities." In Walton's view, this was why no African American entrepreneur had been successful in Gotham for several years. He had no objection to "white managers separating the colored fans from their dimes if they showed a willingness to let some colored manager or managers in on the deal." But the white managers appeared to be "actuated by a spirit of selfishness." Walton concluded with a parting shot at Harlem's black community: "A more desirable and equitable state of affairs can be brought about, but not until the colored people themselves take the matter in hand."[26]

On June 29, 1918, the *Age* reported Strong's response to Williams's accusation. Several of his players reportedly asked for letters of recommendation to seek employment at the New York Central railroad station. After Strong wrote these letters, the players had apparently decided to play for the Red Caps. Strong indicated that Williams had declared there would be no Royal Giants in 1918 and that the players' employment was contingent on their playing ball. Because they had no playing facility, Williams and Earle offered Strong the opportunity to book the club; Strong refused. After being shot down by the Royals' owners, Williams had evidently sent several letters to white managers to schedule games but received no response. Strong concluded his letter in a paternalistic tone. He reminded the *Age*'s readers that he had "been known to colored people who patronize colored amusements for many years . . . [and] have probably more personal friends among your own people than Williams." He added, "No one before has ever pointed a finger at me as not doing what is right." The Royals' owner reminded the *Age* that he was the first manager—"white or colored"—who patronized the paper by purchasing advertising space to publicize his basketball team.[27]

The claim that Nat Strong sought to shut the Grand Central Red Caps out of the New York market was valid. By his own admission, Strong viewed the Red Caps as a threat, and he would not assist Williams in putting "the Lincolns and my club out of business." As president of the Intercity Association, Strong may have persuaded the leading white semipro clubs to refuse to schedule games with the Red Caps. It was not in their best interest to antagonize the IA president. Strong may have coerced the Cuban Stars and the Philadelphia Giants to refrain from playing the Grand Central club by refusing to schedule their games in Gotham. However, Strong's influence in Harlem was due to his business alliance with James Keenan. Like the Royals' owner, Keenan had a vested interest in eliminating any potential competition. With Jess McMahon out of black baseball, Keenan had Harlem to himself.[28]

Throughout the war years, several black baseball clubs confronted challenges to their operational autonomy. In spite of these obstacles, African American entrepreneurs like Charles Mills and C. I. Taylor would persevere. The end of World War I would usher in a new period for black professional baseball. But before getting to that, it is essential to trace the emergence of several new black baseball teams—especially one club in Philadelphia which had its start in the prewar era. These new teams would form the nucleus of the Negro National and Eastern Colored Leagues in the 1920s.

The Hilldale Athletic Club

On May 29, 1910, Austin Devere Thompson, a nineteen-year-old from Darby, Pennsylvania, placed an ad in the *Philadelphia Sunday Item.* Under a column titled "Amateur Base Ball Notes," the following notice appeared: "Hilldale A. C. would like to arrange games with all 14 and 15 year old traveling teams. Pay half expenses. Address Manager A. D. Thompson No. 329 Marks Avenue, Darby, Pa." Along with his brother Lloyd, the team's fourteen-year-old second baseman, the elder Thompson organized a black club composed of fourteen-to-seventeen-year-old players, the majority of them from Darby and nearby communities. Before Hilldale's first season ended, A. D. Thompson had left the club and was replaced by Ed Bolden.[29]

The emergence of Ed Bolden as Hilldale's new manager marked the start of the team's transformation from a local stay-at-home to a black independent team. Bolden followed the fundamental strategy of acquiring top-level players, obtaining a playing facility to build a fan base, and developing barnstorming tours to other regions of the US. Bolden developed a symbiotic business relationship with white semiprofessional teams and, much like Rube Foster and C. I. Taylor, recognized the importance of developing good press relations to gain the support of the black middle class and a source of market promotion. By 1919, the Hilldale AC would become the most successful baseball club that was exclusively black owned and operated.

Ed Bolden was born on January 17, 1881, in Concordsville, Pennsylvania, fifteen miles from Darby. Like John Connor of New York, Bolden was not a former baseball player but a Philadelphia postal clerk, typical of the black professional that emerged in the age of accommodation. He had been in the Central Post Office in Philadelphia as a postal clerk since 1904, and prior to that he had been a butler for three years. The historian Neil Lanctot has pointed out that Bolden was said to possess "an efficiency record for case examination and floor work unsurpassed and seldom equaled" at the post office. Quiet yet ambitious, Bolden began the initial steps to transform the Hilldale AC into a top-level black independent club.[30]

Bolden's transforming efforts coincided with the rise of many of black teams in the Quaker City. Hilldale competed for gate receipts against teams like the Ideal Travelers, Anchor Giants, Norristown, and Ardmore Tigers. The majority of these clubs were essentially local teams passing the hat to meet expenses. Both the urbanization process and the organizational efforts of white semipro teams meant that these black clubs remained essentially local wonders. The gradual process of urbanization in Philadelphia, much slower there than in some other cities, led to white and black semipro clubs playing primarily on open lots rather than enclosed grounds. In 1913, only four out of fifteen leading black teams in the Quaker City possessed their own grounds. The available playing fields were usually inferior. One park at Twenty-Sixth and Allegheny, for example, was located in the middle of a "veritable forest of trees," featuring "wooden blocks for bases."[31]

The organizational efforts of white semiprofessional teams into leagues and associations also contributed to the fact that Philadelphia's black clubs operated essentially as local clubs. Formation of these leagues and associations meant that white semipros scheduled fewer games with local black teams. As a result, several black clubs remained idle two-to-three times a week. Local businesses in Philadelphia were the primary stimulus for league formation. Therefore, no booking agent evolved to provide the service of scheduling black teams.

Pennsylvania Blue Laws contributed to the slowness in the overall development of these local black clubs. Sunday represented a big pay for black independents in Chicago, New York, and Indianapolis. Club owners would schedule two or three games on a single Sunday to maximize revenues. However, the lack of a suitable playing field and fear of prosecution made it difficult for Philadelphia's black clubs to schedule Sunday games. Blue Laws explained why the Philadelphia Giants began scheduling more weekend games in New York and New Jersey.

The configuration of black Philadelphia's community settlement patterns constituted a fourth factor causing these black clubs to develop slowly. Migration led to the disbursement of blacks into various sections of the city, in none of which did they constitute a majority. This scattered population was a central reason why no large concentrated black consumer market evolved, making it problematic for a local promoter to gain overall hegemony. This, combined with the fact that only a handful of teams possessed their own grounds, made black clubs reliant on a number of games with whites in order to survive.[32]

It was within this context that a group of teenage boys, primarily from Darby and nearby communities, formed the Hilldale AC club. The borough of Darby was an African American "community satellite" located southwest of Philadelphia in Delaware County, just across the city line. It was incorporated in 1853 originally as part of Darby Township in Delaware County. Darby was one of several communities partitioned from the area of land that included Upper Darby, Sharon Hill, Collingdale, Alden, Colway, Glenolden, and Folcrot. To escape the congestion of Philadelphia, a handful of black families moved to Darby. By 1910, nearly seven hundred African Americans lived in the conveniently located borough, an approximately forty-five-minute ride from downtown Philadelphia by trolley. Blacks comprised 10 percent of the population and were restricted to living "upon the Hill." White realtors refused to make housing available in other sections of the borough.[33]

The *Philadelphia Tribune* reported that the Hilldale AC played their games on a vacant lot on Tenth Street. In June 1910, a "heated contest" with a black club from Philadelphia led the Hilldale team to ask Ed Bolden to umpire the game. Bolden declined, but he agreed to keep score. After the Darbyites won the game, Bolden congratulated them and promised to purchase equipment for the team. This gesture led two of the players, Lloyd Thompson and George Kemp, to ask Bolden to manage the team. After "much consideration," Bolden agreed. The earliest documented Hilldale game was on June 11, 1910, as the "Hilldale Field Club" lost to Landsdowne, 10-5. In 1911, Bolden's club amassed a 23-6 won-lost record.[34]

With the exception of Rube Foster, no other African American club owner utilized the press better than Bolden. Market promotions were essential for stimulating fan interest and simultaneously constructing an acceptable moral image to appeal to the black middle class. Beginning in 1912, Bolden began bombarding the *Philadelphia Tribune* with constant press releases from March to October. On March 23, 1912, for example, he declared, "we have good grounds, and give a good guarantee for a good attraction." In connection to a game against the Three Links club of the Interborough League, Bolden stated that Hilldale's "highest aim is clean baseball and good umpiring. Our games are won on merit. For our ballplayers the chief requisite is a gentleman in uniform as well as off the ball field." The assertion that Hilldale stood for "clean baseball" became the foundation for Bolden's marketing strategy.[35]

Bolden gained control of Hilldale Park in Delaware County. Obtaining a ballpark allowed the AC to build and sustain a fan base and made the team attractive to white semipros who lacked their own grounds. In 1914, Bolden scheduled three games against white clubs, including a game that featured a minor league pitcher owned by Connie Mack's Philadelphia Athletics. That same year, Bolden's AC defeated the Interborough League champion Three Links club for the championship of Darby.[36]

The press was essential in recruiting sandlot players from other teams. Bolden used the *Philadelphia Tribune* to acquire several players that transformed Hilldale from a club of "small boys" to a prospective black independent team. In the following years, he would obtain players from the Morton Republican Club, the Evergreen Hall team, the Ardmore Tigers, and clubs in Camden and Philadelphia.

The 1914 season provides a glimpse into Hilldale's financial situation. The three primary sources of revenue came from gate receipts (which ranged from twenty to forty dollars), donations (from one to five dollars), and concessions (from six to nineteen dollars). Hilldale paid an annual fee for rent (fifty dollars) and for hiring an umpire (fifty dollars). Team expenses (such as equipment, transportation, accommodations, hiring umpires, park rentals in some cases) or player salaries represented the highest expenditure the team made (from five to nineteen dollars). Overall, the Hilldale AC realized a profit of $219.49.[37]

In 1915, the Hilldale Athletic Club enjoyed another successful season, winning twenty, losing eight, and tying two. Its profits doubled from the previous year, amounting to $569.63. That same year marked the start of an annual practice by Bolden of publishing Hilldale's record in the *Philadelphia Tribune*. As the Great Migration became a mass movement, Bolden began his big push into the world of black professional baseball.[38]

The Hilldale Baseball and Exhibition Company

On January 15, 1916, Ed Bolden held a team meeting at his house on 360 Marks Avenue. At the meeting, Bolden stated his intention "to give the public in general a strictly strong club," and he outlined his plan to accomplish this goal. Over the next three years, the Hilldale Athletic Club would be transformed from a team of "small boys" to one of the leading eastern-based black independent clubs. On February 27, 1916, Bolden began the planning phase of a five-year process to renovate Hilldale Park. He contracted a local construction company to build a new grandstand at a cost of $104 and agreed upon, along with the people who made up the HBEC, a 25-cent admission charge once it was completed. Trees were removed from left and center field, and by 1920 the AC had extended the grandstand and built a roof upon it to protect the patrons. Throughout the planning phase, renovations to Hilldale Park were promoted as a means of providing the fans with "one of the best and most comfortable accommodations available."[39]

Hilldale opened its season in its renovated park with a game against the R. G. Dunn Club of the Main Line League. During the prewar years, R. G. Dunn became Hilldale's chief rival, and Hilldale had yet to defeat R. G. Dunn on the field. The game represented the kind of top-level competition Bolden sought to schedule to maintain his symbiotic business relationship with white semipros. Hilldale played R. G. Dunn tough in their home opener but went down in defeat, 5-4.[40]

Hilldale finished the 1916 season with a 19-9-2 won-lost record, and during the off-season efforts were made to incorporate the club. The team's attorney drew up the necessary papers, and the team was incorporated with a capital investment of ten thousand dollars. A constitution and bylaws were drawn up and adopted. On January 7, 1917, the Hilldale club received a certificate of incorporation and letters of patent and paid a thirty-dollar fee. The corporation adopted the name: Hilldale Baseball and Exhibition Company (HBEC).[41]

The HBEC was a prime example of how African American entrepreneurs developed businesses to advance their own economic interests. Bolden typified the business leaders who deemphasized the fight for integration and contributed to the development of a separate institutional life for Darby's blacks by establishing black businesses, in this case the HBEC. Bolden's marketing ideology leaned toward Booker T. Washington's philosophy of self-help. The Tuskegee ideology did not determine his actions, however. It merely validated what he was already doing.

Bolden continued to formulate an acceptable moral image to appeal to the middle-class spectator. In many ways, he reflected the approach of American League president Ban Johnson. Not only were the players expected to live up to this image, but so were the fans who came to Hilldale Park. On January 13, 1917, the *Philadelphia Tribune* reported that legal warrants had been issues at the behest of the Hilldale management against five men for rowdy behavior at a game. The result was that four of them paid fines and costs. Bolden summed up his actions this way: "Hilldale is out for right and will have a force of efficient uniformed policemen and three special clothes men at the park this year. Pleasure and comfort is [our] first consideration." In addition to developing this acceptable moral image, ensuring the fans' safety was also instrumental in the HBEC's public relations campaign.[42]

On March 10, 1917, the *Tribune* reported that Thomas Mackens, a local Darbyite and physical instructor, was signed as Hilldale's first uniformed officer. The paper described Mackens as a man of "gentlemanly demeanor, neat appearance, and robust physique [who] would add prestige and dignity to the Hilldale machine." James Byrd, William Watson, and other "interested men" were sworn in as special officers. These officers would be augmented by the Darby and Yeadon borough police on holidays. Whereas the primary reason for hiring these officers was to maintain order, putting local men on the payroll also served to stimulate community involvement in the club.[43]

Like his predecessors, Rube Foster and C. I. Taylor, Ed Bolden endeavored to establish community relations among Darby's and Philadelphia's black citizenry. He participated in several black fraternal organizations as an Elk, a thirty-second-degree Mason, and a Shriner and was also a member of the Citizen's [*sic*] Republican Club, a local black business and professional group. Bolden also advocated the philosophy that he was a businessman first and a "Race" man second. In 1925, Bolden characterized his philosophy this way: "Close analysis will prove that only where the color line fades and cooperation is instituted are our business advances gratified. Segregation in any form, including self-imposed, is not the solution."[44]

In addition to signing peace officers and establishing a public relations campaign, Bolden signed Hilldale's first professional player. On March 17, 1917, the *Tribune* announced the signing of Otto Briggs, a native of Kings Mountain, North Carolina. Briggs had developed a reputation as one of the smartest players in the game. He began his career in 1914 as a member of C. I. Taylor's West Baden Sprudels. Briggs followed Taylor to Indianapolis and became the ABCs' backup second baseman. He was named the team's captain and would remain with Hilldale for the next thirteen years.[45]

Other professional signings soon followed. Frank "Doc" Sykes was a pitcher with excellent control who once pitched a perfect game. Sykes got his start in baseball in 1913 as a member of the Philadelphia Giants. He played for both the Lincoln Stars and Brooklyn Royal Giants over the next three seasons. By late July 1917, Bolden had signed McKinley "Bunny" Downs, outfielder; Spots Poles, outfielder; and first baseman Bill Pettus. Since Hilldale continued to play primarily on the weekends, Bolden devised a system whereby the newly signed professional players played for the HBEC on the weekends while playing with other clubs during the week.[46]

Signing professional players led Ed Bolden to schedule some of the top black clubs of the East. On July 7, the *Tribune* reported a three-team doubleheader between Hilldale, Norristown, and the Cuban Stars. After Hilldale defeated the local Norristown club, 4-1, in the first game, Doc Sykes took the mound against the Stars' Rodolfo Fernandez. The Stars took a 3-2 lead into the fifth inning, and a three-run rally in the sixth inning led to a 7-2 Stars win. On August 9, the Lincoln Giants were equally tough. Despite having their newly signed players in the lineup, Hilldale was no match for the Cyclone Joe Williams. Williams was also stellar at the plate, collecting three hits and leading the Lincolns to a 6-1 victory. The HBEC finally prevailed against Nat Strong's Brooklyn Royal Giants. Led by the timely hitting of Spots Poles and Bunny Downs, Hilldale jumped out to an early 3-0 lead in the first inning. It was all Sykes needed, as he scattered five hits and Hilldale coasted to a 9-1 victory.[47]

Hilldale completed its 1917 season with a three-game series against an All-Star team composed of Major League players. Playing under the name the All-Americans, several players from Connie Mack's Philadelphia Athletics formed the nucleus of the club. The team was led by pitcher Bullet Joe Bush, who led the A's with eleven wins, and catcher Wally Schang. Other major leaguers included the Detroit Tigers' second baseman Ralph Young and the Pittsburgh Pirates' reserve outfielder Dan Flinn. Hilldale added third baseman Thomas Kimbrough, hurler Cyclone Joe Williams, shortstop Dick Lundy, and catcher Louis Santop to bolster its lineup, bolster its pitching staff, and generate gate receipts. In the first game, the Cyclone maintained his reputation as a fierce competitor against Major League players. The *Tribune* stated Williams "had plenty of stuff and speed at all times" as he led Hilldale to a 6-2 win. The second game told a different story as the All-Americans hit Doc Sykes early and often, taking a 7-0 lead into the seventh inning. Hilldale drew close with a four-run rally in the bottom of the seventh, but the major leaguers added three runs in the eighth and one in the ninth to win, 11-5. In the rubber match, Cyclone Joe Williams faced Bullet Joe Bush. Williams was off form, as the All-Americans scored five runs in the first three innings. The *Tribune* noted that Bush "simply pitched great ball," giving up six hits, and leading the All-Americans to a 10-4 victory. Despite losing the series, the 1917 season was Hilldale's best in its brief history.[48]

The signing of uniformed officers and professional players, scheduling games against the leading black clubs of the East, and competing against Major League players resulted in a transformation of Hilldale's corporate structure. By 1918, the former ballplayers had, in a sense, been "kicked upstairs" and no local player remained. Referred to as the "old fellows," Lloyd Thompson, Charles Freeman, Thomas Jenkins,

Mark Studevan, George Kemp, William Anderson, and James Byrd became HBEC corporate members. It was unclear in what other occupations outside of baseball these race men were engaged. Every indication suggests they were part of Darby's black middle class. The *Tribune* stated Thompson had architectural experience, and he would play a pivotal role in renovating Hilldale Park.⁴⁹

Hilldale's continued marketing efforts not only served as a public relations campaign to convey an acceptable moral image to attract the middle-class spectator, it also had a practical application. Clean baseball was based on the premise of developing a competitive ball club, maintaining order on and off the field, and providing "one of the best and most comfortable" ballparks for the fans. Prior to start of the 1918 season, Bolden made arrangements with the P. R. T. Company to have all trolley lines on Walnut to run straight to Hilldale Park. The P. R. T. ran extra cars from 1:15 P.M. to 6:15 P.M., making it easier for fans go to and from the ball park. Both the practical improvements and the club's ideological legitimation heightened the Hilldale brand in the mind of the middle-class spectator.⁵⁰

The HBEC's tremendous progress caught the attention of Brooklyn Royal Giants' owner Nat Strong. Strong attempted to absorb Hilldale into his booking service, thus making inroads into the Philadelphia market. The Royals' owner stated if he could not amalgamate the HBEC, he would put a club in the park across the street from Hilldale's. Strong would get his former business associate, H. Walter Schlichter, to manage the club. In essence, Nat Strong endeavored to either establish a business alliance similar to what he had with the Lincoln Giants' owner James Keenan to put the HBEC out of business or absorb Hilldale into his booking agency.⁵¹

In response, Bolden published a letter in the *Tribune* that exemplified the race rhetoric in the age of accommodation. He stated, "The race people of Philadelphia and vicinity are proud to proclaim Hilldale the biggest thing in the baseball world owned, fostered, and controlled by race men." Bolden added that the HBEC was "proud to be in a position to give [Darby's citizens] the most beautiful park in Delaware County, a team that is second to none and playing the best attractions obtainable."

It was not the HBEC's concern that other factions attempted to invade their territory. Bolden concluded by stating, "To affiliate ourselves with other than race men would be a mark against our name that could never be eradicated." The HBEC was "personally responsible for the fame and success of Hilldale [and] to place it in jeopardy would be absurd."[52]

From the outset, Nat Strong's desire to make inroads into Philadelphia's black baseball consumer market was poorly conceived. His move occurred at the same time the HBEC had established a symbiotic business relationship with white semipro teams, and its control of Hilldale Park allowed the club to build and maintain a fan base. In a letter to the *Philadelphia Tribune*, Claude Miller, a Hilldale fan, was confident that Bolden would give the city of Darby a "good if not better entertainment than Mr. Schlichter." He added, "Mr. Bolden being a gentleman of color and an honest promoter, I believe our race will support him." Strong had no influence over Philadelphia's key ballparks, and he was not in a position to arbitrarily keep a team busy or idle. In many ways, Strong's proposed challenge to the HBEC highlighted his arrogant attitude toward African American club owners. Instead of creating a business alliance with Bolden like the one he had with Keenan, Strong sought a more paternalistic business relationship by seeking to absorb the HBEC into his booking agency. When Bolden called his bluff, Strong backed down. There would be no team to compete against Hilldale for gate receipts in Darby.[53]

Hilldale would embark on another excellent season in spite of Nat Strong's proposed challenge. By August, the HBEC's success caught the attention of Rube Foster and his Chicago American Giants. Hilldale's emergence as one of the leading eastern black clubs occurred at the same time Foster was constructing his barnstorming tours of midwestern black teams to the East and Midwest. On August 1, the American Giants made their first visit to Hilldale Park, and they overwhelmed the Darbyites in the first game, coasting to a 9-2 win. The second game was a closely contested affair. The *Tribune* claimed "Hilldale Park was packed to the limit by a crowd of frenzied fans to witness the grueling struggle and many late suppers were served in Phillie and other towns." With the American Giants leading 8-7 in the tenth inning, Bill Pettus led off with a double into the overflow crowd. Louis Santop followed with a game-winning home run to give Hilldale a 9-8 victory. Defeating Rube Foster's Chicago American Giants served to heighten Hilldale's prestige.[54]

In September, the HBEC played a second game against an All-Star team made up of Major League players that ended in controversy. All Americans' hurler Bullet Joe Bush insisted on pitching with a dead ball that had been previously thrown out of the game. Hilldale catcher Louis Santop threw the old ball off the field when the umpire gave Bush a new one. Bush reportedly sat down on the mound and began to rip the baseball with his spikes and refused to let the umpire examine it. The All Americans' second baseman, Sherwood Magee, supposedly took the ball from Bush and threw it "in the woods." The bizarre behavior led the umpire to forfeit the game to Hilldale.[55]

Although they would have preferred to defeat the All Americans on the diamond, the Hilldale Baseball and Exhibition Company did win many games on the field and enjoyed an excellent season. For the first time, the HBEC operated as a full-time ball club. The company had received a good return on its investment in park renovations and on signing professional players. The HBEC generated a gross revenue of $17,233.02 on gate receipts and paid $4,719.72 in salaries. It realized a profit of $3,638.24. As the United States entered the postwar era, the HBEC was ready to expand into new markets. It would benefit from Rube Foster's efforts to expand his influence in the Midwest and the rise of two midwestern black clubs that would become charter members of the Negro National League.[56]

East Meets West

Hilldale's first midwestern barnstorming tour coincided with Rube Foster's attempt to expand his booking service in Chicago. Several black clubs, including two new teams, would use Foster's service to schedule games at Schorling Park. Throughout the 1910s, Joe Green assumed ownership of the Chicago Giants prior to Frank Leland's death. The Giants functioned essentially as a traveling team, playing games throughout the Midwest. Green maintained a group of veteran players that included Bobby Winston, John Beckwith, and Walter Ball.[57]

The Dayton Marcos emerged as one of the new black teams during the war years. The Marcos was organized by John "Big" Matthews and George "Chappie" Johnson. Matthews organized the Marcos in the early 1900s, and they were the only nonwhite team in the Ohio-Indiana League for several seasons. Chappie Johnson was one of the best catchers in black baseball during the first two decades of the twentieth century. In 1896, Johnson began his career as an outfielder and first baseman with the Page Fence Giants. Two years later, the Giants moved to Chicago and Johnson joined Frank Grant and Home Run Johnson to make the Columbia Giants a competitive club. Johnson played on several excellent teams throughout the early twentieth century that included the Cuban X Giants, Leland Giants, and Brooklyn Royal Giants. Characterized as quiet, calm, and dignified, Johnson always showed class and maintained a gentlemanly demeanor, even in protesting to umpires.[58]

In 1917, the then Dayton Giants made their first trip to Schorling Park, bringing with them several excellent players. In addition to Johnson, they had Bobby Williams—the team's second baseman—who was an excellent fielder, albeit a weak hitter. Andrew "Stringbean" Williams was the Giants' top pitcher, formerly with the Brooklyn Royal Giants, St. Louis Giants, and Indianapolis ABCs. On June 3, the Dayton Marcos's debut at Schorling Park was not a pleasant one, with the team facing Cannonball Dick Redding. The game was effectively over in the third inning, when the American Giants scored six times. Redding fanned 12 batters on the way to a 9-2 victory. The following day, Tom Johnson held the Marcos to four hits en route to a 5-0 win. The Marcos had to wait until the 1919 season before they finally prevailed over Foster's American Giants. Stringbean Williams pitched a phenomenal game, giving up only three hits and striking out six batters in a 4-0 shutout win. Defeating the Chicago American Giants at Schorling Park provided the Dayton Marcos with a degree of credibility as they struggled to develop their reputation as a top independent team.[59]

The second new club—the Detroit Stars—bore Rube Foster's stamp of approval. Foster was responsible for selecting the Stars' management team, and he held the lease on Mack Park, where the team would play its home games in the Motor City. Mack Park was located at Mack Street and Fairview Avenue in the middle of a white working-class neighborhood, about four miles from downtown. John "Tenny" Blount served as the Stars' manager and Bert Barton was the club's secretary. Blount was involved in gambling enterprises in Detroit, and was one of several vice leaders who began to emerge in the management and ownership of black baseball teams. Pete Hill was selected as the Stars' field manager, and Foster transferred several of his players to the club. Veteran players Bruce Petway, Jose Mendez, and Joe Hewitt formed the nucleus of a solid team.[60]

On June 17, 1919, the Detroit Stars made their initial appearance at Schorling Park in the first of a three-game series. Frank Wickware held the American Giants scoreless for six innings. The Stars led 3-0 in the seventh inning, but the Giants scored seven runs in the bottom of the frame to win, 7-3. The second game was marred by poor pitching and defense. The Giants took a 6-5 lead into the ninth inning and scored two more runs to win, 8-5. The Stars finally prevailed in the final game with a 5-4 victory.[61]

It was within this context that the HBEC made its first extended midwestern barnstorming tour. The Hilldale AC exemplified the pattern black baseball entrepreneurs endeavored to follow in transforming their clubs into elite touring teams. The AC began by assembling and maintaining a team of talented players. Obtaining a ballpark allowed the team to build a fan base and develop a business relationship with white and black semiprofessional clubs. Developing rivalries, particularly with the leading white semipro clubs, was essential to developing a team's reputation. Scheduling the leading black clubs, and from time to time an all-star team made up major or minor league players, and eventually defeating both of them, was also instrumental in heightening the AC's prestige. The final piece of the puzzle would be embarking on a barnstorming tour outside its region.

In August, Hilldale played a five-game series with the Detroit Stars in the Motor City. The Stars took a 2-0 lead off AC hurler Phil Cockrell. Hilldale tied the score and went on to score three times in the seventh and one in the eighth to win, 6-2. The Stars won two of the next three games. In a rain-shortened fifth game, Phil Cockrell held the Stars to three hits en route to a 6-3 Hilldale win. Hilldale's midwestern tour served to elevate the HBEC to the ranks of an elite black baseball team.[62]

Nothing illustrated this heightened prestige better than the Chicago American Giants' return to Hilldale Park. Darby fans witnessed a classic pitching duel in the first game. Tom Williams held the Giants to two hits, and the AC managed to a score a run in the fourth and sixth innings to win, 2-0. The second game was tied at four until a four-run rally in the ninth inning gave the American Giants an 8-4 win.[63]

The HBEC benefited from Rube Foster's attempt to expand his booking service in Chicago and throughout the Midwest. Conversely, Foster benefited from Ed Bolden's efforts to transform Hilldale into a leading eastern black club. Hilldale's emergence occurred at a time when Foster was organizing barnstorming tours to the East for his American Giants and several other midwestern teams. The midwestern clubs would get an opportunity to barnstorm into New York when a club from Jacksonville, Florida, migrated north for games in Gotham. Its migration led to John Connor's return to black baseball.

An Unexpected Competitor

John Connor's return to black baseball allowed midwestern black clubs to tap into New York's baseball market for the first time since the prewar years. From 1914 to 1918, no midwestern black club played in Gotham. New York's black clubs, under the control of the Strong-Keenan alliance and subjected to the collusive practices of white owners, combined to exclude midwestern clubs out of black baseball's largest consumer market. In many ways, the Strong-Keenan alliance typified how Tammany hacks controlled the park system throughout New York. These politically connected individuals made no efforts to make improvements in parks under their control; they saw these places of recreation as simply a means to generate revenue with minimal expenditures. Permits for athletic fields went to individuals or groups with political clout, and park buildings were leased for nominal fees to politically connected commercial enterprises.[64]

In regards to black baseball, neither Strong nor Keenan attempted to establish community relations with Harlem's black middle-class citizenry. They also failed to develop good press relations to promote their clubs in the black community. During the war years, press coverage of the Brooklyn Royal Giants and the Lincoln Giants declined precipitously. However, by the same token, there was a significant degree of apathy among Harlem's black middle class in regards to recreational enterprises like baseball. In contrast to Chicago, there were no indications that Harlem's black leadership pursued baseball as a business endeavor. Their controlling interest over several baseball parks, combined with this black middle-class apathy, enabled Strong and Keenan to keep black clubs under white control.

It was within this context that the Duval Giants from Jacksonville, Florida, barnstormed their way to Atlantic City, New Jersey. The Giants' first baseman, Napoleon Cummings, correctly claimed that the Duval club was lured to the Seaside City by Tom Jackson and Henry Tucker, two African American politicians. The team was renamed the Bacharach Giants after of the city's mayor, Harry Bacharach. The *Atlantic City Daily Press* reported that Tucker toured the South prior to the start of the regular season in search of good players. He was successful in bringing several talented ones to Atlantic City.[65]

The Bacharach Giants' roster included some players who would emerge as among the top star players in the East. First baseman Napoleon Cummings was compared to the Chicago Cubs' first sacker and manager, Frank Chance. Although big and awkward, Cummings was a hard worker. From his careful scrutiny of batters' tendencies, he developed into a good fielder. He was considered a "bad-ball hitter" and was a good clutch hitter. Catcher James "Yank" Deas was considered a fine hitter and was a highly regarded receiver with a great throwing arm. Shortstop Dick Wallace was a solid hitter and, with blazing speed, was a good base runner and excellent infielder. Arthur Dilworth and Leroy Roberts bolstered the Bacharachs' pitching staff.[66]

Richard "Dick" Lundy was at the beginning of a long, stellar career as a player and manager. Lundy has been categorized as one of the three greatest shortstops in black baseball history, along with John Henry Lloyd and Willie Wells. Born on July 10, 1898, in Jacksonville, Florida, Lundy attended Florida Baptist Academy in St. Augustine, Florida, and later played ball while attending the Cookman Institute for two years in 1914–1915. He began his professional career in 1915 as a third baseman for the Duval Giants and also served as a utility man, playing almost every position, including catcher. A switch hitter who hit for average and with power, Lundy was a smart base runner who posed a threat on the base paths. Because of his sterling ability to hit, the Bacharachs' shortstop became a great gate attraction.[67]

Upon their arrival in Atlantic City, the Bacharach Giants became members of the newly created Atlantic City Baseball League (ACBL). Jackson and Tucker formed this league of local clubs that were sponsored by several businesses and institutions which included the railroad and hotel industries and the YMCA. The league consisted of six teams: the Bacharachs, AC Cyclones, Rudolph, Vandal AC, Manhattan AC, and Big Six. From the outset, the local clubs were no match for Jackson and Tucker's team. By mid-June, the Giants had won ten of their first eleven league games, defeating league clubs by lopsided scores. Despite their dominance, the Bacharach Giants reportedly drew large crowds in the two parks in which they played, Inlet Park and Bacharach Park.[68]

The Bacharachs' overwhelming success in the ACBL led Tucker and Jackson to schedule additional games with the top black and white semipro clubs. In July, the Giants played a two-game series with the Baltimore Black Sox at Inlet Park. The Black Sox would later become a charter member in the Eastern Colored League. However, they were no match for the Seaside club, as the Giants scored four runs in the second inning and three in the seventh while Arthur Dilworth scattered five hits and struck out sixteen batters in an 8-2 Bacharachs' win. The second game was over in the seventh inning when the Bacharachs scored four runs and added five in the eighth. Napoleon Cummings led a twelve-hit attack with four hits en route to a 12-3 victory.[69]

Nat Strong's Brooklyn Royal Giants would serve as the Bacharachs' litmus test in the latter's inaugural season. The Royals were a strong team that included veteran players Frank Earle, Joe Hewitt, Johnny Pugh, and Stringbean Williams. Their dominance was evident from the beginning, when the Royals scored seven times in the first three innings and coasted to an 8-5 victory. The second game was never in doubt. Brooklyn batters hit Dilworth early and often as Johnny Pugh led the hitting assault. Frank Harvey gave up five hits and struck out nine batters, and the Royal Giants demolished the Bacharachs, 12-0. Although it was a disappointing performance, scheduling games with the Baltimore Black Sox and the Brooklyn Royal Giants illustrated Tucker and Jackson's business acumen, and their ability to draw the top black and white semipro teams delighted the Atlantic City fans.[70]

The Bacharach Giants' dominance of ACBL clubs and their scheduling of games with the top black and white semipro teams lead to a controversy over the use of Inlet Park. On June 22, the *Daily Press* reported that the Giants were denied access to the park, resulting in a cancellation of their game with the Pleasantville Regulars, a local white semipro club. Apparently, the Pennsylvania Railroad owned the park and its spokesman, an O. V. Bingham, denied the Giants the use of the diamond when he learned that they were planning to charge admission. The action led to the game being relocated to Pleasantville's home ball park.[71]

A league ruling made it problematic for the Giants to play games at their other home grounds, Bacharach Park. The ACBL passed a rule whereby the Bacharachs could only play once every six Sundays at Atlantic City Park. In other words, out of the twenty-four Sundays during the regular season, the Giants could only schedule six games at that park. There were no stipulations regarding what would occur if a scheduled game were canceled due to inclement weather. The ruling led Tucker and Jackson to reschedule several games to Inlet Park.[72]

The Sunday baseball controversy led to the Bacharach Giants withdrawing from the ACBL. At the same time, ACBL officials attempted to get Tom Jackson arrested for supposedly "not living up to his contract." The specific charge for which Jackson was being indicted was unclear. League officials reportedly sought to compel Jackson to return the Giants' uniforms. The whole affair led the *Daily Press* sports editor to conclude that the ACBL officials were engaging in "desperate efforts" to "check the popularity of the Bacharach Giants."[73]

The ability of the Bacharach Giants to use Inlet Park for the remainder of the season came into question. Supposedly, the grandstand had become a safety hazard for the fans. Inspectors from Atlantic City's City Building Department examined the grandstand, recommending certain repairs at a cost of $150. Jackson reportedly complied with the recommendations and the repairs were made. Despite making these repairs, the Pennsylvania Railroad "refused to accept the responsibility of possible accident to people utilizing the grandstand," leading to the ballpark's closure. The future of the Bacharach Giants in Atlantic City was now in doubt.[74]

To add insult to injury, rumors circulated that efforts were being made to cause dissension among the Bacharach Giants players. On July 21, the *Daily Press* reported that "scouts" from Trenton, New Jersey, had tried to "steal" several Bacharach players. One of the scouts admitted that certain men in Atlantic City were to take several players to upstate New Jersey and "abandon them," making it difficult for them to return to the Seaside City. There was no evidence to suggest that any scouts followed through on this plot.[75]

The Bacharach Giants' success on the field was perceived as a threat to the economic viability of the local ACBL teams. The *Daily Press* reported a rumor that ACBL officials—through Atlantic City mayor William Riddle—had "scored the latest victory by having the Pennsylvania Railroad close Inlet Park." Limiting the number of Sunday games they could play at Bacharach Park made it extremely difficult to turn a profit. To add to the Giants' woes, the nation's entry into World War I would result in losing several players to the war effort.[76]

It was within this context that Tom Jackson and Henry Tucker entered into a business alliance with John Connor and Baron Wilkins. Much like Connor, Wilkins was a café owner who ran one of the most successful establishments in Harlem, the Little Savoy Café located on 137th Street, between Seventh and Eight Avenues. He also ran the Astoria Café, "where dancing and singing attracted hundred[s] nightly who did not want to go home until morning." On October 4, 1917, the *New York Age* reported that Wilkins had assumed the ownership of a café on Seventh Avenue and renamed it the Get What You Want Café. During the prewar years, Wilkins had entered into a partnership with Ed Warren and formed the New York Colored Giants. The club lasted only a year, however.[77]

Tucker and Jackson's alliance with Connor and Wilkins epitomized the cooperative enterprise strategy so prevalent among black baseball club owners. Connor and Wilkins provided the substantial capital investment and Tucker served as booking agent. The alliance provided the Bacharach Giants access to two ballparks—Bacharach Park in Atlantic City, and Dyckman Oval in Harlem. Dyckman Oval placed the Bacharachs in direct competition with the Lincoln Giants for gate receipts in Harlem. To complete this transformation, Connor signed several players from the Lincolns and the Brooklyn Royal Giants, including pitchers Dick Redding and Bill Gatewood.

The ability to sign away players from Strong and Keenan reflected the unrest among black players on New York baseball teams. Previously, several players had left the Brooklyn Royal Giants to play for the Grand Central Baseball Club. Former players of Jess McMahon's Lincoln Stars became members of the Pennsylvania Red Caps. The Red Caps were managed by George Victor, who was apparently affiliated with the railroad industry. The Royal Giants' outfielder Johnny Pugh reflected these black players' dissatisfaction about playing in New York. Pugh was supposedly angered by Cyclone Joe Williams, who reportedly claimed "no Race baseball player is worth over $65 a month." According to Pugh, Williams was partly responsible for the players receiving low salaries from the Lincolns and the Royals. On June 14, 1919, the *Defender* reported that Williams denied making this statement and noted his claim that he didn't know any two players' salaries on his team. This player unrest provided John Connor the opportunity to return to black baseball.[78]

Connor's unexpected return to black baseball shocked Nat Strong and James Keenan. Understandably, both men perceived Connor as a threat, given the fact that the Bacharach's co-owner had signed several of their players and that their lease on Dyckman Oval placed the Giants in direct competition with Keenan. The *Defender* reported that secret meetings were held which included Strong, Keenan's partner Charles Harvey, Joe Williams, and John Henry Lloyd in an attempt to exclude Connor from the New York market. The Bacharach owner reiterated James H. Williams's claim of not securing suitable playing dates. Dick Redding reinforced Connor's allegation. The Cannonball stated in the *Defender that* "I have known Mr. Connor and Mr. Wilkins for a long time and have always found them to be fair and square fellows. . . . I know all about Mr. Connor's trouble with the Royal Giants some years ago. He got a dirty deal in getting his team booked and had to stop doing business. I have had similar trouble myself and quickly made up my mind when Mr. Connor popped the question to me. I have no fear of a square deal now and you can bet he will get the best there is in me too." Furthermore, Connor proclaimed the reason they obtained a lease on Dyckman Oval was to book their own games in Gotham.[79]

Despite Connor's aspirations, Strong made every attempt to block the Atlantic City deal. He began by refusing to allow the Royal Giants or the Cuban Stars to play in Atlantic City. Keenan followed suit and refused to allow his Lincolns to play there either. Strong even tried to create a rift within the Bacharachs' management team. On May 31, 1919, the *Defender* reported that Strong, trying to injure Baron Wilkins's credibility, accused Wilkins of owing him money. The Royals' owner indicated that Ed Warren, Wilkins's former business partner, made a sworn statement to confirm the allegation. In response, Wilkins filed a five-thousand-dollar lawsuit in civil court for defamation of character. Later, Warren denied making any statement validating Strong's claim. Faced with possible litigation, the Royals' owner backed down.[80]

If Strong could not create dissension among the Bacharachs' management team, he could utilize the one resource under his control—colluding with white owners to prohibit scheduling games with the Atlantic City club. However, this tactic was closed off because of Connor's lease on Dyckman Oval in Harlem and access to Bacharach Park in Atlantic City. Access to these parks allowed Henry Tucker to schedule several attractive contests throughout the 1919 season. On June

14, the *Defender* reported that the Bacharach Giants had defeated Hal Chase's All Nationals team at Bacharach Park, 3-2. Chase was regarded as one of the best first basemen in the Major Leagues. He did, however, have a notorious reputation as a gambler and supposedly fixed several games throughout his career. Apart from Chase's reputation, defeating the All Nationals represented a significant accomplishment for the Bacharach Giants. The Bacharachs benefited from Rube Foster's aspiration to create barnstorming tours throughout the East. On September 6, the *Defender* reported the Bacharachs had scheduled games with the American Giants, Hilldale, and Guy Empey's Treat 'Em Roughs, a local black team from New York, at Dyckman Oval.[81]

Connor further nullified Strong's attempt to exclude the Bacharach Giants from New York when he entered into a business agreement with Brooklyn Dodgers' owner Charles Ebbets to rent his ballpark. Hal Chase played a role in establishing this business relationship. Undoubtedly, Wilkins's and Chase's paths intersected, given the nightclub owner's reputation as a gambler and bootlegger and because Chase was a member of the National League's New York Giants. The Bacharach Giants had gained access to three ballparks in New York City to schedule games, thus freeing the team from relying on Strong's booking agency for games in Gotham.[82]

For the first time, the *New York Age* championed the cause of these African American owners in Harlem. Connor also made the first community gesture by donating the Bacharachs' old uniforms to a local YMCA after obtaining new ones. The *Age* admonished the white owners for attempting to exclude Connor and Wilkins from the baseball business. The black newspaper also pointed out that whites had allowed the Lincoln Giants' home field, Olympic Field, to slip away without attempting to buy it, marking the start of the loss of Harlem ballparks as a result of subdivision. It was said that the very existence of black clubs was due to African Americans' patronage of their games, although this claim was somewhat exaggerated. Harlem was large enough to support two black clubs, and a rivalry between the Bacharach and Lincoln Giants would serve to stimulate community interest. Moreover, serving as Harlem's spokesman, the *Age* listed four demands of Gotham's black citizens: (1) a series of games between all semipro teams; (2) no secret meetings as a means of freezing black owners out of black baseball; (3) an end to player raiding; and (4) a legitimate claim to the colored champion of the East meeting a recognized champion of the West.[83]

From May 22 to September 11, 1920, Connor scheduled six games between black clubs at Ebbets Field. The *Age* reported that the Bacharachs were the first black club to play in Ebbets Field, with the Giants taking both games of a doubleheader from Guy Empey's Treat 'Em Roughs. On July 17, sixteen thousand fans watched the Bacharachs play the Lincoln Giants for the eastern colored championship. The first game matched Dick Redding against Joe Williams, and Cannonball Redding defeated the Cyclone, 5-0. The Lincolns won the second game, 7-5. There was no indication of whether a third and deciding game was ever played. In August and September, the Chicago Giants and the Indianapolis ABCs invaded Ebbets Field. In the four games with these midwestern clubs, the Bacharachs won three.[84]

The high water mark of Connor's successful 1920 season would not occur until October. Rube Foster's Chicago American Giants invaded Gotham for a four-game series with the Bacharachs, and three of these games were scheduled in Ebbets Field. Connor's Bacharachs manhandled the Windy City crew, winning three out of four games. On October 15, the *Defender* reported that fifteen thousand fans watched Bacharachs' hurlers Dick Redding and Red Ryan defeat the American Giants by scores of 5-3 and 7-3. At no other time in the early twentieth century did Harlem's black community embrace a ball club that was black owned and operated. Connor undoubtedly got some personal satisfaction, given the way Foster's American Giants had manhandled his Royal Giants in the prewar years. At the end of the 1920 season, John Connor was sitting on top of the black baseball world in New York.[85]

CONCLUSION

John Connor's return to black baseball represented the continued efforts of African American entrepreneurs to develop businesses in order to advance their own economic interests. Much like their predecessors of the late nineteenth century, these early-twentieth-century black entrepreneurs recognized that in order to transact business in the United States, they had to negotiate with the white power structure. They conducted business with white semiprofessional club owners, park managers, and occasionally with a white entrepreneur who served as a business partner. Black clubs scheduled games among themselves and with white and Cuban teams. At times they scheduled games with major and minor league clubs and with all-star teams made up of either major or minor league players or a combination of the two.

By the end of the 1919 season, several teams that were black owned and operated functioned as full-time enterprises, despite challenges to their operational autonomy. These teams reflected the continuity and change that black professional baseball underwent in the early twentieth century. Five teams—the Bacharach Giants, Chicago American Giants, Hilldale AC, Indianapolis ABCs, and St. Louis Giants—utilized the pattern black baseball entrepreneurs employed to transform their clubs into top independent teams. They began by assembling and sustaining a team of talented players. They also gained access to ballparks within a close proximity to large urban areas, which was essential to building a fan base. The ballpark also allowed these black entrepreneurs to maintain a symbiotic business relationship with white semipros and simultaneously to schedule more games among themselves. Sustaining rivalries, the entrepreneurs knew, was essential in stimulating fan interest and developing a team's reputation. They also knew that scheduling exhibition games with all-star teams composed of major and minor league players was instrumental in heightening a black team's prestige. Finally, they understood that extended barnstorming tours outside their respective regions of the country served to elevate a black club to the ranks of an elite touring team.

The rise of black baseball in the early twentieth century was part of the expansion of African American business activity during the period. Much like the more conventional businesses, black team owners had to deal with the ways in which a separate black economy was imposed on them. Since the late nineteenth century, the color line in Organized Baseball had highlighted the ways black clubs operated in a segregated economy. To be sure, the color line served to exclude black players from Organized Baseball's player force, but it also served to exclude blacks from both the managerial and ownership ranks. Also, the exclusion of blacks from the player force meant black clubs would not become members of the National Agreement, or the National Association of Professional Baseball Leagues.

Ballpark ownership remained the biggest obstacle to black baseball's business development and illustrated the ways in which it fell under the rubric of a separate black economy. African American owners did not enjoy the advantages the Major League owners had in terms of building or remodeling ballparks to sustain a fan base and maximize revenues. Direct and indirect connections with urban politicians allowed Major League owners to obtain valuable information on matters like transportation plans and real estate developments. In response, African American club owners entered into partnerships with white businessmen to gain access to suitable playing facilities and maintain business ties with white semipro teams.

Business partnerships with whites did not always serve African Americans' best economic interests. Nat Strong and James Keenan maintained their hegemony over the New York market because they gained access to the better ballparks, allowing them to sign the best players. Until John Connor, Baron Wilkins, and Henry Tucker circumvented their autonomy, the Strong-Keenan business alliance made it problematic for a black owner to operate in New York. The Strong-Keenan alliance also benefited from a lack of interest among Harlem's African American elite in operating sports enterprises like baseball teams. Furthermore, black players were content to play for these owners because of their ability to schedule games with the top white semipros, Major League teams, and all-stars teams composed of Major League players. By 1919, player contentment had turned into player unrest, allowing John Connor to return to black baseball.

In contrast to the more conventional businesses in which African Americans engaged, black baseball did not rely solely on a separate black economy for its economic viability. Both the Chicago American Giants and the Indianapolis ABCs tapped into their respective black consumer markets but also sustained their business ties with white semi-pros, which allowed them to exploit the white baseball market. In this way, the American Giants and ABCs epitomized an elementary form of market segmentation that extended beyond the Chicago and Indianapolis black market. Access to their respective ballparks allowed Rube Foster and C. I. Taylor to develop and maintain a fan base in Chicago and Indianapolis and spread the American Giants' and ABCs' brands to the West and South nationally and internationally to Cuba.

As the United States entered World War I, the Great Migration dramatically expanded the black consumer market, particularly in large cities of the North. Rube Foster, C. I. Taylor, and to a lesser degree Ed Bolden recognized that they could not marginalize this growing consumer market. Establishing civic ties with the black middle class and developing a business relationship with the black press became the vehicles for making inroads into this market. Black club owners used the race rhetoric of self-help and racial solidarity to promote their ball clubs as symbols of race respectability and racial uplift. Race rhetoric not only served to promote a sense of respectability; it also assisted in heightening the brands of their respective clubs. In essence, the extended tours of the Chicago American Giants and the Indianapolis ABCs not only represented these clubs' success on the diamond; it also provided a sense of heightened prestige for their respective communities.

By the end of the 1910s, Rube Foster had emerged as the premier black baseball owner, and his Chicago American Giants became the benchmark that African American team owners endeavored to emulate. His extended tours during the decade surpassed the accomplishments of the Cuban Giants of the late nineteenth century. Operating in the largest baseball market of the Midwest allowed Foster to develop a booking service to maximize revenues and heighten his prestige. The American Giants' magnate created a barnstorming network that allowed him to book games for midwestern black clubs throughout the Midwest and East. Creating this network was possible because several black teams operated on a full-time basis. In many ways, these barnstorming tours represented a dry run for the formation of a Negro league.

As the United States entered the 1920s, black professional baseball was on the verge of entering a new era. Migrations, the rise of several black clubs functioning as full-time enterprises, and the postwar economy combined to create a climate ripe for league formation. Andrew Rube Foster would skip his customary winter tour and use the black press to make his case for Negro league formation.

1. John Henry Lloyd was often referred to as the "Black Honus Wagner." In 1911, Lloyd was named to succeed Sol White as the Lincoln Giants' field manager, marking the start of his long career as one of the leading player-managers in the black game.

2. Philadelphia Giants with co-owner and player-manager Sol White (back row, second from the left). In 1907, White's *History of Colored Baseball* attempted to make black professional baseball a legitimate profession.

3. In 1906, the Philadelphia Giants were the premier club in black baseball. Seated in the middle is the Giants' co-owner, H. Walter Schlichter, and standing behind him on his left is co-owner and player-manager Sol White. Harry Smith (standing in the back row on the far right) rounded out the Giants' management team.

4. The Lincoln Giants in their inaugural season of 1911. The Giants represented the last outstanding black club on which Sol White left his imprint.

5. C. W. "Colonel" Strothers (seated in the middle of the first row) ran the Harrisburg Giants as one of the top independent black clubs in the East. The Giants began as a sandlot team in 1891. In 1924, the Harrisburg Giants became a member of the Eastern Colored League.

6. The Leland Giants were the premier black club in the West in the opening decade of the twentieth century. In 1907, Frank Leland (seated in the front row) hired Andrew "Rube" Foster (standing, back row far left) to serve as player-manager. That same year, they defeated Donlin's All-Stars, which served to heighten the Giants' and Foster's prestige among African American fans. Leland's election as Cook County commissioner led to him establish a coalition among the leading black middle-class professionals in Chicago and form the Leland Giants Baseball and Amusement Association.

7. In 1915, Charles Isham "C. I." Taylor (seated in the center of the second row) moved his club from West Baden, Indiana, to Indianapolis and renamed the team the ABCs. They challenged Rube Foster's Chicago American Giants for black baseball supremacy in the Midwest.

8. In 1912, Nat Strong assumed the ownership of the Brooklyn Royal Giants from John Connor. Strong's alliance with Lincoln Giants' magnate James J. Keenan enabled both men to gain a virtual stranglehold on eastern black baseball in New York.

9. The return to black baseball of John Connor (seated in the center) was the result of a partnership with Bacharach Giants' owners Henry Tucker and Tom Jackson and Harlem café owner Baron Wilkins. In 1919, Connor secured a leasing agreement with Brooklyn Dodgers' owner Charles Ebbets to schedule games in Ebbets Field when the National League club was on the road. The leasing agreement with Ebbets allowed the Bacharachs' management team to sign top-level players away from the Brooklyn Royal Giants and Lincoln Giants and bypass Nat Strong's booking agency for games in Gotham.

10. Rube Foster's Chicago American Giants in 1920, the Negro National League's opening season.

BASE BALL
AT LITITZ

Saturday, May 15, '15

The Game of the Season

LITITZ vs. HARRISBURG GIANTS

THE FAMOUS COLORED NINE

Any one who has never seen the colored team play has missed much. They are full of fun and play the game as good as the best. Our boys will have to step lively if they intend winning this contest. Don't fail to see it.

Game called at 3.00 P. M.

RECORD PRINT, LITITZ, PA.

11. A type of the promotional materials that black baseball club owners used to promote their games. The Harrisburg Giants were scheduled to play against a local white semiprofessional club in Lititz, Pennsylvania.

12. Ed Bolden's Hilldale club prior to the start of the 1924 Colored World Series. Hilldale would lose a tough series to J. L. Wilkinson's Kansas City Monarchs.

13. A souvenir program from the 1924 Colored World Series.

14. The Hilldale Baseball and Exhibition Company promoted the club with the concept of "Clean Baseball." In other words, the Hilldale players were to compete on the diamond on the basis of fair play and good sportsmanship and conduct themselves as gentlemen off the field. The fans were also expected to behave in a manner aligned with black middle-class values.

15. In 1926 and 1927, the Chicago American Giants won both the Negro National League pennant and the Colored World Series. Rube Foster was unable to celebrate his club's success due to his nervous breakdown. In his absence, however, the American Giants continued to play "the Rube Foster way."

16. Oscar Charleston was arguably black baseball's premier star player in the early twentieth century. Charleston was often compared to Babe Ruth, and his defensive prowess in center field was reminiscent of the Cleveland Indians' star outfielder, Tris Speaker. In the 1920s, Charleston was the player-manager of the Harrisburg Giants. He was critical of the way the Eastern Colored League club owners ran the circuit.

17. In the early 1900s, Cap Anson's semiprofessional ballclub, Anson's Colts, played Rube Foster's Leland Giants in several benefit games to raise funds for Provident Hospital in Chicago. Provident Hospital was founded by Daniel Hale Williams, the country's best-known African American surgeon. On August 6, 1909, the two teams amassed revenues in the amount of $2,500 and over 6,000 fans attended the game.

18. Dave Malarcher was one of the Negro Leagues' leading player-managers. In 1926, Malarcher assumed the managerial role for the Chicago American Giants after Rube Foster's illness. He led the American Giants to two consecutive Negro National League pennants and two Colored World Series Championships.

19. Jose Mendez began his baseball career at age fifteen. Also known as *el diamante negro* (the Black Diamond), Mendez compiled a scoreless streak of twenty-five innings against the Cincinnati Reds (1908) and the Detroit Tigers (1909). Mendez was the player-manager for the Kansas City Monarchs when they faced the Hilldale club in the 1924 Colored World Series. He won the tenth game of the series and the Monarchs won the first Colored World Series Championship.

20. In 1929, the Baltimore Black Sox won the first and only American Negro League pennant.

21. Alex Pompez's Cuban Stars East was black baseball's leading club among those composed primarily of players of Cuban descent. Pompez found a way to use his relationship with Brooklyn Royal Giants' magnate and booking agent Nat Strong to his advantage. He possessed access to an untapped market—New York's Latino community as well as the Caribbean. By assembling one of the strongest teams to emerge from Cuba, Pompez was able to develop connections beyond Strong's control that later allowed him to exercise greater independence than other club owners.

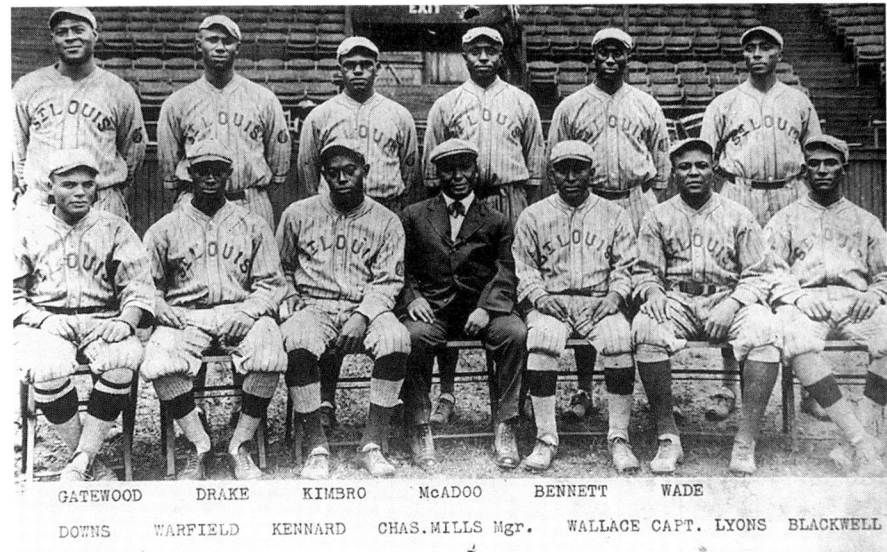

GATEWOOD   DRAKE   KIMBRO   McADOO   BENNETT   WADE
  DOWNS   WARFIELD   KENNARD   CHAS. MILLS Mgr.   WALLACE CAPT. LYONS BLACKWELL

22. St. Louis Giants' magnate Charles Mills assembled one of the strongest black clubs in the Midwest. His Giants were plagued by a constant turnover in ownership, Mills being the sole constant within the club's management team. It was a testament to his business acumen that the club experienced some degree of success.

23. In the 1920s, the St. Louis Stars team was one of the more stable clubs in the Negro National League. In 1928, its defeat of the Chicago American Giants in the Negro National League playoff marked the end of an era in midwestern black baseball.

24. The Kansas City Monarchs in their inaugural season in 1920. The Monarchs were a charter member of the Negro National League, and in 1924, they would defeat the Hilldale club in black baseball's first Colored World Series.

Part Two

The Rise and Fall of the Negro National and Eastern Colored Leagues, 1920–1931

7

Pitfalls of Baseball

The Rise of the Negro National League

From November 1919 to January 1920, Andrew "Rube" Foster made his third, and most passionate, plea for black baseball clubs to organize into professional leagues. Using Organized Baseball's institutional structure as a model, Foster called for a national organization of eastern and western clubs to form into two leagues. He urged the club owners to meet in order to resolve their past differences and to eliminate destructive business practices, like player jumping, to sustain black baseball's future. Foster laid out his vision to place the black game on a sound economic footing that included strong leadership and able lieutenants to carry out the organization's policies. Eastern club owners rejected Foster's call for a national meeting. However, in February 1920, midwestern club owners met and formed the Negro National League (NNL).

The Negro National League enjoyed a good inaugural season, as each club reportedly made a profit. Prior to the start of the season, Foster embarked on what could best be described as a promotional tour of the East to drum up support for league formation. He negotiated a deal with Bacharach Giants' owner John Connor to affiliate with the NNL as an associate member, enabling league clubs to travel to New York and play the Bacharachs at Ebbets Field and Dyckman Oval in Harlem. Foster's trip to Philadelphia, however, marked the start of a conflict between himself and Hilldale magnate Ed Bolden. To tap into the Philadelphia market, Foster supported the newly created Madison Stars and simultaneously boycotted the Hilldale AC by refusing to schedule league clubs to play there. Foster's actions presented a dilemma for Bolden and his HBEC. While the AC continued to schedule games against "outlaw" clubs in New York like the Brooklyn Royal Giants and the Cuban Stars East, the Bacharach Giants refuse to play Hilldale because of the former's affiliation with the NNL. The situation between Bolden and Connor was further aggravated regarding a dispute over players, leading the HBEC to go to court and seek injunctions to prevent several players from jumping to the Giants.

Although Rube Foster's promotional tour of the East yielded mixed results, Negro National League officials took the initial steps to solidify their organization at their 1920 winter meeting. They revised the constitution and secured a working agreement to use a Major League park. The Dayton Marcos were transferred to Columbus, leading to Sol White's return to black baseball. Because the league's teams exhibited a degree of profitability, Ed Bolden's attitude toward the NNL began to change. He applied for and received an associate membership for the AC. With Hilldale and the Bacharach Giants as associate members, Foster's vision of a national organization appeared plausible.

The 1921 season produced mixed results. Whereas gate receipts were reportedly 25 percent lower than the previous season, the East-West association proved to be the NNL's finest hour. It occurred at a time when the Bacharach Giants and Hilldale AC enjoyed spectacular seasons. Both teams began a rivalry that included doubleheaders at Ebbets Field. Although Hilldale and the Bacharachs boycotted the Brooklyn Royal Giants, Lincoln Giants, and Cuban Stars East, Bolden was willing to make this compromise when several NNL clubs barnstormed to Darby for gate receipts for the first time.

At the end of the 1921 season, Rube Foster wrote a series of articles titled, "What Baseball Needs to Succeed." The fundamental underpinning of these articles was what Foster considered the important steps to ensure black baseball's "permanent success." He addressed several issues, including the black game's need to improve its image, the ballpark dilemma, and the hiring of African American umpires. At the outset, Foster wrote that much of what he would say would be controversial. The articles resulted in Foster's alienating the very men he needed to establish a national organization. At no time did he acknowledge the efforts of successful club owners like Bolden and Connor, nor was he willing to recognize the kinds of obstacles his fellow owners faced in their respective league cities. By the time the winter meetings approached, Rube Foster's vision of a national organization became unglued.

Winds of Change: The Rise of the Negro National League

In the *Cleveland Advocate* of January 18, 1919, Sol White outlined a plan for the formation of a black league. Out of black baseball since the early 1910s, White argued that a league be formed consisting of six clubs—three would have ballparks and be home teams, and three teams would operate as traveling teams, or floaters. Two of three traveling teams would play league games in the ballparks of the home teams while the parent club was on the road. The remaining road club could play a home team. White provided a hypothetical situation to illustrate how his scheduling system would work. A home team from Columbus, for example, could play a team from Dayton on the latter's home grounds, while two road teams could play in Columbus. The other floater could play a team in Springfield. White asserted that such a league could be formed and be profitable: "The grounds are available, the players are right here [in Ohio] . . . indeed we have never seen a likelier bunch of ballplayers . . . than the youngsters playing on the teams representing the cities we have mentioned."[1]

On January 25, White continued to discuss the ways in which this compact circuit could function. He utilized the mantra that served as the ideology among African Americans in the development of business enterprises and entrepreneurial activities, namely, economic cooperation. In White's view, a compact circuit would "reduce expenses, engender rivalry and make for the financial and sporting success of the league." "General representation," White concluded, "[would] insure each and every team a square deal in all ways and will make for harmony throughout the season." There were no indications that an Ohio league came to fruition, but White's call for league formation marked the time when several sportswriters and club owners began advocating the need for black clubs to organize.²

On October 4, 1919, Chicago *Defender* sportswriter Carey B. Lewis, in an almost prophetic tone, predicted "a circuit of western clubs" for the 1920 season. Lewis asserted that the 1919 season had been so prosperous "and [the] fans so loyal, [and the] attendance so great in most of the western cities that the circuit [would] become an actuality." Rube Foster would be the man responsible for this proposed western circuit. The league would be owned and controlled by "Race men," and consist of eight teams. Lewis envisioned the western pennant winner traveling east to play the best team there. The league, he said, would create more opportunities for umpires and sportswriters among African Americans. The league would "give a number of our men work and confine a lot of money to the pockets of men of the Race that is now going daily into the pockets of the other fellows."³

In November, Rube Foster began his series of articles titled "Pitfalls of Baseball." Foster's opening article had the character of a presidential State of the Union address. With the exception of one club, the American Giants, black baseball had devolved into a weekend enterprise. Scheduling and an increase in overhead expenses were the root causes for this predicament. Not one club could show a profit of a thousand dollars per season, and not one team knew that it would play ten games the next season. Even with the recent increase in attendance, profits were diminished by the high cost of materials, parks, and "everything connected with baseball." Using his American Giants as an example, the cost to maintain Schorling Park was $945 a week when idle and $1,346 a week when the park was utilized three days a week. After paying the visiting team its 50 percent share of the gate receipts, attendance would have to be doubled to break even. Moreover, should a team experience three rainouts on Sunday during the season, the club owner would operate at a loss. Based on these circumstances, Foster urged club owners to "reconstruct" their business practices to make black baseball a profitable enterprise.⁴

To remedy black baseball's plight, Foster called for strong leadership and used an abridged history of the leading black clubs of the past to validate his claim. In order for these leaders to be successful, he said, they needed able lieutenants who had the confidence of the public. Moral respectability was vital to ensure the support and patronage of the middle-class spectator, whose attendance was needed to pay player salaries. The past salaries of the leading black clubs were used to illustrate this point. The Philadelphia Giants, for example, paid $850 a month in salaries, but the club "had to disband [because] we could not even get the money for such high prices." In other words, the Giants did not generate enough revenue to cover salaries and turn a profit. Player salaries would only increase in the upcoming years, Foster asserted. The American Giants' monthly salary had never been lower than $1,500 a month. Foster provided this analysis to show the need for a strong leader to emerge soon to "reconstruct" black baseball's business practices. The current promoters were blinded to many facts: "They do not realize," Foster added, "that to have the best ball club in the world and no one able to compete with it will lose more money on the season than those that are evenly matched."[5]

In his third article, Foster highlighted the poor business judgment of past black baseball club owners. To assemble the best team possible, club owners, particularly in the East, would offer a player a higher salary as an inducement to leave his current club. Encouraging players to jump their contracts proved to be catastrophic to the team losing the player. This destructive practice could also work in reverse when a talented team offering higher pay failed to generate the revenue necessary to cover salaries and other expenses and, most important, turn a profit. Therefore, Foster concluded, club owners—to ensure the black game's profitability—had to cooperate to eliminate the destructive practice of player jumping.

Foster continued to focus on player jumping in his fourth article, and he simultaneously urged eastern and western club owners to meet to resolve their differences. He began by indicting club owners who advanced players money prior to the start of the season only to watch them move to another club when the season began. This resulted in cutthroat competition among the magnates: "When a player gets money from [an owner]," Foster claimed, "he jumps." He added, "Then the owners writes [sic] and tells you, 'Don't play against so and so, he owes me money.'" This resulted in a lot of good businessmen leaving the black game, he continued. John Connor, for example, was "very ambitious, wanting nothing but the best." "He should not be lost to baseball. His only failure," Foster concluded, was that he had "not been steered right."[6]

In an effort "to let bygones be bygones," Foster proposed that the eastern and western magnates meet in either New York or Chicago. The owners would "pick an arbitration board from experienced men of business" and draw up an agreement that the owners would abide by. Each club owner would make a five-hundred-dollar deposit in good faith that would ensure their adherence to the agreement. Foster was quick to point out that this meeting was not "a proposition to exchange players." Rather, the meeting would mark the start of a partnership "in working for the organized good of baseball." The American Giants' president concluded with a glimpse of his vision of organized black baseball: "This [meeting would] pave the way for such champion team eventually to play the winner among the whites. This is more than possible. Only in uniform strength is the permanent success [plausible]. I invite all owners to write for information on this proposition. It is open to all."[7]

In his fifth article, Foster continued to stress the need to eliminate player jumping and highlighted the necessity for ball clubs to have access to playing facilities. The elimination of player jumping was, in Foster's view, vital to reconstruct black baseball's business practices. The practice led to disreputable behavior among the players and owners, and both sides understandably mistrusted each other. It was problematic for players to be honest when the owners did not respond in kind. Foster stated, "When someone persuades the same man to leave him, disgusted, he will wire you, 'If you play such a club, I will not play you.'" A national organization would ensure that club owners would respect each other's players under contract, thus eliminating player jumping altogether. Much like Sol White before him, Rube Foster urged black club owners to used Organized Baseball as their pattern to place the black game on a sound economic footing.[8]

Playing facilities were crucial to the success of this national organization. Without them, there would be no incentive for either players or owners to choose black baseball as a profession. Essentially, Foster continued to stress the need for club owners to organize because the money for these parks would "naturally come from whites." Foster recognized that black baseball did not rely solely on a separate black economy for its economic and operational viability. By the same token, however, his analysis suggests that, as with more conventional black enterprises, a separate black economy was being impose upon the black game. African American club owners did not enjoy the advantages the Major League owners had in regard to building or remodeling ballparks during the Progressive Era. They did not have the direct and indirect connections with urban politicians that allowed Major League baseball owners to obtain valuable information on matters like transportation plans and real estate developments. This was why black club owners either negotiated with white park managers and major and minor league owners or entered into a partnership with whites in the first place in order to gain access to suitable playing facilities. Foster acknowledged that modern playing facilities had to adhere to building codes which increased the overhead expenses needed to maintain a ballpark. This, Foster said, combined with the expected increase in park rentals and the high cost of real estate, illustrated the monumental task black club owners faced in the pursuit of owning their own parks. Therefore, the remedy to the ballpark dilemma was to focus on what the magnates had the most control over, namely, the reconstruction of the black game's business practices through the creation of a national organization. This was a practical and understandable solution to the Achilles heel that hindered black baseball's business and economic development.

On January 20, 1920, Rube Foster outlined his plan to create a national organization. At the same time, he stated that the attempt to get the eastern and western owners together had ended in failure. The association Foster proposed would be composed of two circuits: the west, to include Chicago; Cincinnati; Detroit; Indianapolis; and Kansas City, Missouri; and the east, to include Pittsburgh, Cleveland, Washington, Baltimore, Philadelphia, and New York. The winners of each league would meet in a world championship series. Such an organization would "have been the salvation of baseball." However, only one eastern owner (from Washington) had written to him to express interest in forming this national association. He reiterated the fact that the substantial investment to build a park, the general maintenance to ensure the facility adheres to building code specifications, and the expense in the day-to-day operations of a club could only be addressed through the creation of a national organization. Organization was also vital to black baseball's future. For the first time, Foster hinted at the possibility of accepting whites as the ownership and management of black teams: "I have fought against delivering Colored baseball into the control of whites, thinking that with a show of patronage from the fans we would get together. The get together effort has been a failure."[9]

In his final article, Foster highlighted his efforts to get the eastern and western owners together and sought to explain why they did not want to join in a national organization. He wrote to Nat Strong in an attempt to get the owners together to reach some agreement. Strong wrote back and supposedly stated he wanted something done. Yet, Strong claimed, there were men "who at present identified with the eastern clubs [that] are [an] IMPOSSIBILITY." In other words, the Lincolns, Cubans, and Royals would refuse to play each other. This appears to be a subtle reference to the Bacharach Giants' club owner, John Connor. To Foster, the "player question [was] the root of all the trouble," resulting in mistrust between player and owner. Given the past negotiations between the players and the owners, the mistrust was understandable. Foster indicted the eastern owners for blocking efforts to create a national association. "Had the eastern men accepted the proposal," he concluded, "the bitter feelings that exist would have been eliminated, a working agreement respecting each other's rights, a chance to see all the clubs meet, the securing of places fit to play, then [the] launching of a league."[10]

While much of Rube Foster's analysis was self-serving, it did reveal that he, and others like him, recognized the need for black baseball to be placed on a sound economic footing. The black game experienced the same kinds of growing pains that Organized Baseball underwent in the late nineteenth century. Player salaries constituted a large percentage of team costs. The free market for players led owners to engage in the destructive promotion of player jumping, which meant higher salaries as teams tried to maintain their competitiveness. Because of this and other overhead costs, Foster advocated for a national organization to place the black game on sound economic ground. Although the eastern owners balked at Foster's call for a national organization, midwestern owners would meet to form a Negro baseball league.

The Rise of the Negro National League

Despite the eastern owners' rejection of his proposal, Rube Foster took the initial steps toward forming a western circuit. Sportswriter Dave Wyatt stated that Foster held two secret meetings in Detroit and Chicago with several midwestern owners and Nat Strong to reach some agreement. It was unclear what both sides agreed to, but Wyatt wrote that the "fans will care little about who got licked and who did the licking. The thing is baseball is once more in for an uplift." Foster then attempted to find a suitable backer for a new Kansas City franchise in Missouri. After considering several proposals, he turned to J. L. Wilkinson.[11]

James Leslie Wilkinson would emerge as a pivotal figure in the proposed new league and would be the circuit's only white owner. The son of the president of Algona Normal College, Wilkinson attended Highland Park College in Des Moines, Iowa. He pitched for a variety of semipro teams under the assumed name of Joe Green. He later signed onto a team sponsored by the Hopkins Brothers Sporting Goods Store in Des Moines. When the manager of that team left, the club voted Wilkinson to assume his responsibilities.[12]

In 1912, Wilkinson—along with J. E. Gall—organized the All Nations team. The All Nations clearly met the standards for multiculturalism. The club had on its roster a mix of whites, blacks, Indians, Mexicans, Cubans, and Asians. Wilkinson even hired a woman, whom he advertised as "Carrie Nation," to play second base. Yet at the same time, the All Nations were fierce competitors, with players like Jose Mendez and John Donaldson providing the club with an awesome pitching staff. The All Nations were a traveling team that rode in a specially built Pullman car along with a host of other entertainers. From

1915 to 1917, the All Nations gained attention by defeating the Chicago American Giants twice and the Indianapolis ABCs. In 1915, Wilkinson moved the club to Kansas City, Missouri. With its meat packing plants and railroad connections, Kansas City had the black population and access to other, larger cities that Des Moines lacked. The club fell on hard times during World War I, but Wilkinson reorganized the All Nations in 1919 for a local season.[13]

At first, Foster attempted to work without Wilkinson, authorizing Dr. Howard Smith, superintendent of Kansas City's black hospital, to form a team. However, Smith had no baseball experience and reportedly lacked the finances to support a team. He also did not hold the lease for the only suitable ballpark in town, the American Association Park. Since Wilkinson held the lease, Foster compromised. Wilkinson had several important links with Kansas City's black community and maintained civic ties with Smith and Quincy J. Gilmore, a well-known businessman. Gilmore may have played a role in negotiating the initial differences between Wilkinson, Foster, and Smith. Gilmore would serve as the traveling secretary for the Kansas City Monarchs. More important, Wilkinson received a nod of approval from the *Freeman* for being an owner who believed in playing clean ball.[14]

On February 13–14, 1920, the midwestern owners met at the YMCA and the Street's Hotel in Kansas City to form the Negro National League. The following club owners were present: Joe Green, Chicago Giants; John Matthews, Dayton Marcos; Tenny Blount, Detroit Stars; C. I. Taylor, Indianapolis ABCs; J. L. Wilkinson, Kansas City Monarchs; Lorenzo S. Cobb, St. Louis Giants; and Rube Foster, Chicago American Giants. Foster also held the proxy for Abe Molina's Cuban Stars. Foster was elected temporary chairman and secretary, and in a move that stunned the owners, he unveiled a charter of incorporation for a Negro National League without their knowledge. The NNL was incorporated in Illinois, Michigan, Ohio, Pennsylvania, New York, and Maryland. Foster then announced that he would leave it to newspapermen to decide all questions, select players for the various teams, and write the bylaws and constitution for the circuit.[15]

The constitution committee consisted of Dave Wyatt of the *Indianapolis Ledger*, Elwood Knox of the *Freeman*; Carey B. Lewis of the *Defender*; and attorney Elisha Scott of Topeka, Kansas. After making several corrections in the document, league owners agreed to pay a fee of five hundred dollars to bind themselves to the terms of the constitution. In an effort to achieve competitive balance, several players were transferred within the new circuit. Foster sent Oscar Charleston back to the ABCs, Sam Crawford to Kansas City, and Dick Whitworth to Detroit. The Monarchs also received Jose Mendez and John Donaldson from Detroit, while Jimmie Lyons was sent from St. Louis to Detroit. League play was not scheduled to begin until April 1, 1921, or until each club owned or leased a park. However, on February 28, for reasons that were unclear, the *Freeman* reported the league would begin play on May 1, 1920, despite the presence of two traveling teams, the Chicago Giants and Cuban Stars, that did not have their own ballparks. The formation of the Negro National League marked a watershed event in the history of black professional baseball.[16]

Throughout the inaugural season, Foster conducted a promotional tour of the East to stimulate support for a national organization. He traveled to New York and negotiated a settlement with John Connor. The *Defender* reported that Connie Savage of the Tesrea Bears, a local black club in New York, "was the prime mover at the peace conference which lasted nearly 24 hours." It resulted in the Bacharach Giants becoming the first associate member of the Negro National League. This meant that NNL clubs could barnstorm to New York for games at either Dyckman Oval or Ebbets Field. Conversely, Connor's Giants could travel westward for games with NNL clubs and the top white semipros. NNL clubs agreed not to tamper with associate members' players under contract and vice versa. Yet the Bacharachs would not compete for the NNL pennant, nor would their record against league clubs factor into the overall standings. They also agreed not to play clubs that were not associate members, most notably the Lincoln Giants, Cuban Stars East, and Brooklyn Royal Giants. Given the fact that Nat Strong and James Keenan had attempted to drive Connor out of the black baseball business, his association with the NNL was understandable. Furthermore, Foster's alliance with Connor allowed the NNL chairman to circumvent the Strong-Keenan alliance that had been so effective in excluding midwestern black clubs from playing in Gotham.[17]

Connor and Foster saw this association as a means of advancing each other's economic interests. It occurred at the same time the management team of Connor, Baron Wilkins, and Henry Tucker transformed the Bacharach Giants into a top-level black baseball club. They had a secured lease on Dyckman Oval and concurrently negotiated a deal with Brooklyn Dodgers owner Charles Ebbets to schedule games in Ebbets Field when the National League club was on the road. The Bacharach Giants benefited from black player unrest in the East, which was a direct result of playing for Nat Strong and James Keenan. This dissatisfaction allowed Connor to sign top-level players like the Cannonball Dick Redding and Bill Gatewood. Foster's alliance with Connor allowed him to establish a barnstorming network that was similar to that of the National Association of Colored Baseball Clubs of the United States and Cuba in the opening decade of the twentieth century. This time the barnstorming link ran from the West to the East instead of the other way around. The Connor-Foster alliance occurred at a time when the Lincoln Giants lost their lease on Olympic Field. The Bacharachs president now had the Harlem market to himself.[18]

Foster's trip to Philadelphia told a different story. What resulted was a feud between Foster and Hilldale owner Ed Bolden. Evidently, Foster was not willing to let bygones be bygones regarding Bolden's signing in 1919 of three American Giants players—Jess Barbour, outfielder; Bill Francis, third baseman; and Dick Whitworth, pitcher—not to mention the near signing of Oscar Charleston. The *Freeman* pointed to the possible signs of "a very stormy session out around Darby . . . and many profuse explanations, no doubt, will be forthcoming." To avoid a potential conflict, Foster instead offered support to the newly formed Madison Stars. The *Philadelphia Tribune* reported that the Madison Park Company had built a new ballpark "with all modern improvements" where the Stars would play their home games. This support was designed to tap into the Quaker City's baseball market and compete against the HBEC for gate receipts.[19]

Incensed by Foster's actions, Bolden published a letter in the *Philadelphia Tribune* calling for cooperation between east and west teams, and claiming that Foster had a "belligerent attitude toward our club" and was attempting to injure the HBEC's reputation. Bolden pointed out that the NNL's reserve clause was not in effect until February 1920. If the NNL chose to boycott Hilldale—which the NNL in fact did during the regular season—then the new league's owners would be hurting themselves financially. Bolden concluded that the Hilldale AC could make more money in a single day in New York than it could in Detroit for one week, and the traveling expenses were cheaper. He wrote, "The cost of traveling expenses make it paramount that no lucrative possibility be overlooked." It is of interest that Bolden found his economic interests being better served by doing business with a club owner who had previously tried to amalgamate the HBEC into his booking agency or compete against the HBEC for gate receipts—namely, Nathaniel Colvin Strong.[20]

Yet the Bacharach Giants' association with the NNL presented a dilemma for Bolden and his HBEC. On the one hand, Hilldale played games throughout the 1920 season with the Brooklyn Royal Giants and the Cuban Stars East, allowing the Darby club access to the New York market. On the other hand, because Hilldale was considered an outlaw club, it lost the opportunity to play the Bacharach Giants in Ebbets Field. The *Philadelphia Tribune* reported that the HBEC attempted to schedule a series of games with the Bacharachs at the Dodgers' home grounds. Because the Giants were an associate member of the NNL, however, they were "unable to play." To add insult to injury, both clubs were involved in a dispute over players. Connor induced catcher Yank Deas, shortstop Dick Lundy, and outfielder Jess Barbour to play for his Bacharachs. The move led the HBEC to file suit in Common Pleas court against Deas and Lundy. The court ruled that Deas could not play for the Giants because he had been contracted to play for Hilldale for the 1920 season. However, the HBEC was not successful in obtaining an injunction against Lundy. It was within Foster's ability to make the

Madison Stars strong enough to compete for gate receipts against the Hilldale AC, a fact undoubtedly not lost on Bolden and the HBEC. Yet at the same time, Foster's feud with Bolden marked the start of a process whereby the NNL chairman alienated the very men who could have helped him to organize a national organization. His personal animosity toward Bolden obviously clouded his better business judgment.[21]

Although the promotional tour produced only mixed results, the Negro National League enjoyed a successful first season. On May 7, 1920, the Chicago Giants played the Indianapolis ABCs in the league's opening game at Washington Park. Joe Green's Giants were a veteran ball club that included Bobby Winston; John Beckwith; and the opening day starter, Walter Ball. Taylor's ABCs were essentially the same club that had risen to the ranks of touring team in the prewar era, witness the presence of Oscar Charleston, George Shively, Ben Taylor, and Paul Powell. Taylor's opening day starter was Ed "Huck" Rile, who was one of the biggest men in the Negro Leagues at six feet six inches and two hundred and thirty pounds. A reported six thousand fans—including a cadre of sportswriters such as Wyatt, Ira Lewis, and Ed Lancaster—watched the ABCs take a 3-1 lead after three innings of play. It was all Rile needed, as he gave up just seven hits, struck out five batters, and collected two hits in a 4-2 victory.[22]

In July 1920, an article in the *Competitor*, an African American periodical, analyzed the NNL's progress to that time. The article declared that the league was "making wonderful progress during its first year, despite many and varied handicaps." The league's competitive balance was suspect, with the American Giants winning thirty-two of its first thirty-seven league games and the Detroit Stars a distant second with an 18-14 won-lost record. The Dayton Marcos had managed only eight wins, while the Chicago Giants could manage only a paltry three victories. There was evidence of players jumping their contracts to play in the East. Huck Rile left the ABCs for the Lincoln Giants, although he reportedly returned to the Hoosier club in late June "and shut out the American Giants . . . much to the delight of 10,000 Indianapolis fans."[23]

The *Competitor* article pointed to the lack of press coverage from black publications as the league's "heaviest handicap." Press coverage was characterized as "unsportsmanlike, unbusinesslike, and weak-kneed," and it was "inconceivable and unbelievable that an effort to promote a colored baseball league would awaken only half-hearted interest." A glaring example of this lack of support was that two months into the regular season, not one league standings had appeared in any of the newspapers published in league cities. Three factors are connected to this state of affairs. First, the papers did not have the wherewithal to either "secure data for themselves when they are deprived of the box score clipped from the white dailies, or they cannot or do not care to figure averages." This circumstance led to the second reason for a lack of information, namely that neither the league nor the individual teams felt they "are remiss in the treatment of the newspapermen in trips with the team and press courtesies."[24]

Black professional baseball did not enjoy the symbiotic business relationship that emerged between the newspapers and white baseball clubs. Dailies within Major League cities acknowledged the economic fact that both sides needed each other. In essence, baseball sold newspapers and newspapers sold baseball. By 1910, whole sections of metropolitan papers were devoted to baseball, complete with features, photos, cartoons, and reminiscences. The scope and dollar value of this newspaper coverage made the majors' advertising expenditures look inconsequential.

In contrast to the white majors, writers did not enter the ownership ranks of black baseball. Former writer Charles Murphy owned the Chicago Cubs during their glorious days of Tinkers, to Evers, to Chance until he made so many enemies with his unsolicited advice that eventually led to his forced retirement. Horace Fogel managed the New York Giants before John McGraw and eventually became president of the Philadelphia Phillies in 1912. In addition, former writers like Ban Johnson and John Heydler succeeded brilliantly as administrators. As president of the American League, Johnson knew the value of newspapers, and he never failed to encourage his clubs to cooperate fully with reporters and photographers.[25]

Nevertheless, the white majors, like black baseball but not nearly to the same degree, devalued this symbiotic business relationship. The historian David Voigt points out that the sportswriters consistently protested baseball's failure to honor them in what he referred to as the construction of the "second dimension" (the baseball press). Nor did the white Major Leagues place a high premium on taking control of marketing and promoting their sport. As historian Harold Seymour accurately points out, professional baseball remained the most highly publicized business in the country, and promoters continued to receive an amazing amount of free publicity the year round. This circumstance reduced the owners' motivation to concern themselves about publicity or to construct innovative ways to promote their product. Public relations and promotion long remained murky concepts for baseball men, who easily slipped into the mindset that all they needed to do was open the gates in order to get fans into ballpark.[26]

Black baseball's relationship with the press was somewhat similar to that of the white majors, but it was also characterized by some stark contrasts. The black game began to receive increased press coverage during the war years at a time when several African American entrepreneurs succeeded in creating a number of politically influential newspapers. Unlike the white dailies, however, the black newspapers varied in the extent to which they expanded their sports sections. A lot of this variation was due to the fact that no black editor rose to the ranks of a William Randolph Hearst or Joseph Pulitzer in the early twentieth century. Also, virtually all black newspapers were weekly publications. They provided little or no feature stories, cartoons, or photos. In the prewar era, only a handful of black journalists provided the black game with consistent coverage, examples being Billy Lewis of the *Freeman*, Dave Wyatt of the *Indianapolis Ledger*, Frank Young of the *Defender*, and Lester Walton of the *New York Age*. During the war years, the *Defender* and the *Philadelphia Tribune* expanded their sports sections while the *Freeman*'s coverage remained the same. At the same time, the *New York Age* drastically reduced its coverage of black baseball. Undoubtedly, Nat Strong's and James Keenan's lack of involvement in the black community contributed to this lack of coverage.

The final point the *Competitor* article raised was that the managers of several clubs marginalized the importance of publicity, which was a valid claim. Throughout the opening decades of the twentieth century, only Sol White, Rube Foster, C. I. Taylor, and Ed Bolden recognized the value of newspapers, and each man served as his own press agent. Not only did they keep the media spotlight on their respective teams; these entrepreneurs used the black press to shape public opinion on a number of issues affecting the black game. By the same token, the absence of published league standings and box scores created a dilemma for the club owners. League standings meant publishing won-lost records, and a losing record reflected poorly on a black club. On the other hand, however, it was essential for a black team to remain on the sports page, and this could only occur by publishing box scores on a regular basis. Thus, in some cases the devaluation of publicity may be attributable to a desire to minimize attention to a club's poor performance on the field. To the owners' way of thinking, such attention would hurt box office receipts.

Despite these many handicaps, the *Competitor*'s overall assessment of the Negro National League's first season was favorable. The mere fact that the teams were trying to operate under an agreement of cooperation should "enlist the aid, support and influence of every contributing power within the race." By the end of the season, Rube Foster reported that the NNL was in a healthy financial condition and that all eight teams had turned a profit. The *Freeman* reported the league played to 616,000 paid admissions. This rosy picture would lead Foster to continue to pursue the formation of a national organization.[27]

The rise of the Negro National League coincided with the remarkable economic growth of the United States during the 1920s. The temporary postwar boom gave way to a depression in 1921, but the economy recovered quickly two years later. With the exception of brief economic downturns in 1924 and 1927, the US economy enjoyed seven prosperous years until the stock market crashed in 1929. The overall standard of living improved as per capita income, which stood at $480 in 1900, leaped to $681 by 1929.

Other demographic trends of the 1920s were favorable to both Organized Baseball and black professional baseball. Baseball's market expanded because of the accelerated growth of cities and small towns as the US was transformed from a rural society to an urban one. By 1930, fewer than 44 percent of the population dwelled in rural areas, compared to 60 percent in 1900. The Great Migration continued to enlarge black communities in the North, particularly in league cities. Chicago's Black Belt continued its tremendous growth; it expanded from 109,458 in 1920 to 233,903 in 1930. Detroit's black population grew precipitously from 48,838 in 1920 to 120,066 ten years later. In St. Louis, the black population grew from 69,854 to 93,580. Nonleague cities grew steadily as the number of African Americans in New York expanded from 152,467 to 327,706 and the figures in Philadelphia rose from 134,229 to 219,599.[28]

Prosperity was more widely distributed in the United States of the 1920s than had been possible in any community of its size previously. Unemployment, for example, declined significantly while wholesale and retail price levels remained stable. As the tools of production became increasingly efficient, output per factory worker-hour climbed nearly 75 percent. Although the expanded product was being assigned in such a way as to widen the gap between rich and poor, the share going to blue- and white-collar workers was enough to produce the world's first excursion into mass affluence. For the first time in world history, numerous people were able to acquire machine products and electronic devices, afford higher education, enjoy extended leisure, and engage in other activities once reserved for a wealthy few.[29]

African Americans embodied the ways in this national prosperity was widespread but not universal. On the one hand, African Americans had no trouble finding jobs. When World War I shut off the flow of southern and eastern European immigrants to mines and mills in Pittsburgh, for example, blacks from the American South stepped in to fill the void. Blacks found employment in Chicago's stockyards, garment factories, hotels, kitchens, and on the railroads. The expansion of the black community contributed to the continued expansion of the African American middle class. Blacks became politicians, firemen, aldermen, precinct captains, lawyers, and teachers. On the other hand, white workers became apprehensive over a large pool of nonunionized blacks that could be used to keep wages low. Three years after the war, a minor depression wiped out most of the gains that African American women had made in light manufacturing and in the garment industry. Concurrently, blacks were used as strikebreakers in Chicago's stockyards. While they became permanently established in that industry, blacks endured the bitter antagonism of the Irish, Polish, and Italian workers. By 1925, however, the economy had recovered and racial conflict in industry subsided as unemployment declined.[30]

It was within this context that the NNL owners met in December 1920 to tighten their organization. Rube Foster was reelected president and secretary of the league. NNL owners were determined to rectify the problems of their inaugural season. New constitutional provisions included these: (1) club owners would be fined for ungentlemanly actions that would hurt the reputation of the game; (2) managers were banned from taking their teams off the field during a game; (3) managers disagreeing with an umpire's decision could finish the game under protest rather than ending the contest in protest, protecting the public from foreshortened games; (4) ballplayers were required to conduct themselves in an exemplary manner on and off the field; (5) infractions against the constitution could result in heavy fines; and (6) players could not accept advance money, that is, money received from an owner prior to playing, and could not report or refuse to pay a fine for conduct unbecoming a player. Several other revisions were made to the constitution. League clubs could refuse to play a team that was not an associate member. Clubs had the right to ask waivers on players, trade players, and sell a player to another club in the league or association. Finally, the deposit to ensure clubs would play the entire season was raised from five hundred to one thousand dollars.[31]

NNL owners also made changes to the league structure and considered applications for teams to become associate members. The Dayton Marcos were transferred to Columbus, where Sol White would manage the club. The re-named Buckeyes would play their home games at the American Association Park when the minor league Columbus club was on the road. To establish a home territory for one of the traveling teams, the Cuban Stars would use Cincinnati's Redland Field when the

National League team was on the road. The use of Redland Field by the Stars provides a glimpse into the kind of rental agreements black clubs made with major and minor league owners. C. I. Taylor was the prime mover in negotiating with the Reds' management. Twenty-five percent of the gate receipts went into the Reds' coffers. The National League club provided police protection and furnished the tickets, ticket sellers, and the groundskeepers, while the NNL furnished the ticket takers. The league also posted a one-thousand-dollar forfeit deposit to ensure the circuit would play all scheduled games throughout the season. In addition, the NNL received applications from clubs in Pittsburgh, Cleveland, and Omaha, but according to the *Defender*, these teams were "turned down for the [1921] season."[32]

The NNL's evidence of stability resulted in Bolden's change of attitude toward the midwestern circuit. He tendered an application to become an associate member because, according to the *Defender*, the HBEC "found several of [their] best men about to be taken over by other clubs." The league accepted the application and allowed the AC to retain Whitworth and Francis. Peace was also restored between Bolden and John Connor. These men had not spoken to each other in years, and the sportswriters at the winter meeting "were more than surprised when they entered the meeting arm in arm." Foster's goal of an East-West association appeared to be heading in the right direction.[33]

Throughout the 1921 season, efforts were made to generate more publicity for the NNL. Dave Wyatt was hired as the league's publicity man, and greater attempts were made to publish league standings—at least in the Chicago *Defender*. On July 30, the *Defender* published league batting averages for the first time. St. Louis Giants' slugger Oscar Charleston led the league in hitting with a .425 average, followed by John Beckwith of the Chicago Giants (.412) and Ben Taylor of the ABCs (.387). No pitching statistics were published. It would be the only time the batting statistics appeared with no indications that any newspapers in the other league cities followed the *Defender*'s lead.[34]

The East-West association was the NNL's finest hour. Both the Bacharach Giants and the Hilldale AC would enjoy a spectacular 1921 season. Connor negotiated several leasing agreements that would enable his Bacharachs to play games in Ebbets Field, Shibe Park in Philadelphia, and Dyckman Oval in Harlem. The Giants would also play in Bacharach Park in Atlantic City, New Jersey, where renovations were being made to improve the overall playing facility and enlarge the seating capacity. Former Cuban X Giants owner E. B. Lamar made arrangements for the Harlem club to tour Cuba during the winter months. Interestingly enough, the team was essentially composed of Cuban players, which is probably what led the *Philadelphia Tribune* to refer to the club as the "so called Bacharach Giants." First baseman Augustin Parpetti provided the Giants with power, while veteran players Dick Redding and Phil Cockerell appeared to be the only American players that accompanied the team.[35]

Much like the Philadelphia Giants in the opening decade of the twentieth century, the Bacharachs found the Cuban teams to be fierce competitors. Of the six games reported in the press, the Giants won two. One of the victories was on a stellar pitching performance by Cannonball Redding. In the opening game of the winter season, Redding was locked into a pitcher's duel with a Havana Reds hurler by the name of Tuero. The Reds took a 1-0 lead in the sixth inning when the center fielder, named Cuerto, singled and scored on third baseman Bienvenido "Hooks" Jimenez's triple. It would be the only hits the Reds would manage. The Giants then scored two runs in the top of the seventh and Redding fanned nine batters in a 2-1 Giants' win. The Cannonball, however, met his match against Reds' pitcher Jose Acosta, who in 1916 had played for the Northwest League's Vancouver club, a single-A minor league team, and later for the Major League Washington Senators and Chicago White Sox over three seasons. The Reds scored three times in the first four innings while Acosta struck out five and scattered eight hits en route to a 4-0 shutout win.[36]

Upon their return to the United States, the Bacharach Giants embarked on a winter tour of the South and began the regular season touring the NNL cities for the first time. They toured the states of Florida, Alabama, and Georgia, playing a series of games against the St. Louis Giants in Montgomery. By April 19, they had toured throughout Virginia in games against the Baltimore Black Sox and the Norfolk Giants.

The team that toured the South was composed players who would make the Bacharach Giants a tough opponent throughout the regular season. Bill Pettus, George Shively, Dick Lundy, and Julio Rojo, who also pitched, would pound the ball during the year. Redding and Cyclone Joe Williams bolstered a pitching staff that was the envy of any black club.[37]

The Bacharach Giants began their regular season with a midwestern tour of NNL clubs. League clubs showed no hospitality to their eastern associate member. Of the seven games reported in the press, the Bacharachs won just two. Yet the games were closely contested. For example, Dick Redding lost a heartbreaker to the Chicago American Giants before a reported crowd of ten thousand fans. Redding took a 1-0 lead into the ninth inning, when American Giants' shortstop Bingo DeMoss doubled to left field. He went to third base on Carlos Torriente's fly ball to right field. Jimmie Lyons reached first base on a slow roller to third base when Bacharach's first baseman Bill Pettus dropped Dave Brown's throw, allowing DeMoss to score. After Dave Malarcher struck out, Lyons stole second; he was almost caught stealing, but catcher Julio Rojo's throw was dropped by second baseman Oliver Marcelle. Redding intentionally walked George Dixon who, after reaching first base, attempted a delayed steal and got caught in a rundown. Meanwhile, Lyons dashed home to score the winning run all the way from second. It was the type of victory the Chicago American Giants were known for; they had a playing style that would eventually be referred to as the "Rube Foster way." The Bacharachs got some satisfaction in beating Sol White's Columbus Buckeyes in the final game of the road trip. In spite of their mediocre performance, the winter tour of Cuba, their spring training tour of the South, and their midwestern road trip elevated the Bacharach Giants to the ranks of a touring team.[38]

The Bacharach Giants engaged in a fierce rivalry with the Hilldale AC. Much like Connor's club, Ed Bolden's AC was enjoying an excellent season. He assembled one of his strongest teams, including veteran players Napoleon Cummings, Bunny Downs, Billy Francis, Louis Santop, and Otto Briggs. Phil Cockerell and Dick Whitworth provided a strong one-two pitching combination. Being an associate member meant Hilldale would boycott the Lincoln Giants, Brooklyn Royal Giants, and

Cuban Stars East. Since the Bacharach Giants had access to Ebbets Field, not to mention Shibe Park in Philadelphia, Bolden appeared more than willing to make this concession. The loss of games with these New York clubs was offset by the barnstorming of NNL clubs to Hilldale Park for gate receipts.

The Hilldale-Bacharach rivalry began on June 2, much to the delight of Darby's fans. The *Tribune* reported that a large crowd was at "fever heat when the two premier colored clubs of the East grappled for supremacy in their first tilt as members of the National Association of Negro Baseball Clubs." Phil Cockerell faced Dick Redding, and Hilldale hit the Cannonball early and often, taking a 7-3 lead into the ninth inning. Despite giving up three runs in the ninth, Hilldale held on to score an 8-6 victory. The Bacharachs were no match for Dick Whitworth in game two. Hilldale scored all of its runs in the first inning and Whitworth scattered eight hits in a 3-0 shutout win.[39]

On June 5, Hilldale invaded Ebbets Field in the first of two doubleheaders on consecutive Sundays. Redding fared no better in his second matchup against Phil Cockerell as Hilldale erupted for nine runs in the fifth inning and coasted to a 12-6 win. Red Ryan turned the tables in the night cap with a 6-5 victory that was called after five innings because of darkness. On the following Sunday, a three-team doubleheader was scheduled between Hilldale, the Bacharach Giants, and the Tesrea Bears. After defeating the Bears in a morning game, the Bacharachs apparently took their frustrations out on Cockerell by scoring eleven times in the first two innings, and they went on to demolish Hilldale, 14-7. In the final game, Giants' pitcher Johnny Pugh held Hilldale to three hits en route to a 5-1 victory. Overall, both teams split the season series with eight victories a piece.[40]

In July, several NNL clubs made their first visit to Hilldale Park. With the HBEC as an associate member, Darby became the gateway for league clubs to travel to New Jersey and New York for games with the Bacharach Giants and the Tesrea Bears. The Detroit Stars, Indianapolis ABCs, Columbus Buckeyes, and Chicago American Giants barnstormed their way to Hilldale Park. Hilldale proved to be a formidable opponent for its midwestern counterparts. Of the seventeen games reported in the press, the Hilldale won twelve of them. The high water mark of the midwestern tour was the four-game series between Hilldale and the Chicago American Giants. Bingo DeMoss, Carlos Torrente, Jimmie Lyons, Dave Malarcher, and George Dixon led the American Giants to their second straight NNL pennant. Tom Johnson, Tom Williams, and Bill Holland bolstered the pitching staff. In the first contest, the American Giants literally stole the game as Lyons and Malarcher combined to steal six bases, including a steal of home by Lyons. The American Giants won the game, 5-2.[41]

The rest of the series belong to Hilldale. The second game was played at the park of the National League Phillies, with the teams tied at two after five innings of play. The American Giants could manage only one more hit off Phil Cockerell and the Hilldale scored one run in the bottom of the sixth inning to win, 4-3. The third game was the Phil Cockerell show. He struck out six batters while hitting a double and a home run as Hilldale destroyed the American Giants, 15-5. The final game was over in the second inning when Hilldale scored four times with a reported five thousand fans watching Dick Whitworth subdue the Windy City club, 7-1. Defeating the Chicago American Giants put an exclamation mark on the HBEC's excellent year.[42]

Overall, the 1921 season proved to be a mixed blessing for Rube Foster's Negro National League. It was a particularly troubling year for Foster due to his arrest for allegedly not paying his players and because of the death of his daughter. The *Defender* reported that the combination of the postwar recession, high travel expenses, and bad weather contributed to a disappointing season for the NNL. Gate receipts were reportedly 25 percent lower than the previous year, and Columbus, Detroit, St. Louis, and Indianapolis fell way below the previous year's revenue mark. Chicago was the only club that finished in good standing.[43]

By the same token, Rube Foster's NNL had made significant progress, and the creation of a national organization appeared plausible. With the Bacharach Giants and Hilldale AC as associate members, Foster was able to reestablish the barnstorming network to the East that he had set out to accomplish during the war years. In spite of the economic recession, an unbalanced schedule, and limited access to suitable playing facilities, the Negro National League completed its second season. It should be noted that Organized Baseball's early years were marred by constant franchise shifting and unbalanced consumer markets, and it would take from 1876 to 1903 before the white majors reached some semblance of economic stability. Black baseball was experiencing the same kinds of growing pains, and black club owners confronted obstacles their white counterparts never had to endure. Viewed within this context, the NNL's East-West association with the Bacharach Giants and the Hilldale AC represented a significant accomplishment in the midst of the various challenges it faced.

The State of Black Baseball according to Rube Foster

From December 10 to December 31, 1921, Rube Foster wrote four articles in the *Defender* titled "What Baseball Needs to Succeed." He assessed the shortcomings of club owners and managers, discussed player behavior, and presented his point of view about hiring African American umpires. From the beginning, the NNL president declared that many would disagree with his perspective, but his long tenure in the black game gave him the credibility to highlight what was necessary to ensure the sport's "permanent success."[44]

In the opening article, Foster stated that the evolution of black professional baseball has been a proverbial roller-coaster ride. Writing two years after the Black Sox scandal of 1919, he said the black game had been placed "in disfavor by the narrow ignorance of leading people all over the country, who [believe] baseball was [a] game to be patronized by the sporting element." In other words, black baseball's image was marred to the extent that middle-class spectators found the sport unappealing. The sport needed to improve its image because "no respectable people would think of inviting a ball player to their home." To remedy the situation, black clubs needed to be owned and operated by men who had the respect of their community.[45]

Foster outlined the familiar strategy of economic cooperation to attract men of good standing to own black clubs. A group of men should form a stock company with either ten men investing one thousand dollars each or twenty men at five hundred dollars apiece. This ten thousand dollars would serve as start-up capital to allow them to obtain a franchise in the league. In this way, a group of "influential men" in any city "would be able to realize at the lowest possible estimate more than 10 percent on [their] investment." This investment was essential because several men who currently owned ball clubs did not have the financial means to operate them. Because of the past season, it was uncertain whether these men could continue "in harmony and work as they previously did."[46]

Foster highlighted the park dilemma the NNL faced in its two years of existence. Only three of the eight clubs—Detroit, St. Louis, and Chicago—had unfettered access to a playing facility. Three teams—Columbus, Indianapolis, and Kansas City—used American Association parks when their respective home teams were on the road. Because the Cuban Stars and Chicago Giants were traveling teams, it was necessary for them to play every Sunday. This predicament made establishing a balanced schedule problematic. Club owners supposedly agreed that only fifteen games between each club would be counted as league games. The other games would be classified as exhibition games. This arrangement worked, and everybody reportedly made money. However, the economic downturn diminished gate receipts, and several owners were unhappy with the scheduling system Foster developed.

In his second article, Foster continued to highlight the shortcomings of black baseball club owners. The American Giants' magnate stated that these owners had "failed" to learn the fundamental principles that would ensure a club's success. They would have been successful had they applied a business system that included managing the day-to-day operations of the team, hiring a good field manager, and allowing the success or failure of the club rest on the shoulders of the manager.

Another shortcoming discussed by Foster dealt with several owners' lack of knowledge of the game itself. There were "only three men who own or control . . . ball clubs . . . [who] know anything about baseball as it should be played, the rules governing it, or the ability of players." The owners, therefore, lost the players' respect, which often led the players to undermine the manager's authority. "With the exception of C. I. Taylor and myself," Foster concluded, "I know of no other man connected with baseball as manager or owner that has the full [authority over] everything pertaining to the club in its [day-to-day-operations]."[47]

Foster targeted the St. Louis Giants as a prime example of club owners exercising poor judgment in operating their teams. The club supposedly accumulated debt due to player salaries, diminishing the club's revenue potential. The Giants' owners wanted to remain in the league but found it problematic to pay the one-thousand-dollar deposit prior to the start of the regular season. The plight of the St. Louis Giants led Foster to focus the remainder of his article on the basic fundamentals an owner should follow—as well as principles managers should adhere to when dealing with players—to ensure the successful operation of a ball club.

As with the majority of Foster's articles, the issues he raised and the possible solutions to address them were valid. However, much of Foster's rhetoric in this series of articles was self-serving and often condescending. The tone of these articles could not have sat well with the owners whose cooperation he sought in establishing a national organization. At no time did Rube Foster acknowledge the numerous obstacles black baseball owners confronted within their respective cities, and one cannot say that he was unaware of them. To be sure, the St. Louis Giants were plagued by the constant turnover in its management and ownership ranks. But throughout the Giants' history, Charles Mills had managed to remain with the team as either a manager or co-owner. The St. Louis Giants and Amusement Association was run by exactly the type of businessmen and professionals that Foster wanted as black team owners. The SLGAA was instrumental in elevating the Giants to the ranks of a touring team. Their first barnstorming tour of the East, however, was blighted by the efforts of eastern clubs, most notably the Lincoln Giants, to induce players to jump their contracts. This experience, evidently, led these black middle-class professionals to abandon the SLGAA, leading Mills to look constantly for a business partner. The Giants' plight was further complicated by the fact that the St. Louis Browns' owner, Phil Ball, used his influence to deny the black club access to Federal League

Park. This St. Louis rivalry led the then Giants' owner, a Mr. Brock, to leave the club because he had invested heavily in ballpark renovations. When the United States entered World War I, the Giants loss several players to the war effort. None of these issues factored into Foster's assessment of the St. Louis Giants.[48]

Foster's underlying assumption that black baseball clubs were run by men who did not have the respect of their community was also problematic. It was hard to claim that Ed Bolden was not a respected African American professional and club owner in Darby, and undoubtedly among baseball fans in black Philadelphia. The Hilldale Baseball and Exhibition Company was composed of black middle-class professionals and, like its president, the HBEC had the respect of Darby's black community. By 1921, these men had effectively transformed the Hilldale AC from a team of "small boys" to one of the leading eastern-based black independent clubs. With the exception of C. I. Taylor, Bolden made concerted efforts to create a positive image that embodied the ideals of the middle-class spectator. HBEC's slogan, "clean baseball," meant that the organization maintained a suitable playing facility for the comfort of the team's fans, hired security officers to ensure their safety, and expected its players to be gentlemanly on and off the field. These were the kinds of practical qualities that Foster apparently looked for in the management and ownership of a black baseball club.

Foster took some jabs at Bolden in his final article, which dealt with the use of African American umpires. The debate over the hiring of black umpires would be hotly contested in the black press in the upcoming years. Foster had indicated that he had received hundreds of letters from people across the country, and from sportswriters as well, urging him to hire African American umpires and "in some cases condemning me because I have not inaugurated Colored umpires at Chicago and in the league." He discussed the qualifications he believed an umpire needed, including an awareness of "the temperament of the players with whom he comes in contact" and knowledge of the playing rules, the interpretation of those rules and, most important, to be "HONEST and SQUARE." The NNL president acknowledged that the league needed "Race umpires," but it would be "unfair to give them positions unless we [the league] were in [a] position to give them the protection they will need in doing their work." The NNL carried over from the independent era the practice of allowing the home team to hire the umpire. This resulted in a conflict of interest. If the umpire wanted to continue working for the home team, close calls and at times controversial decisions would go against the visiting club. Therefore, in Foster's way of thinking, black umpires would be better served when the owners agreed that the men in blue be hired and instructed by the league president.[49]

The Chicago American Giants' series with Hilldale was used by Foster as an example showing why the hiring of umpires by the home team represented a conflict of interest. Undoubtedly, a lot of this analysis was biased because the AC outplayed the American Giants in the series. Bolden evidently hired a black umpire for the series. In the second game of the series, with the score tied at three, the Giants had runners on second base and first. Carlos Torrente hit a fly ball down the left field line "that everybody thought was fair." Both runners scored. However, the umpire called the fly ball foul. When the runners returned to their respective bases, a Hilldale player threw the ball to second base and the umpire called the runner out. Not surprisingly, the American Giants protested the call and convinced the black umpire to go to the umpire in chief for a clarification of the rules. Foster was quick to point out that the umpire-in-chief was white, and that he informed the black arbiter that his call was wrong. The black umpire reportedly was angered by being "showed up" and refused to reverse the decision. This supposedly cost the American Giants the game. In another game in Philadelphia, the umpire reportedly "[played] the game by the rules" and the Windy City club won. "Rules or no Rules," Foster concluded, "it is impossible to get Hilldale to play according to the playing rules."[50]

Rube Foster's series of articles showed the transition the NNL president and his fellow owners underwent to function as a league. If the white Major Leagues served as their model, then these black baseball owners would eventually have to come to grips with the fact that they were both competitors and partners. Cooperation among them had to be much greater within the framework of a league format. As league president, Foster found himself dealing with administrative issues that in some ways were not designed to maximize revenues, but could have an impact—positively or negatively—on those residuals if he did not address them. The transition appeared to be a rocky one for Foster as he bewailed the fact that he could not focus more of his attention on his American Giants, although the team continued to be successful on the field. "I have been so engaged day and night in trying to keep other clubs going," he proclaimed, "that I have not been able to see the American Giants practice this season. All of my time has been taken up trying to do things for the other clubs." To alleviate some of this administrative burden, Foster proposed the creation of an advisory board. However, the current club owners were not responsive regarding the issues that affected the league: "When [consulting] their advice [their response] is always, 'Do as you see fit because you know best.'" Yet surely C. I. Taylor, J. L. Wilkinson, and Charles Mills could have served in this advisory capacity.[51]

Rube Foster's series of articles marked the start of the process by which he alienated the very men he needed to develop a national organization. His self-serving and condescending tone throughout the articles did a disservice to his supposed pursuit of ensuring the NNL's permanent success. Further, at no time did he recognize the efforts of successful club owners like C. I. Taylor, John Connor, and Ed Bolden. His analysis was also marred by his unwillingness to recognize the kinds of obstacles his fellow owners confronted within their respective cities. Much as in the case of his feud with Taylor in the prewar era, Rube Foster let his personal animosity toward Bolden cloud his better business judgment. He had become his own worst enemy. As the winter meetings approached, Rube Foster's vision of a national organization began to unravel.

8

Black Baseball War

The Rise of the Eastern Colored League

Rube Foster's series of articles at the end of the 1921 season undoubtedly irritated his fellow club owners, many of whom could have assisted him in the creation of a national organization. On the other hand, many of the obstacles he highlighted surfaced throughout the 1922 season. Franchise shifting continued, and Charles Mills's St. Louis Giants disbanded due to the apparently insurmountable debt the team accumulated. The franchise was saved, however, when a group of African American businessmen and professionals formed a stock company and renamed the club the St. Louis Stars. The untimely death of C. I. Taylor marked the start of a process whereby the league lost one of its most stable franchises, the Indianapolis ABCs. The season was further aggravated by a rift within the Bacharach Giants' management team, resulting in two clubs under the same name playing during the year.

Other issues emerged during the course of this chaotic year. Chicago *Defender* sportswriter Frank "Fay" Young ratcheted up the pressure on Foster to hire African American umpires. Several fans wrote to the *Defender* pointing out several black arbiters who operated throughout the United States. For the first time, former league officials and sportswriters complained about Foster's scheduling practices. The chief complaint was that the American Giants made fewer road trips than did the other league clubs. The conflict between Foster and Ed Bolden reached its peak, leading to irreconcilable differences. Annoyed by Foster's grabbing of pitcher Dick Whitworth from the ACs, Bolden withdrew as an associate member and asked for the return of his one-thousand-dollar deposit. The prospects of league clubs raiding the Hilldale AC's roster for players led Bolden to remain an associated member for another year. However, at the end of the season, Bolden withdrew from the Negro National League.

Ed Bolden's break with the Negro National League led to the formation of the Eastern Colored League (ECL). Utilizing the cooperative business philosophy as a foundation, Bolden advocated the creation of a board of commissioners to promote and govern the league. Within months of the ECL's formation, eastern owners began inducing NNL players to jump their contracts. The raids crippled John Connor's Bacharach Giants and contributed to the constant shifting of NNL franchises. The presence of two traveling teams, along with Nat Strong's setting a precedent for skipping league games, meant that the ECL confronted the same scheduling dilemma that Foster's NNL experienced. Yet the new league had a relatively excellent inaugural season.

In response to the formation of the "outlaw" league, Rube Foster mounted a propaganda war in the black press to sway public opinion in his favor. The basic premise of this campaign was to take a stance against the destructive practice of player jumping and downplay Bolden's influence in the new league. He raised the issue of race, primarily in the ownership of eastern teams, and indicted Bolden for race abandonment. Bolden mounted a PR campaign of his own. He attacked Foster for raising the issue of race in the ownership of black teams and claimed the NNL was nothing more than a booking agency designed to maximize his revenues. Paying the booking fee, Bolden said. was a primary reason the HBEC had left the NNL.

With Rube Foster losing the propaganda war and while contract jumping threatened to cripple the Negro National League, the NNL confronted internal obstacles. The league continued its practice of franchise shifting, and by July the NNL had begun to unravel. League officials awarded a franchise to Toledo, and the NNL began the season with a compact midwestern circuit. Attempts were made to create a more equitable playing schedule, but the constant franchise shifting made this untenable. Simultaneously, Rube Foster conceded to the fans' and the sportswriters' demand for African American umpires. Seven black umpires were hired, and they represented the silver lining in the dark clouds that hovered over the league.

In the East, the optimism at the end of the 1923 season led the ECL owners to expand their league by two clubs and simultaneously urge NNL players to jump their contracts. The Harrisburg Giants and the Washington Potomacs were selected as the league's new clubs, and attempts were made to standardize the scheduling system and adopt "strict rules to govern [the] game." Several clubs, most notably the Lincoln Giants and the Baltimore Black Sox, aggressively signed NNL players. Both leagues received some unexpected competition for players from Cumberland Posey, owner of the independent club called the Homestead Grays. In mid-May, Nat Strong refused to play James Keenan's Lincoln Giants, and his actions led the commissioners to expel the Royals' owner. When Strong saw that the commissioners would stand by their decision, he lobbied for reinstatement.

Concurrently, Rube Foster continued to deal with the internal problems that plagued his Negro National League. The Birmingham Black Barons and the Cleveland Browns replaced the disbanded franchises in Milwaukee and Toledo. By June, one of the league's strongest franchises, the Indianapolis ABCs, disbanded and was replaced by the Memphis Red Sox. Simultaneously, Foster continued his public relations campaign in the black press. The campaign was in response to the criticism he was receiving for the way he ran the league and was meant to reassure the public that the NNL was on solid ground despite the constant franchise shifting and player defections to the ECL. A counteroffensive to Foster's PR campaign, led by the Baltimore Black Sox management team of George Rossiter and Charles Spedden, refuted much of Foster's claim that the ECL could not long endure the higher salaries the club owners paid. The NNL president's PR campaign was further compromised when the Detroit Stars' owner Tenny Blount began to skip league games on a regular basis. Blount's actions marked an early expression by club owners of their dissatisfaction with Foster's czar-like rule in league affairs.

The Season of Discontent

Franchise shifting would be a constant in the history of Rube Foster's Negro National League. The first order of business at the league's winter meeting was finding replacements for the Columbus Buckeyes and the Chicago Giants. The Cleveland Tate Stars and the Pittsburgh Keystones were selected to replace the Buckeyes, with Joe Green's Chicago Giants being relegated to associate member. The Buckeyes' players were transferred to the other league clubs, with three of them—John Henry Lloyd (shortstop), Leroy Roberts (pitcher), and Bob "High Pockets" Hudspeth (first baseman)—going to the Bacharach Giants. The 1921 season was marred by personal tragedy for Green. Both the illness of his wife and the loss of the couple's first baby, combined with his increased overhead expenses, no doubt were instrumental in Green's decision to remain close to home. Thus, the NNL began the season with the Chicago American Giants, Cleveland Tate Stars, Cuban Stars, Detroit Stars, Indianapolis ABCs, Kansas City Monarchs, and Pittsburgh Keystones. The Bacharach Giants, Hilldale AC, and the Chicago Giants served as associate members. The league did not renew its lease with the Cincinnati Reds, and therefore the Cuban Stars operated as a road club.[1]

A great deal of league business was devoted to the disposition of the St. Louis Giants. Charles Mills's Giants had loss a degree of credibility when the club failed to complete a series with the National League's St. Louis Cardinals. Mills admitted the team was so far in debt that he could not see his way out of it. A group of African American businessmen formed the St. Louis Giants Baseball Club and Amusement Company in an attempt to keep the franchise in the league. Apparently, an intense discussion emerged between the group and Foster that went on "for hours" over whether the Giants should remain in the league. The newly created Board of Directors—consisting of Foster, C. I. Taylor, and J. L. Wilkinson—voted to give the new group a fifteen-day grace period to provide evidence showing why the team should not be expelled.[2]

The St. Louis situation would not be rectified until mid-April, when the *Defender* reported that a new group of businessmen, led by African Americans Richard W. Kent, Samuel Shepard, and Dr. J. W.

McClelland, had formed a new organization and renamed the club the St. Louis Stars. Shepard was named the team's business manager, and pitcher Bill Gatewood would serve as player-manager. The Giants' former players would remain with the new team, including league stalwarts Tully McAdoo and Joe Hewitt. The Stars' new management team also announced a new park would be built at Compton Avenue and Market Street, a location in the heart of St. Louis's black community. Since the park would not be ready at the start of the season, the Stars would begin the year as a traveling team.[3]

The NNL received a serious setback with the untimely death of C. I. Taylor. The *Defender* described Taylor as a man who had lived a life of which anyone should be proud and strive to emulate. He was fearless and upright and had many friends, witnessed by the large turnout at his funeral. Despite the numerous obstacles he confronted, Taylor managed to elevate his Indianapolis ABCs to the ranks of a touring team that competed for midwestern supremacy with the Chicago American Giants in the prewar era. He embodied the ideals that came to describe the new black leadership which emerged in the early twentieth century. The ABCs were to excel on the diamond and simultaneously serve as a symbol of race pride and racial solidarity. Taylor's passing would add to the NNL's franchise woes as the ABCs became entangled in a complicated controversy among his surviving relatives.[4]

The death of C. I. Taylor and the ensuing plight of the St. Louis Giants occurred at the same time that the conflict between Rube Foster and Ed Bolden reached a fever pitch. Bolden became disenchanted with the terms under which he was an associate member in the NNL. Conflict arose over Foster's signing Dick Whitworth away from the ACs, leading the *Defender* to conclude that "the first gun [was] fired in a war between organized baseball and the Hilldale club." Bolden supposedly refused to join the association and requested a return of his $1,000 deposit. The *Defender* alleged the Hilldale president intended to play outlaw clubs during the coming season and, furthermore, had aspirations to raid the NNL for players. The possible retaliation by NNL clubs led Bolden to capitulate, and the HBEC remained as an associate member for another year. However, the American Giants retained

Whitworth because "the league directors decided it would be best for the morale of the league not to return him to the Philadelphia club."[5]

While the HBEC chose to remain an associate member for another season, a rift occurred within the Bacharach Giants' management team, with Connor and Wilkins on one side and Jackson and Tucker on the other. Two factors appeared to have led to this division among the club owners. The transfer of players from the Columbus Buckeyes constituted the first factor. Connor named John Henry Lloyd as the Giants' new manager to the dismay of their former skipper, Dick Redding. The Cannonball reportedly resigned from the club and, along with shortstop Dick Lundy, formed the nucleus of the Original Bacharach Giants. Tom Jackson and Henry Tucker would manage the Original Bacharachs, and they reportedly contacted Nat Strong to schedule games with the Brooklyn Royal Giants and the Cuban Stars East. No doubt this infuriated Connor and Baron Wilkins. In May, the *Baltimore Afro-American* reported that Jackson and Turner were making plans to form an eastern league composed of the Original Bacharachs, the Royal Giants, Lincoln Giants, and the Baltimore Black Sox.[6]

Finally, it appeared that the transformation of the Bacharach Giants' into a touring team contributed to the split within the club's management team. The Giants' entry into the ranks of touring teams occurred at the same time the nation's economy experienced a brief recession. The high cost of railroad travel evidently led Jackson and Tucker to attempt to organize an eastern circuit, with the intent to decrease travel and overhead expenses. Black baseball teams continued to travel by private Pullman car, especially on extended barnstorming tours. This must have become an expensive undertaking. By the 1920s, the railroads were classified as a "troubled industry." A tradition of overcapitalization and mismanagement, unimaginative regulation, and relatively powerful labor unions made it problematic either to meet the competition from newer forms of transportation or to adjust capacity to shrinking demand. Declining consumer demand doubtlessly led to higher rates, which increased the overhead expenses of black clubs.[7]

Despite this breakup, John Connor managed to keep his Bacharach Giants intact. Redding and Lundy must have reconsidered their decision to leave Connor and Wilkins. They played the entire season for the Harlem magnates. The Giants embarked on a second spring training tour of the South and began the regular season in the Midwest against NNL clubs. Upon their return east, the Giants continued their rivalry with Hilldale for eastern supremacy. In July, the Bacharachs made a second midwestern tour, playing against the Detroit Stars, St. Louis Stars, and Kansas City Monarchs. They culminated their second midwestern tour with a 3-2 series defeat of the American Giants at Schorling Park. Keeping the Bacharach Giants together was a testament to John Connor's business acumen. He was an entrepreneur who had endured numerous conflicts—from both inside and outside his organization—as a black baseball club owner.[8]

By the middle of the 1922 season, Chicago *Defender* sportswriter Frank Young had begun mounting a campaign advocating the hiring of African American umpires. Young's campaign was in response to the poor officiating occurring at league games. Hiring black umpires would concurrently serve as an alternative to the predominantly white umpires union, who sent arbiters to Windy City parks to officiate semipro games. Semipro games in Chicago were officiated by members of the Umpires Official Association (UOA). Also referred to as the Baseball Umpires Association, it was customary for park managers to inform this union when games were scheduled. The UOA would send two umpires to arbitrate the game; usually, a given pair of umpires was always sent out to the same park. Park managers tolerated these umpires and their poor officiating primarily because otherwise the union would threaten to boycott their games. A simple solution to this dilemma was for the league to hire its own umpires.[9]

Young highlighted several examples to show how poor umpiring had reached its nadir at league games. In one game, a short fly ball to center field was caught on one bounce by the fielder, yet the umpire called the batter out. In the same game, the home plate umpire called a strike a ball even though the batter had swung at the pitch. When this was brought to the arbiter's attention, he corrected the call. To Young, poor officiating had led the "fans to become dissatisfied and attendance to drop off."[10]

It was within this context that Young made the case for hiring black umpires. Since the NNL was formed, Young and several other sportswriters had conducted a low-level campaign urging league officials to hire black arbiters. They supposedly were informed that "the time wasn't yet ripe." Not only was the time ripe, but, as Young stated, "in the language of the street, 'The darn pot is about to boil over.'" Young pointed to several black umpires throughout the country who should have the opportunity to arbitrate league games. If there were not enough qualified African Americans to serve as officials, then the league should train them. He encouraged his readers to send letters to the *Defender* to discuss the merits of hiring black umpires.[11]

Several readers responded to Young's call to discuss the pros and cons of hiring blacks to arbitrate league games. One fan from St. Louis pondered why former ballplayers did not serve as umpires: "When the president of the Negro baseball association begins to employ . . . [those] who in the past years were some of the best ball players on the diamond . . . then why in Heaven's name such men should not be employed . . . to arbitrate league games." Others recommended black umpires who officiated semipro games across the country. Ed O'Malley, a sportswriter for the *Los Angeles Times*, endorsed Billy Donaldson, who worked games in the City of Angels. Donaldson had officiated in the California Winter League, and he worked with a white umpire in league games. O'Malley found him "to be alert, impartial and fearless." Another fan in Washington, D.C., recommended a "Mr. Despert," a former player who officiated games in the nation's capital. This might have been Denny Despert, an outfielder who had played briefly for the Philadelphia Giants and the Lincoln Giants in the prewar era.[12]

Several sportswriters joined Young's campaign to hire African American umpires. They included J. M. Batchman, who asserted that the clamor for black umpires would not dissipate soon and that the reasons given for why the league had not hired black arbiters were unconvincing. Like the St. Louis fan, Batchman pointed to an increase in the number of former ballplayers leaving the game who could serve as a pool for prospective umpires. Several blacks who officiated college games could "acquaint themselves with credit to the game," he wrote.

Batchman pointed to the fact that a black operating an organization like the Negro National League was in a position to, and should, provide opportunity to a downtrodden people: "An "ump" is a Czar on the field, and it is not any too pleasing a spectacle to the average fan to have to witness this authority vested in white men—and this is said without an iota of prejudice—when capable colored men are denied so many opportunities. It is time for [a] Negro business controlled by Negro capital and seeking Negro patronage . . . to realize that if the Negro is big enough for a venture, there are other Negroes seeking opportunities who are capable of filling the minor positions at his disposal."[13] The call for hiring black umpires presented a dilemma for Rube Foster. In many ways, he was indifferent to their plight. He would deal with their predicament in a manner similar to the way the white Major Leagues dealt with its arbiters. Historian David Voigt stated that by the 1880s and well into the following decade the umpire had become the universal symbol of hate. The owners and administrators allowed this phenomenon to evolve because they discovered that villains, too, could be profitable. The effort to professionalize the status of umpires did not begin until the formation of the National League. Yet in 1882, it was the rival American Association that adopted the first full-time umpiring staff. Only one umpire officiated the game, and he was strictly on his own, at the mercy of rowdy players, ruthless managers, and heartless fans. Although it was apparent that the security of the umpires could have been assured with cooperation from league officials, owners, and sportswriters, at no time during the late nineteenth century was such joint action forthcoming.[14]

American League president Ban Johnson was one of the few administrators who sought to elevate the status of umpires. It began during his tenure as president of the Western League. He repeatedly reminded players that if they did not behave, they would be fined, suspended, or both. Club owners were cautioned to keep a closer rein on their players and managers, but they ignored Johnson's warnings. He discovered that if he suspended every player who deserved it, half the league would be out of business. Furthermore, Johnson was criticized for hiring unqualified people as umpires or assigning biased arbiters to cities where their partisanship affected their judgment. However, as biographer Eugene Murdock has pointed out, Johnson did demonstrate that rowdyism could be reduced and that firm leadership was the only answer to the problem.[15]

By the opening decade of the twentieth century, Ban Johnson had established the principle that league support of umpires was crucial to maintaining discipline on the diamond. By 1906, he had hired a staff of competent arbiters, paid them well, and backed their decisions. Johnson required his umpires to wire reports to him the night following a game in which disputes had occurred. He made his decisions based on this information. The AL president expected his umpires to be neatly attired because they represented the league. Whereas Johnson supported and protected his umpires fully, he was demanding of them and would punish the arbiters for disorderly conduct. Johnson was slow to adopt the double-umpire system, but by 1909 his American League would be employing it.

Rube Foster acknowledged the importance of league support to elevate the status of umpires in the NNL. However, Fay Young's campaign to provide opportunities for African Americans presented another challenge for Foster. Despite the presence of white influence in the NNL, the league was a predominantly black-owned and -operated enterprise. The NNL was in a position to embody the ideals reflected in the rhetoric of the new black leadership of the early twentieth century—the doctrine of self-help and racial solidarity. Foster recognized the need to open doors for blacks, but he felt they were not ready for the job: "The leading thinkers of the country today admit that it was cruel and unjust for four million slaves, uneducated and ignorant, to be turned loose as a free people without safeguarding the necessary things in life for them, preparing . . . them for the duties necessary as citizens and a free people; these same conditions confront baseball as far as umpires of the Race are concerned." Fay Young's campaign appeared to somewhat refute Foster's claim that blacks were not prepared to serve as umpires. More important, hiring black umpires was one of the ways that a black baseball entrepreneur had to address the wants and needs of the black middle-class spectator in order to guarantee continued patronage and increase consumer demand. Rube Foster, and later Ed Bolden, could no longer function as businessmen first and Race men second if they desired black middle-class support. Hiring black umpires was one way to address black consumer demand and simultaneously create a symbol of racial uplift.[16]

While Fay Young ratcheted up the pressure on Foster to hire black umpires, the NNL president had to face other challenges during this season of discontent. For the first time, Foster's scheduling system came under scrutiny in the black press. The primary complaint was against Foster's reluctance to schedule his American Giants away from Schorling Park. In other words, the Chicago American Giants made fewer road trips than the rest of the league clubs. The *Kansas City Call* reported that the American Giants had played only one Sunday game away from the Windy City, while two league clubs "kept the turnstile going for Schorling Park."[17]

Other complaints focused on the fact that several teams remained idle throughout the season because Foster ran the league like a booking agency. A wire service report stated that the Pittsburgh Keystones received "a raw deal" when Foster scheduled no games for the team in Forbes Field in June, when the National League Pirates were on the road. On July 4, both the Keystones and the Cleveland Tate Stars were idle. By September, J. M. Batchman was pointing out that the American Giants had not played in the St. Louis Stars' new ballpark. It led the Stars' management to schedule a lot of exhibition games that drew "only small crowds." Batchman also focused attention upon the disparity in the number of league games played by each club. By September, NNL clubs had played the following number of games:

LEAGUE CLUBS	GAMES PLAYED
Chicago	46
Kansas City	65
Indianapolis	73
Detroit	65
Pittsburgh	37
Cleveland	44
Cuban Stars	37
St. Louis	34

The lack of interest in weekday games was due essentially to this discrepancy in the playing schedule. The league, Batchman wrote, should attempt to create a balanced schedule and, more important, "Mr. Foster ought to get out of town more with his team." "The cry in [St. Louis] is for a game with Mr. Foster's American Giants," he added, "yet [the fans of] St. Louis . . . [have] been denied the sight of Rube's Warriors."[18]

In response, Foster stressed the sacrifice the Chicago American Giants had made as a member of the NNL regarding profits. When the other league clubs traveled, salary and travel expenses were essentially the only expenses they generated. He conveniently neglected to mention his 5 percent booking fee when they were playing league games. However, when the American Giants embarked on a road trip, Foster took "one of the highest paid baseball clubs" and the expenses generated from their home ballpark: "All this expense is on my shoulders together with traveling expenses and I have to accept a 25 percent loss . . . when at home. For any man to [cooperate] on an equal basis with anyone, he must carry equal liabilities." Foster placed his own economic interests above those of the league. He appeared unwilling to recognize that his economic interests and the league's had now become one and the same.[19]

By the same token, some of this expense that Foster incurred was offset by booking additional games at Schorling Park. In addition to league games, he continued to schedule white semipros at the American Giants' home grounds. Combined with operating in the Midwest's largest consumer market, scheduling fewer road trips allowed Rube Foster to leverage his position in the baseball marketplace. This was an advantage that the other league clubs never enjoyed.

The NNL winter meeting marked the beginning of the end of Rube Foster's goal of creating a national organization. Both the Pittsburgh Keystones and the Cleveland Tate Stars were in receivership. The Bacharach Giants failed to send a representative to the league meeting, leading the Board of Directors to believe the club intended "to drift to the outlaws." And then there was Ed Bolden's resignation as an associate member and demand for the return of his deposit. While the Board accepted the Hilldale president's resignation, it refused to return his deposit, citing a recent amendment to the constitution forbidding the refund. Bolden disavowed any knowledge of any recent amendment change or when it had been implemented. This action only served to escalate the conflict between Bolden and Foster.[20]

It appeared that Ed Bolden was already making plans to sever his ties with the NNL. In February 1922, a group of clubs formed the Philadelphia Baseball Association (PBA). In May, more than sixty clubs had joined the PBA, including the HBEC. Bolden played a prominent role in the new organization, and he was elected to the Board of Governors. Other administrators included Eddie Gottlieb, who would become Bolden's business partner in the 1930s, and Art Summers. Affiliating with the PBA seemed to be a response to the high cost of rail travel, a central concern among the club owners as reported in the black press. In essence, the HBEC attempted to create a more compact schedule and eliminate extended barnstorming tours.[21]

Hilldale's year-end book balance influenced Bolden's decision to leave the NNL. At the end of the 1921 season, Hilldale's balance was $13,799.01. The following year it dipped to $10,433.04. On December 23, 1922, the *New York Age* announced the formation of the Mutual Association of Eastern Colored Baseball Clubs. The first shots of the baseball war had been fired.[22]

The Rise of the Eastern Colored League

On December 16, 1922, club owners representing six eastern-based baseball teams met at the YMCA in Philadelphia and formed the Eastern Colored League. Representatives at the meeting included Nat Strong from the Brooklyn Royal Giants; James J. Keenan from the Lincoln Giants; Charles P. Spedden, George Rossiter, and John S. McDevitt from the Baltimore Black Sox; William Weeks, Thomas Jackson, and Henry Tucker from the Original Bacharach Giants; Alex Pompez from the Cuban Stars East; and Ed Bolden and Lloyd Thompson from the Hilldale AC. Six commissioners, one from each club, composed the governing board, while Bolden and Keenan were elected chairman and secretary-treasurer, respectively. On January 20, 1923, the ECL owners met again to tighten their organization. Bolden appointed a committee to draft a playing schedule and establish a policy regarding umpires. The arbiters would come under the commissioner's jurisdiction and would be "vested [with] the authority to run the games without molestation from players or managers of the clubs."[23]

The Baltimore Black Sox's entry into the ECL occurred at the same time its management endeavored to compete against the leading clubs in the East. The Black Sox began as a sandlot club and eventually rose to the ranks of an independent. On July 29, 1921, the *Baltimore Afro-American* reported that the Black Sox Baseball and Exhibition Club had been incorporated and stock in the amount of twenty thousand dollars would be sold at one hundred dollars per share. The following year, the club was sold to George Rossiter, a local white tavern owner, with Spedden retained as business manager. The team moved into a new ballpark, Maryland Park, and plans were made to renovate the grandstand and add box seats. In contrast to Philadelphia and Chicago, African American fan support was lacking in the Monumental City. An editorial in the *Baltimore Afro-American* indicted the city's black businessmen for this fan apathy. Supposedly, Rossiter and Spedden approached several prominent black businessmen to form a partnership but were turned down. Rossiter and Spedden hoped that league affiliation would stimulate local interest through the regular appearance of strong gate attractions.[24]

The Cuban Stars' affiliation with the ECL marked the start of Alejandro Pompez's long career as one of black baseball's leading entrepreneurs. Although raised partly in Key West and Tampa, Florida, Pompez spent his teenage years in Havana before moving to New York City. Upon his arrival there, Pompez secured employment as a cigar maker. Not long after that he opened a cigar store and reportedly started operating his numbers bank. It was during this time that Pompez established a relationship with Nat Strong. Historian Adrian Burgos points out that Pompez found a way to use his relationship with Strong to his advantage. He possessed access to an untapped market, New York's Latino community and the Caribbean as well. In other words, Strong established a business relationship with Pompez that was somewhat similar to the one he had with E. B. Lamar in the opening decade of the twentieth century.

As business manager of the National Association of Colored Baseball Clubs of the United States and Cuba, combined with Lamar's alliance with Abel Linares, Strong had access to the Cuban baseball market. Strong's mentorship prepared Alex Pompez for a career as a sports promoter and a baseball club owner.[25]

By assembling one of the strongest teams to emerge from Cuba, the Cuban Stars East, Pompez was able to develop connections beyond Strong's control that later allowed him to exercise greater independence than at first. The transnational position of his baseball operation was evident in the Stars' inaugural season. Prior to the start of the 1916 regular season, his Cuban Stars toured the Caribbean, including stops in Cuba, the Dominican Republic, and Puerto Rico. These barnstorming tours enabled the Stars' magnate to promote his team, scout new players, and establish a presence in baseball's transnational circuit. The Stars were led on the diamond by two of Cuba's premier players, Luis "El Mulo" Padron and Julio Rojo. In 1909, Padron led the Stars against the Brooklyn Royal Giants in the competition for the eastern colored championship. Although Padron came up on the short end in this series, it marked the beginning of El Mulo's emergence as one of the top left-handed pitchers from Cuba. Known for his excellent change of pace, Padron also possessed an exceptional fastball and a good curve ball; he was also a versatile outfielder and second baseman on the days he was not pitching. Julio Rojo was generally considered one of the best Cuban catchers in the Negro Leagues. Although he acquired a reputation as a "dirty ballplayer," Rojo was endowed with an accurate throwing arm behind the plate and excellent speed on the base paths.[26]

In response to the formation of the ECL, Rube Foster mounted a war of words in the black press. In an article published in several black newspapers, Foster endeavored to diminish Bolden's role in the ECL's organizational effort and place the spotlight on Nat Strong as the real power behind the league. He began by stating it was useless to "camouflage" the real motive for forming the league. Strong had "taken 10 percent from the gross earnings of black clubs for 20 years, and has never built a fence for them to use and never will." The Royals' owner believed in the organization of white clubs and building a fine park for them to use while relegating the Royal Giants to a traveling team. Foster was referring to Dexter Park, the new home of Strong's Bushwicks in Long Island. The NNL president then turned his attention to the reasons why Bolden resigned his associate membership. He reportedly had no objections about the HBEC withdrawing from the NNL. Foster supposedly asked Bolden to get an agreement from the ECL owners not to tamper with the players under contract in the Midwest circuit. If such an agreement were forthcoming, then the league would return Bolden's thousand-dollar deposit. This contradicts the NNL Board's earlier claim that an amendment to the constitution prevented the Board from refunding the Hilldale president's deposit. Nevertheless, the NNL would not schedule games with the eastern clubs nor make it "compulsory for the Eastern clubs to come west." Foster merely wanted an agreement respecting the contracts of players in both leagues.[27]

Foster raised the issue of race regarding the ownership of eastern black clubs. He conveniently neglected the fact that the ECL ownership was a culturally diverse group. With Bolden, Tucker, and Jackson (all black) representing Hilldale and the Original Bacharach Giants respectively, and Pompez (Cuban) running the Cuban Stars, the only white owners in the ECL were Strong (Royal Giants), Keenan (Lincoln Giants), and Rossiter and Spedden (Black Sox).

Foster reminded his readers that he had played in the East under Strong when the players received only one hundred dollars for Sunday games. White owners exploited the players, paying them low salaries and two fifteen-cent meals a day. This, he said, was the primary reason why the Chicago magnate left the Philadelphia Giants for the Leland Giants. "Can you imagine a colored club playing to 10,000 people," Foster added, "and receiving only the limit of five hundred dollars, and then giving 10 percent to Strong to play in New York, and Bolden, to play him, must give him a percentage."[28]

Foster concluded his article by addressing the players leaving the NNL to play in the East. He pointed to Bolden's signing of John Henry Lloyd from John Connor's Bacharach Giants. Foster attempted to establish himself as a man of principle, taking a moral stance against player jumping and stressing that it was a dishonest practice. The NNL had tried to avert a war, but Bolden and Strong were intent on starting one, Foster claimed. He stated that he would not attempt to stop the player exodus, but that he would at the proper time "drive a blow that would not be easy to get rid of."[29]

In response, Bolden mounted his own PR campaign in the black press. He attacked the league president for raising the issue of race regarding the ownership of black clubs. "Why," exclaimed Bolden, "does Mr. Foster not publish the fact that Schorling Park, for whom the park is named, and Foster is but a chattel of his white boss?" Bolden minimized the fact that Schorling Park was the American Giants' home ballpark, allowing Foster to build and maintain a fan base. Foster and Schorling had also expanded the park's seating capacity to accommodate the fans and to further stimulate consumer demand. In contrast, under Strong's reign, the Brooklyn Royal Giants languished as a traveling team, and this would become a source of contention throughout the ECL's history. Nevertheless, Bolden continued to point to the presence of whites in the NNL leadership. The secretary of the league was J. L. Wilkinson of the Kansas City Monarchs. Bolden accurately stated that the HBEC had never paid Strong to book the AC's games, while accusing Foster of "[pillaging] every club in the Western Association for [5] percent of their gross earnings." Paying this booking fee was another reason the HBEC had left the midwestern circuit. Bolden stated that Foster's "Sunday games in the West don't mean anything to us, as we have received more money for a twilight engagement in Philadelphia . . . than a Sunday game in the West, with over a thousand miles of railroad fair [sic] to cover."[30]

Foster challenged either Strong or Bolden to a debate on the "merits and demerits of the two leagues." Bolden accepted, and he suggested that the league president take part of Hilldale's thousand-dollar deposit and rent the Academy of Music in Philadelphia so that thousands of fans may attend and give the balance to help disabled ballplayers. Bolden resumed his verbal assault, indicating that the NNL was nothing more than a booking agency. For example, if the Bacharach Giants played Hilldale in Philadelphia and the Bacharachs amassed a gross revenue of $1,000 and Hilldale $1,200, a 5 percent fee was affixed to the earnings.

The Bacharachs would pay $50, while Hilldale would pay $60, placing $110 in Foster's coffer. This could possibly explain why Tucker and Jackson severed ties with Connor and Wilkins.

The public debate never took place, but Bolden fired one last shot at the NNL president. He asked why NNL clubs play in parks where they give from 20 to 25 percent of the gross receipts to white men and 10 percent to Foster. This was why, Bolden said, four of Foster's clubs had already failed: "Mr. Foster may not fail, but he is digging his own grave through his greed for personal gain, unless he becomes fair and gives the team an even break."[31]

A former NNL official and Charles Spedden also took Foster to task about the way he ran his league. W. S. Ferrance, former secretary of the St. Louis Giants, reinforced Bolden's claim that the NNL was primarily a booking agency. Concurrently, he also criticized the NNL president's czar-like rule in handling league affairs. Trouble began for the Giants at the NNL's inaugural meeting. Due to the illness of Charles Mills, the Giants sent Lorenzo Cobb to represent the team with the instruction not to sign any papers that would bind the organization to the proposed league. Ferrance stated the transfer of Jimmie Lyons to Detroit was "a hard blow" for the St. Louis team. Not only was Lyons the Giants' best player, but also their top gate attraction. Ferrance accurately stated that clubs like St. Louis and Indianapolis had been booking their clubs for years, but league affiliation had placed these clubs under Foster's network. C. I. Taylor and Mills opposed the booking arrangement whereby each club paid a 5 percent fee for each league game played. However, they supposedly agreed to this arrangement with the understanding that a new system would be developed. But the new arrangement never materialized. Foster's booking system resulted in league clubs becoming reliant on Sunday games in Chicago. Ferrance also voiced his frustration with disputes being resolved in a undemocratic manner, especially when the American Giants were accused. A manager filing a protest against the Chicago club would "have to file a complaint against Mr. Foster, mail it to Secretary Foster, and then President Foster would have to decide."[32]

Baltimore Black Sox business manager Charles Spedden attacked Foster for claiming that the formation of the ECL was organized to make war against Foster. "When the men who head the new association met in Philadelphia," replied Spedden, "not once was Foster's name mentioned." Black baseball was too large an enterprise to be controlled by one man, and it would be in Foster's best interests to recognize that. The Black Sox's business manager cleverly suggested that eastern and western clubs play a series of interleague games, with the winner of both leagues to play in a World Series. In regards to player jumping, ECL owners had not induced players to jump, but if dissatisfied players in the NNL left on their accord, Spedden saw no reason why the new league should turn them down. The propaganda war placed the spotlight on the NNL's inner workings, and it reflected badly on Foster. But although he may have lost the battle, he had not totally lost the propaganda war.[33]

In the midst of the propaganda war, the black press reported several NNL players signing with the new league. They embodied John Henry Lloyd's observation that "where the money was that was where I was." John Connor's Bacharach Giants was the first casualty of war, undoubtedly much to the liking of Nat Strong, Ed Bolden, and James Keenan. The Lincolns' owner immediately signed Oliver Marcelle, High Pockets Hudspeth, and Charles Mason. Charles Spedden lured Julio Rojo away from the Bacharachs for his Baltimore Black Sox. Not only did Connor lose his star players, but his business partner, Baron Wilkins, was murdered in a dispute over the sale of bootleg whiskey. It marked the end of John Connor's long and tumultuous career as a black baseball club owner. Connor elevated the Brooklyn Royal Giants to the ranks of a touring team using the familiar strategy of going where the money was and creating a demand for his team in several locales. Cutthroat competition led to his loss of the Royals to Nat Strong and his temporary departure from the black game. Connor's partnership with Wilkins, Thomas Jackson, and Henry Tucker allowed him to spearhead the most successful African American management team to operate a baseball club in the New York market. Connor's leasing agreement with Charles Ebbets exemplified his business acumen and allowed him to undermine the Strong-Keenan alliance that had been effective in marginalizing African American efforts to operate black clubs in Gotham. Connor's business savvy enabled Rube Foster's NNL to tap into baseball's largest market, a fact the league president never acknowledged. With Connor out of black baseball, New York's black baseball market would remain under white control. In 1926, John Connor died.[34]

Several other NNL players migrated east for what they perceived as greener pastures in the ECL. Keenan signed pitchers Dave Brown and Big Ed Rile from the American Giants. The *Defender* reported that Rile had been working as an "agent" in the ECL's pursuit to lure top-level players from the NNL. Bolden added pitchers George Carr and Frank Warfield from the American Giants and Detroit Stars, respectively. Nat Strong snatched Dick Redding from Connor's Bacharach Giants. Ben Taylor, the brother of C. I., jumped to Washington, and along with local businessman George Robinson formed the Potomacs in the nation's capital. Taylor had managed to induce catcher Mark Eggleston, third baseman Harry Jeffries, and shortstop Speco Clark to jump their contracts, marking the beginning of the end for the Indianapolis ABCs.[35]

Throughout the player exodus from the NNL and the propaganda war in the black press, eastern owners worked during the season to tighten their organization. The commissioners initially agreed to a forty-five-game schedule, and a fund was established to purchase a league pennant which the ECL champion would receive. ECL owners made efforts to publish statistics throughout the year to stimulate fan interest. Batting averages and the league standings were published, but the commissioners evidently compiled no pitching statistics.[36]

In spite of this cooperative effort, the ECL proved no more successful than the NNL in obtaining a balanced schedule. The presence of two traveling teams, the Cuban Stars and the Brooklyn Royal Giants, undermined any attempt at schedule balancing. It was apparent from the outset that the commissioner would have trouble getting Nat Strong to abide by the league schedule. By July, his Royal Giants had played only eight league games and only fifteen one month later. The commissioners met several times during the season to adjust the playing schedule to accommodate the disparity in the number of league games played. The Royal Giants improved somewhat and by September had played thirty-six games. Hilldale and the Bacharach Giants came the closest to completing the schedule, playing forty-nine and forty-two games, respectively. At the end of the season, Hilldale was declared the pennant winner.[37]

Overall, the ECL owners appeared to be happy with their inaugural season. The commissioners expressed their intention of remaining in the league and favored expanding to eight clubs. In contrast, the NNL's season was a virtual roller-coaster ride.[38]

Sustaining a Fledgling League

The Negro National League began the 1923 season with its most compact circuit in its brief history. Toledo was awarded a franchise, and players from the disbanded Pittsburgh Keystones and other league clubs were to make up its player roster. The Toledo club would play its games in Toledo's American Association park when the minor league club was on the road. A new team was organized in Milwaukee, composed of the remaining players from John Connor's Bacharach Giants. The revised circuit was made up of the following teams: Chicago American Giants, Cuban Stars, Detroit Stars, Indianapolis ABCs, Kansas City Monarchs, Milwaukee Bears, St. Louis Stars, and Toledo. The revamped league appeared to alleviate some of its overhead expenses brought on by the high cost of rail travel.[39]

With the revised league settled, Rube Foster wrote an article to praise the fans for their support and their patience. The PR move unquestionably served to maintain black-middle class support for Foster and his NNL. He began by citing an increase in attendance throughout the league after the first month of the season. The reports bolstered the league president's "waning spirits" and provided the stimulus to continue to "build up a great league." He added, "[Often times] I've felt that the task was hopeless—I felt ready to give up—yet something kept my feet in the pathway of progress and always onward and upward toward the goal." Foster proceeded to ingratiate the fans for standing by their "home town clubs and [keeping] the turnstiles turning." They deserved all the credit for the success the league enjoyed to that time, he wrote.[40]

Despite this rosy forecast, by July the compact circuit had begun to crumble. On July 15, the Toledo franchise disbanded and its players were turned over to the league. Fans in Milwaukee did not provide adequate support and the Bears were transferred to Toledo, taking on that club's name. At first, a group of African American businessmen from Cleveland lobbied to replace the vacancy left by Milwaukee. The Cleveland Tate Stars were in receivership due to debts accumulated from the previous season. Local businessman George Hooper paid the team's debts; however, the Tate Stars failed to come up with the thousand-dollar deposit to obtain a franchise. Rumors circulated that two southern teams, the Birmingham Black Barons and the Memphis Red Sox, had filed applications for league entry, but the NNL limped through the remainder of the season with only seven clubs.[41]

Franchise shifting contributed to the ongoing scheduling dilemma. Before the season began, the Board of Directors devised a 105-game schedule. The first 15 games between league clubs would count in the standings. The remaining games would be classified as exhibitions.[42] By late July, the disparity in the number of games played between league clubs, combined with franchise shifting, made this aspiration untenable:

LEAGUE CLUBS	GAMES PLAYED
Kansas City	60
Indianapolis	56
St. Louis	49
Chicago	47
Detroit	42
Milwaukee	41
Cuban Stars	37
Toledo	26

By mid-August, another league club had complained about Foster's scheduling practices. On August 17, the *Kansas City Call* reported that the Monarchs would play no more league games until early September. At the same time, the American Giants and Detroit Stars would continue playing league games. League officials supposedly knew that the American Association's Kansas City Blues would be home in the latter part of August. With this information in hand, it would have been an easy matter to switch the Monarchs to Detroit, Chicago, or any other league city. Foster still refused to schedule his American Giants in other league cities. His club had been in Kansas City only two times during the season. Detroit Stars' owner Tenny Blount began to rebel against Foster's scheduling methods. Blount's Stars were scheduled to play the Monarchs in Kansas City, but he refused to make the trip, citing high travel expenses. The editorial in the *Call* demonstrated why there remained a disparity in the number of league games played. The Monarchs had made several road trips during the year to Toledo, Milwaukee, and St. Louis. On the other hand, the Detroit Stars had yet to play in Kansas City. Three clubs—Toledo, Milwaukee, and St. Louis—had played the Monarchs at home twice, and the Cuban Stars had made one appearance at Muehlebach Field. "If the Negro National League is to survive and retain the interest of the fans," the editor concluded, "the schedule should be arranged so that the pennant race is a real one, with all teams playing an equal number of games with each other and with 'feed-box' exhibitions limited to before and after the season."[43]

In contrast to the scheduling dilemma and the constant franchise shifting, the hiring of African American umpires appeared to be the league's saving grace in an otherwise chaotic season. On April 21, 1923, the *Defender* reported the NNL had signed seven black umpires for the upcoming season. It marked the successful end of Faye Young's four-year campaign to urge the league to hire black umpires. Billy Donaldson was the first African American umpire hired. He had worked on the West Coast with an interracial umpiring crew as well as with a fellow black official. Bert Gholston, from Oakland, California, had worked with Donaldson on the West Coast and was highly recommended. Two umpires from New York, Caesar Jamison and William Embry, and two from New Orleans, Leon Augustine and Lucian Snaer, rounded out the umpiring crew that worked the 1923 season. Jamison had reportedly worked games with National League umpire Bill Klem and called balls and strikes for Major League players like Carl Mays and Waite Hoyt. Another umpire, Tom Johnson, a former American Giants pitcher, was held in reserve.[44]

During the course of the season, Fay Young encouraged the fans to give the black umpires their support. He asked the fans to treat the black arbiters "with the same accord that they do a baseball player or an actor who are applauded for their good work." Young reminded his readers that officiating a game is a daunting task for an umpire. Therefore, the fans should applaud them "for good decisions and good work." When the men in blue come onto the field prior to the start of the game, the fans should express their "appreciation by applauding." The approach he urged differed drastically from the way the late-nineteenth-century white sportswriters vilified the umpires on their sport pages. Yet Young's rhetoric reflected the ways in which black middle-class leadership waged another, more subtle kind of battle. Hiring African American umpires exemplified Booker Washington's philosophy of racial advancement through self-help. The Negro National League provided opportunities for blacks, and these African American arbiters would serve as a symbol of racial uplift and race pride.[45]

Reserve umpire Tom Johnson reinforced Young's call for the fans to support the black arbiters. Johnson wrote an article, published in several black newspapers, extolling Rube Foster for his progressive thinking and making the decision to hire black umpires. The majority of the fans did not, Johnson stated, believe that it was possible "for Colored umpires to handle a ball game." The league president was not "discouraged by the many protests that came from the so-called wise ones who only believe in white supremacy and domination." Instead, Foster inaugurated what Johnson called the "Umpire System" and hired arbiters like Donaldson and Jamison, competent officials who could make the system work. Johnson claimed these men were "making good."[46]

Hiring these African American umpires became a source of racial tension. In early August, the American Giants and the Cuban Stars transferred their league game from Schorling Park to Pyott's Park, located on Chicago's West Side. Black umpires officiated the game despite the protest of park manager William Niesen. Since Niesen did not stipulate what color the umpires should be and a rental agreement had been signed, he had to concede. When the white umpires from the Umpires Officials Association arrived at the park, they found that Foster had started the game five minutes early. He stated he did not call for UOA umpires. Foster's actions marked the start of a feud between himself and the UOA.[47]

In mid-October, the American Giants were scheduled to play Niesen's Pyotts at the same location. A near race riot occurred when American Giants catcher John Beckwith was accused of allowing an errant throw to hit the home plate umpire. Pyott outfielder Ray Demmitt, a white southerner, took a swing at Beckwith. A fistfight took place, with both benches and the fans pouring out onto the field. When the police restored order, the game was called because of darkness.[48]

On October 20, the *Defender* reported that the UOA had sent a letter to Foster, stating the union would boycott American Giants games as long as Beckwith was on the roster. Previously, Foster and Niesen had met with UOA officials to protest the game. At that time, the UOA had not made any objections regarding Beckwith. Rather, they sent a letter "at the eleventh hour" stating their intentions and allowing no time for Foster to respond.[49]

Foster phoned Logan Squares' owner James J. Callahan to inform him that the American Giants would not play their scheduled game. Concurrently, he sent a letter to UOA officials stating he would make no effort to protest the union's proposed action. Foster reminded the UOA that at no time in the past had such an organization possessed the authority to carry out the intended actions of the umpires' association. He also stated that there was no agreement that required him to accept umpires from the union to officiate semipro games. Foster berated the UOA for not disciplining Demmitt for attacking Beckwith, the incident which led to the near riot in the first place. These developments led Foster to cancel his game with the Logan Squares. This decision incensed James Callahan, who had sold a substantial number of tickets, and he appealed to Foster to reconsider. After all, both men had been doing business together for over a decade. To remedy the situation, Foster and Callahan chose men from their respective squads to officiate the game, the Logans winning 1-0 in ten innings.[50]

Later in October, the American Giants were scheduled to play a series of games with the American League's Detroit Tigers. Fay Young asked Foster who would arbitrate the games. Foster replied he would get Tom Johnson along with a white umpire to officiate them.[51]

Aside from the worthy introduction of black umpire, the 1923 season was marred by the continuing practice of franchise shifting and by Foster's unwillingness to schedule road trips for his American Giants, each contributing to the league's scheduling dilemma. As the 1924 season approached, the war between the leagues over players resumed.

1924: THE WAR CONTINUES

At the ECL winter meeting, the commissioners adopted the slogan "bigger and better" to mark the league's objective of strengthening their organization. Ed Bolden was reelected as chairman, and the commissioners considered several applications to be one of the two new teams that were going to be added to the circuit. They accepted the applications of the Harrisburg Giants and Washington Potomacs. C. W. "Colonel" Strothers, a former city policeman and a local entrepreneur, ran the Harrisburg Giants. Strothers formed the Giants as a sandlot team in 1908 and eventually transformed it into an independent club. The *Philadelphia Tribune* reported that the Giants won the city championship from the Motive Power Club, one "of the strongest white clubs that . . . represented Harrisburg . . . [in] the Tri-State League." George W. Robinson, a Philadelphia "capitalist," and Ben Taylor operated the Washington Potomacs.[52]

An expanded playing schedule was adopted and a policy designed to govern the players' and umpires' behavior during league games was drafted. Bolden appointed a scheduling committee that included himself, Ben Taylor, Charles Spedden, James Keenan, and Nat Strong. The season was extended from fifty to seventy games, with each club playing each of the others ten times. The presence of two traveling teams made it difficult to draft a schedule to ensure a league club would play an equal number of games at their respective home ballparks. To remedy the situation, the scheduling committee devised the schedule in a way that all clubs would end the season playing seventy league games. Before the start of the season, the ECL owners considered adopting a rotation system for their umpires. However, because the season was about to start, the matter was tabled for future consideration., The league, though, did approve "strict rules" to govern the game. The players must be courteous to the fans, and only the team captain or manager could represent his team if a dispute occurred on the field. Umpire baiting by the players or managers was punishable with a twenty-five-dollar fine for the first offense, fifty dollars for a second offense, and "drastic action" for any further offenses. Finally, umpires were to use discretion in ejecting players, and decisions had to be rendered promptly.[53]

ECL owners continued to lure NNL players to the East. The Lincoln Giants and the Baltimore Black Sox were the most aggressive clubs in signing players from the Midwest. James Keenan had made several improvements to the Protectory Oval, the Lincolns' home ballpark. A new clubhouse was built, and the entrance to the park gave "the appearance of a big league park." Several new players were signed, including Harry Kenyon, an outfielder from the Chicago American Giants, and Gerald Williams, a catcher from the Indianapolis ABCs. Charles Spedden signed Pete Hill as the Black Sox's new manager. Hill had been the player-manager for the Milwaukee Bears before the club was transferred to Toledo. The *Baltimore Afro-American* reported that Hill was given full "authority over the players" and could hire and fire them, provided he made the Sox a winning team. He attracted two players from the ABCs, second baseman Connie Day and third baseman Henry Blackmon. Hill added outfielders Wade Johnson and Jud Wilson from the Detroit Stars and Birmingham Black Barons respectively. The biggest acquisition of the 1924 season was the signing of Oscar Charleston by Colonel Strothers as the player-manager of the Harrisburg Giants. Charleston's ambition to become a manager, along with his unwillingness to play for the ABCs' club owner, Mrs. C. I. Taylor, led to his migration eastward. Whereas Charleston would be the biggest acquisition in 1924, he would soon become the ECL's most outspoken critic.[54]

Both the ECL and the NNL faced an unexpected competitor for the signing of top-level players. On January 4, 1924, the *Baltimore Afro-American* reported that the Homestead Grays had signed American Giants' catcher John Beckwith. The reported signing of Beckwith marked the start of the long career of the Grays' owner, Cumberland "Cum" Posey, as one of black baseball's leading entrepreneurs. Born in 1891 in Homestead, Pennsylvania, Posey gravitated toward sports at a young age, playing sandlot football and baseball. He enrolled at Holy Ghost University (renamed Duquesne University) and Penn State, where he excelled as a basketball player. In 1911, Posey joined the Murdock Grays, a local sandlot baseball team that was later renamed the Homestead Grays. Posey played in the outfield, and in 1916 he became the Grays' manager. In the following years, Posey began to transform the Grays from a local club to a leading independent, competing for the best players in black baseball. In addition to Beckwith, Posey reportedly signed Dizzy Dismukes and Gerald Williams.[55]

Evidently, Posey was unable to retain either Beckwith or Williams. Williams had already signed with the Lincoln Giants and chose to remain with Keenan's club out of a sense of loyalty. Beckwith, on the other hand, was apparently released, and Pete Hill signed the catcher for the Baltimore Black Sox. Later in the year, the Grays' magnate attempted to induce Beckwith to rejoin his club but was unsuccessful. Posey made overtures to several Hilldale players. He attempted to sign catcher Bizz Mackey and pitcher Jesse "Nip" Winters, but both players remained with the AC. Posey was unsuccessful in landing these players, but he would become a thorn in the proverbial side of both leagues in the upcoming years.[56]

In the midst of this unwanted competition from Cumberland Posey, the ECL commissioners had to contend with Nat Strong's unwillingness to abide by the league schedule. In mid-May, conflict arose because Strong wanted Keenan's Lincoln Giants to play Harrisburg in the opening game of the season instead of his Royals. Keenan refused, leading the Royals' owner to declare that he would remain in the ECL but would boycott games with the Lincoln Giants. Strong's proposed boycott led Keenan to take the matter up with the commissioners who, by a unanimous vote, expelled the Royal Giants from the league. When the Royals' magnate saw that the commissioners meant business, he wired Bolden in Philadelphia to get the board to reconsider. Strong's expulsion lasted only two days, and his Royals' participation in league games would increase somewhat. Yet they would play only forty-two of the seventy league games.[57]

The brief expulsion and reinstatement of the Brooklyn Royal Giants was only the beginning of Nat Strong's placing his business interests before those of the league's. Like Foster, Strong was unwilling to recognize the fact that as a member of the ECL, his business interests and the league's were now one and the same. It may be that he remained in the league because of his declining influence over the New York semipro scene. As the *New York Age* pointed out, Strong booked only two black clubs, his Royals and the Cuban Stars, and had control of only two parks. To revive interest in semipro ball, New York City became a member of the National Baseball Federation (NBF), which further undermined Strong's booking control. The NBF's origins were in the Midwest, where cities like Cleveland and Detroit became hotbeds for "amateur" leagues that contained many semipros. New York's affiliation with the NBF led to the formation of the New York Baseball Association, of which the Lincoln Giants became a member. The association controlled several parks throughout the city. The *Age* was critical of Strong as a consequence of his unwillingness to provide a home ballpark for the Royals in New York. This would also become a source of dispute with his fellow ECL owners in the following years. While the ECL commissioners grappled with their maverick owner from Brooklyn, the NNL experienced another chaotic season.[58]

By the 1923 winter meeting, franchise shifting had become commonplace in Negro National League affairs. Applications from teams in several cities, including John Matthews's Dayton Marcos, were considered for league entry. The Marcos were dropped from the league after the inaugural season but continued as an independent. The league accepted the application from the Birmingham Black Barons. The Black Barons were owned by Joe Rush, who purchased the players from the defunct Milwaukee Bears for a reported two thousands dollars and hired Sam Crawford, the former manager of the Kansas City Monarchs, as the team's new skipper. In March, the league added the Cleveland Browns, and for the second time in the league's history, Sol White served as a field manager. Apparently, the Browns had their own ballpark. The

Pittsburgh Courier reported that George Hooper would make improvements on Hooper Field, including the renovation of the clubhouse and the installation showers for the players. Thus, the NNL began the 1924 season with the following teams: the Birmingham Black Barons, Chicago American Giants, Cleveland Browns, Cuban Stars, Detroit Stars, Indianapolis ABCs, Kansas City Monarchs, and St. Louis Stars. The Dayton Marcos were accepted as an associate member.[59]

The league rehired the black umpires for the upcoming season. Foster instructed the club owners to make sure the players did not engage in any "violent or unnecessary" confrontations with the arbiters. Such actions had a tendency to intimidate the umpires and create a false impression among the fans that the arbiters were incompetent. Tenny Blount also stressed the need to curb rowdyism at league games. If rowdyism was not brought under control, he said, the decisions the umpires made would eventually lead the fans to unjustly think the players had good reason to protest. Supposedly, appropriate league regulation was enacted to address the situation.[60]

The 1923 winter meeting provided some information, albeit anecdotal, regarding the league's finances. On December 22, 1923, the *Defender* published the notes of the sportswriter covering the league meeting to reveal the NNL's financial picture. This, no doubt, was part of Foster's overall PR campaign to show the league was on solid economic ground despite the constant franchise shifting and loss of several top players to the ECL. The total paid attendance for the 1923 season was 402,436, and the total receipts were $197,218. The league incurred the following expenses:

Player salaries	$101,000
Railroad Fares	$ 25,212
Board and Street Car Fare	$ 9,136
Balls	$ 7,965
Umpires	$ 7,498
Club Advertising	$ 7,500
Other Expenses	$ 4,164
TOTAL	$162,475

After deducting the expenses, the NNL had a book balance of $34,793, which gave each of the seven clubs $7,439. This must have been a misprint by the *Defender*, because the correct amount should have been $4,970.43 for each club.[61]

Concurrently, Rube Foster resumed his public relations campaign in the black press. The fundamental purposes of this PR campaign were to respond to the criticism he was receiving for the way he ran his NNL and to reassure the public that the league was on solid economic ground, despite the constant franchise shifting and the player defections to the ECL. He began with the familiar tactic of providing a brief financial forecast of the league that differed somewhat from the financial picture the *Defender* presented. According to him, the NNL paid out $423,000 in player salaries and $165,000 for park rental. Travel and accommodations in the form of railroad fares, car fares, and room and board amounted to $130,000. This assessment did not include incidental expenses like advertising, equipment, and umpires' salaries.[62]

Foster then turned his attention to the criticism he received regarding scheduling. Sunday games remained the most profitable for league clubs, and there were only twenty-seven Sundays and holidays in a playing season. Detroit and Chicago had eighteen Sundays during the season, while Kansas City, Indianapolis, and St. Louis had eleven. On several occasions, weekday games had been "a complete loss," and clubs had to cover expenses from their own coffers to pay the additional costs. These comments were Foster's justification for why the NNL could not achieve a balanced playing schedule comparable to the white Major Leagues.[63]

In a second article, Foster addressed the "numerous criticism" of himself that was published in the *Baltimore Afro-American*. He indicted the weekly for allowing several individuals to publish "unreliable" information about himself and the league. These stories, he wrote, created a false impression among the fans about the baseball war. Foster suggested the *Afro-American* should investigate the facts thoroughly prior to publication: "Certainly anyone that wanted to do a beneficial thing for [the] readers or a race, would surely investigate the real facts, rather than abuse what little progress the individual had made." When the investigation was complete," he continued, it would be better for the paper to be discreet in its criticism "if such exposure would do more harm than good." An example of poor investigation, Foster claimed, was a supposed comment attributed to the league president about his refusal to play a series with ECL teams. Foster admitted he received a letter from the *Afro-American* sports editor but did not respond to it because "the men [who] operate the Eastern League know how to do such things." In other words, the ECL owners were responsible for the absence of scheduled games between the East and West.[64]

Rube Foster attempted to downplay player defections to the ECL and simultaneously place the spotlight on Nat Strong as the real authority in the eastern league. The league president had never asked any player to remain in the West and declared there were "more players idle than employed." There existed, he asserted, a reservoir of talent for the NNL club owners to choose from. In an attempt to distinguish himself from Strong, Foster highlighted the opportunities he created for African Americans to learn the business aspects of the sport. He declared, "My men and associates count tickets, schedule games, make all arrangements, carry the money, and know something of the business." In contrast, Foster said, Strong had taken 10 percent from the revenues of black clubs for thirty years and had "never let [blacks] count a ticket, learn anything about the business, and even yet run your league with a club in it, and do not allow them at his own park." No doubt such comments were targeted to the African American middle-class leadership at a time when racial uplift served as its mantra. Hiring African American umpires and putting them on the league's payroll gave Foster the justification to make this claim.[65]

Foster declared there could be "no peace in baseball" as long as there was no agreement between the leagues to respect each other's players under contract. He repeated his assertion about returning Ed Bolden's deposit if the Hilldale president could secure a nontampering agreement. Bolden would not do this because he, along with Strong and Keenan, wanted the NNL's players. A second overture was supposedly made that would have allowed the ECL to keep the players they currently had as long as they agreed not to tamper with players in the future. In Foster's view, the ECL owners did not possess the ability to develop players and so had to steal them.

Finally, Foster suggested that the Eastern Colored League would collapse under the weight of the higher salaries the owners paid as a result of the war. In other words, he was saying, the ECL could not generate enough revenue to cover salary and other expenses and at the same time turn a profit. This was why Foster would not engage the East in a bidding war for players. "I would fight back," he proclaimed, "but there is nothing to gain, [and] I am content to see [the players] go." The higher salaries paid by Bolden and Strother played into the hands of Strong and Keenan. "They [Strong and Keenan] do not care who carries the freight," Foster added, "as long as it does not cost them anything. When they are broke, which is certain, they will have the East as formerly and will pay what they please." Given the fact that Keenan had renovated the Protectory Oval and signed several new players, Foster was engaging in the same tactic of which he accused the *Afro-American* contributors: misrepresenting the facts. Regardless, the existing state of black baseball would not deter Rube Foster, and the league president could "take the medicine." He made no mention of whether his fellow league owners could also take the medicine.[66]

Reaction to Rube Foster's PR campaign from league officials and sportswriters told a different story. It began with rumors circulating that the NNL would employ legal counsel to force players to respect their contracts. Foster reportedly had hired attorneys to seek injunctions to protect the contract rights of the league clubs. The supposed court action led George Rossiter, owner of the Black Sox, to declare that Foster's "back is against the wall." He added, "I have just gotten the signed contract this morning of [William] Force, leading pitcher of the Detroit Stars. We have some six other men signed up and have forwarded them advance money." Rossiter pointed out that these players had signed with the Black Sox before signing with any NNL clubs. He saw no problems involving contract rights.[67]

The Black Sox's business manager, Charles Spedden, mounted a counteroffensive to Foster's PR campaign. He pointed out that salaries in the NNL were "notoriously low" and presented an explanation of why the ECL was able to pay higher salaries. Salaries for star players in the NNL ranged from $150 to $175 a month. The high cost of rail travel made it difficult for the NNL to pay higher salaries. In contrast, the compact ECL circuit reduced the cost of travel, which allowed the club owners to pay $100 a month more "without feeling any strain." Spedden engaged in a PR tactic similar to that used by Foster to show that the Baltimore Black Sox were on solid economic ground. The Black Sox organization owned and operated a ballpark worth $35,000, and the management had never missed a payday. The Black Sox had a twenty-one-man roster for the 1923 season but would have only fifteen players for the 1924 season. This allowed the management to increase the overall team salary by about $100 a month. Spedden was demonstrating that the Baltimore Black Sox would not collapse under the strain of paying higher salaries as Foster had suggested would occur. However, he, like Foster, made no mention of whether his fellow owners could withstand the higher salary demand.[68]

Kansas City Call sportswriter Carl Beckwith offered an insightful assessment of the baseball war. Beckwith stated that the ECL's primary motive for raiding the NNL for players was to cripple the latter league to a point where it could not function. With the NNL out of the way, the eastern owners could drop the Eastern League cloak, have their choice of the best players in the country, and return to independent ball. With the number of players far exceeding demand, salaries would be reduced. For the time being, it was in the ECL owners' best interest to pay higher salaries because they could afford to. Beckwith added that the NNL owners could not stand to lose money indefinitely, and he pointed to J. L. Wilkinson losing a reported eight thousand dollars for the 1923 season.[69]

Two factors were linked to Beckwith's assertion that the NNL owners could not continue to endure these financial losses. First, the Indianapolis ABCs were dropped from the NNL. From the league's inception, the ABCs were one of the league's strongest clubs, but it fell on hard times after the death of C. I. Taylor. A dispute arose within the Taylor family over who would assume the presidency of the club. According to

C. I.'s brother, Ben, he was to take over the club, but the job fell to the late owner's wife. From the outset, Mrs. C. I. Taylor resisted the players' unwillingness to play for her because she was a woman, which resulted in several of them jumping to the ECL. It also led to Ben Taylor leaving the team to become the co-owner of the Washington Potomacs.[70]

A statement published in several black newspapers explained why the Board of Directors expelled the Indianapolis ABCs from the league. Essentially, the ABCs had accumulated so much debt that it was dropped from the NNL to enable the league "to save itself." The ABCs supposedly had no funds to pay the players' salaries, and they had a "personal obligation" to Foster. Outstanding debts were also owed to the league, and the management team could not put together a club that could play "a good brand of semipro ball." These reasons reportedly led the club owners to conclude that "the continuance of the club in the league would prove costly and perhaps disastrous to all the clubs of the league."[71]

Mrs. C. I. Taylor took exception to the press release that explained why the ABCs were expelled from the Negro National League. The fundamental reason why the team was dropped, Mrs. Taylor said, "was to disorganize the club and prevent them from playing any more games." She stated the ABCs did a gross business of twenty-five thousand dollars and was in a position to cover the debt owed to the league. The man responsible for causing this disarray, she stated, was Rube Foster: "When the secretary, president, and treasury happens to be the same person, one dare not dispute the report as sent out, but [an] auditing of the books would throw more light on the status of some of the clubs that are thought to be in good standing." This statement was in reference to the constant franchise shifting that had become commonplace in the NNL. The primary reason for expelling the ABCs was to take the team's players and distribute them among the other league clubs. Apparently, several players were transferred to other teams, which led Mrs. Taylor to conclude that if these players "were good enough for those clubs, why not for the ABCs?" A second reason for expelling the ABCs was to allow the Memphis Red Sox to become a league member. The *Pittsburgh Courier* reported that the Red Sox had long sought entry into the league and that they would assume the ABCs' won-lost record.[72]

Second, and finally, Tenny Blount began to skip league games on a regular basis. On July 19, the *Defender* reported that Blount refused to play a scheduled game with the Cleveland Browns. His actions reportedly led the fans in the Forest City to urge Foster to call a directors meeting and insist that the Stars play the scheduled four-game series. Since the Browns were a weak team, the Stars' expense in traveling there didn't justify making the trip. Blount's rebellious behavior illustrated the growing dissatisfaction with Rube Foster's czar-like rule.[73]

Critics who alleged Rube Foster ran the Negro National League like a booking agency were correct. It was clear from the outset that Foster placed his Chicago American Giants' business interests above the league's interests. In essence, he acted as if what was good for the Chicago American Giants was also good for the Negro National League. He exhibited an unwillingness to acknowledge that his business interests and the league's were now one and the same. Constant franchise shifting, Foster's unwillingness to schedule more road trips for his American Giants, and the disparity in the number of league games played suggest there was no inclination to operate the NNL in a traditional sense. In other words, he did not recognize that the club owners were competitors on the field of play and partners in business who must cooperate to a much greater degree than competitors in other conventional business enterprises. Moreover, the absence of published statistics indicated that promoting the league by pursuing a league pennant and sponsoring a season ending championship series was the furthest thing from Foster's mind.

The scheduling dilemma showed how Foster benefited the most from running the league like a booking agency. On a consistent basis, he used the fact that some clubs did not possess their own parks as an excuse not to achieve a balanced schedule, although his critics in large part refuted the fallacy of the league president's argument. From the outset, club owners like C. I. Taylor and Charles Mills opposed the 5 percent booking fee that Foster assessed for scheduled league games. However, both Taylor and Mills had a history of facing competition from other black clubs and of difficulties in securing suitable playing facilities within their respective cities, Indianapolis and St. Louis. Therefore, they were willing to go along with Foster's arrangement with the understanding that a new scheduling system would be developed. Within a league format, Taylor and Mills could have been led to believe that the American Giants would make more appearances in their respective cities. Theoretically speaking, this would enable Taylor and Mills to gain a hegemony over their respective consumer markets and maximize their revenues. However, Taylor's death and Mills's more or less being ousted from the league meant no further opposition to Foster's scheduling practices until Tenny Blount began to skip league games. Foster's scheduling practices validate W. S. Ferrance's claim that the league clubs became reliant on Sunday games at Schorling Park.[74]

Hilldale president Ed Bolden also showed how Foster benefited from running the league like a booking agency. Hilldale's associate membership allowed Foster to generate additional revenue through his booking fees when he scheduled games in the East for teams like the AC and the Bacharach Giants. Bolden accurately pointed out that such an arrangement was not in the HBEC's best economic interest. Hilldale also lost out when the team was strongly discouraged from scheduling games with outlaw clubs in New York, most specifically Nat Strong's Brooklyn Royal Giants. Therefore, it was understandable when Bolden withdrew as an associate member and became one of the architects of the Mutual Association of Eastern Colored Baseball Clubs.

A combination of factors led to the creation of the Eastern Colored League. The high cost of rail travel led Henry Tucker and Thomas Jackson to split from John Connor and Baron Wilkins and make overtures to eastern-based clubs to form a league. The irreconcilable differences between Bolden and Foster and the Hilldale president's affiliation with the PBA paved the way for the HBEC to become a member of the proposed league. The aspirations of George Rossiter and Charles Spedden to make the Baltimore Black Sox a top-level club also contributed to the formation of the ECL. Finally, the willingness of NNL players to either not re-sign with their current club or jump their contracts presented the eastern owners with an excellent opportunity for league formation. Also, the constant franchise shifting in the NNL resulted in players continuously being transferred to other clubs in their circuit. Without question, this circumstance led to a sense of job insecurity among the players. This provided further motivation for players to bolt the NNL for promises of higher salaries in the ECL.

From its inception, the ECL gave the appearance of club cooperation through the development of a commissioners system to govern the league. Although they made a better effort than the NNL to publish statistics to generate fan interest, ECL owners, like their western counterparts, were less concerned about operating the league in a traditional sense; they felt it was not in their best economic interests to pattern their leagues after the white Major Leagues. Nat Strong undermined any efforts to sustain this cooperative effort. As with Foster, Strong's early actions made it clear that he would place his business interests above the league's, not willing to recognize that his interests and the league's were now one and the same. Strong, however, presented his fellow owners with a fundamental dilemma. Despite his declining influence in New York, Strong was still a more stable club owner from an economic standpoint. As an outlaw, he could have wreaked havoc on the league by enticing away its best players. Cum Posey's intrusion more than validated this concern. On the other hand, the league could benefit from scheduling league games at Dexter Park in an effort to tap into the New York market. Strong refused to do that, and this marked the beginning of an uneasy alliance between the Royals' magnate and the rest of his fellow owners.

By August 1924, Rube Foster had proven George Rossiter's claim that the league president was backed into a corner. He needed an agreement with the ECL to prevent future tampering with players. An opportunity to get an agreement would emerge when the fans and the black press clamored for a Colored World Series.

9

Pursuing Peace

The Colored World Series of 1924 was a response to a supposed demand of the fans and the black press and simultaneously became the means to formalize a peace settlement between the two warring leagues. Rube Foster seized the opportunity to seek a compromise with the ECL commissioners. The Colored World Series did not realize the large profits the black press had projected, but the event was promoted as a symbol of race pride and racial advancement. Black baseball's first world series revealed the contrasting agendas of the black press on the one hand and the Negro League owners on the other regarding the sport's purpose and the ways in which the leagues should operate. The black press believed the Negro Leagues should be patterned after the white Major Leagues, with the postseason series serving as evidence of racial progress. The NNL, on the other hand, utilized the demand for the series to get an agreement from the ECL owners to respect the contracts that the NNL owners had with the players. Once an agreement was reached, each league could run its affairs in a manner it deemed necessary.

The club owners met in the winter of 1924 to ratify the tentative agreement made prior to the Colored World Series. Ed Bolden nominated Rube Foster as chairman of the joint session, and the magnates adopted territorial boundaries and a standard players' contract. A reserve list was drawn up by both leagues to protect the contract rights of league clubs, which placed their players on the list so no other club could tamper with them. A player limit was established, and a discussion ensued over devising a salary limit. The club owners also instituted an arbitration committee to resolve disputes between the two leagues.

At the same time, the leagues met separately to make plans for the 1925 season. Foster was reelected president and treasurer, and he made plans to set his league in order. In concert with Chicago *Defender* sportswriter Frank Young, Foster began a media campaign to discredit Detroit Stars' owner, John Tenny Blount, for his "maverick" ways during the 1924 season. When the NNL owners supported Foster's actions, the Detroit magnate was deposed. Foster also dealt with the familiar challenges of constant franchise shifting and took on the task of formulating a balanced schedule. To stimulate fan interest, the club owners mapped out a one-hundred-game split season, with the winner of each half to play a best four-out-of-seven game series for the NNL pennant. If the same club won in both halves, it would represent the NNL in the Colored World Series. Finally, after a variety of complaints from players, owners, and fans, Foster dismissed several black umpires, marking the end of their short, bittersweet tenure in the NNL.

Much like their midwestern cohorts, the Eastern Colored League underwent a season of transition. The ECL owners reelected Ed Bolden as chairman, and once in office, he began to confront several old and new challenges. The Bacharach Giants began the season under new management, while the Washington Potomacs relocated to Wilmington, Delaware. The league schedule became a source of controversy when it was deliberately left incomplete to allow league clubs to book additional games with white semiprofessional teams. The commissioners adopted a rotating system for their umpires and hired Bill Dallas, a white semipro league official and a sportswriter with the *Philadelphia Public Ledger*, as the arbiters' supervisor. The black press was highly critical of Bolden's decisions regarding the schedule arrangement and the hiring of Dallas. These choices led Oscar Charleston to accuse the commissioners of making decisions that were not in the ECL's best interests. Although Bolden received a lot of unwanted press attention, he did get some satisfaction from the season when his Hilldale Club met the Kansas City Monarchs in black baseball's second Colored World Series.

Addressing the Public Demand: Getting a Tentative Agreement

By August 1924, several black newspapers had reported being besieged by letters asking why there was no Colored World Series. *Kansas City Call* sportswriter Ollie Womack urged black fans in league cities to call for a world championship series. Womack envisioned this series as paralleling the World Series in Organized Baseball. The fans of Kansas City were reportedly "demanding reward for their [Monarchs] in the form of a Championship series at the end of the season with the champions of the Eastern League." He claimed the white Major Leagues provided a high caliber of entertainment because of the economic rewards the winner of the World Series received and the high prestige stakes in competing to be the "world champions." Womack created a scenario whereby the ECL champion Hilldale would play the NNL pennant winner, the Kansas City Monarchs, in a best five out of nine game series. The imagined series would realize a total attendance of 150,000 and generate over $100,000 in gate receipts, with each player receiving over $2,000. "Why," argued Womack, "should not the black players enjoy the advantages as white players in the majors do?" He urged the officials of both leagues to come together and settle their differences.[1]

Despite the Black Sox scandal of 1919, the World Series of the white Major Leagues had been viewed as an important annual event in the lives of Americans. The series was a glamorous culmination of the baseball season, with the entire nation preoccupied with the heroes of the diamond as they vied for the highest prize—the world's championship. At first, scheduling a postseason championship series between the two leagues remained in serious doubt, due primarily to the Great Baseball War. In 1903, the first World Series was played under a simple agreement worked out by the respective league champions, the Pittsburgh Pirates and the Boston Red Sox. Neither of the leagues nor the National Commission was officially connected to it. In 1904, the New York Giants won the National League pennant, but club owner John Brush refused to let his team play the American League champion Red Sox.

Newspapers across the country admonished Brush for his "smallness" and Giants' manager John McGraw for his "malice" and denounced their refusal to participate as a "baby act" and "cowardice."[2]

By 1905, relations between the two leagues had improved and Brush, evidently influenced by the criticism he had received the previous year, relented on the World Series. The National League voted to make participation in the series mandatory for its pennant winners, and Brush even submitted a set of suggestions to NL President Harry Pulliam for conducting the series. The Brush rules, as revised by the National Commission, have remained the core of the World Series rules to this day. He called for a seven-game series to be ended as soon as one of the teams won four games, and in the 1905 series the Giants took the necessary four after playing only five games against the Philadelphia Athletics. After the 1905 World Series, the outcome of the event absorbed the attention of millions. It was promoted as a spectacle that equaled or surpassed the excitement of Independence Day or topping New Year's Eve. AL president Ban Johnson claimed that the prestige and status of "the greatest institution in the world" was on the line during World Series week. In 1911, the popular magazine *Everybody's* declared the series as "the very quintessence and consummation of the Most Perfect Thing in America." Fans congregated in the streets to watch the play-by-play as reported on boards pasted in front of newspaper offices, and reportedly, the series sometimes even delayed the proceedings of the United States Supreme Court.[3]

Several black newspapers in league cities declared they were inundated with letters expressing a desire to see the NNL and ECL champions in a Colored World Series. They deplored the fact that neither of the two leagues appeared willing to resolve their differences for the "betterment of baseball." The fans, said the black press, would not continue to patronize a sport that would not serve their wishes for a postseason classic that was on par with the white Major Leagues. *Defender* sportswriter Frank Young claimed the Colored World Series would "stimulate interest in baseball and would bring back to the game many fans who have been seeking other sports as a recreation."[4]

Rube Foster capitalized on the ostensible clamoring by the fans for a postseason series by stating his terms for peace. Several newspapers claimed that the league president had prevented such a series from taking place the past two years. When Young asked Foster why there was no World Series, the league president answered that the East had not sought such a matchup. Foster was apparently misrepresenting the facts because in 1923, during the course of the propaganda war in the black press, Charles Spedden had suggested the two leagues meet in a World Series. Foster made it clear that he was not opposed to a postseason series, but he stated that it would not occur unless the eastern owners agreed to respect the players' contracts with the NNL teams. The ECL could keep the players who had already defected from the western circuit; however, the eastern league had to agree not to raid the NNL clubs in the future. Other disputes between the leagues would have to be submitted to an arbitration board made up of the leading men in colored baseball, whose decisions would be binding. Finally, the NNL demanded the right to develop and discipline ball clubs and players and emphatically stated it was against contract jumping because it was certain "to ruin colored baseball."[5]

By September, Ed Bolden and the rest of the commissioners had stated their position regarding a Colored World Series. Bolden stated that "if the proposed World Series between colored clubs of the East and West does not materialize in 1924, you may put it down that it will not be due to any obstacle placed in the way by me." Like Foster, Bolden pointed out that many conditions would have to be addressed and an agreement ratified before the series could take place. The ECL chairman added that the "player question" was not the primary cause for the trouble between the leagues. Rather, he claimed, Foster's refusal to return Bolden's one-thousand-dollar deposit when Hilldale resigned as an associate member of the NNL was the primary stumbling block. In spite of this, Bolden claimed the matter was trivial when compared to "public opinion," and he was "far removed from standing in the way of popular sentiment." As a good faith gesture, Bolden waived the thousand-dollar deposit "for the good of the game." He now awaited the actions of his fellow commissioners and "the advance from the West." In other words, Bolden attempted to place the onus on Foster to make the first move for a peace settlement.[6]

Concurrently, Bolden's fellow commissioners expressed their views about the proposed postseason series. As far as they were concerned, a series between the pennant winners could take place, but it was contingent on establishing a method by which the runner-up clubs in each league would share in the profits. They also called for an end to the senseless propaganda, which served primarily to "rattle the time worn skeleton in the closet [that] would never bring the desired results." Finally, in an obvious PR move, the commissioners declared that they were "mindful of [their] duty to the public and [awaited] business advances from the West."[7]

At the same time, rumors circulated that Judge Kennesaw Mountain Landis, the commissioner of Organized Baseball, had offered to arbitrate the two leagues' differences. Landis proposed to draw up an agreement that would settle the differences between the two circuits. Lloyd Thompson considered the idea far-fetched. Even Nat Strong expressed a preference for Foster's judgment over Landis's.[8]

On September 13, 1924, the *New York Age* reported that the ECL commissioners, Foster, and Tenny Blount had met in New York and come to a tentative peace settlement. This temporary agreement would be ratified at a joint meeting of the two leagues in December. Both leagues would respect the other's players contracts and would refrain from any future tampering. The clubs would send a list of players under contract to their respective league secretaries. Players owing money by getting advances from an owner and then jumping to another club would have to compensate the owner they owed. The ECL commissioners were reportedly in a receptive mood to settle all differences in order to get a compromise.[9]

With a tentative settlement out of the way, league officials began making plans for the Colored World Series. The Kansas City Monarchs would face the Hilldale Club in a best five-out-of-nine-game series. A four-man commission—consisting of Alex Pompez and Charles Spedden of the ECL and Rube Foster and Tenny Blount of the NNL—was organized to administer the financial arrangements for the series. The commission attempted to pattern the Colored World Series after the one in Organized Baseball. At first, the players would share in the gate receipts of the first four games. However, in contrast to the white Major Leagues, no fund was created initially to cover operating expenses, and so other residuals were needed to promote the series. Instead, the players would share in all games after the necessary expenses were deducted from the gate receipts. These incidentals included park rental, travel fare, accommodations, umpire salaries, advertising, and commission expenses. After these expenses were deducted, the players would receive 35 percent of the receipts and the clubs another 35 percent. Ten percent would go to the commission. The clubs finishing second and third in each league would share in the remaining receipts, 60 percent to the second-place club and 20 percent to the third-place team. The World Series winner would receive 60 percent of the gate receipts and the loser 40 percent. Finally, ticket prices were set at $1.00 to $1.65, much higher than the typical league levels of 35 to 85 cents.[10]

The schedule format became a source of controversy. Originally, the format called for the series to begin October 3–4 at Hilldale, October 5 at Baltimore, an open date on the sixth, October 7–8 at Chicago, and October 9–11 in Kansas City. If the series went nine games, the commission would decide upon a neutral sight for the final contest. *Kansas City Call* sportswriter Carl Beckwith stated that while the series format might suit Hilldale and Foster, it was not agreeable to Kansas City fans. Philadelphia fans got the only Sunday game, unless the series went the distance. Since the last game held in Kansas City was on Saturday, the logical site for the final game of the series would be Chicago, allowing the Windy City fans to see three games. The proposed format left Beckwith to speculate that the schedule was designed to suit Foster more than the Monarch fans because Foster knew that the Monarch management could not get any dates at their home grounds in October due to a series of local events being held there. Eventually, a compromise was reached. The new schedule assured a Sunday game in Kansas City. The series would begin in Philadelphia on October 3–4 and continue in Baltimore on October 5. October 6–9 were open dates in case of cancellations. The series would resume in Kansas City on October 11–13. If the series was not decided, the remaining games would be played in Chicago.[11]

The stage was now set for black professional baseball's first Colored World Series. The Kansas City Monarchs and the Hilldale Club were equally matched on the diamond. The Monarchs were led by their pitcher-manager Jose Mendez, the Black Diamond. Along with Mendez, Wilber "Bullet Joe" Rogan gave the club a formidable one-two pitching combination. Rogan was an outstanding hurler who possessed an excellent fastball, a fine curve, and good control. A durable workhorse on the mound, he averaged thirty starts a year, fielded his position well, and was a dangerous hitter. Newt Allen, the Monarchs' second baseman, was considered the best at his position in the 1920s. Allen was endowed with great range and quick hands; he was also superb on the pivot in turning a double play. In addition, he was an excellent bunter and a consistent hitter with good bat control who went with the pitch to hit the ball to all fields. Oscar "Heavy" Johnson played right field and was one of the NNL's power hitters during the twenties. He used his 250 pounds to good advantage in generating power at the plate. Also featuring Frank Duncan, Lemuel Hawkins, Dobie Moore, and Newt Joseph, the Monarchs were a formidable opponent.[12]

The ECL champion Hilldale Club was one of the best teams Ed Bolden had ever assembled. Phil Cockerell and Nip Winters led the pitching staff, while veteran players Otto Briggs, Louis Santop, Frank Warfield, and Clint Thomas rounded out the starting lineup. William Junious "Judy" Johnson was Hilldale's shortstop, although he would later make his reputation as a fine third baseman. Johnson played shortstop due to the injury to Hilldale's regular shortstop, Frank Stevens. An excellent defensive infielder with outstanding speed, Johnson was a line drive hitter with an excellent batting eye. Raleigh "Bizz" Mackey played third base and would later become one of the premier catchers in black baseball. Although he was barely literate, Mackey was intelligent, had a baseball mind, and employed a studious approach to the game. The switch-hitting third baseman was one of the most dangerous hitters in black baseball, with power from both sides of the plate.[13]

On October 3, the series began at Baker Bowl, the home of the National League Philadelphia Phillies. Before the start of the game, Rube Foster and Ed Bolden shook hands, ending the proverbial "enmity between the East and West." Phil Cockerell dueled Bullet Joe Rogan to a 0-0 tie until the Monarchs broke the game open in the sixth inning. Lemuel Hawkins led the inning off with a single and advanced to second on Newt Allen's bunt single. The runners moved to second and third on an error committed by Cockerell. After walking leftfielder Hurly McNair, Frank Warfield misplayed Dobie Moore's grounder to second base, allowing two runs to score. Rogan lined a singled past Warfield, and after Heavy Johnson struck out, right fielder George Sweatt singled to right, adding another run. Cockerell committed two additional errors, allowing two more runs. It was all the Monarchs needed to win the first game, 6-2. Hilldale took out its frustrations on Jose Mendez in game two. The AC erupted for five runs in the first inning, two in the second, and two in the third en route to an 11-0 shellacking of the Monarchs. The third game ended in a 6-6 tie when the game was called in the thirteenth inning because of darkness.[14]

Two tightly contested games resulted in Hilldale taking a 3-1-1 series lead. Game four was played in Maryland Park in Baltimore, and the Monarchs took a 2-0 lead in the first inning when Newt Allen doubled and scored on Rogan's two-bagger. Dobie Moore singled to bring Rogan home. The Monarchs added another run in the third inning before Hilldale tied the game in the bottom of the frame. The game remained tied until the ninth inning, when Monarchs' hurler William Bell walked the first two batters he faced. Warfield was safe at first on a close play, loading the bases. Louis Santop hit a hot shot to Allen at second base, and Johnson scored on Allen's wild throw to the plate, giving the AC a 4-3 win.[15]

The series moved to Muehlebach Park in Kansas City. With the Monarchs' Joe Rogan dueling Nip Winters, Kansas City took a 2-1 lead into the ninth inning. In the top of ninth, Otto Briggs of the AC reached first base after being hit by a Rogan fastball. He scored on Biz Mackey's single to left field after the ball got past left fielder Dink Mothel, a late inning replacement for Heavy Johnson. The next batter, Joe Lewis, reached first base on an infield single. Shortstop Judy Johnson stepped to the plate and hit a line drive past right fielder George Sweatt for an inside-the-park home run, leading Hilldale to a 5-2 comeback victory. The Monarchs turned the tables on the ECL champions in game six. With the score tied at five, Dobie Moore singled to right field in the ninth inning and scored on George Sweatt's triple to give the Monarchs a 6-5 win. Game seven was a twelve-inning affair. Whereas the ACs matched the Monarchs on the mound and at the plate, they became their own worst enemy on the field. With the score tied at three in the bottom of the twelfth, George Sweatt tripled to right field, but was injured while sliding into third base. William Bell replaced him and scored the winning run on Judy Johnson's errant throw to first base after fielding Joe Rogan's ground ball.[16]

The final three games were played at Chicago's Schorling Park. The Monarchs won the next two games by scores of 3-2 and 5-3. In the final game, Hilldale sent Holsey "Scrip" Lee to the mound against Jose Mendez. For seven innings, the pitchers were locked into a scoreless pitchers' duel, with Hilldale managing only three singles off Mendez, while the Monarchs were baffled by Lee's submarine delivery. In the bottom of the eighth inning, however, the Monarchs' Dobie Moore led off with a single and went to second on Hurly McNair's sacrifice bunt. Heavy Johnson doubled and Moore scored the game's first run. Lee walked Frank Duncan, and Mendez singled to load the bases. Newt Allen doubled down the third base line and two more runs crossed the plate. Dink Mothel knocked in two more runs with a single, giving the Monarchs a 5-0 lead. It was all Mendez needed, as he shut down the Hilldale batters in the ninth, and the Kansas City Monarchs won the Colored World Series.[17]

Without question, the Kansas City Monarchs and Hilldale played an exciting postseason championship series. With the exception of game two, each game was closely contested, and either team could have emerged the victor. Off the field, however, the rosy financial picture that journalist Ollie Womack had envisioned didn't materialize. In several black newspapers, the World Series commission published a financial report of the series. The total paid attendance for the ten-game series was 45,857, generating $52,113.90 in gate receipts. The Monarchs' players received a total of $4,927.32 Hilldale received the sum of $3,284.88. This averaged out to $335.15 for each Monarch player, while Hilldale players received $193.22. These figures were well below Womack's projection of $2,000 per player. Womack's projected attendance was way off the mark, a full 104,143 less than his prediction. The loser's share led the *Philadelphia Tribune* to conclude that the World Series wasn't a "goldmine." The *Pittsburgh Courier* added that although the series did not live up to expectations financially, it did provide "a definite goal for the contending clubs to shoot at during the months of hot summer conflict."[18]

One sportswriter, Charles A. Starks, viewed the Colored World Series as a symbol of racial progress and advancement. In an editorial in the *Philadelphia Tribune*, Starks asserted that prior to the series, black fans directed their hero worship to white stars like Babe Ruth, Rogers Hornsby, and George Sisler. Such adulation "led eventually to 'white supremacy' and away from Race Idealism that should naturally be focused on black players." White sportswriters marginalized black players' intellectual capacity and consigned blacks "to the mediocre fields of obscurity." The Colored World Series marked one way to shatter the negative psychology fostered by white supremacy. Blacks had made race progress by their indulgence in baseball, and Starks praised C. I. Taylor's and Foster's efforts toward professionalizing the black game. Starks concluded with a more subtle message directed at Organized Baseball: when the Colored World Series was on par with the white one, the fans would, as they had before, clamor for a series between the black champion and the white champion of Organized Baseball.[19]

Carl Beckwith took a different approach to promote the Colored World Series as a symbol of racial advancement. His rhetoric was consistent with that of the new black leadership that emerged in the early twentieth century. Beckwith praised Hilldale for gentlemanly conduct on and off the field. The World Series was a long step forward for organized baseball among blacks. It was a symbol of race progress, and the players' gentlemanly conduct on the field embodied the image the new black middle class sought to project. Moreover, Hilldale had "made many friends for the Eastern league among Western fans."[20]

On November 15, Rube Foster assessed the World Series and the Negro Leagues in general in the Chicago *Defender*. Foster noted that while he had seen most of the World Series during the last twenty years, "never did any of them have anything on our colored series." He described the last eight games as "eight of the best played games of ball I have ever witnessed." Foster praised the Hilldale outfield for working in "unison" and for not committing an error during the entire series. The Monarchs' pitching staff was phenomenal in shutting down Hilldale's strong hitting attack.[21]

Despite the accolades he showered on both clubs, Foster felt that staging the World Series ill-advised at that time. "The big mistake," Foster declared, "came in the anxiety to please the public." He added, "Big leagues operated 40 years without a world series. They played 15 years without sharing with second and third clubs." Foster failed to acknowledge that as early as the 1880s, efforts had been made to stage a postseason series, most notably by Cap Anson's Chicago White Stockings of the National League and Chris Von der Ahe's St. Louis Browns of the American Association. Foster was able, however, to point out that the white World Series drew more fans at higher ticket prices to see one game than the entire attendance at the Colored World Series.[22]

Foster's latter assertion revealed contrasting agendas regarding the ways in which the Negro Leagues should operate. On the one hand, the black press aspired for both leagues to function along the same lines as the white Major Leagues. The fact that the press had to pressure the owners to settle their differences to get them to stage the World Series illustrated this point. It should be noted that the magnates spent little or no time promoting the event. It was left to the black press to stimulate interest. To Foster, on the other hand, the Colored World Series served to get a temporary agreement from the ECL owners to respect the contract agreements between NNL players and owners. He added, "We have played the series and have met the demands of the public. When the two leagues meet at Chicago in December much harsh work has got to be done to meet the demands. It is a true statement and a tough job, and I believe we need more wisdom than the organization possesses." Both the press and the fans would have to wait and see if peace had been restored in black baseball.[23]

Restoring Order

On December 11, 1924, the Negro National League and Eastern Colored League owners met at the Appomattox Club in Chicago to hold their first joint session. When the meeting was called to order, Ed Bolden was granted the floor, and after reviewing the tentative agreement made prior to the World Series, he moved "that through courtesy to Mr. Foster for his experience and untiring efforts in baseball [that] he be made chairman of [the] joint-session." After generous applause, the motion passed by a unanimous vote. Quincy Gillmore was appointed secretary at the joint session.[24]

Bolden submitted a tentative National Agreement, and the owners ratified it after a few minor revisions. Territorial rights were established, giving the ECL from the western boundary of Pennsylvania eastward and the entire East Coast along the Atlantic Seaboard. The NNL's territory extended west of Buffalo and Pittsburgh to the West Coast. A reserve list was submitted by both leagues, and it was agreed that "a player who has played with one club for a season or part of a season shall not be permitted to play with [another] club in either league." Players would also have to clear waivers from all clubs before they could sign with another one. Any disputes between the two leagues would be submitted to a committee of three arbitrators, one to be selected by each league and the third one chosen by those two. The World Series would be played each year under the same arrangement made previously. The second- and third- place clubs would share in the gate receipts. No owner or stockholder on either pennant-winning team could serve on the four-man commission. Finally, the player limit for each team was set at twenty, and while a discussion occurred over devising a salary limit, no definite settlement was made.[25]

Black baseball's first National Agreement recapitulated the similar challenges Organized Baseball had undergone in the late nineteenth century. Introducing restrictive practices in the form of territorial rights and a reserve list to protect the contract rights of league clubs were designed to maximize revenues and gain the owners autonomy over their business enterprise. Much like their white counterparts, these black baseball owners found that consistently following these agreed-on business practices would prove challenging.

Concurrently, both leagues met in separate sessions to make plans for the 1925 season. The NNL club owners reelected Foster president and treasurer, and Birmingham owner Joe Rush was elected secretary. Tenny Blount was dismissed as vice president and replaced by Dr. George Keyes of the St. Louis Stars. Blount was also censured because his players claimed that he had refused to pay their salaries after September 15 although contracts ran until October 1. He was also reprimanded for refusing to play a four-game series in September against the Cleveland Browns. Blount was supposedly given "ample time" to obtain an affidavit signed by the players that they agreed to his proposition to play games booked by him on the co-op plan. At that time, there were no rules in the bylaws or constitution that dealt with a club owner refusing to comply with the schedule, so Blount was not fined. The league officials amended the bylaws so that a five-hundred-dollar fine would apply for future violations. Blount was given a January 1, 1925, deadline to either pay his players or be expelled from the league.[26]

In response, Blount presented his case in the black press. The Stars were not scheduled to play any more league games after September 16, and he resigned from the league. The players then agreed to play games, booked by Blount, in which the Stars' owner would not share in the gate receipts. At the league meeting, Blount asked for a return of his $2,500 deposit minus the expenses owed to the league. The motion to withdraw was reportedly approved. Foster raised the issue about the back pay the players claimed was owed to them. The league president said he had received letters from the Stars' players asking for pay from September 16 to October 1. Blount responded that Foster had treated the Stars unfairly in scheduling league games and that he had it "on good authority that [the league president] intended to break me and put me out of baseball." It was because of this treatment, Blount asserted, that he disbanded his club and resigned from the league. He also pointed out that Birmingham and Cleveland had also disbanded in early September but there was no outcry for their actions. Blount claimed that Foster did not produce any letters written by the Detroit players.[27]

The news of Blount's censure was leaked to the press on the second day of the winter meeting, when the Stars' owners had to return to Detroit on urgent business. The league had no right, Blount said, to issue such a statement because the players had reportedly agreed to finish the season on the co-op plan. Blount stated that Foster had written the players and told them to send in their contracts and he, Foster, would then collect the balance of their money. Foster took steps to discredit Blount and force him out of the league. To validate his charges against Foster, Blount stipulated that if Foster could find one statement that was not true, he would deposit five hundred dollars with any newspaper the league president chose: "Let Frank Young, Ira F. Lewis, and Al Monroe, sports editors of the Chicago *Defender*, *Pittsburgh Courier*, and *Chicago Whip* decide, and if . . . I have misstated one fact in this article, [they] can take the money . . . and give it to any charitable organization that they think worthy of it." Blount concluded that he had lost over $5,000 during the 1924 season, including the $1,100 paid Foster to book the Stars, and that the "money went into his pocket and not into the league treasury."[28]

Tenny Blount underestimated Foster's skill in using the media to sway public opinion in his favor. Chicago *Defender* sports editor and the NNL official scorer Faye Young aided Foster in constructing his effective media strategy. The "World's Greatest Weekly's" wide circulation allowed both men to published a series of articles distributed by Pullman porters throughout the Midwest and East. Since the league's inception, Young had essentially sided with Foster on the controversial issues that arose. He was rarely critical—the hiring of black umpires being the exception—of the way Foster ran the NNL.

On December 27, 1924, both Young and Foster began a media campaign to refute Blount's perspective on the Detroit situation. In an article titled "Negro National League Facing Crucial Period," Young highlighted the financial sacrifices Foster had made to keep the NNL in business. He supposedly advanced money to club owners to keep their franchises from disbanding. The league president covered the salaries and the expenses of the black umpires, reportedly out of his own personal account. Detroit Stars' field manager Bruce Petway was reported as saying that the team's players refused to play unless Foster guaranteed their salaries. Young published another article that claimed the players accused Blount of owing them their salaries from September 16 to October 1. They acknowledged their agreement to play on the co-op plan, but there was no written agreement among the players and the Stars' magnate. Blount had reportedly booked one game for the players against the Detroit Clowns, a local white semipro team. The gate receipts were held to pay the expenses for advertising a game against the American League Cleveland Indians, leaving the players $2.50 each. However, the series with the Indians was never played.[29]

In January 1925, Young continued his media campaign with a series of articles published in eastern black newspapers. He began by highlighting the events that had occurred in the NNL's winter meeting prior to the joint session. Rube Foster returned all franchise deposits to the league clubs, minus the indebtedness to him, and recommended the league appoint a commission to investigate the league books and records. He then vacated the president's chair and made a motion that St. Louis Stars' owner George Keyes take the chair. The league owners refused to accept his resignation. In a show of support for Foster, Kansas City Monarchs' owner J. L. Wilkinson placed his one-thousand-dollar deposit on the table, telling the other owners that under no circumstances could there be an improvement on the present conditions. Chronicling these events of the league meeting was designed to discredit Blount's version of the episode.[30]

Young then turned his attention to Blount's "questionable" business enterprise outside of baseball. Foster supposedly objected to the Stars' players frequenting Blount's gambling houses. In a statement that highlighted the ideals of the new black leadership, Young said that the Stars' magnate "could not go along in a clean game where all cards were played on the table and where a straight deck was set down to be cut by all players and where other men were associated." Young said this to discredit Blount, the only owner at this point to be involved in the numbers racket, an involvement in stark contrast with the ideals of the black middle class. To Young, Foster's biggest mistake was allowing Blount to join the league and "put his feet under the same table with them and dine."³¹

Foster picked up the media campaign with several articles of his own. He began by dispelling rumors that the NNL would disband. Foster used the familiar strategy of publishing facts and figures to show the league was solvent in spite of the numerous problems it faced. In its five years of operation, for example, the NNL had paid over five hundred thousand dollars in player salaries. Over three million people had attended league games. Yet he acknowledged that during the 1924 season, all the league clubs reportedly lost money. Attendance declined during the season, due essentially to inclement weather, he wrote. Weekday games remained a losing proposition for most clubs. Foster used this adverse information to illustrate the difficulties he encountered in running the league. He then turned his attention to Blount's charges. Regarding the one thousand dollars Blount paid Foster to book the Stars' games, Foster said that the deposed owner had failed to acknowledge the twenty thousand dollars the league president gave him in business. Evidently, this was the profit Blount had made over the past five years. Foster concluded, "Fools and their money soon part . . . because they could not handle the vast sums that came into their hands through Foster."³²

The media campaign was effective in ousting John Tenny Blount from the Negro National League. Combined with the refusal of the club owners to accept Foster's resignation as president, the Detroit owner's expulsion was assured. At the league's second winter meeting on January 31, 1925, the owners signed a letter of support for Foster's actions and published it in the black press:

> Therefore, as said owners are part and parcel of said league, collective and individual, we here and now pledge our whole-hearted support to the president, Mr. A. R. Foster, in his efforts to build a bigger and better Negro National League.

We further pledge our support to any movement that has for its purpose the advancement of the game, the players, and the interest in general for which we have banded ourselves together to obtain better baseball and baseball conditions among that portion of the American citizenry known as the Negro.

The show of solidarity among the club owners provided Foster with a significant degree of autonomy and leverage. Having the club owners' backing and his media alliance with Faye Young, the league president now sought to place his proverbial house in order.[33]

On February 2, 1925, the NNL owners met in St. Louis to prepare for the upcoming season. Tenny Blount was voted out of the league and was replaced by a contingent headed by Steve Pierce, an African American entrepreneur from Oakland, California. Pierce had reportedly one of the best semipro clubs on the West Coast. The Cleveland Browns franchise sent no representative to the meeting and was dropped from the league. Two prospective owner groups sought to replace the Browns with a team in Indianapolis. A contingent led by a W. T. Smith paid the one-thousand-dollar deposit, while a former competitor of C. I. Taylor, Warner Jewel, responded in kind. Two weeks later, the league directors awarded Jewel the Indianapolis franchise. Thus, the league began the season with the following teams: the Birmingham Black Barons, Chicago American Giants, Cuban Stars West, Detroit Stars, Indianapolis ABCs, Kansas City Monarchs, Memphis Red Sox, and St. Louis Stars. To ensure each club finished the season, the magnates paid an additional four-thousand-dollar deposit.[34]

The owners devised a new playing schedule that would be revised several times during the year. The season was divided into two halves of fifty games each. If the same team won both halves, it would represent the NNL in the World Series. If the winner of the first half failed to win the second half, the winners of both halves would play a best four-out-of-seven game series to determine the pennant winner. Seeking to play a one-hundred-game split season represented an ambitious undertaking by a league that had yet to complete a balanced schedule. By late May, the new schedule format had evidently proved unworkable.

In a statement released to the press, Foster claimed that league clubs were having trouble playing "an even amount of games." Therefore, only the first ten games among league clubs would count in the standings, with additional games being characterized as exhibitions. It was unclear why the NNL was having a difficult time playing a balanced schedule. Undoubtedly, Foster's unwillingness to schedule his American Giants on road trips was a contributing factor. Apparently, the owners dropped this schedule revision for the second half of the split season. On July 4, the *Defender* reported that the league had dropped the ten-game compromise in favor of all games between league clubs counting in the standings.[35]

A review of the NNL's first split season revealed that the magnates were unsuccessful in their attempt to play a one-hundred-game schedule. The Kansas City Monarchs won the first split season with a 31-9 won-lost record. The American Giants played the most league games (48), followed by the Detroit Stars (46), St. Louis Stars (45), and Memphis Red Sox (42). The Cuban Stars, the only traveling team in the league, played the fewest league games (25). The St. Louis Stars won the second half with a 38-12 won-lost record and played the most league games. They were followed by the Detroit (47), Chicago (46), and Kansas City (42). The Cuban Stars once again played the fewest games (22), with the Birmingham Black Barons next (26).

The root cause for the NNL's scheduling woes was that Rube Foster maintained a scheduling system whereby the majority of league clubs were reliant on Sunday games in Chicago. Other contributors to the scheduling dilemma were the operation of the Cuban Stars as a road club and the fact that of all teams, only one, the St. Louis Stars, owned its ballpark. With the exception of the Chicago American Giants, Memphis Red Sox, and Detroit Stars, the remaining league clubs had to schedule games around their minor league landlords. Midwestern clubs were undoubtedly reluctant to make the extended trips to play their southern counterparts in Birmingham and Memphis. The fact that the Black Barons played only twenty-six league games in the second half validates this point. However, several sportswriters had pointed out previously that with a little creativity, the league could work around these obstacles and still achieve some semblance of a balanced schedule. Rube Foster was unwilling to do this because it was not in his best economic interest to do so. His unwillingness to strive for a balanced schedule revealed that the league president had no intention of modeling his Negro National League after the white majors.

The plight of African American umpires in the NNL further illustrated that Foster had no plans to emulate the white Major Leagues. On August 22, the *Baltimore Afro-American* reported that the umpiring situation had deteriorated to such a state that Foster dismissed most of the black arbiters. Only Caesar Jamison and Billy Donaldson survived the purge. When league owners and managers complained about the black umpires, Foster at first attempted to finish the season with them. The ballplayers and the fans also complained about the umpires' poor officiating, and it led the league president to invite the arbiters to Chicago to work under his watchful eye. Foster made the change after evaluating their work. The umpires' poor mechanics in calling balls and strikes and their supposed inability to control games led to their dismissal.[36]

Several factors contributed to the African American umpires' short and bittersweet tenure in the NNL. First, one arbiter told Carl Beckwith that black umpires were fighting two battles on the diamond. They knew they would struggle for recognition from their white counterparts, but they did not expect to have to fight "for the respect of members of [their] own race and leagues from the President down to the bat-boy." A second factor that evidently led to their dismissal appeared to be the unfavorable working conditions black arbiters faced. The owners supposedly adopted a rule that the league president could not dismiss an umpire. The rule was designed to protect the umpires from retaliation by Foster should they make an unfavorable call against his American Giants. Yet as Beckwith claimed, Foster had indirect ways to rid the league of "undesirable umpires." One umpire by the name of Debow, who reportedly was "one of the best umpires in the game," quit because Foster made his life miserable on the diamond.[37]

The most important factor in the dismissals, however, was that Rube Foster did not support the African American umpires. As the league's chief executive officer, Foster showed no intention of devising a policy to support his arbiters on the field, in contrast to the backing that his white counterpart, American League president Ban Johnson, gave his umpires. It should be noted that external pressure from the black press—most notably Faye Young —was the primary reason Foster hired black umpires in the first place. Foster was, for the most part, ambivalent regarding their plight. He acknowledged having claimed that African Americans were not ready to handle the responsibility of umpiring. The lack of support from the president and the owners would have made it difficult for any umpire to work effectively. Moreover, the black arbiters' biggest cheerleader, Frank Young, was also conspicuous by his silence concerning their fate. Because there was no outcry from either the press or the fans over the discharge of the black umpires, Foster's decision to terminate them was effectively sanctioned.[38]

With the peace settlement between the leagues in place, Rube Foster went about reorganizing his Negro National League in his own image. Complaints and eventual dismissal of black umpires allowed him to return to his philosophy of being a businessman first and a Race man second. The split season and the attempt to play a one-hundred-game season were designed to stimulate fan interest. However, Foster continued to use the scheduling practices that resulted in the reliance of the majority of league clubs on Chicago for Sunday games. While Foster leveraged his position as league president to maintain his autonomy over his NNL, Ed Bolden's ECL would endure a rocky transition that made the league chairman a popular target of criticism.

The Eastern Colored League's Season of Discontent

Prior to the start of the ECL's winter meeting, the league's publicity director, Lloyd Thompson, drew attention to the league's stability since its inception. Thompson pointed out that for the second straight year, the league would start the season with the same eight clubs: the Bacharach Giants, Baltimore Black Sox, Brooklyn Royal Giants, Cuban Stars, Harrisburg Giants, Hilldale Club, Lincoln Giants, and Washington Potomacs. His intent was obviously to highlight the difference between the ECL and its midwestern counterpart, the NNL.

Thompson added that the ECL "holds the distinction of being the only organization of colored clubs that have gone through an entire season without at least one of the member clubs cracking under the strain and dropping out [before] the season closed." He also differentiated the league's governance structure from the NNL by claiming that "the governing powers [were distributed] in such a way that every club has a representative to 'do their bit' in fashioning the destiny of colored baseball here in the East."[39]

Despite the rosy forecast Thompson painted in the black press, two of the ECL's franchises made changes in their managerial ranks. Hammond Daniels succeeded Tom Jackson as the commissioner of the Bacharach Giants. The *Baltimore Afro-American* reported that Daniels had long been identified with the Atlantic City club as a financial backer and president of the Bacharach Giants Athletic Association. He assumed controlling interest of the club and would vote on issues affecting the league. The Washington Potomacs underwent a restructuring in its management team when the partnership of George Robinson and Ben Taylor was dissolved. The rental agreement to play in Griffith Stadium, the home of the American League Washington Senators, and poor patronage were the primary reasons cited for the dissolution. Robinson relocated his Potomacs to Wilmington, Delaware.[40]

The commissioners addressed the schedule for the upcoming season at their second winter meeting. The schedule was described as "one of the most weighty problems that the commissioners have to solve." The scheduling committee, consisting of Bolden, George Robinson, James Keenan, and Charles Spedden, adopted a seventy-game schedule for the 1925 season. The committee left a lot of open dates throughout the season to allow league clubs to book lucrative games with white semipro clubs without forcing the cancellation of league games. The so-called "systematized" schedule the commissioners drafted illustrated that, like Rube Foster in the West, the ECL had no plan to run its league like the white Major Leagues. In essence, the schedule was devised in such a way as to allow Ed Bolden to maintain his business alliance with Nat Strong, much like the association the Royals magnate had with James Keenan in the prewar years. In this way Hilldale could tap into the New

York market to play lucrative games with white semipros and simultaneously play league games. Maintaining this business alliance came at the expense of other league clubs, most notably the Bacharach Giants, Harrisburg Giants, and the Wilmington Potomacs. In defense of this practice, Thompson stated that "with practically only one day per week at the respective cities being a paying proposition, the owners [could] ill afford to pass up lucrative bookings with independent clubs in their adjacent vicinity." To further validate his claim, Thompson pointed out that the Bacharach Giants would play fewer home games in Atlantic City, which "was one of the mistakes of the 1924 schedule." Additional parks were leased not in an effort not to balance the schedule but to schedule as many games as the magnates could muster. In an attempt to complete a balanced schedule, the commissioners agreed that only the first ten games among league clubs would count in the standings. Additional games would be classified as exhibition contests.[41]

The ECL also replaced the home umpire system with a rotation system subject to league authority. The change was in response to the "neutral" arbiters used to work the World Series games in Philadelphia and Baltimore. The basic premise behind the rotation system was that league-controlled umpires would not be subject to reprisals from individual owners, would provide more impartial decision making, and enforce discipline more effectively. In an attempt to "clean up their game," the umpires were instructed to enforce strict discipline, conduct games "as speedily as possible," and enforce penalties handed down by the commissioners whenever necessary. A twenty-five-dollar fine would be imposed on any player ejected from the game for the first time; a second offense would draw a fifty-dollar fine; and succeeding ones would draw an indefinite suspension. Umpire baiting and attacks upon the arbiters would carry a one-hundred-dollar fine and "drastic action by the Commission."[42]

In order for the rotation system to be effective, a supervisor was needed to operate it. To fill this position, Ed Bolden announced the hiring of Bill Dallas, who had served as a supervisor for baseball and basketball leagues and had also supervised umpires in the Pennsylvania–New Jersey League, a low-level minor league, in 1924. Bolden had a second agenda in hiring Dallas. Through Dallas, the ECL would get publicity in the white newspapers.[43]

For black sportswriters, the hiring of Dallas over one of them was a particularly puzzling and offensive episode. The *Baltimore Afro-American* pointed out that the success of the league was due entirely to the publicity given them in Race journals. *Pittsburgh Courier* sportswriter Rollo Wilson, who was unsuccessfully nominated for the position, indicated that, "Yes, this is the Mutual Association of Eastern COLORED Clubs." John Howe of the *Philadelphia Tribune* ran a controversial cartoon depicting Bolden as an "Uncle Tom" groveling for the white man's favor.[44]

Bolden reacted angrily to the Howe cartoon. In a letter to the *Tribune*, the ECL chairman alleged that the cartoon was untimely and unfair and that it undermined the efforts of the commissioners to provide the league with competent umpires. He added that the cartoon tended to inject "race feeling and prejudice into an organization fostered and made successful through cooperation of the two groups." Bolden proceeded to lecture the *Tribune* on the merits of ethical advertising. "Careful thought," he added, "should precede action that may do untold harm and where there is an organization such as the Eastern Colored League fifty percent of which is owned by one group, and having at its head a member of another group, we feel that you can ill afford to publish that which will likely disorganize."[45]

Bolden published a follow-up letter in the *Baltimore Afro-American* to explain the Dallas hiring. To turn some of the responsibility from himself regarding the selection, Bolden pointed out that Dallas could only be appointed by a majority vote of the ECL commissioners. Dallas was appointed primarily because of his previous experience supervising umpires, Bolden stated. Taking a race-neutral stance, Bolden pointed out that the ECL was composed of black and white owners and that this fact "should warrant immunity from the citation of the race question." To evade the issue somewhat, Bolden concluded that "close analysis will prove that only when the color-line fades and [cooperation] instituted are our business advances gratified. Segregation in any form, including self-imposed is not the solution."[46]

The Dallas hiring revealed that the black press's vision for the Negro Leagues and the owners who operated them were not always one and the same. The black press wanted to see the Negro Leagues operating along the same lines as the white Major Leagues. In this way, they would embody the Washingtonian ideal of self-help and racial solidarity. With the Negro Leagues operating on the same level as the white majors, they would compete within the mainstream of the American economy. Thus, baseball would serve as one way that blacks would, theoretically, be integrated into the American mainstream and that prejudice would be eliminated. This was one reason why the black press clamored for a Colored World Series.

On the other hand, the ECL commissioners—primarily Bolden, Strong, and Keenan—sought to recapture the white fans who increasingly abandoned semipro and black baseball games. The Dallas hiring was justified on business grounds. However, it occurred at a time when white semiprofessional baseball began a slow decline. Historian Neil Lanctot cited a lengthy recession in Philadelphia that drastically reduced industrial sponsorship. By 1928, a number of once-powerful industrial teams had disbanded or returned to amateur status. Even Frank Young in Chicago observed that several white semipro clubs, many of which constituted the Chicago City League, started to disappear. Clubs considered to be powerful independents, like Rogers Park and Hammond, had all disbanded or returned to amateur status. Many of the ballparks in the Windy City had been lost to subdivision.[47]

The decline of white semipro ball meant that the Negro Leagues were becoming increasingly reliant on black patronage for their economic existence. By the mid-1920s, black communities throughout the US began to feel the effects of an economic downswing. Whereas black enterprises continued to increase after World War I, the proportion of blacks among all retailers tended to decrease. The success of black businesses depended peculiarly on the income of the working class, which worked primarily for whites and who traded with blacks. When adverse circumstances in the economy caused a curtailment of employment or a reduction of wages, black businesses were affected immediately. When the first signs of recession appeared in the middle of the decade, thousands of blacks lost their jobs. When the stock market crashed in October 1929, many blacks were already suffering from economic depression. Hiring Bill Dallas at a time when blacks were losing jobs, in conjunction with the ECL's becoming reliant on black patronage, was an ill-advised decision on the commissioners' part.[48]

Bolden now became embroiled in another controversy, this one with the league's premier player-manager, Oscar Charleston. In an article published in several black newspapers, Charleston proclaimed that the ECL was a farce: "The fans [were] being hoodwinked and fooled out of hard earned cash by a few men who are thinking of the present only and not the future." The new schedule format had become so confusing for Charleston that he didn't know when his club was playing a league game or an exhibition contest. The owners could manipulate the schedule in such a way that their league clubs would have an advantage in the standings. If their club won the contest it was a league game, but if they lost it was an exhibition. It resulted in several games being played under protest.[49]

Charleston added that the rotating system of umpires served to perpetuate problems rather than eliminate them. The arbiters' decisions were so bad that it would ultimately lead to the death of the league if the situation weren't rectified, he said. On June 14, in a game between Harrisburg and Hilldale at Lancaster, Pennsylvania, the Giants led 6-2 after three innings. The game was delayed by rain, which lasted no longer than fifteen minutes. After efforts were made to repair the field in order to continue play, the umpires postponed the game. Cancellations were rarely rescheduled and since, in Charleston's view, the field was in good condition, the decision angered the Harrisburg manager. Charleston urged black newspapers to denounce the postponement through their columns.[50]

On June 27, the *Philadelphia Tribune* published a response to the Charleston article. In terms of the umpire situation, John Howe stated he did not believe that the umpires were sabotaging league games. However, he did suggest that in the games he had observed, umpiring had deteriorated to a catastrophic state. The umpires exhibited too much uncertainty, Howe concluded; they changed their decisions too frequently. Howe also stated the *Tribune*'s position regarding an umpire baiting and a bullying tactic referred to as the "stall." The stall occurred when an umpire, after making a poor call, was encircled by the players who, hurling insults at him, delayed the game for long periods of time. Howe pointed out that when this behavior was eliminated, league games would become more orderly. Regarding the scheduling dilemma, Howe was as confused as Charleston. Howe suggested that a statement from the commissioners to the press that provided a clear explanation of what constituted a league game would be helpful.[51]

Bolden responded to Charleston's accusations. He charged the Harrisburg manager with spreading "uncalled for lies in an attempt to spread propaganda against the ECL and Hilldale." Bolden had received a letter from one umpire refusing to officiate Harrisburg games. He also claimed that Charleston misrepresented the facts about the Harrisburg-Hilldale game at Lancaster. Bolden stated that it had rained for over a half an hour and that the "pitcher's mound and home plate were a veritable mass of soft mud." The players could hardly walk around the base paths, let alone run. In an attempt to focus attention on Charleston's behavior, Bolden claimed the umpires were "authorized . . . by the Commission to arbitrate league games, and if they are not respected by playing managers and ballplayers the league will not be successful."[52]

Charleston continued his attack in the black press. The fundamental underpinning of his complaint was that the Harrisburg Giants were not getting a "square deal" in the pursuit of the ECL pennant. An unnamed sportswriter in the West claimed that "if Harrisburg should win . . . what a financial flop the World Series would be." In other words, if Harrisburg won the ECL pennant, the World Series games at the Giants' home ballpark would generate less revenue than in Philadelphia or Baltimore. Charleston also indicated that Wilmington would drop out of the league because club owner George Robinson was utterly disgusted with the league schedule. In addition, Charleston also indicted Nat Strong, stating the Royals' owner had little or no interest in the welfare of the league. What frustrated Charleston the most was that the ECL had the potential to be a successful organization that other prospective black leagues could emulate: "The Eastern Colored League with its compact circuit, and with an array of the greatest colored [ballplayers] in the business, with followers in great numbers, from the white race as well as the black race and with a very liberal press has the opportunity of showing the way in organized Negro baseball."[53]

Bolden rejected Charleston's charges, claiming they were "so absurd they are not worth answering." To evade the issue somewhat, Bolden pointed to the rowdy play of Charleston's players at league games. In a game against the Baltimore Black Sox, the Giants' players had supposedly "slammed one of the umpires and fought all over the Baltimore Park." In contrast, no such rowdyism had occurred at Hilldale Park for fifteen years. Bolden took the moral high ground when he stated if his Hilldale club could not win the pennant "through wholesome sportsmanship and clean baseball, I do not want it." He concluded with a peculiar statement: "As long as I can get six teams to work for and back up [the] organization we shall have a league."[54]

Both the Dallas hiring and the Bolden-Charleston controversy revealed the systemic problems that impacted adversely on the operations of the Eastern Colored League. To be sure, the fact that league clubs did not own their ballparks, along with Strong's refusal to allow the Royal Giants to use Dexter Park in Brooklyn, made it difficult to complete a balanced schedule. This provided the commissioners with the justification to lease additional parks to schedule games with white semipros with the potential to generate revenue. This would also allow the league clubs to play their scheduled games with little or no conflict. While this approach sounded commendable in theory, some of the club owners placed a higher premium on exhibition games with white semipros than on league games. An examination of the final league standings of the 1925 season revealed that the Brooklyn Royal Giants (33) played the fewest league games, followed by the Cuban Stars (41) and the Lincoln Giants (46). Hilldale (58) played the most league games, followed by the Harrisburg Giants (55), Bacharach Giants (52), and Baltimore Black Sox (50). The fact that no league club completed the proposed seventy-game schedule suggests that the traditional sense of promoting a league to stimulate fan interest—the pursuit of a pennant and a World Series championship—was the of little or no concern to

ECL owners. There is no evidence that any club owner was reprimanded or fined for skipping league games. It appears that both market size and the owners' lack of intention to place the ECL on a sound economic footing constituted more of a systemic problem than the fact that the teams did not own a ballpark. If the owners invested in leasing additional parks, then it was problematic to suggest that the schedule could not have been arranged in a such a way to accommodate league games. However, as Lloyd Thompson had pointed out previously, scheduling games in Atlantic City—the home of the Bacharach Giants—during the 1924 season was the league's biggest mistake. In other words, league clubs did not want to schedule games in the Bacharach's home park if they could generate more gate receipts against a white semipro team in New York. If this was the case, then it was difficult to explain why the ECL did not attempt to exploit the Washington market with its substantial black population (132,068), not to mention its reputation as a good baseball town. From a business standpoint, it would have been in the ECL's best economic interest to forego profits for a few years to create a demand for its product, ECL baseball. Instead, after only one year, George Robinson moved his Potomacs to Wilmington, Delaware, whose total population (106,597) was smaller than Washington's black population. The ECL owners boycotted the Wilmington Potomacs, and it was no coincidence that Robinson disbanded his club in mid-July. Such decisions appear to validate Charleston's claim that owners like Nat Strong had little or no concern for the ECL's overall welfare. Short-term profits were of greater importance than long-term considerations.[55]

Charleston's comments placed the spotlight on another league club that was having financial difficulties: the Lincoln Giants. In response to Charleston's claim that the Giants could not win games, Lincoln owner James Keenan denied his club would quit the league. Keenan admitted that the Giants were losing money and that the team had lost some of its best players. The Lincolns' owner also appeared to be having trouble with his landlord over the leasing agreement of his home park, the Protectory Oval. The *New York Age* reported that Bronx residents pressured the Catholic diocese to cancel the lease with Keenan. The lease should be terminated, they believed, because the Giants "had not made good and was the cause of occasional racial clashes in the Bronx." In other words, the Lincoln Giants had performed poorly against white semipro teams and this became a source of racial tension. Evidently, local residents wanted a white club, the Bronx Hebrews, to take over the park. To maintain its lease, the Giants met the Bronx team on the field and won, 8-3. To further validate their competence, the Giants defeated another strong club, this one from Philadelphia. Keenan's leasing problems could possibly explain Bolden's statement that the ECL would function as long as it had six clubs. Moreover, Keenan's leasing woes could also illustrate why the Lincoln Giants played only forty-six league games during the regular season. Competing against the leading white semipro clubs may have taken precedence over meeting league opponents, further adding to the ECL's systemic problems.[56]

Finally, hiring Bill Dallas as supervisor of the umpires at a time when African Americans were losing their jobs in other businesses and industries proved to be a poor decision by the ECL chairman. By the mid-1920s, both the ECL and NNL, like other black business enterprises, illustrated the impact of a separate black economy being that was being imposed on them. This, combined with the decline of white semiprofessional baseball, made the Negro Leagues increasingly reliant on black patronage for its economic viability. In comparison to Foster, Ed Bolden's race-neutral rhetoric reflected a more of a public-be-damned sentiment, and when his fellow commissioners did not support his choice of Dallas as supervisor, the ECL chairman faced public scrutiny alone. Dallas's indifferent performance as a supervisor further aggravated Bolden's problems. Dallas was accused by the black press of replacing black arbiters with white officials, and they noted that the league's umpires were frequently as poor as those the respective teams had previously employed. The situation led Rollo Wilson to ponder, "Does the supervisor of umpires ever see his men work and what does he think of them if and when he does?" Finally, the anticipated increase in white press coverage failed to materialize. However, if Ed Bolden felt as if he was left alone to face public criticism, he could at least get some satisfaction from the way his Hilldale Club performed in the World Series.[57]

Hilldale's Finest Hour

After defeating the St. Louis Stars for the NNL pennant, Hilldale would get its chance to avenge its 1924 series defeat against the Kansas City Monarchs. The series would be the best five-out-of-nine games. It would begin on October 1, with the first four games to be played at Muehlenbach Park in Kansas City. The series would then move to Baker Bowl in Philadelphia on October 8, 9, and 10, and because of the Pennsylvania Blue Laws, the eighth game would be played in Jersey City, New Jersey. The series finale, if necessary, would return to Philadelphia. The commission that administered the series consisted of Foster (chairman), Charles Spedden, J. L. Wilkerson, and Ed Bolden. Two umpires from the American Association were hired to arbitrate the series. Due to their second-places finishes in their respective leagues, St. Louis and Harrisburg would share in the gate receipts.[58]

It appeared that the fans would witness a closely contested series after the first two games, in spite of the Monarchs being handicapped by the loss of their pitching ace, Bullet Joe Rogan. In the first game, Hilldale hurler Rube Currie dueled Monarchs right-hander Cliff Bell to a 2-2 tie after eleven innings. Bill Drake relieved Bell in the twelfth inning and promptly hit Hilldale's leadoff hitter, George Johnson, with a pitched ball. Frank Warfield followed with a single, and Otto Briggs drove Johnson home with a single. After Hilldale shortstop Frank Stevens struck out, first baseman Tank Carr singled to center field, driving in Warfield and Briggs. It was all Currie needed, as he shut the Monarchs down in the bottom of the inning to win, 5-2.[59]

In the second game, Hilldale took a 2-1 lead after six innings against Monarchs' starter William Bell. After the Monarchs tied the game in the seventh inning, Newt Allen led off the eighth with a single and reached second base when shortstop Frank Stevens misplayed Newt Joseph's ground ball. Allen scored on Lemuel Hawkins's single past Stevens. The next batter, George Sweatt, walked, and Joseph scored when Judy Johnson could not handle Frank Duncan's line shot down the third base line. Hawkins scored on Nelson Dean's sacrifice fly, and the Monarchs won the second game, 5-3.[60]

The remainder of the series belonged to Ed Bolden's Hilldale Club, although the Monarchs played Hilldale tough throughout. Monarchs' manager Jose Mendez lost a 3-1 heartbreaker to Red Ryan in ten innings. In game four, Nip Winters fanned eight Monarch batters, and Otto Briggs and Frank Warfield led an eleven-hit attack en route to a 7-3 victory.[61]

With Hilldale leading 3-1 after four games, the series moved to Baker Bowl in Philadelphia. A reported 4,200 fans witnessed a classic pitcher's duel between Rube Currie and Cliff Bell in game five. Hilldale scored two runs in the bottom of the fourth inning, and Currie scattered six hits and struck out four batters on the way to a 2-1 win for the Pennsylvania club. Phil Cockerell faced William Bell in game six. Hilldale took a 1-0 lead in the fourth inning when Clint Thomas doubled to right field, and scored on George Johnson's single. In the sixth inning, Cockerell reached first base on Newt Joseph's error. Stevens doubled to right field but Cockerell was thrown out at the plate. With two outs, Stevens scored from third base on Warfield's infield single. In the sixth inning, Tank Carr hit a home run and Biz Mackey followed with a double. Mackey scored on Clint Thomas's double. The game for all intents and purposes was over at that point. Hilldale scored one more run, and while the Monarchs added two, it was not enough to snatch victory from the club from Darby. Hilldale won the 1925 Colored World Series in six games.[62]

Whereas the Hilldale Club was impressive on the diamond, the series' overall financial picture told a different story. The total attendance for the series was 20,867, generating a little over $21,000 in gate receipts. After deducting expenses, the series realized $5,871.95 in total revenue. Hilldale received a winner's share of $1,233.11, while the Monarchs received $822.08. The highest attendance was in game four in Kansas City—7,208. Cold weather impacted the series games in Philadelphia. The financial picture led Frank Young to conclude that the series, financially speaking, was a disaster.[63]

Why didn't the Colored World Series become the predicted goldmine that *Kansas City Call* sportswriter Ollie Womack had envisioned? Certainly, the players on both teams exhibited a high caliber of play on the diamond, even though the Monarchs lost the second series in six games. With the exception of one contest, the games in both series were closely fought. The fundamental reason the Colored World Series did not reap the anticipated financial rewards was an overall lack of commitment to the postseason series by the men who ran the Negro League clubs. After praising the first World Series as the "best" he had ever witnessed, Rube Foster concluded that the event was premature. He stated erroneously that the white Major Leagues had operated for forty years without a fall season classic. The fundamental reason for Foster's involvement in the World Series was to secure an agreement from the ECL to respect the contract rights of NNL teams. This allowed him to gain autonomy over his NNL and simultaneously address the demand from the press and the public for a postseason series.

The Colored World Series further illustrated that the black press's vision regarding the Negro Leagues was not always consistent with that of the men who owned the clubs. To the black press, the World Series was one way to show that African Americans could compete within mainstream America once it was on par with the white World Series. However, the club owners were more concerned with immediate short-term profits rather than their leagues' long-term aspirations. Their lack of commitment to the postseason series was evident when the event did not reap the anticipated financial rewards. Moreover, the black press—the prime mover for the series in the first place—was conspicuous by its lack of postseries assessment of the second Colored World Series.

As the 1925 season came to a close, both the Negro National League and the Eastern Colored League were about to enter a period of uncertainty. The peace settlement after the 1924 World Series placed both leagues in a position to administer their own affairs. They faced the familiar challenges of attempting to complete a balanced schedule; umpiring; and, in the NNL, constant franchise shifting. The economic downturn and the decline of white semiprofessional baseball led both leagues to become more reliant on black patronage for their economic viability. The league owners would attempt to rectify the challenges that the 1925 season presented, but unforeseen consequences frustrated their efforts.

10

Caught in a Rundown

The problems that the Negro National League and the Eastern Colored League confronted during the 1925 season continued to plague both circuits the following year. Several changes were made to address these obstacles at the annual joint winter session. They included a salary cap and a ban on players who jumped their contracts. Rube Foster continued to juggle franchises in his NNL and along with Frank Young made the case for competent businessmen to own and operate league clubs. The senior circuit's season was exacerbated by Foster's nervous breakdown in late July.

Much as with the NNL, the 1926 season of the Eastern Colored League brought with it an air of uncertainty regarding the league's future. Despite the PR campaign that the ECL pursued in the press, the league's commissioners were a divided group. For the first time, rumors circulated that an effort would be made to oust Ed Bolden as ECL chairman. A club owner went on record to declare the ECL was not a "real league." The scheduling dilemma reached its nadir as three league clubs affiliated with a white semiprofessional league in an attempt to recapture the white patronage lost at black baseball games. Also, the ECL season was tarnished when the black press reported several incidents of rowdyism occurring on the diamond.

The air of uncertainty surrounding the Negro Leagues during the regular season continued into the postseason series. Rumors circulated that the World Series would not occur, but a change of heart evidently led to a series between the Chicago American Giants and the Bacharach Giants. The series yielded better financial results than the 1925 World Series, but they were still far below expectations. At the conclusion of the World Series, Frank Young provided a critical assessment of it in the *Defender*. He was particularly critical of the way the World Series commission organized the series. *Kansas City Call* sportswriter Carl Beckwith challenged Young's assessment and claimed the *Defender*'s sports editor was misrepresenting the facts. Beckwith also noted that the importance of a pennant race during the regular season was needed to stimulate fan interest in the Colored World Series. He recommended reform of the existing system to achieve that aim.

To ensure their economic survival, the club owners made several sweeping changes at the joint session of 1927. Both leagues revised their governance structure and elected league presidents with the supposed authority to administer the affairs of their respective circuits. They lowered the salary cap in response to the economic downturn and maintained the ban on contract jumpers. The ban became a controversial issue when several players sought to test it prior to the start of the regular season. The owners' reluctance to follow the ban to the letter led the league presidents to arrive at a compromise solution. An interleague conflict occurred when the Cuban Stars West failed to place Alonzo Montalvo on their reserve list and the outfielder signed with the Lincoln Giants. When James Keenan refused to return Montalvo to the western Cubans, he withdrew his Lincoln Giants from the ECL. At the same time, some internal problems emerged for several clubs in both leagues. To further complicate matters, former ECL chairman Ed Bolden suffered a nervous breakdown that prevented him from handling the affairs of the ECL and his Hilldale Club.

In the midst of this chaotic season, it was amazing that the Colored World Series of 1927 even took place. Like their senior counterparts, the ECL adopted a split season format and the Bacharach Giants won both halves. Although the NNL did not publish standings for the second half, the Birmingham Black Barons were declared the winner, but they lost the league series to the Chicago American Giants in four straight games. For the most part, the World Series was anticlimactic, and the black press paid little or no attention to it. By November, Lloyd Thompson proclaimed that the owners would consider discontinuing the World Series at the joint session after the 1927 season. Thompson's comment revealed the owners' lack of commitment to the postseason series in the first place.

The second annual joint session, held in 1926, was an attempt to rectify the challenges both leagues faced during the 1925 season. The owners elected Ed Bolden chairman of the joint session and Charles Spedden secretary. The magnates adopted a salary cap whereby no club's monthly payroll would exceed three thousand dollars. Players who owed money to a club owner in either league had a July 1 deadline to make restitution. Both leagues agreed that a player jumping his contract would face a five-year suspension from Organized Black Baseball. Finally, both leagues agreed that a league club could play a team outside the association so along as that club did not tamper with players under contract.[1]

The agreement to play clubs outside the association appeared to be in response to the effort of the Homestead Grays' owner, Cumberland Posey, to get an agreement from both leagues to protect the contract rights of his team. Posey supposedly agreed not to tamper with players under contract if both leagues agreed to respond in kind. He reportedly filed an application to become an associate member, but his request was denied because "his joining would be of no benefit" for either league. The *Pittsburgh Courier* told a different story. The *Courier* reported that Charles Spedden had invited Posey to attend the joint session to get an agreement to respect each other's players under contract and sent copies of his letter to Bolden and Foster. Whereas Bolden favored the proposition, Foster rejected it unless the Grays became an associate member of the NNL. Posey rejected Foster's proposal. The owners also requested that the Grays' magnate make some concession to James Keenan for signing Gerald Williams and relinquish claim to Cleo Smith, but Posey refused. When Foster heard of the proposal, he wanted Vic Harris returned to the American Giants and Sam Streeter to the Birmingham Black Barons. The latter proposal ended "all negotiations."[2]

With the failure to secure a working agreement with Posey, both leagues turned their attention to the upcoming regular season. NNL owners reelected Foster as president, Quincy Gilmore as secretary, and J. L. Wilkinson as treasurer. Another round of franchise shifting ensued as Memphis and Birmingham were dropped from the league. At first, attempts were made to retain the Black Barons, but the team would reportedly be under new ownership. The Black Barons were a good gate attraction, amassing a reported $16,694 in gross revenue. Overhead expenses, however, made it problematic for Birmingham owner Joe Rush to turn a profit. Player salaries alone accounted for $12,500 of the total operating expenses. The high cost of rail travel made the midwestern clubs reluctant to travel to the South. The league reportedly paid a little over $25,000 in transportation costs alone. Both the Cleveland Browns and the Dayton Marcos were chosen to replace the southern teams, and the NNL would begin the season as a midwestern circuit in Chicago, Cleveland, Cuban Stars West, Dayton, Detroit, Indianapolis, Kansas City, and St. Louis and with the Cuban Stars West as a traveling team.[3]

During the course of the 1925–1926 winter season, the *Defender* published an article titled, "Foster Seeking System in Business Management of Negro National League." The article was in response to the alleged clamoring by the fans over why so many league clubs failed. The fans were also ostensibly "puzzled" over the lack of published statistics. Newspapers were accused of withholding information, and certain sportswriters were charged with being biased against the league. Individuals who were responsible for compiling league statistics were "roasted" for withholding information to favor a certain club. The primary cause of these deficiencies was supposedly the club owners' lack of business acumen. The owners would hold on to game reports for several days if their club lost but would forward the information immediately when they won. This selective reporting of game results made it difficult for newspapers to print an accurate account of the league standings on the sports pages. To further validate Foster and Young's call for competent businessmen, Faye Young investigated the leagues' ledgers. Four clubs were reportedly in the black: the Chicago American Giants, Detroit, Kansas City, and St. Louis. Since the league's inception in 1920, the Chicago American Giants had generated the most revenue ($514,006.91), followed by Kansas City ($247,735.46), Detroit ($164,881.09), and St. Louis ($152,008.95).[4]

There was probably some validity to the claim that some baseball owners lacked the business savvy necessary to run a successful operation. Both black and white professional baseball has had a history of fly-by-night operators seeking to capitalize on the national game. However, the *Defender* article revealed Rube Foster's familiar strategy of downplaying the heavy-handed tactics that he used to run his NNL. This undoubtedly led to some "competent" businessmen's reluctance to commit to the circuit. Suggesting that baseball owners like Charles Mills, John Connor, and business manager Tenny Blount did not possess the business acumen Foster sought to run league clubs was problematic. By creating a system whereby league clubs and associate members paid a 5 percent booking fee to schedule their games, not to mention those same clubs becoming reliant on Sunday games in Chicago, Rube Foster had essentially alienated the very men he attempted to attract to operate league clubs.

At any rate, the call for competent businessmen to run league clubs was moot due to Foster's illness and subsequent nervous breakdown. He had been showing signs of poor health for several months, and many of his friends suggested he take a long rest. The previous year, he had been severely gassed in a hotel room in Indianapolis because of a leak in the gas pipe of a hot water heater. The cause of his illness was unclear, but contemporaries pointed to the experience in Indianapolis, combined with the burden of operating his club and the league, as contributing to his condition. In mid-August, Foster finally went to Michigan for a two-week vacation before urgent league business brought him back to Chicago. The collapse came within a month of his return to the Windy City.[5]

The black press hailed Foster for his achievement in Organized Black Baseball to that time. They highlighted his brilliant career as a pitcher, manager, and owner of the most prominent black club of the early twentieth century. He was credited for doing "much to make the national pastime a paying business among his race." The *New York Age* proclaimed that "Foster [had] in the past twenty years been able to amass one of the largest fortunes of any member of his race through his ability to make baseball pay." His heavy-handedness alienated several of his fellow owners and, at times, members of the black press. However, one could not fairly marginalize his role in the formation of the Negro Leagues.[6]

Foster's collapse reportedly led Kansas City Monarchs' secretary Quincy Gilmore to lobby for the league's presidency. On September 11, the *Defender* reported that Gilmore had several suggestions regarding league operations, one of which would be a source of controversy. To obtain more publicity for the NNL, Gilmore suggested that the league should "play more to the white papers." This, he said, was where "you've got to center your activities for publicity." He indicated that the *Kansas City Star* gave the Monarchs a good deal of publicity. This suggestion appeared to be an effort to recapture the white fans that had begun to abandon black baseball games.[7]

Predictably, the *Defender* took exception to Gilmore's comments. Frank Young contrasted the kinds of sporting activities on which the press reported in Chicago and Kansas City. The American Giants, he wrote, would never receive a substantial amount of press coverage in Chicago due to the presence of the Cubs and the White Sox. There were also plenty of other sporting activities to report on including horse racing, golf, tennis, boxing, and auto racing. Furthermore, the white papers in Kansas City did not, according to Young, believe the Monarchs were in a real league. How could the Kansas City team play a certain number of games with another league club like Cuban Stars, who played only half the league games that Kansas City did. To the white press in Kansas City, the NNL was merely a booking agency. The white press in neither Detroit nor St. Louis gave much press coverage in their cities. Young accurately stated that Race newspapers had supported the league for six years, providing box scores, batting averages, and photos when they could obtain them. Young said that white attendance had fallen off at Monarchs games despite the alleged publicity from the white press.[8]

Gilmore took exception to the *Defender* article. In a letter written to the paper's editor, Robert Abbott, and published in several black newspapers, Gilmore categorically denied the charges. The league secretary reminded Abbott of a meeting they had in which Gilmore hoped for continued friendly relations with the *Defender*. He added that he was aware of the value "of the *Defender* and other Race papers throughout the country" and knew that the NNL could not have existed without them.[9]

John Howe of the *Philadelphia Tribune* assessed the Gilmore-*Defender* conflict. Howe stated that if Gilmore was misquoted, Abbott owed the league secretary an apology. He added, however, that the desire to seek publicity in the white press illustrated "that many men of color whose weakness for persons and things white [was] the last word in slave psychology." In spite of the controversy, Howe indicated that the black press would continue to boost black sports, giving them publicity and space. The Race papers would also continue to criticize "those weaknesses that were the results of the efforts of selfish individuals."[10]

The Gilmore-*Defender* controversy exemplified the changing business and economic climate in which the Negro Leagues had begun to function by the mid-1920s. In spite of league formation, black baseball teams continued to operate their segregated enterprises within the fabric of a national economy. These clubs would continue to maintain their business ties with white semiprofessional teams. Given the systemic obstacles these entrepreneurs faced, and the fact that they had no intentions of running their leagues like the white majors, it was understandable that they would maintain this method of operation. Yet the decline of white semiprofessional baseball, the economic downturn, and most important of all, the impact of the separate black economy being imposed on them, made this means of doing business impractical. The loss of Rube Foster within this context further illustrated the feeling of uncertainty that surrounded the Negro National League. While the NNL faced an uncertain future, the faction-prone Eastern Colored League commissioners further aggravated the obstacles that impacted their league instead of eliminating them.

A League in Name Only

Using the slogan "bigger and better," the ECL commissioners set out to address the hurdles that had plagued the 1925 season. The commissioners accepted an application from a contingent from Newark to replaced George Robinson's Wilmington Potomacs. The group was led by Wilber

Crelin, who was reportedly a prominent Newark sportsman who had been identified with semiprofessional baseball in Newark for the preceding decade. Several factors contributed to Newark's being selected as the eighth league club. First, it was supposed to receive financial support from Bob Davids, club owner of the International League's Newark franchise. Davids had purchased a minor league club in Reading, Pennsylvania, and relocated it to Jersey City. Second, a new park was being built with a seating capacity of eighteen thousand, and the ECL club would play its home games there when the IL team was on the road. Finally, Newark was chosen because it made the ECL a more compact circuit along the Atlantic Seaboard. The commissioners also censured the managers, players, and "those not financially interested in the ECL from writing [positions] for the press detrimental to the league." This ruling was directed at Oscar Charleston for his outspokenness.[11]

At the same time, rumors circulated about a possible coup to remove Ed Bolden from the chairmanship. Reportedly, several owners had grown disenchanted with Bolden's "narrow, partisan rule as president of their association." Through an alliance of the Lincoln Giants, Baltimore Black Sox, Harrisburg Giants, and the Newark club, an effort was made to replace Bolden at the annual meeting. When Nat Strong heard of the possible coup, he threatened to block any team from playing in New York should Bolden be replaced. The proposed threat proved effective, as two of the teams were reported to have gotten cold feet and backed down. James Keenan denied that such a plot to depose Bolden existed. In a letter to the *Baltimore Afro-American*, Keenan stated that although some of the commissioners had several disagreements with the chairman, there was never an attempt to remove him from office: "Both Mr. Spedden of the Baltimore Black Sox and Colonel Strothers of the Harrisburg Giants denied having any knowledge of this supposed movement to dethrone Mr. Bolden."[12]

Announcement of the proposed palace revolt led *New York Age* sportswriter William Clark to interview Nat Strong about the inner workings of the ECL. The interview allowed Strong to deny that he was the "czar of the Eastern League." Strong stated that the Eastern Colored League was not a league at all, but an alliance of a group of black baseball clubs. "It can't be a league," Strong was reported as saying, "because the majority of the teams play only Saturday and Sunday games." He added that since the association was viewed as a colored league, it was only "proper that a colored commissioner be made the chairman." Since Bolden was an outstanding commissioner, he got the job, Strong said. Much like Bolden, Strong engaged in some race-neutral rhetoric to show how baseball could serve as leveler of racial prejudice and discrimination. "Baseball games of this type are also an educating influence," Strong added, "and do much toward breaking down racial prejudice on the part of the fans who attend." Undoubtedly, the claim was made to justify league clubs playing more games with white semipros than with each other. For the first time, a club owner went on record to show that the Negro Leagues—the ECL in particular—was more of an alliance than an organized league in a traditional sense. It also illustrated that black baseball owners had no intention of running their leagues like the white majors, especially if Nat Strong was involved.[13]

The 1926 season provides the best evidence concerning the factors that influenced the commissioners' thinking in drafting a playing schedule. Essentially, the ECL had six parks for the eight league clubs to use on a regular basis. Scheduling around a minor league club's playing schedule was a daunting task for the commissioners. The *Baltimore Afro-American* reported that Colonel Strothers's Harrisburg Giants used the same park as that used by the white Harrisburg team in the New York–Pennsylvania League. He had to wait for the minor league team's schedule to be released before he could propose home dates for his Giants. Simultaneously, however, two teams—the Baltimore Black Sox and the Lincoln Giants—would only play Sunday games at home. Nat Strong refused to provide home grounds for either the Brooklyn Royal Giants or the Cuban Stars. As the *New York Age* accurately stated, this arrangement presented a "rather complex situation that will take a bit of time and also finance to adjust." This scheduling arrangement validated Strong's assertion that the ECL was essentially an alliance of baseball clubs. Two teams refused to leave home on Sunday, and two teams were regulated to traveling status. With Ed Bolden being more concerned with maintaining his alliance with Strong, it was understandable why the Bacharach Giants, Wilmington Potomacs, and the Newark club fared so poorly financially.[14]

To both alleviate the financial strain on clubs in smaller markets and recapture white patronage at black baseball games, three league clubs joined the Interstate League. The Pennsylvania League consisted of three white and three black clubs, the latter being Hilldale, Harrisburg, and the Bacharach Giants. Affiliation with this league illustrated the efforts of black baseball clubs to continue operating their segregated teams within the fabric of the white semipro scene. A clear indication of this mode of operation was that games played between the black clubs counted in both the ECL and Interstate standings. It also revealed the continued Bolden-Dallas connection, with the white sportswriter being the new league's secretary-treasurer.[15]

By July, the decisions the commissioners had made to deal with the obstacles of the previous season began to unravel. For the second straight year, a league club failed to complete the season. The Newark club disbanded when the reported financial backing from IL owner Bob Davids failed to materialize. This lack of financial support made it impossible for the team to sign top-level players, and the club got off to a disastrous 1-10 start. Even more problematic was that the team played only three home games in the newly built ballpark.[16]

The black press also began to report several incidents of rowdyism at ECL games. Rowdyism has had a mixed legacy in the history of professional baseball. On the one hand, club owners had built in a culture whereby the umpire was demonized by the fans because at times it stimulated spectator interest. Legendary managers like John McGraw had made umpire baiting an art form by the early twentieth century. Ty Cobb had created a persona of someone who was continuing the Civil War on the diamond. All of this conflict helped create a demand for the product of Major League baseball and had, by the early twentieth century, become embedded within baseball culture. On the other hand, when rowdyism was perceived to be out of control, administrators like Ban Johnson developed a policy to curb its excesses but not eliminate it. Whether rowdyism was greater at black baseball games than in Major League contests by the mid-1920s is subject to debate.

What was certain, however, was that the focus of the black press on the perceived rowdy behavior on the field was becoming a public relations nightmare for Ed Bolden's ECL.[17]

Rowdyism had been linked to the poor umpiring on the field. Walter "Rev" Cannady had a reputation as one of the most notorious umpire baiters in black baseball. A good defensive second baseman and a bad ball hitter, Cannady was characterized as quiet but moody and "mean." Other players left him alone due to his unpredictability. On July 3, the *Baltimore Afro-American* reported that Cannady, playing for Harrisburg, had assaulted an umpire in a game against the Lincoln Giants. In the fourth inning, Cannady tried to stretch a single into a double and was caught in a run down. When he attempted to slide back into first base, he was called out. Cannady retaliated by punching the umpire in the jaw and was about to hit him again when Lincoln manager John Henry Lloyd intervened. A special policeman ran onto the field, which led the entire Harrisburg club to do the same. The players thought the officer was about to attack Cannady. Only the coolness of Lloyd averted a near riot. In early August, Cannady was involved in another incident. This time the second baseman attacked an umpire outside of Hilldale Park after a tough 3-0 loss to the Darbyites. Cannady had reportedly thrust a bat through the window of the arbiter's car, shattering the glass.[18]

Rowdyism alone was not enough to undermine the umpires' efforts to maintain order. In a doubleheader between the Bacharach Giants and the Lincoln Giants, minor arguments over decisions made by the arbiters marred the second contest. Abusive remarks by the Lincoln Giants' third baseman Oliver Marcelle led to his ejection from the game. Bacharach catcher William "Fox" Jones was also ordered off the field. When Marcelle refused to leave the field, the umpire threatened to forfeit the game. However, James Keenan exercised his right as a league commissioner to prohibit this action.[19]

Ed Bolden attempted to set an example for the other clubs to follow. He fined and suspended pitching ace Phil Cockerell for attacking an umpire in a game against the Bacharach Giants. Declaring the incident unwarranted, the ECL chairman fined Cockerell one hundred dollars and suspended him for five days. Cockerell had disputed a call by the second base umpire and then decked the arbiter with a right hook.[20]

The combination of rowdiness, the disbandment of the Newark club, and the scheduling debacle served to intensify the internal division among the club owners. On July 28, the owners met in Philadelphia to address rumors about the ostensible disbandment of the ECL and to work out a compromise between James Keenan and Nat Strong. The Royals' owner was conspicuously absent from the meeting. To address the "caustic criticism that has come forth from various sources" about the ECL's status, the commissioners "went on record that the benefit derived from business [relations] along in organization warranted a continuation." In other words, the commissioners agreed to complete the season in the midst of the obstacles that emerged throughout.[21]

Next the commissioners attempted to solve the scheduling dilemma. At the forefront of this quandary was the league clubs who had joined the Interstate League, Nat Strong's refusal to follow the league schedule, and the Royal magnate's antagonistic relationship with Lincolns' owner James Keenan. Strong's unwillingness to provide either the Royal Giants or the Cuban Stars home grounds in New York also contributed to the ECL's malaise. To encourage league clubs to play more league games in an attempt to complete the schedule, the commissioners drafted a policy stipulating that a team had to play at least 50 league games to qualify to compete in the World Series. Only the Bacharach Giants (54) and Hilldale (58) qualified to play in the series. The Royal Giants had played only 14 league games by August and finished the season playing 27. Keenan objected to the Royals' and Cuban Stars' failure to secure home grounds. In an attempt to reach a compromise, Hammond Daniels suggested the Cubans play at Bacharach Park when the Giants were on the road. Keenan refused to list either the Cubans or Royals in the standings and canceled scheduled games with both clubs.[22]

In response, Strong criticized Keenan as well as the overall management of the league. The Royals' magnate stated that the reason he wasn't playing the Lincolns was that Keenan had announced at the start of the season he would not play the Royals due to a previous understanding. This led Strong to book the Royals for several tours through

New York State. Strong also blasted Bolden for his poor leadership, declared the league a "phony," and charged that the Interstate League had taken the best dates for games. In Strong's view, those dates should have gone to the ECL. To further complicate matters, the Interstate League disbanded in August.[23]

The so-called harmony meeting did not reach its intended objectives. On the contrary, *New York Age* sportswriter William Clark stated, the meeting served to widen the breach among the club owners. The meeting did reveal the growing dissatisfaction among the commissioners regarding Nat Strong's "attitudes of indifference and non-cooperation." The fact that Strong was more concerned with maintaining an alliance—particularly with Hilldale—than operating the ECL in a traditional sense only added to the other owners' discontent.[24]

THE 1926 COLORED WORLD SERIES: A "JOKE" OR IN NEED OF REFORM?

On September 25, 1926, the *Baltimore Afro-American* reported that rumors were circulating of a possible cancellation of the Colored World Series. Financial considerations were at the heart of the prospective termination. Three teams were in the hunt for the ECL pennant: the Bacharach Giants, Harrisburg Giants, and Cuban Stars. Harrisburg and the Bacharachs resided in the league's smallest cities, and the Cuban Stars were a traveling team. It was inferred that the gate receipts would not be substantial enough to justify an NNL club to travel east to play the ECL pennant winner. It would cost a reported five thousand dollars to bring a western club to the East. NNL teams were unwilling to travel east given the prospective opponent in the series. However, if the Chicago American Giants won the league playoff, the prospect of the series taking place was promising. The American Giants would "be sure to draw heavy attendance even if Harrisburg wins the pennant."[25]

To the surprise of most observers, the Chicago American Giants defeated the favored Kansas City Monarchs for the NNL pennant, so the World Series would now take place. The series began on October 1–2 at Atlantic City, New Jersey, and moved to Baltimore for a Sunday game on October 3. On October 4, the series moved to Philadelphia and after an open date would resume on October 6 in Atlantic City. October 7–8 were left open for possible makeup games. The series moved to Chicago on October 9, where the remaining games would be played. To alleviate overhead costs, club owners attempted, with apparent success, to reduce umpiring and publicity expenses and deny the second- and third-place clubs a share in the gate receipts.[26]

The Chicago American Giants epitomized the ball clubs Rube Foster had organized in the deadball era of the 1910s. Pitching, defense, baserunning, and timely hitting were the cornerstones of this pennant winning club. They were led by their player-manager and third baseman Dave Malarcher, a speedy switch-hitter who could bunt and run the bases in the Rube Foster style of baseball. He began his career in 1916 as a member of C. I. Taylor's Indianapolis ABCs. Malarcher joined the American Giants in 1920 and began his career on Foster's club by hitting .344. In 1925, he succeeded Bingo DeMoss as the American Giants' team captain and became the manager of the club due to Foster's illness. Floyd "Jelly" Gardner was the American Giants' right fielder, an outstanding defensive player with a good arm and great range. With his blazing speed, excellent bunting ability, and uncanny knack for drawing bases on balls, the punch hitter was an ideal leadoff batter. Willie Foster headed a dominant American Giants pitching staff. He was the half-brother of Rube Foster, and with his pinpoint control and wide assortment of pitches, the tall left-hander was at his best when the game was on the line. He and Willie Powell gave the American Giants a formidable one-two pitching combination. Powell possessed a variety of pitches that included a darting curve ball, blazing fastball, and sharp breaking ball.[27]

The Bacharach Giants similarly reflected the characteristics of a team developed in the deadball era. Dick Lundy was the Giants' shortstop and player-manager. He served as team captain in 1923 through 1925 and was appointed the field manager the following year. Oliver Marcelle was a superb defensive third baseman, and his skillful play earned him the distinction of being the best black third baseman in the 1920s. Marcelle was fast, covered lots of territory, and possessed a quick and snappy arm. Arthur "Rats" Henderson was the Bacharachs' pitching ace. He was endowed with one of the best curveballs of the era, and his right-handed sidearm delivery baffled opposing batters. His career was unfortunately cut short due to arm troubles. Veteran players Napoleon Cummings, Fox Jones, Ambrose Reed, and Chaney White rounded out a solid Bacharachs lineup.[28]

The Bacharach Giants took a 2-1 series lead with two ties. The first game of the series was tied at three after nine innings before the game was called for darkness. The second game was over in the second inning, when the American Giants crossed the plate seven times. Although the Bacharachs would rally, they went down in defeat, 7-6. The series moved to Baltimore, where the fans witnessed a historic pitching performance. The Bacharachs' hurler Claude "Red" Grier pitched a no-hitter, striking out eight batters and walking three. The Giants scored four runs in the first and six in the sixth inning to rout the Windy City club, 10-0. Game four ended in a 4-4 tie after nine innings of play when the game was called for darkness. In game 5, the Bacharachs got the best of American Giants' pitcher Rube Currie, who held the Giants scoreless until the Atlantic City club erupted for six runs in the fifth inning. Catcher Fox Jones led off the inning with a single and scored on Alonzo "Hooks" Mitchell's triple. Left fielder Ambrose Reed continued the hitting assault with a single, followed by base hits from Napoleon Cummings and Oliver Marcelle. A run scored when center fielder Chaney White was safe on a fielder's choice, and Dick Lundy cleared the bases with a double. Bacharachs' hurler Hooks Mitchell gave up four hits on the way to a 7-5 win.[29]

The series moved to Chicago, and after splitting the first two games, the American Giants got the best of Red Grier in the eighth game. Centerfielder George Sweatt doubled in the second inning and scored on Charlie Williams's single to give the American Giants an early 2-0 lead. The American Giants scored one run in the fourth and three in the sixth en route to a 6-3 win. The Bacharachs were never in the ninth game as the American Giants demolished the seaside club, 13-0.[30]

With the American Giants leading the series four games to three with two ties, Willie Foster would live up to his reputation as a big time pitcher in the clutch. Foster was locked into a scoreless tie with Bacharachs' hurler Hubert Lockhart for eight innings. Faye Young reported that Foster did not have his best stuff because he "got in so many tight holes." In the bottom of the ninth, Jelly Gardner led off with a single to left field. Malarcher moved him to second on a sacrifice bunt. American Giants' center fielder Sandy Thompson singled to center and the ball "took a peculiar hop." Gardner rounded third base and scored the winning run, and the Chicago American Giants were the Colored World Series champions. They had won the final game in the typical Rube Foster way.[31]

Attendance and gate receipts were slightly higher than for the 1925 World Series. Total attendance for the series was 20,396, generating $7,733.48 in gross revenue. The American Giants received a winning share of $1,624.04, while the Bacharach Giants received $1,082.68. Interestingly enough, the games at Atlantic City drew the highest attendance in the East. The first game drew 3,158 fans and a gross of $3,386. Game ten in Chicago drew the highest attendance in the series, 3,620 spectators generating $4,068 in ticket revenue.[32]

Frank Young assessed the past two World Series in the *Defender*. The fundamental underpinning of Young's analysis was that both Colored World Series were a "joke." He provided several examples to show that the club owners, park landlords, the railroad industry, and white umpires benefited from the series at the expense of the players. In 1925, the Kansas City Monarchs received a loser's share of $822.08, for example, whereas the commissioners received $400 plus expenses to administer the series. Hilldale, on the other hand, received a winner's share of $1,233.11. Divided by the number of players on the club roster—fifteen—each player received a "little over $80 for his work." The minimal returns led one Monarchs' player to reportedly say, "We could have made more in two games barnstorming than we'll get out of the whole World Series."[33]

Young also highlighted the ways the club owners undermined the series and manipulated the schedule to suit their economic purposes. Ed Bolden scheduled an exhibition contest for his Hilldale club against an All-Star team including five Major League players on the day the

World Series began. The exhibition was played at Wilmington, Delaware, approximately thirty miles away from Atlantic City. Many fans who would have come to the World Series were lured away by the more attractive exhibition game. With the first game ending in a tie, both teams played an additional game in Philadelphia. Bolden scheduled another exhibition contest at Hilldale Park in direct competition with the World Series.[34]

Several other examples illustrate how others rather than the players benefited from the series revenues. Young asked why a series game was scheduled in Baltimore. The answer, Young concluded, was that Black Sox business manager Charles Spedden, who served on the World Series commission, needed an attraction to generate revenues from renting the ballpark. Moving the series to Baltimore increased the travel expenses of both clubs, resulting in the "railroads [getting] theirs." The umpires, Young said, received more than the players "because they were white." According to the commission report, the umpires were paid $1,347, which averaged out to $673 for two arbiters. Conversely, each player on the American Giants received a little over $108. Under these circumstances, Young asserted, the players would rather barnstorm against major leaguers than win a league championship. In Young's view, the Colored World Series—and the Negro National League—faced an uncertain future.[35]

Kansas City Call sportswriter Carl Beckwith challenged Frank Young's analysis of the previous two World Series. Beckwith pointed out how Young conveniently neglected the fact that a portion of the series revenues went to him in his capacity as the NNL publicity director. He also highlighted Young's complicity in protecting the image of Rube Foster, who received four hundred dollars in his position as a World Series commissioner. Beckwith reported that Young, citing Foster's illness, "carefully explained to us in Chicago 'it might hurt the league'" to be critical of his role as a World Series commissioner. What intrigued Beckwith the most was why the sports editor of the *Defender* waited until the end of the 1926 series to conclude that the Colored World Series was a "joke." It could have been due to Young's receiving no compensation for the 1926 series and because of his unsuccessful bid for the NNL presidency. Beckwith astutely noted that the series needed reform before it could be successful. He also linked the series' success to changes needed to the regular season: "The post-season classic is practically new yet and many changes in plans must be made before the affair really gets profitable. Many changes in the regular playing season must be made—all of which will tend to create more interest in the regular games and as a result, in the World Series, before the crowds will storm the turnstiles to see the best of the East and West in action."

Beckwith concluded on a more optimistic tone while taking a final jab at Young: "The Negro National League will not die with the passing of Rube Foster . . . when the playing season for 1927 rolls around the chances are the organization will open the same as ever with just one change—Frank Young will NOT be on the payroll in any capacity."[36]

Carl Beckwith's commentary echoed the call for reform by several sportswriters in the league cities. Numerous changes were needed to both the administrative and financial structure of both leagues. The club owners in both leagues also recognized the need for reform. However, they would commit a series of costly errors that would cause the structure of Organized Black Baseball to crumble at its foundation.

Interleague Woes

On January 11, 1927, the owners of the Negro National League and the Eastern Colored League held their third annual joint session in Detroit, Michigan. An effort was made to secure tighter restrictions on players. The salary cap, including the manager's salary, was reduced from $3,000 to $2,700. The ECL reduced the size of player rosters to fourteen men, while the NNL would keep its roster size at sixteen players. Several changes were made in the World Series arrangements. League umpires would arbitrate the games instead of minor league officials and be paid twenty-five dollars a day plus expenses. Ten percent of the revenues would be allocated for the rental of league parks, whereas 30 percent were allotted to outside parks. A one-hundred-dollar reduction of residuals was designated to compensate officials who served on the World Series commission.[37]

The most sweeping change that occurred at the joint session was the election of presidents for both leagues. ECL publicity director Lloyd Thompson stated that constructive criticism given to the commissioners by several newspapers would be addressed at the league's winter meeting. The commissioners agreed to select an ECL league president and grant him absolute decision-making power regarding questions submitted to him by the various commissioners. To ensure the president's independence, he could not be invested in any way with any of the league clubs. Several candidates were considered for the position, including local park politician Ed Henry, Pennsylvania boxing commissioner Charles Fred White, and Baltimore lawyer Dr. G. A. Robbins. The commissioners eventually chose Isaac Nutter, an attorney from Atlantic City who once had been counsel for John Connor and Baron Wilkins.[38]

Nutter's appointment as ECL president coincided with internal division among the commissioners that would permeate the 1927 season. Prior to the joint session, James Keenan tendered his resignation as secretary-treasurer and announced that the Lincoln Giants would not field a team for the regular season. His primary reason for leaving the ECL was "discrimination on the part of the schedule committee in the matter of dates for games." Keenan alleged inaccurately that Nat Strong was the head of this committee and the Royals' magnate "personally made up the schedule." This was an interesting charge coming as it did from a club owner who refused to leave New York for Sunday games. Evidently, by early January the Lincolns' owner had had a change of heart. The *New York Age* reported that Cuban Stars' owner Alex Pompez served as an unofficial arbitrator to resolve the differences between Keenan and Strong. When the joint session convened, Keenan withdrew his resignation and resumed his duties as secretary-treasurer.[39]

At the same time, the NNL followed the ECL and elected as its president William C. Hueston, an African American municipal judge from Gary, Indiana. Hueston epitomized the type of black professional that emerged in the early twentieth century. Originally from Kansas City, Missouri, Hueston was a district grand master of the Grand United Order of Odd Fellows. This fraternal society had a history of providing assistance to individuals suffering from illness, subsidizing some modest relief to widows, and doing other charitable giving. Hueston was also the head of the New Educational Committee formed by the Elks and a prominent member in AME church circles. At the time of his appointment, he was serving as a municipal judge with criminal jurisdiction in Gary. In addition to Hueston's appointment, Quincy Gilmore was reelected as the league secretary.[40]

The NNL concurrently established a working agreement with the reorganized Negro Southern League (NSL). The NSL was organized one month after the NNL and would operate sporadically throughout the 1920s. It originally began with clubs in eight cities: Birmingham, Nashville, Knoxville, Atlanta, Pensacola, Montgomery, New Orleans, and Jacksonville. As early as 1921, Rube Foster had aspired to make the NSL an associate member of the NNL. On April 10, 1926, the *Pittsburgh Courier* reported that the NSL had reorganized, with Chattanooga and Albany, Georgia, replacing Pensacola and Knoxville.[41]

Bert Roddy was the driving force behind the reorganized Negro Southern League. Roddy attended the NNL winter meetings to help formulate a working agreement between the two leagues. It was a response to the occasional raiding of the southern circuit's player rosters by NNL clubs. A plan was adopted whereby the NSL teams would become associate members of the NNL. Birmingham and Memphis would also become members of the senior circuit. Trades and transfers of players by individual owners had to be ratified by the officials of both leagues, and any grievances had to be brought before the presidents for resolution. All exhibitions games by NNL clubs in the southern league's territories had to be played with NSL teams. If an NNL team played a team that was not a member of the NSL, the league club within the respective territory had the right of first refusal. With the agreement ratified, the NNL began the regular season in the following cities: Birmingham, Chicago, Cleveland, Detroit, Kansas City, Memphis, and St. Louis. The Cuban Stars West would once again function as a traveling team.[42]

The governance structure was in place, but the 1927 season was marred by several interleague squabbles, primarily over players. At first, it appeared that the five-year ban was effective. In January, the *Pittsburgh Courier* announced that Oscar Charleston had signed with the

Homestead Grays. In March, the *Baltimore Afro-American* announced that Charleston would remain with Harrisburg. Initially, Charleston was traded to Baltimore for Jud "Babe Ruth" Wilson. When he informed Baltimore Black Sox owner George Rossiter that he would not report, Harrisburg owner Colonel Strother called off the deal, allowing Charleston to remain with the Giants. The Harrisburg manager changed his mind because he believed that there was a future in what he called, in his words, "Organized Black Baseball," and because Mrs. Charleston did not like the idea of going to Baltimore.[43]

While Charleston decided to remain in the ECL, four highly recognized players attempted to test the five-year ban by failing to report to their clubs. Bizz Mackey of Hilldale, Herbert "Rap" Dixon of Harrisburg, Frank Duncan of Kansas City, and Andy Cooper of Detroit embarked on a barnstorming tour of Hawaii and Japan with Lonnie Goodwin's Philadelphia Royal Giants of the California Winter League. Dixon was considered one of the better power hitters of the 1920s. His nickname was derived from the Rappahannock River in Virginia. Duncan was one of the top receivers in black baseball and appeared in the first two World Series with the Kansas City Monarchs. He was a master at handling pop flies and could cut down would-be base stealers with one of the best throwing arms in the league. Cooper was the Star's pitching ace, with superb control and an exceptional array of breaking pitches, including a great curve ball, changeup, and slider.[44]

The case of the players barnstorming with the Philadelphia Royal Giants would determine the owners' willingness to follow their agreed-on policy regarding contract jumpers and would also show how much authority the magnates would delegate to their newly elected presidents. ECL president Nutter opposed the suspension, stating that the ruling was too drastic and that he would make an effort to modify it. Nutter added that the owners as well as the players were responsible for previous conditions and that it was unjust to bar a repenting player. The ruling on contract jumpers, Nutter said, was adopted by the concerted opinion "of resentful owners" who felt they had made maximum concessions to the players, while they in turn disregarded contracts and the gentlemen's agreement, the unwritten agreement not to employ players of color. In the owners' view, the players, therefore, "turned into which ever avenue their whims desired, mulching from the coffers of the various clubs' cash tills as they jumped from club to club."[45]

Carl Beckwith was suspicious of the way club owners, particularly the ECL magnates, sought to tighten restrictions on players. Bolden had reportedly written a letter to NNL secretary Quincy Gilmore asking what the midwestern league was going to do about its contract jumpers. Gilmore indicated that the NNL would abide by the agreement, and as far as the NNL was concern, the issue was settled. Bolden was looking for a loophole, since the players were not subject to suspension until the season started. Another way the ECL attempted to undermine the ban was through a statement which indicated that the men were "really not subject to suspension because they were not playing with an outlaw." It prompted Beckwith to ask if the Homestead Grays were not outlaws, then what were they. Since the players were not with their league clubs at the start of the regular season, they were suspended, and Bolden had no reason to complain about NNL actions.[46]

Two eastern sportswriters were also suspicious of the way the ECL was attempting to undermine the ban. *Baltimore Afro-American* sportswriter Walter Reeves reported that Bolden had discussed the matter with some of the officials and that they were willing to let Mackey return. This prompted Reeves to argue that the suspended players should be kept out of the games regardless of their ability. "In order to make the league a permanent, stable, and well thought of organization," Reeves added, "the rules and laws must be respected regardless of any individual." As a compromise solution, Judge Hueston recommended a thirty-day suspension as an alternative to the five-year ban. John Howe of the *Philadelphia Tribune* surmised that a thirty-day suspension would mean nothing to a player who was offered even a modest sum of cash to continue playing winter baseball. He believed a much stiffer penalty was advisable. In the end, Nutter suspended Mackey and Dixon for less than two weeks upon their return in July. Judge Hueston suspended Duncan and Cooper for thirty days and tacked on a two-hundred-dollar fine.[47]

Hueston and Nutter were confronted with an interleague dispute involving Lincoln Giants' outfielder Alonzo Montalvo. Montalvo was a star attraction for Abe Molina's Cuban Stars West. He once hit three home runs in a single game against the American Giants and also hit for high average, posting batting averages of .337, .308, and .346 from 1923 to 1925. Montalvo sat out the 1926 season after being denied a pay raise, and he subsequently signed with the Lincoln Giants in 1927. The NNL claimed Montalvo was still the property of the western Cubans, and Keenan refused to return the hard-hitting outfielder, pointing out that his name was omitted from the Cubans' reserve list. In essence, Montalvo was a free agent.[48]

NNL secretary Quincy Gilmore realized that Montalvo's omission from the reserve list was an oversight and that the league was reserving him. Bolden refused to play the Lincoln Giants unless Montalvo was removed from the lineup. Keenan yielded to his request, but the Lincolns' owner suggested that Judge Landis arbitrate this interleague dispute. This request appeared to conflict with the supposed authority granted to the new ECL president Isaac Nutter to "have the power of absolute decision to decide questions submitted to him by the various commissioners." Keenan eventually agreed not to play Montalvo until the two league presidents reached a decision.[49]

On May 14, the *Baltimore Afro-American* reported that Keenan had presented his case to Isaac Nutter. The ECL president decided that since Montalvo's name was not on the reserve list, he was a free agent. One week later, Judge Hueston declared Montalvo was still a member of the western Cubans and that if any team attempted to play the outfielder, it would be considered "by the NNL as an unfriendly act and would be dealt with accordingly."[50]

The Montalvo incident further illustrated the internal division among the faction-prone ECL owners. The *New York Age* reported that at least two owners would oppose Nutter's ruling. Alex Pompez objected to Keenan's signing Montalvo. While the Cubans' owner would not openly admit it, Pompez's objection was based on racial grounds. He felt there were enough American players for the other teams to select without signing Cubans. Pompez evidently had a gentlemen's agreement with his fellow owners that they would not sign Cuban players. He was especially incensed by Julio Rojo's willingness to play with teams other than the Cubans. Ed Bolden also opposed the Lincolns' retaining Montalvo, fearing reprisals by the NNL that could lead to another black baseball war. The NNL was in no position to fight a war over players, but Bolden did not want to take any chances.[51]

The ECL owners urged Keenan to return Montalvo to the Cuban Stars West. He refused and abruptly resigned from the league, indicting Strong and Pompez for allegedly engineering the decision. The Montalvo incident provided Keenan the excuse to withdraw from the ECL. He had also signed Jelly Gardner from the American Giants. Given his disposition prior to the start of the season, James J. Keenan's withdrawing his Lincolns from the Eastern Colored League was predictable.[52]

Whereas the Lincoln Giants' withdrawal wreaked havoc on the ECL playing schedule, in each league four other clubs were also experiencing internal problems. On April 23, the *New York Age* reported that bankruptcy proceedings had been instituted in the Federal District Court in Trenton, New Jersey, against the Bacharach Athletic Association, the principal owner of the Bacharach Giants. The association had accumulated a reported outstanding debt of $30,000. A bankruptcy petition was drawn by Hammond Daniels—who served as an ECL commissioner—and John B. Dykes, who held a joint claim of $13,700 against the athletic club. A judgment of $6,827 was awarded to Daniels and Dykes in an Atlantic County Circuit Court. The Bacharachs had been in financial difficulty for the past two seasons, citing inclement weather as a primary reason for their plight. Although rumors circulated that the club would disband, the Giants managed to finish the regular season.[53]

In Chicago, Rube Foster's illness resulted in a power struggle over control of the Chicago American Giants. Robert Peterson claimed that Foster's failure to make a written contract with John Schorling would cost his wife Sarah dearly. Mrs. Foster was in possession of the player contracts, but Schorling owned the ballpark. She was completely ignorant of her husband's business arrangement and without a written agreement was in an untenable situation. The *Baltimore Afro-American* stated that the league directors considered the American Giants predicament "a local one."[54]

Simultaneously, the Baltimore Black Sox club was also embroiled in an internal dispute. Black Sox business manager Charles Spedden was ousted by George Rossiter after the ECL's World Series share of $385 was reported missing. In August, the Black Sox suffered another mishap when several players were injured in a car accident near Aberdeen, Maryland. Local support dwindled for the club during the 1927 season, leading one observer to ask, "What's the matter with the fans? They don't turn out like they use to!"[55]

Hilldale, too, was hampered by a series of disturbing developments. Declining fan support and the league's unwillingness to resolve the schedule dilemma and umpiring finally took their toll on Ed Bolden. He maintained his full-time job at the post office but had been forced to take several periods of unpaid leave to attend to league matters. In late September, Bolden finally succumbed to the pressure and suffered a nervous breakdown, thirteen months after Rube Foster's mental collapse. Bolden was out of team and league affairs for several months. The HBEC chose Charles Freeman to replace Bolden as president.[56]

Both the Negro National League and Eastern Colored League were like patients in critical condition. Despite the remedies they administered, the owners could not stop the bleeding. Because of the total control over the administration and economics of the NNL by the now-absent Rube Foster, Judge Hueston assumed the presidency of a league that look like a ship that had lost its rudder. In essence, the NNL was dead in the water. Isaac Nutter became the president of a league where some owners were unwilling to abandon their independent ways. As the five-year ban and the Montalvo incident attested, the owners tried to find ways around their own policies instead of abiding by them. Under these circumstances, it was astonishing that the 1927 Colored World Series ever took place.

Farewell to the Postseason Series

The Colored World Series of 1927 began under dark clouds at Schorling Park. It had rained the night before and the skies did not clear until 11 A.M. on game day. The opening day parade was delayed, and the fans were late in arriving to the park because, according to Fay Young, "the owners 'didn't think' there would be a game." They also did not have the presence of mind to "find a nickel to use one of those things Prof. J Graham Bell invented to talk through," an obvious reference to the telephone. Several dignitaries attended the first game, including Mayor William "Big Bill" Thompson, Alderman Louie B. Anderson, and former Chicago Giants' co-owner and alderman Robert Jackson. Anderson and Jackson served as the battery to throw out the ceremonial first ball.[57]

It appeared the Chicago American Giants would win the series in a rout. The first game set the stage for the five games played in the Windy City. With the score tied at one into the fourth inning, back-to-back doubles by Willie Foster and Jim Brown gave the American Giants a 2-1 lead. After Malarcher flied out, Brown scored on right fielder Walter Davis's single. Bacharachs' hurler Luther Farrell hit the next batter, Nat Rogers, with a pitched ball. He was hit in the mouth and had to leave the game. Jumbo Jackson was sent in as a pinch runner and was forced out at second on a fielder's choice while Davis scored. Willie Foster struck out seven batters but gave up thirteen hits and had to wiggle "out of lots of holes" on the way to a 6-2 opening game win.[58]

The Chicago American Giants demolished the Bacharachs in the next three games. The second game was never in doubt, as the American Giants broke the game open with a five-run rally in the fifth inning and routed the Giants, 11-1. Game three was a weekday game, and the fans witnessed an excellent pitching performance by George Harvey. The American Giants' hurler gave up four singles and struck out eight batters in achieving a 7-0 shutout victory. The American Giants continued their hitting assault in the next game. Led by Dave Malarcher, Jim Brown, and Walter Davis, the American Giants would once again break the game open, this time with a five-run rally in the fifth inning en route to a 9-1 win.[59]

With the Chicago American Giants taking a 4-0 series lead, the Bacharach Giants would rally to stay alive. Darkness aided the Bacharachs in their first series win as Luther Farrell held the Chicago club to no hits after six and a half innings, after which the game was stopped.

Three runs in the second inning gave the Atlantic City club a 3-2 victory in this contest. The series moved to Atlantic City, where the sixth game was called after ten innings, ending in a 1-1 tie. The Bacharachs' hitting attack finally got going in the seventh game. They broke the game open with a five-run rally in the fifth inning to defeat the American Giants, 8-1. Jesse Hubbard outdueled Willie Foster in the eighth game, and the Bacharach Giants had now won three straight games. However, in the ninth game, the American Giants' bats came alive again, and Willie Foster held the seaside club in check on the way to an 11-4 win. The Chicago American Giants won the Colored World Series, five games to three.[60]

The lack of press coverage was an indicator that the Colored World Series had reached its nadir. For the first time, the Series commission did not publish a financial report. Postseries analysis by the black press was virtually nonexistent. In addition, the quality of the games themselves was poor, the series being marred by numerous fielding errors by both teams and uninspired play in general.

On November 3, 1927, Lloyd Thompson published an article in the *Philadelphia Tribune* titled "Baseball Heads May Abandon World's Series." Thompson stated one of the issues the owners would consider at the joint session would be whether to eliminate the Colored World Series. The past series in 1927 and the league playoff series between the American Giants and the Birmingham Black Barons that resulted from the split season were a "financial bust." Thompson pointed out that since the first series in 1924, financial revenues had dwindled significantly. Several "handicaps" were attributed to "poor judgment . . . imposed on the series by those who formed the laws and gave momentum to the project." Neither Isaac Nutter nor Judge Hueston was responsible for the postseason muddle, wrote Thompson; rather, they inherited it. Both presidents, however, were wise to eliminate the second- and third-place teams from sharing in the revenues, Thompson continued. The series had never generated enough gate receipts to justify six clubs sharing in them.[61]

Thompson also evaluated the split season that both leagues employed during the regular season. "Instead of intensifying the interest in the race and proving profitable in the playoff," Thompson added, "the irregularity of the schedules in both leagues has caused a lot of friction and ill feelings." He concluded that neither the split season nor the playoff had ever generated "the ever essential lucrative returns." Considering that the ECL had played only one split season, however, Thompson's analysis appeared a bit premature.[62]

Yet Lloyd Thompson's assessment revealed the fundamental reason why the Colored World Series never got off the ground. The fact that the owners would consider eliminating the series after staging only four postseason events was additional evidence of their lack of commitment to it. Creating a demand for the series—not to mention the mystique the World Series had achieved in Organized Baseball—was not compatible with the owners' primary focus on generating short-term profits. The Colored World Series never had a chance to develop memorable moments the fans and the press could talk about for years like the "Miracle Braves" of 1914, Bill Wambsganss's unassisted triple play, or Walter Johnson's memorable appearance in the 1925 World Series in the twilight of his career. For unforgettable events like this to occur, a long-term commitment by the owners was essential, including a consistent effort to make fans and the press see the games as special and deserving of particular attention. Such a commitment by the black baseball club owners was not forthcoming.

The fact that the owners were never proactive in promoting the Colored World Series further revealed their lack of commitment. There were no Ban Johnsons to declare the colored series as "the greatest institution in the world." The owners did not recognize the importance of a pennant race during the regular season as a way to stimulate interest in the postseason series. To some of these magnates, a balanced schedule was not in their best economic interests. At no time did they ever consider that the very thing they sought—amassing short-term profits—could be achieved through the development of a balanced schedule to create consumer demand.

At the end of the Colored World Series of 1927, it was evident that both the Negro National League and the Eastern Colored League had descended from being patients in critical condition to ones surviving on life support. The question was whether to take them off the life support system. One league would give up the ghost prior to the start of the 1928 season. But first, the black press, an independent club owner, and a prominent player-manager would clamor as never before for the reform of both leagues during the off-season.

11

Before the Fall

Beginning in 1925, several members from the black press, a club owner, and a prominent player-manager wrote a series of articles critically assessing the inner workings of the Negro National League and the Eastern Colored League. Some raised the familiar complaint regarding the lack of league statistics, while others focused on the need for both circuits to hire presidents who were unaffiliated with league clubs. Two of the sharpest critiques came from Homestead Grays' owner Cumberland Posey and Lincoln Giants' player-manager John Henry Lloyd. Posey was critical of the business relationship between Nat Strong and Ed Bolden and stressed the need for the ECL to reform the poor umpiring at league games and to eliminate rowdyism on and off the field. Lloyd, on the other hand, suggested a revised Eastern League, including Posey's Homestead Grays, along with a "high commissioner" to govern the league. Few could argue with the critiques these contemporaries raised about the inner workings of both leagues. Nonetheless, they essentially overlooked the club owners' motives that led to the creation of the Negro Leagues from the outset. Those motives made many of the proposed reform measures impractical.

While the commissioners held their annual winter meeting and both leagues conducted their joint sessions, the breakup of the Eastern Colored League was inevitable. Colonel Jacob Strothers's resignation from the league had a domino effect, with other club owners leaving the circuit. Ed Bolden recovered from his illness and assumed control of the Hilldale Corporation. His first official act was to withdraw from the ECL and simultaneously indict some of the former commissioners in the press. Isaac Nutter attempted to hold the league together, but the ECL magnates returned to independent ball. During the course of the season, several sportswriters, led by Rollo Wilson and Bill Gibson, urged the eastern owners to form a new league.

In his second year as president, Judge William Hueston attempted to exert stronger leadership over the NNL's day-to-day operations. He applied many of the black press's recommendations to reform the club owners' business practices. Hueston also sought to improve the league's image by promoting black baseball as a means of self-expression, conducting a series of promotions, and illustrating the ways in which the sport served as a leveler of race prejudice among blacks and whites. The 1928 season was noteworthy for the league championship series between the Chicago American Giants and the St. Louis Stars. The series marked the end of an era in midwestern black baseball.

In January 1929, Ed Bolden invited several former ECL owners and Cumberland Posey to form the American Negro League (ANL). Six clubs constituted the new league: Hilldale AC, Baltimore Black Sox, Bacharach Giants, Cuban Stars, Homestead Grays, and Lincoln Giants. The owners exhibited a willingness to cooperate, as the Lincoln Giants, Hilldale, and Baltimore agreed to play league games away from home. The clubs also tried to improve their relationship with the press by hiring Rollo Wilson as their publicity director and inviting several sportswriters to attend league meetings. Several players tested the owners' resolve when they refused to report to their respective clubs prior to the start of the season. A baseball war almost occurred when Cum Posey lured several players away from NNL clubs. Despite these obstacles, the ANL managed to complete the season, although several owners claimed they had lost money.

The Negro National League, on the other hand, experienced its worst season in its brief history. League secretary Quincy Gilmore resigned his position to organize a league in Texas. Several teams were in transition, such as the Memphis Red Sox, which change ownership for a second time in as many years. The Chicago American Giants lost several key players, including their player-manager, Dave Malarcher. Inclement weather impacted negatively on attendance for a second straight year, leading Judge Hueston to encourage fans to attend league games in the second half of the split season. The season was marred by a fire at the Detroit Stars' home grounds, Mack Park, which injured several fans. The Mack Park fire and declining attendance led many contemporaries to ponder whether the NNL would survive another season.

A Call for Reform: The Black Press Speaks Out

The early relationship between the black press and the Negro Leagues was essentially a neutral one. The press focused primarily on publishing box scores, reporting on the quasi-pennant race that occurred each year, and printing statistics when they were available. Forming public opinion was left to league officials, with Rube Foster and Lloyd Thompson emerging as publicity directors who understandably sought to create an image that was favorable to their respective leagues. As the baseball war of 1923–1924 illustrated, the black press provided space for various club owners and officials to debate among themselves the plethora of issues that arose.

One newspaper, the Chicago *Defender*, was the exception to the rule. The "World's Greatest Weekly" sustained a pro-Rube Foster position throughout his league presidency. Sportswriters Dave Wyatt and Frank Young served as valuable press allies for Foster to shape public opinion in his favor. At no time was either Wyatt or Young critical of the way the league president ran his NNL.

By 1925, a shift in the black press's reporting of both leagues had occurred. They became more critical of the way the club owners ran their teams and leagues. Oscar Charleston's criticism of the ECL led several eastern newspapers to evaluate the league's scheduling practices and umpiring. Rowdyism at league games began to receive increased press attention. One of the league's practices on which the press focused was the need for an administrator not connected with league clubs in any way to run the league's day-to-day operations. Their efforts bore fruit when both leagues elected presidents prior to the start of the 1927 season.

On September 11, 1926, Frank Young wrote an article in the *Defender* titled, "Directors of National League Hold Future of Our Baseball in Their Hands." Young was no longer on the league payroll, and his editorial marked the start of this sports editor's becoming one of black baseball's staunchest critics. He declared it was time for the owners to end "their petty ambition and jealousy . . . and get down to business." Electing a president unaffiliated with a league club was important for the NNL's receiving the respect of the fans and the press. Young turned his attention to scheduling and proclaimed there was too much of a "one-sided arranging of playing dates." The remedy was to draft the schedule prior to the start of the season, with the owners approving it prior to its implementation. For clubs who refused to abide by the schedule, Young stated, a heavy fine should be administered.[1]

Young's analysis used the white Major Leagues as a model to reform black baseball. In his view, there should be no outlaw clubs like the Homestead Grays, Gilkerson's Union Giants, and the Chicago Giants. Instead, a "nation-wide organization" similar to the farm system in Organized Baseball should be established. Working agreements with the outlaw clubs that would compose this national organization should be developed and this would eliminate players jumping their contracts. "By having all clubs in the organization and a man at the head who's nationally known as a square shooter," Young added, "the Southern League and other clubs . . . would act as . . . training or farming out clubs for players." Undoubtedly the man at the top of this proposed organization would be patterned after Commissioner Kennesaw Mountain Landis of Major League baseball. What Young failed to recognize was that Landis opposed the Major Leagues' farm system and sought to eliminate it.[2]

A final issue Young raised dealt with his pet project since the NNL's inception: hiring African American umpires. It was essential, from Young's perspective, to "have umpires of our Race when it is possible to obtain them." Incompetent arbiters should be terminated. To reinforce his claim, Young used the familiar tactic of referring to public opinion: "The public demands them. We mean the man or woman who [pays] to see the game played . . . who is not satisfied with the decisions of either the black or the white officials."[3]

Cumberland Posey offered one of the most compelling critiques of both leagues. He began by critically addressing the business relationship between Nat Strong and Ed Bolden, which favored the Royals' magnate. "Despite the opportunity he has to help colored baseball by placing the Cubans or Royal Giants in one of these parks to use as a home ground," Posey declared, "he will not do this." Rather, Strong sent these clubs for two- and three-game series to Baltimore, Harrisburg, Philadelphia, and Atlantic City. He would send the Royal Giants in May and September to play league clubs with good rain guarantees when there were prospects of inclement weather, but during the "good days" of June, July, and August, the Giants would tour New England. Strong also insisted on a 10 percent booking fee for all the games he scheduled for the Bacharach Giants and the eastern Cubans. Bolden supposedly sanctioned all this "by secret and public dealings with Strong." The Strong-Bolden alliance was a primary reason James Keenan withdrew his Lincoln Giants from the ECL on several occasions.[4]

Posey also turned his attention to ECL publicity director Lloyd Thompson. Thompson was all right personally, according to Posey, but the Grays' magnate described him as a "hindrance to the [advancement] of colored baseball." The press releases Thompson wrote covered up Strong and Bolden's "shady dealings." Posey added that Thompson "should not be permitted to foist the propaganda of these men on the baseball public and call it 'Eastern league Notes.'"[5]

Posey concluded his editorial by addressing the five-year ban on contract jumpers, the impact of poor umpiring, and rowdyism at league games. The policy to ban contract jumpers was not "worth the ink it took to write it." "Five years from now," Posey added, "five-sixths of the magnates now in organized Negro baseball will follow the paths of C. I. Taylor or Rube Foster or will be broke." If the owners allowed their antagonistic relationship with the players to persist and maintained the friction among themselves instead of getting fair umpires and "getting rid of rowdies on the clubs and in the stands," the future of Organized Black Baseball was in jeopardy.[6]

Carl Beckwith followed Posey's analysis with an astute assessment of both leagues. Throughout the 1920s, Beckwith had been black baseball's sharpest critic. At times his analysis was one-sided, and he tended to be uncritical of the way J. L. Wilkinson and Quincy Gilmore ran the

Kansas City Monarchs. However, Beckwith articulated well the black sportswriters' vision whereby the Negro Leagues would incorporate the business characteristics of Organized Baseball. He started by detailing the ways the baseball war negatively impacted on NNL clubs, leading to a high degree of player jumping. The bidding of eastern owners for NNL players led the senior circuit to recruit players from Texas and the South. This recruiting adversely impacted the Negro Southern League, leading President Bert Roddy to secure an agreement with the NNL protecting the contract rights of NSL clubs. Because the NNL owners could not match the salaries the ECL magnates offered, the loss of star players to the eastern league crippled the senior league's financial position.[7]

Despite the higher salaries, bolting to the ECL proved to be a mixed blessing for some of these players. To recover some of the money the ECL owners paid, these owners began scheduling from ten to twelve games a week. The compact circuit allowed the magnates to schedule one league game and an exhibition contest. The players were accustomed to playing five games a week in the NNL. In essence, the higher salaries were counterbalanced by the increased number of games played per week in the ECL.

Beckwith claimed the salary limit was implemented as a cost-cutting measure to favor the ECL. "There was a hook in [the $2,700 salary limit,]" he proclaimed, "but the West failed to see it." ECL magnates were no longer able to maintain their high salary scale and were anxious to reduce it. Concerned over the possibility of losing players to the NNL, the ECL owners convinced the senior league to adopt the salary limit. Given the long jumps some NNL clubs made to the Deep South, their acceptance of the salary limit was understandable. Only one NNL team, the Kansas City Monarchs, did not reduce its salary limit. Instead, Wilkinson took other measures to stay within the salary cap, such as reducing the team's roster size.[8]

In August 1927, Lincoln Giants' player-manager John Henry Lloyd voiced his opinion about the state of the ECL to a group of newspapermen. Lloyd stated that a new eastern league with a "high commissioner not directly invested in a particular club, would be the proper move" for the 1928 season: "The present body [was] a mere association of clubs, controlled by Nat Strong with Bolden. Strong controls two clubs and his unofficial capacity [was] merely that of a booking agent." What disturbed Lloyd most was that the club owners were trying "to make a major issue out of the question of players' salaries." He claimed this issue was blown out of proportion and should have never "entered the discussion" at all. Lloyd pointed to the high salaries Cum Posey and Colonel Strothers paid for the Homestead Grays and the Harrisburg Giants, respectively. "The public [would] always pay to see baseball of high order," Lloyd stated.[9]

Lloyd and *New York Age* sportswriter William Clark discussed the possibility of an eastern league composed of New York, Harrisburg, Philadelphia, Baltimore, Washington, and Pittsburgh. Posey's Grays, located in Homestead, Pennsylvania, appeared to be the most attractive club in this proposed new league. Lloyd claimed that Posey's booking schedule would not be affected because of the Grays' ability to draw big crowds with white semipros in New York, Pennsylvania, and Maryland. The Grays' owner had assembled the best black club in the East, and the ECL in its present state was a "joke." Lloyd concluded by stressing the need for both leagues to be governed "by a high commissioner who knows the game, is a diplomat, and knows the secret of organization." It was an interesting assessment of the state of black baseball from the mild-mannered and often apolitical Lincolns' manager.[10]

Beginning on December 16, 1927, *Kansas City Call* sportswriter A. D. Williams wrote a series of articles titled "Behind the Curtain of Negro Baseball." Williams stated from the outset that he would focus his analysis essentially on the Negro National League. The western "fans" were demanding to know what the owners and league officials would do to "elevate the game." In his opening article, Williams address the financial structure of league clubs and the need to reform the scheduling system. League clubs were underfunded from the NNL's inception. Several clubs were granted charters in the league "without any semblance of finance" and were operated by owners who "knew nothing of the game and who cared less." Status was the primary motive for these magnates' association with the NNL. League officials were warned against placing franchises in Toledo and Milwaukee, for example. Both clubs disbanded in the middle of the season, and their demise created a lot of ill-will among the club owners. The constant franchise shifting led the fans to "feel all was not well with the league."[11]

Williams then turned his attention to the league's scheduling practices. He characterized the league's transportation methods as "criminal," costing the league thousands of dollars annually. The Cuban Stars West was scheduled to jump from Havana to Indianapolis, with no playing dates in between. Given the fact that the Cubans arrived in the United States through Jacksonville, Florida, a series with Birmingham and Memphis would have been feasible prior to their arrival in the Hoosier city. The Indianapolis ABCs were scheduled to play a league game in Kansas City and then an exhibition contest in New York, with no additional games prior to their arrival in Gotham. Due to the high cost of rail travel, Williams's claim that the NNL lost thousands of dollars in transportation costs was valid.

In his next article, Williams focused on the high cost of player salaries, the need to construct a more compact league of clubs, and the importance of publicity. In Williams's view, league clubs had carried too many players on their rosters, and he recommended a roster limit of fourteen men. Williams explained that "if this number had been cut to 14 men at the outset . . . the league would have saved in seven years (at the rate of $150 per month) $84,000 in salaries." Weaker clubs could, theoretically, have had better players, leading to increased spectator interest. The old eight-club format should be replaced with a compact six-club circuit. Seven years with no results, he said, should have convinced these magnates of the need to scrap the eight-team league. The idea was to keep league clubs busy with either league games or plenty of exhibitions. Fewer clubs would reduce travel and overhead expenses and allow the owners to maximize revenues.[12]

With regard to publicity, the NNL underestimated its importance in maximizing profits, Williams asserted. Club owners failed to cooperate with the press in their respective cities and became angry when the sportswriters urged them to send in their game reports each week. They refused to accommodate the press who came out to the park and covered their games. Williams claimed that some owners wanted it both ways: on the one hand, the magnates wanted all the publicity they could get, but on the other hand, they withheld game reports when their clubs were playing poorly. Efforts were made to rectify this strained relationship between the owners and the press. However, a club owner "with more cash than horse sense" defeated this attempt to establish harmony. Such actions led Williams to conclude that "few newspapers in the country really gives 'a tinker's dam' whether they carry any news of league baseball clubs at all." He added that this feeling was "not diminishing with years either."[13]

Williams discussed the ways in which the Foster-Blount controversy and the plight of the Indianapolis ABCs hurt the Negro National League. Tenny Blount had built a solid club in Detroit, and Williams believed the Stars magnate deserved better "than a swift kick from the toe of the league." It should be noted here that Williams served as the Stars' press secretary at the time of the controversy, and so his interpretation of events would naturally favor Blount. Nevertheless, the complaints Blount registered were justified. Blount's replacement, Steve Pierce, had spent a lot of money on the team, but bad management had made the Stars a shell of their former self. Some observers reportedly thought the league made a mistake when they sold the club to Pierce. They felt there were other men in the Motor City more capable of running the Stars. "The Foster-Blount controversy just about wrecked Detroit," Williams declared, "and the attending actions of the president left nothing for Detroit to do but flounder."[14]

The plight of the Indianapolis ABCs was also a bad mark on the league. The ABCs' fall from the ranks of the elite black clubs began with the controversy surrounding C. I. Taylor's successor after his death. It reached its climax when the players refused to play for Mrs. C. I. Taylor. When the matter was brought before the league, the magnates urged Mrs. Taylor to sell the club, but she refused. They also encouraged her to let one of Taylor's brothers run the club. Again she refused, and the ABCs supposedly diminished in drawing power, losing several of its players "until it was a skeleton of the former great ball club." In a rather chauvinistic tone, Williams indicted Mrs. Taylor for the ABCs' demise because she "was allowed to retain her league membership too long."

He added, "She should have been ousted from the league as soon as the officials found that she had no intention of doing anything other than that which she wanted to do regardless to league rules and regulations." Williams did not indicate which "league rules and regulations" Mrs. Taylor was breaking. More important, he provided no concrete evidence to show how Mrs. C. I. Taylor had crippled the ABCs.[15]

With the exception of Williams's analyses of the plight of the Indianapolis ABCs, few could argue with the criticism raised by these contemporaries about black baseball's predicament. Although the owners used the convenient excuse of the lack of park ownership regarding scheduling, the arrangement of playing dates for league clubs was one-sided, favoring some teams over others. This made a mockery of the pennant race and impacted negatively on the Colored World Series. The majority of owners undervalued the importance of publicity in the form of published league standings and player statistics to stimulate spectator interest. The owners' refusal to support their umpires on the field resulted in an increase of reported rowdyism at league games.

Upon close examination of the media critique, however, many of their proposed reform measures were impractical for a number of reasons. First, with the exception of Cum Posey, and to a lesser degree John Henry Lloyd, these sportswriters never considered the primary mode of operation in the way these club owners ran the Negro Leagues. It can best be described as the business alliance model. Of the three principal assets that constitute a professional franchise—the players under contract, the franchise, and the ballpark—the majority of club owners had most control over the first two. In 1919–1920, Rube Foster's series of articles, "Pitfalls of Baseball," spent a great deal of time on the player-owner relationship and, most specifically, the need to eliminate player jumping. Through an association with a few club owners in certain cities, these magnates could collectively eliminate player jumping and allow them to gain tighter control over black baseball's player force. The collusive business relationship among these owners also served to minimize to a certain degree outside competition from prospective entrepreneurs seeking to capitalize on the baseball craze.[16]

In terms of scheduling, the business alliance model enabled the owners to form loose associations among themselves to ensure that their clubs secured the best playing dates and parks to play in. They could play either a league game or an exhibition contest in the pursuit of generating gate receipts. This arrangement, nevertheless, came at the expense of the other league clubs. This led, in most cases, to some clubs relying on additional games booked by Rube Foster and Nat Strong to generate revenue. This arrangement permitted Foster and Strong to leverage their positions in the black baseball marketplace. Also, by charging a 10 percent booking fee, both men earned additional residual income and maximized their profits. Viewed within this context, implementing reform measures would have been a daunting task with Foster and Strong dominating the day-to-day operations of their respective leagues.

Second, the sportswriters used Organized Baseball, and particularly the Major Leagues, as their model for reform. Given the economic prosperity the Major Leagues experienced in the 1920s, it was predictable that sportswriters would urge the Negro Leagues to emulate them. Yet these sportswriters failed to take into account that the Major League owners accepted the fact that they were competitors on the diamond but partners in business. No one owner could run the league by himself, so all had to cooperate to a much greater degree than other business enterprises. Without question, the Major League owners did not always follow the script guiding the competitor-partner model. But they enjoyed considerable advantages—most notably a political and economic climate that allowed them to build lavish stadiums—that black baseball owners never had. These advantages enabled the Major League owners to deviate from the script from time to time with no severe repercussions.[17]

Hiring an administrator not connected with a league club was an impractical reform measure within this context. These presidents or "high commissioners" would only be effective if the owners agreed to grant them the authority over the league's day-to-day operations. The owners would have to cooperate in granting the president the power to impose penalties and sanctions. Without this cooperation from the owners, the presidents would serve essentially as figureheads. The owners, especially in the ECL, exhibited an unwillingness to follow their own policies and procedures on a consistent basis. On the contrary, for the most part the owners tried to undermine them. Hiring a league president sounded commendable in theory, but the suggestion was somewhat of an impractical solution to black baseball's predicament.

Finally, there was one area where the sportswriters should have shouldered some of the responsibility in the effort to reform black baseball—publicity in the form of published statistics. Unlike their white counterparts, African American sportswriters did not view themselves as Organized Black Baseball's "Second Dimension." Undoubtedly, the owners' ambivalence in providing the sportswriters game reports made their job problematic. The writers also appeared to place the primary responsibility for acquiring statistics on the league officials. As historian David Voigt has pointed out, the provision of statistics represented a solid contribution by the white baseball writers of the golden age. In essence, they had taken it upon themselves to compile the statistics for both leagues. It should be noted that Major League officials did not begin to compile statistics until the 1930s, when the American League designated the Howe News Bureau as the league's official compiler of records. The National League followed suit by selecting Al Munro Elias Bureau as its official compiler. By the late 1920s, the relationship between the Negro Leagues and the black press was strained to the point that such a statistical enterprise was untenable.[18]

The call to reform the Negro National League and the Eastern Colored League was not ignored completely. Both league presidents attempted to implement some of the proposed reforms. Several disgruntled owners, however, had a different agenda, marking the start of a brief return to independent ball in the East.

THE ECL DISBANDS

On January 21, 1928, Cumberland Posey continued his analysis on the state of eastern black baseball in the *Pittsburgh Courier*. Posey predicted there would be no eastern league within the next two years, leading to a "mad scramble" for players by eastern and western clubs.

After two years, the eastern league would reorganize "on a sound practical and financial basis." The Grays' magnate offered suggestions to the ECL's current plight. First, the commissioners must insist on Nat Strong providing a home grounds for either the Brooklyn Royal Giants or the Cuban Stars or drop them from the league. If it was necessary to drop the Royal Giants, then the club should be classified as an outlaw. Posey said that as a result, each club, with the exception of the Lincoln Giants and Baltimore Black Sox, would lose one or two good dates in and around New York. He concluded that the amount of revenue loss should be minimal when the clubs keep the money that would have been lost by playing the Royals.[19]

A second suggestion urged by Posey was an assessment of the Bacharach Giants' financial status. Simply put, the Bacharachs needed a financial angel who could be "held responsible for the players' salaries, for the rent of the ballpark, for the actions of fans, players, and umpires at Bacharach Giants' park." The Giants found someone willing to take on this responsibility. Isaac Washington, owner of the Blue Kitten café in Atlantic City, bought out the Bacharach Athletic Association and retained Tom Jackson as his booking agent.[20]

Posey suggested that the Lincoln Giants be brought back into the league. Along with the Baltimore Black Sox, he said, the Lincolns should play more away games on Sundays. Posey acknowledged that the Harrisburg Giants and the Bacharachs needed some home games on the weekends to balance the playing schedule. Both Rossiter and Keenan were proponents of league ball and were willing to abide by the business practices necessary to sustain a circuit.

Another suggestion was directed at both the ECL and NNL. Posey pointed out that rowdyism was ruining the game on the field and urged that the players be fined and suspended for constantly holding up games. League owners should provide the league presidents with an expense account to visit cities where crucial series were being played. After observing games as an unbiased spectator, the presidents could identify the perpetrators of destructive behavior on the field. To ensure their authority, the owners should stick by their selected official or sell their franchise.

Finally, Posey proposed some qualities that would make for a good president. The president did not have to be a well-known judge or leading attorney. What both leagues needed was a fighter who would make a decision and stand by it. Black baseball fans and, apparently, players and owners, had no respect for diplomacy. In Posey's view, "our good black professional men are too diplomatic to cause the best clubs to be without the services of their best players for two weeks in the middle of the season." He suggested that Frank Young in the West and Rollo Wilson in the East "would put more fear in the average club owner and player than all the black attorneys and judges in the US." What is of interest here was that Posey never acknowledged the need for the owners to grant the president the authority needed to "make a decision and stand by it."[21]

An air of uneasiness surrounded the ECL's winter meeting prior to the joint session. From the start, several black newspapers acknowledged the "conspicuous" absence of the Harrisburg owner, Colonel Jacob Strothers. The principal business of the meeting was to elect officers, but even that was shrouded in controversy. The *New York Age* reported that Charles Freeman and Lloyd Thompson appeared on behalf of the Hilldale Club to announce that Ed Bolden was no longer the HBEC president and could not represent the club at the meeting. Bolden replied that he had been defeated for the presidency of the HBEC but that he had secured the majority of the stock and would again be in control by the start of the regular season. After a considerable debate among the commissioners, Bolden was elected secretary-treasurer.[22]

When the two leagues held their joint session, all ECL clubs were represented except the Harrisburg Giants. Several proposals were adopted by both leagues, including a revised World Series format, a provision for both circuits to utilize a rotating umpire system, and a rewriting of the reserve rule to ensure another Montalvo incident would not occur. James Keenan was welcomed back into the ECL after agreeing to return Alonzo Montalvo to the Cuban Stars West and Jelly Gardner to the Chicago American Giants. For the first time, the press was invited to attend the joint session. The move led Rollo Wilson to declare that the "atmosphere was cleared of all suspicion on the part of both the owners and the press." It was tacitly understood that nothing would be published without the consent of the leagues. Wilson optimistically concluded that the year would be a "season of friendship between the writers and the owners."[23]

At the conclusion of the joint session, the Eastern Colored League began to unravel. On March 3, 1928, the *New York Age* reported that the Harrisburg Giants had withdrawn from the ECL. Strothers gave several reasons for quitting the league. One was that the Bacharach Giants refused to play games in Harrisburg. Also, a dispute occurred over the winner of the second half of the 1927 split season. Strothers claimed his Giants won the second half and should have played the Bacharachs for the league title. However, President Nutter ruled in favor of the Atlantic City club. Harrisburg was supposed to receive the second-place money from the World Series, but Nutter once again ruled in favor of the Bacharachs, giving them all the series revenue. Nutter rightly claimed that the financial residuals were not substantial enough to award a share to the second-place finisher. These reasons, combined with the "considerable money" lost to run the Giants, which was affecting his other business activities, meant the end of Colonel Jacob Strothers's eighteen-year reign. His withdrawal led to a virtual fire sale for his former players. Oscar Charleston reportedly signed with the Bacharach Giants, while John Beckwith donned a Hilldale uniform. Fats Jenkins and Rap Dixon signed with the Baltimore Black Sox, and the Lincoln Giants grabbed Rev Cannady and Sam Cooper.[24]

The ECL received another blow when Nat Strong withdrew his Brooklyn Royal Giants. President Nutter heeded Posey's advice regarding Strong's providing a home grounds for his Royals. When informed of Nutter's decision that Strong provide this, Strong chose to withdraw. The Royals' magnate was also opposed to the new way the teams would share the gate receipts on a percentage basis.[25]

Concurrently, Ed Bolden had fully recovered from his physical and mental difficulties and had gradually become active in league affairs. In February, Bolden was reelected president of the HBEC, and at the same time he announced that Hilldale would leave the ECL. Bolden's reelection led Charles Freeman to resign from the corporation, and after a stormy session, Lloyd Thompson submitted his resignation as secretary. George Mayo was named vice president of Hilldale and would also serve as its field manager, following the same policy in handling players that Bolden had employed. Thomas Jenkins replaced Thompson as HBEC secretary and Mark Studevan was named treasurer.[26]

In response to reported queries from the fans, Ed Bolden explained why he had withdrawn his Hilldale Club from the ECL. In a letter to the editor, Bolden claimed that it was never his policy "to enter into [a] discussion or to offer a public criticism of the acts of individual or an organization." Due to misunderstanding about the HBEC's withdrawal from the ECL, he felt obligated to state the reasons that precipitated this action. Bolden was in favor of organized baseball and for implementing a system of rotating umpires. Yet some "selfish commissioners" with a sinister motive had objected, thereby succeeding in making the league accept the old umpire system. The lack of cooperation among the commissioners led some of them to refuse to play their schedule. "One club becomes dissatisfied because it cannot have everything its own way," Bolden proclaimed, "and jumps out of the league when it sees fit, and jumps back again when it feels like it." Some clubs "come to your park, and during the season take away thousands of dollars," he said, "yet they never have a park to give you anything in return," an obvious reference to James Keenan and Nat Strong. It was due to these circumstances, he explained, that the HBEC would return to independent ball. Bolden concluded that "in independent baseball we booked the best attractions obtainable, and the club grew and grew until we were big financially and otherwise."[27]

While Harrisburg, Brooklyn, and Hilldale bolted from the league, Isaac Nutter attempted to hold the circuit together. The Baltimore Black Sox, Lincoln Giants, and Bacharach Giants agreed to remain in the league. Two new clubs—the Eastern All Stars of Philadelphia and the Brooklyn Stars—were granted league franchises. The All Stars were organized by gambler Smithie Lucas. Renamed the Philadelphia Tigers, Lucas attempted to secure Elk Park, located at Forty-Eighth and Spruce Streets in the Quaker City, as the team's home grounds. Bolden, however, still well connected with white park owners, blocked the move and secured the park for Hilldale. Lucas managed to obtain a playing facility for his Tigers at Penncoyld Park, located at Ridge Avenue and Lincoln Drive, approximately ten miles outside of Philadelphia. It was unclear, however, who would own the Brooklyn Stars. Rumors circulated that the Washington Potomacs would be brought back into the league. Nutter predicted that Hilldale and the Royal Giants would seek readmission once they saw that the league could function without them. Other league members felt Strong's exit from the ECL was the best thing that could happen to the circuit. Strong blocked numerous proposals designed to enhance the league, and his loss, they believed, would not be felt.[28]

On April 19, in a meeting attended by Bolden, Pompez, Keenan, Rossiter, and Washington, it was decided to disband the Eastern Colored League and return to independent ball. The *Baltimore Afro-American* reported that Isaac Nutter was "mysteriously absent" from the meeting and that Smithie Lucas was not invited. Overtures were made to lure Hilldale back into the ECL, but Bolden had already scheduled games with independent clubs. A financial backer for the Brooklyn club failed to materialize. Black Sox owner George Rossiter claimed the teams would continue as an "association" with each team having the latitude to "schedule as many games as profitable with teams in the association." Cum Posey's Homestead Grays would possibly be a part of this arrangement.[29]

Despite the announcement of the ECL's disbanding, the circuit refused to die. On April 29, the ECL began its season with five clubs: the Baltimore Black Sox, Lincoln Giants, Bacharach Giants, Philadelphia Tigers, and Cuban Stars. Within three weeks, however, Pompez withdrew his Stars and the Lincoln Giants soon followed. Nutter insisted the league would continue and attempted to find replacements, but in June 1928, less than five and a half years after its formation, the Eastern Colored League collapsed.[30]

The ECL's collapse led sportswriters Bill Gibson and Rollo Wilson to evaluate the return to independent ball and urge the eastern magnates to form a new league for the 1929 season. On April 28, Gibson published an article titled "Eastern League Collapse Far-Reaching in

Effects," and after briefly highlighting the league's demise, he stated that scheduling would be no easy task for the former league clubs. His assertion was supported by Rollo Wilson, who declared that white clubs were refusing to play the black clubs because the latter were "too weak to offer an attractive opposition to generate gate receipts." Twilight games which were formerly used to cover the overhead expenses for black teams were scheduled infrequently. A return to independent ball would lead some owners to enter into a bidding war for players. Field managers would find it difficult to discipline players without an organization to enforce rules. Such matters were difficult enough when the ECL was in existence. The situation would only worsen with a return to independent ball.[31]

Wilson reinforced Gibson's call for the eastern magnates to organize into a new league. The fans wanted to look at league averages and know how their favorite teams fared in competition against the other league clubs. He added, "You can't kid [the fans] into believing that a game between independent clubs means the same as a game between league outfits." Black teams were scheduling lucrative Sunday games with subpar white clubs. "Imagine if you please," Wilson declared, "the Baltimore Black Sox being forced to schedule such a club as the Kensington Congs . . . in their park on a Sunday." There were also incidents of black clubs luring top players away from black teams to make them more attractive to white semipros. The Bacharach Giants snatched George Carr and Fats Jenkins from the Lincoln Giants. Both men were reported to be gate attractions for James Keenan's club in Gotham.[32]

Wilson continued his evaluation of independent ball in the East and encouraged Ed Bolden to serve as the catalyst for the formation of a new eastern league. By late July and mid-August, it was apparent to Wilson that the fans would not embrace a return to independent ball. Low attendance, undoubtedly influenced also by an economic downturn, apathetic players, and disgruntled fans were reasons for the owners to come together. The Eastern Sports Writers Association (ESWA) exhorted the magnates to form a new league for the 1929 season and anointed Ed Bolden to lead the effort. Despite the press criticism Bolden had endured as ECL chairman, the ESWA acknowledged the fact that the Hilldale president could "work order out of the present chaos." After highlighting his stellar career as "Clan Darby's" leader, Wilson declared that Bolden was "to the east what Rube Foster was to the west." The success of the Hilldale Club, along with his long-standing business relationship with black and white club owners and park managers, made Bolden the logical choice to organized "an honest-to-goodness league." Moreover, Wilson stated that the *Courier* would assist in promoting a sound organization in an attempt to preserve eastern black baseball. He also encouraged NNL president Hueston to appeal to the eastern moguls to organize, although no formal statement to that end was made.[33]

Cum Posey was also receptive to the idea of a new league. The Grays' successful barnstorming tour in the East facilitated this positive response. A prospective league featuring Hilldale and Homestead was enthusiastically promoted in the black press. By December, Ed Bolden was now amenable to the reorganization of the ECL.

Providing Stronger Leadership

While efforts were made to reorganize the eastern black clubs into a new league, Judge William Hueston attempted to exhibit stronger leadership at the NNL's winter meeting. He delivered a fiery speech that stunned the older members of the league, stating that he had not been as "dumb" in baseball matters as some had thought. The league president recommended a series of reforms, many of which were advocated by the black press. The reform included fining players for rowdy behavior on the field, reducing the size of player rosters, increasing the entry fee to ensure that a team would finish the season, and improving the league's umpiring. He called for the player roster to be reduced to fourteen, including the manager, and said that to reduce travel expenses, exhibition games with white semipro teams should be played to and from league cities whenever possible. Hueston's speech was reportedly met with five minutes of applause.[34]

At the same time, three league clubs underwent a transition in ownership. John Schorling sold the Chicago American Giants to William Trimble, a white florist from Princeton, Illinois. Schorling sold the club because he believed the other owners were conspiring to keep the best teams away from Chicago. In Memphis, a group of businessmen purchased the Red Sox from R. S. Lewis. It is unclear who these businessmen were, but the *Pittsburgh Courier* reported they were "enthusiastically devoting themselves to the task of making Memphis one of the best black baseball towns in the league." They also predicted that the Red Sox would win the 1928 pennant.[35]

In Detroit, Steve Pierce sold his interest in the club to a contingent headed by Mose L. Walker and John Roesink. Walker had served in the United States Customs Service for twenty-three years and had been located in Detroit since 1915. Roesink, a forty-five-year-old clothier, became the third white owner in the NNL, along with J. L. Wilkinson and William Trimble. He already owned Mack Park, the Stars' home grounds, and had made a fortune during Detroit's boom decade, operating three successful downtown stores. Although Roesink would later inspire the wrath of many black Detroiters, the players generally considered the haberdasher a first-class owner. The Stars would be well paid and continue to travel by train under Roesink's regime.[36]

To improve the league's image, Hueston promoted the NNL in a race rhetoric that personified the ideals of Booker T. Washington. When asked, "What docs baseball mean to the American Negro as played in the National League?," Hueston replied, "First, American life so far as spirit is concerned is based on competition. To pit ones self against another is the thrill which enables the average American to carry on. Second, civilization has demonstrated that sports, in the form of games, are a necessary essential in nation building. Third, baseball is the national game of this great country. Fourth, art and athletics furnished the greatest opportunity for the American Negro to demonstrate that he acts and re-acts to all human activities just the same as all other people. Baseball gives a great opportunity for the Negro to demonstrate the above rule, and in our league, I state without hesitation, we are showing that we can and are carrying our end." In response to the economic downswing, Hueston pointed out with great pride that the NNL furnished employment to five hundred people, 97.5 percent of whom were black, at a cost of nearly four hundred thousand dollars. Much like Bolden, the league president argued that baseball had done more to break down racial barriers than any other institution in American society.[37]

Hueston's statement, printed in several black newspapers, served to exhort blacks to increase their patronage of league games. Outside of park expense, it cost roughly five thousand dollars a month to operate a league club. Both employment conditions and inclement weather affected a club owner's ability to turn a profit. The league depended heavily on weekend and holiday games to boost gate receipts. Hueston explained that "with 10 Sundays in our first half [of the season], we have had six Sundays upon which it either rained or was too cold to play in most of the area[s] where our teams are located." Profitability was furthered compromised by the increased travel expenses required to go to the South for games with Birmingham and Memphis and back. Therefore, Hueston encouraged the fans in league cities to attend "at least one of our games" during the second half of the split season.[38]

Promotional events were organized to improve the league's image. On August 11, the *Defender* reported that the Detroit Stars would play the Chicago American Giants at Comiskey Park as part of Elks Field Day. The league game was part of the field day activities of the Elks, who were gathering for their annual convention. Preceding the game, a band contest for prizes totaling one thousand dollars would also be held. This event featured a band from New York, called the Mighty Monarchs, which had previously won the contest three times. Unfortunately for the league president, rain canceled the game with the scored tied at one in the third inning.[39]

In spite of the poor weather conditions, the NNL endured. The 1928 season was noteworthy for the league championship series between the Chicago American Giants and the St. Louis Stars. To be sure, the American Giants were the New York Yankees of black baseball, and they were the odds on favorite to defeat the Stars. The Mound City crew won the first half of the split season, while the Windy City club captured the second half. A best five-out-of-nine-game series was organized to determine the NNL pennant winner.[40]

The St. Louis Stars combined power, speed on the base paths, and solid pitching to be a worthy opponent for the American Giants. They were led by their manager and third baseman "Candy Jim" Taylor, the younger brother of C. I. Taylor. Taylor began his playing career with the St. Paul Gophers in 1909 and had brief stints with the American Giants and the Indianapolis ABCs. As a manager, Taylor piloted several of the franchises that slipped in and out of the NNL. He guided the Dayton Marcos in the senior circuit's inaugural season, and by 1922 he had signed on to manage the Cleveland Tate Stars. In 1923, Taylor was hired to manage the St. Louis Stars, and after a dismal first season, they competed for the NNL pennant every year. In 1925, the Stars won the second half of the split season and lost a tough series to the Kansas City Monarchs for the pennant. George "Mule" Suttles was the Stars' power-hitting first baseman who used a fifty-ounce bat to drive the ball. A free swinger who struck out a lot, Suttles was a low-ball hitter with a big, powerful swing who hit towering, tape measure home runs. Shortstop Willie Wells was an outstanding player on the field and at the plate. He possessed good range, sure hands, and an accurate throwing arm and compiled batting averages of .378 and .346 in 1926–1927. In 1926, he hit twenty-seven home runs in eighty-eight games. Ted "Highpockets" Trent bolstered the Stars' pitching staff, baffling hitters with a big curve ball and a good slider, posting a 21-2 won-lost record.[41]

Stars' center fielder James "Cool Papa" Bell was at the beginning of a long, stellar career that would eventually land him in the Baseball Hall of Fame in Cooperstown. Bell used his speed and daring to become black baseball's foremost base stealer. Numerous stories are told of his feats on the base paths, like constantly hitting two hoppers to the infield and beating the throw to first base for a hit or going from first to third on a bunt. Cool Papa also used his speed in the field, with his great range allowing him to play a shallow center field. His defensive prowess robbed hitters of would-be base hits, and he ran down pitchers' mistakes. The switch-hitting Bell had good bat control and hit for high average, leading the Stars with a .332 batting average.[42]

Dave Malarcher's American Giants, on the other hand, still maintained the winning strategy of pitching, defense, baserunning, and timely hitting. The Giants' one-two pitching combo of Willie Foster and Willie Powell, along with Eddie "Buck" Miller, remained the most formidable staff in the NNL. Veteran players Lemuel Hawkins, Charlie Williams, Jumbo Jackson, and Walter Davis rounded out a solid hitting attack. Shortstop Pythias Russ gave the Giants power at the plate and outstanding speed on the base paths. He won the league's batting title in the second half with a .401 batting average. Russ's career was unfortunately cut short the following year due to his untimely death from tuberculosis.[43]

The American Giants got off to a 2-0 series lead. Willie Foster took a 5-0 lead into the eighth inning before a three-run rally put the Stars back into the game. However, the American Giants added two insurance runs in the bottom of the eighth on the way to a 7-3 win. Game two was a pitcher's duel between Ted Trent and Willie Powell. The Giants hurler overpowered the Stars, giving up only three hits and striking out eight batters en route to a 3-0 shutout victory.[44]

The Stars rallied to tie the series. They scored first in game three when Cool Papa Bell reached first base on a bunt single and went to second on a balk. Bell made it to third on Willie Wells's infield single and scored on Mule Suttles's base hit to center field. The Stars added two runs in the second inning, one in the fourth, and two in the sixth to defeat the American Giants, 6-4. Game four was a closely contested affair with the Giants taking a 3-2 lead into the fourth inning. In the top of the fourth, the Stars' catcher by the name of Palms was hit by a pitched ball and reached third base on second baseman John Henry Russell's double to right field. Willie Foster struck out the next two batters before right fielder Branch Russell singled past shortstop Pythias Russ to score Palms and John Russell. Branch Russell reached second on the throw to the plate and scored on Willie Wells' base hit. Ted Trent shut down the American Giants hitters for the rest of the game on the way to a 5-4 victory.[45]

The series seesawed back into the American Giants' favor. After they won an 8-7 squeaker in game five, the next contest illustrated how closely contested the series had become. Stars' pitcher Logan Hensley dueled Willie Foster to a 3-3 tie into the eighth inning. In the top of the eighth, Pythias Russ hit a home run to give the Windy City club the lead. The Giants added another run in the ninth when Charlie Williams tripled to deep right-center field and scored on Willie Foster's single en route to a 5-3 win.[46]

At this point, many observers believed the American Giants were in the proverbial catbird seat, but the Stars performed the unthinkable. They rallied to win the next two games to set up the final contest for the pennant. It was only fitting that the leading pitchers for both teams, Ted Trent and Willie Foster, would face each other to determine the NNL champion. The game was anticlimactic, however. The Stars took an early 3-0 lead. Willie Wells led their ten-hit assault with a two-run home run in the fourth inning. His round tripper in the seventh marked the start of a four-run rally that broke the game open. It was all Trent needed as he struck out seven batters on the way to a 9-2 win and the Negro National League pennant.[47]

The Chicago *Defender* marveled that the St. Louis Stars had dethroned the team "that had been considered unbeatable." The statement, though somewhat exaggerated, had some merit. From 1911 to 1928, the Chicago American Giants were the cream of the black baseball crop. The team had been the club that other black baseball entrepreneurs aspired to emulate, both on and off the field. The American Giants exemplified the personality of their founder and architect, Andrew "Rube" Foster. Pitching, defense, baserunning, and timely hitting was the Rube Foster way in black baseball. The series defeat to the St. Louis Stars marked the end of an era for black baseball in the Windy City.[48]

More important, Judge William Hueston's endeavor to furnish stronger leadership in his second year as league president was somewhat effective. Unlike their eastern cohorts, NNL owners exhibited a willingness to delegate the authority that Hueston needed to administer the league's day-to-day affairs. Undoubtedly, Rube Foster's autocratic rule over league operations created the spirit of compliance among the magnates that allowed this delegation of power to occur. Hueston used the press to promote the league through race rhetoric designed to attract black middle-class patronage. The judge, unfortunately, had no control over the weather conditions that impacted negatively on the league's profitability. The fact that the league remained intact and that there were no reported incidents of player misconduct reflected favorably on

Hueston's leadership. The NNL could look to the 1929 season with a cautious optimism, while Ed Bolden would make an attempt to organize the eastern owners into a new league.

A Chance for Redemption: The American Negro League

On January 17, 1929, former ECL owners, along with Cumberland Posey, met at the Citizens Republican Club in Philadelphia and formed the American Negro League. Six clubs constituted the new league: Hilldale, Baltimore, Lincoln, Cubans, Homestead, and Atlantic City. Ed Bolden was elected as the league's first president. The other officers included James Keenan, vice president; Rollo Wilson, secretary; and George Rossiter, treasurer. Wilson would also handle the league's statistics, publicity, and various other administrative functions. Nat Strong was invited to the league meeting, but he declined to attend. Strong was in favor of a mutual association, but he would not provide a home grounds for the Brooklyn Royal Giants.[49]

Attempts were made by the magnates to cooperate within the parameters of the competitor-partner model. Achieving a balanced schedule was one area in which the owners endeavored to cooperate. No league club would have a monopoly on certain days of the week as in the past. Hilldale, the Baltimore Black Sox, and the Lincoln Giants would make road trips on weekends. To accommodate the two traveling teams in the league, Homestead and the eastern Cubans, the Grays would use Forbes Field when the National League Pirates were on the road and Hooper Field in Cleveland. The Cuban Stars, on the other hand, would use Baltimore, Darby, and Lincoln when their parks were available, or neutral grounds like Dexter Park in Brooklyn or Island Park in Harrisburg. To improve press relations, Bolden invited several members of the press to attend league meetings. The *Pittsburgh Courier* reported that the league president acknowledged the "Fourth Estate [was] a mighty factor in the development and life of the game." Several invitations were sent to sports journalists like William Clark of the *New York Age*, Bill Dallas of the Philadelphia *Evening Ledger*, Bill Gibson of the *Baltimore Afro-American*, and Randy Dixon of the *Philadelphia Tribune*. Finally, the owners adopted an eighty-game split season, a reserve clause in player contracts, a system of fines and suspensions, and a plan for rotating umpires.[50]

Opposition to the formation of the ANL surfaced but was not taken seriously. Former ECL president Isaac Nutter threatened to file an injunction if the ANL used former ECL players. In a statement released to the press, Nutter declared he would "not tolerate any player belonging to the Eastern Colored League playing in the American Negro League." Nutter stated his reasons for the collapse of the ECL: "The trouble with the owners of Negro baseball clubs of the Eastern League [was] that [the black magnates permitted] two white owners to run the league for their own personal benefit, allowing the Negro owners to receive such crumbs as may be left," an obvious reference to Nat Strong and James Keenan. The white owners opposed a balanced schedule and demanded "the appointment of their own umpires." With that said, Nutter declared he would bring an injunction against the player and the team using a former ECL player. If an ANL club played any team in the state of New Jersey, the former ECL president would attach the gate receipts to "pay for any and all protested checks given by former secretaries or due club owners in the [ECL]." The proceeds would also pay back the money "that was stolen by one of the former secretaries who now lives in Baltimore," an obvious reference to Charles Spedden. Nutter concluded that if the owners decided that they had a "moral obligation" to meet as members of the ECL to resolve their "differences," they could reorganize under any name they so chose. Otherwise, the "battle" was on, and the former ECL president would thrive "on fighting whenever it [was] justifiable."[51]

In spite of the proposed court action, Isaac Nutter's threat was never taken seriously. *Baltimore Afro-American* sports editor Bill Gibson stated that Nutter's intended actions "got the merry ha-ha." He pointed out that the principal reason for this injunction was to force a settlement regarding economic residuals due to the "shore attorney." The players became free agents when the ECL collapsed, which would nullify any court action Nutter proposed. "Even if he obtained the injunction,"

Gibson added, "Mr. Nutter would find it rather hard to dispose of the players he would automatically have on his hands."⁵²

Simultaneously and throughout the ANL's winter meetings, rumors circulated about several players going to Honolulu, Hawaii, and not returning until late May. It led the magnates to adopt a resolution which stated that any player who failed to report before the start of the season would be suspended for as many days as they were absent. Exceptions would be made for players who were in school. For a second time, Bizz Mackey of Hilldale and George Carr and Ping Gardner of the Bacharach Giants failed to report at the start of the season. It was unclear when these players returned to their respective clubs, but on June 8, the *Pittsburgh Courier* reported that the players would be eligible to return to their clubs after June 24. Three weeks later, the *Afro-American* declared that Mackey, Carr, and Gardner had served their suspensions and were eligible to play league games. Thus, all clubs could begin the second half at full strength.⁵³

The rule suspending players who failed to report had a nearly devastating impact on Alex Pompez's Cuban Stars. Several players, including Pelaro Chacon, Alejandro Oms, Eustaquio Pedroso, and Augustin Bejerano, went to Santo Domingo following the close of the Cuban Winter League and refused to report to Pompez at the start of the regular season. Their suspension led Chacon to organize an outlaw club that was supposedly backed by Nat Strong. Booking agents throughout the East were advised of the league ruling that no club would play any team using a suspended player. Apparently, the owners' actions proved effective. On August 10, the *Afro-American* reported that the suspended players had made their peace with Pompez and returned to the eastern Cubans. At the same time, Bolden announced the ban against the players had been lifted.⁵⁴

In mid-July, Posey was at the center of a controversy that could have resulted in a war between the ANL and the NNL. The senior circuit was already incensed over the Homestead owner's leasing of Hooper Field in Cleveland. On July 13, the *Defender* reported that Grays' pitcher Sam Streeter was in the stands at American Giants Park, watching a doubleheader between the Giants and the Birmingham Black Barons. Streeter was reportedly there to induce Black Barons' pitcher Leroy "Satchel" Paige to go east. The rumor intensified when Paige left the pitcher's mound in the sixth inning. However, the rumor was squelched the following day when Paige appeared in the Black Barons lineup playing right field. Two players who had been suspended by American Giants' manager, Jim Brown—third baseman Stanford Jackson and pitcher Buck Miller—left the club and signed with Posey. Since there was no agreement between the leagues protecting players under contract, the Grays' magnate had no qualms about strengthening his ball club "at the other fellow's expense." Rumors circulated that the American Giants would retaliate by signing Bacharach Giants' players Clint Thomas and Hubert Lockhart, but there is no indication that such an action was ever taken.[55]

Posey's actions nullified any attempt to organize a World Series championship between the pennant winners of both leagues. In an interview with the *Baltimore Afro-American*, former Kansas City Monarchs' co-owner Howard Smith declared that the East-West series would not take place because the eastern owners failed to "keep its contract agreement" with the NNL. Evidently, Smith was suggesting that a "gentlemen's agreement" not to tamper with players under contract existed among the owners. He cited the case of Jelly Gardner signing with the Bacharach Giants and Jackson jumping to the Homestead Grays. Judge Hueston echoed Smith's sentiment. He charged Posey specifically for encouraging NNL players to jump their contracts. The league president concluded that "several matters between the two leagues" must be adjusted before a postseason series could take place.[56]

Despite the controversy involving players, the American Negro League managed to complete its inaugural season. On average, league clubs played sixty-six games on the drafted schedule, with Hilldale playing the most league games (seventy-four) and the Cuban Stars the fewest (fifty-four). The Baltimore Black Sox won both halves of the split season and were declared the pennant winner. Rollo Wilson attempted to put a positive spin on the ANL's first season. "Viewed in an artistic sense," Wilson declared, "the season was successful but the financial angle [was] something else again." With most clubs losing money, six teams played out the schedule except when rain interfered. Although there were incidents of "malingering and indifference" among some of the players, Eastern Seaboard fans were still treated to some "high class baseball." Wilson concluded that the owners, to their credit, "took their medicine like men and stuck to the end." As the ANL owners endured the 1929 season with mixed results, their western counterpart would experience its worst season in league history.[57]

Transiton and Catastrophe

From the start of its annual winter meetings, the Negro National League was a circuit in transition. Quincy Gilmore left the NNL to become the president of a new league composed of clubs from Texas, Oklahoma, and Louisiana. The Chicago American Giants' fall from prominence continued, as five players left the club. Four of these players, Pythias Russ, George Hamey, George Sweat, and Willie Himes were employed by the post office, and they did not want to relinquish their full-time jobs to play baseball. They joined the Quincy Street station in the post office league, playing only weekend games. Dave Malarcher resigned as player-manager, essentially over a salary dispute. The *Defender* reported Malarcher complained that he functioned more in the role of team captain rather than the field manager. In other words, Malarcher was a manager in name only.[58]

The Memphis Red Sox changed ownership for a second straight year. The *Defender* reported that a corporation led by Dr. J. B. Martin and W. S. Martin purchased the club and the Red Sox's ballpark. J. B. Martin's involvement with the Red Sox marked the start of his long career as one of black baseball's most influential club owners. Born in northeast Mississippi, Martin moved to Memphis at age twelve and later attended Lemoyne High School in Memphis and Walton University at Nashville. He earned a degree in pharmacy from Meharry Medical College in Memphis in 1910 and borrowed $250 to open a drugstore in Memphis. Martin became active in politics under the auspices of Robert Church Jr., a black Republican leader and the son of one of the South's first black millionaires. Martin's brother, W. S. Martin, was a physician who operated Collins Chapel Hospital in Memphis.[59]

The NNL would begin the season as a six-team league, consisting of Kansas City, Chicago, St. Louis, Birmingham, Memphis, and Detroit. The Cuban Stars, Indianapolis ABCs, and the Elite of Nashville, Tennessee, were taken in as associate members. The Cleveland club was dropped from the league because the ownership was reportedly engaged in "poor business methods" and because the Homestead Grays scheduled several of their Sunday games there.[60]

For a second straight season, inclement weather was cited for the league's declining attendance. Judge Hueston stated that four of six games played by league clubs were either rained out or called because of cold weather. He went on to explain that league clubs depended on three of the seven days a week to generate gate receipts, and the loss of weekend games was hard on them. Citing these losses as part of his case, Hueston argued that the fans should support league clubs in the second half of the split season: "The league furnishes employment to several young men each playing [the] season at a cost to the joint team owners of well over $200,000." Many of these young men were college students, and they earned money for their education. The owners "put themselves to great disadvantage in permitting the players to report several weeks late each season in order to keep up with their studies."[61]

It was because of these sacrifices that the NNL deserved the fans' support, Hueston stated. "Our league has given evidence sufficient to be depended upon fan support," he added, "and we come now to the place where we feel that we have justified the right to appeal to the public for support." The league president stated three reasons why the fans should patronize the Negro National League. First, the league "had kept the faith" for ten years by completing each season which cost some owners thousands of dollars. Second—a claim that would be disputed later—the league, according to the judge, had improved its image to the point that it adhered to the ideals of the middle-class spectator. Gambling had been eradicated, and profanity and alcohol consumption had been reportedly reduced immensely at league games. Finally, the owners, managers, and players "have submitted themselves to rules of discipline, which assures that the games are played under pleasant and comfortable conditions." For these stated reasons, Hueston posed the question, "What more could the public demand?"[62]

William Hueston's PR campaign was designed to drum up support from the black middle-class spectator. By stressing the sacrifice of the owners, the fact that some players were going to college, and the improvement of the league's image, Hueston was citing ideals the black middle-class could embrace. However, the situation in Detroit told a different story. Spectators began turning out in smaller numbers, due primarily to the behavior of the Stars' white owner, John Roesink. Allowing Mack Park to deteriorate and his use of racial slurs had all but completely alienated black Detroiters. For example, Roesink attempted to have Stars' manager, Bingo DeMoss, arrested when the latter admonished the park owner for using abusive language because some of the fans requested a drinking fountain. For years, former owners Tenny Blount and Steve Pierce pleaded with Roesink to renovate the park to justify an increase in ticket prices. The presence of white umpires, white concessionaires, and white ticket takers, particularly at a time when blacks were losing their jobs, further incensed African American fans.[63]

Roesink was involved in several other incidents that turned off black Detroiters. Dislike for the haberdasher escalated when he began greeting black fans with pet remarks like "shines" and "coons." In 1923, Roesink attempted to segregate black fans into certain boxes while reserving others for whites, but Tenny Blount intervened to prevent the move. It was only after a heated argument that Blount convinced Roesink that attendance would decline if he practiced racial discrimination at the park. The Stars' owner had become so obnoxious that Blount had to bar him from the park for a month.[64]

On July 7, 1929, a tragic event occurred that intensified the hostility between Roesink and Detroit's black fans. The Stars were scheduled to play a doubleheader with the Kansas City Monarchs. When both teams arrived at Mack Park, they discovered that rain, which had canceled Saturday's game, had made the field a soggy mess, so the doubleheader was rescheduled for Sunday. It was customary for club officials to dry out the infield and base paths by pouring gasoline over the dirt and then lighting it. After spreading two five-gallon cans of gas over the infield, a sudden commotion took place under the right field stands, where several hundred early arrivals were sitting out a brief rain shower. Apparently, a cigarette had ignited the debris beneath the grandstand. Fire investigators concluded that park employees had left a trail of flammable liquid while carrying the cans of gas onto the field.[65]

Reportedly, many were injured in the Mack Park fire. While some spectators leaped from the back of the stands, others—making a hurried exit below the stands—were struck by those who leaped from above. The fire had spread so rapidly that the roof of the stands fell in and collapsed, injuring many who were still attempting to escape through the exits below. According to investigators, it was remarkable that no one was killed.[66]

With roughly 220 people injured, the fire inflicted permanent damage to Roesink's reputation. All but one of the casualties was black. Injuries ranged from severe skull and spinal fractures to broken limbs and severe burns. The fire was declared an accident, but many black Detroiters blamed Roesink for the tragedy, who—they suspected—was lying when he insisted that no gas cans had been carelessly stowed under the stands. Fueling their anger was an incident that occurred shortly before the fire. Convinced that the intermittent rain would cancel the game, many of the fans descended on the box office to demand refunds. Roesink refused and then put in a riot call to the police.[67]

The tragedy at Mack Park undermined Judge Hueston's effort to increase spectator interest at league games. More important, the Mack Park fire specifically and the treatment of black fans in general revealed the fundamental dilemma the league president faced in running the NNL's day-to-day operations. Generally speaking, the club owners exhibited a willingness to delegate the authority Hueston needed to run the league's affairs. In spite of the presence of a traveling team and two clubs—Birmingham and Kansas City—using minor league parks, the owners granted the league president the authority to draft the playing schedule. Referred to as the "equalization plan," scheduling was based on the premise of filling open dates with exhibition games to alleviate the traveling expenses that league clubs accumulated when they made extended jumps to the Deep South and vice versa. The equalization plan permitted the league to come close to playing a balance schedule. On average, six clubs played seventy-seven league games out of the proposed ninety-game schedule, with St. Louis and Chicago playing the most games (eighty-six) and Memphis the fewest (sixty-three).[68]

On the other hand, the treatment of black fans in Detroit and the Mack Park fire showed the limits of Hueston's influence over league operations. It should be noted that as president, Judge Hueston was an employee who could be hired and fired by the owners. Without developing a consensus among the magnates, Hueston had no control over an owner's behavior toward his club; ballpark; and, more importantly, the treatment of his consumers—the fans. Roesink's behavior toward them suggests that the economic downturn, the lack of statistics, and rowdyism were not the only factors contributing to declining attendance at league games. It would be of interest to see the kind of customer service the fans experienced in the other league cities.

As the 1929 season came to a close, the air of uncertainty that came to define the Negro Leagues during the decade intensified. Would the eastern black clubs continue their affiliation in the American Negro League, or would they return to independent ball? Despite the numerous obstacles the league constantly confronted, could the Negro National League exhibit its uncanny staying power and last another season? What was clear was that Organized Black Baseball in the East and West was functioning in survival mode.

12

The End of an Era

The 1930 season proved cataclysmic for the majority of eastern black baseball clubs. The American Negro League disbanded, resulting in a return to independent ball. Hilldale experienced another hostile takeover, marking the start of the decline of Ed Bolden's status as one of black baseball's most prominent owners. Sagging attendance led to a call for the formation of a new league, although no action was taken. In response to the declining attendance, a series of benefit games was staged by the Lincoln Giants and the Baltimore Black Sox to raise funds for the Brotherhood of Sleeping Car Porters. In August, a ten-game series was organized by James Keenan and Cumberland Posey throughout New York and Pennsylvania. The series marked the close of one era and the beginning of a new one in eastern black baseball.

As eastern black baseball underwent its painful transition, the Negro National League experienced a similar fate. A sense of urgency filled the air at the NNL's winter meeting when Judge Hueston declared the owners had to address some pressing concerns. Birmingham's and Memphis's status as league clubs received considerable attention, meaning that the southern contingent faced an uncertain future in the NNL. Several contemporaries expressed the need for a "house cleaning" of the black game. Hueston responded to charges against his league, claiming there was nothing wrong with the NNL. At the same time, Kansas City Monarchs' owner J. L. Wilkinson was quietly making plans to leave the league and embark on a new undertaking—night baseball. During the course of Wilkinson's experiment, two events occurred which signaled that the demise of the NNL was inevitable. Reports of rowdyism at league games and a boycott of Detroit Stars' home games by the black fans undermined Hueston's claim that there was nothing wrong with the NNL, and the league limped through the remainder of the 1930 season. The following year, the Negro National League would be a circuit in name only. NNL club owners never officially disbanded the league, but when J. L. Wilkinson withdrew his Monarchs from the NNL, followed by the St. Louis Stars, it did not take long for the other league clubs to respond in kind. Moreover, when Judge Hueston resigned the league presidency in October 1931, the western teams followed their eastern counterparts in a return to independent ball.

In mid-February 1930, American Negro League club owners met in a special session to disband the circuit. The *Baltimore Afro-American* reported that the decision to dissolve the ANL came as no surprise, "having been foreseen for some time." The reasons given for this action included high salaries, lack of discipline on the part of players and owners, poor umpiring, and faulty scheduling practices. In his evaluation of the ANL's demise, Bill Gibson claimed that several owners opposed league baseball because some of the restrictions imposed on the magnates were "peculiarly irksome to them."[1]

At the same time, Hilldale underwent another hostile takeover of the team's management. At the special session, Ed Bolden announced that the Hilldale Baseball Corporation would disband because it had lost its ballpark in Darby. High salaries and internal dissension among the corporate members were also cited for the decision to dissolve the ball club. Bolden stated there was a possibility he would operate an independent team to represent Philadelphia.[2]

The announcement to disband the Hilldale Club was, however, premature. The board members defeated Bolden's attempt to dissolve the team at their annual stockholders meeting and demanded the election of new officers. Three former officers—Jim Byrd, Charles Freeman, and Lloyd Thompson—led the fight to oust Bolden and his allies. The Thompson contingent was successful in garnering enough support to depose the longtime Hilldale president. The *Pittsburgh Courier* reported that the stockholders elected Thompson to succeed Bolden, with Freeman chosen as secretary and Byrd as treasurer. The directors were determined to field a team in spite of the fact that they had lost the lease to Hilldale Park. Also, with Bolden having shipped the team's property to Passion Field at Forty-Eighth and Spruce Streets, the directors stated they would take legal action to recover the possessions. There were no indications that they followed through with this intention.[3]

The Hilldale situation and the disbanding of the ANL led to a rush by clubs to sign top-level players to make their teams better gate attractions. A return to independent ball meant no agreement existed with the Negro National League to protect the contract rights of their respective clubs. It did not take long for Cum Posey to load up his roster with blue chip ballplayers. He reportedly signed Oscar Charleston, Paul Stevens, and Judy Johnson to play for his Grays. James Keenan grabbed Detroit Stars' outfielder Norman "Turkey" Stearns to play for his Lincoln Giants. The left-handed power hitter had led the NNL with twenty-four home runs in 1928 and had never hit below .320 in his nine years with the Stars.[4]

Concurrently, rumors circulated that Bolden would form a club called "Ed Bolden's Hillsdale Club." He reportedly signed longtime captain and outfielder Otto Briggs to manage the team. The club would be composed of such veteran players as Biz Mackey, Chaney White, and Rev Cannady. Phil Cockerell and McDonald Cooper would lead the pitching staff, which also included Porter Charleston, reported to be "one of the best of the younger twirlers." Hillsdale would play its home games at Passion Field, and Nat Strong would reportedly book the team throughout New England and New York.[5]

Ed Bolden's attempt to field a team for the 1930 season was undermined by Lloyd Thompson and the old Hilldale Corporation. Otto Briggs was released from his verbal agreement with Hillsdale and signed with Clan Darby. This appeared to be a package deal because Mackey and Cannady joined the Hilldale Club and Phil Cockerell was hired as player-manager. Several other veteran players were signed, including Ambrose Reid and Ping Gardner from the Bacharach Giants and Jess Hubbard from the Homestead Grays. Reportedly, the directors had "leased the old Darby grounds and [were] building a new fence and stands on the familiar spot." It was unclear whether they had purchased the old ballpark or signed a new lease. In a phone conversation with Rollo Wilson,

Thompson claimed the Hilldale Club would "measure up to the standard of other years and that the fans will be proud of the team."[6]

The inability of Bolden to dissolve the Hilldale Corporation and the loss of the players he needed to start his new club was a devastating blow to Ed Bolden's reputation as one of black baseball's leading club owners. To add to his woes, in August, Bolden received news of a possible demotion from his position as a special clerk at the post office. His annual efficiency rating dropped from 100 percent in 1926 to 91.9 percent in 1930. This was below the necessary 95 percent to retain his position as special clerk. Bolden cited his prior excellent record in a letter to the Philadelphia postmaster and asked for a chance to redeem himself. Congressman James Wolfenden in Bolden's voting district wrote a letter on his behalf, characterizing him as an "outstanding man in the community in which he lives and, in fact, a leader in civic affairs among his people." Bolden was placed on probationary status at the post office for six months. He would eventually be allowed to retain his position with no loss of pay.[7]

Over nineteen years, Ed Bolden transformed the Hilldale Baseball and Exhibition Company from "a team of small boys" to one of black baseball's premier clubs in the early twentieth century. His motto, "Clean Baseball," was not only a PR campaign to sell the HBEC to the middle-class spectator; it embodied the ideals of the African American leadership in the age of Booker T. Washington. Simultaneously, Bolden employed a race-neutral rhetoric in the pursuit of operating his segregated enterprise, the HBEC, within the fabric of a national economy—white semiprofessional baseball. Ed Bolden's administrative talents were pivotal in the formation of the Eastern Colored League. His alliance with Nat Strong, a direct result of his antagonistic relationship with Rube Foster, resulted in some of the ECL clubs being amalgamated into Strong's booking agency. Many were critical of Bolden's business dealings with Strong, a valid criticism. By the same token, it was a testament to Bolden's business acumen that he kept the faction-prone ECL together for five and one-half years. Ed Bolden remained in black baseball throughout the 1930s and 1940s, but he would never reach the height he attained in the 1920s.

With Ed Bolden temporarily absent from the eastern black baseball scene, reportedly sagging attendance led to calls for the organization of a new league. Sportswriter Bill Gibson claimed the fans were staying away because there was no league. Competing for the pennant and comparing player statistics, he said, "has meant more to many fans than this writer ever dreamed of." The inability to schedule the top teams on a regular basis was another reason cited for the low fan turnout. The Baltimore Black Sox, for example, had won thirty-one out of thirty-four games in 1930, but precisely for this reason, they had difficulty scheduling teams that would give them some "worthwhile opposition." The Lincoln Giants would not leave New York without a league, and it was unlikely the Homestead Grays would travel east late in the season.[8]

In response, Gibson led a virtual one-man campaign urging the owners to form a new league. He floated the rumor that Hilldale, Baltimore, the Lincolns, and the Bacharachs, and possibly teams in Norfolk and Richmond, Virginia, would form a new circuit. Gibson admitted this proposal sounded "rather flimsy," since the season was approaching its second half. In July, the *Afro-American* reported that Judge Hueston had proposed the formation of an East-West League composed of eastern and western clubs for the 1931 season. Black Sox owner George Rossiter declared that the proposal was feasible and that it would bolster baseball as it now existed in both regions of the country. The Hueston plan demonstrated that there existed a feeling that "something must be done" to elevate black baseball's status.[9]

Special exhibition games were staged to stimulate fan interest. On July 10, a benefit doubleheader was played at Yankee Stadium between the Lincoln Giants and the Baltimore Black Sox to raise funds for the Brotherhood of Sleeping Car Porters. The Brotherhood represented a significant step toward the unionization of African Americans. Organized by A. Philip Randolph, co-publisher of the *Messenger*, it represented an attempt to secure better working conditions and higher wages from the Pullman Company. When Pullman would have nothing to do with the Brotherhood, it attacked the union as a dangerous radical organization, and Randolph was condemned as a professional agitator. Considerable opposition toward the Brotherhood arose from black and white groups, but the Brotherhood's endorsement by the American Federation of Labor, the NAACP, and the National Urban League bolstered its fight considerably. Ray Lancaster, secretary of the Brotherhood, was the driving force behind the benefit game, along with James Keenan.[10]

In addition to this doubleheader, several other activities were included as part of the overall event. A special half-mile race featuring Phil Edwards, an intercollegiate half-mile champion, against the best runners in the New York area was also scheduled. Reportedly, Eddie Tolan, an Olympic champion, also competed in the race. Entertainment was also provided by Bill Robinson, who commonly went by his stage name, Bojangles. Eighteen thousand fans witnessed the Lincolns split a doubleheader with the Black Sox. Bill Riggins and Charlie "Chino" Smith led a thirteen-hit attack with three hits each as the Giants scored six runs in the seventh inning to win, 13-4. In the second game, Norman Yokely scattered nine hits and Rap Dixon hit two home runs en route to a 5-3 Black Sox victory. *Pittsburgh Courier* sportswriter William Nunn sang the praises of Lancaster and Keenan for staging the event and proclaimed the affair as a "red letter day."[11]

What was of interest about this doubleheader was that it represented one of the few times black teams owned exclusively by whites involved themselves in issues affecting African Americans specifically. It should be noted that since Keenan lost the lease on Olympic Stadium in Harlem, the Lincolns had played their home games in New York in a predominantly white and Jewish neighborhood. In essence, the Lincolns magnate had neglected the largest black consumer market in Gotham, which had patronized his club in the 1910s. Keenan was constantly having problems sustaining the leasing agreements at the places where the Giants played at a time when black clubs were becoming more reliant on a black consumer market for their economic viability. This could possibly explain the financial woes the Lincolns owner claimed he endured throughout the decade. There were no indications that Keenan attempted to attract black fans to the Lincoln Giants games in the 1920s. The doubleheader, therefore, appeared to be a last-ditch effort to salvage something from an otherwise dismal season.

James Keenan was also involved in organizing a ten-game series with Cumberland Posey's Homestead Grays. On August 9, the *Pittsburgh Courier* reported that "considerable discussion by the press and fans [took place regarding] the possibility of a series between" the Grays and the Giants. In a letter to the *Courier*, Posey stated that his club was anxious to play the Lincolns "because we think [the series] would pay financially." Keenan responded to Posey's challenge, and after both men haggled over the terms on which the series would occur, an agreement was reached. The series would be played at Forbes Field in Pittsburgh, Yankee Stadium in New York, and Passion Field in Philadelphia.[12]

Without question, the Lincoln Giants were an awesome club. Player-manager John Henry Lloyd manned the first-base bag due to an injury to John Beckwith. Despite losing their regular first baseman, the Giants still had veteran players Rev Cannady, Fats Jenkins, Clint Thomas, and Bill Yancy to make the lives of opposing pitchers miserable. The mound crew was led by Bill Holland, Luther Farrell, and Connie Rector.

Cum Posey's Grays were a worthy adversary, and they were led by black baseball's Babe Ruth, Oscar Charleston. A strong supporting cast surrounded Charleston, including Jake Stephens, Judy Johnson, and Chaney White. Left fielder Vic Harris was at the beginning of a long career with the Homesteads. Cyclone Joe Williams and George Britt gave Posey a one-two pitching combination that was second to none.

Grays' catcher Josh Gibson was at the beginning of a long career that led him to an iconic status. Along with Satchel Paige, Gibson would become the poster child of black baseball in the 1930s and 1940s. His indomitable presence in the batter's box personified power and electrified crowds. In 1927, he began his career with the Pleasant Valley Red Sox, a sandlot team in Pittsburgh. Later that year Gibson joined the Pittsburgh Crawfords, and there he first caught the eye of Cum Posey. He signed with the Grays in July 1929, and due to the injury to starting catcher Buck Ewing late in the 1930 season, Gibson was pressed into duty. Immediately, his impact was felt, and he helped transform a good team into a great team.[13]

The Homesteads took a 3-1 series lead. After the Grays won a doubleheader at Forbes Field to start the series, both teams headed to

Yankee Stadium for a twin bill. The first game matched the Cyclone against Bill Holland. After taking a 1-0 lead into the fourth inning, the Lincolns broke the game open with a triple by Lloyd and a home run by Cannady. It was all Holland needed, as he gave up six hits and struck out four batters on the way to a 6-2 win. The second game was a pitcher's duel between George Britt and Luther Farrell. With the score tied at two in the tenth inning, Farrell walked Jake Stephens, who promptly stole second base. Stephens scored on Farrell's throwing error to give the Grays a 3-2 victory.[14]

The Lincoln Giants were down, but not out. The Grays won two of the next three games to take a commanding 5-3 series lead. The Lincolns would have to sweep the doubleheader at Yankee Stadium to salvage at least a tie. They pinned their hopes on their staff ace Bill Holland performing a herculean task: winning both games of the doubleheader. Holland was unbeatable in the first game, throwing eight shutout innings before the Homesteads scored two runs in the ninth. Led by Lloyd and Cannady at the plate, the Lincolns crossed the plate six times to seal the victory. In the second game, Holland actually pitched seven scoreless innings! But George Britt matched him, and in the eighth, Holland began to struggle. With two outs, Britt doubled to right field when Cannady and Chino Smith misjudged a fly ball and collided with each other, knocking the outfielder unconscious. Smith had to [be] carried off the field, and Luther Farrell replaced him. Unfortunately for Farrell, he misplayed Vic Harris' line drive, resulting in a double for the left fielder. The Giants were now their own worst enemy on the field. Center fielder Clint Thomas and Farrell misjudged Judy Johnson's hit, which resulted in a triple. Chaney White walked and George Scales singled to knock in another run. Josh Gibson followed Scales and hit a two-run double. Before the inning was over, the Grays had scored five times. The Lincolns managed to score two runs in the ninth before bowing in defeat, 5-2.[15]

Rollo Wilson declared the better team won because the Grays exhibited "better team work, smarter judgment on the bases, stronger and superior handicraft [in the field]." More importantly, the series defeat to the Homestead Grays marked the end of an era for black baseball in New York. The Lincoln Giants represented the last team on which

Sol White had left his imprint. The Giants were a by-product of the efforts of White and the other black entrepreneurs in the early twentieth century who attempted to professionalize the black game. Their defeat of the Chicago American Giants in the 1913 Colored Championship Series and subsequent tour of Cuba elevated their status among the elite black clubs at that time. Under Keenan's ownership, the Lincoln Giants gained control of Harlem's baseball market through a business alliance with Nat Strong. A rift occurred between Keenan and Strong after the Lincolns' owner lost the lease to Olympic Field. Nevertheless, James Keenan was one of the leading commissioners in the ECL, and he received favorable coverage in the black press because of his reputation as a square shooter. The 1930 season had not been kind to Keenan and his Lincolns. Within six months after losing the series to the Homestead Grays, the Lincoln Giants would disband after losing their grounds at the Catholic Protectory Oval.[16]

The series victory by the Homestead Grays symbolically represented the beginning of a new period in eastern black baseball. The torch had been past to Cumberland Posey and his generation of owners, who shaped the black game's direction in the 1930s and 1940s. The winds of change that were blowing in the East would also make its presence felt in the West.

THROWN OUT AT HOME PLATE: THE COLLAPSE OF THE NEGRO NATIONAL LEAGUE

On January 16, 1930, the NNL club owners met in Detroit for their annual winter meeting where, according to Judge Hueston, "one of the most important missions in the history of the organization" would be undertaken. This sense of urgency was due, in part, to the need to drum up fan support for the upcoming season, to devise ways to reduce travel expenses, and to discuss the fate of the league's two southern franchises, Birmingham and Memphis. Several franchises applied for league entry, including Cleveland, Indianapolis, and Nashville. Finally, Judge Hueston stressed the need for the owners to give the league "their undivided attention." He asserted the game could not be handled as a "side issue" but must have the "whole hearted support and attention of the owners."[17]

The plight of both Birmingham and Memphis received considerable attention during the meeting. Both clubs had been a target of criticism since 1925 because traveling to the Deep South had caused "much grief" for the northern clubs in the league. League officials acknowledged that the Black Barons were a good gate attraction at home and on the road. This was not the case for Memphis, however. For reasons unclear, attendance declined at Black Barons and Red Sox home games after July 4. In 1929, Mose Walker claimed his Detroit Stars had amassed only four hundred dollars on a road trip to the South and was obligated to pay salaries, traveling expenses, and "other items" out of this amount. The Stars' co-owner objected, along with the other owners, to carrying out the schedule in the second half of the split season. It was due to this circumstance that the club owners considered dropping Birmingham and Memphis from the league, much to the dismay of the southern magnates.[18]

It appeared that Birmingham and Memphis were constantly victimized by player raiding. Since 1925 the Red Sox, for example, had lost star players like shortstop Charlie Williams, second baseman John Russell, and shortstop Pythias Russ. In 1926, Russ and Williams donned an American Giants uniform and Russell landed in St. Louis. Losing players of this caliber resulted in both clubs being dropped from the league, but they were reinstated for the 1927 season. However, the players were not returned to their respective clubs, and losing these stars had a negative impact on attendance in these southern cities. Not only did the league clubs raid the Red Sox's and Black Barons' player rosters, the newly created Texas-Oklahoma-Louisiana League (TOL) grabbed their players as well. A result of this situation was that a representative from the TOL League negotiating a working agreement with the NNL. The southern loop would serve as farm clubs, and the senior circuit could draft their players for a "small cash consideration." The agreement appeared to be the saving grace for Birmingham and Memphis, and both clubs, having been in the league since 1927, remained for the 1930 season.[19]

During the course of the winter meetings, several contemporaries began to critically assess the state of black baseball specifically and the NNL in general. Candy Jim Taylor made one of the most stinging indictments. After the St. Louis Stars captured the 1928 pennant, Taylor emerged as the league's premier player-manager. "One of the main reasons for lack of interest in baseball among fans of our group," Taylor explained, "[was] that the players don't care enough for the game to stay in condition." In regards to the owners, the Stars' manager said, "The club owners failed to co-operate in the establishment of ball clubs in each city. Limiting the number of men a team can carry to 14 [was] bad. Umpires who do not give fair decisions and who were paid by the club instead of by the league; dirty parks and uniforms and the failure of the clubs to give their teams good publicity, all these are bad." Taylor had reportedly made a careful study of the game's conditions and the player-managers of the league clubs. Player-managers like Bruce Petway, Dizzy Dismukes, and Dave Malarcher should, Taylor said, be given the authority to run their clubs and hold their players accountable: "We have as club owners men who have made their mark in all businesses of life, and only one man who [was] a real baseball man." Undoubtedly, this was in reference to Monarchs' owner J. L. Wilkinson.[20]

Another contemporary, James Newton, echoed many of Taylor's sentiments. His primary focus, however, was on how rowdyism was ruining the game on the field. Newton added his voice to Taylor's and Wilkinson's by stating that unruly players were alienating the fans and reinforcing the league's negative image. Money was the players' primary concern, and they "expect the fans to turn out to see them just because they are stars." Newton claimed he saw players walk off the field to take a drink of "bootleg whiskey" with some unruly fan. Such behavior led him to conclude that the players' behavior was the primary reason for the low fan turnout.[21]

In response, Judge Hueston claimed there was nothing wrong with his league. To counter the criticism, he used a tactic similar to one Rube Foster used: presenting statistical information to make the case that the NNL was in good shape. First, he highlighted the new ballparks built by John Roesink and Tom Wilson, the owner of the Elite of Nashville, an associate member. Roesink, the Stars' owner, built his new ballpark in the ethnic enclave of Hamtramck at a reported cost of $100,000. This twenty-one-square-mile village, located within Detroit's city limits, was the home to more than 56,000 Poles, most of them foreign born. Conversely, Tom Wilson built his park at a cost of $75,000, marking the third league club that had a ballpark which was black owned and operated, along with St. Louis and Memphis. The Mound City ballpark was valued at $150,000 and the Red Sox park at $75,000. Chicago American Giants' owner William Trimble controlled a park with an estimated value of $300,000. The league president boasted that the players were the best, and they were well compensated and always paid. "There is only one thing left for me to do," Hueston concluded, "and that is to say 'PLAY BALL!'"[22]

Despite the rosy picture Hueston sought to paint in the press, one club owner appeared to be making preparations for a quiet exodus from the league. J. L. Wilkinson had remained neutral regarding the league's day-to-day operations. Although he served on the NNL's Board of Directors, he had, for the most part, followed Rube Foster's lead in the way the league president ran the circuit. Next to the American Giants, Wilkinson's Kansas City Monarchs club was the league's most stable franchise, and this worked to Wilkinson's advantage. He was a keen observer of the sports scene, and he witnessed the onset of nighttime activities in the cities of the Midwest and saw that colleges were beginning to adopt electric lights in their recreational facilities and playing fields. In the fall of 1929, Wilkinson took his Monarchs to Lawrence, Kansas, where they practiced under the newly installed lights at the Haskell Institute for Indians. He along with the team recognized that playing under artificial lights was a workable proposition.[23]

That same year, Wilkinson commissioned the Grant Manufacturing Company of Omaha, Nebraska, to build a portable lighting system. It consisted of telescoping poles, elevated forty-five to fifty feet above the playing field. Each pole supported six floodlights measuring four feet across. The poles fastened on a pivot to truck beds and were raised by means of a derrick. The whole system took approximately two hours to assemble.[24]

On April 23, the portable lights were erected for their initial test at Union Pacific Park in Kansas City. After the game, Wilkinson pronounced his experiment ready for implementation. The Monarchs' owner intended to play his first night game on April 26 in Arkansas City, but fierce thunderstorms canceled the contest. Two days later, the Monarchs would play their first night game in Enid, Oklahoma, in an exhibition game against Philips University.[25]

Night baseball also had a debut in the Negro National League. On May 12, the Monarchs defeated the Memphis Red Sox in both the league's and the state of Tennessee's first night game. Next, the Monarchs traveled to St. Louis to play a five-game series with the Stars. Two of the games were played at night, and once again the Monarchs made history with the first night baseball games in Missouri.[26]

Simultaneously, two events revealed that the Negro National League had reached its nadir, and they appeared to validate Wilkinson's plan to leave the league. On August 23, the *Defender* described a doubleheader between the American Giants and the Birmingham Black Barons. The were virtually no fans except for the players' immediate families. An umpire called Rap Dixon of the American Giants out at the plate and then reversed his decision. Predictably, the American Giants utilized "the stall"—circling the umpire to intimidate him—and held up the game for ten minutes. The Black Barons threatened to walk off the field, and there were reportedly more white fans in the stands than blacks. Most of the fans informed Frank Young that they would not return. In the second game, American Giants' players were incensed at Satchel Paige's throwing at hitters. Twice American Giants' shortstop Eddie "Buck" Miller avoided being hit. When Paige threw at him again, Miller charged the mound and attacked the Black Barons' hurler. Paige ran and Miller began chasing him, resulting in more fans leaving the game. Finally, the players intervened and two or three more fights were narrowly avoided.[27]

Finally, the relationship between John Roesink and Detroit's black fans reached an all-time low. When Roesink built his new park, he undoubtedly envisioned attracting spectators and factory teams from

Dodge Main's workforce. What he overlooked was that by the late 1920s, white semipros had begun playing fewer games with black teams. Roesink also neglected the fact that black clubs were becoming more reliant on black patronage for their economic survival. The Stars' owner had alienated this black consumer group with his behavior over the decade. On August 9, 1930, the *Baltimore Afro-American* reported that the fans had organized a boycott of Hamtramck Stadium. The boycott proved effective, as less than five hundred fans witnessed a doubleheader between Louisville and Detroit.[28]

These games undermined Judge Hueston's claims that there was nothing wrong with his NNL. The critics' claim that the players' behavior alienated fans appeared validated, and the owners' ambivalence towards the league's day-to-day operations seemed validated as well. Herein lay a fundamental weakness in Hueston's leadership: his unwillingness to impose penalties and sanctions. There was no evidence that the league president levied a fine or suspension on the players involved in the American Giants-Black Barons doubleheader. Given the fact that the owners did not heed Cum Posey's advice to provide the president with an expense account so he could attend league games, Hueston's inaction was understandable. Newspaper accounts could not be used to justify levying penalties or sanctions. Hueston undoubtedly did not want to incur the wrath of the owners by suspending a star player, especially before or during an important series. Yet with the fans leaving the doubleheader and claiming they would not return and the boycott by Detroit's black fans, things did not bode well for Hueston and his NNL.

Although the Negro National League did not officially disband, the withdrawal of two of the circuit's most stable franchises sealed its fate. In 1931, the NNL was a league in name only. Wilkinson withdrew his Monarchs at the end of the summer. Dr. G. Bernard Key sold his interest in the St. Louis Stars and sold the ballpark to the city. Finally, on October 30, 1931, Judge William Hueston resigned as president of the league to devote his attention to his job as solicitor general at the post office. After twelve years of operation, Rube Foster's Negro National League faded into the dustbin of history.

Conclusion: Extra Innings

On December 30, 1930, Andrew Rube Foster died. The Chicago *Defender* declared Foster a national celebrity, second only in the sporting world to Babe Ruth, and his death was mourned by thousands. Two automobiles filled with flowers preceded the hearse, which was followed by a funeral procession a half mile long. Floral arrangements included a huge baseball made up of small white chrysanthemums with roses for the seams, weighing over two hundred pounds. The baseball was sent by the NNL club owners. A large piece of white and yellow chrysanthemums that covered the coffin was donated by Chicago American Giants' owner William Trimble.[29]

Rube Foster's death marked the end of a generation of African American entrepreneurs who sought to professionalize the black game and place it on a sound economic footing. Foster—along with Sol White; C. I. Taylor; Ed Bolden; Frank Leland; and to a lesser degree John Connor, Henry Tucker, and Tom Jackson—embodied the continued efforts of African American entrepreneurs to develop businesses to advance their economic interests. They exhibited a willingness to work within the parameters of a biracial institutional structure. Early-twentieth-century black baseball entrepreneurs recognized that in order to conduct business in the United States, they had to negotiate with the white power structure. This meant transacting business with white semiprofessional club owners, park managers, and in some cases establishing partnerships with white entrepreneurs. They scheduled games with white semipros, African American clubs, and Cuban teams. At times they also played against major and minor league clubs and all-star teams composed of major or minor league players. They used the business practices established by the successful black baseball clubs of the late 1880s and 1890s, like going where the money was and creating a demand for their teams in several locales. Keeping a talented player force intact, securing a suitable playing facility to generate gate receipts, and mastering the barnstorming schedule allowed several teams to elevate their status to an elite touring team. Teams that reached this height included the

Philadelphia Giants, Leland Giants, Chicago American Giants, Lincoln Giants, Indianapolis ABCs, and Bacharach Giants.

Early-twentieth-century black baseball entrepreneurs embodied the ideals of the new black leadership that emerged in urban cities in the North and South. Unlike the old elite, the new leaders rarely articulated a racial ideology, and many of them shunned racial activities altogether. These men left their imprint through the creation of businesses, institutions, and organizational politics. To the degree to which they were involved in ideological battles, they tended to favor Booker T. Washington's doctrine of self-help. Yet the Tuskegee ideology did not determine their actions. It essentially validated what they were already doing.

In the opening decade of the twentieth century, black baseball experienced tremendous growth. Several black and Cuban clubs emerged to challenge established teams like the Philadelphia Giants, Leland Giants, and Cuban X Giants for players and gate receipts. Black baseball's expansion occurred at the same time as the emergence of black corporate America. Much like more conventional businesses, black team owners dealt with the ways in which a separate black economy was being imposed on them. Ballpark ownership remained the biggest hurdle to the black game's business development. African American owners did not enjoy the advantages the Major League owners had in terms of building or remodeling ballparks to sustain a fan base and maximize revenues. This led several African American club owners to enter into partnerships with white businessmen to gain access to suitable playing facilities and maintain business ties with white semipro teams.

Black baseball's tremendous growth led to concerted efforts to form leagues and associations. League formation represented an attempt to place the black game on a sound economic footing. Understandably, African American club owners used the white Major Leagues as their model for organization. However, they did not run their leagues in a traditional sense: there was no pursuit of a pennant or sponsorship of a postseason championship series. They also did not embrace the concept that they were competitors on the field but partners in business who had to cooperate to a much greater degree than other, more conventional business enterprises. Rather, they endeavored to maintain their symbiotic business relationships with white semipro clubs and concurrently schedule games with black and Cuban teams. In this way, black club owners developed a barnstorming schedule that was both regional and national in scope. Ideally, a black team would expand their barnstorming network internationally to Cuba.

Early attempts to form leagues and associations informed the way Rube Foster, Ed Bolden, and Nat Strong ran the Negro Leagues in the 1920s. In what can best be described as the business alliance model, this approach was based on the premise that black club owners would have the maximum control over their players under contract and the franchise. Through an association of a few club owners in certain cities, these magnates could collectively eliminate contract jumping and gain tighter control over black baseball's player force. This collusive business relationship among these owners also served to minimize to a certain degree outside competition from prospective entrepreneurs seeking to capitalize on the baseball craze.

In regards to scheduling, the business alliance model enabled the owners to form loose associations among themselves to ensure that their clubs secured the best playing dates and parks to play in. They could play either a league game or an exhibition contest in the pursuit of generating gate receipts. Yet this arrangement came at the expense of some of the other league clubs. In most cases, some of the league clubs became reliant on Rube Foster and Nat Strong to book additional games for them to generate gate receipts. This arrangement allowed Foster and Strong to leverage their position in the black baseball marketplace. By charging a 10 percent booking fee, both men earned additional residual income and maximized their profits.

By the 1920s, several forces had made league formation plausible. The Great Migration dramatically expanded the black communities in which several black baseball teams resided. It created an African American consumer market that club owners could no longer minimize. The expansion of the black press provided the means for these magnates to tap into this growing market. The economic situation of African Americans showed that while US prosperity was widespread in the 1920s, it was not universal. On the one hand, African Americans had no trouble finding jobs, which helped to enlarge the black middle class. On the other hand, even a minor depression could wipe out most of the gains African Americans made in certain fields, including manufacturing. Elsewhere, as in the stockyards of Chicago, blacks became a permanent presence, but they had to endure bitter antagonism from several ethnic groups. The Negro Leagues did benefit, however, when the economy recovered in the mid-1920s and unemployment subsided.

Several teams that were black owned and operated functioned as full-time enterprises, in spite of challenges to their operational autonomy. Five owners—those of the Bacharach Giants, Chicago American Giants, Hilldale AC, Indianapolis ABCs, and St. Louis Giants—used the pattern black baseball entrepreneurs used to transform their clubs into a top independent club. The organization of a league would allow these owners to gain a hegemony over their growing industry and protect their economic investment.

By the same token, the business-alliance approach was somewhat problematic because of the ways in which these club owners ran the Negro Leagues in the 1920s. To be sure, ballpark ownership, or rather the lack of it, was the Achilles heel of black baseball's business and economic development. Only two league clubs—the St. Louis Stars and the Memphis Red Sox owned their parks—while the remaining clubs leased their ballparks from minor league teams or local park managers. Traveling teams like the Cuban Stars East and West and the Brooklyn Royal Giants further hampered attempts to achieve a balanced schedule. For these clubs, it was difficult to earn residual income like sales from concessions, parking, and other miscellaneous sources.

Certain club owners, by placing their interests above the league's, made the business-alliance approach problematic for the Negro Leagues. Rube Foster, Ed Bolden, and Nat Strong believed it was not in their best economic interests to pattern their leagues after the white Major Leagues. They refused to acknowledge that their leagues' overall economic interests and their interests were one and the same. These men were satisfied so along as they minimized player jumping and maintained their hegemony over their respective consumer markets. Looking out for their own economic interests first was understandable, but it came at the expense of their fellow owners. More importantly, this approach made it difficult for both leagues to expand into new markets like Washington, D.C.; Cleveland; and Milwaukee.

The business-alliance approach was further compromised by the separate black economy that was imposed on these club owners. I have argued from the outset that black baseball as a business enterprise did not rely solely on the black consumer market for its economic viability. Black club owners continued to maintain their symbiotic business relationship with white semipros because it was in their best economic interest to do so. By the mid-1920s, however, this relationship became impractical due to the decline of white semiprofessional baseball. In spite of this, these magnates continued to make attempts to recapture the white fans they had lost. It was as if they were trying to recapture a bygone era that was highly unlikely to return.

Like more conventional black enterprises, the Negro Leagues could not escape the fact that they were becoming increasingly reliant on the black consumer dollar. The business-alliance approach conflicted with the black press's wish that the black leagues be patterned after the white Major Leagues. To the black press, the pennant race and a postseason championship series would stimulate interest in the black game, a valid and logical assumption. If the Negro Leagues operated on the same level as the white Major Leagues, this would, theoretically at least, elevate the race from its political, economic, and social plight.

The black press's desire for the Negro Leagues to be on par with the white majors was understandable and, most importantly of all, a practical approach to the Negro National League's and Eastern Colored League's business and economic predicament. Because of the economic prosperity the Major Leagues experienced in the 1920s, the competitor-partner model became the ideal for all sports leagues to emulate. As indicated previously, the Major League owners did not always follow the script that guided the competitor-partner model. Nevertheless, they enjoyed considerable advantages that black baseball owners could never capitalize on. It was because of these advantages that Major League owners could deviate from the script from time to time with no severe repercussions.

To the Negro League owners, the competitor-partner approach was, as sportswriter Bill Gibson described it, "particularly irksome." To their way of thinking, that approach was impractical as long as the lack of ballpark ownership impacted on their ability to obtain a balanced schedule. What was more revealing, however, was that the Negro League owners gave priority to the pursuit of short-term profits over long-term considerations. This, more than anything else, nullified the competitor-partner approach among the black baseball club owners.

The collapse of the Negro National and Eastern Colored Leagues left entrepreneurs like Pittsburgh Crawfords' owner Gus Greenlee struggling to keep their enterprises alive. In 1933, Greenlee led an effort to form a new Negro National League. The NNL consisted of six clubs: the Baltimore Elite Giants, Chicago American Giants, Columbus Blue Birds, Detroit Stars, Nashville Elite Giants, and Pittsburgh Crawfords. Constant franchise shifting defined the NNL throughout the Depression decade. Three franchises joined the league; they were Cumberland Posey's Homestead Grays; Alex Pompez's New York Cubans; and the Philadelphia Stars, co-owned by Eddie Gottlieb and Ed Bolden. Greenlee dealt with obstacles including a weak administration, individualistic owners, and inadequate financing. Also, a strained relationship persisted between black baseball, the black press, and a public that was critical of flawed black institutions and of players defecting to foreign countries like Mexico. Also, the growing appeal of Joe Louis overshadowed black baseball.[30]

One of Greenlee's remarkable achievements during this troubled decade was the creation of the East-West All-Star game. The All-Star game featured black baseball's finest players selected by the vote of the fans, and it would quickly increase in prestige. The *Pittsburgh Courier*'s Bill Nunn identified the game as "our connecting link with organized baseball. It's our big opportunity to show . . . under perfect conditions . . . just what we are capable of producing through the years." While the originators of the East-West game remained obscure, Greenlee's role in the execution of the game was particularly crucial. Whereas club owners Tom Wilson (Baltimore Elite Giants) and Robert Cole (Chicago American Giants) shared equally in the promotional expenses with Greenlee, the Crawfords' owner reportedly took the greatest risk by paying $2,500 in advance for the exorbitant rental of Comiskey Park. His risk paid dividends, because the East-West All-Star game exposed black players to a larger audience because daily newspapers, particularly in Chicago, provided generous coverage. Moreover, the All-Star game not only evolved into a superior moneymaking proposition for league teams and a showcase for black talent to white America, but also demonstrated the financial potential of the industry.[31]

The Negro American League was founded in 1937. The wartime economy improved African Americans' financial plight. The Negro National League was revived in the early 1940s. Several black teams were able to attract a plethora of fans with discretionary income to spend. Increased profits generated a significant degree of anxiety over the involvement of white promoters, because white booking agents were also club owners, and it was easier for them to cut deals with white park owners. Additional concerns were raised over the changing of racial perspectives during World War II, resulting in increased advocacy for integration in all facets of American life.

The gradual progress of African Americans into the American mainstream marked the start of black professional baseball's decline. Black clubs could not compete with the enormous appeal of Jackie Robinson's crossing the color line in Organized Baseball in 1947. African Americans were indifferent to arguments claiming the continued usefulness of black teams. Instead, they gravitated toward Major League Baseball, a better-financed institution that was becoming increasingly available through radio and television. The sale of players to Organized Baseball and the scheduling of games in the segregated South enabled several black clubs to survive into the early 1950s. By 1960, however, many African Americans viewed the Negro Leagues as an unfortunate reminder of the segregated past.

The Negro National League and Eastern Colored League have left a lasting imprint on the African American experience specifically and

American baseball in general. The Negro Leagues not only inform us of the ways African Americans endeavored to compete within the framework of the US economy; they also represented the overall pursuit of both freedom and self-determination. Baseball as a professional enterprise was born in the womb of community building during the antebellum era. It evolved as a commercialized amusement at a time when segregation shaped the relationship between black and white people. African Americans made it clear that in spite of their exclusion from mainstream America, they would develop their own institutions and shape their own sporting patterns. They transformed the black game into a commercial enterprise, sought to advance their own business interests, and symbolically "elevated the race" through their success. More importantly, black baseball entrepreneurs were among those African Americans who sought inclusion in mainstream America through economic advancement.

The remarkable accomplishments of African American ballplayers who followed Jackie Robinson in crossing the color line to the Major Leagues clearly revealed the Negro Leagues' lasting imprint on American baseball culture. Willie Mays, Henry Aaron, Larry Doby, Ernie Banks, and Monte Irvin had phenomenal careers in the Major Leagues made possible by the efforts of Rube Foster; Ed Bolden; C. I. Taylor; and to a lesser degree, John Connor, Henry Tucker, and Tom Jackson. These men operated by any means necessary to transform the Negro Leagues into a commercial enterprise that would be inherited by a new generation of African American entrepreneurs. The black baseball entrepreneurs of the late nineteenth and early twentieth centuries were not merely passive participants responding to forces that impacted them. They sought to form black baseball as a business enterprise according to their view of what baseball as a profession should be.

Notes

Bibliography

Index

Notes

1. Continuity and Change

1. *Evening Item* (Philadelphia), April 24, 1902. For a secondary account of the Philadelphia Giants, see Michael E. Lomax, "Black Baseball Entrepreneurship in the Quaker City: The Philadelphia Giants and the Rise and Fall of the NACBC," *Sport History Review* 37 (2006): 100–29.

2. Biographical data is derived from Sol White, *Sol White's Official Base Ball Guide*, 2nd ed. (Philadelphia: H. Walter Schlichter, 1984), 1–4; John Holway, *Blackball Stars: Negro League Pioneers* (New York: Carroll and Graff, 1988), 1–7; and James A. Riley, *The Biographical Encyclopedia of the Negro Baseball Leagues* (New York: Carroll and Graf, 1994), 836–37. I would like to thank Jacqueline Brown, archivist at Wilberforce University, for providing me with Sol White's college transcript. Apparently, White spent only one year at the university. He was a private in the Organization of Corps of Cadets while attending there. *Wheeling Daily Intelligencer* (WV), May 10, July 26, October 13, 1886.

3. For a secondary account of the National League of Colored Base Ball Players, see Michael E. Lomax, *Black Baseball Entrepreneurs, 1860–1901: Operating by Any Means Necessary* (Syracuse, NY: Syracuse University Press, 2003), 63–70. *Sporting Life* 18 (January 12, 1887): 8; Ibid., 18 (February 16, 1887): 8. *Wheeling Daily Intelligencer*, July 2, 1887. For White's end-of-season statistics, see *Sporting Life* 19 (January 25, 1888): 4.

4. For the Ohio League's reorganization into the Tri-State League and its repeal of the provision in its constitution to sign black players, see *Sporting Life* 19 (February 29, 1888): 1. Moses Fleetwood Walker's brother, Weldy, wrote an open letter about the Tri-State League's ban on black players. This letter was reprinted in Sol White's *History of Colored Baseball*. He complimented White and proclaimed him to be "one, if not the surest hitter in the Ohio League." See *Sporting Life* 19 (March 14, 1888): 5.

5. *Evening Item*, September 29, 1902. For Smith's conception of the idea of a black club representing Philadelphia, see Sol White, *History of Colored Baseball: With Other Documents on the Early Black Game, 1886–1936* (Lincoln: University of Nebraska Press, 1995), 31.

6. In 1919, White wrote a series of articles in the *Cleveland Advocate* on the early history of the Philadelphia Giants. See *Cleveland Advocate*, June 14, 21, 1919. For an account of Schlichter's managing of boxing clubs and boxers, see *Amsterdam News* (NY), December 18, 1930.

7. To describe black baseball's business practices, I am drawing heavily from my work on late-nineteenth-century black baseball. See Lomax, *Black Baseball Entrepreneurs, 1860–1901*.

8. The management position held by these men was drawn from a photo published in the *Evening Item* on August 18, 1903. In 1896, Connie Mack began his career as a manager and entrepreneur with Milwaukee in Ban Johnson's Western League. In 1901, Mack and club owner Matt Killilea moved the team to Philadelphia to compete against the National League Phillies. The move took a tragic turn when Killilea died of tuberculosis the same year. Mack held only a quarter of the stock, but Johnson came to the rescue by persuading Benjamin Shibe to purchase the majority of the stock. The venture was successful because Shibe was a partner of Albert Reach, who for years had backed the Phillies. See Harold Seymour, *Baseball: The Golden Age* (New York: Oxford University Press, 1970), 137–39; David Q. Voigt, *American Baseball: From the Commissioners to Continental Expansion* (University Park, PA: Pennsylvania State University Press, 1983), 7; and Robert F. Burk, *Never Just a Game: Players, Owners, and American Baseball to 1920* (Chapel Hill: University of North Carolina Press, 1994), 148.

9. *Evening Item*, April 15, May 22, 1902. According to White, one of the primary reasons for forming the Giants was to place the players on salary and establish individual contracts, as opposed to the co-op plan. On the co-op plan, gate receipts were divided among the management and the players from each game. See *Cleveland Advocate*, July 12, 1919.

10. *Fifteenth Census of the United States: 1930* (Washington, DC: Government Printing Office, 1933), 71. For an account of Columbia Park, see Bruce Kuklick, *To Every Thing a Season: Shibe Park and Urban Philadelphia, 1909–1976* (Princeton, NJ: Princeton University Press, 1991), 15.

11. For an account of the Giants winning fifteen out of their first nineteen games, see *Evening Item*, May 21, 1902. For the night game against the Cosmopolitans, see ibid., June 3, 4, 1902.

12. The Colored Championship Series had its roots in baseball's amateur era in the 1860s. The series emulated the championship system devised by white amateur baseball clubs. For an account of the championship systems of the 1860s, see Melvin Adelman, *A Sporting Time: New York and the Rise of Modern Athletics, 1820–1870* (Urbana: University of Illinois Press, 1986), 146–47. For secondary accounts dealing with the rise of the Colored Championship Series, see White, *History of Colored Baseball* (1995), 35–49; Lomax, *Black Baseball Entrepreneurs*, 74–79; and Michael E. Lomax, "Black Baseball's First Rivalry: The Cuban Giants versus the Gorhams of New York and the

Birth of the Colored Championship," *Sport History Review* 28 (November 1997): 134–45.

13. *Evening Item,* June 2, 15, 23, 1902.

14. For secondary accounts regarding the rise of the Philadelphia Athletics and their war over players with the National League, see Seymour, *Baseball: The Golden Age,* 156–57; Burk, *Never Just a Game,* 153–54; and Charles C. Alexander, *Our Game: An American Baseball History* (New York: Henry Holt, 1991), 80–81.

15. Buck Freeman's statistics for the 1902 season are in David S. Neft and Richard M. Cohen, *The Sports Encyclopedia: Baseball,* 16th ed. (New York: St. Martin's Griffin, 1996). *Evening Item,* September 26, 27, 29, 1902.

16. For an account of the backgrounds of Harry Buckner, William Binga, Robert Footes, and John Patterson, see Riley, *Biographical Encyclopedia,* 83–84, 131, 286, 609–10. For accounts regarding the 1896 Colored Championship Series between the Cuban X Giants and the Page Fence Giants, see Lomax, *Black Baseball Entrepreneurs,* 135–39, and Thomas E. Powers, "The Page Fence Giants Play Ball," *Chronicle: The Quarterly Magazine of the Historical Society of Michigan* 19 (Spring 1983): 14–18.

17. *Evening Item,* May 31, July 18, August 3, 21, September 8, 1903.

18. Ibid., May 11, 1903.

19. Ibid., May 4, 18, July 3, 31, August 23, September 4, 11, 13, 14, October 8, 1903. Average ticket prices are based on the prices of Cuban Giants games reported in the press. See, for example, *Trenton True American* (NJ), June 4, 5, 1888.

20. *Evening Item,* September 6, 12, 13, 14, 19, 26, 1903.

21. Ibid., April 6, 1904. For accounts regarding the Morrow club playing at the Giants' new grounds, see Ibid., May 8, 22, 31, August 14, 24, 26, 31, 1904.

22. For accounts of games against the Murray Hills, see *New York Sun,* April 4, May 9, June 27, August 29, 1904. For an account regarding Bill Duggleby pitching against the Giants, see *Evening Item,* August 1, 1904. Ibid., April 11, August 9, 18, 1904.

23. *Evening Item,* July 28, August 2, 4, 5, 7, 16, 25, 30, 1904.

24. Ibid., September 2, 3, 6, 1904.

25. Ibid., September 28, 30, October 5, 1904. For a secondary account of Douglass Hospital, see Roger Lane, *William Dorsey's Philadelphia and Ours: On the Past and Future of the Black City in America* (New York: Oxford University Press, 1991), 174–75, 181. Some of the members who made up the hospital's board of directors were undoubtedly part of the "colored aristocracy." They included prominent members of the African American elite such as Jacob White, who was a member of the Pythians baseball club of the late 1860s.

26. For secondary accounts regarding the Eastern League, Ed Barrow, and the Newark Eagles, see James M. DiClerico and Barry J. Pavlec, *The Jersey Game: The History of Modern Baseball from Its Birth to the Big Leagues in the Garden State* (New Brunswick, NJ: Rutgers University Press, 1991), 77–79, 207, and Robert Obojski, *Bush*

League: A History of Minor League Baseball (New York: Macmillan, 1975), 94–99. *Evening Item,* April 7, 8, 9, 1905. On May 12, the Giants played the Eagles a fourth time, defeating them 4-0. See *Evening Item*, May 13, 1905.

27. *Evening Item*, May 12, 1905.

28. Ibid., April 24, May 22, June 5, 12, 19, July 13, 17, 21, 23, 24, August 14, 15, 19, 28, 30, 31, September 1, 2, 18, 25, October 2, 16, 1905.

29. For games in New York, see *Evening Item*, April 24, May 22, June 5, 12, 19, July 24, August 28, September 18, 25, October 2, 16, 1905. Games in New Jersey include those covered in *Evening Item,* July 17, August 14, 15, 19, 30, 31, September 1, 2, 15, 17, 1905.

30. For games against the Ridgewoods, see *Evening Item*, April 24, May 22, June 12, September 18, 1905. Games against the Atlantic City club include those reported in ibid., August 15, 19, 30, 31, September 1, 2, 1905.

31. Ibid., August 3, 4, 1905.

32. Ibid., September 15, 16, 17, 1905.

33. *Trenton Times*, May 10, 1886. Lomax, *Black Baseball Entrepreneurs*, 56; Riley, *Biographical Encyclopedia*, 847–48.

34. See Lomax, *Black Baseball Entrepreneurs*, regarding the rift between the Cuban Giants' players and their owner, J. M. Bright, that led to the formation of the Cuban X Giants.

35. Throughout the late 1880s and the 1890s, the *New York Sun* provided the best coverage of the Cuban Giants and Cuban X Giants. By 1900, press coverage had begun to decline significantly. The *Sun* printed only line scores on a sporadic basis. See *New York Sun*, August 18, September 18, 1902; April 13, May 4, 8, 11, 12, 13, 25, 29, June 1, 5, 6, 9, 29, July 13, 20, 27, August 3, 1903; and April 11, May 2, Jun 13, 20, 27, 29, 30, July 10, August 8, 15, October 3, 1904. For accounts of the rivalry between the X Giants and Ridgewoods, see *New York Times*, April 12, May 3, July 19, 1903; April 14, 18, 29, May 2, June 20, July 1, 1904; and May 12, 15, October 2, 1905. For accounts of the 1904 colored championship with the Chicago Union Giants, see *Chicago Tribune*, September 11, 12, 18, 19, 25, 26, 1904. On September 22, the Cuban X Giants played the Chicago Union Giants in Polo, Illinois. This game was apparently not billed as a colored championship game. The Union Giants defeated the Cubans, 3-0.

36. *Sporting Life* 31 (January 4, 1902): 1.

37. For the All Cubans' 1899 tour and the Cuban X Giants' tour of Cuba the following year, see Lomax, *Black Baseball Entrepreneurs*, 163–65, 167–68. In 1904, *Spalding's Official Base Ball Guide* published a series of articles on the history of baseball in Cuba up to that time. See "History of Base Ball in Cuba," in *Spalding's Official Base Ball Guide, ed. Albert Spalding* (New York: America Sports Pub. Co., 1904), 282–83. For the All Cubans' barnstorming tours of 1900 and 1902, see H. D. Ramsey, "Base Ball in Cuba," *Spalding's Official Base Ball Guide*, 234–35.

38. Adrian Burgos Jr., "Playing America's Game: Latinos and the Performance and Policing of Race in North American Professional Baseball, 1868–1959" (PhD diss., University of Michigan, 2000), 118–20; Adrian Burgos Jr., "Entering Cuba's Other Playing Field: Cuban Baseball and the Choice between Race and Nation, 1887–1912," *Journal of Sport and Social Issues* 29 (February 2005): 9–40.

39. I am drawing from the work by Burgos that was part of an in-depth study of black baseball funded by the National Baseball Hall of Fame and Museum. See Lawrence D. Hogan, *Shades of Glory: The Negro Leagues and the Story of African American Baseball* (Washington, DC: National Geographic, 2006).

40. Ramsey, "Base Ball in Cuba," 235. The majority of the games listed are line scores. See, for example, *New York Sun*, May 25, August 3, 10, 1903; May 2, 23, September 26, 1904; and August 21, 1905. The Philadelphia *Evening Item* did, however, provide some box scores of All Cuban games. See *Evening Item*, May 2, July 22, August 9, 18, 21, September 5, 28, 1904, and July 30, 1905.

41. I would like to thank Larry Hogan for providing me with a photocopy of a baseball guidebook published by the Chicago Giants in 1910: *Frank Leland's Chicago Giants Baseball Club*, Baseball Hall of Fame and Museum, Cooperstown, NY. *Defender* (Chicago), November 21, 1914.

42. Lomax, *Black Baseball Entrepreneurs*, 160–61.

43. *Chicago Tribune*, May 4, 1902; Riley, *Biographical Encyclopedia*, 501, 885.

44. *Chicago Tribune*, June 23, July 28, 1902.

45. For a secondary account of Chicago's semiprofessional baseball infrastructure, see Raymond Schmidt, "The Golden Age of Chicago Baseball," *Chicago History* 29 (Winter 2000): 38–59.

46. *Chicago Inter Ocean*, March 22, April 7, May 10, 26, June 2, 16, 23, July 14, August 11, 1903.

47. *Chicago Tribune*, June 15, July 19, 20, 1903.

48. *Chicago Inter Ocean*, April 3, 1904; *Chicago Tribune*, May 17, 1904.

49. *Chicago Tribune*, June 7, 1904.

50. For an account of Peters's son, Frank, managing the Union Giants in the 1910s, see *Defender*, March 27, 1915.

51. *Frank Leland's Chicago Giants Baseball Club*.

2. Black Professional Baseball's Growth and Expansion, 1906–1907

1. John Whiteclay Chambers II, *The Tyranny of Change: America in the Progressive Era, 1890–1920*, 2nd ed. (New Brunswick, NJ: Rutgers University Press, 2000); Paul Johnson, *A History of the American People* (New York: HarperPerennial, 1997); Charles N. Glaab, ed., *The American City: A Documentary History* (Homewood, IL:

Dorsey Press, 1963); Blake McKelvey, *The Urbanization of America, 1865–1915* (New Brunswick, NJ: Rutgers University Press, 1963); Sam Bass Warner Jr., *The Private City: Philadelphia in Three Periods of Its Growth* (Philadelphia: University of Pennsylvania Press, 1968); Alexander Callow, *American Urban History: An Interpretive Reader with Contemporaries* (New York: Oxford University Press, 1973); Alexander Callow, *The Urban Wilderness: A History of the American City* (New York: Harper and Row, 1972).

2. *Defender* (Chicago), July 17, 1926; *Pittsburgh Courier*, July 17, 1926; *Philadelphia Tribune*, July 24, 1926.

3. For secondary accounts regarding the rise of the new black middle class and the Tuskegee ideology at the turn of the twentieth century, see W. E. B. Du Bois, *The Souls of Black Folk* (New York: Penguin Books, 1996); E. Franklin Frazier, *Black Bourgeoisie* (New York: Free Press, 1957); August Meier, *Negro Thought in America, 1880–1915* (Ann Arbor: University of Michigan Press, 1964); Allan H. Spear, *Black Chicago: The Making of a Negro Ghetto, 1890–1920* (Chicago: University of Chicago Press, 1967); David M. Katzman, *Before the Ghetto: Black Detroit in the Nineteenth Century* (Chicago: University of Illinois Press, 1973); Kenneth L. Kusmer, *A Ghetto Takes Shape: Black Cleveland, 1870–1930* (Chicago: University of Illinois Press, 1976); Manning Marable, *How Capitalism Underdeveloped Black America: Problems in Race, Political Economy, and Society* (Boston: South End Press, 1983); Bart Landry, *The New Black Middle Class* (Berkeley: University of California Press, 1987); and Kevin K. Gaines, *Uplifting The Race: Black Leadership, Politics, and Culture in the Twentieth Century* (Chapel Hill: University of North Carolina Press, 1996).

4. While Harris focused primarily on amusement enterprises like theaters, dance halls, poolrooms, and cabaret, baseball also fell within this category. See Abram L. Harris, *The Negro as Capitalist: A Study of Banking and Business among American Negroes* (Philadelphia: American Academy of Political and Social Science, 1936), 53–56. See also J. H. Harmon, Arnett G. Lindsey, Carter G. Woodson, *The Negro as a Business Man* (College Park, MD: McGrath, 1929), 1–36, and Vishnu V. Oak, *The Negro's Adventure in General Business* (Yellow Springs, OH: Antioch Press, 1949), 48. For an account of the proliferation of black teams in the 1900s, see Robert Peterson, *Only the Ball Was White* (New York: Oxford University Press, 1970), 59–72, and Phil Dixon and Patrick J. Hannigan, *The Negro Baseball Leagues, 1867–1955* (Mattituck, NY: Amereon House, 1992), 31–56. For the increase in bankers, undertakers, and retail merchants, see Meier, *Negro Thought*, 140. For the increase in printing companies and real estate companies, see Seth M. Scheiner, *Negro Mecca: A History of the Negro in New York City, 1865–1920* (New York: New York University Press, 1965), 78.

5. *New York Sun*, April 25, 1904. See chapter 1 regarding the colored championship with the Philadelphia Giants.

6. For a secondary account of the backgrounds of Jap Payne, Billy Holland, Gus James, Al Robinson, Lefty Andrews, and Jack Emery, see James A. Riley, *The*

Biographical Encyclopedia of the Negro Baseball Leagues (New York: Carroll and Graff, 1994), 36, 267, 387–88, 419, 669–70. *Chicago Tribune*, May 7, 1906.

7. *Evening Item* (Philadelphia), June 1, 5, August 26, September 13, 1906.

8. For an account of welfare capitalism, see Daniel T. Rodgers, *The Work Ethic in Industrial America, 1850–1920* (Chicago: University of Chicago Press, 1978), 154–56, and Stuart Brandes, *American Welfare Capitalism* (Chicago: University of Chicago Press, 1970), 16, 20.

9. See any edition of the Philadelphia *Evening Item* from May to October 1905.

10. For an account of the playground movement, see Dominick Cavallo, *Muscles and Morals: Organized Playgrounds and Urban Reform, 1880–1920* (Philadelphia: University of Pennsylvania Press, 1981).

11. *New York Times*, March 3, 1906. For an account of Sunday ball in New York and the ways in which baseball magnates circumvented the Blue Laws, see Steven A. Riess, *Touching Base: Professional Baseball and American Culture in the Progressive Era* (Westport, CT: Greenwood Press, 1980), 121–50.

12. Riess, *Touching Base*, 121–50; *New York Times*, March 16, 26, 27, 1905.

13. *New York Times*, March 2, 1907, January 11, 1935; *New York Tribune*, January 11, 1935; *Baltimore Afro-American*, February 11, 1921; *Philadelphia Tribune*, April 12, 1928.

14. For professional baseball's connections to Tammany Hall in New York, see Riess, *Touching Base*, 66–75.

15. Ibid. See also M. R. Werner, *Tammany Hall* (New York: Doubleday, Doran, 1928), 303–482. For black baseball games scheduled at the New York Highlanders' home facility, see, for example, *New York Age*, June 23, 1910, August 11, 1911, August 8, 1912.

16. Sol White, *History of Colored Baseball: With Other Documents on the Early Black Game, 1886–1936* (Lincoln: University of Nebraska Press, 1995), 33, 91; John Holway, *Blackball Stars: Negro League Pioneers* (New York: Carroll and Graff, 1988), 1–7; Riley, *Biographical Encyclopedia*, 6–7.

17. White, *History*, 33, 106, 113. *Evening Item*, May 10, 11, June 19, 1906.

18. *Evening Item*, July 24, 1906.

19. Ibid., April 15, 18, 19, 20, 21, 25, 27, 1906. *The Reach Official American League Guide* (Philadelphia: A. J. Reach, 1907), 177.

20. *Chicago Tribune*, May 16, 20, 21, 26, 1906.

21. *Evening Item*, August 7, 9, 19, 28, September 3, 6, 7, 1906.

22. Ibid., October 13, 14, 1906.

23. Ibid., October 29, 1906.

24. Ibid.

25. For secondary accounts of major league baseball's competitor-partner model, see Harold Seymour, *Baseball: The Early Years* (New York: Oxford University Press,

1960); Harold Seymour, *Baseball: The Golden Age* (New York: Oxford University Press, 1970); Walter C. Neale, "The Peculiar Economics of Professional Sports: A Contribution to the Theory of the Firm in Sporting Competition and in Market Competition," *Quarterly Journal of Economics* 1 (1964): 1–14; and David Q. Voigt, *American Baseball: From Gentlemen's Sport to the Commissioner System* (Norman: University of Oklahoma Press, 1966).

26. Lloyd quote in Dixon and Hannigan, *Negro Baseball Leagues*, 89, and Peterson, *Only the Ball*, 77. White, *History*, 68.

27. *Chicago Tribune*, April 24, 28, 1906. For information on the San Francisco earthquake of 1906, see http://quake.wr.usgs.gov/info/1906/.

28. The majority of the games reported in the *Chicago Tribune* were weekend games, mostly played in Chicago.

29. *Chicago Tribune*, June 4, 8, 11, 1906.

30. Ibid., September 27, 1906.

31. Ibid., June 13, 1904, May 5, 1907. Raymond Schmidt, "The Golden Age of Chicago Baseball," *Chicago History* 29 (Winter 2000): 49–50. For Jimmy Callahan's background, see David S. Neft, Richard M. Cohen, and Michael L. Neft, *The Sports Encyclopedia: Baseball*, 24th ed. (New York: St. Martin's Griffin, 2004), and *Reach's Official American League Guide* (Philadelphia: A. J. Reach, 1902), 58.

32. Ibid. *Chicago Tribune*, June 2, 1912.

33. For Jake Stahl's background, see D. Neft et al., *Sports Encyclopedia: Baseball*, and *Chicago Tribune*, October 1, 1912.

34. *Defender*, November 29, 1919.

35. See chapter 1 regarding the estimates.

36. *Defender*, February 20, 1915.

37. Ibid. Secondary accounts of Rube Foster's career include Robert Charles Cottrell, *The Best Pitcher in Baseball: The Life of Rube Foster, Negro League Giant* (New York: New York University Press, 2001); Holway, *Blackball Stars*; Charles E. Whitehead, *A Man and His Diamonds* (New York: Vantage Press, 1980); and Peterson, *Only the Ball*.

38. For Talbert's background, see Riley, *Biographical Encyclopedia*, 758–59. *Frank Leland's Chicago Giants Baseball Club* (n.p.), in Baseball Hall of Fame and Museum, Cooperstown, NY.

39. *Freeman* (Indianapolis), February 20, 1907.

40. *Broad Ax*, June 29, July 6, 1907.

41. For Donlin's statistics, see D. Neft et al., *Sports Encyclopedia*. For Donlin's vaudeville career and marriage to Mabel Hite, see Seymour, *Baseball: The Golden Age*, 118–19.

42. D. Neft et al., *Sports Encyclopedia*; *Chicago Tribune*, July 11, 1907.

43. *Chicago Tribune*, August 7, 8, 9, 1907.

44. Ibid., August 28, 29, 31, 1907; *Chicago InterOcean*, August 28, 1907; *Freeman*, September 7, 1907.

45. *Broad Ax*, August 17, 1907; *Freeman*, September 7, 1907.

46. *Freeman*, September 21, 1907. For a secondary account about how black baseball entrepreneurs catered their clubs to the white consumer market in the late nineteenth century, see Michael E. Lomax, *Black Baseball Entrepreneurs, 1860–1901: Operating by Any Means Necessary* (Syracuse, NY: Syracuse University Press, 2003). For Chicago's black population, see *Fifteenth Census of the United States: 1930* (Washington, DC: Government Printing Office, 1933), 67.

47. For an interpretation of Booker T. Washington and W. E. B. Du Bois's economic philosophy, see Oaks, *The Negro's Adventure*, 9–25; Wilson Jeremiah Moses, *The Golden Age of Black Nationalism, 1850–1925* (Hamden, CT: Archon Books, 1978), 83–102; and Juliet E. K. Walker, *The History of Black Business in America: Capitalism, Race, Entrepreneurship* (New York: Macmillan Library Reference, 1998), 184–87.

48. Spear, *Black Chicago*, 41–42.

49. Harold F. Gosnell, *Negro Politicians: The Rise of Negro Politics in Chicago* (Chicago: University of Chicago Press, 1935), 67–68; *Broad Ax*, March 30, 1901, December 27, 1902, December 29, 1906.

50. Ibid.

51. *Freeman*, October 19, 1907; *Broad Ax*, October 12, November 2, 1907.

52. *Broad Ax*, November 2, 1907.

53. *Freeman*, November 9, 1907.

54. Ibid., November 9, 16, 23, December 7, 28, 1907.

55. Ibid., December 28, 1907, January 11, 25, 1908.

56. Ibid., December 28, 1907, February 15, 1908.

57. *Chicago Tribune*, August 13, 1906, July 28, 29, 1907; *Freeman*, December 28, 1907.

58. *Freeman*, February 15, 1908.

59. Biographical profiles of the Cuban players are drawn from Riley, *Biographical Encyclopedia*; *Chicago Tribune*, May 29, 1907.

60. *Chicago Tribune*, May 31, June 2, 9, 10, 1907; *Chicago InterOcean*, May 29, 30, June 2, 9, 10, 1907.

61. For secondary accounts of baseball guidebooks, see Voigt, *American Baseball: From Gentleman's Sport to the Commissioner System*, 91, 195; Peter Levine, *A. G. Spalding and the Rise of Baseball: The Promise of American Sport* (New York: Oxford University Press, 1985), 75–77; Stephen Hardy, "Entrepreneurs, Organizations, and the Sport Marketplace: Subjects in Search of Historians," *Journal of Sport History* 13 (Spring 1986): 14–33.

62. White, *History of Colored Baseball*, 3.

63. Ibid., 35.

64. David Q. Voigt, *American Baseball: From the Commissioners to Continental Expansion*, vol. II (University Park, PA: Pennsylvania State University Press, 1983), 64–65; Seymour, *Baseball: The Golden Age*, 172–73; Steven A. Riess, *Touching Base: Professional Baseball and American Culture in the Progressive Era*, rev. ed. (Urbana: University of Illinois Press, 1999), 169–70.

65. Robert F. Burk, *Never Just a Game: Players, Owners, and American Baseball to 1920* (Chapel Hill: University of North Carolina Press, 1994), 159–61.

66. Lomax, *Black Baseball Entrepreneurs*, 74–79.

67. White, *History of Colored Baseball*, 71, 74.

68. William A. Sutton, "Marketing Principles Applied to Sport Management," in *Principles and Practice of Sport Management*, ed. Lisa P. Masterlexis, Carol A. Barr, and Mary A. Hums (Gaithersburg, MD, 1998), 51–52. See also Bernard J. Mullin, Stephen Hardy, and William A. Sutton, *Sport Marketing*, 2nd ed. (Champaign, IL, 2000).

69. For secondary accounts of "inside baseball," see Alexander, *Our Game*, 86–87, and Voigt, *American Baseball*, II, 39. See also *Spalding's Official Base Ball Guide* (New York: American Sports Pub. Co., 1915), 23–26.

70. White, *History of Colored Baseball*, 76–77.

71. Lomax, *Black Baseball Entrepreneurs*, 41–46, 79–88, 118–22.

72. Michael E. Lomax, "Black Baseball, Black Community, Black Entrepreneurs: The History of the Negro National and Eastern Colored Leagues, 1880–1930" (PhD diss., Ohio State University, 1996), 181–84; Burk, *Never Just a Game*, 130–32. For an account of the number of blacks who played in the white leagues in the late nineteenth century, see Merl F. Kleinknecht, "Blacks in 19th Century Organized Baseball," *Baseball Research Journal*, May 1977, 118–27.

73. White, *History of Colored Baseball*, 78. For Matthews's plight in the Vermont League, see Peterson, *Only the Ball*, 57–59.

74. Secondary accounts that address the Charlie Grant affair include Michael E. Lomax, "'If He Were White': Black and Cuban Players in Organized Baseball, 1880–1920," *Journal of African American Men* 3 (1998): 31–44; Lee Allen, *The American League Story* (New York: Hill and Wang, 1962), 21–22; Peterson, *Only the Ball*, 54–57; and Charles C. Alexander, *John McGraw* (Lincoln: University of Nebraska Press, 1988), 75–76.

75. White, *History of Colored Baseball*, 67.

76. Secondary accounts of John Henry Lloyd include Peterson, *Only the Ball*, 74–79; Holway, *Blackball Stars*, 36–49; and Riley, *Biographical Encyclopedia*, 486–89. According to Peterson, Lloyd's widow claimed that her husband went north at the urging of his fellow porters in Jacksonville and that he arrived in Philadelphia with total assets of $1.50 and a pocket watch and no assurance of employment.

77. *Evening Item*, October 20, 30, 1907.

78. Ibid., April 21, 1907; Riley, *Biographical Encyclopedia*, 33, 514–15, 573–74.

79. *Evening Item*, October 20, 21, 29, November 2, 7, 11, 14, 20, December 14, 17, 18, 22, 29, 1907.

80. *Evening Item*, October 20, 24, 30, November 2, 9, 11, December 16, 22, 29, 1907, January 5, 7, 1908.

81. The estimates were drawn from the *Evening Item* from October 20, 1907, to January 7, 1908.

82. Seymour, *Baseball: The Golden Age*, 7–8.

3. Striving for Professionalism

1. *Evening Item* (Philadelphia), March 16, 18, 1908.

2. Harold Seymour, *Baseball: The Early Years* (New York: Oxford University Press, 1960), 223; David Q. Voigt, *American Baseball: From Gentleman's Sport to the Commissioner System* (Norman: University of Oklahoma Press, 1966), 290; Robert F. Burk, *Never Just a Game: Players, Owners, and American Baseball to 1920* (Chapel Hill: University of North Carolina Press, 1994), 96. *Evening Item*, March 11, 16, 20, 1908.

3. *Evening Item*, January 24, March 7, 17, 29, 1908.

4. Ibid., April 11, 30, May 31, June 5, 1908.

5. Ibid., June 4, 1908.

6. Ibid., June 4, July 12, 14, 1908.

7. *Chicago Tribune*, May 31, 1908. It should be noted that the *Chicago Tribune* and the *Chicago InterOcean* referred to this Cuban club as either the All Havanas or the Cuban Stars. A close examination of the box scores reveals that the same players played for the team whether they were called one or the other. For biographical information on Jose Mendez, see John Holway, *Blackball Stars: Negro League Pioneers* (New York: Carroll and Graf, 1988), 50–60; James A. Riley, *The Biographical Encyclopedia of the Negro Baseball Leagues* (New York: Carroll and Graf, 1994), 545–46; Adrian Burgos Jr., "Playing America's Game: Latinos and the Performance and Policing of Race in North American Professional Baseball, 1868–1959 (PhD diss., University of Michigan, 2000), 181–85; and Lawrence D. Hogan, *Shades of Glory: The Negro Leagues and the Story of African-American Baseball* (Washington, DC: National Geographic, 2006), 116.

8. *Chicago Tribune*, June 2, 3, 10, 15, 17, 18, 1908. Games played against Chicago's white semipros are in recorded in ibid., June 7, 8, 9, 12, 16, 19, 20, 21, 22, 1908.

9. Ibid., July 2, 7, 8, 9, 12, 13, 1908. Games against Chicago's white semipros include those recorded in ibid., July 5, 6, 10, 11, 19, 20, 1908.

10. Ibid., July 28, 29, 30, August 3, 1908. Games against Chicago's white semipros include those cited in ibid., July 26, 27, 31, August 1, 2, 4, 5, 9, 10, 1908.

11. Ibid., August 7, 8, 1908.

12. *New York Age*, February 18, March 25, April 8, 15, 1909.

13. *Baltimore Afro-American*, February 11, 1921; *Philadelphia Tribune*, April 12, 1928.

14. *New York Age*, April 15, April 22, July 18, 1909.

15. See, for example, *Chicago Tribune*, June 8, 11, 14, 21, 22, 23, 24, 25, 26, 27, 28, July 5, 11, 12, 18, 19, 25, 26, 28, 29, 31, August 9, 1909.

16. Ibid., June 15, 16, 17, 18, 19, 1909. The Cubans played a second series of games with the Lelands. It was noteworthy because Rube Foster broke his leg in the first game in the series. The Giants won the series, four games to one. See ibid., July 13, 14, 15, 16, 17, 1909.

17. Ibid., June 29, 30, July 1, 2, 3, 4, 1909.

18. Ibid., August 2, 3, 4, 5, 7, 8, 10, 11, 12, 13, 14, 1909.

19. *New York Age*, August 19, 1909. *Chicago Tribune*, August 10, 11, 12, 1909.

20. *Chicago Tribune*, August 17, 18, 19, 20, 25, 1909.

21. Ibid., August 24, 1909.

22. *New York Age*, September 2, 9, 16, 23, 30, 1909.

23. Ibid., February 24, 1910.

24. Ibid., February 24, 1910; March 31, 1910. Connor's quote is in ibid., April 14, 1910.

25. Ibid., May 5, 1910. For Lloyd's leaving the Philadelphia Giants, see *New York Age*, February 24, 1910, and *Broad Ax*, April 23, 1910.

26. See, for example, *Chicago Tribune*, May 7, 10, 13, 14, 15, 17, 19, June 5, 6, 9, 11, 14, 15, 17, 18, 21, 22, 23, 26, 27, 28, 30, July 1, 10, 1910. The Philadelphia Giants' barnstorming tour is reported in the *Chicago Tribune*, May 24, 26, 27, 28, 30, 31, June 2, 8, 10, 20, 1910.

27. *New York Age*, August 18, 1910.

28. *Broad Ax*, October 12, 1907, June 13, December 5, 1908, January 30, March 13, May 1, May 15, 1909.

29. *Chicago InterOcean*, April 4, 18, 26, May 3, 1908; *Chicago Tribune*, June 4, 1908.

30. *Chicago InterOcean*, May 4, 11, 18, 25, June 1, 15, 22, 1908; *Chicago Tribune*, May 4, 11, 18, 25, June 1, 29, 1908; *Freeman* (Indianapolis), August 1, 1908.

31. *Chicago Tribune*, September 22, 23, 24, 25, 1908; Neil Sullivan, *The Minors: The Struggle and the Triumph of Baseball's Poor Relation from 1876 to the Present* (New York: St. Martin's Press, 1990).

32. *Broad Ax*, October 10, 1908.

33. *Freeman*, April 13, May 15, 1909; *Chicago Tribune*, April 11, 12, 13, 16, 22, 23, 1909.

34. *Freeman*, February 13, 1909; *Chicago Tribune*, April 4, 10, 18, 25, 26, 30, May 2, 3, 9, 17, 23, 24, 30, 31, June 1, 6, 7, 13, 20, July 6, 24, August 16, 29, 30, September 5, 6, 7, 13, 19, 20, 27, October 3, 4, 1909.

35. *Chicago Tribune*, October 18, 19, 22, 23, 1909.

36. *Defender* (Chicago), January 22, 1910.

37. *Chicago Tribune*, May 2, 1910. For a secondary account about Williams's background, see Riley, *Biographical Encyclopedia*, 854–56.

38. *Defender*, April 2, 16, 1910; *Chicago Tribune*, April 5, 8, 11, 12, 13, 14, 16, 19, 1910.

39. *Broad Ax*, April 23, 1910; *New York Age*, April 21, 28, 1910.

40. *Defender*, February 5, June 4, 1910; *Chicago Tribune*, February 8, April 7, 18, 20, 24, 27, 1910.

41. *Defender*, February 5, 1910.

42. *Chicago Tribune*, July 19, 1910; *Defender*, July 23, 1910; *New York Age*, July 21, 28, August 4, 1910.

43. For Chicago Giants Rooter's Club, see *Broad Ax*, May 14, 1910. Harold Seymour, *Baseball: The Golden Age* (New York: Oxford University Press, 1970), 63. For the Giants' move into their new park, see *Defender*, June 25, 1910, and *Chicago Tribune*, June 14, 1910.

44. *Chicago Tribune*, August 23, 24, 27, 30, September 1, 2, 1910.

45. *Defender*, August 10, 27, October 29, 1910; *Los Angeles Times*, November 19, 1910. For a secondary account of the California Winter League, see William F. McNeil, *The California Winter League: America's First Integrated Professional Baseball League* (Jefferson, NC: McFarland, 2002). McNeil states that Rube Foster's Leland Giants played in the CWL in 1910. A close examination of the box scores, however, indicates that it was Frank Leland's Chicago Giants who played in that league. As will be shown, the Lelands embarked upon an eastern barnstorming tour that took them through New York, New Jersey, and Florida. They eventually traveled to Cuba and played in the winter league there.

46. *Los Angeles Times*, November 21, 1910.

47. Ibid., November 21, December 5, 12, 17, 19, 31, 1910, January 1, 2, 7, 8, 9, 23, 1911.

48. *Broad Ax*, March 12, 1910.

49. Ibid., May 7, 1910. The LGBBA also staged several promotions during the 1910 season, including "Jack Johnson Day" and "Kentucky Day." For these, see *Broad Ax*, August 6, 20, 1910, and *Chicago Tribune*, August 6, 1909. For other benefit games, see *Broad Ax*, August 20, 1910. The Lelands also played a benefit game for Spanish War Veterans. See *Broad Ax*, September 3, 1910. For a secondary account about Daniel Hale Williams and Provident Hospital, see Allan H. Spear, *Black Chicago: The Making of a Negro Ghetto: 1890–1920* (Chicago: University of Chicago Press, 1967), 97–100. It should be noted that Dr. Williams sponsored the dinner for the Leland Giants in 1908.

50. *Defender*, May 14, 1910; Vincent Harding, *The Other American Revolution* (Los Angeles: Center for Afro-American Studies, 1980), 30.

51. *Broad Ax*, August 27, 1910.

52. *Chicago Tribune*, September 23, 25, 28, October 3, 5, 1910. *Broad Ax*, October 8, 1910; *Defender*, October 8, 1910; *New York Age*, December 8, 1910.

53. *Broad Ax*, January 21, 1911.

54. Ibid., November 26, December 17, 31, 1910, January 21, 1911; *Defender*, December 31, 1910, January 7, 21, February 25, 1911.

55. *Fifteenth Census of the United States: 1930* (Washington, DC: Government Printing Office, 1933), 67, 69, 71.

4. Years of Transition, 1911–1913

1. *New York Age*, February 16, 1911.

2. For an account of Spotswood Poles, see James A. Riley, *The Biographical Encyclopedia of the Negro Baseball Leagues* (New York: Carroll and Graf, 1994), 631–32.

3. Ibid., 654–55; Robert Peterson, *Only the Ball Was White* (New York: Oxford University Press, 1970), 213–14; John B. Holway, *Blackball Stars: Negro League Pioneers* (New York: Carroll and Graf, 1988), 79–87; *New York Times*, August 19, 1911.

4. *New York Age*, April 20, 1911.

5. *New York Times*, June 18, July 2, 1911.

6. Harold Seymour, *Baseball: The Early Years* (New York: Oxford University Press, 1970), 328; *New York Times*, July 4, 13, 18, 1911.

7. Lawrence D. Hogan, *Shades of Glory: The Negro Leagues and the Story of African-American Baseball* (Washington, DC: National Geographic, 2006), 135–36; *New York Age*, February 9, June 29, 1911. For the Giants' 1910 series with the Chicago Giants, see *Chicago Tribune*, September 25, 26, 1910.

8. *New York Age*, July 13, 1911.

9. Ibid., August 10, 17, 1911.

10. Ibid., August 17, September 7, 1911.

11. Ibid., September 14, 1911; *Philadelphia Tribune*, March 16, 1912.

12. *New York Age*, October 19, 1911; *New York Times*, October 12, 15, 16, 1911. On October 28, the *New York Times* reported a contest between the Lincolns and Baker's All Stars. The All Stars were organized by Philadelphia Athletics third baseman Frank "Home Run" Baker, who received his nickname for hitting two home runs in the 1911 World Series against the New York Giants off Rube Marquard and Christy Matthewson. McMahon offered a "special prize" for every home run Baker hit.

13. *New York Age*, March 30, May 11, 1911; *Chicago Tribune*, June 21, 1911.

14. *New York Age*, July 20, 1911.

15. Seth Scheiner, *Negro Mecca: A History of the Negro in New York City, 1865–1920* (New York: New York University Press, 1965); Gilbert Osofsky, *Harlem: The Making of a Ghetto* (New York: Oxford University Press, 1966); *Thirteenth Census*

of the United States: Taken in the Year 1910 (Washington, DC: Government Printing Office, 1913), 95; "The Wealthiest Negro Colony in the World," *New York Times Magazine* (September 2, 1917): 10; "The Negro in the Cities of the North," in *Charities* (New York: The Charity Organization Society, 1905), 1–2; W. A. Domingo, "The Tropics in New York," *Survey Graphic* 53 (1925): 648–50.

16. *New York Age*, August 3, 10, 1911.

17. Ibid., May 9, 1912.

18. *Chicago Tribune*, May 19, 20, 22, 23, 24, 27, 1912.

19. Ibid., May 26, 31, June 3, 1912.

20. *New York Age*, November 9, 1911.

21. Ibid., April 11, 1912; *Philadelphia Tribune*, April 27, 1912. The *Tribune* claimed Lloyd was a figurehead who was content to manage the game on the field. Apparently, this was the type of manager the McMahons sought to replace Sol White. It is unclear why Lloyd changed his mind and managed the Lincolns or how these "agreements" resulted in the Giants' shortstop remaining as field manager.

22. *New York Age*, March 28, April 11, 1912.

23. Riley, *Biographical Encyclopedia*, 695–97; Peterson, *Only the Ball*, 224; Holway, *Blackball Stars*, 88–95.

24. Cogan's major league record is in Hy Turkin and S. C. Thompson, *The Official Encyclopedia of Baseball*, 10th ed. (New York: Doubleday, 1979), 133. *New York Age*, May 30, 1912; *Philadelphia Tribune*, June 8, 1912.

25. *New York Age*, May 2, June 13, August 8, 15, 1912.

26. Ibid., May 2, 1912.

27. Ibid., May 2, August 1, 1912, July 19, 1913.

28. Ibid., October 31, November 7, December 12, 1912; *New York Times*, October 28, 1912.

29. *New York Age*, June 5, 19, 1913; *New York Times*, February 20, 1913.

30. *New York Age*, August 21, September 4, 1913. On December 29, 1913, the *New York Times* reported that the McMahons were supposedly involved in obtaining a franchise for New York in what eventually became the Federal League. Although they did not deny the rumor that they were involved, Jess McMahon declared their "friendship with John McGraw and Frank Farrell would not permit us to have a hand in the local outlaw club."

31. *New York Age*, October 9, 1913; *Defender* (Chicago), October 11, 1913.

32. *New York Age*, October 16, 23, November 6, 1913.

33. *Freeman* (Indianapolis), December 23, 1911.

34. The Moseley quote is in "Rube Foster—The Master of Baseball," Rube Foster file, Ashland Collection, Baseball Hall of Fame, Cooperstown, NY.

35. Michael E. Lomax, "Black Entrepreneurship in the National Pastime: The Rise of Semiprofessional Baseball in Black Chicago, 1890–1915," *Journal of Sport History*

25 (Spring 1998): 58. Schorling's securing a lease on the old White Sox ballpark was reported in *Chicago Tribune*, June 16, 1910.

36. Riley, *Biographical Encyclopedia*, 381–82, 623–24; Peterson, *Only the Ball*, 223.

37. Riley, *Biographical Encyclopedia*, 464. In 1914, Lindsay died only a few days before the American Giants' Colored Championship Series with the Brooklyn Royal Giants.

38. *Chicago Tribune*, June 21, 1911. For Williams's duel with Redding, see *Chicago Tribune*, May 29, 1911.

39. Foster quote in *Freeman*, December 23, 1911. *Chicago Tribune*, July 3, 4, 5, 6, 1911. *Defender*, July 8, 1911.

40. *Chicago Tribune*, July 7, 1911.

41. Ibid., July 30, 1911.

42. Ibid., August 14, 21, September 18, 1911.

43. *New York Age*, April 18, 1912; *Defender*, November 21, 1914.

44. *Chicago Tribune*, August 29, September 6, 1911; *New York Age*, August 24, 31, September 7, 1911.

45. For the activities and membership of the booster coalition, see any issue in either Chicago's *Defender* or the *Broad Ax* from May to June 1911.

46. *Defender*, May 20, 27, 1911.

47. *Broad Ax*, June 3, 1911; *Defender*, May 13, June 3, 10, 1911.

48. *Chicago Tribune*, May 7, 8, June 5, 11, 12, 20, 26, July 10, 16, 17, 23, August 1, 20, 28, 31, September 3, 4, 10, 1911.

49. *Freeman*, December 23, 1911; *Chicago Tribune*, June 2, 1912.

50. *Chicago Tribune*, June 2, October 1, 1912.

51. *Freeman*, December 23, 1911.

52. *Broad Ax*, May 18, 1912.

53. Schorling's Auburn Park club played there for several years until the Leland Giants moved there in 1905.

54. For benefit games on behalf of Provident Hospital, see *Chicago Tribune* August 11, 1911, August 23, 1912. For some of the other fund-raising events, see *Defender*, May 10, August 16, 1913.

55. *Chicago Tribune*, July 4, 1912.

56. For a comprehensive overview of the California Winter League's 1912 season, see William F. McNeil, *The California Winter League: America's First Integrated Professional Baseball League* (Jefferson, NC: McFarland, 2002), 40–43. The statistics of the Giants' players are in David S. Neft, Richard M. Cohen, and Michael L. Neft, *The Sports Encyclopedia: Baseball 2006*, 26th ed. (New York: St. Martin's Griffin, 2006). The infamous Merkle boner occurred in a game between the Giants and Chicago Cubs on September 23, 1908, at the Polo Grounds in upper Manhattan. The Giants had

Moose McCormick on third base, representing the potential winning run, and Merkle on first. Al Bridwell had made an apparently safe hit to center field, and McCormick scored. Excited at their assumed victory, the Giants players, including Merkle, raced across the field for the clubhouse in deep center field. According to Harold Seymour, precisely what happened next will never be known. Cubs' second baseman Johnny Evers, realizing that Merkle had not touched second base before running off the field, supposedly ran over to second, shouting to the Cubs outfielder to throw in the ball hit by Bridwell. Outfielder Solly Hofman returned the ball to the infield, but Giants pitcher Joe McGinnity dashed from the coach's box, wrestled the ball away from some of the Cubs players, and threw it into the stands. Evers either recovered the original ball or must somehow have got hold of another one and touched second. Merkle was called out on a force play. The controversial play was instrumental in the Cubs' winning the National League pennant in 1908 and eventually the World Series. See Harold Seymour, *Baseball: The Golden Age* (New York: Oxford University Press, 1970), 147–48.

57. *Los Angeles Times*, November 2, 3, 4, 1912. Coverage of the CWL by the black press includes articles in *Defender*, December 14, 1912, and *Freeman*, November 9, 16, December 7, 1912.

58. McNeil, *California Winter League*, 42.

59. *Seattle Post-Intelligencer*, April 5, 6, 7, 1913. Coverage of the American Giants' winter tour by the black press includes articles in the *Defender*, April 12, 19, 26, 1913. *Freeman*, April 19, 26, 1913. *New York Age*, April 3, 1913.

60. *Defender*, April 5, 26, 1913; *Freeman*, April 5, 12, 1913.

61. *Defender*, July 12, August 2, 1913.

62. Ibid., July 5, 1913.

63. *New York Age*, July 24, 1913; *Chicago Tribune*, July 19, 21, 1913.

64. *New York Age*, July 24, 1913; *Chicago Tribune*, July 19, 21, 1913.

65. *Chicago Tribune*, July 29, 30, 31, August 1, 1913.

66. *Defender*, August 9, 1913; *Chicago Tribune*, August 10, 13, 14, 1913. In addition to playing the championship series, the Lincolns played games against the Windy City's white semipros. See *Chicago Tribune*, August 7, 8, 9, 1913.

67. *Defender*, April 5, 9, 1913.

68. *Freeman*, December 23, 1913.

5. Black Baseball and the Separate Black Economy

1. Juliet E. K. Walker, *The History of Black Business in America: Capitalism, Race, Entrepreneurship* (New York: Macmillan Library Reference USA, 1998), 183–87. For contemporary accounts of Washington's and DuBois's promotion of black economic nationalism, see W. E. B. DuBois, ed., *The Negro in Business: Report of a Social Study Made under the Direction of Atlanta University* (Atlanta: Atlanta University,

1899), and Booker T. Washington, *Up from Slavery: An Autobiography* (New York: Doubleday, Page, 1902), 217–37.

2. DuBois, *Negro in Business*, 50.

3. Walker, *History of Black Business*, 186.

4. Ibid., 213–14; John Sibley Butler, *Entrepreneurship and Self-Help among Black Americans: A Reconsideration of Race and Economics* (Albany, NY: State University of New York Press, 1991), 175–84; Charles Ashley Hardy III, "Race and Opportunity: Black Philadelphia during the Era of the Great Migration, 1916–1930 (PhD diss., Temple University, 1989), 15–18.

5. Allan H. Spear, *Black Chicago: The Making of a Negro Ghetto, 1890–1920* (Chicago: University of Chicago Press, 1967), 112–13.

6. Ibid. For a definitive account of the business career of Jesse Binga, see Carl R. Osthaus, "The Rise and Fall of Jesse Binga, Black Financier," *Journal of Negro History* 58 (January 1973): 39–60.

7. Gilbert Osofsky, *Harlem: The Making of a Ghetto; Negro New York, 1890–1930* (New York: Harper and Row, 1965), 94–96.

8. Walker, *History of Black Business*, 209–10.

9. Ibid., 215.

10. Harold Seymour, *Baseball: The Golden Age* (New York: Oxford University Press, 1970), 49–50. For a comprehensive account of stadium building in the Progressive Era, see Robert C. Trumpbour, *The New Cathedrals: Politics and Media in the History of Stadium Construction* (Syracuse, NY: Syracuse University Press, 2007).

11. Steven Riess provides a definitive account of the link between baseball and urban politics in *Touching Base: Professional Baseball and American Culture in the Progressive Era*, rev. ed. (Urbana: University of Illinois Press, 1999), 99–133. For secondary accounts on ballpark construction in the Progressive Era, see Michael Gershman, *The Evolution Diamonds of the Ballpark* (Boston: Houghton Mifflin Co., 1993), and Ted Vincent, *Mudville's Revenge: The Rise and Fall of American Sport* (New York: Seaview Books, 1981).

12. See, for example, Walker, *History of Black Business*; Spear, *Black Chicago*; Earl Ofari, *The Myth of Black Capitalism* (New York: Monthly Review Press, 1970); W. E. B. Du Bois, *Dusk of Dawn* (New York: Harcourt, Brace, 1940); and Booker T. Washington, *The Negro in Business* (1907; reprint, Chicago: Afro-American Press, 1969).

13. For an account of market segmentation, see Bernard J. Mullin, Stephen Hardy, and William A. Sutton, *Sport Marketing*, 3rd ed. (Champaign, IL: Human Kinetics, 2007), 101–14. A discussion of Rube Foster's barnstorming tours will be provided below.

14. *St. Louis Argus*, January 29, February 5, 19, March 19, 26, April 2, 9, 16, 23, 1915.

15. *New York Age*, April 9, 1914, March 4, 1915.

16. Seth M. Scheiner, *Negro Mecca: A History of the Negro in New York City, 1865–1920* (New York: New York University Press, 1965), 80. In 1916, the *New York Age* ran a series of articles on the plight of black businesses in Harlem. See *New York Age*, March 9, 16, 23, 30, April 4, 1916.

17. See any issues of the *New York Age* from 1914 to 1916. Although the coverage was sporadic, the *New York Times* printed the box scores of games between the black clubs and white semipros, major league clubs, and all-star teams composed of major league players. See *New York Times*, May 29, July 12, October 18, 1915.

18. See any issues of the *New York Age* from 1914 to 1916.

19. The *New York Age* was used to develop this interpretation.

20. See chapter 4 regarding the St. Louis Giants' plight in New York.

21. *Indianapolis Ledger*, February 21, 1914.

22. James A. Riley, *The Biographical Encyclopedia of the Negro Baseball Leagues* (New York: Carroll and Graf, 1994), 763–64; C. I. Taylor file, Baseball Hall of Fame and Museum, Cooperstown, NY; *Freeman* (Indianapolis), March 18, 1911; *Defender* (Chicago), March 4, 1922; *Indianapolis Ledger* September 26, 1914. For games between the West Baden Sprudels and the Leland Giants and the Chicago American Giants, see *Chicago Tribune*, June 22, July 18, 20, 21, 1910, June 30, September 8, 9, 1913.

23. Riley, *Biographical Encyclopedia*, 712–13, 761–63, 767–68.

24. Although the book has several drawbacks, Paul Debono discusses the evolution of the Indianapolis ABCs in *The Indianapolis ABCs: History of a Premier Team in the Negro Leagues* (Jefferson, NC: McFarland, 1997).

25. *Freeman*, April 18, 1914.

26. Ibid.

27. This assessment is based on the examination of several newspapers that include the *Defender*, *New York Age*, *Chicago Tribune*, *Indianapolis Star*, and *Indianapolis Ledger*.

28. *Chicago Tribune*, June 1, 2, 3, 1914; *Indianapolis Ledger*, June 6, 1914.

29. *Indianapolis Ledger*, August 1, 1914; *Chicago Tribune*, August 25, 1914; *Indianapolis Star*, July 28, 29, 30, 1914.

30. *Indianapolis Ledger*, August 29, 1914; *Chicago Tribune*, August 24, 27, 1914.

31. For secondary accounts of the Federal League, see Seymour, *Baseball: The Golden Age*, 196–213; David Q. Voigt, *American Baseball: From the Commissioners to Continental Expansion* (University Park: Pennsylvania State University Press, 1983), 114–20; Charles C. Alexander, *Our Game: An American Baseball History* (New York: Henry Holt, 1991), 102–7.

32. David S. Neft, Richard M. Cohen, and Michael L. Neft, *The Sports Encyclopedia: Baseball 2006*, 26th ed. (New York: St. Martin's Griffin, 2006).

33. *Indianapolis Ledger*, October 24, 31, 1914.

34. Ibid., February 13, 27, March 6, 1915.

35. Riley, *Biographical Encyclopedia*, 228–29, 236–37.

36. Ibid., 164–66.

37. Ibid., 787–88; *Indianapolis Ledger*, June 19, July 17, August 7, September 11, 1915.

38. The first series between the American Giants and the ABCs is reported in the *Chicago Tribune*, June 22, 23, 24, 1915; *Defender*, June 26, 1915; and *Indianapolis Ledger*, June 26, 1915. *Defender*, July 24, 1915. *Indianapolis Ledger*, July 24, 1915.

39. *Defender*, July 31, 1915; *Indianapolis Ledger*, July 31, 1915.

40. *Defender*, July 31, 1915; *Indianapolis Ledger*, July 31, 1915.

41. *Defender*, July 31, 1915; *Indianapolis Ledger*, July 31, 1915.

42. *Freeman*, August 7, 1915.

43. Ibid., August 14, 1915. *Indianapolis Ledger*, August 14, 1915.

44. *Freeman*, August 14, 1915. *Indianapolis Ledger*, August 14, 1915.

45. *Freeman*, August 14, 1915. *Indianapolis Ledger*, August 14, 1915.

46. *Freeman*, September 18, 1915.

47. Ibid.; *Defender*, August 28, 1915; *Freeman*, August 28, 1915; *Chicago Tribune*, August 24, 1915.

48. *Freeman*, September 18, 1915. In 1914, Strong sent his Brooklyn Royal Giants to Chicago to play the American Giants. The series was for the World's Colored Championship. The series was marred by rowdyism on and off the field. The *Defender* reported that in the first game, some fans used "foul language," and the paper indicted the police for not escorting them from the grandstand (see ibid., September 5, 1914). In the third game, a disputed call led to an assault on the umpire by members of the Royal Giants. To add insult to injury, the American Giants swept the series, seven games to none. It was the last time Strong sent his Royals to the Midwest in the pre–World War I years. See *Chicago Tribune*, September 1, 2, 3, 4, 7, 8, 1914. *New York Age*, September 3, 1914.

49. *Indianapolis Ledger*, September 25, 1915.

50. *Freeman*, October 30, 1915. For the ABCs' barnstorming tour, see *ibid.*, October 16, 1915.

51. Ibid., December 11, 1915.

52. Ibid., March 25, April 29, 1916.

53. *Defender*, October 21, 1916.

54. Ibid., October 28, November 4, 11, 1916; *Freeman*, October 28, November 4, 1916.

55. *Freeman*, November 18, 1916; *Defender*, November 18, 1916.

56. *Freeman*, November 18, 1916; *Defender*, November 18, 1916. Foster published a second article in the *Defender* on November 25.

57. For accounts regarding branding, see Mullin et. al., *Sport Marketing*, 174–86, and George R. Milne and Mark A. McDonald, *Sport Marketing: Managing the Exchange Process* (Boston: Jones and Bartlett, 1999), 39–52. For accounts of black

teams using the nickname "Giants," see Robert Peterson, *Only the Ball Was White* (New York: Oxford University Press, 1970); Janet Bruce, *The Kansas City Monarchs: Champions of Black Baseball* (Lawrence, KS: University Press of Kansas, 1985); and Phil Dixon and Patrick Hannigan, *The Negro Baseball Leagues: A Photographic History* (Mattituck, NY: Amereon House, 1992).

58. For an account of Foster's donation of Schorling Park for philanthropic activities, see *Defender*, August 8, 1914.

59. For accounts on market reach, see Matthew D. Shank, *Sports Marketing: A Strategic Perspective* (Upper Saddle River, NJ: Prentice-Hall, 2002), 240–41, and Sam Fullerton, *Sports Marketing* (Boston: McGraw-Hill Irwin, 2007), 245.

60. James R. Grossman, *Land of Hope: Chicago, Black Southerners, and the Great Migration* (Chicago: University of Chicago Press, 1989), 74.

61. William F. McNeil, *The California Winter League: America's First Integrated Professional Baseball League* (Jefferson, NC: McFarland, 2002), 51–57; *Defender*, November 6, 20, 27, December 4, 11, 25, 1915, January 1, 8, 1916.

62. *Defender*, January 22, March 11, April 8, 15, 29, May 3, 1916; *Freeman*, March 25, 1916; *Chicago Tribune*, April 30, 1916.

6. The War Years: Toward the Rise of the Negro Leagues

1. Edward N. Akin provides a comprehensive account about the rise of the resort system in Florida in *Flagler: Rockefeller Partner and Florida Baron* (Kent, OH: Kent State University Press, 1988). See also Gary R. Mormino, *Land of Sunshine, State of Dreams: A Social History of Modern Florida* (Gainesville: University Press of Florida, 2005), 301–54. For black baseball's link to Florida's resort system, see Michael E. Lomax, *Black Baseball Entrepreneurs, 1860–1901: Operating by Any Means Necessary* (Syracuse, NY: Syracuse University Press, 2003).

2. Akin, *Flagler*, 143–45.

3. *Defender* (Chicago), January 27, February 10, 1917.

4. See Spalding's comments in Akin, *Flagler*, 157. *Defender*, February 17, 24, 1917.

5. Theodore G. Vincent, ed., *Voices of a Black Nation: Political Journalism in the Harlem Renaissance* (San Francisco: Ramparts Press, 1973), 22. In his foreword, Vincent provides an excellent overview of the black press during the era of the Harlem Renaissance. Other secondary sources that analyze the early-twentieth-century black press in the United States include Henry Lewis Suggs, ed., *The Black Press in the Middle West, 1865–1985* (Westport, CT: Greenwood Press, 1996). Juliet E. K. Walker provides a business analysis of the *Defender* in chapter 1 of her *History of Black Business in America: Capitalism, Race, Entrepreneurship* (New York: Macmillan Library Reference, 1998). Todd Vogel, ed., *The Black Press: New Literary and Historical Essays* (New Brunswick, NJ: Rutgers University Press, 2001); Charles Pete

Banner-Haley, "*The Philadelphia Tribune* and the Persistence of Black Republicanism during the Great Depression," *Pennsylvania History* 65 (Spring 1998): 190–202. A secondary source that examines the mainstream press and includes an analysis of the early-twentieth-century black press is Edwin Emery, *The Press and America*, 3rd ed. (Englewood Cliffs, NJ: Prentice-Hall, 1972), 207–30, 617–52. Foster's telegram is in *Defender*, March 17, 1917. For examples of press coverage in black newspapers other than the *Defender*, see *Freeman* (Indianapolis), January 27, 1917, and *Philadelphia Tribune*, February 10, 17, 24, 1917.

6. *Defender*, March 29, 1917; James A. Riley, *The Biographical Encyclopedia of the Negro Baseball Leagues* (New York: Carroll and Graf, 1994), 63–64, 325, 454, 676–77.

7. *Chicago Tribune*, June 17, August 20, September 3, 1917.

8. *Freeman*, May 12, 19, 1917.

9. *Chicago Tribune*, July 18, 20, 21, August 4, 5, 21, 25, 26, September 2, 1917.

10. William Cohen, "The Great Migration as a Lever for Social Change," in *Black Exodus: The Great Migration from the American South*, ed. Alferdteen Harrison, 72–82 (Jackson: University Press of Mississippi, 1991). *Fifteenth Census of the United States: 1930* (Washington, DC: Government Printing Office, 1933), 67–73

11. *Defender*, September 16, 1916.

12. Ibid., April 21, 28, 1917.

13. For secondary accounts that examine the impact of the work-or-fight order on major league baseball, see Harold Seymour, *Baseball: The Golden Age* (New York: Oxford University Press, 1970), 248–49, and Charles C. Alexander, *Our Game: An American Baseball History* (New York: Henry Holt, 1991), 112. *Freeman*, February 9, October 12, November 16, 1918; *New York Age*, March 16, 1918; *Defender*, September 8, 1917, March 30, May 25, July 13, 20, 27, August 17, 1918; *Philadelphia Tribune*, March 30, June 1, July 20, 1918.

14. For accounts of the Hotel League, see the *Defender*, January 5, February 2, March 9, 16, 1918. *Freeman*, January 12, February 2, 1918, and *Philadelphia Tribune*, February 2, 1918. For the American Giants and ABCs midwestern and eastern barnstorming tour, see *Chicago Tribune*, August 2, 9, 11, 18, 1918. *Defender*, August 3, 10, 17, 1918; *New York Age*, August 3, 1918. *Freeman*, August 3, 1918.

15. *Freeman*, March 10, 1917; *St. Louis Argus*, April 6, 1917.

16. *St. Louis Argus*, April 6, 1917. For accounts of Phil Ball, see Seymour, *Baseball: The Golden Age*, 200, and Alexander, *Our Game*, 104.

17. *St. Louis Argus*, May 4, 11, 25, June 22, 1917.

18. *Freeman*, April 28, 1917. On December 22, *Freeman* sportswriter Billy Lewis wrote a feature article on Taylor that highlighted the ABCs' successful pool hall. According to Lewis, Taylor gave "his patrons, his Colored patrons, the very best he can afford." He added, "And when I say he has something like $5,000 invested in this establishment it will appear that he can afford to do quite a great deal."

19. Ibid., April 21, 1917.

20. Ibid., September 29, 1917. For box scores on the two-game series with the Indianapolis Indians, see *Indianapolis Star*, September 23, 24, 1917.

21. *Defender*, October 6, 1917. See chapter 2 regarding the assessment of Sol White's *History of Colored Baseball*.

22. See preceding note.

23. *Freeman*, July 6, 1918.

24. Ibid., July 20, 1918.

25. *New York Age*, April 6, 1918. Riley, *Encyclopedia of the Negro Baseball Leagues*, 367, 824–25.

26. *New York Age*, June 8, 1918.

27. Ibid., June 29, 1918.

28. Ibid.

29. The *Sunday Item* ad is in Neil Lanctot, *Fair Dealing and Clean Playing: The Hilldale Club and the Development of Black Professional Baseball, 1910–1932* (Jefferson, NC: McFarland, 1994), 16.

30. Ibid., 17–18.

31. For a description of the inferior parks, see *Philadelphia Tribune*, February 21, 1914.

32. For secondary accounts on black Philadelphia's urban development, see W. E. B. Du Bois, *The Philadelphia Negro: A Social Study* (1899; reprint, New York: Schocken Books, 1967); Richard R. Wright, *The Negro in Pennsylvania: A Study in Economic History* (Philadelphia: A. M. E. Book Concern, 1909); Charles Ashley Hardy, "Race and Opportunity: Black Philadelphia during the Era of the Great Migration" (PhD diss., Temple University, 1989); and Robert Gregg, *Sparks from the Anvil of Oppression: Philadelphia's African Methodists and Southern Migrants, 1890–1940* (Philadelphia: Temple University Press, 1993).

33. To provide a sketch of Hilldale's origins in order to trace the club's transformation, I draw primarily from Neil Lanctot's work. See *Fair Dealing*, 16–26. On April 8, 1916, the *Philadelphia Tribune* provided a brief portrait of Hilldale's early history.

34. See preceding note.

35. *Philadelphia Tribune*, March 23, 30, September 14, 21, 1912.

36. Lanctot, *Fair Dealing*, 22; *Philadelphia Tribune*, October 17, 1914.

37. For the 1914 Hilldale Ledgers, see Lloyd Thompson-Bill Cash Collection, Afro-American Historical and Cultural Museum, Philadelphia, PA.

38. For the 1915 Hilldale Ledgers, see ibid.

39. *Philadelphia Tribune*, January 15, 1916; Minutes from HBEC Meeting, January 23, 1916, in Lloyd Thompson-Bill Cash Collection; Minutes from HBEC Meeting, February 27, 1916, ibid. For an example concerning the promotion of Hilldale Park, see *Philadelphia Tribune*, February 12, 1916.

40. *Philadelphia Tribune*, October 21, 1916.

41. Ibid.; Minutes from HBEC Meeting, October 22, 1916, December 10, 1916, January 7, 1917, Lloyd Thompson–Bill Cash Collection.

42. *Philadelphia Tribune*, January 13, 1917. On February 10, 1917, the *Philadelphia Tribune* reported that the HBEC had adopted the slogan "Bigger and better" for the upcoming season. The *Tribune* was also complicit in accentuating Hilldale's marketing efforts. See ibid., February 17, 24, 1917.

43. Ibid., March 10, 1917.

44. The Bolden quote is in *Baltimore Afro-American*, April 11, 1925.

45. *Philadelphia Tribune*, March 17, 1917; Riley, *Encyclopedia of the Negro Baseball Leagues*, 108.

46. *Philadelphia Tribune*, March 24, June 30, 1917.

47. Ibid., June 9, 23, July 7, August 18, 25, September 15, 22, 1917.

48. David S. Neft, Richard M. Cohen, and Michael L. Neft, *The Sports Encyclopedia: Baseball 2006*, 26th ed. (New York: St. Martin's Griffin, 2006), 80–83; *Philadelphia Tribune*, October 13, 20, 27, 1917.

49. A reference to Thompson's architectural skills is in *Philadelphia Tribune*, April 14, 1917.

50. Ibid., March 2, April 6, 1918.

51. Ibid., April 13, 1918.

52. Ibid.

53. Ibid., April 20, 1918.

54. Ibid., July 6, August 10, 1918.

55. *Ibid.*, September 14, 21, 1918.

56. For the 1918 Hilldale Ledgers, see the Lloyd Thompson–Bill Cash Collection.

57. Newspaper coverage on the Chicago Giants was sporadic after Frank Leland's death. See box scores for Chicago Giants game in *Chicago Tribune*, May 14, 21, June 24, 25, July 23, 30, August 4, 13, 20, September 3, 17, 1917, May 6, June 10, July 22, 29, August 26, 1918, May 19, 26, June 22, 30, July 8, 14, 21, 27, 28, 1919. For examples of Foster booking games at Schorling Park, see *Chicago Tribune*, July 13, August 8, 1915, July 29, August 5, 12, 1918. *Defender*, August 18, September 1, 1917.

58. Phil Dixon and Patrick J. Hannigan, *The Negro Baseball Leagues, 1867–1955: A Photographic History* (Mattituck, NY: Amereon House, 1992), 140. Riley, *Encyclopedia of the Negro Baseball Leagues*, 432–34.

59. Riley, *Encyclopedia of the Negro Baseball Leagues*, 844–45, 860–61; *Chicago Tribune*, June 4, 5, 1917, June 22, August 30, 1919; *Defender*, April 20, 1918.

60. For a secondary account of the rise of the Detroit Stars, see Richard Bak, *Turkey Stearnes and the Detroit Stars: The Negro Leagues in Detroit, 1919–1933* (Detroit: Wayne State University Press, 1994). *Defender*, March 1, April 19, 1919.

61. *Chicago Tribune*, June 18, 19, 20, July 8, 1919.

62. *Philadelphia Tribune*, July 12, 26, August 16, 1919.

63. Ibid., August 30, 1919.

64. For a discussion of how Tammany hacks managed the park system in New York, see Robert A. Caro, *The Power Broker: Robert Moses and the Fall of New York* (New York: Alfred A. Knopf, 1974), 323–46. See also Steven A. Riess, *City Games: The Evolution of American Urban Society and the Rise of Sports* (Urbana: University of Illinois Press, 1991), 140–45.

65. Robert Peterson, *Only the Ball Was White: A History of Legendary Black Players and All-Black Professional Teams* (New York: Oxford University Press, 1970), 67; James M. DiClerico and Barry J. Pavelec, *The Jersey Game: The History of Modern Baseball from Its Birth to the Big Leagues in the Garden State* (New Brunswick, NJ: Rutgers University Press, 1991), 140; *Atlantic City Daily Press*, May 8, 1916.

66. Riley, *Encyclopedia of the Negro Baseball Leagues*, 204–5, 226, 668, 812.

67. Ibid., 496–98.

68. *Atlantic City Daily Press*, May 4, 8, 1916. For examples of box scores of league games, see *ibid.*, May 9, 13, 19, June 5, 12, 1916.

69. For accounts of the Bacharach Giants playing against white semipros, see *ibid*, May 20, June 12, 26, July 2, 1916. Ibid., July 4, 5, 1916.

70. *Ibid.*, July 18, 19, 1916.

71. Ibid., June 22, 1916.

72. Ibid., July 6, 1916.

73. Ibid., July 12, 14, 1916.

74. Ibid., July 19, 1916.

75. Ibid., July 21, 1916.

76. Ibid., July 20, 1916.

77. *New York Age*, October 4, 1917.

78. Press coverage of the Pennsylvania Red Caps was sporadic. See *Philadelphia Tribune*, April 1, October 14, 1916. *New York Age*, September 13, 1917. The Pugh comment is in the *Defender*, May 31, 1919. Williams's retraction of Pugh's comments is in the *Defender*, June 14, 1919. The *Defender* provided a brief account for players demanding higher pay on February 22, 1919.

79. *Defender*, April 26, 1919. Cannonball Redding's comments are in ibid., May 31, 1919.

80. Ibid., May 17, 31, June 7, 1919.

81. Ibid., June 14, September 6, 1919; *New York Age*, August 2, 1919.

82. For Connor's and Wilkins's connection to Hal Chase, see *New York Age*, May 15, 1920. For a secondary account about Hal Chase, see Seymour, *Baseball: The Golden Age*, 288–93.

83. *New York Age*, May 15, 1920. For the subdivision of Olympic Field, see *Defender*, March 13, 1920.

84. *New York Age*, May 22, July 10, 17, August 28, September 11, 1920.

85. *Defender*, October 16, 1920.

7. Pitfalls of Baseball: The Rise of the Negro National League

1. *Cleveland Advocate*, January 1, 1919.

2. Ibid., January 25, 1919.

3. *Defender* (Chicago), October 4, 1919. C. I. Taylor once again advocated the need for black clubs to organize in "The Future of Colored Baseball," *Competitor* (February 1920): 76–78.

4. *Defender*, November 29, December 13, 20, 27, 1919, January 3, 19, 17, 1920.

5. Ibid., December 13, 1919. See chapter 2 for my assessment of Rube Foster's analysis of why a black club was unable to meet its monthly payroll.

6. Ibid., December 20, 1919.

7. Ibid., December 27, 1919.

8. Ibid., January 3, 1920.

9. Ibid., January 10, 1920.

10. Ibid., January 17, 1920.

11. *Freeman* (Indianapolis), February 28, 1920.

12. Janet Bruce, *Kansas City Monarchs: Champions of Black Baseball* (Lawrence: University Press of Kansas, 1985), 14–18.

13. Background on the All Nations team is drawn primarily from Bruce, *Kansas City Monarchs*, 14–18. See also Robert Peterson, *Only the Ball Was White* (New York: Oxford University Press, 1970), 70–72; James A. Riley, *The Biographical Encyclopedia of the Negro Baseball Leagues* (New York: Carroll and Graf, 1994), 842–43; and Phil Dixon and Patrick J. Hannigan, *The Negro Baseball Leagues, 1867–1955* (Mattituck, NY: Amereon House, 1992), 116–20.

14. Bruce, *Kansas City*, 22. *Freeman*, February 28, 1920.

15. *Defender*, February 14, 1920; *Freeman*, February 14, 1920; *New York Age*, February 28, 1920; Ira F. Lewis, "National Baseball League Formed," *Competitor* (March 1920): 66–67.

16. *Defender*, February 21, March 20, 27, 1920; *Freeman*, February 21, 28, 1920; *Baltimore Afro-American*, February 27, 1920.

17. *Defender*, April 24, May 8, 1920; *Freeman*, April 24, 1920; *New York Age*, May 22, 1920; Dave Wyatt, "National League of Colored Clubs Prepare for Season's Opening," *Competitor* (April 1920): 73–74.

18. See chapter 6 regarding Connor's leasing agreement to use Ebbets Field. The Lincoln Giants' losing their lease on Olympic Field is covered in *Defender*, March 13, 1920.

19. *Freeman*, April 24, 1920; *Philadelphia Tribune*, March 6, 1920.

20. *Philadelphia Tribune*, August 21, 1920.

21. Ibid., September 18, 1920. For the dispute over players between Bolden and Connor, see *Baltimore Afro-American*, June 11, 1920, and *Defender*, June 12, 1920. For Hilldale playing games in New York against the Brooklyn Royal Giants and Cuban Stars East, see *Philadelphia Tribune*, June 17, 24, August 14, September 25, October 9, 23, 1920.

22. *Defender*, May 8, 1920; *Freeman*, May 8, 1920; Riley, *Negro*, 665.

23. "Big League Making Progress," *Competitor* (July 1920): 69.

24. Ibid. NNL standings were published in *Defender*, July 31, 1920, and *St. Louis Argus*, July 30, 1920.

25. For an account of major league baseball's relationship with the press, see David Q. Voigt, *American Baseball: From the Commissioners to Continental Expansion* (University Park: Pennsylvania State University Press, 1983), 94–101.

26. Ibid.; Harold Seymour, *Baseball: The Golden Age* (New York: Oxford University Press, 1970), 59–60.

27. *Freeman*, December 11, 1920.

28. Seymour, *Baseball*, 344; *Fifteenth Census of the United States: 1930* (Washington, DC: Government Printing Office, 1933), 67–72.

29. Ellis W. Hawley, *The Great War and the Search for a Modern Order: A History of the American People and Their Institutions, 1917–1933* (New York: St. Martin's Press, 1992), 67–70; Paul Johnson, *A History of the American People* (New York: HarperPerennial, 1997).

30. Rob Ruck, *Sandlot Seasons: Sport in Black Pittsburgh* (Urbana: University of Illinois Press, 1987); St. Clair Drake and Horace R. Cayton, *Black Metropolis: A Study of Negro Life in a Northern City* (New York: Harper and Row, 1945); Charles Ashley Hardy III, "Race and Opportunity: Black Philadelphia during the Era of the Great Migration, 1916–1930" (PhD diss., Temple University, 1989).

31. *St. Louis Argus*, December 10, 1920; *Defender*, December 11, 1920; *Freeman*, December 11, 1920; *Baltimore Afro-American*, December 24, 1920.

32. *St. Louis Argus*, December 10, 1920; *Defender*, December 11, 1920; *Freeman*, December 11, 1920; *Baltimore Afro-American*, December 24, 1920; Letter from C. I. Taylor to Karl C. Finke, November 28, 1920, Ashland Collection, Baseball Hall of Fame and Museum, Cooperstown, NY; Letter from C. I. Taylor to Karl Finke, December 5, 1920, ibid.

33. *Defender*, December 11, 1920.

34. For Dave Wyatt as NNL publicity man, see ibid., November 27, 1920. Ibid., June 11, 25, July 2, 30, 1921. The *Baltimore Afro-American* published the NNL final standings on October 21, 1921.

35. *Defender*, February 19, 1921; *Philadelphia Tribune*, January 8, 1921.

36. *Philadelphia Tribune*, January 8, 1921; *Defender*, January 15, 22, 1921.

37. *Defender*, March 26, 1921; *New York Age*, April 16, 1921.

38. *Defender*, May 14, 21, 28, June 4, 1921.

39. *Philadelphia Tribune*, May 21, June 11, 1921.

40. Ibid., June 11, 18, 25, July 2, October 1, 1921. *Defender*, June 18, 1921.

41. *Philadelphia Tribune*, July 23, 30, August 6, 20, 27, September 27, 1921.

42. Ibid., October 15, 22, 1921.

43. *Defender*, November 12, 28, 1921; *Baltimore Afro-American*, November 11, 1920.

44. *Defender*, December 10, 17, 24, 31, 1921.

45. Ibid., December 10, 1921.

46. Ibid.

47. Ibid., December 17, 1921.

48. See chapters 4 and 6 regarding the plight of the St. Louis Giants.

49. *Defender*, December 31, 1921.

50. Ibid. The *Philadelphia Tribune* made no mention of the disputed play to which Foster referred. See the issue for October 15, 1921.

51. *Defender*, December 10, 1921.

8. Black Baseball War: The Rise of the Eastern Colored League

1. *Defender* (Chicago), January 7, February 4, 1922; *Kansas City Call* (Missouri), January 21, February 4, 11, 1922; *Baltimore Afro-American*, January 20, February 10, 1922; *New York Age*, February 4, 1922.

2. *Defender*, January 14, 1922; *Baltimore Afro-American*, March 31, April 21, 1922.

3. *Defender*, April 15, 1922; *Kansas City Call*, April 22, 1922.

4. *Defender*, March 4, 1922; *Kansas City Call*, March 4, 1922; *New York Age*, March 11, 1922.

5. *Defender*, March 4, 11, 1922.

6. Ibid., March 18, May 6, 1922; *Baltimore Afro-American*, May 19, 1922.

7. For the railroads as a troubled industry, see Ellis W. Hawley, *The Great War and the Search for a Modern Order: A History of the American People and Their Institutions, 1917–1933* (New York: St. Martin's Press, 1992), 73.

8. The Bacharachs' second southern spring training tour is reported in *Defender*, May 6, 13, 1922. For the Bacharachs' start of the regular season against NNL clubs, see *ibid.*, May 20, June 3, 17, 1922. For the Bacharach-Hilldale rivalry, see ibid., May 20, June 10, 15, 1922. For the Bacharachs' second midwestern tour, see ibid., July 15, 22, 30, August 12, 19, 1922.

9. Young's assessment of the umpire situation and a brief account of the UOA are in ibid., August 19, 1922. Other accounts regarding the hiring of black umpires are in

ibid., October 9, 1920, April 9, 1921, *Freeman* (Indianapolis), March 27, 1920, and *Kansas City Call*, January 7, July 26, 1922.

10. *Defender*, August 19, 1922.

11. Ibid.

12. Ibid., September 2, 16, 23, October 7, 1922.

13. *Kansas City Call*, September 9, 1922.

14. Secondary accounts of the evolution of major league umpires are in David Q. Voigt, *American Baseball: From Gentlemen's Sport to the Commissioner System* (Norman: University of Oklahoma Press, 1966); David Q. Voight, *American Baseball: From the Commissioners to Continental Expansion* (University Park: Pennsylvania State University Press, 1983); Eugene C. Murdock, *Ban Johnson: Czar of Baseball* (Westport, CT: Greenwood Press, 1982); and Charles C. Alexander, *Our Game: An American Baseball History* (New York: Henry Holt, 1991).

15. Murdock, *Ban Johnson*, 39–41. Murdock devotes all of chapter 9 to his endeavor to elevate the status of umpires in the American League.

16. *Defender*, December 31, 1921.

17. *Kansas City Call*, August 5, September 9, 1922.

18. Ibid.

19. *Defender*, December 10, 1922.

20. Ibid., October 28, November 18, December 2, 16, 1922; *Kansas City Call*, October 27, December 15, 1922; *Baltimore Afro-American*, December 15, 1922. On Bolden withdrawing from the NNL, see *Baltimore Afro-American*, December 8, 1922.

21. The HBEC's affiliation with the PBA is discussed in Neil Lanctot, *Fair Dealing and Clean Playing: The Hilldale Club and the Development of Black Professional Baseball* (Jefferson, NC: McFarland, 1994), 49–72.

22. Hilldale's year-end book balance is found in the Lloyd Thompson-Bill Cash Collection, Afro-American Historical and Cultural Museum, Philadelphia, PA. *New York Age*, December 23, 1922.

23. *Baltimore Afro-American*, December 1, 22, 1922; *New York Age*, December 23, 1922, January 27, 1923; *Kansas City Call*, December 22, 1922.

24. *Baltimore Afro-American*, July 29, November 18, 1921, March 10, June 2, 9, 1922. In 1887, Baltimore was represented in the National League of Colored Base Ball Clubs. The Lord Baltimores also endured low fan turnout and would disband along with the league in May of that year. See Michael E. Lomax, *Black Baseball Entrepreneurs, 1860–1901: Operating by Any Means Necessary* (Syracuse, NY: Syracuse University Press, 2003), 63–70.

25. Adrian Burgos Jr., *Playing America's Game: Baseball, Latinos, and the Color Line* (Berkeley: University of California Press, 2007), 111–16. See chapter 2 of Burgos's book regarding Strong's association with the NACBC and the Lamar-Linares

connection. *New York Age*, May 17, 24, 31, June 28, August 16, September 13, 1917, May 25, August 3, June 7, 1918.

26. See preceding note. James A. Riley, *The Biographical Encyclopedia of the Negro Baseball Leagues* (New York: Carroll and Graff, 1994), 594–95, 680–81. See chapter 4 for Padron pitching against the Brooklyn Royal Giants in the Colored World Series.

27. *Baltimore Afro-American*, January 12, 1923; *Kansas City Call*, January 19, 1923.

28. *Baltimore Afro-American*, January 12, 1923; *Kansas City Call*, January 19, 1923.

29. *Baltimore Afro-American*, January 12, 1923; *Kansas City Call*, January 19, 1923.

30. *Baltimore Afro-American*, January 26, 1923; *Pittsburgh Courier*, January 20, 1923.

31. *Baltimore Afro-American*, February 16, 1923.

32. Ibid., February 2, 1923; *Kansas City Call*, February 9, 1923.

33. *Baltimore Afro-American*, March 23, 1923.

34. *Defender*, February 17, 1923; *New York Age*, February 24, 1923; *Baltimore Afro-American*, March 16, April 6, 1923. For Wilkins's death, see *Pittsburgh Courier*, May 31, October 25, 1924.

35. *Defender*, February 17, March 10, 1923.

36. *New York*, April 21, 1923; *Pittsburgh Courier*, April 14, 1923; *Baltimore Afro-American*, March 2, 1923. For published statistics in the black press, see *Baltimore Afro-American*, June 29, 1923. *New York Age*, July 7, August 11, 25, September 15, October 6, 1923; *Pittsburgh Courier*, September 6, 1923.

37. *New York Age*, July 7, August 11, 25, September 15, October 6, 1923; *Pittsburgh Courier*, September 6, 1923.

38. *New York Age*, October 6, 1923.

39. *Defender*, February 17, 1923; *Kansas City Call*, February 23, 1923.

40. *Pittsburgh Courier*, June 2, 1923.

41. *Kansas City Call*, July 6, August 3, 1923; *Defender*, July 7, 14, 28, 1923; *Pittsburgh Courier*, July 7, August 4, 1923.

42. *Defender*, April 21, 28, July 28, 1923.

43. *Kansas City Call*, August 17, 1923.

44. *Defender*, April 7, 21, 1923; *Baltimore Afro-American*, April 27, 1923; *Kansas City Call*, March 30, April 27, 1923.

45. *Defender*, May 5, 12, 1923.

46. Ibid., August 25, 1923; *Pittsburgh Courier*, August 25, 1923.

47. *Defender*, October 20, 1923.

48. Ibid., October 13, 1923.

49. Ibid., October 20, 1923.

50. Ibid.

51. Ibid., October 27, 1923.

52. *Philadelphia Tribune*, December 1, 15, 1923; *Baltimore Afro-American*, December 7, 14, 1923; *Pittsburgh Courier*, December 15, 1923; *The Reach Official American League Guide* (Philadelphia: A. J. Reach, 1910), 496.

53. *Baltimore Afro-American*, January 18, February 27, April 18, 1924; *Philadelphia Tribune*, February 23, March 1, 15, 1924; *New York Age*, March 8, 1924.

54. *Baltimore Afro-American*, January 11, 25, March 21, 1924; *Kansas City Call*, January 25, 1924; *New York Age*, March 15, 1924.

55. *Baltimore Afro-American*, January 4, 1924; *Kansas City Call*, February 1, 1924; Robert Peterson, *Only the Ball Was White* (New York: Oxford University Press, 1970); Rob Ruck, *Sandlot Seasons: Sport in Black Pittsburgh* (Urbana: University of Illinois Press, 1987).

56. *Pittsburgh Courier*, June 21, 28, 1924; *Baltimore Afro-American*, August 8, 1924.

57. *Baltimore Afro-American*, May 30, June 6, 1924; *Pittsburgh Courier*, May 31, June 7, 1924; *Kansas City Call*, May 30, 1924; *New York Age*, May 31, 1924; *Philadelphia Tribune*, May 31, June 7, 1924.

58. *New York Age*, May 31, 1924. For a discussion of the National Baseball Federation, see Harold Seymour, *Baseball: The People's Game* (New York: Oxford University Press, 1990), 270–75. For semipros organizing a new body in New York, see the *New York Times*, April 17, 1921.

59. *Defender*, November 17, December 1, 8, 15, 1923; *Kansas City Call*, December 14, 1923; *Pittsburgh Courier*, December 15, 1923, March 22, 1924; *Philadelphia Tribune*, December 22, 1923.

60. *Kansas City Call*, January 25, 1924; *Defender*, February 2, 9, 16, 1924; *Pittsburgh Courier*, February 16, 1924.

61. *Defender*, December 22, 1923.

62. Ibid., January 5, 1924. Kansas City Monarchs' business manager Quincy Gilmore extolled the progress the NNL had made in *Kansas City Call*, February 15, 1924.

63. *Baltimore Afro-American*, February 8, 1924.

64. Ibid.

65. Ibid.

66. Ibid.

67. Ibid., February 22, 1924.

68. Ibid.

69. *Kansas City Call*, February 29, 1924.

70. *Defender*, March 11, 1922; *Baltimore Afro-American*, March 30, 1923; *Kansas City Call*, March 9, 1923; *Pittsburgh Courier*, April 7, 1923; *New York Age*, April 7, 1923. Mrs. C. I. Taylor had the player salaries of the ABCs for the 1923 season published in *Defender*, January 19, 1924.

71. *Baltimore Afro-American*, July 18, 1924; *Defender*, July 19, 1924.

72. *Pittsburgh Courier*, June 28, July 26, 1924; *Defender*, June 21, July 5, 19, 1924; *Kansas City Call*, June 27, 1924.

73. *Defender*, July 19, 1924.

74. Taylor also pointed out that the American Giants made only a few appearances in Indianapolis in the 1910s. See chapter 6.

9. Pursuing Peace

1. *Philadelphia Tribune*, August 16, 1924.

2. For secondary accounts of the origins of Major League Baseball's World Series, see Harold Seymour, *Baseball: The Golden Age* (New York: Oxford University Press, 1970); Eugene C. Murdock, *Ban Johnson: Czar of Baseball* (Westport, CT: Greenwood Press, 1982); David Q. Voigt, *American Baseball: From the Commissioners to Continental Expansion* (University Park: Pennsylvania State University Press, 1983); Charles C. Alexander, *Our Game: An American Baseball History* (New York: Henry Holt, 1991); and Benjamin G. Rader, *Baseball: A History of America's Game* (Urbana: University of Illinois Press, 1992).

3. The Johnson comment is found in Murdock, *Ban*, 87. The excerpt from *Everybody's* is in Alexander, *Our Game*, 93. The 1905 World Series was unique because each game ended in a shutout victory.

4. *Pittsburgh Courier*, August 16, 30, September 13, 1924; *Defender* (Chicago), August 30, September 6, 1924; *Philadelphia Tribune*, September 6, 1924; *Baltimore Afro-American*, September 5, 1924.

5. See chapter 8 for Spedden's comments regarding a proposed World Series. *Defender*, August 30, 1924.

6. *Baltimore Afro-American*, September 5, 1924; *Philadelphia Tribune*, September 6, 1924.

7. *Philadelphia Tribune*, September 6, 1924.

8. *Baltimore Afro-American*, September 5, 1924; *Philadelphia Tribune*, September 6, 13, 1924.

9. *New York Age*, September 13, 1924.

10. *Philadelphia Tribune*, September 13, 1924; *Defender*, September 20, 1924. Evidently, there was a dispute over who should represent the ECL on the World Series commission. In an article printed in the *Pittsburgh Courier*, Washington Potomacs' magnate George Robinson claimed that Nat Strong objected to his serving on the commission. The situation was further complicated when Robinson found out that his Potomacs were an "associate" member of the ECL and not a league club. This was the primary reason Strong objected to Robinson serving on the commission. See *Pittsburgh Courier*, September 26, 1924.

11. *Kansas City Call*, September 12, 1924.

12. James A. Riley, *The Biographical Encyclopedia of the Negro Baseball Leagues* (New York: Carroll and Graf, 1994), 31–32, 440–41, 677–79.

13. Ibid., 444–45, 502–4.

14. *Baltimore Afro-American*, October 10, 1924; *Pittsburgh Courier*, October 11, 1924; *Kansas City Call*, October 10, 1924.

15. *Kansas City Call*, October 17, 1924; *Pittsburgh Courier*, October 18, 1924; *Philadelphia Tribune*, October 18, 1924.

16. *Kansas City Call*, October 24, 1924; *Pittsburgh Courier*, October 25, 1924; *Philadelphia Tribune*, October 25, 1924.

17. *Kansas City Call*, October 24, 1924; *Pittsburgh Courier*, October 25, 1924; *Philadelphia Tribune*, October 25, 1924.

18. *Baltimore Afro-American*, October 31, 1924; *Philadelphia Tribune*, November 1, 1924; *Pittsburgh Courier*, November 1, 1924; *Defender*, November 1, 1924.

19. *Pittsburgh Courier*, October 16, 1924.

20. *Kansas City Call*, October 31, 1924.

21. *Defender*, November 15, 1924.

22. Ibid. For an account of the Chicago White Stockings' and St. Louis Browns' attempts to organize a championship series in the 1880s, see Larry G. Bowman, "Christian Von der Ahe, the St. Louis Browns, and the World's Championship Playoffs, 1885–1888," *Missouri Historical Review* 91 (July 1997): 385–405.

23. *Defender*, November 15, 1924.

24. Ibid., November 22, December 6, 1924; *Kansas City Call*, December 12, 1924; *Philadelphia Tribune*, December 13, 1924; *Pittsburgh Courier*, December 13, 1924; *New York Age*, December 13, 1924; *Baltimore Afro-American*, December 13, 1924.

25. Ibid.

26. *Defender*, December 13, 1924.

27. Ibid., December 20, 1924; *Pittsburgh Courier*, December 20, 1924; *Baltimore Afro-American*, December 27, 1924.

28. *Pittsburgh Courier*, December 20, 1924.

29. *Defender*, December 27, 1924.

30. *Baltimore Afro-American*, January 10, 1925; *Philadelphia Tribune*, January 10, 1925.

31. *Baltimore Afro-American*, January 10, 1925; *Philadelphia Tribune*, January 10, 1925.

32. *Philadelphia Tribune*, November 29, 1924, January 10, 1925; *Baltimore Afro-American*, February 28, 1925.

33. *Defender*, February 7, 1925; *Pittsburgh Courier*, February 14, 1925.

34. *Defender*, February 7, 1925; *Philadelphia Tribune*, February 14, 1925; *New York Age*, February 14, 1925; *Pittsburgh Courier*, February 14, 1925.

35. *Pittsburgh Courier*, April 11, 1925; *Baltimore Afro-American*, May 23, 1925; *Defender*, July 4, 1925.

36. *Baltimore Afro-American*, August 22, 1925; *Pittsburgh Courier*, August 22, 1925.

37. The umpire's comment to Carl Beckwith is in Leslie Heaphy, "The Growth and Decline of the Negro Leagues," (MA thesis, University of Toledo, 1989), 45. *Kansas City Call*, July 11, 1924.

38. See chapter 8 regarding Rube Foster's perspective on African American umpires.

39. *Baltimore Afro-American*, November 22, 1924.

40. Ibid.; *New York Age*, November 22, 1924; *Pittsburgh Courier*, November 22, 1924; *Philadelphia Tribune*, November 22, 1924. On the dissolution of the Robinson-Taylor partnership, see *Baltimore Afro-American*, October 17, 1924. On Robinson's relocation to Wilmington, see *ibid.*, January 31, 1925.

41. *Baltimore Afro-American*, January 31, 1925; *Pittsburgh Courier*, January 31, 1925; *Philadelphia Tribune*, January 31, 1925; *New York Age*, January 31, 1925.

42. *Baltimore Afro-American*, March 28, June 20, 1925; *Philadelphia Tribune*, March 28, 1925; *New York Age*, April 11, 1925.

43. *Baltimore Afro-American*, March 28, June 20, 1925; *Philadelphia Tribune*, March 28, 1925; *New York Age*, April 11, 1925.

44. *Baltimore Afro-American*, March 28, June 20, 1925; *Philadelphia Tribune*, March 28, 1925; *New York Age*, April 11, 1925. ; *Pittsburgh Courier*, March 28, 1925.

45. *Philadelphia Tribune*, April 4, 1925.

46. *Baltimore Afro-American*, April 11, 1925.

47. Neil Lanctot, *Fair Dealing and Clean Playing: The Hilldale Club and the Development of Black Professional Baseball, 1910–1932* (Jefferson, NC: McFarland, 1994), 70; *Defender*, September 17, 1927.

48. John Hope Franklin, *From Slavery to Freedom: A History of Negro Americans*, 5th ed. (New York: Alfred A. Knopf, 1980), 357–60.

49. *Philadelphia Tribune*, June 20, 1925; *Pittsburgh Courier*, June 20, 1925.

50. *Philadelphia Tribune*, June 20, 1925; *Pittsburgh Courier*, June 20, 1925.

51. *Philadelphia Tribune*, June 27, 1925.

52. *Baltimore Afro-American*, June 27, 1925; *Philadelphia Tribune*, June 27, 1925; *Pittsburgh Courier*, July 4, 1925.

53. *Pittsburgh Courier*, July 25, 1925.

54. Ibid., August 1, 1925; *Baltimore Afro-American*, August 1, 1925.

55. *Fifteenth Census of the United States: 1930* (Washington, DC: Government Printing Office, 1933), 73; *New York Age*, July 18, 25, 1925; *Baltimore Afro-American*, July 25, 1925; *Philadelphia Tribune*, July 25, August 1, 1925.

56. *Baltimore Afro-American*, August 1, 1925; *Philadelphia Tribune*, August 1, 1925. *Pittsburgh Courier*, August 1, 1925; *New York Age*, August 1, 1925.

57. The Wilson comment is in *Pittsburgh Courier*, September 12, 1925.

58. *Defender*, September 19, 26, October 3, 1925.

59. *Philadelphia Tribune*, October 10, 1925; *Defender*, October 10, 1925; *New York Age*, October 10, 1925.

60. *Philadelphia Tribune*, October 10, 1925; *Defender*, October 10, 1925; *New York Age*, October 10, 1925.

61. *Philadelphia Tribune*, October 10, 1925; *Defender*, October 10, 1925; *New York Age*, October 10, 1925.

62. *Philadelphia Tribune*, October 17, 1925; *Defender*, October 17, 1925.

63. *Defender*, October 17, 1925; *Pittsburgh Courier*, October 24, 1925.

10. Caught in a Rundown

1. *Philadelphia Tribune*, October 10, 1925; *Defender* (Chicago), October 10, 1925; *New York Age*, October 10, 1925.

2. *Philadelphia Tribune*, October 10, 1925; *Defender*, October 10, 1925; *New York Age*, October 10, 1925. See Posey's side of the story in the *Pittsburgh Courier*, January 16, 1926.

3. *Defender*, December 26, 1925. On Birmingham and Memphis being dropped from the league, see *Baltimore Afro-American*, January 2, 1926, and *Pittsburgh Courier*, January 9, 1926. Regarding Cleveland's entry into the NNL, see *Defender*, March 13, 1926.

4. *Defender*, January 30, 1926. This article also appeared in the *Philadelphia Tribune*, January 30, 1926.

5. Regarding Foster's being gassed in Indianapolis, see *Baltimore Afro-American*, June 8, 1925; *Philadelphia Tribune*, June 6, 1925; and *Pittsburgh Courier*, June 6, 1925. *Pittsburgh Courier*, July 24, 1926; *New York Age*, July 24, 1926; *Baltimore Afro-American*, September 4, 11, 18, 1926; *Philadelphia Tribune*, September 4, 18, 1926; *Kansas City Call* (Missouri), September 10, 1926; *New York Age*, September 11, 1926.

6. See preceding note. *New York Age*, September 11, 1926.

7. *Defender*, September 11, 1926.

8. Ibid.

9. *Philadelphia Tribune*, September 18, 1926.

10. Ibid.

11. *Baltimore Afro-American*, November 14, 1925, January 16, 1926; *New York Age*, November 14, 1925; *Defender*, January 9, 1926.

12. *New York Age*, January 23, 1926; *Baltimore Afro-American*, March 6, 1926.

13. *New York Age*, February 6, 1926.

14. *Baltimore Afro-American*, February 27, 1926; *New York Age*, February 27, 1926; *Philadelphia Tribune*, March 6, 1926.

15. *Baltimore Afro-American*, March 20, 1926; *New York Age*, March 20, 1926; *Kansas City Call*, March 19, 1926.

16. *Baltimore Afro-American*, July 10, 1926; *New York Age*, July 10, 1926; *Philadelphia Tribune*, July 10, 1926.

17. See chapter 8 on the history of umpires in Major League Baseball.

18. *Baltimore Afro-American*, July 3, August 7, 14, 1926; *Pittsburgh Courier*, August 14, 1926. For accounts on the black press's focus on rowdyism at black baseball games, see *Pittsburgh Courier*, July 18, August 1, 1925, and *Baltimore Afro-American*, August 8, 1925.

19. See preceding note.

20. *Pittsburgh Courier*, August 14, 1926.

21. *Baltimore Afro-American*, August 7, 1926.

22. On the drafting by the commissioners of a policy for league clubs to play fifty games to qualify for the World Series, see *New York Age*, April 24, 1926. *Philadelphia Tribune*, August 7, 1926. *Baltimore Afro-American*, August 7, 14, 1926.

23. *New York Age*, August 7, 1926.

24. Ibid.

25. *Baltimore Afro-American*, September 25, 1926.

26. Ibid., October 30, 1926.

27. James A. Riley, *The Biographical Encyclopedia of the Negro Baseball Leagues* (New York: Carroll and Graf, 1994), 292–94, 305–6, 506–7, 640–41.

28. Ibid., 374, 496–98, 511–12; *Baltimore Afro-American*, October 2, 1926.

29. *Kansas City Call*, October 8, 1926; *Baltimore Afro-American*, October 9, 1926; *Defender*, October 9, 1926.

30. *Kansas City Call*, October 15, 1926; *Defender*, October 16, 1926.

31. *Defender*, October 16, 1926.

32. *Baltimore Afro-American*, October 30, 1926.

33. *Defender*, October 23, 1926. For the 1925 World Series commission report, see ibid., October 17, 1925. *Pittsburgh Courier*, October 24, 1925.

34. See preceding note. For Bolden's staging of exhibition games in conflict with World Series games, see *Defender*, October 9, 1926.

35. *Defender*, October 23, 1926.

36. *Kansas City Call*, October 29, 1926.

37. *Philadelphia Tribune*, January 15, 1927; *Kansas City Call*, January 21, 1927; *Pittsburgh Courier*, January 22, 1927; *Baltimore Afro-American*, January 22, 1927; *New York Age*, January 15, 1927.

38. *New York Age*, January 22, 1927; *Philadelphia Tribune*, January 22, 1927; *Defender*, January 22, 1927.

39. *New York Age*, January 8, 15, 1927.

40. *Kansas City Call*, February 4, 1927; *Baltimore Afro-American*, February 5, 1927; *Pittsburgh Courier*, February 5, 1927; *Philadelphia Tribune*, February 5, 1927.

41. Robert Peterson, *Only the Ball Was White* (New York: Oxford University Press, 1970), 101; *Defender*, March 6, April 17, 1920; *Pittsburgh Courier*, April 10, 1926.

42. *Kansas City Call*, February 4, 1927; *Baltimore Afro-American*, February 5, 1927; *Pittsburgh Courier*, February 5, 1927; *Philadelphia Tribune*, February 5, 1927; *Defender*, February 5, 1927.

43. *Pittsburgh Courier*, January 1, March 19, 1927; *Philadelphia Tribune*, January 8, 1927; *Defender*, March 19, 1927; *Baltimore Afro-American*, March 12, 1927.

44. *Kansas City Call*, March 25, 1927; Riley, *Biographical Encyclopedia*, 190–91, 239–40, 253–54.

45. *New York Age*, March 19, 1927; *Philadelphia Tribune*, March 26, 1927; *Baltimore Afro-American*, March 26, 1927.

46. *Kansas City Call*, May 13, 1927.

47. *Baltimore Afro-American*, June 4, 1927; *Philadelphia Tribune*, June 23, 1927.

48. Riley, *Biographical Encyclopedia*, 561–62; *Pittsburgh Courier*, April 30, 1927.

49. *Kansas City Call*, May 8, 1927; *Baltimore Afro-American*, May 14, 1927.

50. *Pittsburgh Courier*, May 21, 1927.

51. *New York Age*, May 21, 1927.

52. *Baltimore Afro-American*, June 25, 1927; *New York Age*, July 2, 1927; *Defender*, April 9, 1927; *Philadelphia Tribune*, July 21, 1927.

53. *Baltimore Afro-American*, April 23, 1927; *New York Age*, April 23, 1927; *Pittsburgh Courier*, April 23, 1927.

54. Peterson, *Only the Ball*, 114–15; *Defender*, February 5, 1927; *Baltimore Afro-American*, April 16, 1927.

55. Neil Lanctot, *Fair Dealing and Clean Playing: The Hilldale Club and the Development of Black Professional Baseball, 1910–1932* (Jefferson, NC: McFarland, 1994), 157.

56. *Philadelphia Tribune*, September 29, 1927; *New York Age*, October 1, 1927; *Kansas City Call*, December 2, 1927.

57. *Defender*, October 8, 1927.

58. Ibid.; *Baltimore Afro-American*, October 8, 1927.

59. *Defender*, October 8, 1927; *Baltimore Afro-American*, October 8, 1927.

60. *Defender*, October 15, 1927; *Baltimore Afro-American*, October 15, 1927.

61. *Philadelphia Tribune*, November 3, 1927; *Defender*, November 3, 1927.

62. *Philadelphia Tribune*, November 3, 1927; *Defender*, November 3, 1927.

11. Before the Fall

1. *Defender* (Chicago), September 11, 1926.
2. Ibid. For secondary accounts of Landis's opposition to the farm system, see Harold Seymour, *Baseball: The Golden Age* (New York: Oxford University Press, 1970); Lee Lowenfish, *The Imperfect Diamond: A History of Baseball's Labor Wars*, rev. ed. (New York: Da Capo Press, 1980); and Robert F. Burk, *Much More Than a Game: Players, Owners, and American Baseball since 1921* (Chapel Hill: University of North Carolina Press, 2001).
3. *Defender*, September 11, 1926.
4. *Pittsburgh Courier*, January 29, 1927.
5. Ibid.
6. Ibid.
7. *Kansas City Call*, May 13, 1927.
8. Ibid.
9. *Pittsburgh Courier*, August 20, 1927.
10. Ibid.
11. *Kansas City Call* (Missouri), December 16, 1927.
12. Ibid., December 23, 1927.
13. Ibid.
14. Ibid., December 30, 1927.
15. Ibid.
16. See chapter 7 regarding Rube Foster's series of articles titled "Pitfalls of Baseball."
17. See chapter 5 regarding the advantage major league owners had in terms of remodeling and building new ballparks. The major league owners and officials looked the other way in terms of gambling, which eventually led to 1919 Black Sox scandal. This represented one way the magnates deviated from the competitor-partner model.
18. For an account of the white sportswriters' contribution in terms of statistics, see David Q. Voigt, *American Baseball: From the Commissioners to Continental Expansion* (University Park: Pennsylvania State University Press, 1983).
19. *Pittsburgh Courier*, January 21, 1928.
20. Ibid.
21. Ibid.
22. *Philadelphia Tribune*, February 16, 1928; *New York Age*, February 18, 1928.
23. *Defender*, February 18, 1928; *Baltimore Afro-American*, February 20, 1928; *Pittsburgh Courier*, March 5, 1928.
24. *New York Age*, March 3, 1928; *Baltimore Afro-American*, March 10, 1928.
25. *New York Age*, March 10, 1928.

26. *Philadelphia Tribune*, February 2, 1928; *Defender*, March 17, 1928; *Pittsburgh Courier*, March 17, 1928; *Baltimore Afro-American*, March 17, 1928.

27. *Philadelphia Tribune*, March 24, 1928; *Baltimore Afro-American*, March 31, 1928.

28. *Pittsburgh Courier*, March 24, 1928; *Baltimore Afro-American*, March 24, April 21, 1928.

29. *Philadelphia Tribune*, April 19, 1928; *Baltimore Afro-American*, April 21, 1928; *Pittsburgh Courier*, April 21, 1928; *Defender*, April 21, 1928.

30. *Pittsburgh Courier*, April 28, June 2, 1928; *Defender*, April 28, May 5, 26, 1928; *Baltimore Afro-American*, June 2, 1928.

31. *Baltimore Afro-American*, April 28, 1928; *Pittsburgh Courier*, June 16, 1928.

32. *Pittsburgh Courier*, June 9, 16, July 28, 1928; *Defender*, June 9, 1928; *Baltimore Afro-American*, June 9, 1928.

33. *Pittsburgh Courier*, August 18, 25, 1928; *Baltimore Afro-American*, August 18, December 29, 1928.

34. *Defender*, January 7, 14, 1928.

35. Ibid., February 18, 1928; *Pittsburgh Courier*, April 7, 1928.

36. *Baltimore Afro-American*, March 10, 1928; Richard Bak, *Turkey Stearnes and the Detroit Stars: The Negro Leagues in Detroit, 1919–1933* (Detroit: Wayne State University Press, 1994), 179–81.

37. *Defender*, July 7, 1928; *Baltimore Afro-American*, July 14, 1928; *Pittsburgh Courier*, July 14, 1928.

38. *Defender*, July 7, 1928; *Baltimore Afro-American*, July 14, 1928; *Pittsburgh Courier*, July 14, 1928.

39. *Defender*, August 11, 1928. Although the evidence is limited, two additional promotional events included Rube Foster Day and President's Day. See *Philadelphia Tribune*, March 15, 1928, and *Defender*, August 25, 1928.

40. *Defender*, September 29, 1928.

41. James A. Riley, *The Biographical Encyclopedia of the Negro Baseball Leagues* (New York: Carroll and Graff, 1994), 753–55, 764–66, 789–90, 826–28.

42. Ibid., 72–74.

43. Ibid., 685–66; *Defender*, September 29, 1928.

44. *Defender*, September 29, 1928.

45. Ibid., September 29, October 6, 13, 1928.

46. Ibid.

47. Ibid.

48. Ibid., October 13, 1928.

49. *Baltimore Afro-American*, January 5, 1929; *Pittsburgh Courier*, January 5, 19, 1929.

50. *Pittsburgh Courier*, January 26, February 23, 1929; *Baltimore Afro-American*, March 2, 1929.

51. *Pittsburgh Courier*, January 26, 1929.

52. *Baltimore Afro-American*, March 2, 1929.

53. *Defender*, March 2, 1929; *Pittsburgh Courier*, March 2, June 8, 1929; *Baltimore Afro-American*, May 4, June 24, 1929.

54. *Baltimore Afro-American*, June 24, August 10, 1929.

55. *Defender*, July 13, 1929; *Baltimore Afro-American*, July 20, 1929.

56. *Baltimore Afro-American*, August 24, 1929; *Defender*, August 31, 1929; *Pittsburgh Courier*, August 31, September 7, 1929.

57. *Pittsburgh Courier*, September 28, 1929.

58. *Defender*, January 12, March 16, April 6, 1929. Two of Dave Malarcher's contracts are in the Baseball Hall of Fame and Museum at Cooperstown, NY. However, they contain no stipulations spelling out Malarcher's managerial duties. In 1926, Malarcher's salary called for $225 per month, and he received a $50 raise the following year. He received a $500 bonus at the end of each season.

59. *Defender*, April 6, 1929. For a secondary account of J. B. Martin's background, see Neil Lanctot, *Negro League Baseball: The Rise and Ruin of a Black Institution* (Philadelphia: University of Pennsylvania Press, 2004), 123–25.

60. *Defender*, April 6, 1929.

61. *Baltimore Afro-American*, June 15, 1929.

62. Ibid.

63. Ibid., August 2, 1930.

64. Ibid., August 9, 1930.

65. Bak, *Turkey Stearnes*, 184.

66. Ibid., 185–87.

67. Ibid., 187.

68. For accounts of Hueston's equalization plan for scheduling, see *Defender*, April 27, 1929, and *Pittsburgh Courier*, April 27, 1929.

12. The End of an Era

1. *Baltimore Afro-American*, March 1, 1930.

2. Ibid.

3. *Pittsburgh Courier*, February 22, April 12, 1930; *Baltimore Afro-American*, April 5, 12, 1930; *Defender* (Chicago), April 12, 1930.

4. *Baltimore Afro-American*, March 1, 1930; *Defender*, April 5, 1930.

5. *Pittsburgh Courier*, April 19, 1930.

6. Ibid., April 19, 26, 1930.

7. Neil Lanctot, *Fair Dealing and Clean Playing: The Hilldale Club and the Development of Black Professional Baseball, 1910–1932* (Jefferson, NC: McFarland, 1994), 209–11.

8. *Baltimore Afro-American*, June 7, 1930.

9. Ibid., June 7, July 12, 19, 1930.

10. For accounts of the plight of the Brotherhood of Sleeping Car Porters, see Herbert R. Northrup, *Organized Labor and the Negro* (New York: Harper and Brothers, 1944), and Philip Foner, *Organized Labor and the Black Worker, 1619–1973* (New York: International Publishers, 1974).

11. *Pittsburgh Courier*, June 28, July 5, 12, 1930.

12. Ibid., August 9, 1930. A disagreement occurred between Posey and Keenan regarding the division of gate receipts. See *Pittsburgh Courier*, August 16, 23, 30, 1930.

13. James A. Riley, *The Biographical Encyclopedia of the Negro Baseball Leagues* (New York: Carroll and Graf, 1994), 312–15.

14. *Baltimore Afro-American*, September 27, 1930; *Pittsburgh Courier*, September 27, 1930.

15. *Baltimore Afro-American*, October 4, 1930; *Pittsburgh Courier*, October 4, 1930.

16. *Pittsburgh Courier*, October 4, 1930.

17. Ibid., January 11, 18, 1930.

18. *Defender*, January 25, March 22, 1930; *Pittsburgh Courier*, January 25, 1930; *Baltimore Afro-American*, January 25, 1930.

19. *Defender*, January 25, March 22, 1930; *Pittsburgh Courier*, January 25, 1930; *Baltimore Afro-American*, January 25, 1930.

20. Taylor's commentary was published in several newspapers. See, for example, *Defender*, February 1, 1930; *Pittsburgh Courier*, February 1, 1930.

21. *Defender*, March 1, 1930.

22. *Baltimore Afro-American*, April 5, 1930.

23. For an account of the advent of night baseball and the Kansas City Monarchs, see Larry G. Bowman, "The Monarchs and Night Baseball," *National Pastime* 16 (1986): 80–84. For examples of night games as reported in the press, see *New York Times*, September 29, October 4, 1929, and *Washington Post*, September 29, 1930.

24. Janet Bruce, *The Kansas City Monarchs: Champions of Black Baseball* (Lawrence: University of Kansas Press, 1985), 68–70.

25. Bowman, "Monarchs," 81.

26. Ibid., 82.

27. *Defender*, August 23, 1930.

28. *Baltimore Afro-American*, August 2, 9, 1930.

29. *Defender*, December 13, 20, 1930.

30. For an account of the history of the Negro Leagues after 1931, see Neil Lanctot, *Negro League Baseball: The Rise and Ruin of a Black Institution* (Philadelphia: University of Pennsylvania Press, 2004).

31. Ibid. For an account of the East-West All-Star game, see Larry Lester, *Black Baseball's National Showcase: The East-West All-Star Game, 1933–1953* (Lincoln: University of Nebraska Press, 2001).

Bibliography

Manuscript Collections

The Ashland Collection. National Baseball Hall of Fame and Museum, Cooperstown, NY.
Frank Leland's Chicago Giants Baseball Club. National Baseball Hall of Fame and Museum, Cooperstown, NY.
Lloyd Thompson-Bill Cash Collection. Afro-American Historical and Cultural Museum, Philadelphia, PA.

Newspapers

Atlantic City Daily Press, 1915–17
Baltimore Afro-American, 1920–1931
Broad Ax, 1906–15
(Chicago) *Defender*, 1905–31
Chicago InterOcean, 1901–10
Chicago Tribune, 1901–20
Cleveland Advocate, 1919–20
(Indianapolis) *Freeman*, 1904–26
Indianapolis Ledger, 1913–15
Indianapolis Star, 1913–15
Kansas City Call, 1920–28
New York Age, 1907–30
New York Sun, 1901–10
New York Times, 1905–20
(Philadelphia) *Evening Item*, 1901–10
Philadelphia Tribune, 1912–30
Pittsburgh Courier, 1920–32

Sporting Life, 1901–10
St. Louis Argus, 1919–28

BOOKS AND ARTICLES

Alexander, Charles C. *Our Game: An American Baseball History*. New York: Henry Holt, 1991.
Bowman, Larry G. "The Monarchs and Night Baseball." *National Pastime* 16 (1986): 80–84.
Bruce, Janet. *The Kansas City Monarchs: Champions of Black Baseball*. Lawrence, KS: University Press of Kansas, 1985.
Burgos, Adrian. *Playing America's Game: Baseball, Latinos, and the Color Line*. Berkeley: University of California Press, 2007.
——— . "Entering Cuba's Other Playing Field: Cuban Baseball and the Choice between Race and Nation, 1887–1912." *Journal of Sport and Social Issues* 29 (February 2005): 9–40.
Butler, John Sibley. *Entrepreneurship and Self-Help among Black Americans: A Reconsideration of Race and Economics*. Albany, NY: State University of New York Press, 1991.
Dixon, Phil, and Patrick J. Hannigan. *The Negro Baseball Leagues 1867–1955*. Mattituck, NY: Ameron House, 1992.
Du Bois, W. E. B. *The Souls of Black Folk*. Rev. ed. New York: Penguin Books, 1996.
——— . *Dusk of Dawn*. New York: Harcourt, Brace, 1940.
——— , ed. *The Negro in Business: Report of a Social Study Made under the Direction of Atlanta University*. Atlanta, GA: Atlanta University, 1899.
Echevarria, Roberto Gonzalez. *The Pride of Havana: A History of Cuban Baseball*. New York: Oxford University Press, 1999.
Emery, Edwin. *The Press and America*. 3rd ed. Englewood Cliffs, NJ: Prentice-Hall, 1972.
Franklin, John Hope. *From Slavery to Freedom: A History of Negro Americans*. 5th ed. New York: Alfred A. Knopf, 1980.
Frazier, E. Franklin. *Black Bourgeoisie*. New York: Free Press, 1957.
Fullerton, Sam. *Sports Marketing*. Boston: McGraw-Hill Irwin, 2007.
Gaines, Kevin K. *Uplifting the Race: Black Leadership, Politics, and Culture in the Twentieth Century*. Chapel Hill: University of North Carolina Press, 1996.

Gosnell, Harold F. *Negro Politicians: The Rise of Negro Politics in Chicago.* Chicago: University of Chicago Press, 1935.

Gregg, Robert. *Sparks from the Anvil of Oppression: Philadelphia's African Methodists and Southern Migrants, 1890–1940.* Philadelphia: Temple University Press, 1993.

Grossman, James R. *Land of Hope: Chicago, Black Southerners, and the Great Migration.* Chicago: University of Chicago Press, 1989.

Harding, Vincent. *The Other American Revolution.* Los Angeles: Center for Afro-American Studies, 1980.

Hardy, Charles Ashley III. "Race and Opportunity: Black Philadelphia during the Era of the Great Migration, 1916–1930." PhD diss., Temple University, 1989.

Hardy, Stephen. "Entrepreneurs, Organizations, and the Sport Marketplace: Subjects in Search of Historians." *Journal of Sport History* 13 (Spring 1986): 14–33.

Harmon, J. H., Arnett G. Lindsey, and Carter G. Woodson. *The Negro as a Business Man.* College Park, MD: McGrath Publishing, 1929.

Harris, Abram L. *The Negro as Capitalist: A Study of Banking and Business among American Negroes.* Philadelphia: American Academy of Political And Social Science, 1936.

Harrison, Alferdteen, ed. *Black Exodus: The Great Migration from the American South.* Jackson: University Press of Mississippi, 1991.

Hogan, Lawrence D. *Shades of Glory: The Negro Leagues and the Story of African American Baseball.* Washington, DC: National Geographic, 2006.

Holway, John. *Blackball Stars: Negro League Pioneers.* New York: Carroll and Graff, 1988.

Katzman, David M. *Before the Ghetto: Black Detroit in the Nineteenth Century.* Chicago: University of Illinois Press, 1973.

Kusmer, Kenneth L. *A Ghetto Takes Shape: Black Cleveland, 1870–1930.* Chicago: University of Illinois Press, 1976.

Lanctot, Neil. *Fair Dealing and Clean Playing: The Hilldale Club and the Development of Black Professional Baseball, 1910–1932.* Jefferson, NC: McFarland, 1994.

Landry, Bart. *The New Black Middle Class.* Berkeley: University of California Press, 1987.

Lomax, Michael E. "Black Baseball Entrepreneurship in the Quaker City: The Philadelphia Giants and the Rise and Fall of the NACBC." *Sport History Review* 37 (2006): 100–29.

———. *Black Baseball Entrepreneurs, 1860–1901: Operating by Any Means Necessary.* Syracuse, NY: Syracuse University Press, 2003.

———. "'If He Were White': Black and Cuban Players in Organized Baseball, 1880–1920." *Journal of African American Men* 3 (1998): 31–44.

———. "Black Entrepreneurship in the National Pastime: The Rise of Semiprofessional Baseball in Black Chicago, 1890–1915." *Journal of Sport History* 25 (Spring 1998): 43–63.

———. "Black Baseball's First Rivalry: The Cuban Giants versus the Gorhams of New York and the Birth of the Colored Championship." *Sport History Review* 28 (November 1997): 134–45.

Marable, Manning. *How Capitalism Underdeveloped Black America: Problems in Race, Political Economy, and Society.* Boston: South End Press, 1983.

Masterlexis, Lisa P., Carol A. Barr, and Mary A. Hums, eds. *Principles and Practice of Sport Management.* Gaithersburg, MD: Aspen Pub. Inc., 1998.

Meier, August. *Negro Thought in America, 1880–1915.* Ann Arbor: University of Michigan Press, 1964.

Milne, George R., and Mark A. McDonald. *Sport Marketing: Managing the Exchange Process.* Boston: Jones and Bartlett, 1999.

Moses, Wilson Jeremiah. *The Golden Age of Black Nationalism, 1850–1925.* Hamden, CT: Archon Books, 1978.

Mullin, Bernard J., Stephen Hardy, and William A. Sutton. *Sport Marketing.* 3rd ed. Champaign, IL: Human Kinetics, 2007.

Neale, Walter C. "The Peculiar Economics of Professional Sports: A Contribution to the Theory of the Firm in Sporting Competition and in Market Competition." *Quarterly Journal of Economics* 1 (1964): 1–14.

Oak, Vishnu V. *The Negro's Adventure in General Business.* Yellow Springs, OH: Antioch Press, 1949.

Ofari, Earl. *The Myth of Black Capitalism.* New York: Monthly Review Press, 1970.

Osofsky, Gilbert. *Harlem: The Making of a Ghetto.* New York: Oxford University Press, 1966.

Osthaus, Carl R. "The Rise and Fall of Jesse Binga, Black Financier." *Journal of Negro History* 58 (January 1973): 39–60.

Peterson, Robert. *Only the Ball Was White.* New York: Oxford University Press, 1970.

Riley, James A. *The Biographical Encyclopedia of the Negro Baseball Leagues.* New York: Carroll and Graff, 1994.

Riess, Steven A. *Touching Base: Professional Baseball and American Culture in the Progressive Era.* Urbana: University of Illinois Press, 1999.

Ruck, Rob. *Sandlot Seasons: Sport in Black Pittsburgh.* Urbana: University of Illinois Press, 1987.

Scheiner, Seth M. *Negro Mecca: A History of the Negro in New York City, 1865–1920.* New York: New York University Press, 1965.

Schmidt, Ray. "The Golden Age of Chicago Baseball." *Chicago History* 29 (Winter 2000): 38–59.

Seymour, Harold. *Baseball: The Golden Age.* New York: Oxford University Press, 1970.

Shank, Matthew D. *Sports Marketing: A Strategic Perspective.* Upper Saddle River, NJ: Prentice Hall, 2002.

Spear, Allan H. *Black Chicago: The Making of a Negro Ghetto, 1890–1920.* Chicago: University of Chicago Press, 1967.

Suggs, Henry Lewis, ed. *The Black Press in the Middle West, 1865–1985.* Westport, CT: Greenwood Press, 1996.

Vincent, Ted. *Mudville's Revenge: The Rise and Fall of American Sport.* New York: Seaview Books, 1981.

Vincent, Theodore G., ed. *Voices of a Black Nation: Political Journalism in the Harlem Renaissance.* San Francisco: Ramparts Press, 1973.

Vogel, Todd, ed. *The Black Press: New Literary and Historical Essays.* New Brunswick, NJ: Rutgers University Press, 2001.

Voigt, David Q. *American Baseball: From the Commissioners to Continental Expansion.* University Park: Pennsylvania State University Press, 1983.

Walker, Juliet E. K. *The History of Black Business in America: Capitalism, Race, Entrepreneurship.* New York: Macmillan Library Reference, 1998.

Washington, Booker T. *The Negro in Business.* 1907. Reprint, Chicago: Afro-American Press, 1969.

———. *Up From Slavery: An Autobiography.* New York: Doubleday, Page, 1902.

Index

Aaron, Henry, 425
Abbott, Robert, 123, 168, 179, 347
AC Cyclones, 203
Acosta, Jose, 261
Afro-American Realty Company, 142
Akin, Edward N., 175
Alexander, Grover Cleveland, 116
Algona Brownies, 24
All Cubans, 4, 13, 14, 15, 19, 20, 21, 432
Allen, Newt, 316, 317, 318, 339
Allen, Thomas W., 123, 124
All-Havanas, 57, 70, 77, 78, 80, 95, 439
All Leaguers, 110
All Nationals team, 208
All Nations team, 177, 249–50, 454
Almeida, Rafael, 57, 67
Almendares Blues, 67, 115, 177
Amateur Manager's Baseball League (AMBL), 24, 45
American Association (AA), 90, 162, 293,
American Federation of Labor, 409
American Negro League (ANL), 372, 397, 398, 403, 404, 406; disbands, 405; formation, 395
Anchor Giants, 189
Anderson, Bert, 54
Anderson, Louie, 179, 367

Anderson, William, 196
Andrews, Lefty (Pop), 31, 434
Anson, Cap, 44, 63, 320; forms Anson's Colts, 45
Anson's Colts, 44, 48, 57, 58, 91
Ardmore Tigers, 189, 191
Armbruster, Harry, 37
Armour, Philip, 98
Artesians, 44
Athletics club, 89
Atlantic City Baseball League (ACBL), 203, 204, 205
Attel, Abe, 107
Augustine, Leon, 293
Avendorph, Julius, 23, 130, 133

Bacharach, Harry, 202
Bacharach Giants, xiii, xvi, 173, 202–10, 242, 253, 260–65, 272, 274, 276, 282, 283, 286, 289, 290, 291, 310, 329, 331, 336, 337, 342, 351, 353–56, 365, 367, 372, 375, 383, 385–88, 397, 398, 406, 419, 421, 453, 456; 1926 Colored World Series, 357; 1927 Colored World Series, 368; named after Mayor Harry Bacharach, 202
Bacharach Giants Athletic Association, 330, 365, 383

477

Baldwin, F. D., 33, 34, 35
Ball, Phil De Catesby, 180–81, 267; blocks St. Louis Giants from using Federal League Park, 181
Ball, Walter, 19, 47, 77, 93, 96, 108, 120, 121, 122, 199, 254
Baltimore Black Sox, xvi, 203, 204, 261, 273, 276, 283, 303, 307, 329, 336, 349, 350, 372, 383, 386, 387, 388, 395, 404, 408; ANL pennant, 398; benefit game with Lincoln Giants, 408; in car accident, 366; early origins, 284
Baltimore Elite Giants, 423, 424
Baltimore Giants of Newark, 36
Baltimore Orioles, 64
Banks, Ernie, 425
Barber, Jesse, 130, 154, 155
Barbour, Jess, 252, 253
Barnett, Richard, 181
Baro, Bernardo, 177
Barrow, Ed, 15, 431
Bartley, Bill, 37
Barton, Bert, 200
Barton, Sherman, 43, 122, 124
Basken, Harry, 179
Batchman, J. M., 278–79, 281–82
Bauchman, Harry, 158, 159
Bayside club, 12
Beadle Dime Baseball Player, 58
Beckwith, Carl, 304, 315, 319–20, 328, 342, 362, 462; assessment of Negro Leagues, 375–76; critiques Frank Young's assessment of Colored World Series, 358–59
Beckwith, John, 199, 254, 260, 295, 297, 298, 385, 410; signs with Baltimore Black Sox, 298
Bejerano, Augustin, 397
Bell, Cliff, 339, 340

Bell, James (Papa), 392, 393; early background, 392
Bell, William, 12, 317, 318, 339, 340
Bender, Charles (Chief), 117
Bernhard, Bill, 10
Big Six, 203
Binga, Jesse, 142, 446
Binga, William, 11, 26, 43, 66, 431
Birmingham Black Barons, 273, 292, 297, 299, 300, 326, 327, 343, 345, 397, 413, 416, 417
Birmingham Giants, 48
Blackmon, Henry, 297
Black Sox Baseball and Exhibition Club, 284
Blount, John (Tenny), 172, 250, 273, 293, 300, 307, 310, 313, 314, 322, 323, 324, 326, 346, 379, 401; censured by NNL, 322–23; Detroit Stars' manager, 200; skips league games, 306
Board of Trade League, 24
Bolden, Ed, xv, xvi, xvii, 172–73, 188, 190, 193–94, 201, 241–43, 252–54, 257, 260, 262–63, 268, 271–72, 275, 280, 283, 285–87, 289, 296, 302, 303, 307, 309, 310, 313–14, 317, 321, 329, 338–40, 342, 343, 344, 350, 352, 354, 357–58, 363, 365, 371, 372, 375, 377, 384, 385, 387–90, 395, 397, 404–8, 418, 420, 421, 423, 425, 455, 457, 464; attempts to remove from chairmanship, 349; business alliance with Nat Strong, 330; challenged by Nat Strong, 196–97; Charleston's criticism, 335–36; criticized for Dallas hiring, 332–33; early background, 188–89; ECL Chairman, 283; Foster's critique of ECL, 287–88;

HBEC, 192–93; hires Bill Dallas as supervisor of umpires, 331–32; nervous breakdown, 366; president of ANL, 395; president of HBEC, 385; resignation as NNL associate member, 282–83; secretary-treasurer of ECL, 384; withdraws Hilldale A. C. from ECL, 385, 386
Bolling, Jesse, 123, 124
Booker, Pete, 47, 77–78, 83, 99, 106
Boston Beaneaters, 74
Boston Monarchs, 6
Boston Red Sox, 10–11, 15, 45, 311
Bowman, Emmett, 17, 66, 77, 86, 90, 110
Bowser, Thomas, 150, 152, 158, 163–64
Boyd, Ben, 59
Bradley, Phil, 106, 113, 114
Branding, 167, 448
Breakers Hotel, 155, 175
Briggs, Otto, 194, 262, 316, 317, 339, 340, 406; signed as Hilldale's first professional player, 194
Bright, John (J. M.), 18, 19, 39, 59, 73, 77, 81, 87, 88, 111, 114
Britt, George, 410, 411
Brooklyn Dodgers, 146, 173
Brooklyn Royal Giants, 17, 28, 32, 37, 39, 43, 46, 69, 72, 76, 77, 80, 84, 86, 88, 104, 105, 111, 112, 116, 117, 132, 135, 147, 149, 156, 161, 170, 172, 185, 194, 195, 199, 202, 204, 206, 242, 251, 253, 262, 276, 283, 286, 287, 289, 290, 299, 307, 329, 336, 350, 353, 375, 383, 387, 395, 421, 444, 448; expelled from ECL then reinstated, 298; and Nat Strong, 115
Brooklyn Stars, 386, 387

Brotherhood of Sleeping Car Porters, 404, 408–9, 469
Brown, Dave, 262, 290
Brown, George, 154
Brown, Jim, 367, 398
Brown, Mordecai (Three Finger), 92, 120
Brush, John, 311–12
Buckner, Harry, 11, 14, 84, 86, 106, 113, 114, 431
Burk, Robert, 61
Bush, Joe (Bullet), 195, 198
Bush, Joseph (Ownie), 155, 162–63
Bushwicks club, 286
business-alliance model, 380, 420, 422; defined, 380–81
Bustamente, Luis, 57, 68, 82
Butler, Randolph (Ran), 54
Byrd, James, 196; attempts to oust Bolden, 405

California Winter League (CWL), 73, 96–97, 102, 105, 118, 120, 129, 166, 168, 278, 362, 441, 444; early origins, 97
Callahan, Jimmy, 38, 44, 49, 58, 82, 125, 295; early background, 44
Camden club, 59
Campbell, Andrew, 23
Camps, Manuel, 37, 39
Cannady. Walter (Rev), 352, 385, 410, 411
Capital City club, 5, 22
Carey, Archibald, 142
Carr, George, 290, 388, 397
Carr, Tank, 339, 340
Carter, Charles (Kid), 8, 11, 12, 13
Cedars, 34
Central Islip, 107

Chacon, Pelayo, 157, 397
Chalmers, George, 117
Chance, Frank, 82, 92, 202, 255
Charleston, Oscar, xi, 157, 163, 175, 179, 182, 251, 252, 254, 260, 310, 337, 349, 361–62, 373, 385, 406, 410; criticism of ECL, 334–36; early background, 156; player-manager of Harrisburg Giants, 297
Charleston, Porter, 406
Chase, Hal, 60, 97, 115, 208, 453
Chateau De La Plaisance, 54, 88, 92
Chicago Amateur Baseball Association (CABA), 24
Chicago American Giants, xiii, xiv, 104, 105, 109, 110, 112, 116, 120–22, 127–29, 135, 136, 139, 143, 150, 151, 153, 155, 162, 167, 170–72, 175–79, 183, 185, 197–201, 208–12, 245, 250, 254, 262–64, 269, 274, 275, 277, 281, 291–94, 296, 297, 299, 306, 326, 327, 342, 343, 345, 347, 354–56, 364, 365, 367, 372, 384, 391, 398, 399, 412, 413, 415–19, 421, 423, 424, 444, 447, 448, 450, 460; 1915–16 barnstorming tour, 166–69; 1926 Colored World Series, 357; 1927 Colored World Series, 368; against Lincoln Giants for colored championship, 132–33; rivalry with Indianapolis ABCs, 157–61, 164–67; against St. Louis Stars for NNL league championship, 391–94
Chicago City League, 73, 89, 90, 91, 92, 94, 95, 97, 102, 333; bans playing black and Cuban clubs, 95; lawsuit with Chicago Giants, 94
Chicago Cubs, 73, 92, 102, 444

Chicago Giants, 26, 73, 94, 95, 96, 98, 102, 105, 108, 112, 118, 119, 120–24, 127, 129, 135, 178, 198–99, 250, 251, 254, 266, 274, 367, 441, 442, 452
Chicago Giants Rooter's Club, 96, 441
Chicago Union Giants, 4, 11, 22, 24, 32
Chicago Unions, 3, 4, 11, 24, 98, 144, 146, 432
Chicago White Sox (White Stockings), 44, 49, 92, 146, 261, 320, 461
Chicopee Falls club, 177
Cincinnati Reds, 57, 274
Clark, C. T., 174
Clark, Speco, 290
Clark, William, 349, 354, 377, 395
Cleveland Americans, 10
Cleveland Browns, 273, 299, 300, 322, 326, 344
Cleveland Indians, 324
Cleveland Tate Stars, 274, 280, 282, 292, 392
Cobb, Lorenzo S., 250, 288
Cobb, Ty, 60, 72, 75, 119, 155, 351
Cockerell, Phil, 261, 263, 264, 316, 317, 340, 352–53, 406
Cogan, Dick, 114, 443
Cogan's Smart Set, 114, 134, 136
Cole, Robert, 424
Collins, Eddie, 75
Colored World Series, 308–12, 314, 315, 319, 320, 340, 341, 343, 354, 366, 368, 369, 380
Columbia Giants, 4, 11, 23, 24, 65
Columbia League, 45
Columbus Blue Birds, 423
Columbus Buckeyes, 259, 262, 263, 274, 276
Comiskey, Charles, 23, 65, 146

Commercial League, 24, 25
Connor, John, xvii, 29–30, 31, 36, 39, 72, 81, 84, 86, 87, 104–6, 110, 112, 114, 115, 117, 170, 173, 186, 188, 201, 209, 211, 242–42, 248, 251, 252, 260–61, 270, 272, 276, 277, 286, 289, 290, 291, 307, 346, 418, 425, 440, 454, 455; alliance with Tucker and Jackson, 205; death, 290; denies Grant Johnson partnership, 86–87; early background, 30; lease on Harlem Oval, 110–11; negotiation with Charles Ebbets to use Ebbets Field, 208;
Cook, Walter, 59
Cooper, Andy, 362, 363; test five-year suspension from Organized Black Baseball, 362
Cooper, McDonald, 406
Cooper, Sam, 385
Cosmopolitans, 9, 37
Coveleski, Frank, 75
Cravath, Gavy, 116
Crawford, Sam, 110, 161, 251, 299
Crelin, Wilbur, 348–49
Croker, Richard, 35
Cuba libre, 20
Cuban Giants (Genuine), 6, 7, 19, 23, 37, 39, 59, 62, 69, 76, 77, 78, 80, 86, 87, 144, 185, 212, 431, 432; disbands, 114
Cuban National League (CNL), 19
Cuban Stars (East), 37, 39, 76, 80, 82–84, 87, 88, 95, 109, 111, 135, 136, 139, 149, 150, 161, 170, 171, 175, 180, 185, 187, 194, 242, 251, 253, 263, 276, 283, 285, 290, 299, 329, 350, 353, 354, 360, 372, 375, 387, 395, 397, 398, 421, 439

Cuban Stars (West), 129, 156–57, 161, 176–77, 178, 184–85, 251, 259–60, 266, 274, 291, 294, 300, 326, 327, 343, 345, 347, 361, 364, 377, 378, 421
Cuban Stars of Santiago de Cuba, 36
Cuban Winter League, 397
Cuban X Giants, xiii, 3, 4, 6–9, 14, 15, 17–23, 26, 28, 34, 37, 39, 41, 43, 46–48, 59, 66, 69, 144, 167, 199, 261, 419, 432; against Philadelphia Giants for colored championship, 9, 12, 16
Cummings, Napoleon, 202, 203, 262, 355
Currie, Rube, 339, 340, 356
Cusack, George S., 24

Dallas, Bill, 310, 332, 333, 334, 338, 351, 395; supervisor of ECL umpires, 331–32
Daniels, Hammond, 330, 353, 365; Bacharach Giants' commissioner, 330
Daus, George, 155
Davids, Bob, 349, 351
Davis, Walter, 367, 393
Day, Connie, 297
Dayton Marcos, 199, 242, 250, 254, 259, 299, 344, 390; formation of, 199
Dean, Nelson, 339
Deas, James (Yank), 202, 253
Demmitt, Ray, 295
DeMoss, Elwood (Bingo), 156, 163, 175, 262, 264, 355
DePriest, Oscar, 179
Despert, Denny, 278
Detroit Clowns, 324

Detroit Stars, xv, 172, 250, 254, 263, 273, 274, 277, 291, 293, 297, 303, 306, 324, 326, 327, 372, 391, 404–5, 413, 423, 452; formation of, 199–200
Detroit Tigers, 92, 100, 295–96
Devery, William, 35
Dilworth, Arthur, 202, 203
Dimick, E. N., 174
Dismukes, William (Dizzy), 156, 157, 179, 183, 298, 414
Dixon, George, 179, 264
Dixon, Herbert (Rap), 362, 385, 409, 416; test five-year suspension from Organized Black Baseball, 362
Dixon, Randy, 396
Doby, Larry, 425
Donahue's Red Sox, 94, 95
Donaldson, Billy, 278, 327; first African American umpire, 293
Donaldson, John, 249, 251
Donigan, Al, 98
Donlin, Mike, 49, 436
Donlin's All-Stars, 49, 50, 106
Doughtery, Pat, 92, 99, 120, 121, 122, 129, 130
Douglass, Frederick, 51
Downs, McKinley (Bunny), 194, 195, 262
Doyle, Larry, 115
Doyles, 97
Drake, Bill, 339
Drucke, Louis, 115
Du Bois, W. E. B., 51, 140, 141, 152; Negro National Business League, 140–41
Duggleby, Bill, 13
Duncan, Frank, 119, 122, 132, 316, 318, 339, 363; test five-year suspension from Organized Black Baseball, 362
Duval Giants, 202
Dykes, John B., 365

Earle, Frank, 84, 85, 86, 110, 112, 132, 185, 204
Earl Mack's All Stars, 116
Eastern All Stars of Philadelphia, 386; renamed Philadelphia Tigers, 386
Eastern Colored League (ECL), xv, 187, 203, 272, 273, 290, 291, 296–97, 299, 302–4, 307–12, 314, 321, 329–31, 334, 336–38, 341–43, 348–50, 352, 354, 359, 360, 366, 369–71, 373, 376, 382, 384, 388, 396, 422–24, 460; disbands, 382–87; formation of, 283–91; luring players from NNL, 289–90, 297–98. *See also* Mutual Association of Eastern Colored Baseball Clubs
Eastern League, 15, 44, 431
Eastern Sports Writers Association (ESWA), 388
Ebbets, Charles, 146, 173, 208, 289
Ebbets Field, 173, 208, 209, 241, 251–53, 261, 263, 454
Eclipse, 125
economic cooperation, 6
Ed Bolden's Hillsdale Club, 406
Edwards, Phil, 409
Eggleston, Mark, 290
Elias Bureau, 382
Elite of Nashville, Tennessee, 400, 414–15
Elmwood F. C., 33
Emanuel, William, 124
Embry, William, 293

Emery, Jack, 31, 32, 434
equalization plan, 402–3, 468
Evergreen Hall club, 191
Evers, Johnny, 82, 92, 255, 445

Falls City Club, 5
Farrell, Frank J. 35, 443
Farrell, Luther, 367, 410, 411
Fe club, 47
Federal League, 153, 154–55, 181, 443
Federal League All-Stars, 168
Fernandez, Rodolfo, 194
Ferrance, W. S., 288, 307
Figarola, Jose, 57, 157
five-year suspension from Organized Black Baseball, 344, 366, 375
Flagler, Henry Morrison, 173–76
Flag Raising Day, 96
Flemings' ABCs, 177, 182
Flinn, Dan, 195
Fogel, Horace, 255
Footes, Robert, 11, 431
Force, William, 303
Foster, Andrew (Rube), xi, xiv–xvii, 12–14, 23, 29, 38, 45, 46, 49–50, 51, 53, 59, 70, 73, 77, 78, 83, 89, 90, 92, 93, 99, 104, 105, 109, 110, 119–23, 125, 128, 130–31, 139–40, 146–47, 150, 153, 157–58, 160, 162, 164–65, 170–172, 175, 176, 178–83, 188, 190, 193, 197–99, 201, 208, 209, 212, 213, 241–43, 250, 252–54, 257, 259, 264, 271, 272, 274, 275, 279–82, 290, 291, 293, 295, 296, 299, 301–10, 313–15, 317, 319, 322–24, 327, 328, 339, 341, 342, 344, 346, 348, 355, 361, 365, 366, 373, 375, 379, 380, 381, 394, 407, 417, 420, 421, 425, 436, 440, 441, 444, 446, 449, 452, 454, 456, 462, 466; assessment of 1924 Colored World Series, 320–21; barnstorming tours, 166–69, 178; booking agent, 129; call for black clubs to organize, 125–26, 134–37; death of, 418; early background, 46–48; fires African American umpires, 328–29; forms Chicago American Giants, 117–19; media campaign to oust Tenny Blount, 325; nervous breakdown, 346–47; peace settlement with ECL, 314; "Pitfalls of Baseball," 244–49; propaganda war against ECL, 285–87; and state of black baseball (1921), 265–70
Foster, Sarah, 365
Foster, Willie, 355, 356–57, 367, 368, 392, 393, 394
Fowler, Bud, 15, 24, 63
Francis, Billy, 66, 106, 113, 252, 260, 262
Fraser, Chick, 10
Frederick Douglass Hospital, 14–15
Freedman, Andrew, 35
Freeman, Buck, 11, 431
Freeman, Charles, 195, 384; attempts to oust Bolden, 405; replaces Ed Bolden as HBEC chairman, 366; resigns from HBEC, 385
Freihoffer, William, 37, 79
French, Charlie, 155, 168
French Lick Plutos, 129, 136

Gaillard, Edward S., 55
Gal, J. E., 249
Gans, Jude, 114, 132, 133, 167, 179

Gardner, Floyd (Jelly), 355, 357, 365, 384, 398
Gardner, Ping, 397, 406
Garrett, Alvin H., 23, 73, 93, 94
Gatewood, Bill, 43, 46, 47, 83, 107–8, 120, 130, 133, 206, 252, 275
Gholston, Bert, 293
Gibson, Bill, 387–88, 395–96, 405, 408, 423; attempts to form new league, 408
Gibson, Josh, 410, 411; early career, 410
Gillmore, James, 154
Gilmore, Quincy J., 250, 344, 361, 363, 364, 372, 459; conflict with (Chicago) *Defender*, 347–48; leaves NNL, 399
Gonzales, Geravacio (Strike), 177
Goodgame, John, 112
Goodwin, Lonnie, 362
Gorhams of New York, 6, 59
Gottlieb, Eddie, 283, 423
Govantes, Manuel, 82
Govern, S. K., 59
Grace Sunday School, 128
Grand Central Baseball Club (Red Caps), 185–86, 187, 206
Grant, Charlie, 12, 64–65, 438
Grant, Frank, 7, 8, 63, 199
Grant, Leroy, 119, 133, 179
Grant Manufacturing Company, 415
Great Depression, 138, 176, 423, 450
Great Migration, xiv, xv, 172, 178–79, 180, 191–92, 258, 420
Green, Charles (Joe), 26, 92, 93, 120, 198, 250, 254; ownership of Chicago Giants, 136
Greenlee, Gus, 423; East-West All-Star game, 423–24

Grier, Claude (Red), 356
Griffith, Clark, 20
Grossman, James, 168
Gunther, Charles F., 44, 82, 112
Gunthers, 38, 44, 48, 82, 91, 94, 95, 112, 124, 125
Guy Empey's Treat 'Em Roughs, 208, 209

Haddington, 33
Hal Chase's All Stars, 115
Hall, Blainey, 175
Hamey, George, 399
Hammond club, 333
Harding, Vincent, 99
Hardy, Bill, 185–86
Hardy, Stephen, 58
Harris, Nate, 25–26, 43, 46, 47, 93, 124
Harris, Vic, 344, 410, 411
Harrisburg Giants, 273, 296, 329, 331, 334, 336, 349–52, 354, 377, 383; withdrawal from ECL, 385
Harrison, Abe, 59
Harvey, Charles, 148, 207
Harvey, Frank (Lefty), 185, 204
Harvey, George, 367
Haskell Institute for Indians, 415
Havana Cubans, 177
Havana Reds, 57, 66, 67, 115, 119
Havana Stars of Cuba, 37
Hawkins, Lemuel, 316, 317, 339, 393
Haynes, J. H., 181
Hearst, William Randolph, 256
Henderson, Arthur (Rats), 356
Henry, Ed, 360
Hensley, Logan, 393
Herrmann, August, 172

Hewitt, Joe, 107, 175, 200, 204, 275
Heydler, John, 255
Hicaugo Giants, 177
Hildalgo, Heliodoro, 67
Hill, Pete, 13, 15, 66, 99, 119, 121, 130, 157, 167, 172, 298; Baltimore Black Sox manager, 297; Detroit Stars' field manager, 200
Hilldale Athletic Club, xiii, 241–42, 172, 188–92, 198, 200–201, 208, 210, 253, 260, 262, 263–64, 265, 269, 272, 274, 275, 277, 283, 290–91, 302, 307, 310, 314–16, 319, 329–31, 334, 336, 339, 340, 343, 351, 353, 357, 366, 372, 384, 387, 397, 398, 404, 421; 1924 Colored World Series, 318; 1925 Colored World Series, 340; hostile takeover of, 405. *See also* Hilldale Baseball and Exhibition Company
Hilldale Baseball and Exhibition Company (HBEC), xviii, 173, 198, 200, 242, 253, 254, 275, 276, 283, 286, 307, 366, 384, 386, 407, 452, 457; formation of, 192–93; NNL associate member, 260
Hillebrand, Arthur (Doc), 49
Himes, Willie, 399
History of Colored Baseball, 37, 41, 57, 58, 80; analysis of, 58–66
Holland, Billy, 26, 31, 43, 46, 264, 410, 411, 434
Holt, George, 179
Homestead Grays, 273, 297–98, 344, 362, 363, 371, 372, 377, 387, 400, 406, 408, 410–11, 412, 423
Hooper, George, 292, 300
Horn, Will, 14, 43
Hornsby, Rogers, 319

Hotel League, 180, 450
Howe, John, 332, 334–35, 363; assessment of Gilmore/*Defender* conflict, 348
Howe News Bureau, 382
Hoyt, Waite, 293
Hubbard, Jesse, 368, 406
Hudspeth, Bob (High Pockets), 274, 289
Hueston, William C., 360–61, 363, 364, 366, 372–73, 389, 394, 398, 400–405, 408, 412–13, 417, 468; answers critics about state of NNL, 414–15; NNL president, 360–61; promotion of NNL, 390–91; resigns from NNL, 417
Hughes Tom (Long), 44
Hutchinson, Fred, 121, 130, 133

Ideal Travelers, 189
Indianapolis ABCs, xiii, 55, 76, 136, 150, 170–72, 175, 177–80, 194, 199, 210–12, 250, 254, 263, 271, 273–75, 291, 297, 300, 326, 355, 378, 379, 400, 419, 421, 447, 448, 450, 459; dropped from NNL, 304–5; rivalry with Chicago American Giants, 157–61, 164
Indianapolis Feds, 155
Indianapolis Indians, 162, 183, 451
Interborough League, 191
Intercity Association (IA), 33, 34, 35, 70, 80, 149, 187
Intercity Baseball Association (IBA), 4, 24, 42, 43, 45; Unions-Union Giants dispute, 25
Inter-City League, 101
International League (IL), 15, 349

International League of Colored Baseball Clubs in America and Cuba (ILBCAC), 37, 79, 80, 81
Interstate League, 351; disbands, 354
Irvin, Monte, 425
Irwin, Arthur, 74–75

Jackson, Jumbo, 367, 393
Jackson, Ollie, 107
Jackson, Robert R., 52, 73, 89, 93, 94, 95, 118, 122, 367; early background, 52–53
Jackson, Stanford, 398
Jackson, Thomas, xvii, 173, 204, 205, 276, 283, 286, 289, 307, 418, 425; alliance with Connor and Wilkins, 205; lures Duval Giants to Atlantic City, 202; replaced by Hammond Daniels, 330
James, Gus, 31, 84, 86, 114, 434
Jamison, Caesar, 293, 328
Jefferson Grays, 23
Jeffries, Harry, 290
Jeffries, Jim, 126
Jenkins, Fats, 385, 388, 410
Jenkins, Horace, 153
Jenkins, Thomas, 195; replaces Lloyd Thompson as HBEC secretary, 386
Jewel, Warner, 326
Jewel's ABCs, 182
Jimenez, Bienvenido (Hooks), 261
Jimmy Callahan's All Star team, 96
Johnson, Byron Bancroft (Ban), 5, 10, 35, 44, 154, 193, 255, 312, 329, 351, 369, 430, 460; elevated status of umpires, 279–80
Johnson, George, 339, 340
Johnson, George (Chappie), 13, 93, 108; early background, 199

Johnson, Grant (Home Run), 15, 31, 73, 86, 95, 99; 115, 122, 149, 199; refused partnership of Brooklyn Royal Giants, 86–87
Johnson, Jack, 16, 126
Johnson, Louis (Dicta), 153
Johnson, Oscar (Heavy), 316, 317, 318
Johnson, Tom, 175, 199, 264, 293
Johnson, Wade, 297
Johnson, Walter, 75, 97, 110, 369
Johnson, William Junious (Judy), 316, 318, 339, 406, 410, 411
Jones, Fielder, 44
Jones, William (Fox), 352, 355
Joseph, Newt, 316, 339, 340
Junco, Jose, 177

Kansas City Blues, 293
Kansas City Giants, 111–12, 136
Kansas City Monarchs, xv, 250, 274, 277, 287, 291, 292, 299, 300, 310, 311, 314, 316, 319, 326, 327, 339, 347, 354, 357, 362, 376, 392, 401, 416, 459; 1924 Colored World Series, 318; 1925 Colored World Series, 340
Keary, Jack, 22, 42
Keenan, James J., 139, 170, 187, 197, 201, 202, 206–7, 211, 251–52, 256, 273, 283, 286, 289, 290, 296, 330, 333, 337–38, 342, 344, 349, 352, 353, 360, 364, 383, 386, 387, 388, 396, 404, 409, 412, 469; alliance with Nat Strong, 149; ECL Secretary, 283; ownership of Lincoln Giants, 148; refuses to return Alonzo Montalvo to NNL, 364; remodels Protectory Oval, 297; returns to ECL, 384; rift with Nat

Strong, 353–54; ten-game series with Cumberland Posey, 410; vice-president of ANL, 395; withdrew Lincoln Giants from ECL, 365
Kemp, George, 190, 196
Kennedy, M. J., 146
Kensington Congs, 388
Kent, Richard W., 274
Kenyon, Harry, 297
Keyes, George Barnard, 322, 324; sold interest in St. Louis Stars, 417
Keystone Giants of Philadelphia, 36
Killilea, Matt, 430
Kimbrough, Thomas, 195
Kindle, Bill, 132–33
Kirke, Jay, 183
Klem, Bill, 293
Knox, Elwood C., 54, 55, 251
Kuebler, Conrad, 147

Ladies Day, 107
Lajoie, Napoleon, 10
Lake Shore League, 45
Lamar, Edward B. (E. B.), 4, 7, 9, 10, 16–17, 18, 19, 26, 39, 66–67, 79, 81, 82, 111, 261, 284; partnership with Linares, 21
Lambert, Doc, 80
Lancaster, Edward, 55, 254
Lancaster, Ray, 409
Lanctot, Neil, 188, 333
Landis, Kennesaw Mountain, 314, 364, 466
Landsdowne club, 190
Lang, John, 59
Langford, Sam, 107
Lawson, Al, 74
Leach, Tommy, 75
Lee, Holsey (Scrip), 318

Leland, Frank, 4, 21, 23, 26, 28, 42, 46, 52, 53, 54, 56, 70, 73, 89, 95–96, 97, 101, 102, 108, 118, 119, 120, 122, 198, 418, 441; death of, 122; early background, 22; formation of Chicago Giants, 93; formation of National Colored League, 55; split with William Peters, 22; sued by LGBBA, 94; Unions-Union Giants dispute, 25
Leland Giants, xiii, xiv, 4, 25, 28, 29, 31, 32, 38, 42, 44, 46, 48, 50, 51, 55, 66, 70, 71, 72, 74, 76, 77, 82, 83, 85–88, 90–92, 95, 99, 101, 105, 122, 124, 125, 127, 128, 135, 167, 199, 286, 419, 441, 447; benefit game for Provident Hospital, 98. *See also* Leland Giants Baseball and Amusement Association
Leland Giants Baseball and Amusement Association (LGBBA), 29, 42, 53, 56, 71, 73, 74, 88, 92–93, 98, 99, 101, 105, 118, 119, 122, 124, 128, 131, 146, 441; court case against Leland, 94; early formation, 53
Leland Giants Booster Club (LGBC), 123
Leland Giants Rooters Club, 98
Lewis, Billy, 161, 164, 182, 183, 184, 450
Lewis, Cary B., 55, 244, 251
Lewis, Ira, 254, 323
Lewis, Joe, 318
Lewis, R. S., 390
Linares, Abel, 4, 19, 21, 36, 67, 87; partnership with Lamar, 21; *Sporting Life*, 20
Lincoln Giants, xvi, 104, 106–9, 111–16, 120, 131, 135–36, 144, 147, 149, 155, 170, 175, 180, 202, 206,

Lincoln Giants (*cont.*)
208, 209, 251, 254, 262, 267, 273, 276, 278, 283, 298, 329, 336, 337, 338, 343, 349, 350, 352, 364, 371, 372, 376, 383, 386, 387, 388, 395, 404, 406, 408, 410–12, 419, 442, 445, 454; against American Giants for colored championship, 132–33; benefit game with Baltimore Black Sox, 408; disbands, 412

Lincoln Stars, 139, 147–50, 155, 194, 206

Lindsey, Bill (Kansas Cyclone), 120, 121, 122, 130, 133, 444

Lloyd, John Henry, xi, 41, 78, 83, 86, 87, 95, 99, 106, 132, 155, 167, 170, 175, 179, 207, 274, 276, 286, 289, 352, 371, 380, 410, 411, 436, 438, 440, 443; assessment of ECL, 376–77; early background, 66; Lincoln Giants manager, 109; Lincoln's player-manager, 112–13

Lockhart, Hubert, 357, 398

Logan Squares, 38, 44, 48, 57, 82, 89, 91, 95, 125, 295

Loughlin, 109

Louis, Joe, 423

Louisville Giants, 48, 55, 85

Lucas, Smithie, 386, 387

Lundy, Richard (Dick), 195, 253, 262, 276, 355; early career, 203

Lyons, Jimmie, 107, 108, 251, 262, 264, 288

Lytle, Clarence, 23

Mack, Connie, 7, 10, 37, 60, 151, 191, 195, 430

Mack, Earl, 116

Mackens, Thomas, 193

Mackey, Raleigh (Bizz), 298, 316, 317, 340, 397, 406; test five-year suspension, 362

Mack Park fire, 401–3

Madison Park Company, 252–53

Madison Stars, 252, 254

Magee, Sherwood, 198

Magrinat, Hector, 57, 82, 83

Malarcher, Dave, 179, 182, 262, 264, 357, 367, 372, 392, 399, 414, 468; early background, 355

Manhattan AC, 203

Marcelle, Oliver, 262, 289, 355–56

Maroons, 147

market reach, 167–68, 449

Marquette club, 22, 42, 89

Marsans, Armando, 67

Marshall, Bob, 93

Marshall, Charles, 55

Martin, J. B., 399, 468; purchases Memphis Red Sox, 399

Martin, J. S., 399

Marx, Karl, 58

Mason, Charles, 289

Matthews, William Clarence, 64

Matthews, John (Big), 199, 250, 299

Matthewson, Christy, 60, 75, 442

Mayo, George, 386; vice-president of HBEC, 386

Mays, Carl, 293

Mays, Willie, 425

McAdoo, Tully, 108, 275

McAllister, A. M., 95

McCarthy, Jack, 44

McClellan, Danny, 13, 15, 17, 59, 66, 77, 83, 106, 110, 113, 114

McClelland, J. W., 274–75

McCormick, Robert R., 174

McCormick of Los Angeles, 129

McCormick Shamrocks, 97

McGraw, John, 57, 62, 64, 116, 155, 255, 312, 351, 443
McKeever, Steve, 146
McMahon, Ed, 106; forms Lincoln Giants, 106, 107, 443
McMahon, Roderick (Jess), 106, 107, 111, 113, 132, 148–50, 172, 187, 206, 442, 443; controversy over use of Olympic Field, 116; formation of Lincoln Giants, 133; formation of Lincoln Stars, 148
McNair, Hurly, 112, 317, 318
McNeil, William, 130
Memphis Red Sox, 273, 305, 326, 327, 372, 390, 399, 413, 416
Mendez, Jose, 77, 82, 83, 85, 95, 200, 249, 251, 316, 317, 318, 340, 439; early background, 77
Mercantile League, 24, 25
Merkle, Fred, 129, 445
Miller, Claude, 197
Miller, Eddie (Buck), 392–93, 398, 416
Mills, Charles, 107, 108, 110, 111, 147, 150, 180, 181, 182, 185, 187, 267, 270, 271, 274, 288, 306–7, 346
Milwaukee Bears, 291, 292, 297, 299
Milwaukee White Sox, 91, 273
Minneapolis Millers, 73, 90, 101
Mitchell, Alonzo (Hooks), 356
Mohawk Giants, 134, 136
Molina, Abe, 364
Molina, Augustin (Tinti), 161, 177
Monroe, Al, 323
Monroe, Bill, 13, 15, 16, 84, 86, 110, 112, 129
Montalvo, Alonzo, 343; early background, 363–64, 366, 384; omitted from NNL's reserve list, 364
Moore, Dobie, 316, 317, 318

Moore, Harry, 47, 83, 93, 96, 115, 120, 121, 124
Moran, Carlos, 57
Morrow, 33
Morton Republic Club, 191
Moseley, Beauregard, 53, 73, 74, 89, 93, 99, 118, 119, 122, 124–25, 179, 443; attempts to organize black league, 100–101; early background, 53
Mossell, Nathan, 15
Mothel, Dink, 317–18
Motts, R. T., 124
Munch, Gus, 49, 50
Munoz, Jose, 14, 15, 67, 82, 83
Munro, Al, 382
Murdock, Eugene, 280
Murray, Red, 115
Murray Hills club, 13, 70, 80, 431
Murphy, Charles, 255
Murphy, Danny, 10
Mutual Association of Eastern Colored Baseball Clubs, 283, 307, 332
Myers, John (Chief), 129

NAACP, 409
Nashville Elite Giants, 423
National Agreement, 154, 211
National Agreement (Black Baseball), 321–22
National Association of Colored Baseball Clubs of United States and Cuba (NACBC), 28, 46, 55–57, 61, 66, 68–73, 76, 78–80, 82, 83, 85, 87, 88, 95, 100, 102, 104, 114, 117, 144, 252, 285, 457; ends booking control, 111; formation of, 39–42
National Association of Professional Baseball Leagues, 211

National Baseball Federation (NBF), 299, 459
National Colored League of Professional Ball Clubs, 29, 54, 55
National Commission, 312
National League of Colored Baseball Players (NCL), 5, 22, 457
National Registration Day, 171
Navin, Frank, 172
Negro American League, 424
Negro National Business League (NNBL), 140
Negro National League (NNL), xv, 26, 187, 241, 253, 254, 257, 259, 262–67, 272, 274, 275, 278, 281, 282, 286–87, 290, 291, 293, 299–301, 303, 305, 309, 311, 312, 321, 322, 325–27, 329, 338, 341–43, 345, 346, 348, 354, 359, 363, 365, 366, 369–72, 376, 377, 382, 383, 390, 394–95, 397, 400, 402–6, 413, 417, 422, 423, 424, 455, 457, 459; formation of, 243–51; loses players to ECL, 289–90, 297–98, 307–8, 316, 327, 330, 417
Negro Southern League (NSL), 361
Nelson, John, 8, 77
Newark club, 348, 349, 351; disbands, 353
Newark Eagles, 15
New Londons, 107
Newton, James, 414
New York Baseball Association, 299
New York Colored Giants, 206
New York Cubans, 423
New York Giants (African American), 36
New York Giants, 35, 57, 60, 62, 115, 116, 129, 255, 311, 444–45
New York Highlanders (Yankees), 13, 15, 35, 156

New York–Pennsylvania League, 350
Niagara Movement, 141
Niesen, William, 295; protests use of African American umpires, 294
Niesen's Pyotts, 295
Norfolk Giants, 261
Normals, 44, 125
Norman, Billy, 99
Norristown club, 189, 194
Northwest League, 261
Northwestern League, 130, 134
Nunn, William, 409
Nutter, Isaac, 360, 364, 366, 371–72, 385, 387; attempts to hold ECL together, 386; ECL president, 360; on five-year suspension, 362–63; lawsuit against ANL, 396–97

Oak Leas, 57
Ohio-Indiana League, 199
Ohio League, 5, 429
O'Malley, Ed, 278
Oms, Alejandro, 397
Organized Baseball, 51, 61, 63, 66, 68, 181, 211, 241, 248, 257, 265, 311, 314, 315, 319, 321–22, 369, 381, 424
Organized Black Baseball, 344, 346, 359, 362, 375, 382, 403
O'Rourke, John, 9, 37, 79
Overall, Orvie, 92
Ownie Bush's Federal League All-Stars, 162

Pacific Coast League, 134
Padron, Luis (El Mulo), 85, 175, 177, 285
Page Fence Giants, 6, 11, 15, 26, 59, 65, 144, 167, 199

Paige, Leroy (Satchel), 398, 416
Palm Beach Inn, 174
Palomino, Emilio, 77
Park Owners Association (POA), 44, 45, 48, 52, 89, 94, 95
Parks, James, 130
Parks, William (Bubber), 121
Parpetti, Augustin, 82, 157, 261
Patterson, John, 11, 431
Payne, Andrew (Jap), 8, 31, 49, 68, 99, 119, 434
Payne, Felix, 100
Payton, Jr., Phillip, 142
Pedroso, Eustaquio, 397
Pennsylvania–New Jersey League, 331
Pennsylvania Red Caps, 206, 453
Peters, Frank, 25
Peters, William, 4, 21, 23, 46; split with Frank Leland, 22; Unions-Union Giants dispute, 25
Pettus, Bill, 120, 121, 122, 175, 194, 197–98, 262
Petway, Bruce, 43, 66, 99, 112, 121, 130, 133, 155, 167, 200, 324; early background, 119
Philadelphia Athletics, 6, 8, 9, 10, 11, 13, 39, 151, 191, 195, 312, 442
Philadelphia Baseball Association (PBA), 283, 307, 457
Philadelphia Giants, xiii, xviii, 3, 4, 10, 12–14, 17, 18, 25, 28, 29, 31, 37–39, 41, 43, 46, 47, 57, 66, 69, 70, 72, 76–80, 83–85, 88, 117–18, 120, 136, 143, 149, 156, 167, 187, 245, 278, 286, 419, 440; against Cuban X Giants for colored championship, 9, 12, 16; origins of, 6–8; tour of Cuba, 67–68
Philadelphia Phillies, 10, 13, 44, 116, 255, 264, 317

Philadelphia Professionals, 33, 37, 109
Philadelphia Quaker Giants, 37
Philadelphia Royal Giants, 362
Philadelphia Tigers, 386–87
Pierce, Bill, 112, 122, 130
Pierce, Steve, 326, 379, 401; Detroit Stars interest and Mose L. Walker, 390
Pittsburgh Crawfords, 423
Pittsburgh Keystones, 5, 6, 59, 274, 280, 282, 291
Pittsburgh Pirates, 311
Plank, Eddie, 10, 39
Poles, Spotswood, 83, 106, 113, 117, 132, 175, 183, 194, 195, 442
Pompez, Alex, 283, 286, 314, 360, 364–65, 387, 397, 423; early background, 284–85; withdrawal from ECL, 387
Ponce de Leon Hotel, 174
Posey, Cumberland (Cum), 273, 308, 344, 371, 372, 377, 380, 385, 387, 395, 397, 398, 404, 406, 412, 417, 463, 469; early background, 298; on Negro Leagues, 374–75; on state of eastern black baseball, 382–84; ten-game series with James Keenan, 410
Powell, Paul, 254
Powell, Russell, 154, 182
Powell, Willie, 355, 390, 393
Provident Hospital, 98, 99, 441, 444
public relations (PR), 98–99, 272, 273, 287, 300, 303, 304, 314, 342, 401, 407
Pugh, Johnny, 204, 206, 263, 453
Pulitzer, Joseph, 256
Pullman, Florence, 98

Quaker Giants of New York, 36, 48, 80

Randolph, A. Philip, 408
Raymond, Charles (Bugs), 83–84
Reach, Albert, 7
Rector, Connie, 410
Redding, Dick (Cannonball), xi, 106, 109, 113, 120, 175, 177, 179, 199, 206, 209, 252, 261, 262, 263, 276, 290, 444, 453; early background, 106; support of John Connor, 207
Redland Field, 259–60
Red Stockings of Norfolk, Virginia, 59
Reed, Ambrose, 356
Reeves, Walter, 363
Reid, Ambrose, 406
Reulbach, Ed, 92
R. G. Dunn Club, 192
Riddle, William 205
Ridgewood club, 13, 18, 70, 80, 84, 99, 432
Rieger, Elmer, 97
Riggins, Bill, 409
Rile, Ed (Huck), 254, 290
Rios, Herman, 157
Riverton Palmyra, 37
Riverview club, 77, 89
Robbins, G. A., 360
Roberts, Leroy, 202, 274
Roberts, William, 55
Robinson, Al, 31, 86, 112, 434
Robinson, Bill (Bojangles), 409; partnership with Ben Taylor, 330; George Robinson, 290, 296, 348, 460, 462
Robinson, Jackie, 424, 425
Roddy, Bert, 361
Rodriquez, Jose, 177
Roesink, John, 390, 402, 403, 415; with African American fans, 401, 416–17; Detroit Stars, 390

Rogan, Wilbur (Bullet Joe), 316, 317, 318, 339
Rogers, Nat, 367
Rogers Park, 44, 95, 125, 333
Rojo, Julio, 262, 285, 289, 364–65
Rossiter, George, 273, 283, 284, 286, 303, 307, 308, 383, 387, 408; Charles Spedden, 366; treasurer of ANL, 395
Royal League, 45
Royal Poinciana Hotel, 151, 155, 171, 174
Rush, Joe, 299, 322, 344
Russ, Pythias, 393, 399, 413
Russell, Branch, 393
Russell, John Henry, 393, 413
Ruth, Babe, 156, 319, 410
Ryan, Jimmy, 44, 49
Ryan, Red, 209, 263, 340

San Diego Griefers, 97
Santop, Louis, 113, 175, 183, 195, 198, 262, 316, 317; early background, 113
Savage, Connie, 251
Scales, George, 411
Scanlon, James, 163
Schang, Wally, 195
Scheiner, Seth, 148
Schlicther, H. Walter (Slick), 4, 6, 7, 16–17, 26, 36, 39, 71, 72, 75, 78, 79, 80, 81, 88, 101, 149, 196; Union League manager, 76
Schmidt, Fred, 44
Schorling, John, 119, 127, 128, 131, 146–47, 444; sale of Chicago American Giants to William Trimble, 389–90

Schulte, Frank (Wildfire), 82, 92
Scott, Elisha, 251
Scott, Emmett, 142
Seattle Steelheads, 130
separate black economy, 138–70, 210
Seybold, Socks, 10
Seymour, Harold, 60, 68, 96, 256
Shepard, Samuel, 274
Shibe, Benjamin, 7
Shibe Park, 261, 263
Shipp, Jesse, 110
Shively, George, 151–52, 154, 157, 183, 254, 262
Sisler, George, 319
Skillem, Percy, 49
Smith, Charlie (Chino), 409, 411
Smith, Cleo, 344
Smith, Harry, 4, 6, 7, 26
Smith, Howard, 250, 398
Smith, W. T., 326
Snaer, Lucian, 293
Snodgrass, Fred, 97, 129
Soto, A. M., 176–77
South Atlantic League, 25
South Chicagos, 38, 44, 48, 57, 58, 89, 125
Spalding, Albert, 58
Spalding, Arthur, 175, 449
Spaulding club, 89, 95, 125
Speaker, Tris, 156
Spedden, Charles, 273, 283, 284, 286, 289, 296, 297, 303–4, 307, 313, 314, 330, 339, 344, 396, 460; and Foster's critique of ECL, 288–89; and George Rossiter, 366
Stahl, Jake, 38, 49, 125–26, 179, 436; early background, 45
stall, 335, 416; defined, 335
Starks, Charles A., 319

Stars of Cuba, 95
Stearns, Norman (Turkey), 406
Stephens, Jake, 410, 411
Sterry, Fred, 175
Stevens, Frank, 316, 339, 340
Stevens, Paul, 406
St. Louis Browns, 60, 180, 320, 461
St. Louis Cardinals, 274
St. Louis Giants, xiii–iv, 107, 108, 110, 111–12, 126, 129, 134, 136, 147, 180, 271; early origins, 107, 151, 156, 172, 177, 185, 199, 210, 250, 261, 267, 274, 288, 421, 447, 456; renamed St. Louis Stars, 275. *See also* St. Louis Giants and Amusement Association
St. Louis Giants and Amusement Association (SLGAA), 108, 112, 146, 267
St. Louis Giants Baseball Club and Amusement Company, 274
St. Louis Maroons, 5
St. Louis Stars, xv, 271, 275, 277, 281, 291, 300, 322, 326, 327, 339, 372, 405, 416; against Chicago American Giants for NNL league championship, 391–94; withdrew from NNL, 417
St. Louis Terriers, 181
St. Paul Gophers, 76
Streeter, Sam, 344, 397–98
Strong, Nathaniel (Nat), xv, xvi, 36, 39, 70, 73, 79–81, 99, 105, 106, 111, 116, 117, 139, 149, 161–62, 170, 172, 173, 176, 195, 201, 202, 204, 206–7, 211, 252, 253, 256, 272, 273, 276, 283–87, 289, 290, 296, 298, 299, 302, 307, 308, 314, 333, 336, 337, 349, 353, 354, 360,

Strong, Nathaniel (Nat) (*cont.*) 371, 375, 377, 381, 383, 386, 387, 395–97, 406, 407, 412, 420, 421, 448, 457, 460; alliance with Ed Bolden, 330; alliance with James Keenan, 149; and Brooklyn Royal Giants, 115; early background, 34–35; against HBEC, 196–97; Intercity Association president, 35; interview by *New York Age*, 349–50; refusal to book games for Grand Central club, 186–87; rift with James Keenan, 353–54; withdraws Brooklyn Royal Giants from ECL, 385

Strothers, C. W. (Colonel), 296, 303, 349, 350, 362, 371; withdraws from ECL, 384, 385

Studevan, Mark, 196; named treasurer of HBEC, 386

Suburban League, 101

Sullivan, Neil, 90

Summer Garden and Peruvian Gallery, 89

Summers, Art, 283

Suttles, George (Mules), 392, 393

Sutton, Bill, 62

Sweatt, George, 317, 318, 339, 356, 399

Sweeney, Dennis, 116

Sykes, Frank (Doc), 194, 195

Talbert, Danger, 43, 47, 124, 436

Tammany Hall, 35

Taylor, Ben, 108, 151, 154, 155, 157, 254, 260, 290, 296, 462; conflict with Mrs. C. I. Taylor over ABCs, 305; partnership with George Robinson, 330

Taylor, Charles Isham "C. I.," xiv, xvii, 139–40, 150–66, 172, 181–85, 187, 188, 193, 194, 212, 257, 260, 267, 268, 270, 271, 274, 288, 304, 306–7, 319, 326, 355, 375, 379, 392, 418, 425, 450, 454, 459, 460; calls for black clubs to organize, 152–53; early background, 151–52; Rube Foster's criticism, 159–61; on moving his ABCs, 183–84; death, 275

Taylor, C. I. (Mrs.), 297, 379; conflict with Ben Taylor over ABCs, 305; on expulsion of ABCs, 305–6

Taylor, James, 93

Taylor, Jim (Candy), 151, 469; early background, 392; on NNL, 414

Taylor, John (Steel Arm), 96, 108, 130, 151, 152, 155, 182

Taylor, Julius, 54, 127–28, 131

Terpsichorean Parlors, 88

Tesrea Bears, 251, 263

Texas-Oklahoma-Louisiana League (TOL), 413

Thatcher, John, 146

Thomas, Bill, 110, 123

Thomas, Clint, 316, 340, 398, 410, 411

Thomas, Jules, 84

Thompson, Austin Devere, 188

Thompson, Frank, 59, 174

Thompson, Lloyd, 190, 195, 196, 283, 329, 330, 331, 337, 343–44, 360, 373, 375, 384, 406, 407, 452; attempts to oust Bolden, 405; on discontinuation of Colored World Series, 368–69; resignation from ECL, 386

Thompson, Sandy, 357

Thompson, William (Big Bill), 367

Three Links club, 191

Tinker, Joe, 60, 92, 255
Tolan, Eddie, 409
Toledo club, 272, 273, 291, 292
Topeka Giants, 56
Torrenti, Christobal (Carlos), 157, 161, 262, 264
Torrey, Will, 82
Traveling Managers Association, 45
Trent, Ted (Highpockets), 392, 393, 394
Trice, Sandy, 142
Tri-County League, 14
Trimble, William, 389, 390, 415, 418; purchase of Chicago American Giants, 389–90
Tri-State League, 5, 38, 429
Trolley League, 107, 147
Tucker, Henry, xvii, 173, 207–8, 211, 252, 276, 283, 289, 307, 418, 425; alliance with Connor and Wilkins, 205; lures Duval Giants to Atlantic City, 202
Tuft Lyons, 129
Tyree, Ruby, 175

Umpires Official Association (UOA), 277, 294–95, 456
Union Association, 134
Union League, 72; disbands, 75; early formation, 74
U. P. team, 128

Valdes, P. S., 176–77
Valdes, Rogelio, 67
Vancouver club, 261
Vandal, 203
Vermont League, 64

Victor, George, 206
Vincent, Theodore, 176
Voigt, David, 256, 279, 382
Von der Ahe, Chris, 320

Waddell Rube, 10, 39
Wade, Lee, 132, 154
Wagner, Honus, 75, 76, 110
Walker, C. J., 142–43
Walker, Fleet, 63
Walker, Juliet E. K., 143
Walker, Mose L., 390, 413; purchase interest in Detroit Stars, 390
Walker, Weldy, 63
Walker Manufacturing Company, 143
Wallace, Bobby, 60
Wallace, Felix, 93, 108
Walton, Lester, 114–15, 132, 186, 256
Wambsganss, Bill, 369
Warfield, Frank, 290, 316, 317, 339, 340
Warren, Ed, 207
Warrington, Noah, 108
Washington, Booker T., 50, 128, 140, 141, 142, 193, 294, 407, 419, 437; Negro National Business League, 140–41
Washington, Isaac, 383
Washington Potomacs, 273, 290, 296, 329, 387; relocation, 330
Washington Senators, 45, 261, 330
Watkins, John (Pop), 80, 81
Webster, Pearl (Speck), 185
Weeks, William, 283
Wells, Willie, 392, 393
West Baden Sprudels, 129, 136, 151, 156, 194, 447
West End League, 25

West Ends, 44, 89, 91, 95, 124, 125
Western Interstate League, 6
Western League, 44, 279
Wheeling Green Stockings, 5
White, Chaney, 356, 406, 410, 411
White, Jacob, 431
White, Solomon (Sol), 3, 7, 8, 11, 13, 26, 36, 37, 41, 59, 66, 69, 72, 73, 76, 78, 79, 80, 81, 86, 88, 104, 106, 126, 149, 182, 242, 243–44, 246, 257, 262, 412, 418, 429, 430, 443; early background, 4–6; forms Lincoln Giants, 106; *History of Colored Baseball*, 58–66; manager of Cleveland Browns, 299; manager of Columbus Buckeyes, 259; manager of Lincoln Giants, 109
Whitworth, Dick, 157, 167, 251, 252, 260, 264, 271, 275–76
Wickware, Frank, 97, 115, 121, 124, 132, 154, 155, 157, 167, 179, 200
Wilkins, Baron, 211, 252, 276, 277, 307, 458; business alliance with Tucker and Jackson, 205; death, 289; early background, 205–6
Wilkinson, James Leslie (J. L.), 249–50, 270, 274, 287, 304, 324, 339, 344, 390, 404, 405, 414, 415; introduces night baseball in NNL, 416; withdrew his Kansas City Monarchs from NNL, 417
Williams, A. D., 377; assessment of NNL, 377–80
Williams, Andrew (Stringbean), 199, 204
Williams, A. W., 124
Williams, Bobby, 199
Williams, Charlie, 356, 393–94, 413
Williams, Clarence, 7, 8, 26, 59, 67, 79, 441; early background, 18

Williams, Daniel Hale, 98, 441
Williams, George, 7, 8
Williams, Gerald, 297, 298, 344; remained with Lincoln Giants, 298
Williams, Henry, 129
Williams, James, 172
Williams, James Byrd, 193
Williams, James H. 185, 207; and Grand Central club, 186–87
Williams, Joseph (Cyclone), 93, 96, 97, 113, 115, 116, 117, 120, 121, 122, 132, 133, 152, 167, 175, 183, 194–95, 206, 207, 209, 262, 410, 411, 444; early background, 93–94
Williams, Tom, 154, 155, 201, 264
Wilmington Giants, 36, 37
Wilmington Potomacs, 330, 331, 337, 348, 351
Wilson, Jud (Babe Ruth), 297, 362
Wilson, Rollo, 332, 338, 372, 384–85, 387, 388, 398–99, 406–7, 411; Ed Bolden and new league, 388–89; secretary of ANL, 395
Wilson, Tom, 414–15, 424, 463
Winston, Bobby, 78, 93, 96, 120, 121, 254
Winters, Jesse (Nip), 298, 316, 317, 340
Womack, Ollie, 311, 318–19, 340
World's Colored Championship, 4, 11, 14, 19, 23, 43, 116, 133, 135, 165, 430, 448; defined, 9
World Series, 126, 369; early origins, 311–12
World War I, 171, 176, 180, 187, 205, 258, 267, 333, 448
World War II, 424
Wolfenden, James, 407
Wright, Edward H., 54, 179
Wright, George, 46, 47, 93, 113
Wright, Richard, Jr., 142

Wyatt, Dave, 23, 50–51, 251, 254, 256, 373, 455; NNL publicity director, 260

Yancy, Bill, 410
York Colored Monarchs, 6
Young, Frank (Faye), 169, 256, 271, 293, 294, 295, 310, 312, 313, 323, 329, 333, 342, 343, 345, 347, 357, 359, 367, 373, 384, 416, 456; assessment of Colored World Series, 357–58; assessment of NNL, 373–74; campaign to hire African American umpires, 277–81; campaign to oust Tenny Blount, 323–25
Young, Ralph, 195